THE CATECHETICAL DOCUMENTS
A PARISH RESOURCE

THE CATECHETICAL DOCUMENTS
A PARISH RESOURCE

Liturgy Training Publications

Editor: Martin Connell
Production editor: Pedro A. Vélez
Designer: Barb Rohm
Production artist: Mark Hollopeter
Indexer: Mary Laur

Cover art: *Mother of God of the Sign* (two-sided processional icon), mid-16th century, in the Moscow State Museum of History. Reproduced with the permission of Associazione Pubblica di Fedeli, Via Ponzio 11, Milan 20133.

This book was typeset in Trump Mediaeval and Gill Sans.
Printed in the United States of America

Library of Congress Cataloging-in-Publications Data
The catechetical documents: a parish resource.
   p. cm.
   Includes index.
   ISBN 1-56854-113-9
   1. Catholic Church—Doctrines. 2. Catholic Church—Education. 3. Catechetics—Catholic Church.
BX1747.5.C36 1996
268'.82—dc20
      95-52014
      CIP

CATDOC

CONTENTS

ABBREVIATIONS

AA   *Apostolicam actuositatem:* The Decree on the Apostolate of the Laity (Vatican II, November 18, 1965)

AAS   *Acta Apostolicae Sedis*

ACCC   Adult Catechesis in the Christian Community: Some Principles and Guidelines (International Council for Catechesis, 1992)

AG   *Ad gentes divinitus:* The Decree on the Church's Missionary Activity (Vatican II, December 7, 1965)

BT   Basic Teachings for Catholic Religious Education

CA   *Centesimus annus* (John Paul II, May 1, 1991)

CAC   The Challenge of Adolescent Catechesis: Maturing in Faith (The National Federation for Catholic Youth Ministry, 1986)

CCC   Catechism of the Catholic Church (John Paul II, October 11, 1992)

CCL   Corpus Christianorum, Series Latina

CD   *Christus dominus:* The Decree on the Pastoral Office of Bishops in the Church (Vatican II, October 28, 1965)

CL   *Christifideles laici:* The Vocation and the Mission of the Lay Faithful in the Church and in the World (John Paul II, December 30, 1988)

CIC   *Codex iuris canonici:* Code of Canon Law

CSEL   Corpus Scriptorum Ecclesiasticorum Latinorum

CSL   *Sacrosanctum concilium:* Constitution on the Sacred Liturgy (Vatican II, December 4, 1963)

CT   *Catechesi tradendae:* On Catechesis in Our Time (John Paul II, October 16, 1979)

DH   *Dignitatis humanae:* The Declaration on Religious Liberty (Vatican II, December 7, 1965)

DS   Denziger-Schönmetzer, *Enchiridion Symbolorum, definitionum et declarationum de rebus fidei et morum*

DV   *Dei verbum:* The Dogmatic Constitution on Divine Revelation (Vatican II, November 18, 1965)

EJFA   Economic Justice for All: Pastoral Letter on Catholic Social Teaching and the U.S. Economy (NCCB, 1986)

EN   *Evangelii nuntiandi:* On Evangelization in the Modern World (Paul VI, December 8, 1975)

ES   *Ecclesiae sanctae* (Congregation for the Doctrine of the Faith, June 24, 1973)

FC   *Familiaris consortio:* On the Family (John Paul II, November 22, 1981)

GC   Guide for Catechists: Document of Vocational, Formative and Promotional Orientation of Catechists in the Territories Dependent on the Congregation for the Evangelization of Peoples (Congregation for the Evangelization of Peoples, 1993)

GCD   General Catechetical Directory (Sacred Congregation for the Clergy, 1971)

GDSCM   Guidelines for Doctrinally Sound Catechetical Materials (USCC, 1990)

GE	*Gravissimum educationis:* The Declaration on Christian Education (Vatican II, October 28, 1965)	RCIA	Rite of Christian Initiation of Adults
GNLY	General Norms for the Liturgy Year and the Calendar	RDECS	The Religious Dimension of Education in a Catholic School (Congregation for Catholic Education, 1988)
GS	*Gaudium et spes:* The Pastoral Constitution on the Church in the Modern World (Vatican II, December 7, 1965)	RM	*Redemptoris missio:* On the Permanent Validity of the Church's Missionary Mandate (John Paul II, December 7, 1990)
IM	*Inter mirifica:* The Decree on the Means of Social Communication (Vatican II, December 4, 1963)	SC	*Sacrosanctum concilium:* The Constitution on the Sacred Liturgy (Vatican II, December 4, 1963)
JJPC	*Notes on the Correct Way to Present the Jews and Judaism in Preaching and Catechesis of the Roman Catholic Church* (Commission for Religious Relations with the Jews, 1985)	SCh	*Sources chrétiennes,* ed. H. deLubac and J. Danielou
		SD	*Salvifici doloris:* On the Christian Meaning of Human Suffering (John Paul II, February 11, 1984)
LG	*Lumen gentium:* The Dogmatic Constitution on the Church (Vatican II, November 21, 1964)	SRS	*Sollicitudo rei socialis:* On Social Concern (John Paul II, December 30, 1987)
NA	*Nostra aetate:* The Declaration on the Church's Relations with non-Christian Religions (Vatican II, October 28, 1965)	TLCJ	To Live in Christ Jesus: A Pastoral Reflection on Moral Values (NCCB, 1978)
NCCB	National Conference of Catholic Bishops	TJD	To Teach as Jesus Did: A Pastoral Message on Catholic Education (NCCB, 1972)
NCD	Sharing the Light of Faith: National Catechetical Directory for Catholics of the United States (NCCB, 1978)	UR	*Unitatis redintegratio:* The Decree on Ecumenism (Vatican II, November 21, 1964)
OE	*Orientalium ecclesiarum:* The Decree on Catholic Oriental Churches (Vatican II, November 21, 1964)	USCC	United States Catholic Conference
OT	*Optatam totius:* The Decree on the Training of Priests (Vatican II, October 28, 1965)		
PC	*Perfectae caritatis:* The Decree on the Appropriate Renewal of the Religious Life (Vatican II, October 28, 1965)		
PG	J.P. Migne, *Patrologiae cursus completus: Series Graeca*		
PL	J.P. Migne, *Patrologiae cursus completus: Series Latina*		
PO	*Presbyterorum ordinis:* The Decree on the Life and Ministry of Priests (Vatican II, December 7, 1965)		

GENERAL INTRODUCTION TO THE CATECHETICAL DOCUMENTS

by John E. Pollard, Director, Office for the Catechism, NCCB

Twenty years ago the pastor of the parish to which I was appointed as a newly ordained priest issued an edict upon my arrival that was to have a profound impact on my life. In the midst of a rather heated discussion, he threw up his hands and said, "If you can show it to me in the documents of the church, you can do it." I took his words to heart and began "showing him in the documents of the church" that the Apostles' Creed could replace the Nicene Creed in Masses with children (*Directory for Masses with Children*, 49) and that the parish really was required to have a finance council (*Code of Canon Law*, 537). He retracted his edict quickly, but I have been dedicated to the careful study of the church's official documents ever since.

Since *The Liturgy Documents* was published some years ago by Liturgy Training Publications, I have urged consideration of a companion volume containing introductions and texts of catechetical documents. Given the interdependent relationship of liturgy and catechesis in the church's pastoral ministry, this seemed a self-evidently appropriate project. With the encouragement of Liturgy Training Publications and the contributions of several distinguished catechetical scholars and practitioners, *The Catechetical Documents* has become a reality. I am personally and professionally delighted to introduce the volume to the reader.

Before attending to each of the introductory essays, some general commentary on five fundamental themes that run through the documents and essays seems useful. This general commentary aims to relate the documents and essays to one another in an effort to trace the contours of catechetical thought since the Second Vatican Council.

THE GENERAL THEMES

First, and perhaps most obvious, the mere collection of these documents and essays emphasizes the influential position that the church's documentary tradition holds within its pastoral mission. The heritage of faith has been entrusted to the whole church in a living tradition. Together with sacred scripture, that living tradition forms the deposit of faith that has been handed on for two millennia with the guidance of the Holy Spirit. First orally and subsequently both orally and in writing, the deposit of faith has been authentically and authoritatively communicated and interpreted through the church's teaching office in the name of Jesus Christ. Much of this living tradition has taken the form of official church documents on both the universal and local levels. The church is a people of the Word and a people of the word. Thus both sacred scripture and the church's living tradition as articulated in its official documents nourish God's people and guide their pastoral mission.

Second, the documents that are treated in this volume represent several centers of authority within the church's teaching office. Each is a valuable articulation of the church's teaching on catechesis, but they are of unequal authority. For example, the *Catechism of the Catholic Church* was promulgated by Pope John Paul II by an apostolic constitution in which he "orders its publication by virtue of my apostolic authority" and "declares it to be a sure norm for teaching the faith" (*Fidei depositum,* 3). The *Rite of Christian Initiation of Adults* was issued by the Congregation for Divine Worship, approved by Pope Paul VI, and its use is "mandatory in the dioceses of the United States of America" (*Rite of Christian Initiation of Adults,* Decree of the NCCB). Two documents are examples of apostolic exhortations, *On Evangelization in the Modern World* and *On Catechesis in Our Time.* These compelling papal appeals were issued in light of the collaboration of the Synods of Bishops in 1974 and 1977 respectively. Three other documents were issued by dicasteries of the Holy See, namely, the *General Catechetical Directory* (Congregation for the Clergy), *The Religious Dimension of Education in the Catholic School* (Congregation for Catholic Education) and the *Guide for Catechists* (Congregation for the Evangelization of Peoples). Four were issued by the bishops of the United States, namely, *To Teach as Jesus Did, Basic Teachings for Catholic Religious Education, Sharing the Light of Faith: National Catechetical Directory for Catholics of the United States* and *Guidelines for Doctrinally Sound Catechetical Materials. Adult Catechesis in the Christian Community* was sponsored by the International Council for Catechesis (COINCAT), an advisory panel of the Congregation for the Clergy established by Pope Paul VI in 1975. And one, *The Challenge of Adolescent Catechesis,* is not an official document of the church. It was published by the National Federation for Catholic Youth Ministry in collaboration with the Desk for Youth and Young Adult Ministry, Department of Education, United States Catholic Conference, the National Catholic Educational Association and the National Conference of Catechetical Leadership.

Third, the relatively large number of catechetical documents issued since the Second Vatican Council indicates the church's solicitude for the catechetical ministry. The teaching office of the college of bishops in union with the pope, the pope's ordinary teaching office as well as the teaching ministry of the National Conference of Catholic Bishops have each contributed to building the church's documentary tradition of catechesis. This documentary tradition has taken the forms of apostolic constitutions and exhortations, universal rites and local instructions, general and national directories, pastoral letters and messages, episcopal statements and instructions, and curial guidelines. These documents also represent a wide range of styles and tones from the exacting rhetoric of the *General Catechetical Directory* and the *National Catechetical Directory* to the more evocative and inspiring tenor of *On Evangelization in the Modern World* and *On Catechesis in Our Time* to the *Catechism's* harmonization of a relatively straightforward presentation of doctrine with consistently encouraging illustrations from life experience.

Fourth, most of the documents treated in this collection represent the outcome of the postconciliar preference for the process of consultation. In fact, they represent several forms of the process of consultation. The Second Vatican Council was itself a primary example of the process of consultation in the particular form of an ecumenical council. *On Evangelization in the Modern World* and *On Catechesis in Our Time* are both the result of a synod of bishops, a specific kind of consultation that was initiated at the Second Vatican Council. A unique form of episcopal collegiality, the synod of bishops is an assembly of representative bishops from all parts of the world gathered to discuss and debate a particular topic. Ordinarily the documentary outcome of such discussion and debate is an apostolic exhortation. In addition, these two apostolic constitutions in particular were significantly influenced by another form of consultation, the International Catechetical Study Weeks of the 1960s and 1970s.

The origin of the *General Catechetical Directory* is the Second Vatican Council's *Decree on the Bishops' Pastoral Office* in the church. In addition, however, participants in national episcopal conferences along with various catechetical experts were involved in the process of consultation that eventually produced the document. *To Teach As Jesus Did* "reflects a painstaking effort to obtain the views of persons from a variety of backgrounds and interests — priests, religious men and women, lay people, professional educators at all levels of education, parents [and] students. Much of this consultation took place at the national level, but even more occurred at the local diocesan level" (1). *Sharing the Light of Faith: National Catechetical Directory for Catholics of the United States* was the object of the widest possible consultation that encouraged the participation of all the faithful and spanned several years. "The process of dialogue included three extensive consultations with the church at large and with scholars, involving hundreds of thousands of people and resulting in tens of thousands of recommendations" (4). *Adult Catechesis in the Christian Community* is the product of the International Council for Catechesis, whose precise purpose is to provide consultation to the Congregation for the Clergy on catechetical matters of international consequence. And finally, the *Catechism of the Catholic Church* is partially the result of a worldwide consultation that involved all bishops, national episcopal conferences and catechetical institutes. Such a comprehensive consultation, because it is a distinct form of episcopal collegiality evident in ecumenical councils or synods of bishops, is unprecedented in the history of the church. This consultation produced over 24,000 "modi," or suggestions for changes, in the text.

Fifth, the documents in this collection represent the trajectory of the development of catechetical thought since the Second Vatican Council. To many, it was surprising that the Council participants did not agree to suggest the composition of a catechism. There was considerable discussion of the issue. The participants at both the Council of Trent and the First Vatican Council strongly favored such catechisms. But the directive from the Second Vatican Council was the publication of a catechetical directory rather than a catechism. The genre "directory" is quite different from the genre "catechism." A catechetical directory by its nature and form contains directives, guidelines, exhortations, proposals, recommendations and procedures. A catechism by its nature and form contains a complete and faithful presentation of the fundamental Christian truths formulated in a way that facilitates their understanding. Thus it is significant that the postconciliar trajectory of catechetical thought began with the publication of the *General Catechetical Directory* in 1971.

Shortly thereafter, Pope Paul VI issued *On Evangelization in the Modern World*. It can be seen in retrospect as the theological and motivational springboard for the catechetical thought of the following 25 years. The document asserts that "the church exists to evangelize" (14). This bold proclamation reoriented the pastoral mission of the church. Even today we hear echoes of this proclamation in Pope John Paul II's preoccupation with the "new evangelization" and especially in his consistent encouragement to prepare for the coming of the third millennium of Christianity. More immediately, *On Evangelization in the Modern World* situated catechesis as a crucial component within the wider scope of the ministry of evangelization. Paul VI was working on the sequel to *On Evangelization in the Modern World*, what we now know as *On Catechesis in Our Time*, when he died. Following quickly on his predecessor's initiative, John Paul II issued *On Catechesis in Our Time* as the first apostolic exhortation of his pontificate. It specified and developed the relationship between evangelization and catechesis and has since become the mission statement for the church's catechetical ministry. Its first line insists that "the church has always considered catechesis one of her primary tasks" (1). These two documents, then, form the energizing center for the development of catechetical thought since the Second Vatican Council.

During this same period, the bishops of the United States issued *To Teach As Jesus Did*, a pastoral message in support of all forms of Catholic education; *Basic Teachings for Catholic Religious Education*, a statement of the principal elements of the Christian message; *Sharing the Light of Faith: National Catechetical Directory for Catholics of the United States* and *Guidelines for Doctrinally Sound Catechetical Materials*. These four documents teased out some of the practical implications for the ministry of catechesis in the United States that were implied in the Holy See's more universal and visionary texts.

Perhaps the document that has had the single greatest impact on the development of catechetical thought during this period is the *Rite of Christian Initiation of Adults*. Because of this document, contemporary catechetical thought began to employ the language, methods and paradigms from the church's ancient liturgical and catechetical texts. Initiation, conversion, inquiry, catechumenate, enlightenment, election and mystagogia were incorporated into the catechetical vocabulary. When the *National Catechetical Directory* was issued, it recognized that the *Rite of Christian Initiation of Adults* was "the norm for catechetical and liturgical practice" (115).

But the notion of a catechism resurfaced again during the Extraordinary Synod of Bishops in 1985. This Synod was called to celebrate the twentieth anniversary of the closing of the Second Vatican Council. The Synod participants revisited the discussion about a catechism that had been part of earlier conciliar and synodal deliberations. The participants in the Synod suggested that "a catechism or compendium of all Catholic doctrine regarding both faith and morals be composed, that it might be, as it were, a point of reference for the catechisms or compendiums that are prepared in the various regions" (*Message to the People of God*, Final Report, 4). The same day on which the Synod's Final Report was issued, Pope John Paul II accepted the suggestion regarding the composition of a catechism. He said:

The desire to prepare a compendium or catechism of all Catholic doctrine to serve as a point of reference for catechisms or compendia on this theme in all the particular churches . . . responds to a real need both of the universal church and of the particular churches (Closing Talk, 6).

After numerous drafts over a nine-year period under the guidance of a Commission of Cardinals and Bishops, Pope John Paul II promulgated the *Catechism of the Catholic Church* in December 1992.

The church remains in a postconciliar period. No doubt there will continue to be further development of catechetical thought during this postconciliar period. But the event of the *Catechism of the Catholic Church* represents a defining moment in the history of the church's catechetical mission. In the *Catechism*, the trajectory of postconciliar catechetical thought has matured to include in its documentary tradition "an organic synthesis of the essential and fundamental contents of Catholic doctrine, as regards both faith and morals, in light of the Second Vatican Council and the whole of the church's tradition" (*Catechism of the Catholic Church*, 11).

THE PARTICULAR DOCUMENTS

The Second Vatican Council called for the renewal of catechesis and prescribed that a directory be prepared that articulated the fundamental principles of catechesis. In response to this directive, the *General Catechetical Directory* was published in 1971 by the Congregation for the Clergy. "The immediate purpose of the *Directory* is to provide assistance in the production of catechetical directories and catechisms" (foreword).

Michael Horan's helpful introduction to the document provides some interesting historical information about the development of the concept of a catechetical directory. He emphasizes the fact that a directory represents a new genre for catechesis. Dr. Horan contrasts the genre "directory" with the genre "catechism" and points out the inherent tension between the two. It is interesting to note that the *General Catechetical Directory* itself claims to assist in the production of catechisms and includes in part III, chapter II, its longest section, "The More Outstanding Elements of the Christian Message" (preface).

To Teach As Jesus Did is a pastoral message on Catholic education issued by the National Conference of Catholic Bishops in 1972. They indicated at that time that "it will serve a useful purpose if it proves a catalyst for efforts to deal realistically with problems of polarization and of confusion now confronting the educational ministry."

Richard Walsh's well-balanced introduction notes the document's affinity with other ecclesial texts, especially those of the Second Vatican Council, and the comprehensive process of consultation that preceded its publication. He reminds the reader that *To Teach As Jesus Did* made a strong case for what is now known as "total Catholic education" and introduced the categories of message, community and service into contemporary catechetical language. Fr. Walsh highlights the thorny treatment of the proper relationship between the Catholic university and the diocesan bishop. He concludes with a sobering and challenging caution that, with all the church's efforts in its educational ministries, perhaps half of the baptized children and young people are not receiving the benefit of any of the forms of Catholic education.

Basic Teachings for Catholic Education is a statement that the National Conference of Catholic Bishops issued in 1973. It draws substantially from the documents of the Second Vatican Council and the *General Catechetical Directory*. In fact, *Basic Teachings* served as a quasi-interim national catechetical directory while the *National Catechetical Directory* was being prepared. It intended "to set down the principal elements of the Christian message," ensure "that these teachings be central in all Catholic religious instruction, be never overlooked or minimized and be given adequate and frequent emphasis" (introduction).

Jane Regan's insightful introduction makes note of the historical context of *Basic Teachings*. She sees *Basic Teachings* as an adaptation of the *General Catechetical Directory* and an integral part of the *National Catechetical Directory*. Dr. Regan emphasizes the document's insistence on a balance between the content of faith and the experience of the believer. She critiques *Basic Teachings'* instruction on the sacraments, especially in light of the *Rite of Christian Initiation of Adults*, but finds its timeliness in its emphasis on doctrinal substance and stability, the importance of the role of the catechist and the broader catechizing community and its reliance on the teachings of the Second Vatican Council.

Issued in 1975, *On Evangelization in the Modern World* is an apostolic exhortation of Pope Paul VI. It followed the 1974 Synod of Bishops that focused on the topic of evangelization. While the document is quite broad in the scope of its presentation, it belongs in a collection of catechetical documents because it provides the fundamental motivation and direction for the development of catechetical thought after the Second Vatican Council. *On Evangelization in the Modern World* links catechesis closely to evangelization when it says that "catechesis occupies such an important place in evangelization that it has often been synonymous with it; and yet it is only one aspect of evangelization" (23).

Thomas Walters' introductory essay underscores the centrality of Christ in the process of evangelization and urges the reader to note the pope's treatment of the process of inculturation, an issue that has become a major concern for the contemporary church. In the spirit of the document, he cautions the reader "that in growing numbers, Catholics no longer stand over against the secular culture; they have become the culture." This in turn becomes a challenge for church leaders to provide for the formation and training of its evangelizers and catechists, who must act "in communion with the church and her pastors" (60).

Eight years after the publication of the *General Catechetical Directory*, the U.S. bishops issued *Sharing the Light of Faith: National Catechetical Directory for Catholics of the United States*. The *National Catechetical Directory* was intended primarily for those responsible for catechesis. It "is an official statement of the National Conference of Catholic Bishops of the United States and has been reviewed by the Sacred Congregation for the Clergy according to established norm" (6).

John Zaums' thorough introduction expresses the document's relationship to the Second Vatican Council in general and the *General Catechetical Directory* in particular. He traces its historical development, emphasizing the extraordinary process of consultation that preceded its publication and its practical use especially for catechetical planning and evaluation. Among its strengths, Dr. Zaums suggests that it has become a touchstone for catechetical programming; it stresses both the "what" of catechesis as well as the "why," "how," "when" and "where"; it is balanced and holistic.

Following the Synod of Bishops of 1977, Pope John Paul II issued his apostolic exhortation *On Catechesis in Our Time*. The purpose of the document is that "the whole church should strengthen the solidity of the faith and of Christian living, should give fresh vigor to the initiatives in hand, should stimulate creativity—with the required vigilance—and should help spread among the communities the joy of bringing the mystery of Christ to the world" (4). In fact, the document has become a significant source of inspiration and motivation for the renewal of catechesis called for by the Second Vatican Council. If *On Evangelization in the Modern World* is the charter for the "new evangelization," *On Catechesis in Our Time* is the charter for the "new catechesis."

Jane Regan's discerning introduction highlights the document's treatment of the fundamental relationship of evangelization and catechesis. She advises the reader to reflect with the document on the relationship between culture and tradition and message and experience. While noting the document's advocacy for systematic catechesis and the understanding that catechesis is an essential ecclesial action, Dr. Regan points out what she perceives to be the weakness of the document in the areas of sacramental catechesis and adult catechesis.

The *Rite of Christian Initiation of Adults* was first published in 1972, and it became mandatory for use in the dioceses of the United States in 1988. It is the result of the Second Vatican Council's directive for a revision of the Rite of Baptism and the restoration of the catechumenate. The ancient practices of the catechumenate have been retrieved and the values inherent in their celebration have been represented in the RCIA. Among these are the involvement of the faith community in the catechumen's journey of conversion and the interplay of ritual celebration and catechetical instruction in the catechumenal process. The RCIA has had a profound impact on both the content and methodology of catechesis in general and on initiatory catechesis in particular.

Anne Marie Mongoven has provided a meticulous overview in her introduction to the RCIA. She sets forth the structure of the rite, emphasizes the need for an unhurried pace throughout the stages of the catechumenate and links these stages to the paschal mystery. She cautions that catechesis is more than instruction and insists that it is a proclamation of faith to be lived. Emphasizing the centrality of the creed, Dr. Mongoven demonstrates how catechesis is woven throughout the process of initiation. She stresses the significance of the faith community indicating that the believers' initiation is by the community and for the community. She wisely calls for the continued collaboration of liturgists and catechists in the pastoral implementation of the RCIA, recognizing that the process of conversion is simultaneously catechetical and liturgical.

The *Religious Dimension of Education in the Catholic School* was issued by the Congregation for Catholic Education in 1988. The purpose of the document is to present a reflection on "what makes the Catholic school distinctive in its religious dimension" (1). While it is not an overtly catechetical document, among its sources are listed the *General Catechetical Directory, On Evangelization in the Modern World* and *On Catechesis in Our Time*. In addition, the effectiveness of the catechetical component of education in a Catholic school at this time in this country is becoming an increasingly engaging topic. For example, the document terms the Catholic school "one of the ways for evangelization to take place." And "the quality of the religious instruction integrated into the overall education of the students" is the underlying reason for the Catholic school's existence (66).

Fayette Veverka's introduction provides a useful overview of the document. She adequately summarizes its audience, scope, purpose and thesis, articulates the principles of a Catholic philosophy of education it sets forth and reviews its recommendations for implementing its vision of a Catholic school. She concludes by posing two questions that urge the reader to reflect on the contrasting visions of education/catechesis that at times form a point of tension within the church.

The Challenge of Adolescent Catechesis was published by the National Federation of Catholic Youth Ministry in collaboration with the Desk for Youth and Young Adult Ministry; Department of Education, United States Catholic Conference; the National Catholic Educational Association and the National Conference of Catechetical Leadership. While this paper is not an official document of the church, its widespread acceptance and use among the community of diocesan and parish youth ministers argue for its inclusion in this collection. "By proposing the aim, process and principles for adolescent catechesis and a framework of key faith themes for younger and older adolescents, and by identifying the roles and responsibilities of key leaders in ministry with youth, the paper sets forth a vision and direction for adolescent catechesis" (3).

Carole Eipers presents a thoughtful overview of this paper. She summarizes the context for the paper and reviews the process of consultation through which it was refined. She reminds the reader of this paper on adolescent catechesis that the catechesis of adults is primary. Dr. Eipers advocates for the interrelatedness of ministries in general and for an integrated approach to ministry with youth in particular. After noting the paper's reliance on official church documents, she underscores its argument for the continuity and complementarity of all forms of catechetical ministry.

Published in 1990, *Adult Catechesis in the Christian Community* represents the efforts of the International Council for Catechesis. Citing Pope John Paul ii's assertion in *On Catechesis in Our Time* that adult catechesis "is the principal form of catechesis" (43), the document "touches on common issues, common problems and probable solutions, which seem prevalent throughout the world, fully recognizing that inculturation will have to be made in the local churches" (7). Among adult religious educators, this document has quickly become a frequent and reliable reference point as well as a source of encouragement.

Margaret Ralph's splendid introduction emphasizes the main themes of the document: the priority of adult catechesis, the place of catechesis in adult formation, the consistent invitation to become adult in faith, the call to discipleship and the challenge to ecumenism. Noting the document's recognition of the catechumenal model for adult catechesis, she urges the involvement of the whole community. Dr. Ralph concludes by echoing the document's challenge to the church to harmonize what it says about adult catechesis with what it does.

The *Guide for Catechists* was issued by the Congregation for the Evangelization of Peoples in 1993. Its subtitle indicates that it is intended for catechists in missionary lands, but the appeal and scope of the document encompasses all catechists. Ultimately an unequivocal and enthusiastic affirmation of catechists, it "treats in a doctrinal, existential and practical way the principle aspects of the catechists' vocation, identity, spirituality, selection and training, missionary and pastoral tasks, and remuneration, along with the responsibility of the people of God toward them, in today's conditions and those of the immediate future" (1).

Marina Herrera's introduction recognizes the similarity between catechists in missionary lands and those in the well-established churches. She underscores the document's unswerving conviction about the richness of native resources in the ministry of catechesis. Since the document terms the catechist the "apostle ever relevant," Dr. Herrera rightly emphasizes the dignity of the catechist, the importance of the catechist as a community leader, the high standards for catechists, the primacy of spiritual formation for the catechist and the respect, appreciation and remuneration due the catechist. She notes also the document's treatment of inculturation and calls the reader's attention to the crucial relationship of faith and culture in catechesis.

The *Guidelines for Doctrinally Sound Catechetical Materials* was approved by the general membership of the United States Catholic Conference in 1990. It was prepared by a task force of the Bishops' Committee on Education that was chaired by Bishop John Leibrecht and on which I served. In the few years since it was issued, *Guidelines* has been used extensively by the publishers of catechetical materials in the preparation of their texts and by diocesan educational and catechetical offices for the evaluation of those texts.

Eva Marie Lumas also served on the task force that prepared the drafts of *Guidelines for Doctrinally Sound Catechetical Materials*. Her introduction sketches for the reader what she considers the basic strengths and weaknesses of the document. She points out that the document provides publishers and catechists with a clear statement of the general principles and guidelines for doctrinal soundness as well as a common frame of reference for determining the doctrinal merit of catechetical texts. Dr. Lumas also underscores the document's positive treatment of the relationship between faith and culture. She cautions that the document's emphasis on the priority of doctrine could be interpreted by some as an implicit reduction for the role of methodology in the catechetical process. She concludes by reminding the reader that the "vast quantity and diversity of catechetical materials give evidence of the vast and divergent spiritual sensibilities of contemporary Catholics."

/

GENERAL CATECHETICAL DIRECTORY

SACRED CONGREGATION FOR THE CLERGY
1971

OVERVIEW OF THE *GENERAL CATECHETICAL DIRECTORY*: HISTORICAL CONTEXT AND LITERARY GENRE

by Michael P. Horan

Nearly 25 years have passed since the publication of the *General Catechetical Directory* (GCD), prepared by the Sacred Congregation for the Clergy.[1] As the first international catechetical directory, it stands as a marker on the map of the catechetical journey which, during the past century, has been anything but slow or smooth. This essay reviews the context for the proposal for the new genre of "directory" and offers an overview of the structure of the document itself. It draws attention also to the usefulness of consulting the *Directory* for help in charting the course for the present and future church in light of the more recently published *Catechism of the Catholic Church.*

THE BACKGROUND AND THE CONTEXT: A NEW GENRE FOR THE AGE OF VATICAN II

The GCD is the product of the Second Vatican Council in at least two ways: first, in its underlying principle of historical consciousness, and, second, in its understanding of catechesis as a ministry of the word. The document known as the GCD came from the discussions on the floor of the Council and as such reflects the Council's concern to function as a creative (rather than a reactive) Council in forging an ecclesiology that institutes a dialogue with the modern world. Related to that function, the Council rehabilitated the notion of episcopal collegiality and subsidiarity, which would inform the way in which national catechetical directories emerged in various countries, taking their lead from the GCD. In the process, the Council leaders and the documents that they produced clearly reinvested authority in the bishop for the catechesis of people in the church, challenging bishops to share responsibility for catechesis in the local church. Equally important for our consideration 30 years after the close of the Council, the GCD symbolizes a sea change in thought about the kind of printed matter that might aid the tasks of catechesis as undertaken by the various leaders of catechesis who work in concert with the bishop.

BISHOPS, CATECHISMS AND DIRECTORIES: A REVIEW

The Second Vatican Council made clear in *Christus Dominus* (CD), the document on the *Pastoral Office of Bishops,* that the bishop has the principal responsibility for overseeing the aims and content of catechesis in a particular diocese (CD, 44). This document, when read in light of the documents from Vatican I (the council that preceded Vatican II by some 90 years), signals an advance over that earlier council in its restoration of the ancient church's understanding of the role of the bishop in catechesis. In light of this advance, it is possible to imagine the freshness of the insight that captured the bishops' imaginations and eventuated in a directory — rather than a catechism — at the Council. Some contextual history may illumine this point and thus paint the backdrop for viewing the distinctive features of the GCD.

Since the sixteenth-century Christian Reformation, the catechism genre was presumed to be that medium through which catechists communicated content. Martin Luther had composed a large catechism for the clergy and leaders and a small catechism for children and the unlearned. Other reformers followed his lead. The Catholic reformers at Trent crafted a large catechism but did not write a universal small catechism.

The bishops at Vatican Council I took up the unfinished task of the small catechism but never completed their own mission. In 1870, they deliberated at great length over the feasibility of crafting a uniform small catechism for use in the Catholic Church.[2] The catechism proposal received approval at Vatican I, but the bishops never actually wrote the catechism described in *De Parvo Catechismo*.[3]

At Vatican II, four centuries after the Council of Trent, the conciliar proposal for a catechetical directory furnished a solution to the problem of composing either a large or a small catechism. At the beginning of Vatican Council II, Bishop Pierre Lacointe of Beauvais, France, anticipated the concerns of some Council members regarding the unfinished agenda of Vatican I. He urged the composition of a catechetical directory, one that would offer directives and guiding principles about the context for catechesis and a variety of catechetical issues aimed at serving a diversity of age groups.[4] Lacointe's suggestion came from his experience of success in France where, in 1957, the hierarchy had commissioned a directory for catechesis. Lacointe's proposal represented a grand departure from the unexamined assumptions that a catechism is the necessary medium for catechesis, assumptions revealed in the following statement, made in 1951 by the apostolic delegate to the United States, Archbishop (later Cardinal) Cicognani:

> No human book can compare with the catechism in certitude or in power.
> It transforms tender children into sure theologians, . . . a fortress against
> atheism and a bulwark for the freedom and the life of man.[5]

Lacointe's proposal, while prophetic, was not without a context, nor did it result in instant solutions. The actual composition of the *Directory* did not occur overnight or in a catechetical vacuum. The history of the development of the document is itself quite significant, and the story of its composition is inextricably bound to the larger narrative of the history of catechesis that unfolded in the century of activity between the two Vatican Councils. One obvious and proximate source for the development of catechetical theory in the years prior to Vatican II was the international catechetical study weeks. These study weeks, which were organized by Johannes Hofinger and others through the East Asian Pastoral Institute, functioned as think tanks for catechetical theorists and practitioners during the preconciliar years, as they reflected on pastoral experience, crafted theories and tested ideas among peers.[6] In his analysis and official commentary on the GCD, Berard Marthaler notes that the fingerprints of the catechetical study weeks can be found on the *Directory*; the study week at Medellin (1968) functioned as the principal source for part one of the *Directory*, while conclusions to the study weeks held at Katigando (1964) and Manila (1967) "furnish much of the vocabulary found in part two."[7]

More than vocabulary, the *Directory* represents a new genre for catechesis. Having received its impetus from the Council document on the pastoral office of bishops, the *Directory* does not offer content so much as orientation to the ministry of the word, and it locates catechesis within that ministry. Moreover, it assumes a broad understanding of the human being (more than one's cognition) as the person experiences and expresses faith in the context of modern culture. A review of the structure of the document demonstrates these emphases.

THE STRUCTURE AND THE PURPOSE

The document underwent several revisions in the process of preparation through the auspices of the Sacred Congregation for the Clergy. The *Directory* is divided into six basic sections. Part one outlines the "Reality of the Problem," with an overview of the situation in the world and within the church. This section illustrates the orientation of the Second Vatican Council with respect to the ongoing recognition that the church and the world must be in dialogue, as each enriches and challenges the other. Part two of the *Directory* locates catechesis as a "Ministry of the Word" alongside evangelization, liturgy and theology. Part three outlines the content of catechesis and does so from the perspective of the mystery of salvation found in scripture and the continuing tradition of the church. The explanation of content is redolent of what one theologian has called the historical event approach to revelation.[8]

Part four considers "Elements of Methodology" with a bias toward the importance of the catechist. The catechist functions in the dual role of a model of faith as well as a professional who understands the proper place of memory and memorization, the distinctions between inductive and deductive reasoning, and the contemporary trends that inform the culture of the learners. Part five is fresh in its insistence that catechesis occurs in successive age levels that correspond to the successive growth and maturation of the hearers of the word, who apprehend the faith and existential questions in various ways according to their level of development. Part six, the last major section, is a reworking of the earlier *Directory* draft of 1969 on catechetical aids and resources that would enhance the tasks; it also proceeds from the Vatican II concern to secure interaction between the world church and episcopal conferences in the design of catechetical programs for the future. The final section is an addendum that deals with the controversy over the order of reception of first eucharist and penance, based in the varying interpretations and practices in the years following the International Catechetical Congress held in Rome in 1971.[9]

THE LEGACY OF THE GCD — THE AIM OF CATECHESIS: MATURE FAITH

The conciliar document *Christus Dominus* identifies the role of the bishop as essential to the vitality of catechesis.[10] That same document contains a challenging and often quoted exhortation for catechists about the real aim of catechesis: the fostering of a faith that is "living, conscious and active, through the light of instruction."[11] While it is clear that the development of living conscious and active faith is a lifelong pursuit, the text of the GCD emphasizes the need to present the unity of the content of catechesis in order to reach the goal; hence the authors of the *Directory* also press the point that the content of the faith needs to be presented as an organic whole, initially as a simple presentation of the entire structure of the Christian message (GCD, 38).

The GCD paints a portrait of the personal face of faith as that profound and mysterious gift that is present in the life of the Christian without willing or expecting it. The mystery of faith functions in the life of the Christian in a holistic way in the person. The *Directory* integrates the insights from social science research that analyze the many ways in which the human being matures. Faith apprehension and expression are among those items that are subject to the process of development, the theorists concurred. This truth is generally accepted in current church and university discussion but quite new when the GCD was composed. The *Directory*'s treatment of faith development reveals an advance in the fundamental description of the human being as one who grows in faith. The theory of faith development also follows upon the nuanced understanding of faith as a response to revelation in the human being's life, as found in the conciliar Constitution on Divine Revelation, *Dei verbum*.

THE CONTENT OF AND THE GENRE FOR CATECHESIS: MORE THAN A CATECHISM

Perhaps more immediate to our current situation in the church, the GCD is fresh in its offering the church a new genre for catechetics, resulting from the gradual acceptance in the twentieth century of a new way of imagining the ministry of catechesis. The ministry of catechesis, rediscovered as a ministry of the word, expands the apprehension of the term catechesis. By the very use of the ancient term, the activity of sharing faith no longer can be equated simply and exhaustively with the word "catechism." The *Directory*, in representing a new genre, also articulates a sea change in thought about the constitutive elements of sharing faith. As a product of the thinking of the Second Vatican Council, the GCD assumes that a "return to the sources" of scripture and liturgy (that many theologians and ecclesial voices prior to Vatican II had called for) decidedly informs and radically reforms the method as well as the content of catechesis. The renewal of the church's catechumenate is one example of the functional difference that this essential change in approach caused in the postconciliar church. The *Directory* offers a similar example on the level of theory to the catechumenate on the level of practice. Both stand as witnesses to the insights shared by catechetical prophets in the church before the Council and the official acceptance of those insights in documents such as the GCD: The act of sharing faith cannot and should not be reduced, either in practice or in theory, to the sharing of intellectual knowledge as summarized in a catechism. As the *Catechism of the Catholic Church* finds a place in the practice of catechesis in the postconciliar era, the GCD will help to provide the context for its reception. The *Directory* can aid the next generation of catechists, who will learn much from the generation that gave us the *Directory*.

NOTES

1. Congregatio pro Clericis, *Directorium Catechisticum Generale*. AAS 64 (1972): 97–176. The official commentary, prepared by Berard L. Marthaler, "situates the General Directory in the context of present-day catechetics out of which it came and to which it is addressed." Berard L. Marthaler, *Catechetics in Context: Notes and Commentary on the General Catechetical Directory Issued by the Sacred Congregation for the Clergy* (Huntington IN: Our Sunday Visitor, 1973): xiii.

2. A detailed study of the deliberations about the catechism at Vatican I can be found in Michael Donnellan, *Rationale for a Universal Catechism* (PhD dissertation, The Catholic University of America, 1972).

3. Interestingly, the minority voice argued that the preparation of a universal small catechism constituted, among other things, an infringement on the rights and responsibilities of the bishops in their local dioceses. For example, see Michael Donnellan, "Bishops and Uniformity in Religious Education: Vatican I to Vatican II," *The Living Light* 10 (1973): 237–48, especially 239–42.

4. *Acta et documenta* I, vol. 11, app. 11, 482; as cited in Michael Donnellan, "Bishops and Uniformity in Religious Education: Vatican I to Vatican II," *The Living Light* 10 (1973): 237–48; the note is on 248. Lacointe's contribution to the discussion of directories is narrated in Berard L. Marthaler, *Catechetics in Context* (as above); Marthaler's study also offers historical context for this discussion.

5. Sermon to the delegates at the CCD Congress, Chicago, 1951, *The Confraternity Comes of Age* (Paterson NJ: Confraternity Publications, 1956), quoted in Michael Donnellan, "Bishops and Uniformity," *The Living Light* 10 (1973): 248.

6. Luis Erdozain, "The Evolution of Catechetics: A Survey of Six International Study Weeks on Catechetics," *Lumen Vitae* 25 (1970): 7–31, which reports the emphases and the conclusions of the meetings that took place from 1959 through 1968.

7. Berard L. Marthaler, *Catechetics in Context:* xxvii. For an exposition of the event and significance of the catechetical study weeks, see Luis Erdozain, "The Evolution of Catechetics," *Lumen Vitae* 25 (1970): 7–13.

8. Avery Dulles, *Models of Revelation* (Garden City NY: Doubleday and Company, 1983): 53–67.

9. The 1971 International Congress recommendation that each child be treated as an individual and that parents of the child help to determine the child's readiness for the reception of the sacraments was interpreted differently in a variety of dioceses and touched off a debate about the proper order of reception. See Marthaler, *Catechetics in Context:* 261–79, especially 273ff.

10. CD, 44.

11. CD, 14.

OUTLINE

FOREWORD

This *General Catechetical Directory* is published in accord with the directive in the *Decree on the Bishops' Pastoral Office in the Church*, n. 44.

Considerable time was spent in the preparation of this document, not only because of the difficulties involved in a work of this sort, but also because of the method which was used in producing it.

Thus, after a special Commission was set up consisting of men truly expert in catechesis — they were of various nationalities and had been selected after consultation with certain episcopates — the first thing done was to seek the advice and opinions of the various episcopates.

With that advice and those opinions in mind, a first draft of the *Directory* was worked up in an outline form showing only the principal features. This was examined at a special plenary session of the Sacred Congregation for the Clergy. After that, a longer draft was prepared, and once again the Conferences of Bishops were queried so that they might express their opinion about it. In accord with the advice and observations given by the bishops in this second consultation, a definitive draft of the *Directory* was prepared. Even so, before this was published, it was reviewed by a special theological commission and by the Sacred Congregation for the Doctrine of the Faith.

The intent of this *Directory* is to provide the basic principles of pastoral theology — these principles have been taken from the Magisterium of the Church, and in a special way from the Second General Vatican Council — by which pastoral action in the ministry of the word can be more fittingly directed and governed. This explains why the theoretical aspect is given primary emphasis in this *Directory*, although, as will be evident, the practical aspect is by no means neglected. Such a course of action was adopted especially for the following reason: the errors which are not infrequently noted in catechetics today can be avoided only if one starts with the correct way of understanding the nature and purposes of catechesis and also the truths which are to be taught by it, with due account being taken of those to whom catechesis is directed and of the conditions in which they live. Moreover, the specific task of applying the principles and declarations contained in this *Directory* to concrete situations properly belongs to the various episcopates, and they do this by means of national and regional directories, and by means or catechisms and the other aids which are suitable for effectively promoting the work of the ministry of the word.

It is clear that not all parts of the *Directory* are of the same importance. Those things which are said about divine revelation, the criteria according to which the Christian message is to be expounded, and the more outstanding elements of that same message, are to be held by all. On the other hand, those things which are said about the present situation, methodology, and the form of catechesis for people of differing ages, are to be taken rather as suggestions and guides, for a number of them are of necessity taken from the human sciences, theoretical as well as practical, and these are indeed subject to some evolution.

The *Directory* is chiefly intended for bishops, Conferences of Bishops, and in general all who under their leadership and direction have responsibility in the catechetical field. The immediate purpose of the *Directory* is to provide assistance in the production of catechetical directories and catechisms. Indeed, it is for this reason, that is, to help in the preparation of these tools, that the following have been done. Some basic features of present-day conditions have been set forth, so as to stimulate studies in the various parts of the Church, studies which should be carried out with careful and diligent effort, with regard to local conditions and local pastoral needs. Some general principles of methodology and catechesis for different age groups have been noted, so as to highlight how necessary it is to learn the art and wisdom of education. Special pains have been taken in the composition of Part Three, where the criteria which should govern the presentation of the truths to be taught through catechesis are set forth and where a summary of essential elements of the Christian faith is also given, so as to make fully clear the goal which catechesis must of necessity have, namely, the presentation of the Christian faith in its entirety.

Since the *Directory* is intended for countries which differ greatly in their conditions and pastoral needs, it is obvious that only common or average conditions could be considered in it. Therefore, in judging and evaluating the *Directory*, one will have to give due consideration to this particular feature as well as to the structure. The same thing must be said about the description of pastoral work given in Part Six. It deals with the plan of pastoral action that is to be promoted, and this is described only in general outlines. This will perhaps be inadequate for those areas in which catechesis has already made great strides, while, on the other hand, in those places where catechesis has not yet advanced very far, it will perhaps seem to demand too much.

With the publication of this document the Church gives new evidence of her concern for a ministry which is absolutely necessary for proper fulfillment of her mission in the world. It is prayerfully hoped that this document will be accepted and be carefully studied and weighed, with attention to the pastoral needs of the individual ecclesial communities. It is similarly hoped that this document will be able to stimulate new and more vigorous studies that faithfully respond to the needs of the ministry of the word and to the norms of the Magisterium of the Church.

PART ONE
THE REALITY OF THE PROBLEM

1.   Since the essential mission of the Church is to proclaim and promote the faith in contemporary human society, a society disturbed by very great socio-cultural changes, it is appropriate here, with the declarations of the Second Vatican Council in mind, to sketch some features and characteristics of the present situation by pointing out the spiritual repercussions they have and the new obligations the Church has as a result. The discussion here is not meant to be exhaustive, because the subject covers points which are unique and often very much different in the various parts of the Church. National directories will have the task of filling out this outline and applying it to the circumstances of individual countries and regions.

THE WORLD

THE MODERN WORLD IN CONTINUAL DEVELOPMENT

2.   "Today, the human race is passing through a new stage of its history. Profound and rapid changes are spreading by degrees around the world. . . . Hence we can already speak of a true social and cultural transformation, one which has repercussions on man's religious life as well" (GS, 4).

As examples, two repercussions on the life of faith which more directly affect catechesis can be cited:

a) In times past, the cultural tradition favored the transmission of the faith to a greater extent than it does today; in our times, however, the cultural tradition has undergone considerable change, with the result that less and less can one depend on continued transmission by means of it. Because of this, some renewal in evangelization is needed for transmitting the same faith to new generations.

b) It should be noted that the Christian faith requires explanations and new forms of expression so that it may take root in all successive cultures. Though the aspirations and basic needs peculiar to human nature and the human condition remain essentially the same, nevertheless, men of our era are posing new questions about the meaning and importance of life.

Believers of our time are certainly not in all respects like believers of the past. This is why it becomes necessary to affirm the permanence of the faith and to present the message of salvation in renewed ways.

Today one must also keep in mind the very great diffusion of the instruments of social communication, the influence of which extends beyond national boundaries and makes individual persons citizens as it were of human society as a whole (cf. IM, 22).

Such instruments exert very great influence on the lives of Christians, whether because of the things they teach or because of the style of thinking and mode of behavior they introduce among these same Christians. It is necessary to take account of this fact and to give it all due attention.

PLURALISM TODAY

3.   "By this very circumstance, the traditional local communities such as father-centered families, clans, tribes, villages, various groups and associations stemming from social contacts experience more thorough changes every day" (GS, 6).

In Christianity of old, religion was regarded as the chief principle of unity among peoples. Things are otherwise now. The cohesion of peoples which stems from the phenomenon of democratization promotes harmony among various spiritual families. "Pluralism," as it is called, is no longer viewed as an evil to be eliminated, but rather as a fact which must be taken into account; anyone can make his own decisions known without becoming or being regarded as alien to society.

Therefore, those engaged in the ministry of the word should never forget that faith is a free response to the grace of the revealing God. And to an even greater extent than this was done in the past, they should present the good news of Christ in its remarkable character both as the mysterious key to understanding of the whole human condition and as a free gift of God which is to be received by means of heavenly grace upon admission of one's own insufficiency (cf. GS, 10).

THE DYNAMISM OF OUR AGE

4.   The building up of human society, human progress, and the ongoing execution of human plans stimulate the concern or the men of our era (cf. GS, 4). Faith should by no means keep itself as it were outside that human progress. Joined with that progress there are indeed even now serious aberrations. Accordingly, the Gospel message should pass judgment on this state of affairs and tell men what it means.

The ministry of the word, through an ever-deeper study of the divine and human calling of man, must permit the Gospel to spread its own vital seeds of genuine freedom and progress (cf. AG, 8,12) and to stimulate a desire for promoting the growth of the human person and for contending against that way of acting and thinking which tends toward fatalism.

What has been said above is meant merely to show how today's ministry of the word ought to direct its activity toward this world: ". . . it is demanded from the Church that she inject the perennial, vital, divine power of the Gospel into the human society of today" (John XXIII, Apost. Const. *Humanae salutis*, AAS, 1962, p. 6).

5.   That form of civilization which is called scientific, technical, industrial, and urban not infrequently diverts the attention of men from matters divine and makes their inner concerns with regard to religion more difficult. Many feel that God is less present, and less needed, and God seems to them less able to explain things in both personal and social life. Hence a religious crisis can easily arise (cf. GS, 5, 7).

The Christian faith, as are the other religious confessions, is experiencing a crisis of this sort among its followers. It has an urgent duty, therefore, to manifest its true nature, by virtue of which it transcends every advancement of culture, and to show forth its newness in cultures which have been secularized and desacralized.

It is a function of the ministry of the word to uncover, purify, and develop the authentic values which are found in the spiritual heritage of those human cultures wherein a religious sense remains alive and operative and is all-pervasive in human life.

In times past, faulty opinions and errors about the faith and the Christian way of life generally reached a comparatively small number of people, and were to a greater extent than is so today confined within groups of intellectuals. Now, however, human progress and the instruments of social communication are having this effect: faulty opinions are being spread abroad with greater speed and are exerting an ever-wider influence among the faithful, young adults especially, who suffer grave crises and are not infrequently driven to adopt ways of acting and thinking that are hostile to religion. This situation calls for pastoral remedies that are truly adapted to the circumstances.

THE CHURCH

The particular characteristics of the spiritual condition of the world are also found in the life of the Church herself.

"TRADITIONAL" FAITH

6.   The faith of many Christians is strained to a critical point in those places where religion was seeming to favor the prerogatives of certain social classes to an excessive degree, or where it was depending too much on ancestral customs and on regional unanimity in religious profession.

Great numbers are drifting little by little into religious indifferentism, or are continuing in danger of keeping the faith without the dynamism that is necessary, a faith without effective influence on their actual lives. The question now is not one of merely preserving traditional religious customs, but rather one of also fostering an appropriate re-evangelization of men, obtaining their reconversion, and giving them a deeper and more mature education in the faith.

By no means, however, is the above to be interpreted in such a way that it results in neglect of the genuine faith which is preserved within groups in a culture that is traditionally Christian, or in a low estimation of the popular religious sense. Despite the growth of secularization, a religious sense continues to flourish in the various parts of the Church. No one can fail to note it, for it is expressed in ordinary life by a very large number of people, and for the most part in a sincere and authentic way. In fact, the popular religious sense provides an opportunity or starting point for proclaiming the faith. The question is, as is clear, only one of purifying it and of correctly appraising its valid elements, so that no one will be content with forms of pastoral act on which today have become unequal to the task, altogether unsuitable, and perhaps even irrelevant.

RELIGIOUS INDIFFERENTISM AND ATHEISM

7.   Many baptized persons have withdrawn so far from their religion that they profess a form of indifferentism or something close to atheism. "Still, many of our contemporaries recognize in no way this intimate and vital link with God, or else they explicitly reject it. Thus atheism must be accounted among the most serious problems of this age, and must be subjected to closer examination" (GS, 19).

The Second Vatican Council gave the matter careful consideration (cf. GS, 19 – 20) and dealt expressly with remedies to be applied: "The remedy which must be applied to atheism, however, is to be sought in a proper presentation of the Church's teaching as well as in the integral life of the Church and her members. For it is a function of the Church to make God the Father and his incarnate Son present and in a sense visible by ceaselessly renewing and purifying herself under the guidance of the Holy Spirit. This result is achieved chiefly by the witness of a living and mature faith, namely, one trained to see difficulties clearly and to master them" (GS, 21).

There are also cases in which the Christian faith is found contaminated with a new form of paganism, even though some religious sense and some faith in a Supreme Being persist. A religious disposition can exist far from the influence of the word of God and from the practice of the sacraments, but be nourished by the practice of superstition and magic; moral life can fall back into pre-Christian ethics. Sometimes elements of nature worship, animism, and divination are introduced into the Christian religion, and thus in some places a lapse into syncretism can occur. Moreover, religious sects are being propagated which mingle together the Christian mysteries and elements of fables from antiquity.

In these cases, there is the greatest possible need for the ministry of the word, especially evangelization and catechesis, to be renewed in accord with the *Decree on the Missionary Activity of the Church*, 13, 14, 21, 22.

FAITH AND VARIOUS CULTURES

8.   There are some members of the faithful who have had an excellent Christian education who are having difficulty with regard to the way of expressing the faith. They think it is bound up too much with ancient and obsolete formulations and too much tied to Western culture. They are, therefore, seeking a new way of expressing the truths of religion, one which conforms to the present

human condition, allows the faith to illumine the realities pressing upon men today, and makes it possible for the Gospel to be brought over to other cultures. The Church certainly has a duty to give all possible consideration to this aspiration of men.

What is declared in the *Decree on the Missionary Activity of the Church* for recently established churches is also valid for all who labor in the ministry of the word: "From the customs and traditions of their people, From their wisdom and their learning, from their arts and sciences, these churches borrow all those things which can contribute to the glory of their Creator, the revelation of the Savior's grace, and the proper arrangement of Christian life" (AG, 22; cf. AG, 21; Paul VI, Alloc., August 6, 1969).

Consequently, "by presenting the Gospel message to men in a renewed way, the ministry of the word should show clearly the unity of the divine plan of salvation. Avoiding confusions and simplistic identifications, the message should always show clearly the deep and intimate harmony that exists between God's salvific plan, fulfilled in Christ the Lord, and human aspirations, between the history of salvation and human history, between the Church, the People of God, and human communities, between God's revelatory action and man's experience, between supernatural gifts and charisms and human values" (Comm. 5-s/comm. 2 General Conference of Bishops of Latin America, 1968).

THE WORK OF RENEWAL

9.   In this new state of affairs, it is possible for one to suppose that the apostolic fervor which the Church is now striving to promote is being impeded. Certainly neither the shepherds nor the faithful should be faulted on zeal, which they in fact have in large measure. The impediments seem rather to result either from a widespread failure to prepare suitably for the new and difficult tasks, or from a kind of thinking, as yet not fully developed, which is at times expressed in theories that hinder rather than help evangelization.

Having duly considered these things, the Sacred Synod of Vatican II time and again urged renewal of the ministry of the word in the Church. This renewal seems today to be entering a period of crisis, being led there especially by:

— *those who are unable to understand the depth of the proposed renewal*, as though the issue here were merely one of eliminating ignorance of the doctrine which must be taught. According to the thinking of those people, the remedy would be more frequent catechetical instruction. Once the matter has been considered that way, that remedy is immediately seen to be altogether unequal to the needs. In fact, the catechetical plan is to be thoroughly renewed, and this renewal has to do with a continuing education in the faith, not only for children but also for adults.

— *those who are inclined to reduce the Gospel message to the consequences it has in men's temporal existence.*

The Gospel and its law of love do, of course, demand that Christians, each according to his strength, work together—fulfilling their secular duties and responsibilities—to restore justice and brotherhood among men more and more. That, however, does not in any way satisfy the need to give due witness to Jesus Christ, God's Son and our Savior, whose mystery, which revealed God's ineffable love (cf. 1 John 4:9), must be proclaimed openly and in its entirety to those being evangelized, and must be examined by them.

The teaching of the *Pastoral Constitution on the Church in the Modern World* and the *Declaration on Religious Freedom* countenance no "minimalism" in explaining the service of the faith directed through the ministry of the word. Both these documents show concern for providing a remedy for the state of affairs described above. Renewal in the ministry of the word, especially in catechesis, can in no way be separated from general pastoral renewal.

Steps which are effective and indeed of the greatest importance for good results must be taken: promoting the growth of the customary forms of the ministry of the word and stimulating new ones; evangelizing and catechizing men of lower cultural levels: reaching the educated classes and taking care of their needs; improving the traditional forms of the Christian presence and finding new ways; gathering together all the practical aids of the Church and at the same time avoiding forms which are not in accord with the Gospel.

In carrying out this task, the Church places her hope in all members of the People of God. Everyone—bishops, priests, men and women religious, lay people—should by all means fulfill his mission, each according to his responsibilities. And indeed each should fulfill his mission with attention to the state of the world which profoundly affects the life of faith.

So that effective help may be given these workers in the service of the Gospel, the catechetical renewal ought to use the help which can be given by the sacred sciences, theology, bible studies, pastoral thought, and the human sciences, and also the instruments by which ideas and opinions are spread, especially the social communications media.

PART TWO
THE MINISTRY OF THE WORD
CHAPTER I
THE MINISTRY OF THE WORD AND REVELATION

REVELATION: GOD'S GIFT

10. In the *Dogmatic Constitution on Divine Revelation,* the General Council looked at revelation as the act by which God communicates himself in a personal way: "In his goodness and wisdom, God chose to reveal himself and to make known the hidden purpose of his will . . . so that he may invite and take men into fellowship with himself" (DV, 2). God appears there as one who wishes to communicate himself, carrying out a plan which proceeds from love.

Catechesis, then, ought to take its beginning from this gift of divine love. Faith is the acceptance and coming to fruit of the divine gift in us. This characteristic, by which faith is to be considered as a gift, has a direct bearing on the whole subject-matter of the ministry of the word.

REVELATION: DEEDS AND WORDS

11.   So that men may come to a knowledge of his plan, God works in this way, namely, through events in the history of salvation and through the divinely inspired words which accompany these events and clarify them: "This plan of revelation is realized by deeds and words having an inner unity: the deeds wrought by God in the history of salvation manifest and confirm the teaching and realities signified by the words, while the words proclaim the deeds and clarify the mystery contained in them" (DV, 2).

Revelation, therefore, consists of deed and words, the ones illuminating, and being illuminated by, the others. The ministry of the word should proclaim these deeds and words in such a way that the loftiest mysteries contained in them are further explained and communicated by it. In this way the ministry of the word not only recalls the revelation of God's wonders which was made in time and brought to perfection in Christ, but at the same time, in the light of this revelation, interprets human life in our age, the signs of the times, and the things of this world, for the plan of God works in these for the salvation of men.

JESUS CHRIST: MEDIATOR AND FULLNESS OF ALL REVELATION

12.   "By this revelation, then, the deepest truth . . . is made clear to us in Christ, who is the Mediator and at the same time the fullness of all revelation" (DV, 2).

Christ is not only the greatest of prophets, who by his teaching fulfilled those things which had been said and done by God in earlier times. He himself is the eternal Son of God, made man, and thus the last event to which all events in the history of salvation look and which fulfills and manifests the final plans of God. "For this reason he . . . perfected revelation by fulfilling it . . . " (DV, 4; cf. LG, 9).

The ministry of the word ought to direct attention to this wonderful characteristic peculiar to the economy of revelation. The Son of God inserts himself into the history of men, takes to himself the life and death of a man, and in this history fulfills his plan of the Covenant.

In the same way as does the Evangelist Luke, the ministry of the word ought first to recall the event of Jesus for believers, by manifesting its meaning and by searching more and more into this unique and irreversible fact: "Many have undertaken to compile a narrative of the events which have been fulfilled in our midst. . . . I too have carefully traced the whole sequence of events from the beginning, and have decided to set it in writing for you" (Luke 1:1–3).

Therefore, the ministry of the word should be based on the divinely inspired exposition regarding the redemptive incarnation, the exposition which has been given us by Jesus himself and by the first disciples and especially the apostles, who were witnesses of the events. "It is common knowledge that among all [the Scriptures] . . . the Gospels have a special pre-eminence, and rightly so, for they are the principal witness of the life and teaching of the incarnate Word, Our Savior" (DV, 18).

Moreover, it is to be recalled that Jesus, the Messiah and Lord, is through his Spirit always present to his Church (cf. John 14:26; 15:26; 16:13; Revelation 2:7). Accordingly, the ministry of the word presents Christ not only as its object but also as the one who opens the hearts of hearers to receive and understand the divine proclamation (cf. Acts 16:14).

MINISTRY OF THE WORD OR PREACHING OF THE WORD OF GOD:
ACT OF LIVING TRADITION

13. "Now what was handed on by the apostles includes everything which contributes to the holiness of life and the increase in faith of the People of God; and so the Church, in her teaching, life, and worship, perpetuates and hands on to all generations all that she herself is, all that she believes" (DV, 8).

This tradition is bound up with things that have been said. In scope and depth, however, it is more than these sayings. It is a living tradition, since through it God continues his conversation. "And thus God, who spoke of old, uninterruptedly converses with the Bride of his beloved Son; and the Holy Spirit, through whom the living voice of the Gospel resounds in the Church, and through her, in the world . . ." (DV, 8).

This is why the ministry of the word can be considered as that which gives voice to this living tradition, within the totality of tradition. "This tradition which comes from the apostles develops in the Church with the help of the Holy Spirit. For there is a growth in the understanding of the realities and the words which have been handed down. This happens through the contemplation and study made by believers, who treasure these things in their hearts, through the intimate understanding of spiritual things they experience, and through the preaching of those who have received through episcopal succession the sure gift of truth" (DV, 8).

On the one hand, the divine revelation which constitutes the object of the Catholic faith and which was completed at the time of the apostles, must be clearly distinguished from the grace of the Holy Spirit, without whose inspiration and illumination no one can believe. On the other hand, God, who formerly spoke to the human race by revealing himself through divine deeds together with the message of the prophets, of Christ, and of the apostles, even now still secretly directs, through the Holly Spirit, in sacred tradition, by the light and sense of the faith the Church, his bride, and he speaks with her, so that the People of God, under the leadership of the Magisterium, may attain a fuller understanding of revelation.

The Church's shepherds not only proclaim and explain directly to the People of God the deposit of faith which has been committed to them, but moreover they make authentic judgments regarding expressions of that deposit and the explanations which he faithful seek and offer. They do this in such a way that "in holding to, practicing, and professing the heritage of the faith, there results on the part of the bishops and faithful a remarkable common effort" (DV, 10).

From this it follows that it is necessary for the ministry of the word to set forth the divine revelation such as it is taught by the Magisterium and such as it expresses itself, under the watchfulness of the Magisterium, in the living awareness and faith of the People of God. In this way the ministry of the word is not a mere repetition of ancient doctrine, but rather it is a faithful reproduction of it, with adaptation to new problems and with a growing understanding of it.

SACRED SCRIPTURE

14.   Under special inspiration of the Holy Spirit, divine revelation has also been expressed in writings, that is, in the sacred books of the Old and New Testaments, books which contain and present divinely revealed truth (cf. DV, 11).

The Church, guardian and interpreter of the Sacred Scriptures, learns from them, by constantly meditating on and penetrating more and more into their teaching. Remaining faithful in tradition, the ministry of the word finds its nourishment and its norm in Sacred Scripture (cf. DV, 21, 24, 25). For in the sacred books the Father, who is in heaven, very lovingly meets with his children and speaks with them (cf. DV, 21).

But if it takes its norm for thinking from Sacred Scripture, the Church, inspired by the Spirit, interprets that same Scripture: "and the sacred writings themselves are more profoundly understood and unceasingly made active in her" (DV, 8).

The ministry of the word, therefore, takes its beginning from Holy Writ and from the preaching of the apostles, as these are understood, explained, and applied in concrete situations by the Church.

FAITH: RESPONSE TO THE WORD OF GOD

15.   By faith man accepts revelation, and through it he consciously becomes a sharer in the gift of God.

The obedience of faith must be offered to the God who reveals. By this, man, with full homage of his mind and will, freely assents to the Gospel or the grace of God (cf. Acts 20:24). Instructed by faith, man, through the gift of the Spirit, comes to contemplate and savor the God of love, the God who has made known the riches of his glory in Christ (cf. Colossians 1:26). Indeed, a living faith is the beginning in us of eternal life in which the mysteries of God (cf. 1 Corinthians 2:10) will at last be seen unveiled. Informed of God's plan of salvation, faith leads man to full discernment of the divine will towards us in this world, and to cooperation with his grace. "For faith throws a new light on everything, manifests God's design for man's total vocation, and thus directs the mind to solutions which are fully human" (GS, 11).

16.   To put the whole matter in a few words the minister of the word should be honestly aware of the mission assigned to him. It is to stir up a lively faith which turns the mind to God, impels conformance with his action, leads to a living knowledge of the expressions of tradition, and speaks and manifests the true significance of the world and human existence.

The ministry of the word is the communication of the message of salvation: it brings the Gospel to men. The mystery which has been announced and handed down deeply influences that will to have life that innermost desire for attaining fulfillment, and that expectation of future happiness which God has implanted in the heart of every man and which by his grace he raises to the supernatural order.

The truths to be believed include God's love. He created all things for the sake of Christ and restored us to life in Christ Jesus. The various aspects of the mystery are to be explained in such a way that the central fact, Jesus, as he is God's greatest gift to men, holds first place, and that from him the other truths of Catholic teaching derive their order and hierarchy from the educational point of view (cf. 43, 49).

CHAPTER II
CATECHESIS IN THE PASTORAL MISSION OF THE CHURCH
(NATURE, PURPOSE, EFFICACY)

MINISTRY OF THE WORD IN THE CHURCH

17.   The ministry of the word takes many forms, including catechesis, according to the different conditions under which it is practiced and the ends which it strives to achieve.

There is the form called evangelization, or missionary preaching. This has as its purpose the arousing of the beginnings of faith (cf. CD, 11, 13; AG, 6,13, 14), so that men will adhere to the word of God.

Then there is the catechetical form, "which is intended to make men's faith become living, conscious, and active, through the light of instruction" (CD, 14).

And then there is the liturgical form, within the setting of a liturgical celebration, especially that of the Eucharist (e.g., the homily) (cf. SC, 33, 52; *Inter Oecum.* 54).

Finally, there is the theological form, that is, the systematic treatment and the scientific investigation of the truths of faith.

For our purpose it is important to keep these forms distinct, since they are governed by their own laws. Nevertheless, in the concrete reality of the pastoral ministry, they are closely bound together.

Accordingly, all that has so far been said about the ministry of the word in general is to be applied also to catechesis.

18.   Catechesis proper presupposes a global adherence to Christ's Gospel as presented by the Church. Often, however, it is directed to men who, though they belong to the Church, have in fact never given a true personal adherence to the message of revelation.

This shows that, according to circumstances, evangelization can precede or accompany the work of catechesis proper. In every case, however, one must keep in mind that the element of conversion is always present in the dynamism of faith, and for that reason any form of catechesis must also perform the role of evangelization.

FORMS OF CATECHESIS

19.   Because of varied circumstances and multiple needs, catechetical activity necessarily takes various forms.

In regions which have been Christian from of old, catechesis often takes the form of religious instruction given to children and adolescents in schools or outside a school atmosphere. Also found in those regions are various catechetical programs for adults. There are also various catechumenate programs for those who are preparing themselves for the reception of baptism, or for those who have been baptized but lack a proper Christian initiation. Very often the actual condition of large numbers of the faithful necessarily demands that some form of evangelization of the baptized precede catechesis.

In churches that have been established recently, special importance is placed on the work of evangelizing in the strict sense. Accordingly, they have the well-known form of the catechumenate for those who are being initiated in the faith so that they may prepare themselves for receiving baptism (cf. AG, 4).

In a word, catechetical activity can take on forms and structures that are quite varied, that is to say, it can be systematic or occasional, for individuals or for communities, organized or spontaneous, and so on.

20.   Shepherds of souls should always keep in mind the obligation they have of safeguarding and promoting the enlightenment of Christian existence through the word of God for people of all ages and in all historical circumstances (cf. CD, 14), so that it may be possible to have contact with every individual and community in the spiritual state in which each one is.

They should also remember that catechesis for adults, since it deals with persons who are capable of an adherence that is fully responsible, must be considered the chief form of catechesis. All the other forms, which are indeed always necessary, are in some way oriented to it. In obedience to the norms of the Second Vatican Council, shepherds of souls should also strive "to reestablish or better adapt the instruction of adult catechumens" (CD, 14; cf. AG, 14).

21. Within the scope of pastoral activity, catechesis is the term to be used for that form of ecclesial action which leads both communities and individual members of the faithful to maturity of faith.

With the aid of catechesis, communities of Christians acquire for themselves a more profound living knowledge of God and of his plan of salvation, which has its center in Christ, the incarnate Word of God. They build themselves up by striving to make their faith mature and enlightened, and to share this mature faith with men who desire to possess it.

For every man whose mind is open to the message of the Gospel, catechesis is a particularly apt means for him to understand God's plan in his own life and to examine the highest meaning of existence and history so that the life of individual men and of society may be illumined by the light of the kingdom of God and be conformed to its demands, and the mystery of the Church as the community of those who believe in the Gospel may be able to be recognized.

All these things determine the functions proper to catechesis.

CATECHESIS AND THE GRACE OF FAITH

22. Faith is a gift of God which calls men to conversion. "For this faith to be given, the grace of God and the interior help of the Holy Spirit must precede and assist, moving the heart and turning it to God, opening the eyes of the mind and giving joy and ease to everyone in assenting to the truth and believing it" (DV, 5).

The Christian community, listening to the word of God religiously, lives in a mature faith, constantly strives for conversion and renewal, and gives diligent ear to what the Spirit says to the Church.

Catechesis performs the function of disposing men to receive the action of the Holy Spirit and to deepen their conversion. It does this through the word, to which are joined the witness of life and prayer.

CATECHESIS AND PERFORMANCE OF THE DUTIES OF THE FAITH

23. A person mature in the faith fully accepts the Gospel invitation by which he is impelled to communion with God and with his brothers; he takes on in his life the duties that are connected with this invitation (cf. AG, 12).

Catechesis performs the functions of helping men make this communion with God a reality, and of presenting the Christian message in such a way that it is clear that the highest value of human life is safeguarded by it. All this requires that catechesis keep in mind the legitimate aspirations of men, as also the progress and success of the values contained in these aspirations.

Communion with God and adherence to him entail the carrying out of human responsibilities and the duty of solidarity, since all these things are in keeping with the will of God the Savior (cf. GS, 4).

Catechesis, therefore, must foster and illumine the increase of theological charity in individual members of the faithful as well as in ecclesial communities, and also the manifestations of that same virtue in connection with the duties that pertain to individuals and to the community.

CATECHESIS AND KNOWLEDGE OF THE FAITH

24.   A person mature in the faith knows the mystery of salvation revealed in Christ, and the divine signs and works which are witnesses to the fact that this mystery is being carried out in human history. It is, therefore, not sufficient for catechesis merely to stimulate a religious experience, even if it is a true one; rather, catechesis should contribute to the gradual grasping of the whole truth about the divine plan by preparing the faithful for the reading of Sacred Scripture and the learning of tradition.

CATECHESIS AND THE LIFE OF LITURGICAL AND PRIVATE PRAYER

25.   "Every liturgical celebration, because it is an action of Christ the priest and of his Body the Church, is a sacred action surpassing all others. No other action of the Church can match its claim to efficacy, nor equal the degree of it" (SC, 7). And the more mature a Christian community becomes in faith, the more it lives its worship in spirit and in truth (cf. John 4:23) in its liturgical celebrations, especially at the Eucharist.

Therefore, catechesis must promote an active, conscious, genuine participation in the liturgy of the Church, not merely by explaining the meaning of the ceremonies, but also by forming the minds of the faithful for prayer, for thanksgiving, for repentance, for praying with confidence, for a community spirit, and for understanding correctly the meaning of the creeds. All these things are necessary for a true liturgical life.

"The spiritual life, however, is not confined to participation in the liturgy. The Christian is assuredly called to pray with his brethren, but he must also enter into his chamber to pray to the Father in secret (cf. Matthew 6:6), indeed, according to the teaching of the Apostle Paul (cf. 1 Thessalonians 5:17), he should pray without ceasing" (SC, 12).

Therefore, catechesis must also train the faithful to meditate on the word of God and to engage in private prayer.

CATECHESIS AND CHRISTIAN LIGHT ON HUMAN EXISTENCE

26.   A person mature in the faith is able to recognize in various circumstances and encounters with his fellowman the invitation of God whereby he is called to work toward the fulfillment of the divine plan of salvation.

Catechesis has the task, then, of emphasizing this function by teaching the faithful to give a Christian interpretation to human events, especially to the signs of the times, so that all "will be able to test and interpret all things in a wholly Christian spirit" (GS, 62).

27.   Communities of the faithful should according to the circumstances in which they live, take part in ecumenical dialogue and the other undertakings for the restoring of Christian unity (cf. UR, 5).

Catechesis should, therefore, assist in this cause (cf. UR, 6) by clearly explaining the Churches doctrine in its entirety (cf. UR, 11) and by fostering a suitable knowledge of other confessions, both in matters where they agree with the Catholic faith, and also in matters where they differ. In doing this. it should avoid words and methods of explaining doctrine that could "lead separated brethren or anyone else into error regarding the true doctrine of the Church" (LG, 67). The order or hierarchy of the truths of Catholic teaching should be kept (cf. UR, 11; AG, 15; *Ad Ecclesiam totam*, May 14, 1967, AAS, 1967, pp. 574–592). However, the case for Catholic doctrine should be presented with charity as well as with due firmness.

CATECHESIS AND THE MISSION OF THE CHURCH IN THE WORLD

28.   The Church is in Christ like a sacrament or sign and an instrument of the salvation and of the unity of the whole human race (cf. LG, 1). It will be more noted as such, however, the more mature in faith the individual communities of the faithful become.

Catechesis should help these communities to spread the light of the Gospel and to establish a fruitful dialogue with men and cultures that are not Christian, preserving here religious freedom correctly understood (cf. DH; AG, 22).

CATECHESIS AND ESCHATOLOGICAL HOPE

29.   A person mature in the faith directs his thoughts and desires to the full consummation of the kingdom in eternal life.

Catechesis, therefore, performs the function of directing the hope of men in the first place to the future goods which are in the heavenly Jerusalem. At the same time, it calls men to be willing to cooperate in the undertakings of their neighbors and of the human race for the improvement of human society (cf. GS, 39, 40–43).

CATECHESIS AND DEVELOPMENT OF THE LIFE OF FAITH

30.   Among the faithful the one faith is found to be more or less intense according to the grace that is given to each one by the Holy Spirit, grace which must constantly be asked for in prayer (cf. Mark 9:23), and according to the response that each one gives to this grace. Moreover, the life of faith passes through various stages, just as does man's existence while he is attaining maturity and taking on the duties of his life. Consequently, the life of faith admits of various degrees, both in the global acceptance of the total word of God and in the explanation of that word and the application of it to the different duties of human life, according to the maturity of each and the differences of individuals (cf. 38). Certainly, the acceptance of this faith and its explanation and application to the

life of man are different according to whether there is question of the very young, children, adolescents, young adults, or adults. Catechesis has the function of lending aid for the beginning and the progress of this life of faith throughout the entire course of a man's existence, all the way to the full explanation of revealed truth and the application of it to man's life.

RICHNESS OF CATECHETICAL WORK

31. Catechesis is concerned with the community, but it does not neglect the individual believer. It is linked with the other pastoral functions of the Church, but it does not lose its own specific character. At one and the same time it performs the functions of initiation, education, and formation.

It is very important that catechesis retain the richness of these various aspects in such a way that one aspect is not separated from the rest to the detriment of the others.

EFFICACY OF THE WORD OF GOD IN CATECHESIS

32. This sentence from Sacred Scripture is pertinent also to catechesis: "Indeed, God's word is living and effective" (Hebrews 4:12).

The divine word becomes present in catechesis through the human word. So that it may bear fruit in man and generate inner movements which expel indifference or uncertainty and lead him to embrace the faith, catechesis ought to express the word of God faithfully and present it suitably. Furthermore, the witness given by the life of both the catechist and the ecclesial community contributes very much to the efficacy of catechesis (cf. 35).

Catechesis, therefore, should convey the word of God, as it is presented by the Church, in the language or the men to whom it is directed (cf. DV, 13; OT, 16). When God revealed himself to the human race, he made the human word the sign of his word, expressing his word in a language that belonged to a particular culture (cf. DV, 12). The Church, to whom Christ entrusted the deposit of revelation, strives until the consummation of the world to transmit, explain, and interpret this word in a lively manner for the peoples of every culture and for men of every condition.

PEDAGOGY OF GOD IN REVEALING AND OF THE CHURCH IN CATECHIZING

33. In the history of revelation God used pedagogy in such a way that he announced his plan of salvation in the Old Covenant prophetically and by means of figures, and thus prepared the coming of his Son, the author of the New Covenant and the perfecter of the faith (cf. Hebrews 12:2).

Now, however, after the consummation of revelation, the Church has the obligation of sharing the entire mystery of our salvation in Christ with the people to be instructed. Mindful of the pedagogy used by God, she too uses a pedagogy, a new one, however, one that corresponds to the new demands of his message. The Church sees to it, of course, that this message, when it has been presented without adulteration or mutilation, is accommodated to the ability of the people to be taught.

On the one hand, in order to take account of the limited ability of some, the Church explains matters rather simply and briefly, using even suitable summary formulas, which may be explained further later. On the other hand, she tries to satisfy the requirements of the more lively and capable minds by using more profound explanations.

PRESERVING FIDELITY TO GOD AND HAVING CONCERN FOR MEN

34. The Church performs this kind of function chiefly by means of catechesis (cf. DV, 24). By drawing the truth from the word of God and faithfully adhering to the secure expression of this word, catechesis strives to teach this word of God with complete fidelity. The function of catechesis, however, cannot be restricted to repetition of traditional formulas; in fact, it demands that these formulas be understood, and be faithfully expressed in language adapted to the intelligence of the hearers, using even new methods when necessary. The language will be different for different age levels, social conditions of men, human cultures, and forms of civil life (cf. DV, 8; CD, 14).

THE NECESSITY OF ECCLESIAL WITNESS

35. Catechesis, finally, demands the witness of faith, both from the catechists and from the ecclesial community, a witness that is joined to an authentic example of Christian life and to a readiness for sacrifice (cf. LG, 12,17; NA, 2).

Man encounters Christ not only through the sacred ministry, but also through individual members of the faithful and their communities (cf. LG, 35), and these accordingly have a duty to give witness. If such witness is lacking, there arises in the listeners an obstacle to the acceptance of God's word.

Catechesis must be supported by the witness of the ecclesial community. It speaks more effectively about those things which in fact exist in the community's external life as well. The catechist is in a certain way the interpreter of the Church among those who are to be instructed. He reads the signs of faith and he teaches others how to read them. The chief of these signs is the Church herself (see First Vatican Council, Dogm. Const. *Dei Filius*, DS 3014).

Hence it is clear how necessary it is that the ecclesial community, according to the mind of the Church and under the guidance of her bishops, remove or correct things that mar the appearance of the Church and constitute an obstacle for men to embrace the faith (cf. GS, 19).

Catechists, therefore, have the duty not only to impart catechesis directly, but also to offer their help in making the ecclesial community come alive, so that it will be able to give a witness that is authentically Christian.

Catechetical action, therefore, fits into that general pastoral action in which all elements of ecclesial life are properly ordered and bound together (cf. GS, 4, 7, 43).

PART THREE
THE CHRISTIAN MESSAGE

36.   Faith, the maturing of which is to be promoted by catechesis (cf. 21), can be considered in two ways, either as the total adherence given by man under the influence of grace to God revealing himself (the faith *by which* one believes), or as the content of revelation and of the Christian message (the faith *which* one believes). These two aspects are by their very nature inseparable, and a normal maturing of the faith assumes progress of both together. The two can, however, be distinguished for reasons of methodology.

The subject of this third part is the content of the faith, and it is treated in the way indicated here. The first chapter points out the norms or criteria which catechesis must observe in the discovery and exposition of its content. The second chapter will deal with that content itself. This second chapter is by no means intended to set forth each and every one of the Christian truths which constitute the object of faith and of catechesis. Nor is it desired here to present an enumeration of the chief errors of our age, or of the truths of the faith which today are being more sharply denied or neglected. The ordinary or extraordinary Magisterium of the Church provides for this point authoritatively by its public pronouncements.

Much less is there an attempt in that second chapter to show a suitable way for ordering the truths of faith according to an organic plan in a kind of synthesis which would take just account of their objective hierarchy, or of the needs more intensely felt by the men of our age, whether men are considered in the context of their age or in the perspective of their social and cultural formation. This is the task of sacred theology and of the various other kinds of exposition of Christian doctrine.

Rather, it has seemed opportune to expound in that chapter—by means of those broad formulations which encompass fuller explanations—some of the more outstanding elements contained in the saving message, elements which certainly are organically interrelated, especially in those particular features which must be brought out more clearly in a new, adapted catechesis which pursues its goal faithfully.

CHAPTER I
NORMS OR CRITERIA

THE CONTENT OF CATECHESIS IN RELATION TO THE VARIOUS FORMS
OF ECCLESIAL LIFE, IN RELATION TO DIFFERING CULTURES, AND IN RELATION
TO DIFFERENT LANGUAGES OF MEN

37.   Revelation is the manifestation of the mystery of God and of his saving action in history. It takes place through a personal communication from God to man. The content of this communication constitutes the message of salvation which is to be preached to all men.

It is, consequently, the supreme and absolutely necessary function of the Church's prophetic ministry to make the content of this message intelligible to men of all times, in order that they may be converted to God through Christ, that they may interpret their whole life in the light of faith, having considered the special conditions of events and times in which that life develops, and that they may lead a life in keeping with the dignity which the message of salvation has brought them and that faith has revealed to them.

To achieve this end, catechesis, is a most excellent opportunity for the prophetic ministry of the Church, must not only foster a strong and continuous contact with the various forms of life in the ecclesial community, but it must strive to promote a greater accord between the possible formulations of the divine message and the various cultures and diverse languages of peoples.

THE GOAL OF CATECHESIS IS TO PRESENT THE ENTIRE CONTENT

38.   The content of the message of salvation is made up of parts that are closely interrelated, even though its revelation was given by God gradually, in times past through the prophets, last of all in his Son (cf. Hebrews 1:1). Since the purpose of catechesis, as was said, consists in leading individual Christians and communities to a mature faith, it must take diligent care faithfully to present the entire treasure of the Christian message. This must surely be done according to the example of the divine pedagogy (cf. 33), but with the full store of revelation that has been divinely communicated being taken into account, so that the People of God may be nourished by it and live from it.

Catechesis begins, therefore, with a rather simple presentation of the entire structure of the Christian message (using also summary or global formulas), and it presents this in a way appropriate to the various cultural and spiritual conditions of those to be taught. By no means, however, can it stop with this first presentation, but it must be interested in presenting the content in an always more detailed and developed manner, so that individuals among the faithful and the Christian community may arrive at an always more profound and vital acceptance of the Christian message, and may judge the concrete conditions and practices of Christian life by the light of revelation.

This task of catechesis, not an easy one, must be carried out under the guidance of the Magisterium of the Church, whose duty it is to safeguard the truth of the divine message, and to watch that the ministry of the word uses appropriate forms of speaking, and prudently considers the help which theological research and the human sciences can give.

THE CONTENT OF CATECHESIS FORMS A CERTAIN ORGANIC AND LIVING BODY

39.   The object of faith embraces a content which of its very nature is complex, namely, God in his own mystery and in his saving intervention in history. All these things are known through what God himself has revealed about himself and about his works. Christ has central importance both in the salvific intervention of God and in the manifestation of him to men. Catechesis, therefore,

has as object God's mystery and works, namely the works that God has done, is doing and will do for us men and for our salvation.

A catechesis that neglects this interrelation and harmony of its content can become entirely useless for achieving its proper end.

CHRISTOCENTRISM OF CATECHESIS

40.   Christ Jesus, the incarnate Word of God, since he is the supreme reason why God intervenes in the world and manifests himself to men, is the center of the Gospel message within salvation history.

He is "the image of the invisible God, the firstborn of all creation. In him everything . . . was created" (Colossians 1:15). For he stands out as the one mighty mediator through whom God draws near to man and man is led to God (cf. 1 Timothy 2:5). In him the Church has its foundation. In him all things are brought together (cf. Ephesians 1:10). For this reason, created things and the conscience of men and the genuine values which are found in other religions and the diverse signs of the times are all to be thought of, though not univocally, as paths and steps by which it is possible to draw near to God, under the influence of grace and with an ordering to the Church of Christ (cf. LG, 16).

Hence catechesis must necessarily be Christocentric.

TRINITARIAN THEOCENTRISM OF CATECHESIS

41.   Just as Christ is the center of the history of salvation, so the mystery of God is the center from which this history takes its origin and to which it is ordered as to its last end. The crucified and risen Christ leads men to the Father by sending the Holy Spirit upon the People of God. For this reason the structure of the whole content of catechesis must be theocentric and trinitarian: through Christ, to the Father, in the Spirit.

Through Christ: The entire economy of salvation receives its meaning from the incarnate Word. It prepared his coming; it manifests and extends his kingdom on earth from the time of his death and resurrection up to his second glorious coming, which will complete the work of God. So it is that the mystery of Christ illumines the whole content of catechesis. The diverse elements — biblical, evangelical, ecclesial, human, and even cosmic — which catechetical education must take up and expound are all to be referred to the incarnate Son of God.

To the Father: The supreme purpose of the incarnation of the Word and of the whole economy of salvation consists in this: that all men be led to the Father. Catechesis, therefore, since it must help to an ever-deeper understanding of this plan of love of the heavenly Father, must take care to show that the supreme meaning of human life is this: to acknowledge God and to glorify him by doing his will, as Christ taught us by his words and the example of his life, and thus to come to eternal life.

In the Spirit: The knowledge of the mystery of Christ and the way to the Father are realized in the Holy Spirit. Therefore, catechesis, when expounding the content of the Christian message, must always put in clear light this presence of the Holy Spirit, by which men are continually moved to have communion with God and men and to fulfill their duties.

If catechesis lacks these three elements or neglects their close relationship, the Christian message can certainly lose its proper character.

FOR US MEN AND FOR OUR SALVATION

42.   The theocentric-trinitarian purpose of the economy of salvation cannot be separated from its objective, which is this: that men, set free from sin and its consequences, should be made as much like Christ as possible (cf. LG, 39). As the incarnation of the Word, so every revealed truth is for us men and for our salvation. To view the diverse Christian truths in their relation to the ultimate end of man is one of the conditions needed for a most fruitful understanding of them (cf. First Vatican Council, Dogm. Const. *Dei Filius*, DS 3016).

Catechesis must, then, show clearly the very close connection of the mystery of God and Christ with man's existence and his ultimate end. This method in no way implies any contempt for the earthly goals which men are divinely called to pursue by individual or common efforts; it does, however, clearly teach that man's ultimate end is not confined to these temporal goals, but rather surpasses them beyond all expectation, to a degree that only God's love for men could make possible.

HIERARCHY OF TRUTHS TO BE OBSERVED IN CATECHESIS

43.   In the message of salvation there is a certain hierarchy of truths (cf. UR, 11), which the Church has always recognized when it composed creeds or summaries of the truths of faith. This hierarchy does not mean that some truths pertain to faith itself less than others, but rather that some truths are based on others as of a higher priority, and are illumined by them.

On all levels catechesis should take account of this hierarchy of the truths of faith.

These truths may be grouped under four basic heads: the mystery of God the Father, the Son, and the Holy Spirit, Creator of all things; the mystery of Christ the incarnate Word, who was born of the Virgin Mary, and who suffered, died, and rose for our salvation; the mystery of the Holy Spirit, who is present in the Church, sanctifying it and guiding it until the glorious coming of Christ, our Savior and Judge; and the mystery of the Church, which is Christ's Mystical Body, in which the Virgin Mary holds the preeminent place.

HISTORICAL CHARACTER OF THE MYSTERY OF SALVATION

44.   The economy of salvation is being worked out in time: in time past it began, made progress, and in Christ reached its highest point; in the present time it displays its force and awaits its consummation in the future. Hence in the exposition of the content of catechesis, memory of the past, awareness of the present, and hope of the future life ought to be evident by all means.

Therefore, catechesis recalls the supreme event of the whole history of salvation, the event with which Christians are united by faith, namely, the incarnation, passion, death, and resurrection of Christ.

Moreover, catechesis enables the faithful to recognize how the saving mystery of Christ works today and throughout the ages through the Holy Spirit and the ministry of the Church, and leads them to understand their duties toward God, themselves, and their neighbors.

Finally, catechesis rightly disposes hearts to hope in the future life that is the consummation of the whole history of salvation. Towards this goal Christians ought to tend with filial confidence, but not without a holy fear of divine judgment. Through this hope the Christian community is deeply filled with an inner eschatological expectation which enables it to think correctly about human and earthly goods by keeping them in proper perspective, while not despising them as worthless.

These three main viewpoints are to be kept in mind continuously and practically in the exposition of the content of catechesis.

SOURCES OF CATECHESIS

45.   The content of catechesis is found in God's word, written or handed down; it is more deeply understood and developed by the people exercising their faith under the guidance of the Magisterium, which alone teaches authentically; it is celebrated in the liturgy; it shines forth in the life of the Church, especially in the just and in the saints; and in some way it is known too from those genuine moral values which, by divine providence, are found in human society.

Catechesis has all these as its sources. These sources are either principal or subsidiary, and so they are by no means all to be taken as sources in exactly the same sense. In using them, the catechist must first and always look to the unquestionable preeminence of revelation, written or handed down, and to the authority of the Magisterium of the Church in matters connected with faith.

Moreover, in regard to any particular part of the content of faith that is to be explained, the catechist should carefully note how the mystery of Christ is the center of that part; how the Church interprets and defines that part, and how she celebrates it and puts it into practice, sharing it in her liturgy and in the practice of the Christian life. Finally, the catechist must consider how, with the aid of the Holy Spirit, the plan of God can be fulfilled in the present era.

GENERAL PRINCIPLES OF CATECHETICAL METHODOLOGY

46.   The norms pointed out above, about the exposition of the content of catechesis, must be applied in the various forms of catechesis, that is to say, in biblical and liturgical catechesis, in doctrinal summaries, in the interpretation of the conditions of human existence, and so on.

It is not possible, however, to deduce from those norms an order which must be followed in the exposition of the content. It is right to begin with God and proceed to Christ, or to do the reverse; similarly, it is permissible to begin with man and proceed to God, or to do the reverse; and so on. In selecting a pedagogical method, one ought to take into account the circumstances in which the ecclesial community or the individuals among the faithful to whom the catechesis is directed live. From this there arises the need to use great diligence in looking into and finding ways and methods which better respond to the various circumstances.

The Conferences of Bishops have the task of giving more specific norms in this matter and of applying them by means of catechetical directories, of catechisms for various age levels and cultural conditions, and of the other helps that seem appropriate for the task (cf. below, Part Six).

CHAPTER II
THE MORE OUTSTANDING ELEMENTS OF THE CHRISTIAN MESSAGE

THE MYSTERY OF THE ONE GOD: FATHER, SON, HOLY SPIRIT

47. The history of salvation is identical with the history of the way and the plan by which God, true and one, the Father, the Son, the Holy Spirit, reveals himself to men, and reconciles and unites with himself those turned away from sin.

The Old Testament, while clearly affirming the unity of God in a polytheistic world, already gives some foreshadowings of the mystery of the Trinity. These are completely explicitated, however, in the person, the works, and the words of Jesus Christ. Indeed, when he reveals himself as the Son of God, he at the same time reveals the Father and the Holy Spirit. An intimate knowledge of the true God imbues the whole mind of the Divine Teacher, and he shares it with his disciples, calling them to become sons of God, through the Gift of his filial Spirit, which he bestows on them (cf. John 1:12; Romans 8:15).

In catechesis, therefore, the meeting with the Triune God occurs first and foremost when the Father, the Son, and the Spirit are acknowledged as the authors of the plan of salvation that has its culmination in the death and resurrection of Jesus (cf. Irenaeus, *Proof of the Apostolic Preaching*, n. 6, *Sources chretiénnes*, 62, pp. 39 ff.). In this way the growing awareness of the faithful responds to the revelation of the mystery transmitted by the Church; for the faithful understand through faith that their life, beginning at baptism, consists in acquiring a more intimate familiarity with the three divine Persons, inasmuch as the faithful are called to share in their divine nature. Finally, Christians, through the gift of the Holy Spirit, can already now contemplate with eyes of faith and cherish with filial love the Most Holy Trinity of Persons, as it is from eternity in God's intimate life.

48. "The God and Father of our Lord Jesus Christ" (Ephesians 1:3) is "the living God" (Matthew 16:16). He is a holy, just, and merciful God; He is God the author of the covenant with men; God who sees, frees, and saves; God who loves as a father, as a spouse. Catechesis joyfully proclaims this God who is the source of our every hope (cf. 1 Peter 1:3 – 4).

Catechesis, however, cannot ignore the fact that not a few men of our era strongly sense a remoteness and even absence of God. This fact, which is part of the process of secularization, surely constitutes a danger for the faith; but it also impels us to have a purer faith and to become more humble in the presence of the mystery of God, as we ought: "Truly you are a hidden God, the God of Israel, the Savior" (Isaiah 45:15). With this perspective, it is possible also to understand more easily the true nature of the worship which God demands and which glorifies him, a worship, that is, which includes a resolve to fulfill his will in every field of activity, and faithfully to increase in charity the talents given by the Lord (cf. Matthew 25:14 ff.). In the sacred liturgy the faithful bring the fruits of every kind of act of charity, of justice, of peace, in order to make a humble offering of them to God, and to receive in return the words of life and the graces they need to enable them in the world to profess the truth in love (cf. Ephesians 4:15) in communion with Christ, who offers his Body and Blood for men.

KNOWLEDGE OF GOD AND THE WITNESS OF CHARITY

49. The greatest way the faithful can help the atheistic world for coming to God is by the witness of a life which agrees with the message of Christ's love and of a living and mature faith that is manifested by works of justice and charity (cf. GS, 21).

However, the right use of human reason may not be neglected; for, as the Church holds and teaches, from created things this reason can come to a knowledge of God as the beginning and the end of all things (cf. First Vatican Council, Dogm. Const. *Dei Filius*, DS 3004 – 3005, 3026). This knowledge of God not only does no harm to human dignity, but rather gives it a basis and strength.

Though the eternal salvation of men is the objective of the Church, nevertheless faith in the living God carries with it the urgent duty of collaborating in the solution of human questions (cf. 1 John 4:20 – 21). In this area the faithful must give witness by their works to the value of the Lord's message.

JESUS CHRIST, SON OF GOD, THE FIRSTBORN OF ALL CREATION AND SAVIOR

50. The greatest of God's works is the incarnation of his Son, Jesus Christ. Being the Firstborn of all creation, he is before all and all things hold together in him (cf. Colossians 1:15 – 17). All things have been created in him, through him, and for him (cf. Colossians 1:15 ff.).

Having become obedient unto death, he was exalted as Lord of all things, and was manifested to us through his resurrection as God's Son in power (cf.

Romans 1:4). Being the Firstborn of the dead, he gives life to all (cf. 1 Corinthians 15:22): in him we were created new men (cf. Ephesians 2:10); through him all creatures will be liberated from the slavery of corruption (cf. Romans 8:19 – 21). "There is no salvation in anyone else" (Acts 4:12).

CREATION, THE BEGINNING OF THE ECONOMY OF SALVATION

51.   The entire world created out of nothing is the world in which salvation and redemption are in fact accomplished through Jesus Christ.

Already in the Old Testament the truth of God's creative action is not presented as an abstract philosophical principle; rather, it enters the minds of the Israelites, with the help of a notion of the oneness of God, as a message declaring the power and victory of Yahweh, as the basis for showing that the Lord remains always with his people (cf. Isaiah 40:27 – 28; 51:9 – 13). The omnipotence of God the Creator is also manifested in a splendid way in Christ's resurrection, wherein is revealed "the immeasurable scope of his power" (Ephesians 1:19).

For this reason the truth of creation is not to be presented simply as a truth standing by itself, torn from the rest, but as something which is in fact ordered to the salvation wrought by Jesus Christ. The creation of visible and invisible things, of the world and of angels, is the beginning of the mystery of salvation (cf. DV, 3); the creation of man (cf. Pius XII Encycl. *Humani generis*, AAS, 1950, p. 575; GS, 12, 14) is to be regarded as the first gift and the first call that leads to glorification in Christ (cf. Romans 8:29 – 30). When a Christian hears the explanation of the doctrine about creation, besides thinking about the first act whereby God "created the heavens and the earth" (Genesis 1:1), he should turn his mind to all the salvific undertakings of God. These things are always present in the history of man and of the world; they also shine forth especially in the history of Israel; they lead to the supreme event of Christ's resurrection and, finally, they will be brought to completion at the end of the world, when there will be "new heavens and a new earth" (cf. 2 Peter 3:13).

JESUS CHRIST, THE CENTER OF THE ENTIRE ECONOMY OF SALVATION

52.   A Christian recognizes that in Jesus Christ he is linked with all of history and is in communion with all men. The history of salvation is being accomplished in the midst of the history of the world. By this history of salvation God fulfills his plan, and thus the People of God, that is, "the whole Christ," is being perfected in time. The Christian acknowledges with simplicity and sincerity that he has a role in such work, which through the power of Jesus the Savior is aimed at having creation give the greatest possible glory to God (cf. 1 Corinthians 15:28).

JESUS CHRIST, TRUE MAN AND TRUE GOD IN THE UNITY OF THE DIVINE PERSON

53.   This great mystery, namely, Christ as Head and Lord of the universe, "has been manifested in the flesh" (1 Timothy 3:16) to men. The man, Jesus Christ, who dwelt among men — the one who as man worked with his hands, thought

with a human mind, acted with a human will, loved with a human heart—he is truly the Word and the Son of God, who through the incarnation in a certain way joined himself with every single man (cf. GS, 22).

Catechesis must proclaim Jesus in his concrete existence and in his message, that is, it must open the way for men to the wonderful perfection of his humanity in such a way that they will be able to acknowledge the mystery of his divinity. Christ Jesus, for a fact, who was united with the Father in a constant and unique practice of prayer, always lived in close communion with men. By his goodness he embraced all men, the just and the sinners, the poor and the rich, fellow-citizens and foreigners. If he loved some more particularly than others, this predilection was showered on the sick, the poor, the lowly. For the human person he had a reverence and a solicitude such as no one before him had ever manifested.

Catechesis ought daily to defend and strengthen belief in the divinity of Jesus Christ, in order that he may be accepted not merely for his admirable human life, but that men might recognize him through his words and signs as God's only-begotten Son (cf. John 1:18), "God from God, light from light, true God from true God, begotten not made, consubstantial with the Father" (DS 150). The correct explanation of the mystery of the Incarnation developed in Christian tradition: through a diligent understanding of the faith, the Fathers and the Councils made efforts to determine more precisely the concepts, to explain mere profoundly the peculiar nature of Christ's mystery, to investigate the hidden connections that bind him to his heavenly Father and to men. Besides, there was the witness of the Christian life about this truth—a witness that the Church presented throughout the centuries: that God's communion with men, which is had in Christ, is the source of joy and inexhaustible hope. In Christ there is all fullness of divinity; through him God's love for men is shown forth.

St. Ignatius wrote to the Ephesians: "There is only one physician, both in body and in spirit, born and unborn, God become man, true life in death; sprung both from Mary and from God, first incapable of suffering and then capable of it, Jesus Christ our Lord" (*Enchiridion patristicum*, 39).

JESUS CHRIST, SAVIOR AND REDEEMER OF THE WORLD

54. The mystery of Christ appears in the history of men and of the world—a history subject to sin—not only as the mystery of the incarnation but also as the mystery of salvation and redemption.

God so loved sinners that he gave his Son, reconciling the world to himself (cf. 2 Corinthians 5:19). Jesus therefore as the Firstborn among many brethren (cf. Romans 8:29), holy, innocent, undefiled (cf. Hebrews 7:26), being obedient to his Father freely and out of filial love (cf. Philippians 2:8), on behalf of His brethren, sinners that they were, and as their Mediator, accepted the death which is for them the wages of sin (cf. Romans 6:23; GS, 18). By this his most holy death he redeemed mankind from the slavery of sin and of the devil, and he poured out on it the spirit of adoption, thus creating in himself a new humanity.

55.   The mystery of Christ is continued in the Church, which always enjoys his presence and ministers to him. This is done in a specific way through the signs that Christ instituted, which signify the gift of grace and produce it, and are properly called sacraments (cf. Council of Trent, *Decree on the Sacraments*, DS 1601).

The Church herself, however, is in some way to be considered the primordial sacrament, since she is not only the People of God but also in Christ and a kind of "sign and instrument of the intimate union with God, and of the unity of the entire human race" (LG, 1).

Sacraments are the principal and fundamental actions whereby Jesus Christ unceasingly bestows his Spirit on the faithful, thus making them the holy people which offers itself, in him and with him, as an oblation acceptable to the Father. The sacraments are surely to be considered inestimable blessings of the Church. To her, then, belongs the power of administering them; and yet they are always to be referred to Christ, from whom they receive their efficacy. In reality it is Christ who baptizes. It is not so much a man who celebrates the Eucharist as Christ himself; for he it is who offers himself in the sacrifice of the Mass by the ministry of the priests (cf. Council of Trent, *Decree on the Sacrifice of the Mass*, DS 1743). The sacramental action is, in the first place, the action of Christ, and the ministers of the Church are as his instruments.

FULL MEANING OF THE SACRAMENTS

56.   Catechesis will have the duty of presenting the seven sacraments according to their full meaning.

First, they must be presented as sacraments of faith. Of themselves they certainly express the efficacious will of Christ the Savior; but men, on their part, must show a sincere will to respond to God's love and mercy. Hence, catechesis must concern itself with the acquisition of the proper dispositions, with the stimulation of sincerity and generosity for a worthy reception of the sacraments.

Second, the sacraments must be presented, each according to its own nature and end, not only as remedies for sin and its consequences, but especially as sources of grace in individuals and in communities, so that the entire dispensation of grace in the life of the faithful may be related in some way to the sacramental economy.

CATECHESIS ON THE SACRAMENTS

57.   Baptism cleanses man from original sin and from all personal sins, gives him rebirth as a child of God, incorporates him into the Church, sanctifies him with the gifts of the Holy Spirit, and, impressing on his soul an indelible character, initiates him in Christ's priestly, prophetic, and kingly roles (cf. 1 Peter 2:9; LG, 31).

Confirmation binds the Christian more perfectly to the Church and enriches him with a special strength of the Holy Spirit, that he may live in the world as a witness of Christ.

Since the life of Christians, which on earth is a warfare, is liable to temptations and sins, the way of the sacrament of Penance is open for them, so that they may obtain pardon from the merciful God and reconcile themselves with the Church.

Holy Orders in a special way conforms certain members of the People of God to Christ the Mediator by conferring on them a sacred power, that they may shepherd the Church, nourish the faithful with the word of God, and make them holy, and, in the first place, that they, representing Christ's person, may offer the Sacrifice of the Mass and preside at the Eucharistic banquet.

"By the sacred anointing of the sick and the prayer of her priests, the whole Church commends those who are ill to the suffering and glorified Lord, that He may lighten their sufferings and save them" (LG, 11; cf. James 5:14–16).

In catechesis on the sacraments, much importance should late placed on the explanation of the signs. Catechesis should lead the faithful through the visible signs to ponder God's invisible mysteries of salvation.

THE EUCHARIST, CENTER OF THE ENTIRE SACRAMENTAL LIFE

58.   The primacy of the Eucharist over all the other sacraments is unquestionable, as is also its supreme efficacy in building up the Church (cf. LG, 11, 17; Instruction, *Eucharisticum mysterium*, 5–15).

For in the Eucharist, when the words of consecration have been pronounced, the profound (not the phenomenal) reality of bread and wine is changed into the body and blood of Christ, and this wonderful change has in the Church come to be called "transubstantiation." Accordingly, under the appearances (that is, the phenomena reality) of the bread and wine, the humanity of Christ, not only by its power but by itself (that is, substantially), united with his divine Person, lies hidden in an altogether mysterious way (cf. Paul VI, Encycl. *Mysterium fidei*, AAS, 1965, p. 766).

This sacrifice is not merely a rite commemorating a past sacrifice. For in it Christ by the ministry of the priests perpetuates the sacrifice of the Cross in an unbloody manner through the course of the centuries (cf. SC, 47). In it too he nourishes the faithful with himself, the Bread of Life, in order that, filled with love of God and neighbor, they may become more and more a people acceptable to God.

Having been nourished with the Victim of the sacrifice of the Cross, the faithful should by a genuine and active love remove the prejudices because of which they are at times accused of a sterile worship that keeps them from being brotherly and from cooperating with other people. By its nature the Eucharistic banquet is meant to help the faithful to unite their hearts with God more each day in frequent prayer, and thence to acknowledge and love other men as brothers of Christ and sons of God the Father.

59.   In our hearts, With the pre-eminence that the Christian message ascribes to consecrated virginity being preserved (cf. 1 Corinthians 7:38; Council of Trent, *Canons on the Sacrament of Matrimony*, DS 1810), a special importance must be assigned to religious education on matrimony, which the Creator himself instituted and endowed with various blessings, purposes, and laws (cf. GS, 48).

Supported by the words of faith and by the natural law, under the guidance of the Magisterium of the Church, which is responsible for authoritative interpretation of both the moral and the natural law (cf. Paul VI, Encycl. *Humanae vitae*, 4, AAS, 1968, p. 483), and at the same time taking due account of contemporary advances in the anthropological sciences, catechesis must make matrimony the foundation of family life, with regard to its values and its divine law of unity and indissolubility, and with regard to its duties of love, which by its natural character has been ordered towards the procreation and education of offspring. In regulating procreation, conjugal chastity must be preserved in accord with the teaching of the Church (cf. Encycl. *Humanae vitae*, 14, AAS, 1968, p. 490).

Since Christ elevated matrimony to the dignity of a sacrament for the baptized, the spouses, who are the ministers of the sacrament when they give personal and irrevocable consent, living in Christ's grace imitate and in a certain way represent the love of Christ himself for his Church (cf. Ephesians 5:25). Christian spouses are strengthened and as it were consecrated by this special sacrament for fulfilling the duties of their state and for upholding its dignity (cf. GS, 48).

Finally, it is part of the family's vocation to become a community, one which is also open to the Church and to the world.

THE NEW MAN

60.   When man accepts the Spirit of Christ, he establishes a way of life that is totally new and gratuitous.

The Holy Spirit, present in the soul of the Christian, makes him a partaker of the divine nature and intimately unites him to the Father and Christ in a communion of life which not even death can break (cf. John 14:23). The Holy Spirit heals man of his spiritual weaknesses and infirmities, frees him from the slavery of his passions and of immoderate self-love, by giving him power to keep the divine law, strengthens him with hope and fortitude, enlightens him in the pursuit of the good, and infuses in him the fruits of charity, joy, peace, patience, kindness, goodness, longanimity, humility, fidelity, modesty, continence, and chastity (cf. Galatians 5:22–23). This is why the Holy Spirit is invoked as the guest of the soul.

Justification from sin and God's indwelling in the soul are a grace. When we say a sinner is justified by God, is given life by the Holy Spirit, possesses in himself Christ's life, or has grace, we are using expressions which in different words mean one and the same thing, namely, dying to sin, becoming partakers of the divinity of the Son through the Spirit of adoption, and entering into an intimate communion with the Most Holy Trinity.

The man belonging to the history of salvation is the man ordered to the grace of filial adoption and to eternal life. Christian anthropology finds its own proper character in the grace of Christ the Savior.

HUMAN AND CHRISTIAN FREEDOM

61.   The divine call of man requires him to give a free response in Jesus Christ.

It is not possible for man to be unfree. It is also very much part of his dignity and duty, since he has dominion over his actions, to keep the moral law in the order of nature and in the order of grace, and thus to adhere closely to God who revealed himself in Christ. The freedom of fallen man has been so weakened that he would be unable for long to observe even the duties of the natural law without the help of God's grace; but, when he has received grace, his freedom is so elevated and strengthened that the life he lives in the flesh, he is able to live holily in the faith of Jesus Christ (cf. Galatians 2:20).

The Church has a duty to defend and promote a true sense of freedom and its right use against every kind of unjust force. She also protects freedom against those who deny it, who think man's activity is wholly dependent on psychological determinism and on economic, social, cultural, and such other conditions.

The Church is by no means unaware that freedom, even when assisted by divine grace, is liable to grave psychological difficulties and to the influence of external conditions in which each one lives, with the result that human responsibility is not rarely diminished, and indeed in some cases is barely preserved, and in some cases it is not preserved at all. The Church likewise takes note of the researches and modern progress in the anthropological sciences concerning the use and limits of human freedom. For this reason she is solicitous both to educate for and to foster genuine freedom, and also to bring about suitable conditions in the psychological, social, economic, political, and religious fields, so that freedom will be able to be truly and justly exercised. Christians, therefore, must work sedulously and sincerely in the temporal sphere, so that as far as possible the best conditions may be established for the right exercise of freedom. They have this duty, of course, in common with all men of good will; yet Christians know they are bound to the same duty because of a more important and more urgent reason. For here it is question not only of promoting a good that belongs to this life on earth, but also of a duty which ultimately serves the acquisition of the inestimable good of grace and of eternal salvation.

SIN OF MAN

62.   Nevertheless, the conditions of history and of life are not to be considered the main impediment to human freedom. When man freely applies himself to the work of salvation, he finds sin the greatest obstacle.

"Although he was made by God in a state of holiness, from the very dawn of history man abused his liberty, at the urging of the Evil One. Man set himself against God and sought to find fulfillment apart from God" (GS, 13). "Through one man sin entered the world, and with sin death, death thus coming to all men inasmuch as all sinned" (Romans 5:12). "It is human nature so fallen, stripped of the grace that clothed it, injured in its own natural powers, and subjected to the dominion of death, that is transmitted to all men, and it is in this sense that every man is born in sin" (Paul VI, *Professio fidei*, 16, AAS, 1968, p. 439).

The multitude of sins, then, has become a sorrowful experience for mankind, and it is also the cause of manifold sorrows and ruin. One must not neglect the teaching on the nature and effects of personal sins, whereby man, acting knowingly and deliberately, by his act violates the moral law, and in a serious matter also seriously offends God.

The history of salvation is also the history of liberation from sin. Every intervention of God both in the Old and in the New Testament was to give guidance to men in the struggle against the forces of sin. The role entrusted to Christ in the history of salvation relates to the destruction of sin, and is fulfilled through the mystery of the cross. The profound reflections found in St. Paul (cf. Romans 5) concerning the reality of sin and Christ's consequent "work of justice" must be numbered among the principal points of the Christian faith, and it is not right to pass over them in silence in catechesis.

But the salvation brought by Jesus Christ involves much more than redemption from sin. For it fulfills the plan begun by God that he would communicate himself in Jesus with such fullness that it utterly transcends human understanding. The plan in question does not come to an end because of men's transgressions, but it confers a grace that is superabundant compared to the death which sin brought (cf. Romans 5:15–17). This plan, which has proceeded from love, by virtue of which men are called by the Holy Spirit to share in divine life itself, is always in force and belongs to all times. Even though man is a sinner, he always remains in the one order which God willed, namely, in the order in which God mercifully shares himself with us in Jesus Christ, and man can, therefore, under the impulse of grace, attain salvation through repentance.

MORAL LIFE OF CHRISTIANS

63.   Christ commissioned his apostles to teach the observance of everything that he had commanded (cf. Matthew 28:20). Catechesis, therefore, must include not only those things which are to be believed, but also those things which are to be done.

The moral life of Christians, which is a way of acting that is worthy of a man and an adopted son of God, is a response to the duty of living and growing, under the guidance of the Holy Spirit, in the new life communicated through Jesus Christ.

The moral life of Christians is guided by the grace and gifts of the Holy Spirit. "The love of God has been poured out in our hearts through the Holy Spirit who has been given to us" (Romans 5:5).

The docility with which the Holy Spirit must be obeyed entails a faithful observance of the commandments of God, the laws of the Church, and just civil laws.

Christian freedom still needs to be ruled and directed in the concrete circumstances of human life. Accordingly, the conscience of the faithful, even when informed by the virtue of prudence, must be subject to the Magisterium of the Church, whose duty it is to explain the whole moral law authoritatively, in order that it may rightly and correctly express the objective moral order.

Further, the conscience itself of Christians must be taught that there are norms which are absolute, that is, which bind in every case and on all people. That is why the saints confessed Christ through the practice of heroic virtues; indeed, the martyrs suffered even torture and death rather than deny Christ.

THE PERFECTION OF CHARITY

64. The action of the Spirit of Christ is made clear when the peculiar characteristic of Christian moral teaching is brought to light; all precepts and counsels of this moral teaching are summarized in faith working through charity (cf. Galatians 5:6), and this is as it were its soul.

Man is called to adhere freely to the will of God in all things; this is "the obedience of faith by which man entrusts his whole self freely to God" (DV, 5). However, since God is love, and his plan calls for communicating his love in Jesus Christ and for uniting men in mutual love, it follows that adhering freely and perfectly to God and to his will is the same as following a way of life in which love reigns in the keeping of the commandments; in other words, it is identical with embracing and putting into practice the precept of charity as a new precept.

Man, therefore, is called to embrace, in faith, a life of charity toward God and other men; in this lies his greatest responsibility and his exalted moral dignity. The holiness of a man, whatever his vocation or state of life may be, is nothing other than the perfection of charity (cf. LG, 39 – 42).

THE CHURCH, PEOPLE OF GOD AND SAVING INSTITUTION

65. The Church, instituted by Christ, had its origin in his death and resurrection. She is the new People of God, prepared for in the course of the history of Israel; a people to which Christ gives life and growth through the outpouring of the Spirit, and which he perpetually renews and directs by his hierarchical and charismatic gifts; "a people made one with the unity of the Father and the Son and the Holy Spirit" (LG, 4).

The Church, therefore, inasmuch as she is the People of God, the society of the faithful, and the communion of men in Christ, is the work of God's saving love in Christ.

And the principles which give birth to Christians, form them, and establish them as a Community (namely, the deposit of faith, the sacraments, and the apostolic ministries) are found in the Catholic Church. To her they have been entrusted, and from them spring the ecclesial activities. In other words, in the Church there are all the means necessary for assembling herself and guiding herself to maturity as the communion of men in Christ. This work is the fruit not only of the action of a transcendent God, and of the invisible working of Christ and of his Spirit, but also of the institutions, offices, and saving actions of the Church. The Church, therefore, besides being a society of the faithful, is also mother of the faithful because of her ministerial and salutary work.

The Church is the holy People of God which shares in the prophetic office of Christ (cf. LG, 12). Assembled by the word of God, it accepts it and gives witness to it throughout the world. She is a priestly people: "Christ the Lord, High Priest taken from among men, 'made a kingdom and priests to God his Father'" (Revelation 1:6) out of this new people. The baptized, by regeneration and the anointing of the Holy Spirit, are consecrated into a spiritual house and a holy priesthood. Thus, through all those works befitting Christian men they can offer spiritual sacrifices and proclaim the power of him who has called them out of darkness into his marvelous light" (LG, 10). The Church, however, is essentially a hierarchical society; it is a people guided by its Shepherds, who are in union with the Supreme Pontiff, the Vicar of Christ, and who are under his direction (cf. LG, 22). To them the faithful look with filial love and obedient homage. The Church is a people on pilgrimage toward fullness of the mystery of Christ.

The Holy Spirit's presence in the Church, on the one hand, safeguards in her, in an indefectible manner, the objective conditions required for her sanctifying meeting with Christ; on the other hand, the Holy Spirit's presence brings it about that the Church strives for continual purification, and renewal in her members, and for the sake of her members, and in her changeable structures.

THE CHURCH AS COMMUNION

66. The Church is a communion. She herself acquired a fuller awareness of that truth in the Second Vatican Council.

The Church is a people assembled by God and united by close spiritual bonds. Her structure needs a diversity of gifts and offices; and yet the distinctions within her, though they can be not only of degree but also of essence, as is the case between the ministerial priesthood and the common priesthood of the people, by no means takes away the basic and essential equality of persons. "The chosen People of God is one: 'one Lord, one faith, one baptism' (Ephesians 4:5). As members, they share a common dignity from their rebirth in Christ. They have the same filial grace and the same vocation to perfection. They possess in common one salvation, one hope, and one undivided charity. . . . And if by the will of Christ some are made teachers, dispensers of mysteries, and shepherds on behalf of others, yet all share a true equality with regard to the dignity and the activity common to all the faithful for the building up of the Body of Christ" (LG, 32).

In the Church, therefore, every vocation is worthy of honor and is a call to the fullness of love, that is, to holiness; every person is endowed with his own supernatural excellence, and must be given respect. All gifts and charisms, even though some are objectively more excellent than others (cf. 1 Corinthians 12:31; 7:38), work together for the good of all members by means of the provident multiplicity of forms, which the apostolic office must discover and coordinate (cf. LG, 12). This holds also for all particular churches individually; for in each one, though it be small and poor or living in dispersion, "Christ is present, and by his power the one, holy, catholic, and apostolic Church is gathered together" (LG, 26).

The Catholic faithful ought to be solicitous for the separated Christians who do not live in full communion with the Catholic Church, by praying for them, communicating with them about Church matters, and taking the first steps toward them. First of all, however, each one according to his condition, should weigh sincerely and attentively the things in the Catholic family itself which ought to be renewed and achieved, in order that its life might bear a more faithful and clear witness to the doctrine and institutions handed down by Christ through the apostles (cf. UR, 4, 5).

THE CHURCH AS SAVING INSTITUTION

67. The Church is not only a communion among brothers, whose head is Christ, but she manifests herself also as an institution to whom the universal saving mission has been entrusted. The People of God, established by Christ "as a communion of life, of charity, and of truth, is also used by him as an instrument for the redemption of all, and is sent forth into the whole world as the light of the world and the salt of the earth" (LG, 9).

For this reason the Church is shown by the Second Vatican Council as a reality that embraces all history, accepts all its different cultures and directs them to God; and by virtue of the action of Christ's Spirit is constituted "the universal sacrament of salvation." Likewise, she is shown as the Church that is engaged in dialogue with the world. Taking note of the signs of the times, she discovers what men are considering important and on what things she is in agreement with them. Moreover, she takes pains to be understood and recognized by the world, striving to divest herself of those external forms which seem less Gospel-like, and in which traces of eras already ended appear all too clearly.

The Church, of course, is not of this world, she is "inspired by no earthly ambition" (GS, 3) and she will be perfect only in heaven, or which she has her eyes fixed and toward which she is journeying. And yet she is connected with the world and its history. However, "the deep solicitude of the Church, the Spouse of Christ, for the needs of men, for their joys and hopes, their griefs and efforts, is nothing other than her great desire to be present to them, in order to illuminate them with the light of Christ and to gather them all in him, their only Savior. This solicitude can never mean that the Church conform herself to the things of this world, or that she lessen the ardor of her expectation of her Lord and of the eternal Kingdom" (Paul VI, *Professio fidei*, 27, AAS, 1968, p. 444).

68.   Mary is united in an ineffable manner with the Lord, being his Ever-Virgin Mother, who "occupies in the Holy Church the place which is highest after Christ and yet very close to us" (LG, 54).

The gift of Christ's Spirit is manifested in her in an altogether singular manner, because Mary is "full of grace" (Luke 1:28), and is "a model of the Church" (LG, 63). In her, who was preserved from all stain of original sin, who was freely and fully faithful to the Lord, and who was assumed body and soul into heavenly glory, the Holy Spirit has fully manifested his gift. For she was completely conformed "to her Son, the Lord of lords, and the Conqueror of sin and death" (LG, 59). Because she is the Mother of God and "mother to us in the order of grace" (LG, 61), the type of the virginity and motherhood of the total Church (cf. LG, 63–65), and the sign of a secure hope and solace for the pilgrim People of God (cf. LG, 69), Mary "in a certain way unites and mirrors within herself the central truths of the faith," and she "summons the believers to her Son and to his sacrifice, and to love for the Father" (LG, 65). Therefore, the Church who honors the faithful and the saints who are already with the Lord and are interceding for us (LG, 49, 50), venerates in a most special way Christ's Mother, who is also her mother.

FINAL COMMUNION WITH GOD

69.   In Christ Jesus and through this mystery, the faithful already in this earthly life hopefully await "our Lord Jesus Christ, who will give a new form to this lowly body of ours and remake it according to the pattern of his glorified body" (Philippians 3:21; cf. 1 Corinthians 15). The very last realities, however, will become manifest and perfect when and only when Christ comes with power, as Judge of the living and the dead, to bring history to its end and to hand over his people to the Father, so that "God may be all in all" (1 Corinthians 15:24–28). Until "the Lord comes in his majesty, and all the angels with him, and until death is destroyed and all things are subject to him, some of his disciples are pilgrims on earth, some have finished this life and are being purified, and others are in glory, beholding clearly God himself three and one, as he is" (LG, 49).

On the day of the Lord's coming, the entire Church will reach her perfection and enter into the fullness of God. This is the very foundation of the hope and prayer of Christians ("Thy kingdom come"). Catechesis on the subject of the last things should, on the one hand, be taught under the aspect of consolation, of hope, and of salutary fear (cf. 1 Thessalonians 4:18), of which modern men have such great need; on the other hand, it should be imparted in such a way that the whole truth can be seen. It is not right to minimize the grave responsibility which every one has regarding his future destiny. Catechesis can not pass over in silence the judgment after death of each man, or the expiatory punishments of Purgatory, or the sad and lamentable reality of eternal death, or the final judgment. On that day each man will fully arrive at his destiny, because all of us will be revealed "before the tribunal of Christ, so that each one may receive the recompense, good or bad, according to his life in the body" (2 Corinthians 5:10), and "those who have done right shall rise to live; the evildoers shall rise to be damned" (John 5:29; cf. LG, 48).

PART FOUR
ELEMENTS OF METHODOLOGY

NATURE AND PURPOSE OF THIS PART

70. Within our present century, catechists have thoroughly investigated questions raised by the psychological, educational, and pedagogical sciences. Indeed, studies have been undertaken with regard to the method to be used in the catechism lesson; the role of activity methods in the teaching of catechesis has been pointed out; the act of catechesis has been investigated in all its parts according to the principles which govern the art of teaching (experience, imagination, memory, intelligence); and finally, a differential methodology has been worked out, that is, a methodology which varies according to the age, social conditions, and degree of psychological maturity of those who are to be taught.

Not all problems of this sort are considered here; rather, here are set forth only certain points to which great importance is being attributed today. Attacking these problems in an appropriate and specific way in individual countries will be the task of the various directories and the other tools.

FUNCTION OF THE CATECHIST

71. No method, not even one much proved in use. frees the catechist from the personal task of assimilating and passing judgment on the concrete circumstances, and from some adjustment to them. For outstanding human and Christian qualities in the catechists will be able to do more to produce successes than will the methods selected.

The work of the catechist must be considered of greater importance than the selection of texts and other tools (cf. AG, 17).

The importance and magnitude of the work to be done by catechists does not prevent the necessary establishing of boundaries around the role of catechists. They are responsible for choosing and creating suitable conditions which are necessary for the Christian message to be sought, accepted, and more profoundly investigated. This is the point to which the action of catechists extends — and there it stops. For adherence on the part of those to be taught is a fruit of grace and freedom, and does not ultimately depend on the catechist; and catechetical action, therefore, should be accompanied by prayer. That remark is self-evident, but it is nevertheless useful to recall it in present-day conditions, because today much is being demanded of the talent and of the genuine Christian spirit of the catechist, while at the same time he is being urged to have the greatest possible regard for the freedom and "creativity" of those to be taught.

72. The method called inductive offers great advantages.

It serves in the presentation of facts (such as biblical events, liturgical actions, the life of the Church, and daily life) and in the consideration and examination of those facts in order that in them may be recognized the meaning they have in the Christian mystery. This method is in harmony with the economy of revelation and with one of the fundamental processes of the human spirit, one that comes to grasp intelligible realities through visible things, and also with the particular characteristic of knowledge of the faith, that is, a knowing through signs.

The inductive method does not exclude the deductive, but rather even requires it. The deductive method is used in interpreting and explaining the facts by proceeding from their causes. The deductive synthesis usually manifests its full force, however, when the inductive process has already been carried out.

FORMULATIONS

73. The advantages of the inductive method, chief among which are the active exercise of the spiritual faculties and the constant reference to concrete things in the explanation of intellectual concepts, must in no way lead to a forgetting of the need for and the usefulness of formulas.

Formulas permit the thoughts of the mind to be expressed accurately, are appropriate for a correct exposition of the faith, and when committed to memory, help toward the firm possession of truth. Finally, they make it possible for a uniform way of speaking to be used among the faithful.

Formulas are generally presented and explained when the lesson or inquiry has reached the point of synthesis.

To be selected in preference to the others are those formulas which, while expressing faithfully the truth of the faith, are adapted to the capacity of the listeners. It must not be forgotten that dogmatic formulas are a true profession of Catholic doctrine, and are accordingly to be accepted as such by the faithful in the sense in which the Church has understood and does understand them (cf. First Vatican Council, Dogm. Const. *Dei Filius,* DS 3020, 3043). The traditional formulas for professing the faith and for praying, such as the Apostles' Creed, the Lord's Prayer, the Hail Mary, and the like, are to be taught with special care.

EXPERIENCE

74. a) Experience begets concerns and questionings, hopes and anxieties, reflections and judgments; these merge and there results a certain desire to steer the human way of life.

Therefore, catechesis should be concerned with making men attentive to their more significant experiences, both personal and social; it also has the duty of placing under the light of the Gospel the questions which arise from those experiences, so that there may be stimulated within men a right desire to transform their ways of life.

In this fashion, experience also makes men respond in an active way to the gift of God.

b) Experience can also help make the Christian message more intelligible.

Christ himself preached the kingdom of God by illustrating its nature with parables drawn from the experience of human life. He recalled to mind certain human situations (the merchant who carries on a good business, the servants who to a greater or lesser extent increase the talents given to them, and so forth) in order to explain eschatological and transcendent realities, and then to teach the way of life which these realities demand of us.

Thus it is that experience serves in the examination and acceptance of the truths which are contained in the deposit of revelation.

c) Experience, considered in itself, must be illumined by the light of revelation. By recalling to mind the action of God who works our salvation, catechesis should help men to explore, interpret, and judge their own experiences, and also to ascribe a Christian meaning to their own existence.

In this aspect, experience is as it were an object to be interpreted and illumined by the catechist. This task, even though it is not without its difficulties, must not be overlooked.

STIMULATING THE ACTIVITY OR CREATIVITY OF THOSE CATECHIZED

75. All human education and all real communication require first of all that interior activity be made possible and be stimulated in the one to whom they are directed. In catechesis, therefore, one must stir up the activity of faith (of hope, too, and of charity); for correctness and vigor of judgment, which are to be stimulated by an active style of instruction, here help to bring about acceptance or the word of God. But the confidence which inspires active education should never lead one to forget that the act of faith necessarily involves a conversion of the one making it.

From what has been said it is evident that this active way of catechizing is in complete harmony with the economy of revelation and salvation. The pedagogical art which promotes an active response on the part of those to be catechized is in harmony with the general condition of the Christian life in which the faithful actively respond to God's gifts through prayers, through participation in the sacraments and the sacred liturgy, through acceptance of responsibilities in the Church and in social life, and through the practice of charity.

Those to be taught, especially if they are adults, can contribute in an active way to the progress of the catechesis. Thus, they should be asked how they understand the Christian message and how they can explain it in their own words. Then a comparison should be made between the results of that questioning and what is taught by the Magisterium of the Church, and only those things which are in agreement with the faith should be approved. In this way powerful aids can be found to hand on effectively the one true Christian message.

76.   In catechesis, the importance of the group is becoming greater and greater.

In the catechesis of children, the group helps to further their education for social life, both in the case of children who attend catechism classes together, and in the case of those brought together in a small number to engage in some activities.

For adolescents and young adults, the group must be considered a vital necessity. In a group, the adolescent or the young adult comes to know himself and finds support and stimulation.

In the case of adults, the group can today be considered a requisite for catechesis which aims at fostering a sense of Christian co-responsibility.

In groups which include adolescents or adults, catechesis takes on the character of a joint study.

Such joint study aims at exploring the mutual relationships and ties between the content of the Christian message, which is always the norm for believing and acting, and the experiences of the group.

The catechist should take part in the joint study, but in such a way as to maintain his particular place in the group. For in the name of the Church he acts as a witness of the Christian message, one who ministers to others, shares with them the fruits of his own mature faith, and wisely orders the joint study toward the accomplishment or its purpose.

This function of the witness of the message does not necessarily mean that the catechist must be set over the group as its director.

A group which has achieved a high degree of perfection in carrying out its task will be able to give its members not only an occasion for religious education, but also an excellent experience of ecclesial life.

Catechesis performed in this way will be able to show the young that the Church is not at all something unrelated to their own existence, but is rather a great reality for which all, each in keeping with his own calling and service, have some responsibility.

PART FIVE
CATECHESIS ACCORDING TO AGE LEVELS

NATURE AND PURPOSE OF THIS PART

77.   There are many methods and plans by which the Christian message is made to meet the various needs of men.

If missionary activity is considered, there is the method of evangelization, and of the initiation of catechumens and neophytes.

If the physical and spiritual development of those who are to be taught is considered, there is catechesis according to age levels.

If the sociological and cultural conditions in which men live are considered, there is catechesis suited to various mental outlooks (catechesis for workers, for technicians, and so on).

Finally, if the various stances which those who have been baptized can take towards the faith are considered, there is catechesis for believers who desire to obtain a fuller and more profound knowledge of the faith, and there is a catechesis for those who still lack the very basics of the faith.

Each of these methods, which are interconnected and interdependent, obviously has its own value and importance.

National or regional catechetical directories will have the task of providing specific and definite norms in this whole area, in accord with concrete local conditions and needs.

Here, for the sake of an example, are presented only some general principles of a catechesis adapted to various age levels, to show the force and importance of such a catechesis.

INFANCY AND ITS IMPORTANCE

78.   The first roots of religious and moral life appear at the very beginning of human life. In the families of believers the first months and years of life, which are of the greatest importance for a man's balance in the years to come, can already provide the right conditions for developing a Christian personality. The baptism of infants takes on its full meaning when the Christian life of the parents, of the mother especially but not exclusively, makes it possible for the baptismal grace to produce its fruits. For the infant absorbs into himself, as though through an "osmosis" process, the manner of acting and the attitudes of the members of his family. And so it is that the immense number of his experiences will be, as it were, pressed together within him to form a foundation of that life of faith which will then gradually develop and manifest itself.

The right orientation of a trusting spirit depends at first on a good relationship between the infant and his mother, and then also on one between him and his father; it is nourished by sharing their joyfulness and by experiencing their loving authority. The theological virtues depend in part upon the growth of that healthy orientation for their own unimpeded development, and at the same time they tend to strengthen that orientation. At this time, too, there arises the affirmation of personality, or autonomy; this is needed for the acquisition of the moral virtues and for leading a life in community. It itself demands a balance between firmness and acceptance. Next, the capacity for spontaneous action can gradually develop; this will be most necessary for beginning social life as well as for promoting and strengthening the service of God and of the Church.

An education in prayer must accompany all these acquisitions, so that the little child may learn to call upon the God who loves us and protects us, and upon Jesus, the Son of God and our brother, who leads us to the Father, and upon the Holy Spirit, who dwells within our hearts; and so that this child may also direct confident prayers to Mary, the Mother of Jesus and our mother.

If these foundations are lacking, catechesis must determine whether there are any insufficiencies as a result, what they may be, and how they may be compensated. Suitable assistance on the part of Christian parents must be supported by giving the parents an adequate formation. This formation must be given to them by competent educators, even though it is to be simple and adapted to the cultural level of the parents. This task of pastors is not supererogatory; for when parents are helped to perform their duties rightly, the Church is being built up. This also provides a splendid occasion for catechizing adults.

CHILDHOOD AND ITS IMPORTANCE

79. When the child goes to school he enters a society wider than that of his family, and he is initiated into the society of adults in an intensive way that absorbs a great part of his resources and concerns. He gets his first experience of working in school (cf. GE, 5).

Before this point, the family served a mediating role between the child and the People of God. But now the child is ready to begin sharing directly in the life of the Church, and can be admitted to the sacraments.

The child's intelligence develops gradually. Catechesis must be adapted to this mental development. The child seeks to understand the religious life of adults. Accordingly, the genuine Christian life of the adult community helps very much toward giving the children a solid formation, and it does this in a truly instructive way when it explains the religious life of adults and the activities of the People of God suitably in the light of salvation history.

The initial experience of working should not be thought unrelated to the aim of catechesis. The joy of doing things and doing them well, cooperation with others, discipline arising out of this as something easy to understand and reasonable—in all this one finds many experiences which are useful not only for sharing in social life but also for active participation in the life of the Church.

With these things in mind, catechetical pedagogy, whatever method it follows, should stimulate activity on the part of the children. If it should fail to do so, catechesis could not satisfy its obligation to teach the believer to give an ever more personal response to the word and the gift of God. This active pedagogy should not be satisfied with external expressions only, however useful they may be, but it should strive to bring forth a response from the heart and a taste for prayer. This interior education is indeed rendered more difficult, but also more necessary, because of the character of contemporary civilization which tends to disperse spiritual energies.

Cooperation between catechists and parents (sharing with one another their opinions about programs, about methods, and about difficulties which arise) is necessary if the education of the children is to proceed in a suitable and harmonious way. This kind of cooperation is useful for both the catechists and the parents and helps them in carrying out their own specific duties.

CHILDREN WHO DO NOT ATTEND SCHOOL

80. There are also regions, even very large and sometimes heavily populated areas, in which there are not enough schools. Where this is so, earnest pastoral action should be directed to the families themselves, and, to the extent that it is possible, various associations should be set up to take care of the children. These associations should be set up in such a way that they can take account of the local circumstances and meet the spiritual needs of the children.

CHILDREN WHO GROW UP IN FAMILIES AFFECTED BY RELIGIOUS INDIFFERENCE

81. The difficulty of giving catechesis to children living in families who do not practice their religion at all or do so in an entirely inadequate way is becoming more and more marked. Sometimes questions are raised about the very possibility and appropriateness of giving them a catechesis.

Catechesis is certainly not to be omitted for such children; rather, it is to be planned and carried out in a way that fits in with actual circumstances and conditions. In these cases there is need to establish contact with the families and to study their mental attitudes and styles of life, so that some means can be found to open a dialogue with them. It is also necessary that catechesis present its material in a way that really responds to the concrete possibilities of these children.

ADOLESCENCE AND EARLY ADULTHOOD, AND THEIR IMPORTANCE

82. The period of adolescence and, in a larger sense, the so-called "phenomenon of youth" have very great importance (cf. AA, 12). in pre-industrial societies which have only a smaller number of schools, the transition from childhood to the adult community takes place as it were directly. In our time the custom is spreading more and more of extending the time of education in schools for adolescents. This custom creates in society a generation which is not immediately occupied with gainful labor, and which, though it already enjoys physical and intellectual vitality, is engaged in no activity other than study and preparation for a future profession. This social class has a great impact on adult society; and this creates no small problem.

This problem is also found in the Church, and although it takes different forms here, it is just as serious. Adolescents and young adults are less exposed to the danger of violently opposing the Church than they are to the temptation of leaving it. The fact that it is often difficult for adults to acknowledge that adolescents and young adults can contribute anything worthwhile is a further reason why this is a very serious problem in catechesis.

But the young will be less distrustful, the more the catechists show an ability to understand their roles and to accept them.

83. National directories should distinguish pre-adolescence, adolescence, and early adulthood.

Here it can only be pointed out that in sophisticated regions where the point is raised, the special difficulties of pre-adolescence are in practice not sufficiently nor always recognized. The educator can be tempted to treat pre-adolescents in the same way as children, and thus it is to be feared that he will not win their attention; or he can treat them as adolescents, and in that case give them themes and methods of working which presuppose a maturity of personality and of experience that they have not yet attained.

The age of pre-adolescence has as its peculiar note the troublesome beginning of concern with one's self. Hence it is important not to continue at this age the simple and objective kind of instruction which is appropriate for children; at the same time, however, one must be careful not to propose problems and themes that belong properly to adolescence.

A concrete type of instruction which would explain the lives and works of the Saints and of other outstanding person, together with reflections on the actual life of the Church, could provide catechetical students of this age with wholesome nourishment.

The time of young adulthood, taken strictly, which follows adolescence, is also a period of life which has not yet been sufficiently studied and investigated, and its special characteristics are not yet sufficiently known.

Some think that theological instruction should begin at this age. Others believe that human and social questions should be presented for study, together with simple theological explanations and with certain encouragements to Christian behavior. The method that seems most desirable is that of treating fundamental problems and problems of most concern to this age with the serious, scholarly apparatus of the theological and human sciences, using at the same time a suitable group-discussion method.

SEARCHING INTO THE MEANING OF LIFE

84. The adolescent notices profound physical and psychological changes within himself. He is looking for his place in society. Although he is no longer content with the religious forms of his childhood, he has not yet reached the maturity of faith proper to an adult; and therefore he seeks a basic orientation by which he can unify his life anew. But this searching often leads to a religious crisis.

The principal task of catechesis in adolescence will be to further a genuinely Christian understanding of life. It must shed the light of the Christian message on the realities which have greater impact on the adolescent, such as the meaning of bodily existence, love and the family, the standards to be followed in life, work and leisure, justice and peace, and so on.

FOCUSING ATTENTION ON GENUINE VALUES

85. The adolescent makes an effort to direct the vision of his life and the course of his existence according to certain principal and primary values. Today, however, the adolescent feels himself immersed in "values" that are opposed to one another. This fact sharpens the conflict within the adolescent among the various values which he is in search of, and he persuades himself to reject those values which he does not find expressed in the way adults live.

Catechesis must help him more and more to discover genuine values and to put them in order.

PERSONAL AUTONOMY

86. In order to attain the autonomy which he very much desires, the adolescent often exaggerates his self-expression and at times finds fault with the pattern of life which he has received from adults.

Adults must realize that adolescents hold fast to the faith and strengthen themselves in it, not because of any identification with adults, but because of their own convictions as these are gradually explored.

From this kind of autonomy there arises what can be called a "temptation to naturalism," which makes adolescents tend to perform their actions and to seek their salvation by their own powers. The bolder the personality, the stronger will be an inclination of this sort.

It is, therefore, the task of catechesis to bring the adolescent to that personal maturity which will allow him to overcome subjectivism and to discover a new hope in the strength and the wisdom of God.

GROUPS OF ADOLESCENTS

87. In order to maintain their autonomy adolescents seek to form associations among themselves, so that they may be able to follow out more easily their own ideas and talents, and so that by means of groups they may protect their own autonomy from adult groups. Again within the orbit of these groups the adolescent is urged on by various life values and is moved to live in accordance with them. In daily life practice adolescents communicate more easily with young people of their own age than with adults.

Catechesis has the task of working with these youth groups, which can serve to mediate between young people and the whole community of the Church (cf. AA, 12).

Youth groups do not always have positive values. For this reason there is an urgent need to promote relationships between them and Christian communities, so that the human and Christian values of the latter may be duly recognized and appreciated by the adolescents (cf. AA, 12).

INTELLECTUAL DEMANDS

88.   The adolescent possesses essentially the "formal" use of reason. He is learning how the intellect is to be used rightly, and is discovering that the culture set before him demands reflection and must be actively applied in his own life.

If catechesis is to be able to awaken an experience of the life of faith, it simply cannot neglect the formation of a religious way of thinking which will show the connection of the mysteries with one another and with man's final end (cf. First Vatican Council, Dogm. Const. *Dei Filius*, IV, DS 3015–3020). To make firm the inner coherence of this kind of religious thinking, witnessing is not enough. Today scientific strictness is demanded everywhere; hence catechesis must also provide the rational foundations for faith with the greatest care.

The intellectual building up of the faith of adolescents must by no means be considered as merely a kind of addition, but rather it should be counted as an essential need for the life of faith. The manner of teaching is of special importance. The catechist, in dialogue with the adolescent, must stimulate the mind of the adolescent.

ACTION

89.   Action is necessary for the development of the adolescent's personality. Freedom from egocentrism and subjectivism demands dealing with reality itself, whether with success or with failure.

Catechesis, which should encourage personal experience of faith and at the same time well-ordered reflection on religious matters, is brought to perfection when it leads to the fulfillment of religious duties. Christian catechesis should educate adolescents to assume the responsibilities of faith and gradually make them capable of upholding their Christian profession before all men.

ADOLESCENTS WHO DO NOT ATTEND SCHOOL

90.   An immense number of young people who are engaged in the manual or professional skills are drawn into an accelerated development of their personality. This accelerated development of personality may turn out to be favorable or unfavorable, complete or incomplete.

It follows, then, that it is necessary to establish a special catechesis for such adolescents. This will have to consider the immediate problems of everyday life, support the young as they begin working and help them, in accordance with their individual capacities, to carry on their activity by working together with Catholic associations.

Moreover, since the special characteristics and needs of adolescents remain present in the young worker, it will be the task of catechesis not only to shed light on his concrete activity, but also to lead him to embrace the whole of God's plan.

91. The duty here cannot be considered one that is secondary or one that is taken care of elsewhere. Maladjusted children and adolescents make up no small part of the citizenry. The conditions of society today not infrequently make it difficult for young people to have a harmonious life development and to have a suitable adjustment to society.

Catechesis must provide for these young people the possibility of living a life of faith in accordance with their own state. This is an eminently evangelical task and a witness of great value, which the Church has carried on in every age.

The education of these young people in the faith has a pastoral value, and indeed one of great importance, also because it offers the possibility of reaching very many families.

Finally, the peculiar difficulty in performing this task and the necessity of imparting to such young people only the essential elements can give catechesis in general the benefit of employing the methods and ways which pedagogical research discovers and makes available for the sake of these young people.

ADULTHOOD

92. This *General Directory* earnestly affirms the need of catechesis for adults, for these reasons:

a) The undertaking of tasks in social life, and the responsibilities of family, professional, civic, and political life demand of adults that they complete their Christian formation according to the norm of the word of God in a special and suitable way (cf. AA, 29–32). Cooperation should be promoted between those who catechize adults and those who take part in the various forms of the apostolate of the laity.

b) Aptitudes and capacities which reach their full development in adult life, such as the experience of life, maturity of personality, and so on, must be cultivated and illumined by the word of God.

c) The adult, moreover, must successfully pass through certain periods of life which are full of crises. Although these crises are less obvious than those experienced by adolescents, they are not to be considered less dangerous or less profound; in these times the adult's faith must be constantly illumined, developed, and fortified.

DYNAMIC NOTES OF ADULTHOOD — FELLOWSHIP AND LONELINESS

93. When a person arrives at adult age, he ordinarily becomes more capable of having fellowship with others and of establishing mutual relationships with them.

This capacity and the need for fellowship come into play within the framework of family duties and within the relationships of social life; and all these things serve at times to promote this fellowship and at times to hinder it.

As a matter of fact, people, especially in contemporary society, often experience too much loneliness.

Catechesis ought to show that God, who is love, is really the author of the community of faith, which is the Church, and at the same time it should enkindle a desire for entering into fellowship with every man. It reminds married couples that their intimate union is, in virtue of the sacrament of matrimony, a sign of the mystery of unity and fruitful love between Christ and the Church, and that it shares in that mystery (cf. Ephesians 5:32).

Within the frame of small groups of the faithful, catechesis will help adults to live Christian charity to the full. Indeed, this charity, as the sign of a certain common experience, makes them be of assistance to one another in the faith.

FULL DEVELOPMENT OF THE PERSONALITY

94. Adult age is distinguished chiefly by the awareness of having achieved a fully developed personality.

The man who has successfully passed through each stage of his development and who has been able to enter into fellowship with others and to exercise creative ability, tries, when he has reached adult age, to reduce to a unified whole all the experiences of his personal, social, and spiritual life. A danger lies in the fact that the adult, especially if he belongs to an industrial society, may think that he can obtain this unity merely by conforming himself to the society in which he lives. But the perfect attainment of personality does not consist in a merely exterior balance between personal life and its social context, but it looks especially toward the attainment of Christian wisdom.

For this reason catechesis must strive to lead man to observe the order of priority among ends, that is, to perceive more fully the meaning of life and death, in the light of the death and resurrection of Christ.

OLD AGE

95. The importance of old age is still not sufficiently recognized in the pastoral ministry.

In our times the number of the aged is increasing more and more. The aged are often neglected by contemporary society, however, and this fact must be carefully noted for its relevance to pastoral activity.

As a matter of fact, the aged can contribute no small benefit to the community both by their work, which is not always justly appreciated, and by the witness that flows from their experience.

Moreover, there is a duty in justice to help the aged by a catechesis that has reference to death, which biologically is near at hand, and socially is to some extent already present, since almost nothing is expected any more from their activity.

Catechesis should teach the aged to have supernatural hope, by virtue of which death is considered a crossing over to true life and as a meeting with the divine Savior. In this way old age can become a sign of the presence of God, of immortal life, and of the future resurrection. This will, indeed, be an eschatological witness that the aged can bear by their patience toward themselves and toward others, by their benevolence, by their prayers poured out in praise of God, by their spirit of poverty and the trust that they put in God.

Unquestionably, it would be a serious loss to the Church if the great number of the aged who have been baptized were not to show that their faith shines with a brighter light when death approaches.

SPECIAL FORMS OF CATECHESIS FOR ADULTS

96.   There are conditions and circumstances that demand special forms of catechesis.

a) There is the catechesis of Christian initiation or the catechumenate for adults.

b) There is the catechesis for those who are involved in the lay apostolate in a special way. Clearly catechesis must provide for a deeper study of the Christian message in these cases.

c) There is a catechesis which is to be given on the occasion of the principal events of life, such as marriage, the baptism of one's children, first communion and confirmation, the more difficult periods of the children's education, one's illness, and so forth. These are times when people are moved more strongly than ever to seek the true meaning of life.

d) There is a catechesis which is to be given on the occasion of some change in the circumstances of one's life, as for example on the occasion of starting work, on entering military life, when migrating, or when changing one's profession or social status. These changes can indeed increase one's spiritual goals, but they can also disturb the spirit and snatch away hope. The Christian community has a duty to supply those who experience them with necessary helps in fraternal love. The word of God, which in these circumstances is sometimes more readily accepted, ought to be a light and an aid to them.

e) There is the catechesis which is concerned with a Christian use of leisure, and that which is to be given on the occasion of recreational traveling (cf. *Directorium Generale pro ministerio pastorali quoad "turismum,"* 19, 25).

f) There is the catechesis which is to be given on the occasion of special events touching the life of the Church or of society.

These special forms of catechesis in no way lessen the need for establishing catechetical cycles which are devoted to a systematic study of the entire Christian message. This organic and well-organized formation is certainly not to be reduced to a simple series of conferences or sermons.

97.   So that it will always be able to respond to the more urgent demands of our time, a catechesis for adults should:

a) *Teach them to evaluate correctly, in the light of faith, the sociological and cultural changes in contemporary society.* The Christian people are becoming more and more aware of the necessity of examining where the contemporary development of society may be leading and of distinguishing between true blessings and the dangers of our present human civilization. They desire help in evaluating the changes which are constantly taking place, and they want to be enlightened about the styles of behavior which they can and should make their own.

b) *Explain contemporary questions in religious and moral matters.* Catechesis must make its own the new questions which men of this age are asking themselves. For example, today great importance is attached to questions that deal with social relations. Man wishes to imprint a new form on the society in which he lives. Such attempts at renewal, in which the responsibilities and also the limits of man are clearly evident (cf. Encycl. *Populorum progressio*, AAS, 1967, pp. 257–299), simply cannot escape the interest of catechesis.

c) *Shed light on the relations between temporal action and ecclesial action.* Catechesis should educate Christians to perceive the mutual relations between temporal duties and ecclesial duties. Catechesis should make it clear that the performance of temporal duties can have a useful influence on the ecclesial community itself, when it makes it more aware of its transcendent goal and of its mission in the world, and that the performance of ecclesial duties serves in turn to benefit human society (cf. GS, 40–45).

d) *Develop the rational foundations of the faith.* The Church has always guarded the rational foundations of the faith against fideism. Catechesis must develop more and more a correct understanding of the faith, and thereby show that the act of faith and the truths which are to be believed are in conformity with the demands of human reason. Catechesis must show that the Gospel is always contemporary and always relevant. For this reason pastoral action must be promoted in the area of Christian doctrine and Christian culture.

PART SIX
PASTORAL ACTIVITY IN THE MINISTRY OF THE WORD

PASTORAL ACTION

98.   Those things which have been explained about the catechetical act and the content of catechesis provide the basis for a plan of pastoral action, the main points of which are treated in this part.

This pastoral action requires appropriate organs on the national level, to be set up by the Conferences of Bishops, for the purpose of planning or research and for administration. Generally these organs include: (a) an episcopal commission for catechesis on which work selected *ex officio* members and experts; and (b) a permanent executive structure (office, center, and so on).

So that with the aid of these organs the pastoral action in the ministry of the word can be carried out in an efficient and coordinated way, it is necessary that:

1) a report be prepared about the actual state of affairs and the place, and about what it is possible to achieve through the ministry of the word under those conditions;

2) a program of the action to be carried out be published:

3) attention be given to the formation and instruction of those who have responsibility in this matter;

4) appropriate aids for the work be rightly planned and made available;

5) organizational structures suitable for catechesis be promoted;

6) pastoral action in catechesis be coordinated with the other fields of pastoral work;

7) provision be made for research; and

8) international cooperation be encouraged.

The guides and suggestions presented in this part cannot be implemented always and all at the same time in all parts of the Church. In the case of countries or regions where catechetical action is not yet sufficiently advanced, the purpose of these suggestions and guides is to point out goals which are to be accomplished gradually.

CHAPTER I
ANALYSIS OF THE SITUATION

PURPOSE

99. It is necessary that there be within a Conference a clear knowledge of the situation in which the ministry of the word is exercised.

The analysis aims at bringing out to what extent the Church's evangelical activity is at attaining the goals that have been set for it. Careful study must be made of the way in which the ministry of the word is being practiced and of the results — to the extent that these can be ascertained by human knowledge — which have been obtained by catechesis or by other ways of presenting the Christian message. To be subjected to examination are the undertakings of the Church and how they have seen received, where and by what persons, with what results, and so on.

100. The object of this investigation is multiple. Included are examination of pastoral action and analysis of the religious situation as well as of the sociological, cultural, and economic conditions, to the extent that these facts of collective life can greatly influence the success of evangelization.

METHODS

101. Since this work is rather arduous, it is necessary that two dangers be avoided, that is to say, one must guard against:

a) considering principles and indications which have not been sufficiently tested and proved as though they were certain;

b) demanding a degree of scientific accuracy so high that it cannot be attained.

It must also be rightly noted that technical research carried out by means of questionnaires or interviews is of little value unless preceded by diligent consideration of the various forms of pastoral action that can be chosen. It seems necessary, then, for the Conferences of Bishops to have a complete picture of the situation. This can be obtained by consulting experts truly skilled in examining the evidence available and by drawing conclusions from pastoral action which has already been started. Monographs can be of very useful help in this regard.

The entire Christian community should share in the study of the situation, so that the people may be made aware of the questions and be disposed to action.

EFFECTS

102. An investigation of this sort is not its own end. Rather, it should bring to light the more effective activities and pave the way for the undertaking of them, both by intensifying the works and undertakings that have already been proved effective and by promoting others. For it deals with foreseeing and preparing for those things that will necessarily have to be done in the future.

An investigation of this sort should also convince those who work in the ministry of the word that, so far as pastoral action is concerned, human situations are ambivalent. Therefore, workers in the service of the Gospel should learn to note the many possibilities that are opening up for their action in new and diverse circumstances. There is a danger that knowledge of difficulties might lead one to conclude that pastoral action is impossible. On the contrary, everyone should be convinced that cultural realities are not inert, immutable, univocal principles which have the effect of reducing grace and pastoral action to impotence as it were in their regard. For always possible is a process of change which can make clear the way to the faith.

CHAPTER II
PROGRAM OF ACTION

103. After the situation has been carefully examined, it is necessary to proceed to the publishing of a program of action, especially by means of a catechetical directory. This program determines the objectives, the tools for pastoral catechetical action, and the guiding norms for that same action, and these are determined in such a way that they are altogether in harmony with the objectives and norms of the universal Church and at the same time they fully respond to the local needs.

In proposing a program of action, one should carefully bear in mind the functions of strictly ecclesial institutions, such as parishes, special communities of the faithful, and societies devoted to the apostolate; of the institution of the family; of educational institutions, such as school, both Christian and neutral; and of all other forms of social and cultural groups.

The goals to be attained and the means to be used should be considered the cardinal points of any program of action.

GOALS TO BE ATTAINED

104. The goals to be attained in the field of pastoral action may differ in degree and style according to differences of place and of needs. Nevertheless, all must pertain to the growth of faith and morality among Christians and to a strengthening of their relationships with God and neighbor. They should, for example, have the objectives that adults achieve a mature faith, that Christian teaching reach scientific and technical groups, that the family be able to carry out its Christian duties, that the Christian presence exert an influence on the work of social transformation.

Since the goals are generally numerous, it is altogether advisable that they be determined in due time and according to an order of priority for the objectives to be accomplished.

It is also helpful for the pastoral goals established in one region to be opportunely compared with those established by the Conferences of Bishops that are closest to it geographically or culturally.

MEANS TO BE USED

105. The chief means to be used are: catechetical institutes, which are to be promoted or supported; programs; texts (cf. Chapter 5 of this part); working tools; instructions on methods (cf. Part Four). The area of research on means can hardly be defined. Yet this is always to be carefully borne in mind: the means proposed should always respond appropriately to the spiritual objectives that are to be attained.

106. The norms that can be given with regard to catechesis are many and they vary with the ends to be attained. In comparison with the others, the norms for preparing the faithful for the sacraments have a special importance. These include, for example, norms for the catechumenate of adults, for the sacramental initiation of children, and for the preparation of families for the baptism of their children.

To be effective, all such norms should be few in number, simple in character, and set external rather than internal criteria.

As is obvious, no particular norm can derogate from the Church's general laws and common practice without the approval of the Apostolic See.

DISTRIBUTION AND PROMOTION OF RESPONSIBILITIES

107. First of all, attention must be given to a clear and effective distribution of tasks and responsibilities. It is very important, for example, to clarify and put in their proper light the responsibilities of Christian families, of associations of the faithful, of the clergy, and of catechists. Nevertheless, it is not enough to rest content with the distribution of forces already existing; it is also necessary that effort on the part of all Christians be more and more stimulated and promoted. Care must be taken to make the Christian community every day conscious of its duty, which is to be a sign of the wisdom and love of God that was revealed to us in Christ. For this, it is expedient that the entire community and each of its members as far as possible always be informed at the proper time about what things are to be done, and also that all be invited to take an active part in the undertaking of projects, in the making of decisions, and in the carrying out of what has been decided.

In preparing programs of catechetical activity, one must consider well the fact that various undertakings can at times give rise to inconveniences and disputes. For example, difficulties can arise from the changes in terminology and from the new opinions on the relationship between education and the apostolate. In these cases, every effort should be made to avoid all those things, which can unduly disturb people.

Finally, it is necessary that all catechetical activities be provided with suitable financial support.

CHAPTER III
CATECHETICAL FORMATION

CATECHETICAL FORMATION

108. Any pastoral activity for the carrying out of which there are not at hand persons with the right formation and preparation will necessarily come to

nothing. The working tools themselves cannot be effective unless used by catechists who have been rightly formed. Hence, the suitable formation of catechists must come before reform in texts and strengthening of the organization for handling catechesis.

First of all, it is necessary that attention be given to the formation of those who carry out catechetical activities on the national level. The duty here belongs to the Conferences of Bishops. Nevertheless, the formation of those who direct catechetical activities on a national level should be joined, as it were with an extension and completion of itself, with the formation of the catechists who carry out this activity on regional and diocesan levels. Responsibility for this latter formation belongs to the regional Conferences of Bishops, where such exist, and to the individual bishops.

HIGHER INSTITUTES AND CATECHETICAL SCHOOLS

109. Higher institutes for training in pastoral catechetics should be promoted or founded, so that catechists capable of directing catechesis at the diocesan level, or within the area of activities to which religious congregations are dedicated, may be prepared. These higher institutes can be national or even international. They ought to function as a university so far as curriculum, length of courses, and requisites for admission are concerned.

Schools of religious education should also be founded within individual dioceses, or at least within the area of regional Conferences, in order that, through a curriculum that is less advanced but still effective, full-time catechetical personnel may be prepared.

CONTINUING FORMATION

110. Continuing formation includes diverse methods and grade levels. It is necessary that this formation be continued over the entire time that the catechists remain committed to their functions. Thus this pertains to directors of catechesis as well as to ordinary catechists.

Continuing formation cannot be entrusted to the central offices alone. Rather, Christian communities on lower levels must also give attention to it, also for the reason that the conditions and needs for catechesis can vary from place to place. The clergy and all who have responsibilities for supervising and directing catechesis have a duty to see to the continuing formation of all their co-workers in catechesis.

OBJECTIVE OF CATECHETICAL FOMATION

111. The summit and center of catechetical formation lies in an aptitude and ability to communicate the Gospel message. This formation requires, therefore, an accurate formation in theological doctrine, in anthropology, and in methodology, geared to the level of knowledge that is to be attained. The formation does not end, however, with the acquisition of doctrinal knowledge. The formation is complete when the catechist becomes competent to select the most

suitable method for communicating the Gospel message to groups and individuals who live in circumstances always different and singular.

112. a) *Doctrine.* That a strong doctrinal heritage must be acquired is self-evident. This must always include adequate knowledge of Catholic doctrine, together with a degree of scientific theology obtained at higher catechetical institutes. Sacred Scripture should be as it were the soul of this entire formation.

In any case, the doctrine ought to be mastered in such a way that the catechist will be able not only to communicate the Gospel message accurately, but also to make those being taught capable of receiving it actively and of discerning what in their spiritual journey agrees with the faith.

b) *Human sciences.* Our era is marked and distinguished by a very great growth in the sciences about man. These sciences are no longer reserved for the learned and the specialists. They penetrate the awareness that modern man has of himself. They influence social relationships and shape a cultural pattern, as it were, for humanity today, even that not very sophisticated.

In the teaching of human sciences, given their very great number and diversity, there are difficult problems in regard to choosing from among them and in regard to the method of teaching them. Since the question here is one of training catechists, not experts in psychology, the norm to be followed is this: determine and choose that which can directly help them to acquire facility in communication.

c) *Methodological formation.* Methodology is by its very nature nothing other than careful consideration of means that have stood the test of experience. Therefore, more importance is to be attributed to practical exercises than to theoretical instruction on pedagogy. Still, theoretical instruction is necessary for helping the catechist to meet various situations appropriately, for avoiding an empirical form of teaching catechesis, for grasping the changes found in educational reports, and for directing future work correctly.

Careful attention should be given to the fact that, when it is a question of training ordinary catechists (that is, those who teach the primary elements of catechesis), the principles we have considered above can be acquired better if they are taught at the same time the work is being performed (for example, during sessions in which lessons of catechesis are being prepared and tested).

LEARNING THE ART OF CATECHESIS

113. The preparation of the catechist must be such that he will be able accurately to interpret the reactions of each person or group, and thus be able to discern their spiritual capacities and choose the means by which the Gospel message can be received fruitfully and effectively. Many methods for this can be given: practical exercises, working in groups, analysis of cases, and so on.

The whole question here turns on weighing well and understanding the communicative power of the Christian message. Catechesis, which is the Church's practice, is not learned in a merely theoretical way. The art of teaching catechesis is acquired from experience, from the guidance of skilled teachers, and from actually performing the function. An aptitude for apostolic action and knowledge of the faith, of men, and of the laws that govern the development both of individual men and of communities, contribute to the acquisition of skill in this art.

SPIRITUAL LIFE OF CATECHESIS

114. The function entrusted to the catechist demands of him a fervent sacramental and spiritual life, a practice of prayer, and a deep feeling for the excellence of the Christian message and for the power it has to transform one's life; it also demands of him the pursuit of the charity, humility, and prudence which allows the Holy Spirit to complete his fruitful work in those being taught.

FORMATION OF CATECHISTS

115. It is necessary that ecclesiastical authorities regard the formation of catechists as a task of the greatest importance.

This formation is meant for all catechists (cf. AG, 17, 26), both lay and religious, and also for Christian parents, who will be able to receive therefrom effective help for taking care of the initial and occasional catechesis for which they are responsible. This formation is meant for deacons, and especially for priests, for "by the power of the sacrament of Orders, and in the image of the Eternal High Priest (cf. Hebrews 5:1 – 10; 7:24; 9:11 – 28), they are consecrated to preach the Gospel, shepherd the faithful, and celebrate divine worship as true priests of the New Testament" (LG, 28). Indeed, in individual parishes the preaching of the word of God is committed chiefly to the priests, who are obliged to open the riches of Sacred Scripture to the faithful, and to explain the mysteries of the faith and the norms of Christian living in homilies throughout the course of the liturgical year (cf. SC, 51, 52). Hence it is of great importance that a thorough catechetical preparation be given students in seminaries and scholasticates, which should he completed afterwards by the continuing formation mentioned above (cf. 110).

Finally, the formation is meant for teachers of religion in public schools, whether these belong to the Church or to the state. To carry out a task of such great importance, only persons should be selected who are distinguished for talent, doctrine, and spiritual life (cf. GS, 5).

It is highly desirable that in this area of formation there be genuine cooperation between the various apostolic activities and catechesis, because they are performing, although under different aspects, a common task, that of communicating the Christian message.

CHAPTER IV
CATECHETICAL AIDS

AIDS

116. Of the chief working tools for catechesis, the following are considered here:

—directories of the Conferences of Bishops;

—programs;

—catechisms;

—textbooks;

—audiovisual aids.

CATECHETICAL DIRECTORIES

117. Directories are concerned with promoting and coordinating catechetical action in the territory of a region or nation, or even of several nations of the same sociocultural condition. Before they are promulgated, every local Ordinary should be heard, and then should be submitted to the Apostolic See for approval (cf. 134).

PROGRAMS

118. Programs set up the educational goals to be attained according to ages or places or set times, the methodological criteria to be used, and the content to be taught in catechesis. By all means care must be taken that the mysteries of faith to be believed by adults are already indicated in the programs for children's and adolescents' catechisms in a way adapted to their age (cf. n. 134).

CATECHISMS

119. The greatest importance must be attached to catechisms published by ecclesiastical authority. Their purpose is to provide, under a form that is condensed and practical, the witnesses of revelation and of Christian tradition as well as the chief principles which ought to be useful or catechetical activity, that is, for personal education in faith. The witnesses of tradition should be held in due esteem, and very great care must be taken to avoid presenting as doctrines of the faith special interpretations which are only private opinions or the views of some theological school. The doctrine of the Church must be presented faithfully. Here the norms set forth in Chapter i of Part Three are to be followed.

In view of the great difficulties in putting these works together and the great importance of these witnesses, it is most expedient that:

a) there be collaboration by a number of experts in catechetics and in theology;

b) there be consultation with specialists in other religious and human disciplines, and also with the other pastoral organizations;

c) individual local Ordinaries be consulted and their opinions be carefully considered;

d) limited experiments be tried before definitive publication; and

e) these texts be duly reviewed after a certain period of time.

Before promulgation, these catechisms must be submitted to the Apostolic See for review and approval (cf. 134).

TEXTBOOKS

120. Textbooks are aids offered to the Christian community that is engaged in catechesis. No text can take the place of a live communication of the Christian message; nevertheless, the texts do have great value in that they make it possible to present a fuller exposition of the witnesses of Christian tradition and of principles that foster catechetical activity. The putting together of these texts requires a cooperative effort by a number of catechetical experts, and also consultation with other experts.

MANUALS FOR CATECHISTS

121. These books should contain:

—an explanation of the message of salvation (constant reference must be made to the sources, and a clear distinction must be kept between those things which pertain to the faith and to the doctrine that must be held, and those things which are mere opinions of theologians);

—psychological and pedagogical advice;

—suggestions about methods.

Books and other printed materials intended for study and activity by those being taught should also be provided. These printed materials can be made part of the books for the use of those being taught, or they can be published as separate booklets.

Finally, care should be taken to publish books for the use of parents, if the question is one of giving catechesis to children.

AUDIOVISUAL AIDS

122. Audiovisual aids are used especially:

a) as resources for enriching catechetical instruction with objective elements; for this use, they should excel in truthfulness, careful selection of ideas, and pedagogical clarity; and

b) as images for properly cultivating the powers of the senses and the imagination; for this use they should have real beauty and be effective in moving people.

In regard to these aids, the following are necessary functions:

—fostering studies concerning the criteria which should guide the production and selection of these aids in keeping with the particular aspects of the Christian message that are to be presented and the particular groups of people for whom they are intended; and

—instructing catechists in a right use of these aids (it often happens that catechists are ignorant of the proper nature of visual language; it happens more often that audiovisual aids used improperly lead to passive rather than active behavior; and so on).

MASS MEDIA

123. The mass media have the effect, among other things, of giving an aura of reality and actuality to the events, undertakings, and ideas about which they speak, and, contrariwise, of diminishing in popular estimation the importance of the things they are silent about.

The message of salvation, therefore, must have a place among the media of social communication (cf. IM, 3). It is not enough to perfect the media that the Church already possesses in this field, but rather it is necessary to promote cooperation among the producers, writers, and actors who offer their services for this purpose. Such cooperation requires that on the national and international levels there be set up groups of experts who can give genuine assistance if consulted about programs of activities that pertain to religion.

Also, it is the function of catechesis to educate the faithful to discern the nature and value of things presented through the mass media. This, as is obvious, demands a technical knowledge of the language proper to these media.

PROGRAMMED INSTRUCTION

124. Catechesis can and should use audiovisual aids so that it will be better able to achieve its goal. In this area there is a new method which is gaining ground more and more today and which in the educational field is called "programmed instruction." It ought not to be ignored.

In this matter, however, one must consider the difficulties which arise, either from the truths to be taught, or from the purpose of catechesis itself. Unprepared explanations are to be avoided. Rather, both for preparing the programs, as well as for expressing truths with the help of pictures, one should call upon the joint effort of experts in sacred theology, in catechetics, and in the art of audiovisual teaching.

CHAPTER V
ORGANIZATION FOR CATECHESIS

ORGANIZATION FOR CATECHESIS

125. The organization for catechesis within the area of every Conference of Bishops consists chiefly of diocesan, regional and national structures.

The principal purposes of these structures are:

a) to promote catechetical activities; and

b) to cooperate with other apostolic undertakings and works (for example, with the liturgical commission, with associations for the lay apostolate, with the ecumenical commission, and so on), because all these activities of the Church have a part, even though in different ways, in the ministry of the word.

DIOCESAN STRUCTURES

126. The Decree *Provido sane* (cf. AAS, 1935, pp. 151 ff.) established the Diocesan Catechetical Office, the function of which is to supervise the entire catechetical organization. This diocesan office should have a staff of persons who have special competence. The extent and diversity of the problems which must be handled demand that the responsibilities be divided among a number of truly skilled people.

It is also the task of the diocesan office to promote and direct the work of those organizations (such as the parish catechetical center, the Confraternity of Christian Doctrine, and so on) which are as it were the basic cells of catechetical action.

Permanent centers for training catechists should be set up by local communities. It will thus become clear among Christian people that the work of evangelization and the teaching of the message of salvation pertain to all.

The Catechetical Officer, therefore, which is part of the diocesan curia, is the means which the bishop as head of the community and teacher of doctrine utilizes to direct and moderate all the catechetical activities of the diocese.

No diocese can be without its own Catechetical Office.

REGIONAL STRUCTURES

127. It is useful for a number of dioceses to combine their actions, bringing together for common benefit their experiences and undertakings, their offices and equipment; for the dioceses that are better provided for to give help to the others; and for a common action program to be prepared for the region as a whole.

NATIONAL STRUCTURES

128. It is by all means necessary that the Conferences of Bishops, and more directly, the Bishops' Catechetical Commission, be equipped with a permanent structure.

This National Catechetical Office or Center has a twofold task:

— to serve the catechetical needs of the country as a whole. The effort here would extend to publications of national importance, national congresses, relations with the mass media, and generally all those works and projects which are beyond the powers of individual dioceses and regions;

—to serve dioceses and regions by publicizing catechetical ideas and undertakings, by coordinating action, and by giving assistance to those dioceses that are less advanced in catechetical matters.

Another function of the National Office or Center is to coordinate its own work with the action of the rest of the national pastoral undertakings, and also to cooperate with the international catechetical movement.

CHAPTER VI
COORDINATION OF PASTORAL CATECHETICS
WITH ALL PASTORAL WORK

CATECHESIS AND PASTORAL ACTION

129. Since every important act in the Church participates in the ministry of the word, and since catechesis always has a relation to the universal life of the Church, it follows that catechetical action must necessarily be coordinated with the overall pastoral action. The aim of this cooperation is to have the Christian community grow and develop in a harmonious and orderly fashion; for, surely, although it has distinct aspects because of the various functions, it nevertheless strives toward a single basic goal.

It is necessary, therefore, that catechesis be associated with other pastoral activities (cf. *Motu proprio, Ecclesiae sanctae*, 17), that is, with the biblical, liturgical, and ecumenical movements, with the lay apostolate and social action, and so on. Besides, it must be kept in mind that this cooperation is necessary from the very outset, that is, from the time that studies and plans for the organization of pastoral work are started.

CATECHUMENATE FOR ADULTS

130. The catechumenate for adults, which at one and the same time includes catechesis, liturgical participation, and community living, is an excellent example of an institute that springs from the cooperation of diverse pastoral functions. Its purpose is to direct the spiritual journey of persons who are preparing themselves for the reception of baptism, and to give direction to their habits of thought and changes in moral living. It is a preparatory school in Christian living, an introduction to the religious, liturgical, charitable, and apostolic life of the People of God (cf. AG, 13–14; SC, 65; CD, 14). Not only the priests and catechists, but the entire Christian community, through sponsors who act in its name, is engaged in this work.

CHAPTER VII
NECESSITY OF PROMOTING SCIENTIFIC STUDY

SCIENTIFIC STUDY

131. Because of the rapid development in present-day culture, the catechetical movement will in no way be able to advance without scientific study.

Hence it is necessary that the national organs of the Conferences of Bishops promote joint research projects. Clearly it is necessary that a program of questions to be researched be determined, that there be awareness of the questions already under study and occasional consultation with the experts who are working on them, and that a study be undertaken of questions that have not yet been researched, the necessary financial support for this having been provided.

There can be subjects for research that have universal importance: for example, the relations between catechesis and modern exegesis, between catechesis and anthropology, between catechesis and the mass media, and so on. Because of the nature and difficulties of such kinds of research, international cooperation is often advisable.

CHAPTER VIII

INTERNATIONAL COOPERATION AND RELATIONS
WITH THE APOSTOLIC SEE

INTERNATIONAL COOPERATION

132. The Apostolic College performs its function in a closely cooperative way (cf. LG, 22–23; AG, 38; CD, 2, 4). Consequences of this solidarity which affect catechesis have been considered a number of times in this part of the *Directory* (for example, Chapter II: comparing pastoral goals among neighboring countries; Chapter III: establishing higher institutes; Chapter IV: working out common aids; Chapter VII: doing scientific research).

International cooperation is also required in the ministry of the word for immigrants.

The task to be accomplished is twofold. On the one hand, the word of God must be brought to the immigrants. Because of the differences in language, culture and customs, this requires an exchange both of information and of persons between the churches of the countries from which the immigrants come and the churches of the countries which accept them. On the other hand, it is necessary that this ministry of the word make the Christians of the host countries aware of the pressing problems of the immigrants, and ready to welcome them out of brotherly love.

International cooperation is also required for the catechesis of tourists. It is clear that "tourism," as it is called, is spreading more and more among all nations (cf. *Directorium Generale pro ministerio pastorali quoad "turismum,"* passim).

International cooperation must show regard for the tasks and conditions of the local churches. Hence, those countries that have made greater advances in personnel, in economic goods, and in scientific research, should assist the other countries that have not progressed that far, but should not impose their own styles of thinking and acting, nor their own methods.

133. Just as Peter was made the head of the Apostolic College and the foundation upon which the Church is built, so the Successor to Peter, namely, the Roman Pontiff (cf. LG, 22), is the visible head of the College of Bishops and of the entire People of God. He fulfills his universal office of teaching and of ruling as Vicar of Christ and Shepherd of the whole Church (cf. LG, 22), always for the welfare and spiritual development of the People of God. He can, however, freely carry out this office according to the needs of the Church, either in a personal way, or in a strictly collegial way, that is, together with the bishops of the entire Church. The personal way he exercises either by his own acts or through acts of his ministers, principally by acts of the Offices of the Roman Curia.

SACRED CONGREGATION FOR THE CLERGY

134. The central responsibility for catechesis in territories of so-called common law has been entrusted to the Sacred Congregation for the Clergy (Second Office). This Congregation has the task of working out, of coordinating, and of moderating matters that have to do with promoting the preaching of the word of God and the works of the apostolate; it also has the task of publishing information, and of promoting, as much as possible, collaboration among the various countries.

This Office assists the development of and gives guidance to offices that are in charge of catechesis.

It reviews and approves catechetical directories, catechisms, and programs for preaching the word of God produced by Conferences of Bishops. It encourages national catechetical congresses, or it approves or calls international ones (cf. Const. Apost., *Regimini Ecclesiae universae*, 69; Letter of the Secretariat of State, August 20, 1969, N. 143741).

ADDENDUM
THE FIRST RECEPTION OF THE SACRAMENTS OF PENANCE AND THE EUCHARIST

Among the tasks of catechesis, the preparation of children for the sacraments of Penance and the Eucharist is of great importance. With regard to this, it is held opportune to recall certain principles and to make some observations about certain experiments that have been taking place very recently in some regions or places of the Church.

THE AGE OF DISCRETION

1. The suitable age for the first reception of these sacraments is deemed to be that which in documents of the Church is called the age of reason or of discretion. This age "both for Confession and for Communion is that at which the child begins to reason, that is, about the seventh year, more or less. From that time on the obligation of fulfilling the precepts of Confession and Communion

begins" (Decree *Quam singulari*, I, AAS, 1910, p. 582). It is praiseworthy to study by research in pastoral psychology and to describe this age which develops gradually, is subject to various conditions, and which presents a peculiar nature in every child. One should, however, be on guard not to extend beyond the above-mentioned limits, which are not rigid, the time at which the precept of Confession and Communion begins to oblige *per se.*

FORMATION AND GROWTH OF THE MORAL CONSCIENCE OF CHILDREN

2.   While the capacity to reason is evolving gradually in a child, his moral conscience too is being trained, that is, the faculty of judging his acts in relation to a norm of morality. A number of varying elements and circumstances come together in forming this moral conscience of a child: the character and discipline of his family, which is one of the most important educative factors during the first years of a child's life, his associations with others, and the activities and the witness of the ecclesial community. Catechesis, while carrying out its task of instructing and forming in the Christian faith, puts order into these various factors of education, promotes them, and works in conjunction with them. Only in this way will catechesis be able to give to the child timely direction toward the heavenly Father and correct any goings astray or incorrect orientations of life that can occur. Without doubt children at this age should be told in the simplest possible way about God as our Lord and Father, about his love for us, about Jesus, the Son of God, who was made man for us, and who died and rose again. By thinking about the love of God, the child will be able gradually to perceive the malice of sin, which always offends God the Father and Jesus, and which is opposed to the charity with which we must love our neighbor and ourselves.

IMPORTANCE OF EXPLAINING THE SACRAMENT OF PENANCE TO CHILDREN

3.   When a child begins to offend God by sin, he also begins to have the desire of receiving pardon, not only from parents or relatives, but also from God. Catechesis helps him by nourishing this desire wholesomely, and it instills a holy aversion to sin, an awareness of the need for amendment, and especially love for God. The special task of catechesis here is to explain in a suitable way that sacramental Confession is a means offered children of the Church to obtain pardon for sin, and furthermore that it is even necessary *per se* if one has fallen into serious sin. To be sure, Christian parents and religious educators ought to teach the child in such a way that above all he will strive to advance to a more intimate love of the Lord Jesus and to genuine love of neighbor. The doctrine on the sacrament of Penance is to be presented in a broad framework of attaining purification and spiritual growth with great confidence in the mercy and love of God. In this way, children not only can little by little acquire a delicate understanding of conscience, but do not lose heart when they fall into some lesser fault.

The Eucharist is the summit and center of the entire Christian life. In addition to the required state of grace, great purity of soul is clearly fitting for the reception of Communion. One must be very careful, however, that the children do not get the impression that Confession is necessary before receiving the Eucharist even when one sincerely loves God and has not departed from the path of God's commandments in a serious way.

CERTAIN NEW EXPERIMENTS

4.   In very recent times in certain regions of the Church experiments relative to the first reception of the sacraments of Penance and of the Eucharist have been made. These have given rise to doubt and confusion.

So that the Communion of children may be appropriately received early, and so that psychological disturbances in the future Christian life which can result from a too early use of Confession may be avoided, and so that better education for the spirit of penance and a more valid catechetical preparation for Confession itself may be fostered, it has seemed to some that children should be admitted to first Communion without first receiving the sacrament of Penance.

In fact, however, going to the sacrament of Penance from the beginning of the use of reason does not in itself harm the minds of the children, provided it is preceded, as it should be, by a kind and prudent catechetical preparation. The spirit of penance can be developed more fully by continuing catechetical instruction after first Communion; likewise, there can be growth in knowledge and appreciation of the great gift that Christ has given to sinful men in the sacrament of the pardon they will receive and of reconciliation with the Church (cf. LG, 11).

These things have not prevented the introduction in certain places of a practice in which some years regularly elapse between first Communion and first Confession. In other places, however, the innovations made have been more cautious, either because first Confession was not so much delayed, or because consideration is given the judgment of the parents who prefer to have their children go to the sacrament of Penance before first Communion.

THE COMMON PRACTICE IN FORCE MUST BE HIGHLY ESTEEMED

5.   The Supreme Pontiff, Pius X, declared, "The custom of not admitting children to Confession or of never giving them absolution, when they have arrived at the use of reason, must be wholly condemned" (Decree *Quam singulari*, VII, AAS, 1910, p. 583). One can scarcely have regard for the right that baptized children have of confessing their sins, if at the beginning of the age of discretion they are not prepared and gently led to the sacrament of Penance.

One should also keep in mind the usefulness of Confession, which retains its efficacy even when only venial sins are in question, and which gives an increase of grace and of charity, increases the child's good dispositions for receiving the Eucharist, and also helps to perfect the Christian life. Hence, it appears the usefulness of Confession cannot be dismissed in favor of those forms of penance or those ministries of the word, by which the virtue of penance is aptly fostered in children, and which can be fruitfully practiced together with the sacrament of Penance, when a suitable catechetical preparation has been made. The pastoral experience of the Church, which is illustrated by many examples even in our day, teaches her how much the so-called age of discretion is suited for effecting that the children's baptismal grace, by means of a well-prepared reception of the sacraments of Penance and of the Eucharist, shows forth its first fruits, which are certainly to be augmented afterwards by means of a continued catechesis.

Having weighed all these points, and keeping in mind the common and general practice which *per se* cannot be derogated without the approval of the Apostolic See, and also having heard the Conferences of Bishops, the Holy See judges it fitting that the practice now in force in the Church of putting Confession ahead of first Communion should be retained. This in no way prevents this custom from being carried out in various ways, as, for instance, by having a communal penitential celebration precede or follow the reception of the sacrament of Penance.

The Holy See is not unmindful of the special conditions that exist in various countries, but it exhorts the bishops in this important matter not to depart from the practice in force without having first entered into communication with the Holy See in a spirit of hierarchical communion. Nor should they in any way allow the pastors or educators or religious institutes to begin or to continue to abandon the practice in force.

In regions, however, where new practices have already been introduced which depart notably from the pristine practice, the Conferences of Bishops will wish to submit these experiments to a new examination. If after that they wish to continue these experiments for a longer time, they should not do so unless they have first communicated with the Holy See, which will willingly hear them, and they are at one mind with the Holy See.

The Supreme Pontiff, PAUL VI, by a letter of his Secretariat of State, n. 177335, dated March 18, 1971, approved this General Directory together with the Addendum, confirmed it by his authority and ordered it to be published.

Rome, April 11, 1971, Feast of the Resurrection of Our Lord.

John J. Cardinal Wright, Prefect

+ Pietro Palazzini, Secretary

TO TEACH
AS
JESUS DID

A PASTORAL MESSAGE ON CATHOLIC EDUCATION
1972

OVERVIEW OF *TO TEACH AS JESUS DID*

by Richard W. Walsh

In 1972, the National Conference of Catholic Bishops (NCCB) offered its first pastoral letter completely devoted to the concern of Catholic education. The bishops spoke in the language emerging out of the Second Vatican Council. They spoke in the words of *To Teach as Jesus Did* (TJD). The voice was substantial and sent three clear messages. First, the very process that produced TJD was highly consultative. Second, its 150 paragraphs, covering just 42 pages, echoed the immediate preconciliar, conciliar and postconciliar documents: *Mater et Magistra, Dogmatic Constitution of the Church, On Christian Education, On Human Life, On the Apostolate of the Laity, On the Ministry of Bishops,* and the *General Catechetical Directory.* Finally, the content and tone of the document is directed to immediate concerns of a particular church realizing the vision of the conciliar decrees. *To Teach as Jesus Did* was intended specifically not to be timeless; it gave prophetic voice to concerns that are just as real more than two decades after its publication.

To Teach as Jesus Did can claim a special relationship to Vatican II through the *Declaration on Christian Education (Gravissimum Educationis),* which offered fresh perspectives and directions for the mission of education. With these perspectives and directions, American bishops returned from the Council to find a substantial measure of ecclesial controversy concerning the future of the foundational education/catechetical unit of the church in America: the Catholic schools. To respond to the looming crisis, the emerging NCCB issued a strong statement in November 1967 in support of Catholic schools and stated their intention to address the larger question of the "comprehensive obligation to education," which would apply the *Declaration on Christian Education* to this particular national setting. While the intent of the bishops was to support leaders in Catholic schools, the feedback of these leaders called for wider consultation and collaboration in future statements. Because of the complexities of building a national ecclesial infrastructure, it was 1970 before the reorganized Education Committee of the United States Catholic Conference (USCC) began the preparation of a draft of this statement and, in January 1972, such a resource was shared with the bishops. The response was some 500 pages of *modi:* suggestions, requests for clarification and modification, and so on. The most interesting dynamic in the consultation process included a February 1972 consultation with 20 delegates of the then Leadership Conference of Major Superiors of Women. The revision in spring 1972 brought new direction to the document in a focus on message, community and service. Through the following summer, bishops and USCC staff members rewrote the document, and in September bishops were consulted again, now offering 50 pages of *modi.* Presented to the NCCB in November 1972, TJD was accepted in a vote of 197 to 29.

To Teach as Jesus Did has a particular relationship to two other documents of the NCCB: *Basic Teachings for Catholic Religious Education* and *Sharing the Light of Faith: National Catechetical Directory for Catholics of the United*

States. The bishops gathered at the Second Vatican Council made a clear decision that they would produce no catechism and intentionally opted for a process shaped by the currents of renewal. National hierarchies were called to develop detailed directories that would be modeled on the *General Catechetical Directory,* for use in their own countries. These directories, or commentaries, would serve as the foundation for catechetical resources. By the issue date of TJD and *Basic Teachings,* the *National Catechetical Directory* was already in formation. Still, the NCCB published both TJD and *Basic Teachings for Catholic Religious Education.* These two projects would demonstrate two divergent views of catechesis, one in which process and content are treated as separate concerns (TJD and *Basic Teachings*) and another that intentionally demonstrates the essential interaction of process and content (the *National Catechetical Directory*). *To Teach as Jesus Did* holds the perspective that the content of faith is alive within the faith community and articulates a general vision and direction for the method through which this content can be shared most effectively.

MISSION, MINISTRY, ACTION

The goal of TJD was threefold: to articulate the mission, to identify those ministry areas clearly identified with this mission and to set an agenda for action. The mission was articulated as a lifelong process of "integrated ministry embracing three interlocking dimensions: the message revealed by God *(didache)* which the church proclaims; fellowship in the life of the Holy Spirit *(koinonia)*; service to the Christian community and the entire human community *(diakonia).* . . . Each educational program or institution under church sponsorship is obliged to contribute in its own way to the realization of the threefold purpose within the total educational ministry" (14). Within the context of this catechetical theology, which so highly values inculturation into the lived experience of faith, TJD would offer a blueprint for action shared by the NCCB. The importance of this articulated mission can be neither underestimated nor overappreciated.

Identifying ministry areas, TJD chooses to emphasize the lifelong nature of the mission of Catholic education by beginning with the fullness of Christian maturation in adulthood, viewing other areas as part of this developmental process. While excluding none, the document specifically identifies the ministry areas of adult education, Catholic higher education, Catholic colleges and universities, campus ministry, family involvement, youth ministry, religious education of children in public schools, Catholic schools and the Christian community.

Oriented to action and desiring to build an agenda, TJD offers general direction in all the areas noted. Still, these directions become quite specific in a number of ministry areas and this specificity may reveal particular comfort zones. To imply that the greater degree of attention given to these ministry areas denotes a preference would be unfair to the document. The document simply reveals the existence of an infrastructure that was both in existence and available to bishops in setting the agenda for some ministry areas. *To Teach as Jesus Did* is particularly specific in its treatment of diocesan educational structures shaped to facilitate this direction for total Catholic education, adult formation in the areas that treat Christian parenting and concerns in the area of higher education, religious education of children not enrolled in parochial schools, and Catholic elementary and secondary schools. In its treatment of each area TJD is consistently and honestly challenging. The document is comfortable in noting that these are "crisis" areas. Because of its specificity in these areas, they are worthy of particular note.

GENEROUS IN CONCERN: HIGHER EDUCATION, RELIGIOUS EDUCATION, CATHOLIC SCHOOLS

To Teach as Jesus Did is particularly generous in its treatment of the topics of higher education, Catholic colleges and universities, campus ministry, and theology and the Catholic university. In the two other areas where TJD is as generous in its treatment—religious education and Catholic schools—the agenda is specific and directed. In this area there is a particular delicacy that avoids this measure of specific direction founded in two possible realities: Section II of the document, entitled "A World in Transition," and the complex relationship between bishops and such institutions of higher learning. "A World In Transition" is a short section, revealing the awareness of a "knowledge explosion" in which the very enterprise of education is changing. This section notes that "faithful to the past and open to the future, we must accept the burden and welcome the opportunity of proclaiming the gospel of Christ in our times" (41). *To Teach as Jesus Did* seems aware that in the light of this world in transition, Catholic higher education, and all higher education, will have a profound and lasting effect on the church and that the church has an authentic responsibility to impact Catholic higher education profoundly, and all higher education. At the same time, in the midst of both a desire to influence awareness and of rapid change, only the general spheres of influence have become clear for TJD.

Aware that "historically, Catholic colleges and universities have had varying degrees of relationship to ecclesiastical authority" (76), TJD seeks to offer broad but real parameters for the development of the ministry of higher education. While addressing campus ministry, a responsibility related directly to diocesan responsibilities, the text is more specific. When addressing concerns more clearly in the realm of the governance systems of such institutions, TJD seems aware that there is an infrastructure in place that abuts episcopal teaching but maintains its independence. The delicate but directed invitation of TJD concerning these areas continues to be a worthy resource for reflection, and definition of the exact relationship between bishops and Catholic scholarship in higher education is an issue for continued discussion.

The document notes the importance of parish programs for young people not attending Catholic schools, stating that "among the pastoral issues in education [that] today challenge the Catholic community in our nation, none is more pressing than providing Catholic education for these young people" (84). The analysis of the situation is bluntly honest. Parish programs of religious education have inherent limitations and suffer because of parental and pastoral indifference, the lack of systematic programs and skilled leadership, and poorly trained volunteers. Underfunded and understaffed, parish religious education is not realizing the threefold purpose, or plan, of Catholic education in deepening the experience of Christian community, sharing the message and going forth in service to transform the world in word and action: "Merely teaching religion is not enough" (87). Further, this area of ministry is failing to reach out to the large numbers of young people and families not involved in any religious education. Finally, minorities and the disabled are being overlooked.

The action plan is correlated closely to the critique: Use apparent weaknesses as strengths. Leadership is called to recognize and support this ministry. The resources and models employed should manifest the threefold mission: message, community and service. Adequately paid professionals should be placed in key positions, and volunteers should be well formed for ministry. Parental roles should be expanded and enhanced. New resources should be infused, and the use of media should be implemented, even when this calls parishes to collaborate to provide the necessary fiscal resources. Minorities and persons with disabilities should be included fully. Outreach should be initiated for those who are not experiencing the ministry of our church. Research what is perceived as the "best" in this area of ministry, and share those models throughout local churches; generate the data needed to move forward. The insight of this critique and agenda is worthy of praise, and the enthusiasm for ministry it generated is legendary.

A recent study might illustrate that the urgency of TJD was quite appropriate. In "Serving American Catholic Children and Youth: A Study of the Number of School Age Children Enrolled in Catholic Schools and Parish Religious Education Programs" (1992), prepared for the USCC Department of Education by Maryelle Schaub and David Baker, it was estimated that in 1970, two years before the promulgation of TJD, approximately 35 percent of our youth were not being served actively by the catechetical mission. The study also identifies that in 1991, of children between the ages of five and seventeen, 33 percent were taking part in parish religious education ministries, 18 percent were enrolled in Catholic schools and 49 percent of our young people were baptized but not served actively by the catechetical mission of our church. In short, while TJD sounded an alarm concerning our lack of outreach within our own community, the percentage of those not served by the mission of Catholic education in this particular age group rose from 35 percent in 1970 to 49 percent in 1990.

Approximately 20 percent of the document addresses the issues of Catholic schools, and section 84 contains the often quoted statement that "Catholic elementary and secondary schools are the best expression of the educational ministry to youth." *To Teach as Jesus Did* roots the ministry of Catholic schools in the American experience, states clearly our common debt to the past and commitment to the future, and articulates the challenge of maintaining schools without state assistance. As a letter of the bishops, TJD calls for local leadership to act upon the mission, especially through building ownership on the local level. Catholic schools are to be truly Catholic, parents are to take up new roles of support, experimentation is to be invited—sharing insight into a great many educational fads that have most often passed their prime—and close collaboration with the public schools is considered essential.

UNFINISHED BUSINESS: TOTAL CATHOLIC EDUCATION, CATECHETICAL THEOLOGY AND NEW DIRECTIONS

The concept and practice of total Catholic education is a preoccupation of TJD, which offers a vision that formational ministries are covenanted to one another in a common mission and should act upon this mission in complementarity with these other ministries. The document does not address how the many parts of the mission have developed in isolation from one another or why complementarity might elude us. There are compelling reasons why this particular ecclesial vision might be evasive. Each of the ministries that are called to common mission in total Catholic education have a unique history. In the context of that history, these ministries have developed their own vision, vocabulary and foundational understandings. Each of these ministries states its mission—and communicates internally—with its own vocabulary and from its foundational understandings. And each of these ministries has called forth leadership committed to this history, vocabulary and mission. To challenge the situation further, early experiments in total Catholic education resulted frequently in unhealthy competition for resources, unfair comparisons and unwelcome interventions. Even at this time, the church that received TJD in 1972 has, at best, a complex response to the notion of total Catholic education.

In this "totality" there are missing pieces essential for integral unity. Immediate critique of TJD noted the consistent reference to individual and communal prayer and worship but the absence of reference to this essential element along with community, message and service. This exclusion, then, results in the inability of TJD to describe the necessary collaboration of the catechetical and liturgical community in the many expressions that have emerged in the intervening years. These include the Order of Christian Initiation for Children and Adults, the impact of the *Directory for Masses with Children,* the Liturgy of the Word with Children, renewed processes of sacramental catechesis, the development of lifelong lectionary-based resources for small communities, and reflection upon the interrelationship of catechesis and worship at every level.

The many divergent traditions and vocabularies gathered as total Catholic education are reconciled in TJD by using the term "religious education" interchangeably with "catechesis," a process that continues in the popular Catholic tradition. This practice may have been used in order to build bridges, for catechesis is a term that unites sacramental, formational and initiatory theology, while religious education is a term that can unite scholastic and quasi-scholastic processes. Still, religious education has been identified with the scholarly discipline of reflection on the nature and practices of religious traditions, while catechesis is a term that is rooted in our particular tradition and, though historically having multiple definitions, reflects an intentional process of sharing the Christian message and mission in the context of a lived community of faith. The result often enough has been a road that changes signs so often that people lose track of exactly where they are and what they are about.

To Teach as Jesus Did reflects solid conciliar teaching, wide consultation, an articulate direction for the wide enterprise of lifelong formation in faith that is founded in building Christian community, sharing the message, going forth in service and—implicitly—gathering in worship. It sets an agenda for the work as yet unfinished, which ensures its place as a contemporary, prophetic voice.

OUTLINE

Preface

I. To Teach as Jesus Did
        Message
        Community
        Service

II. A World in Transition: Faith and Technology

III. Giving Form to the Vision
    1. The Educational Ministry to Adults
        Adult Education
            Adult Religious Education
            Education for Family Life
            Parents as Educators
            Adult Education and Social Problems

        Higher Education
            Campus Ministry
            Catholic Colleges and Universities
            Theology and the Catholic University

    2. The Educational Ministry to Youth
        Religious Education Outside the Catholic School
            Doctrine, Community and Service
            Problems and Policies
            Guidelines for the Future

        Catholic Schools
            Doctrine, Community and Service
            The Crisis of Catholic Schools
            Action Needed Now
            Catholic Schools Called to Reorganization

        Youth Ministry

IV. Planning the Educational Mission
        An Invitation to Cooperation

V. A Ministry of Hope

PREFACE

1.   This pastoral message is the product of wide consultation involving many individuals and groups. It reflects a painstaking effort to obtain the views of persons from a variety of backgrounds and interests — priests, religious men and women, lay people, professional educators at all levels of education, parents, students. Much of this consultation took place at the national level but even more occurred at the local diocesan level, where bishops sought out the views of the people regarding various drafts of the document. While, in the last analysis, the pastoral represents the views of the American bishops and only they are responsible for what it says, grateful recognition is due the indispensable contributions of all those who participated in the collaborative effort involved in its preparation, itself in many ways a model of the shared responsibility for educational ministry which the document envisions and warmly recommends.

2.   The pastoral is also written against the background of the Second Vatican Council's *Declaration on Christian Education* which requested national hierarchies to issue detailed statements on the educational ministry considered in the context of the Church and society in their own countries.

3.   The pastoral's scope is broad but not all-encompassing. A virtually endless catalogue of programs, institutions, and activities could be gathered together under the rubric of "education." It was therefore necessary to employ some principles of exclusion to avoid producing a treatise of excessive length and, perhaps, superficiality. This document is concerned in the main with those agencies and instruments under Church sponsorship which are commonly recognized as "educational" by professional and layman alike and through which a deliberate and systematic effort is made to achieve what are commonly recognized as "educational" objectives. This is not to discount the educational/formational role played by communications media, liturgy — indeed one of the most powerful and appropriate educative instruments at the disposal of the Church — and countless other familial, social, and pastoral efforts, but only to state that they could not be considered in depth in this particular document. In addition, some extremely important educational programs are not treated here because they have already received detailed attention by the bishops elsewhere (for example, the education of priests, which is the subject of the National Conference of Catholic Bishops' recently published *Program of Priestly Formation*).

4.   As the concluding section of this document states, the pastoral is not to be regarded as the "final word" on its subject on either the theoretical or practical level. It will serve a useful purpose if it proves a catalyst for efforts to deal realistically with problems of polarization and of confusion now confronting the

educational ministry. Thus one hopes that the ideas it contains will be studied closely, criticized intelligently, and, where possible, implemented successfully. In the years ahead American Catholics should continue to articulate and implement their commitment to the educational ministry in ways suited to their times and circumstances. Within both the Christian community and the educational ministry the mission to teach as Jesus did is a dynamic mandate for Christians of all times, places, and conditions.

I. TO TEACH AS JESUS DID

5.   *"Lord," said Thomas, "we do not know where you are going. How can we know the way?" Jesus told him: "I am the way, and the truth, and the life; no one comes to the Father but through me. If you really knew me, you would know my Father also. From this point on you know him; you have seen him"* (John 14:5 – 7).

6.   Proclaiming the Gospel is a perennial task and joy for the Church of Jesus Christ. Rarely if ever has it been more pressing a need, more urgent a duty, and more ennobling a vocation than in these times when mankind stands poised between unprecedented fulfillment and equally unprecedented calamity.

7.   Catholic education is an expression of the mission entrusted by Jesus to the Church He founded. Through education the Church seeks to prepare its members to proclaim the Good News and to translate this proclamation into action. Since the Christian vocation is a call to transform oneself and society with God's help, the educational efforts of the Church must encompass the twin purposes of personal sanctification and social reform in light of Christian values.

8.   Thus one crucial measure of the success or failure of the educational ministry is how well it enables men to hear the message of hope contained in the Gospel, to base their love and service of God upon this message, to achieve a vital personal relationship with Christ, and to share the Gospel's realistic view of the human condition which recognizes the fact of evil and personal sin while affirming hope.

9.   Christian hope is of special importance today when many people express a naive optimism which fails to admit the reality and effects of sin upon the individual and society, and when many others, fully aware of evil in themselves and society, are tempted to indulge in crippling despair. In face of these two attitudes the Church can make a unique contribution by preaching the Gospel of hope. The Gospel proclaims the dignity and freedom of each person and gives assurance that men are right to hope for personal salvation and for the ultimate conquest of sin, isolation, injustice, privation and death because these evils have already been conquered in the person of Jesus Christ.

10.   The success of the Church's educational mission will also be judged by how well it helps the Catholic community to see the dignity of human life with the vision of Jesus and involve itself in the search for solutions to the pressing

problems of society. Christians are obliged to seek justice and peace in the world. Catholics individually and collectively should join wherever possible with all persons of good will in the effect to solve social problems in ways which consistently reflect Gospel values.

11.   Since special knowledge and skills are needed for the effective pursuit of justice and peace, Christian education is basic to the effort to fulfill the demands of the Gospel in many different communities: family, church, neighborhood, working world, civic arena, international scene. To discern the practical demands of justice is often difficult. Yet Christians must be prepared to perform these difficult tasks of discernment; social needs "must in the years to come take first place among (their) preoccupations" (Pope Paul VI, *A Call to Action*, 7).

12.   The Church is an instrument of salvation and a sign of Christ in the world today. His mission is the Church's mission; His message is the Church's message. Jesus was sent to reveal the deepest truth about God and at the same time reveal "man to himself and make his supreme calling clear" (*The Church Today*, 22). He commissioned His Church to do the same; to teach men and women about God and themselves, to foster their love of God and one another.

13.   Education is one of the most important ways by which the Church fulfills its commitment to the dignity of the person and the building of community. Community is central to educational ministry both as a necessary condition and an ardently desired goal. The educational efforts of the Church must therefore be directed to forming persons-in-community; for the education of the individual Christian is important not only to his solitary destiny but also to the destinies of the many communities in which he lives.

14.   The educational mission of the Church is an integrated ministry embracing three interlocking dimensions: the message revealed by God (*didache*) which the Church proclaims; fellowship in the life of the Holy Spirit (*koinonia*); service to the Christian community and the entire human community (*diakonia*). While these three essential elements can be separated for the sake of analysis, they are joined in the one educational ministry. Each educational program or institution under Church sponsorship is obliged to contribute in its own way to the realization of the threefold purpose within the total educational ministry. Other conceptual frameworks can also be employed to present and analyze the Church's educational mission, but this one has several advantages: it corresponds to a long tradition and also meets exceptionally well the educational needs and aspirations of men and women in our times.

MESSAGE

15.   *"For I have not spoken on my own; no, the Father who sent me has commanded me what to say and how to speak. Since I know that his commandment means eternal life, whatever I say is spoken just as he instructed me"* (John 12:49–50).

16.   Revelation is the act by which God unfolds to mankind the mystery of Himself and His plan for salvation. In Jesus, the Son of God, the message of the Old Law was fulfilled and the fullness of God's message was communicated. At the time of the Apostles the message of salvation was completed, and we therefore "await no further new public revelation before the glorious manifestation of our Lord Jesus Christ" (DV, 4). It is this message, this doctrine, which the Church is called to proclaim authentically and fully.

17.   This does not preclude development in doctrine, properly understood, or change in the forms in which it is expressed. The tradition handed on by the Apostles is a "living tradition" through which God continues His conversation with His people. God "still secretly directs, through the Holy Spirit, in sacred tradition, by the light and sense of the faith, the Church, His bride, and speaks with her, so that the People of God, under the leadership of the magisterium, may attain a fuller understanding of revelation" (GCD, 13). There is, then, a growth in understanding of the message which has been handed down (DV, 8).

18.   In proclaiming all things which His Father commanded Him to reveal, Jesus used images from the lives of His hearers and spoke in the idiom of His day. The Church, too, must use contemporary methods and language to proclaim the message of Christ to men and women today. The proclamation of the message is therefore "not a mere repetition of ancient doctrine" (GCD, 13). Furthermore, within the fundamental unity of the faith, there is room for a plurality of cultural differences, forms of expression, and theological views. But what is taught and how it is expressed are subject to the magisterium, the teaching authority of the Church, as guarantor of authenticity.

19.   The teaching Church calls upon each of us to have an active faith in God and His revealed truth. Under the influence of the Holy Spirit, man gives total adherence to God revealing Himself. Faith involves intellectual acceptance but also much more. Through faith men have a new vision of God, the world, and themselves. They must not only accept the Christian message but act on it, witnessing as individuals and a community to all that Jesus said and did. Catechesis thus "gives clarity and vigor to faith, nourishes a life lived according to the spirit of Christ, leads to a knowing and active participation in the liturgical mystery, and inspires apostolic action" (GE, 4).

20.   In sum, doctrine is not merely a matter for the intellect, but is the basis for a way of life as envisioned by St. Paul: "Let us profess the truth in love and grow to the full maturity of Christ the head" (Ephesians 4:15).

COMMUNITY

21.   *"I give you a new commandment: Love one another. Such as my love has been for you, so must your love be for each other. This is how all will know you for my disciples: your love for one another" (John 13:34–35).*

22.   As God's plan unfolds in the life of an individual Christian, he grows in awareness that, as a child of God, he does not live in isolation from others. From the moment of Baptism he becomes a member of a new and larger family, the Christian community. Reborn in Baptism, he is joined to others in common faith, hope, and love. This community is based not on force or accident of geographic location or even on deeper ties of ethnic origin, but on the life of the Spirit which unites its members in a unique fellowship so intimate that Paul likens it to a body of which each individual is a part and Jesus Himself is the Head. In this community one person's problem is everyone's problem and one person's victory is everyone's victory. Never before and never since the coming of Jesus Christ has anyone proposed such a community.

23.   Community is at the heart of Christian education not simply as a concept to be aught but as a reality to be lived. Through education, men must be moved to build community in all areas of life; they can do this best if they have learned the meaning of community by experiencing it. Formed by this experience, they are better able to build community in their families, their places of work, their neighborhoods, their nation, their world.

24.   Christian fellowship grows in personal relationships of friendship, trust and love infused with a vision of men and women as children of God redeemed by Christ. It is fostered especially by the Eucharist which is at once sign of community and cause of its growth. From a Christian perspective, integral personal growth, even growth in grace and the spiritual life, is not possible without integral social life. To understand this is a high form of learning; to foster such understanding is a crucial task of education.

25.   In the family children learn to believe what their parents' words and example teach about God, and parents enrich their own faith by participating in the formal religious education of their children: for example, by preparing them to receive the Sacraments of Penance, Eucharist and Confirmation. The members of a parish grow in fellowship by coming together to worship God and by making a shared response of faith on occasions of joy and stress. Creating readiness for growth in community through worship and through the events of everyday life is an integral part of the task of Catholic education, which also seeks to build community within its own programs and institutions.

26.   Our nation, blessed by God with enormous resources, has a heavy responsibility in the larger community of people on this planet. Christian educational ministry includes as a dimension of high importance the education of our own people to the imperatives of justice which should direct our national political, military, cultural and economic policies. In the absence of justice no enduring peace is possible. Thus the teaching of recent Popes, the Council and the Synod of Bishops concerning peace and justice for all nations and peoples must be communicated effectively and accepted fully. In this task we invite the collaboration of mission-sending societies whose apostolate includes educating American Catholics regarding their international responsibilities.

27.   *"You address me as 'Teacher' and 'Lord,' and fittingly enough, for that is what I am. But if I washed your feet — I who am Teacher and Lord — then you must wash each other's feet. What I just did was to give you an example: as I have done, so you must do"* (John 13:13 – 15).

28.   The experience of Christian community leads naturally so service. Christ gives His people different gifts not only for themselves but for others. Each must serve the other for the good of all. The Church is a servant community in which those who hunger are to be filled; the ignorant are to be taught; the homeless to receive shelter; the sick cared for; the distressed consoled; the oppressed set free — all so that men may more fully realize their human potential and more readily enjoy life with God now and eternally.

29.   But the Christian community should not be concerned only for itself. Christ did not intend it to live walled off from the world any more than He intended each person to work out his destiny in isolation from others. Fidelity to the will of Christ joins His community with the total human community. "Thus the mission of the Church will show its religious, and by that very fact, its supremely human character" (*The Church Today*, 11). No human joy, no human sorrow is a matter of indifference to the community established by Jesus. In today's world this requires that the Christian community be involved in seeking solutions to a host of complex problems, such as war, poverty, racism, and environmental pollution, which undermine community within and among nations. Christians render such service by prayer and worship and also by direct participation in the cause of social reform.

30.   It is imperative that the Church render the service of educational ministry today. Many institutions in society possess much larger material resources and thus can do far more to meet the material needs of man. None, however, has the unique resources of vision and values entrusted to His community by Jesus Christ. To suppose that the Church's mission of service is somehow less urgent in today's world than in the past is to fail to recognize mankind's enduring spiritual need and the unique capacity for meeting that need possessed by the Christian community.

31.   Beyond question the vision of the threefold educational ministry presented here is an ambitious one. Were it of human origin, one might well despair of its attainment. But since it represents God's plan, it must be energetically pursued.

32.   Even now it is being realized in many places. All three aspects of the educational mission are present, for example, in a well organized, comprehensive parish program of education where the teaching of authentic doctrine supports and is supported by the building of community, and teaching and fellowship in turn support and are supported by Christian service through sharing spiritual and temporal goods with those in need. In such a parish Catholic education's lessons are learned in classroom and pew; yet not only there, but also in the

experience of living in a Christian community of faith actively engaged in service of God, Church and neighbor.

II. A WORLD IN TRANSITION: FAITH AND TECHNOLOGY

33. Underlying virtually all of the changes occurring in the world today, both as instrument and cause, are technology and the technological worldview. Technology is one of the most marvelous expressions of the human spirit in history; but it is not an unmixed blessing. It can enrich life immeasurably or make a tragedy of life. The choice is man's, and education has a powerful role in shaping that choice.

34. Technological progress equips man with sophisticated means of communication, analysis and research. The speed and ease of travel, the marvel of instantaneous communication via satellite, television and telephone, the "transistor revolution" which carries new information and ideas to the most remote corners of the earth — these and many other developments foster growth in awareness that the human family is one, united though diverse.

35. Scientific tools or research and analysis like the computer have created a knowledge explosion. The past itself is more accessible to people and they are able to understand it far better than before. Thus not only does the present generation of mankind experience powerful influences toward unity but its bonds with earlier cultures also grow stronger. In this context the continuity of God's living revelation and of teaching based on the enduring deposit of faith is more apparent; the beauty of God's plan for community among all His scattered children can be more readily appreciated, and the plan itself can be more easily realized.

36. On the other hand, one must acknowledge a distressing paradox: this same technology threatens the unity and even the future of mankind. Its instruments destroy ancient patterns of life and uproot peoples from their traditions and history. Values cherished for centuries are abruptly challenged, and the stability of the social order is weakened if not destroyed. If this generation is, as some suggest, moving into a new era of global culture, it simultaneously risks losing the values of particular cultures which deserve to be preserved.

37. Although technology can create unparalleled material prosperity for all men, its abuse can be a tool of human selfishness. At present, technologically advanced nations are accumulating wealth at a rate which widens the gap between themselves and the poor nations of the world. The same phenomenon — a tragic gulf between rich and poor — is also present within many technologically developed nations, including our own. Our readiness for sharing has not kept pace with our skill at acquiring.

38. Technology poses new threats to the dignity of the person. It makes possible violence and destruction on a scale hitherto undreamed of. In our own nation's wealthy society the immense output of goods and services too often

distracts its citizens from awareness of their duty to God and their fellows, without satisfying their deepest needs for stability, friendship and meaning.

39.   Faith suffers in the resulting climate of uncertainty and alienation. Torn between the appeals of idealism and reform on the one hand, and the seductions of greed and self-indulgence on the other, many people drift on the surface of life, without roots, without meaning, without love.

40.   Yet profound human needs endure, and the educational mission of the Church must use old ways and new to meet them. This task is more difficult today than at many times in the past, precisely because turbulence and uncertainty bring with them skepticism toward the institutions of society, including those of the Church. In evaluating and responding to this contemporary phenomenon, it would be a serious mistake to identify mere externals with essential faith, or to confuse rejection of what is merely familiar with repudiation of our basic heritage. This underlines the need for balanced discernment in place of simplistic solutions.

41.   Faithful to the past and open to the future, we must accept the burden and welcome the opportunity of proclaiming the Gospel of Christ in our times. Where this is a summons to change, we must be willing to change. Where this is a call to stand firm, we must not yield. In this spirit, our discussion turns now to the concrete forms and structures of the educational mission.

III. GIVING FORM TO THE VISION
1. THE EDUCATIONAL MINISTRY TO ADULTS

42.   The Church's educational mission takes form in many different programs and institutions adapted to the needs of those to be educated. We shall first consider those directed to adults, including in this category both adult or continuing education and also the various forms of the ministry in higher education.

Adult Education

43.   Today, perhaps more than ever before, it is important to recognize that learning is a lifelong experience. Rapid, radical changes in contemporary society demand well planned, continuing efforts to assimilate new data, new insights, new modes of thinking and acting. This is necessary for adults to function efficiently, but, more important, to achieve full realization of their potential as persons whose destiny includes but also transcends this life. Thus they will also enjoy ever deepening fellowship within the many communities to which each of them belongs. Consequently the continuing education of adults is situated not at the periphery of the Church's educational mission but at its center. Like other church-sponsored educational efforts, adult programs should reflect in their own unique way the three interrelated purposes of Christian education: the teaching of doctrine, the building and experiencing of community, and service to others.

44.   It is essential that such programs recognize not only the particular needs of adults, but also their maturity and experience. Those who teach in the name of the Church do not simply instruct adults, but also learn from them; they will only be heard by adults if they listen to them. For this reason adult programs must be planned and conducted in ways that emphasize self-direction, dialogue, and mutual responsibility.

45.   There are many instruments of adult education, and the Church itself sponsors many such activities and programs. Their full potential in this area should be recognized and used effectively. The liturgy is one of the most powerful educational instruments at the disposal of the Church. The fact that homilies can be effective tools of adult education lends urgency to current efforts to upgrade preaching skills and to improve the entire homiletic process. The Catholic press and other communications media should be utilized creatively for continuing education.

46.   Finally, formal programs of adult education at the parish and diocesan levels deserve adequate attention and support, including professional staffing and realistic funding. Adult education should also have a recognized place in the structure of church-sponsored education at all levels, parish, diocesan and national.

ADULT RELIGIOUS EDUCATION

47.   The gradual manner of God's self-revelation, manifested in Scripture, is a model for the catechetical efforts of the Church. The full content of revelation can be communicated best to those able by reason of maturity and prior preparation to hear and respond to it. Religious education for adults is the culmination of the entire catechetical effort because it affords an opportunity to teach the whole Christian message (GCD, 20). Catechetics for children and young people should find completion in a catechetical program for adults.

48.   The content of such a program will include contemporary sociological and cultural developments considered in the light of faith, current questions concerning religious and moral issues, the relationship of the "temporal" and "ecclesial" spheres of life, and the "rational foundations" of religious belief (GCD, 97). Adult religious education should strive not only to impart instruction to adults but to enable them better to assume responsibility for the building of community and for Christian service in the world.

EDUCATION FOR FAMILY LIFE

49.   Like many institutions in society, the family is under severe pressure today. Challenges to accepted values, changing sexual mores, new ideas about marriage and especially about the sanctity of life — these and other factors can threaten family life and unity.

50.   To respond creatively to such pressures and to build a healthy family life, Catholic adults who have assumed or are about to assume the responsibility of marriage must see the family as an image of the Church itself and base their

marriage and family life on Christian values taught by the Church in the name of Jesus. As the Church struggles to fulfill Christ's mandate to sanctity and teach men and women in the difficult circumstances of life today, so should a man and a woman, united in marriage and imbued with the Gospel ideal, seek mutual growth in Christ and strive to form, in light of Christian values, the children whom God entrusts to their care. But as all the people of the Church are imperfect human beings who live their vocations imperfectly, so parents approach their vocation conscious of their limitations but aware also that by persevering effort to meet their responsibilities, even in the face of failure and disappointment, they help their children learn what faith, hope and love mean in practice. Finally, as the Church, in imitation of Christ, must constantly seek to be more sensitive and responsive to the needs of the poor among us, so must each Christian family see Christ in those who are less fortunate and, at cost to its own convenience and comfort, strive to be Christ to them, in the parish, the neighborhood, and the larger communities of the nation and world.

51.   In seeking to instill this understanding of the Christian family's role, family life education must employ such means as premarital instruction and marriage counseling, study, prayer and action groups for couples, and other adult programs which married persons themselves may plan and conduct in collaboration with Church leadership.

PARENTS AS EDUCATORS

52.   While it was relatively easy in more stable times for parents to educate their children and transmit their values to them, the immense complexity of today's society makes this a truly awesome task. Without forgetting, then, that parents are "the first to communicate the faith to their children and to educate them" (AA, 11), the Christian community must make a generous effort today to help them fulfill their duty. This is particularly true in regard to two matters of great sensitivity and importance, religious education and education in human sexuality.

53.   Although religious education should foster unity within the family and the Church, today at times it causes division instead. There are several reasons for this. Changes in religious education in recent years have disturbed many parents, in part at least because the training their children now receive seems to bear little resemblance to their own. To the extent that this problem relates to valid pedagogical methods, it may be resolved as parents come to understand better the techniques of contemporary religious education. However, the difficulty also touches at times on more basic issues involving the orthodoxy and authenticity of what is taught.

54.   Religious truth must be communicated in a relevant manner which gives each student a vital experience of faith. But it must also be transmitted fully and accurately. There is no opposition between orthodox and relevance. Religious truth is itself supremely relevant, and the manner in which it is presented must make this manifest. The Catholic community today faces the challenge of combining these complementary values — orthodoxy and relevance — in viable programs of religious education for the young. The steps to achieving this cannot

be spelled out in the abstract but must instead be worked out in dialogue and cooperation on the parish, diocesan and national levels. Parents, religious educators, including authors and publishers of textbooks, pastors, bishops, must seek together, in a spirit of mutual respect and shared commitment to the values of orthodoxy and relevance, to solve the problems and ease the tensions that now exist. They will find guidance in such sources as the *General Catechetical Directory* issued by the Holy See, "The Basic Teachings of Catholic Religious Education" to be issued by the American bishops, and the projected U.S. national catechetical directory.

55.   Continuing education will help parents understand the approach, content and methods of contemporary religious education. At the same time, however, parents must not only be helped to understand the aims and methods of catechesis; they must also be involved in planning and evaluating the catechetical programs provided for their children (GCD, 79). And in order that this evaluation may be realistic and informed, parents and other members of the Christian community have a right to expect at least that the content of these programs will be expressed in doctrinally adequate formulae as an assurance that the programs are indeed capable of transmitting the authentic Christian message.

56.   If neglecting parental involvement can only contribute to further misunderstanding and polarization in catechetics, the same is equally true of the sensitive subject of education in human sexuality. In 1968 we affirmed the "value and necessity of wisely planned education of children in human sexuality" and acknowledged our "grave obligation" to assist parents, who are "primarily responsible for imparting to their children an awareness of the sacredness of sexuality" (*Human Life in Our Day*, 61). We continue to regard this as an important priority in Christian education, met in part through diocesan-approved family life education in Catholic schools and other instructional programs.

57.   These efforts presuppose parental understanding and approval and require parents' cooperation with classroom teachers. The aim is no to supplant parents but to help them fulfill their obligation. They have a right to be informed about the content of such programs and to be assured that diocesan-approved textbooks and other instructional materials meet the requirements of propriety. But when these reasonable conditions have been met, parents should not allow continuing anxiety to be translated into indiscriminate opposition to all forms of classroom education in sexuality. Such opposition would be contrary to the teaching of Vatican Council II and the pastoral policy of the American bishops. Also, to the extent that it might disrupt responsible efforts to provide formal education in sexuality for the young, it would violate the rights of other, no less conscientious, parents who ask for such instruction for their own children.

58.   The child's need for and right to adequate knowledge and guidance, adapted to his age and individual maturity are the paramount considerations. In all programs proper emphasis must be given to the spiritual and moral dimensions of

sexuality. The child's reverence for the God-given dignity and beauty of sex is an effective safeguard of purity; it should be cultivated from the earliest years.

59.   These remarks all underline the fact that a "parent component" must be part of many different church-sponsored educational programs. Where appropriate, Catholic schools can offer courses for parents. School-related parent organizations should provide opportunities for adults to learn more about child development and pedagogical method. Similar provision for educating and involving adults should be made by parish religious education programs. All this requires teachers professionally educated for work in this area.

ADULT EDUCATION AND SOCIAL PROBLEMS

60.   "The constant expansion of population, scientific and technical progress, and the tightening of bonds between men have not only immensely widened the field of the lay apostolate . . . These developments have themselves raised new problems which cry out for the skillful concern and attention of the laity" (AA, 1). Adult education must therefore deal with the critical issues of contemporary society. "The role of the Church today is very difficult; to reconcile man's modern respect for progress with the norms of humanity and of the gospel teaching" (*Mater et Magistra*, 256). Applying the Gospel message to social problems is a delicate but crucial task for which all members of the Church are responsible but which is entrusted in a specific way to lay people.

61.   In proclaiming the social doctrine of the Gospel, the aim is not to antagonize but to reconcile. But the proclamation must be forthright, even where forthrightness challenges widely accepted attitudes and practices. Even though Christians may at times err in their facts, interpretations, and conclusions about social issues, they must not fail to apply the Gospel to contemporary life. Adult programs which deal with social problems in light of Gospel values thus have an extremely important place in the Church's educational mission. And, as in other areas of adult education, participants in such programs must be encouraged to bring their insights and experiences to planning and conducting them.

Higher Education

62.   While higher education has always been important in the United States, our rapid evolution as a technological society since World War II has given universities and colleges an even more prominent role in American life. Americans look to them for expert knowledge in a multitude of fields and depend on them for many functions which powerfully affect social and economic life. This is reflected in the remarkable growth of college and university enrollment. Today more than half of American young people of college age attend institutions of post-secondary education. The nation should be aware, however, that many private institutions, including Catholic ones, are not now sharing in this growth. For many, rising costs and dependence on tuition have caused a student shortage which threatens their survival.

63. Like the nation, the Church is greatly influenced by higher education and indebted to it in many ways. Cooperation between these two great institutions, Church and university, is indispensable to the health of society.

64. Everything possible must be done to preserve the critically important contribution made by Catholic institutions through their commitment to the spiritual, intellectual, and moral value of the Christian tradition. Their students have a right to explore the distinctively Catholic intellectual patrimony which affirms, among other things, the existence of God and His revelation in Jesus Christ as ontological facts and essential elements in seeking and sharing truth. The Church itself looks to its colleges and universities to serve it by deep and thorough study of Catholic beliefs in an atmosphere of intellectual freedom and according to canons of intellectual criticism which should govern all pursuit of truth. The Catholic community should therefore fully support practical efforts to assure the continued, effective presence of distinctively Catholic colleges and universities in our nation.

65. The same support and concern should be extended to all of higher education. The Church desires a commitment in every college and university to the full and free pursuit and study of truth, including the place of religion in the lives of individuals and society. Catholics are further called to give their support to all of higher education by the fact that the great majority of Catholics who enter college enroll in non-Catholic institutions. These young men and women have a strong claim on the service and affection of the entire Catholic community; among them are many future leaders of the nation and the Church.

CAMPUS MINISTRY

66. The Second Vatican Council urged all "pastors of the Church" not only to seek the spiritual welfare of students in Catholic institutions of higher education, but also to ensure that "at colleges and universities which are not Catholic, there are Catholic residences and centers where priests, religious and laymen who have been judiciously chosen and trained can serve on campus as sources of spiritual and intellectual assistance to young people" (GE, 10). While the Council's emphasis reflected conditions as they were up to that time, developments since then point to the importance of campus ministry in Catholic institutions as well. These developments include a decline in the number of priests and religious engaged in Catholic higher education, the increasing number of students who have not attended church-sponsored elementary and secondary schools, and some strong pressures to secularize Catholic institutions.

67. Wherever exercised, campus ministry has a number of distinct but related goals. These include promoting theological study and reflection on man's religious nature so that intellectual, moral and spiritual growth can proceed together; sustaining a Christian community on campus with the pastoral care and liturgical worship it requires; integration of its apostolic ministry with other ministries of the local community and the diocese; and helping the Christian community on campus to serve its members and others, including the many non-students who gravitate toward the university. Campus ministry thus involves far more

than pastoral care given by chaplains to students. It is pastoral, educational and prophetic, including a complex of efforts to give witness to the Gospel message to all persons within the college or university. It is conducted not only by priests and religious, but also by lay faculty and administrators, students and members of the local community.

68. Among the challenges facing campus ministry today are the special problems posed by "commuter" colleges and universities and the rapidly growing number of two-year colleges, whose enrollment is expected to reach five million by the middle of this decade. Students in these schools differ greatly from students in four-year, largely residential institutions, since most of them live at home and have jobs and many are married.

69. The work of campus ministry requires continual evaluation of traditional methods of ministry and also of new approaches which are licitly and responsibly employed. These latter can be highly appropriate in the campus setting, where there exists an audience receptive to the kind of sound innovation which may in the future prove beneficial to the larger Catholic community.

70. Religious studies, formal or informal, should be part of every campus ministry program. Neglect of such studies would risk a growth in religious indifferentism. Today, when the importance of reason and rational discourse is questioned and frequently slighted in favor of the affective side of life, there is need for emphasis on the relationship of faith and reason.

71. At the same time campus ministry must reflect the fact that young people, while deeply concerned about personal holiness and salvation, also seek meaning and values thorough the life of community. A community of believers engaged in analysis and practice of their faith is a sign of the continuing vitality of the Church. Such a community is sympathetic to all who search sincerely for the meaning of life and seek a foundation for values which will guide them in the pursuit of their destiny.

72. Campus ministry must have its proper place in the educational and financial planning of every diocese. The selection, preparation and continuing education of the men and women of campus ministry should have a high priority in educational planning. Regional and national programs must be developed to promote the development of campus ministry not only for its own sake but for the sake of increased dialogue between the Church and the university.

CATHOLIC COLLEGES AND UNIVERSITIES

73. The Catholic college or university seeks to give the authentic Christian message an institutional presence in the academic world. Several things follow from this. Christian commitment will characterize this academic community. While fully maintaining the autonomy concomitant to its being a college or university, the institution will manifest fidelity to the teaching of Jesus Christ as transmitted by His Church. The advancement of Christian thought will be

the object of institutional commitment. The human sciences will be examined in light of Catholic faith. The best of the Christian intellectual and spiritual tradition will be blended with the special dynamism of contemporary higher education in a way that enriches both.

74. The Catholic college or university must of course be an institution of higher education according to sound contemporary criteria. It will therefore be strongly committed to academic excellence and the responsible academic freedom required for effective teaching and research.

75. For a Catholic institution, there is a special aspect to academic freedom. While natural truth is directly accessible to us by virtue or our innate ability to comprehend reality, the datum or raw material from which theological reflection arises is not a datum of reality fully accessible to human reason. The authentic Christian message is entrusted by Jesus Christ to His community, the Church. Theological research and speculation, which are entirely legitimate and commendable enterprises, deal with divine revelation as their source and material, and the results of such investigation are therefore subject to the judgment of the magisterium.

76. Historically, Catholic colleges and universities have had varying degrees of relationship to ecclesiastical authority. The concern of Vatican Council II with these institutions centered on their nature or function, their faculty, and their role in Christian formation (GE, 10). At present, cordial, fruitful and continuing dialogue on the complex question of the relationship of the Catholic college or university to the Church is proceeding between representatives of such schools and of others officially concerned with Catholic education. The entire Catholic community stands to benefit from this continued exploration.

THEOLOGY AND THE CATHOLIC UNIVERSITY

77. As an institution committed to examination of the full range of human existence, the university should probe the religious dimension of life. Scholars engaged in theological and religious studies should thus be part of the academic community.

78. A department of theology, conceived and functioning as an integral part of the Catholic university, can encourage scholars in other disciplines to examine more deeply their own fields of study. The theological scholar himself is enriched by participating in such discussion.

79. The department of theology also encourages students to confront religious questions and explore beyond the limits of a narrow vision of life which excludes the religious dimension. At the same time, interaction with students obliges scholars to respond to the healthy challenge of reexamining their insights and modes of expression.

80. Finally, the department of theology is a vital resource to the Catholic community outside the university and must be aware of its responsibility to that

community. Its scholarship can provide support to the pastoral ministry of the Church and help deepen the Church's understanding of the Gospel message. Theologians can render special assistance to bishops, whose role, like theirs, includes both the development and the defense of Christian truth.

81.   While no aspect of genuine religious experience is beyond the scope of concern of the department of theology or religious studies in a Catholic university, its characteristic strength appropriately lies in the presence of scholars whose professional competence and personal commitment are rooted in the Catholic tradition. In such an institution every scholar, Catholic or not, is also obliged to respect its spirit and purpose.

2. THE EDUCATIONAL MINISTRY TO YOUTH

82.   "The future of humanity lies in the hands of those who are strong enough to provide coming generations with reasons for living and hoping" (*The Church Today*, 31). Here as in other areas of educational ministry the threefold purpose of Christian education provides a guide for developing and evaluating programs. Educational programs for the young must strive to teach doctrine, to do so within the experience of Christian community, and to prepare individuals for effective Christian witness and service to others. In doing this they help foster the student's growth in personal holiness and his relationship with Christ.

83.   This ideal of Christian education will best be realized by programs which create the widest opportunities for students to receive systematic catechesis, experience daily living in a faith community, and develop commitment and skill in serving others. All who share responsibility for educational ministry should support programs which give promise of realizing this threefold purpose which is the guide and inspiration of all the Church's educational efforts.

84.   The history of American education is testimony to the deeply held conviction of American Catholics that Catholic elementary and secondary schools are the best expression of the educational ministry to youth. As we shall explain at length later, this remains our conviction today, one shared, we believe, by the great majority of American Catholics. Yet we choose to deal here first with religious education programs for children and young people who attend public and other non-Catholic schools not because Catholic schools are any less important than in the past—their importance is in fact greater now than ever before—but because the urgency and the difficulty of the educational ministry to the students outside them warrant this emphasis. Among the pastoral issues in education which today challenge the Catholic community in our nation, none is more pressing than providing Catholic education for these young people.

Religious Education Outside The Catholic School

85.   Confraternity of Christian Doctrine and other parish programs of religious education are essential instruments of catechesis. Besides enrolling some five

and a half million students, they have an even larger potential outreach among the many Catholic children and young people who attend neither Catholic schools nor out-of-school religious education programs. These students, both present and potential, are the youth of whom the Second Vatican Council spoke in urging the Catholic community to be "present" to them with its "special affection and helpfulness" (GE, 2).

86.   Obviously a part-time, out-of-school program of religious education labors under special handicaps in attempting to achieve the threefold purpose of Christian education. Yet we have a grave duty toward the students for whom such programs now represent the only means of formal religious instruction available to them. Parents, educators, and pastors must do all in their power to provide these children and young people with programs which correspond as fully as possible with the ideal of Catholic education.

DOCTRINE, COMMUNITY AND SERVICE

87.   Pastoral programs of religious education for young people outside Catholic school is must be developed and conducted within the framework or the threefold purpose of Christian education. Merely "teaching about" religion is not enough. Instead such programs must strive to teach doctrine fully, foster community, and prepare their students for Christian service. Whether it takes place in a Catholic school or not, it is essential that the Catholic community offer children and young people an experience of catechesis which indeed gives "clarity and vigor" to faith, fosters living in the spirit of Christ, encourages participation in the liturgy and sacraments, and motivates involvement in the apostolate (GE, 4).

88.   Although there are inherent limitations in out-of-school programs, there are also considerable strengths which should be recognized and built upon. A limitation, which is also a potential source of strength, is their voluntary character, which, while making it more difficult to secure participation, also offers significant opportunities for the building of Christian community. The fact that participants in leadership, teaching or student roles, are volunteers provides creative planners with opportunity to develop esprit among them, and indeed, to foster a stronger sense of community within the entire parish. This is simply to apply to the out-of-school program what has long been recognized as true of the parish school, namely that the hard work and sacrifice required for success can be powerful forces for Christian fellowship.

89.   In regard to service, administrators and teachers in such programs offer personal witness to the meaning of Christian service by their dedicated effort to impart Christian truth and values to the young. This must be carried further, however, by giving the programs themselves an orientation to service of both the parish community and the community outside the parish. For service is itself an efficacious means of teaching doctrine, and thus these programs should include opportunities for service as part of the educational experience they seek to provide the young. Today, when many people have more leisure time than in the past, it is appropriate that a parish increasingly turn its attention to the task

of preparing its members, young and old, for service within and beyond the Christian community.

90.   In many places pastoral programs of religious education are now demonstrating vitality and effectiveness in achieving the threefold purpose at Christian education, especially in parishes which are true communities of faith. Their success deserves recognition, praise and imitation. The achievements of some innovative and imaginative programs for high school students offer a bright ray of hope in a particularly difficult area. Some parishes have made substantial progress in becoming centers for the religious education of all parishioners, young and old. In short, there now exist across the nation a variety of successful models which should be studied and translated into similar efforts elsewhere.

PROBLEMS AND POLICIES

91.   Despite their achievements and bright hopes, such programs face serious problems which should concern the entire Catholic community. These programs do not reach large numbers of Catholic young people not in Catholic schools. Many of them may simply not be accessible or receptive to any systematic, organized program of religious education now available to the Church. There are many reasons for this: parental indifference; problems of scheduling; pressures of time; demands on and appeals to their loyalty by other communities of which they are members; the inadequacy of some religious education programs, an inadequacy often due to insufficient financing and reliance on personnel who have not had proper training and support. But practical difficulties, frustrations and disappointments accentuate the need for the Catholic community to increase its effort in this crucial area. As a matter of policy, religious education programs for Catholic students who attend public and other non-Catholic schools should receive high priority everywhere, a priority expressed in adequate budgets and increased service from professional religious educators. In this light we offer the following pastoral guidelines.

GUIDELINES FOR THE FUTURE

92.   The essential unity of the educational ministry should be reflected in its programmatic expressions. The educational mission of the Church is one. It takes form in many institutions, programs and activities which, different as they are, all derive inspiration, rationale and purpose from the same source: the one educational mission of the Church which is essentially a continuation in our times of the mission of Jesus Christ. Far from competing with one another for money, personnel, students, etc., they must function together harmoniously and efficiently, complementing and supplementing one another in order to achieve jointly the fullest possible realization of the threefold aim of Christian education: teaching doctrine, building community, and serving others.

93.   Since religious education programs for Catholic students who do not attend Catholic schools are an essential part of the Church's total educational ministry, their staff and students should be integrated fully into the unified educational ministry of the local Christian community. In parishes this calls for

efforts to draw together these programs and the Catholic schools in closer working relationships: for example, by including "CCD" students in school and parish organizations and activities to the greatest extent possible, and, in parishes which have no schools, by doing the same for students who attend Catholic schools outside the parish. The objective—integration of all pastoral and educational programs into a unified whole whose components complement and assist one another—should be a major concern of parish leadership. In this regard, consideration should be given to common funding of all catechetical education in a parish for both the school and out-of-school programs.

94. Parishes which have Catholic schools should explore new ways of placing them more directly at the service of the entire parish community. The school should be a focal point for many educational efforts on behalf of children, young people, and adults. Where there is no parish school a parish educational center should serve the same function of drawing together programs and people.

95. Where a parish school must be closed, there should be careful advance planning to provide funds and personnel for such a center.

96. Parishes without parochial schools must not limit their programs to the bare essentials of religious instruction. Their children and young people deserve Catholic education in as full a sense as possible. This suggests that traditional programs be enriched with a variety of informal experiences to help pupils discover the meaning of Christian community life and its potential for service to others. New study and effort are needed to utilize communications media and modern technology in religious education. In areas where parishes and missions confront the problems of isolation and limited resources, regional catechetical centers, either drawing together students from a broad geographical area or sending out teams of skilled catechists into the parishes of the region, may help meet the need for high quality, comprehensive religious education. In short, far from being an excuse for an inferior program, the absence of a parochial school simply challenges a parish, either alone or in cooperation with other parishes, to expand its efforts to give its children and young people as broad a Catholic educational experience as it possibly can.

97. The effectiveness of voluntary service in religious education programs must be strengthened. Parish leadership should give recognition and moral support to the volunteers engaged in this work, but, more than that, it should provide adequately financed opportunities for their professional preparation and in-service training. Furthermore, these programs, while retaining their distinctive voluntarism, must at the same time be reinforced by the increased use of well trained, adequately paid professionals in key positions. Organizations which serve the professional needs of personnel working in this field should receive official recognition and encouragement.

98. Careful attention should be given to providing religious education for members of minority groups and to involving them in the mainstream of the catechetical effort.

99. The right of the handicapped to receive religious education adapted to their special needs also challenges the ingenuity and commitment of the Catholic community.

100. Planning is essential to create a unified system of religious education accessible and attractive to all the People of God. We must continue to explore new ways of extending the educational ministry to every Catholic child and young person. In doing so, we must be open to the possibility of new forms and structures for all Catholic education in the years ahead. With regard to the "tasks and responsibilities" of catechesis, "it is not enough to rest content with the distribution of forces already existing; it is also necessary that effort on the part of all Christians be more and more stimulated and promoted. Care must be taken to make the Christian community every day conscious of its duty" (GCD, 107). A comprehensive vision of the Christian ministry in education, and integrated structures to embody it, seem now to offer the best hope for achieving the greatest success with the largest number of Catholic children and young people, both those who attend Catholic schools and those who do not.

Catholic Schools

101. Of the educational programs available to the Catholic community, Catholic schools afford the fullest and best opportunity to realize the threefold purpose of Christian education among children and young people. Schools naturally enjoy educational advantages which other programs either cannot offer or can offer only with great difficulty. A school has a greater claim on the time and loyalty of the student and his family. It makes more accessible to students participation in the liturgy and the sacraments, which are powerful forces for the development of personal sanctity and for the building of community. It provides a more favorable pedagogical and psychological environment for teaching Christian faith. With the Second Vatican Council we affirm our conviction that the Catholic school "retains its immense importance in the circumstances of our times" and we recall the duty of Catholic parents "to entrust their children to Catholic schools, when and where this is possible, to support such schools to the extent of their ability, and to work along with them for the welfare of their children" (GE, 8).

DOCTRINE, COMMUNITY, SERVICE

102. Christian education is intended to "make men's faith become living, conscious, and active, through the light of instruction" (CD, 14). The Catholic school is the unique setting within which this ideal can be realized in the lives of Catholic children and young people.

103. Only in such a school can they experience learning and living fully integrated in the light of faith. The Catholic school "strives to relate all human culture eventually to the news of salvation, so that the life of faith will illumine the knowledge which students gradually gain of the world, of life, and of

mankind" (GE, 8). Here, therefore, students are instructed in human knowledge and skills, valued indeed for their own worth but seen simultaneously as deriving their most profound significance from God's plan for His creation. Here, too, instruction in religious truth and values is an integral part of the school program. It is not one more subject alongside the rest, but instead it is perceived and functions as the underlying reality in which the student's experiences of learning and living achieve their coherence and their deepest meaning.

104. This integration of religious truth and values with the rest of life is brought about in the Catholic school not only by its unique curriculum but, more important, by the presence of teachers who express an integrated approach to learning and living in their private and professional lives. It is further reinforced by free interaction among the students themselves within their own community of youth.

105. This integration of religious truth and values with life distinguishes the Catholic school from other schools. This is a matter of crucial importance today in view of contemporary trends and pressures to compartmentalize life and learning and to isolate the religious dimension of existence from other areas of human life. A Catholic for whom religious commitment is the central, integrative reality of his life will find in the Catholic school a perception and valuation of the role of religion which matches his own.

106. More than any other program of education sponsored by the Church, the Catholic school has the opportunity and obligation to be unique, contemporary, and oriented to Christian service: unique because it is distinguished by its commitment to the threefold purpose of Christian education and by its total design and operation which foster the integration of religion with the rest of learning and living; contemporary because it enables students to address with Christian insight the multiple problems which face individuals and society today; oriented to Christian service because it helps students acquire skills, virtues, and habits of heart and mind required for effective service to others. All those involved in a Catholic school—parents, pastors, teachers, administrators, and students—must earnestly desire to make it a community of faith which is indeed "living, conscious, and active."

107. The program of studies in a Catholic school reflects the importance which the school and sponsoring community attach to Christian formation. Basic to this task, as we have said earlier, is instruction which is authentic in doctrine and contemporary in presentation. Failure on either side renders the instruction ineffective and can in fact impede the growth of living faith in the child. Thus the proper use of new catechetical methods designed with these objectives in view is to be applauded, as are many new programs for the professional development of religion teachers. They can contribute to making Catholic schools true communities of faith in which the formational efforts of Catholic families are complemented, reinforced and extended. Within such communities teachers and pupils experience together what it means to live a life of prayer, personal responsibility and freedom reflective of Gospel values. Their fellowship helps

them grow in their commitment to service of God, one another, the Church, and the general community.

108. Building and living community must be prime, explicit goals of the contemporary Catholic school. Community is an especially critical need today largely because natural communities of the past have been weakened by many influences. Pressures on the family, the basic unit of society, have already been noted. Urbanization and suburbanization have radically changed the concept of neighborhood community.

109. Racial and ethnic tensions and other conflicts reflect an absence of local and national community. War and the exploitation of poor nations by the rich dramatize the same tragic lack of community on the international level. Today's Catholic school must respond to these challenges by developing in its students a commitment to community and to the social skills and virtues needed to achieve it. Participation together in the liturgy and in paraliturgical activities and spiritual exercises can effectively foster community among students and faculty. Since the Gospel spirit is one of peace, brotherhood, love, patience and respect for others, a school rooted in these principles ought to explore ways to deepen its students' concern for and skill in peacemaking and the achievement of justice. Here young people can learn together of human needs, whether in the parish, the neighborhood, the local civic community, or the world, and begin to respond to the obligation of Christian service through joint action.

110. At the level of institutional commitment, too, service of the public interest is a notable quality of Catholic and other non-public schools in America. "Private education has played and is playing a significant and valuable role in raising national levels of knowledge, competence and experience" (Justice Byron White in Board of Education v. Allen [392 U.S. 236]). Countless men and women have been better able to contribute to the political, social and economic life of the nation as a result of their education in nonpublic schools. This service has been extended not only to those already in the mainstream of social life, but also to many suffering special disadvantages, including in a notable way the physically and mentally handicapped.

111. Other benefits flow from the private educational effort into the lifeblood of the nation. These schools supply a diversity which the American educational system would otherwise lack. They provide desirable competition for the public schools, not as antagonists, but as partners in the total American educational enterprise. In a unique way they serve the community by keeping viable the right to freedom of choice under law among educational alternatives. Most important, the commitment of Catholic schools to Christian values and the Christian moral code renders a profound service to society which depends on spiritual values and good moral conduct for its very survival.

THE CRISIS OF CATHOLIC SCHOOLS

112. It will perhaps be objected that much of what has been said up to now paints an ideal picture of the Catholic school and its purposes. Truly it is an

ideal, but little is achieved without ideals to strive for. Furthermore, Catholic schools have realized and continue to realize this ideal more successfully than is sometimes acknowledged today.

113. Of the Catholic school in America we say humbly, and with gratitude for the grace of God manifested in it, that it has nurtured the faith of Jesus Christ in millions of men and women who have lived vibrantly Christian lives and have given themselves generously in service to others. Scarcely a man or woman in the Church in America today has not benefitted either directly or indirectly from the sacrifices of his fellow Christians in creating the Catholic school system. A full measure of gratitude is due to the dedicated teachers who have expressed their Christian vocation through the apostolate of Catholic education. All deserve the thanks of the Catholic community, especially the religious women whose resourceful leadership has been at the heart of the Catholic school effort in the United States throughout its history.

114. Today this school system is shrinking visibly. The reasons are many and include complex sociological, demographic and psychological factors. Some believe there has been an excessive effort in formal education and too much concentration on schools at the expense of other educational programs. Some are convinced that other forms of Christian service take unequivocal priority over service rendered in the classroom. Some feel American Catholics no longer have the material resources to support so ambitious an educational enterprise.

115. Financial problems have contributed significantly to the present crisis. Burdened by the spiraling costs of both public and nonpublic education, those who support nonpublic schools have placed their cause before them fellow Americans. While legislators have responded in many instances, courts have often rejected laws favorable to nonpublic education, sometimes on grounds which many find extremely difficult to understand or accept.

116. The chief obstacle to meaningful public aid to nonpublic elementary and secondary schools continues to be the United States Supreme Court's interpretation of the First and Fourteenth Amendments. The Court, however, has decided only the cases brought before it; it has not rendered judgment on every conceivable plan. To some it appears that the Court has raised an impenetrable barrier between government and church-sponsored schools; but to others, who are knowledgeable about its jurisprudence and procedures, it appears that the Court, having acknowledged that it is walking a tightrope between the First Amendment's free exercise and establishment clauses, may eventually see a way to give realistic support to parents' freedom to choose a nonpublic school.

117. The words of Pope Pius xi, written some 40 years ago in the encyclical on Christian education, afford timely encouragement to those seeking justice for Catholic schools. "Catholics will never feel, whatever may have been the sacrifices already made, that they have done enough, for the support and defense of their schools and for the securing of laws that will do them justice" (*Christian Education of Youth*).

118. We are well aware of the problems which now face the Catholic school system in the United States. We also wish our position to be clear. For our part, as bishops, we reaffirm our conviction that Catholic schools which realize the threefold purpose of Christian education — to teach doctrine, to build community, and to serve — are the most effective means available to the Church for the education of children and young people who thus may "grow into manhood according to the mature measure of Christ" (GE, 2; cf. Ephesians 4:13). We call upon all members of the Catholic community to do everything in their power to maintain and strengthen Catholic schools which embrace the threefold purpose of Christian education.

ACTION NEEDED NOW

119. Specific steps can and should he taken now by concerned parents, educators, pastors and others to ensure the continuance and improvement of Catholic schools. (Cf., for example, *Nonpublic Schools and the Public Good*, Final Report: The President's Panel on Nonpublic Education.)

120. These will include such things as stating clearly and compellingly the distinctive goals of the Catholic school; increasing associations with other nonpublic and public schools; practicing fiscal, professional, academic and civic accountability; conducting vigorous programs of student recruitment; joining with other nonpublic schools in public relations efforts; exercising firm control over operating costs and practicing greater efficiency in the use of facilities and personnel; intensifying efforts to increase income from private sources, including those which have generally gone untapped up to now; entering into partnership with institutions of higher learning; undertaking school consolidations at the elementary and secondary levels where circumstances make this educationally desirable; and participating fully in the search for solutions to the racial crisis in American education.

121. The unfinished business on the agenda of Catholic schools, like many other schools, also includes the task of providing quality education for the poor and disadvantaged of our nation. Generous, sustained sacrifice is demanded of those whom God has favored in order to make available educational programs which meet the need of the poor to be self-determining, free persons in all areas of individual and social life. Recognition of past failures should not obscure the fact that the Church in many places does provide a wide variety of services for the poor, including schools of high quality, often at the cost of heroic sacrifice and with encouraging success. What is now being accomplished, however, should serve only as a spur to renewed commitment and continued effort in this area so crucial to the good of society and so central to the mission of the Church.

122. If the Catholic community is convinced of the values and advantages of Catholic schools, it must and will act now to adopt such measures and face such challenges as these. In particular all those involved in the Catholic school effort should avoid a defeatist attitude which would regard present problems as a prelude to disaster. Difficult as they may be, they are not insoluble, given the will and the intelligence to seek and adopt solutions.

123. Like other schools in our nation, Catholic schools are called to a renewal of purpose, and some to reorganization. The goals appropriate to today's Catholic educational effort, and thus to today's Catholic schools, are in some ways more challenging than in the past, including as they do the need to prepare young men and women to be witnesses to faith during an era of instability and at the same time to act as agents of creative institutional change for which adequate models hardly exist. While the Christian purpose of the Catholic school must always be clearly evident, no one form is prescribed for it.

124. The search for new forms of schooling should therefore continue. Some may bear little resemblance to schooling as we have known it: the parish education center; the family education center; the school without walls, drawing extensively on community resources; the counseling center; etc. We do not mention these new forms to canonize what some may regard as educational fads or to presume a kind of knowledge we do not possess The point is that one must be open to the possibility that the school of the future, including the Catholic school, will in many ways be very different from the school of the past. Consideration should also be given to the relationship of parish and school where circumstances suggest that the traditional parish may no longer provide the best framework for formal schooling.

125. New forms require pilot programs along with study and evaluation. Catholic schools have the capacity and freedom to experiment. Administrators and teachers should therefore cooperate with parents in designing experimental models or pilot programs to improve educational standards and results.

126. Reorganization may also involve new models of sponsorship and collaboration. Various forms of cooperation with public schools should be explored. In supporting a school system which provides an alternative to the system sponsored by the state, the Catholic community does not wish to ignore or be isolated from public schools. On all levels of education, and particularly on a system-wide basis, Catholic educators should seek actively to cooperate with their public school counterparts and their colleagues in other nonpublic schools, sharing ideas, plans, personnel, technology, and other resources where mutually feasible and beneficial. The possibility of institutional cooperation with other Christian groups in the field of education should be explored. Approached with candor and intelligence, cooperative planning need not threaten the identity or independence of any school system and can benefit all.

Youth Ministry

127. Youth ministry today faces challenges created by the problems and needs of youth in our society. Mirroring to a great extent the alienation and uncertainty of adults, many young people in this country, as well as in other nations of the world, feel estranged both from traditional values and from an adult society whose actions often belie its own professed commitment to these values.

These young people grope for the deeper meaning of life and for roles consonant with their sense of human dignity. The Christian community should be anxious to understand the causes of their uncertainty and eager to respond to what is often an unvoiced cry for help.

128. Other young people, more positively oriented toward society, exhibit encouraging energy and optimism. But even many of them feel unrest and apathy as a result of a socially imposed prolonged adolescence during which they are impeded in their growth to adulthood and frustrated in their efforts to act as responsible persons.

129. Disenchantment with organized religion is often part of the alienation of the young today. This seems in many instances not to be disenchantment with God or with the spiritual dimension of life but with some institutional forms and functions. Even as society grows more secularistic, many young people, reflecting genuine religious concern, express growing interest in Jesus Christ. Their quest for authentic values by which to live has urgency and commendable authenticity.

130. Christians should be sensitive and discerning in their approach to the young, who through their Baptism and Confirmation have been incorporated into full membership in the Christian community. This community does have solutions to many of the questions which trouble today's youth, but it cannot realistically expect young people to accept them unless it, for its part, is willing to listen to their problems. Thus it must strive not only to teach the young but to learn from them and to see its own institutions through their eyes and to make prudent changes which this insight may suggest.

131. There are thus three distinct tasks for the ministry to youth: to enable young people to take part in the Church's mission to the world in ways appropriate to their age and responsive to their interests; to give a specific dimension — education in service — to religious education; and to interpret young people, their problems and their concerns to the Christian and general communities.

132. Youth have a right and duty to be active participants in the work of the Church in the world. Obviously, however, they face certain obstacles because they are young and lack experience, organizational skills, and other necessary abilities. Adults engaged in youth ministry therefore should function mainly as guides and helpers by giving young people direction and support.

133. Those engaged in youth ministry are by that fact involved in religious education. Their efforts complement the formal religious education carried on in Catholic schools and out-of-school programs. They bring a specific focus to the work of religious education, namely, education for mission. This is done through programs which provide young people with opportunity to engage in action projects exemplifying what it means to be a Christian in the world today. Such projects should be designed and conducted in a way that helps youth see their participation as a true expression of Christian concern and not simply as a natural response to human needs.

134. The youth ministry should also provide for another educational need of the young, education in community. As maturing Christians, young people need to experience a wide variety of communities. They particularly need the experience of being in a community which brings together young people from both Catholic and public schools. Youth programs under Church sponsorship should base their concept of "community" upon the Gospel values proclaimed by Jesus Christ.

135. Among the major responsibilities of a diocesan youth director and others engaged in youth ministry is that of interpreting youth and advocating their legitimate causes to the Christian community and to other communities to which the young belong. Their informal and immediate contact with the young often gives those engaged in youth work a deep insight into the needs and concerns of youth. It is appropriate that they share these concerns with other adults and plead youth's cause with them.

136. Finally, all those involved in Catholic youth work should recognize the value of what is called peer group ministry. Young people themselves "must become the first and immediate apostles to youth exercising their apostolate among themselves and through themselves" (AA, 12). Young people should be welcomed as co-workers in this genuinely prophetic form of education, and programs which develop their leadership talents should have a central place in the youth ministry.

IV. PLANNING THE EDUCATIONAL MISSION

137. This pastoral message has stressed the need of many different educational programs and institutions and insisted that each is an important part of the total educational ministry. This may seem of questionable value at a time when the material resources available to the Church for education are limited and, perhaps, diminishing. But only if the Catholic community of our nation is fully aware of and committed to various elements of the educational ministry is it likely to provide the resources which are needed. The cooperation of all is vital if the vision sketched here is to be a reality now or in the future.

138. While it is difficult to define and plan the Church's educational mission in this period of rapid institutional change, the effort must continue. Educational needs must be clearly identified; goals and objectives must be established which are simultaneously realistic and creative; programs consistent with these needs and objectives must be designed carefully, conducted efficiently and evaluated honestly.

139. Under the leadership of The Ordinary and his priests, planning and implementing the educational mission of the Church must involve the entire Catholic community. Representative structures and processes should be the normative means by which the community, particularly Catholic parents, addresses fundamental questions about educational needs, objectives, programs and resources.

Such structures and processes, already operating in many dioceses and parishes in the United States, should become universal.

140. Vatican Council II urged the establishment of agencies by which the laity can "express their opinion of things which concern the good of the Church" (LG, 37). One such agency, long a part of the American experience and in recent years increasingly widespread in Catholic education, is the representative board of education, which, acting on behalf of the community it serves, seeks patiently and conscientiously to direct the entire range of educational institutions and programs within the educational ministry.

141. On the diocesan level, the educational mission can best be coordinated by a single board of education concerned with the needs of the entire local church. Many such boards have already been established and are now rendering important service to the Church and education. They work best when they are broadly representative of all the people of the diocese, laity, priests and religious. Membership should be open to people of many points of view, including those who may perceive needs and advocate approaches different from those expressed in this pastoral.

142. Participatory approaches to decision making are desirable not only in regard to educational policy but in the entire area of pastoral need. Although the Ordinary has ultimate responsibility for coordinating pastoral programs in the diocese, a significant role in setting priorities can be played by the diocesan pastoral council, itself a structure strongly recommended by Vatican II (CD, 27).

143. Much progress has already been made in educational planning by the Church in the United States. Many dioceses and institutions, for example, have sponsored valuable educational research carried out by professional agencies. Sharing the results of these studies through a national clearinghouse would make it easier to exchange data, provide guidance for new studies, help avoid duplication, and assist planning.

An Invitation to Cooperation

144. The planning and collaboration invited here will only come about through the active cooperation of all involved in the educational apostolate. We especially seek the collaboration of the teachers—priests, religious, and laity—who serve in Catholic schools and other educational programs. If the threefold purpose of Christian education is to be realized, it must be through their commitment to give instruction to their students, to build community among them, and to serve them. Furthermore, teachers bring insights and experience to planning the total educational mission of the Church. We invite and urge their creative contribution to the effort of the entire community to meet the current challenges.

145. The involvement of religious men and women in educational ministry has long provided example and support to the Christian community. They are

publicly identified as persons committed to giving witness to Gospel values, notably the value of community. The stability which religious communities have brought to the apostolate has made it possible to continue many schools and programs which could hardly have survived otherwise. Their witness, always valuable, is needed more than ever today. The entire Church will be enriched by authentic renewal of religious communities. All Catholics look forward to their continued presence as a vital force in the total teaching mission of the Church.

146. The number of religious teachers, upon whom Catholic education has historically depended, is declining at present. The entire Catholic community should seek to understand the causes of this phenomenon and should adopt appropriate measures in an attempt to reverse the trend. Clarification of the ecclesial role of women could be a factor in the solution of the much deplored vocations crisis among religious communities of women.

147. A continuing shortage of religious teachers now is one of those signs of the times which Catholics must confront realistically in carrying on the educational ministry. It emphasizes the fact that reliance on lay persons in the work of Catholic education will not only continue in the years ahead but will certainly increase. This is not to suggest, however, that the presence of lay teachers and administrators in Catholic schools and other educational programs is merely a stopgap. They are full partners in the Catholic educational enterprise, and the dramatic increase of their numbers and influence in recent years is welcome and desirable in itself. As with religious, so with lay teachers and administrators, the Catholic community invites not only their continued service but also their increased participation in planning and decision making and their continued emergence in leadership roles.

148. It is also imperative that the Catholic community collaborate with all Americans committed to educational freedom. The right of parents to exercise genuine freedom of choice in education in ways consistent with the principles of justice and equality must be recognized and made operative. In this connection one must hope that our nation will arrive at a satisfactory accommodation on the role of religion in public education, one which respects the rights and legitimate interests of all parents and students.

149. While steps must be taken to ensure legitimate freedom of choice in education for all, special attention should be given to extending it to those in our country who suffer most from educational disadvantage. Efforts at educational self-determination already undertaken by some members of such groups are truly a significant manifestation of man's struggle to be free, akin to the Catholic community's historic effort to be free to direct its educational destiny. Incompatible with such freedom is a philosophy which would demand, in effect, that all educational efforts be subsumed in one educational system. In an area so intimately related to fundamental human needs and rights as is education, coercive theory or practice which results in the elimination of viable educational alternatives is intolerable, however it may be rationalized.

150. The development of Catholic education in this country up to now reflects the religious freedom which Catholics enjoy in the United States. For its part the Catholic community has a long tradition of cooperating with public authority in promoting civic interests in many fields including education. Thus it is important that persons in government and public service, who influence and regulate the educational activities of the state, understand our convictions about what church-sponsored, faith-inspired education contributes to the general good of the nation.

V. A MINISTRY OF HOPE

151. This pastoral document is not the final word on Christian education. In a sense the final word has already been spoken by Jesus Christ whose mission the Christian community continues today in many ways, including the educational ministry. In another sense the final word will never be spoken; it is the task of each generation of Christians to assess their own times and carry on the mission of Christ by means suited to the needs and opportunities they perceive.

152. The educational mission is not exhausted by any one program or institution. By their complementary functions and cooperative activities all programs and institutions contribute to the present realization of the Church's educational mission. All should remain open to new forms, new programs, new methods which give promise of fuller realization of this mission in the future.

153. The educational mission is not directed to any single group within the Christian community or mankind. All have a role to play; all should have a voice in planning and directing.

154. Like the mission and message of Jesus Christ, the Church's educational mission is universal—for all men, at all times, in all places. In our world and in our nation, the mission of Christian education is of critical importance. The truth of Jesus Christ must be taught; the love of Jesus Christ must be extended to persons who seek and suffer.

155. The Christian community has every reason to hope in confronting the challenge of educational ministry today. To all our efforts we join prayer for God's help, and for the intercession of Mary, the Mother of Jesus. We face problems; so did those who came before us, and so will those who follow. But as Christians we are confident of ultimate success, trusting not in ourselves, but in Jesus Christ, who is at once the inspiration, the content, and the goal of Christian education: "the way, and the truth, and the life."

BASIC TEACHINGS
FOR
CATHOLIC RELIGIOUS
EDUCATION

1973

OVERVIEW OF *BASIC TEACHINGS FOR CATHOLIC RELIGIOUS EDUCATION*

by Jane E. Regan

The decade of the 1970s saw the preparation and publication of several documents examining the focus and process and content of the catechetical enterprise. The sources of these documents range from Vatican commissions to the United States bishops' conference to the pope as he wrote in response to synod discussions. In many ways, it was with these documents that attempts were made to define the implications of the Second Vatican Council for contemporary catechesis. In the midst of these is a document prepared under the direction of the National Conference of Catholic Bishops and published in January, 1973: *Basic Teachings for Catholic Religious Education* (BT).

It is worth noting that BT was written in the years between the promulgation of the *General Catechetical Directory* [GCD (1971)] and *Sharing the Light of Faith: National Catechetical Directory for Catholics of the United States* [NCD (1978)]. As is made clear in BT, the document is to "be read in the light of the *General Catechetical Directory*, by which its admittedly limited scope can readily be understood."[1] A comparison of the headings present in BT with those used in chapter II of part three of the GCD makes evident BT's reliance on the *Directory*: With few variations the topic headings are identical, and the content of each topic is very similar. It is also worth noting that these same topics serve to organize the presentation of the "Principal Elements of the Christian Message for Catechesis," chapter V of the NCD. At some level, BT can be seen as an "excerpt" of the GCD and a guide for one chapter of the NCD. As such it must be read within the broader context set out by these directories; it must be seen as only one element of catechesis.

One of the concerns in the area of religious education during the years leading up to the publication of BT was the need to balance a focus on an experiential approach to the process of faith formation with a concern for the presentation of Catholic teaching. Catechetical documents written through the decades of the 1970s recognize the need to balance the life experience of the learner with the systematic presentation of the Christian message.[2] Those who composed BT had as their task the compilation of those teachings that were to be considered central to catechesis, those teachings that needed to be present for the realization of authentic catechesis.[3]

BASIC TEACHINGS: STRUCTURE AND CONTENT

This brief document contains an introduction, a presentation of church teaching discussed under 25 different headings and appendices that include the Decalogue, the Beatitudes and the church precepts.

Beginning with a discussion of the nature of religious education, the introduction sets out the fundamental framework within which the presentation of church teachings is to be situated. Citing the GCD, the opening paragraphs of BT describe the nature of religious education. "All religious education is formative in Christ, given to make 'faith become living, conscious and active, through the light of instruction'" (BT, Introduction). In doing this, the authors of this document make clear that no list of teachings can be equated to the whole of religious education. While these teachings "are necessary for doctrinal substance and stability," the role of the teacher is central to effective religious education (BT, Introduction).

With this in mind, the introduction continues with a discussion of the importance of the use of effective methodology and the necessity that "the authentic teachings of the church, and those [teachings] only be presented in religious instruction as official church doctrine" (BT, Introduction). The scope, use and audience of BT is then set out:

> This text does not give guidance concerning a hierarchical order of importance of doctrines or concerning methods of religious instruction. This only specifies the doctrinal basics which the bishops expect in teaching Catholic doctrine. This is intended for parents and catechists, for priests, deacons and religious, for writers and publishers of catechetical texts — to use as adult study and in reviewing the content of religious education programs.

The introduction concludes with a discussion of "three themes, chosen from others, which carry through all religious education." At the heart of all religious education activities rests the importance of prayer, participation in the liturgy and familiarity with the scriptures. As each theme is discussed, it is evident that there is a desired interplay between learning about these elements of Catholic life and being engaged actively in them. Instruction in prayer leads to more mature prayer, an understanding of the eucharistic celebration makes one a more active participant, and knowledge of the Bible leads to a love and respect for the scriptures. Engagement with these fundamental expressions of the Christian tradition enhances one's faith and formation in Christ, the goal of all religious education.

The majority of the text examines the series of basic teachings that the United States bishops expect to be present in all Catholic religious education. Although the 25 headings are listed without indication of subheadings or association among the topics, the flow of these themes and their interrelationship is generally clear.[4]

The text begins with a discussion of the mystery of God and the nature of the relationship between God and humankind (1–3). It is here that the overarching category for presenting Catholic teaching is set out: the action of God and the response of humans in the history of salvation. It is in this context that the person of Jesus is examined (4–8) and the role of the Holy Spirit is described (10). In this journey of salvation history, the church and the sacraments serve as the primary expression and source of God's grace (11–13).

The reality of human sinfulness and the enduring presence of God's grace serve to introduce the discussion of morality (14–16). Following this a rather lengthy section sets out the basic elements of moral thinking and emphasizes the importance of conscience formation (17–20). In this context, the church is presented as the community striving for holiness and called to reflect the unity of God (21–23). This presentation of the basic teachings concludes with a section on Mary as mother of God and model of the church (24) and one on the "last things" (25).

At the end of the BT text are two appendices. The first includes the Ten Commandments and the Beatitudes; the second contains a list of duties Catholics should strive to fulfill with reference to the traditional precepts of the church.

BASIC TEACHINGS: DOCUMENT OF ITS TIME

As we read BT today, some 20 years after its publication, it is clear that the document reflects its own time. While the themes that are presented in BT remain at the core of the Christian message and are essential components of Catholic teaching, the way in which some of the elements are presented date the text somewhat. Although evident in a few places in terms of emphases or specific lacunae, the primary example of the dated nature of the presentation is the discussion of sacraments and particularly sacramental catechesis. After discussing the nature of sacraments as actions of Christ in the church (10), the document proceeds with a section entitled "Religious Instruction on the Sacraments" (11). Here emphasis is placed on the individual nature of each sacrament, on an explanation of the external ritual and on each sacrament's effect on the individual. Not discussed adequately is the fundamental unity of the sacraments and their relationship to the self-expression of the church and faith community. Also lacking is the more experiential dimension of sacramental formation: We "learn" most about the sacraments through celebrating them and reflecting back on that celebration rather than through prior explanations and instruction. Clearly, in reading the sections on the sacraments, one would want to argue for a more mystagogical approach to sacramental catechesis. Because this document predates the general use of the Order of Christian Initiation of Adults and the discussion of liturgical formation that followed, this observation is less a critique of the text and more a caution as we attempt to explore its usefulness for today.

BASIC TEACHINGS: DOCUMENT FOR THE PRESENT

So, what is the usefulness of this text for contemporary religious education? What role can it serve in the consideration of the reality of parish catechesis into the future? While the content is obviously still useful in naming those elements that give shape to the Christian message today, its more significant contribution rests with the understanding of the complexity of catechesis that is implicit in the text.

First, the document makes clear that essential to religious education and necessary for addressing its goals is what BT refers to as "doctrinal substance and stability." In more recent times, this has been spoken of as "Catholic literacy." However it is named, it is clearly necessary that each generation and all maturing Catholics engage in conversation and instruction about key Catholic teaching. A document such as this provides straightforward access to the basic outline of such teaching.

Second, BT, both in the introduction and in its reference to the GCD as the context for its reading, makes clear the important role of the catechist and of the faith community. The process of catechesis extends far beyond the transmission of a set of propositions. Catechesis is fundamentally about initiating people into a faith community and strengthening that bond. The lived faith of the catechist and the very life of the community serve as the primary expressions of the meaningfulness of these basic church teachings.

Finally, a review of the works cited in BT reveals that all but a handful of the one hundred-plus footnotes are to documents approved at Vatican II or to those that derived directly from Council directives. At essence, the teachings of Vatican II are not "new teachings"; they reflect core, basic Catholic teaching expressed anew for this generation. As such, contemporary Catholic catechesis turns to the documents as the primary source of the church's tradition.

In these times, as discussions related to catechesis are shaped by the publication of the *Catechism of the Catholic Church,* these three themes that are presumed in BT — the importance of doctrinal stability, the role of the catechist and the broader catechizing community, and the prominence of the teaching of Vatican Council II — are of great significance. They serve as indispensable guides as we chart the course of catechesis into the twenty-first century.

NOTES

1. NCCB, *Basic Teachings for Catholic Religious Education* (Washington, DC: Publication Office, USCC, 1973); reprint Chicago, Liturgy Training Publications, 1996, Introduction. All further citations will be given in the text.

2. See, for example, the GCD's discussion of the role of the inductive method of learning (72) and the importance of both formulations (73) and the learners' experience (74) to the process of catechesis. Some years later, the *Apostolic Exhortation on Catechesis* makes the importance of this balance even more explicit: "Nor is any opposition to be set up between a catechesis taking life as the point of departure and a traditional, doctrinal and systematic catechesis" (CT, 22).

3. In a helpful article entitled "The Background and Development of the *Basic Teachings* Document," *The Living Light* 11 (1973): 264–277, Charles C. McDonald argues that BT was the final result of a series of proposed documents that included a small catechism in the tradition of the *Baltimore Catechism*, a narrative resource text or sourcebook and an American catechetical directory.

4. In the presentation of the principle elements of the Christian message in the NCD, these same themes are rearranged slightly and divided into ten topics. See NCD, 83–111.

OUTLINE

Introduction

1. The Mystery of the One God—Father, Son, Holy Spirit

2. True Worship of God in a World Which Ignores Him

3. Knowledge of God and the Witness of Christian Love

4. Jesus Christ, Son of God, the Firstborn of all Creation, and Savior

5. Creation, the Beginning of the History of Man's Salvation

6. Jesus Christ, the Center of all God's Saving Works

7. Jesus Christ, True Man and True God in the Unity of the Divine Person

8. Jesus Christ, Savior and Redeemer of the World

9. The Holy Spirit in the Church and in the Life of the Christian

10. The Sacraments, Actions of Christ in the Church (the Universal Sacrament)

11. Religious Instruction on the Sacraments

12. The Eucharist, Center of all Sacramental Life

13. The Sacrament of Matrimony

14. The New Man in the Spirit

15. Human and Christian Freedom

16. The Sins of Man

17. The Moral Life of Christians

18. The Perfection of Christian Love

19. Specifics in the Teaching of Morality

20. The Church, People of God and Institution for Salvation

21. The Church as a Community

22. The Quest for Unity

23. The Church as the Institution for Salvation

24. Mary, Mother of God, Mother and Model of the Church

BASIC TEACHINGS
FOR CATHOLIC RELIGIOUS EDUCATION

INTRODUCTION

All religious education is formation in Christ, given to make "faith become living, conscious and active, through the light of instruction."[1] Religious education is proclaiming to others the Gospel of the risen Lord, while showing that this "Good News" alone gives meaning to life. So the faith, prayer and lived example of the teacher are of great importance.

No list of documents can bring about real religious education, but certain basic teachings are necessary for doctrinal substance and stability.

This text sets down the principal elements of the Christian message. These basic teachings are here specified by the American Bishops, who as bishops hold in the Church special responsibility for determining the content of faith instruction.[2] It is necessary that these basic teachings be central in all Catholic religious instruction, be never overlooked or minimized, and be given adequate and frequent emphasis.

This text makes clear what must be stressed in the religious formation of Catholics of all ages. The Bishops have in mind every type of religious education: in the home, in Catholic schools, in programs of the Confraternity of Christian Doctrine, in courses of adult education in religion.

The most effective methodology is expected in teaching these basic beliefs. Due consideration should be shown for the listener's level of maturity and understanding.[3] "In this instruction a proper sequence should be observed, as well as a method appropriate to the matter that is being treated, and to the natural disposition, ability, age and circumstances of life of the listener."[4]

It is necessary that the authentic teachings of the Church, and those only be presented in religious instruction as official Catholic doctrine. Religion texts or classroom teachers should never present merely subjective theorizing as the Church's teaching.

"For this reason, a distinction must be borne in mind between, on the one hand, the area that is devoted to scientific investigation and, on the other, the area that concerns the teaching of the faithful. In the first, experts enjoy the freedom required by their work and are free to communicate to others, in books and commentaries, the fruits of their research. In the second, only those doctrines may be attributed to the Church which are declared to be such by her authentic Magisterium."[5]

This document is not to be confused with either the *General Catechetical Directory* or the planned *National Catechetical Directory* (to which this document will be helpful input). This document should however be read in the light of the *General Catechetical Directory*, by which its admittedly limited scope can readily be understood.

This text does not give guidance concerning a hierarchical order of importance of doctrines, or concerning methods of religious instruction. This only specifies the doctrinal basics which the bishops expect in teaching Catholic doctrine. This is intended for parents and catechists, for priests, deacons and religious, for writers and publishers of catechetical texts — to use as adult study and in reviewing the content of religious education programs.

John Henry Cardinal Newman described the knowledge of religion expected in his day: "We want a laity . . . who know their religion, who enter into it, who know just where they stand, who know what they hold and what they do not, who know their creed so well that they can give an account of it, who know so much history that they can defend it."[6]

A century later, the Bishops want all this. But they ask and pray for much more — or a laity transformed by the Gospel message, who put the Gospel to work in every action of their daily lives, whose joy and simplicity and concern for others are so radiant that all men recognize them as Christ's disciples by the love they have for one another.

There are three themes, chosen from others, which carry through all religious education. These are:

FIRST THEME: THE IMPORTANCE OF PRAYER

The People of God have always been a praying people. Religious educators then, who are mature in the faith and faithful to this tradition, will teach prayer. This teaching will take place through experiences of prayer, through the example of prayer, and through the learning of common prayers. Religious education, at home or in the classroom, given by a teacher who values prayer, will provide both the instruction and the experience.

People can pray together as a community when they share some common prayers. So it is important that some of the Church's great prayers be understood, memorized and said frequently. Among these are the Sign of the Cross, the Our Father, the Hail Mary, the Apostles Creed, an Act of Contrition, and the Rosary.[7]

But there is more to prayer than memorized formulas. Talking with God spontaneously and familiarly, and listening to him, is prayer. Informal prayer, suited to the person's age and capacity, should be explained and encouraged. Praise and thankfulness in prayer bring balance and strength in the difficulties, as well as the joys of life.

By instruction in prayer, through all levels of religious education, the learner is gradually led on to a more mature prayer — to meditation, contemplation, and union with God.

As members of the Christian community, all are called to participate actively in the liturgical prayer of the Church. Religious education therefore must involve the student in his faith community and in that community's liturgy.

Liturgy itself educates. It teaches, it forms community, it forms the individual. It makes possible worship of God and a social apostolate to men.

The Mass, the Church's "great prayer," is the highest, most noble form of the Church's liturgy. Effective instruction will therefore help every Christian participate actively in the Eucharistic celebration of his own witnessing faith community.

It is especially important, therefore, that the Eucharistic celebration engage younger members of the parish in genuine worship. The parish community takes on new dimension and vitality from their participation in every Mass, especially when the community comes together on Sundays and Holy Days. The young of the parish are influenced by the example of their elders, and grow by their own full sharing in the Sacrifice of the Mass.

THIRD THEME: FAMILIARITY WITH THE HOLY BIBLE

A life of prayer is nourished by reading the Bible, which is in itself a form of prayer.

The Word of God is life giving. It nourishes and inspires, strengthens and sustains. It is the primary source, with Tradition, of Church teaching.

Religious education should encourage love and respect for the Scriptures. This will happen as one is gradually introduced to the Scriptures and given a background knowledge which will prepare him for reading and understanding them. At an appropriate level, each one should have his own copy of the Bible.

In studying and teaching the Bible, the instructor should follow the approach of the Second Vatican Council.[8] The Bible has God as its author and helps us to know and love Jesus Christ.

The Bible is likewise to be taught as a collection of divinely inspired books, each with its human author, its history of composition, and type of literature (or literary form). These help us understand "what meaning the sacred writers really intended, and what God wanted to manifest by means of their words."[9]

The words of St. Paul should describe the Catholic student of religion: "From your infancy you have known the Sacred Scriptures, the source of the wisdom which, through faith in Jesus Christ, leads to salvation. All scripture is inspired of God and is useful for teaching—for reproof, correction, and training in holiness, so that the man of God may be fully competent and equipped for every good work" (2 Timothy 3:15–16).

Scripture and Tradition stand together as the "one sacred deposit of the word of God, which is committed to the Church."[10] The importance of Tradition is described by the Second Vatican Council: "This Tradition, which comes from the apostles, develops in the Church with the help of the Holy Spirit. For there is a growth in the understanding of the realities and the words which have been handed down. . . . "[11] Catholics therefore should be well instructed in Tradition as well as Scripture.

BASIC TEACHINGS FOR CATHOLIC RELIGIOUS EDUCATION

1. THE MYSTERY OF THE ONE GOD—FATHER, SON, HOLY SPIRIT

The "history of salvation" is the story of God's dealing with men. Through it, the one true God in three Persons—the Father, the Son, the Holy Spirit—reveals himself to man and saves man from sin.

In the Old Testament God revealed himself as the one true personal God, transcendent above this world. By these Old Testament words and actions, God prepared for the later revelation of the Trinity.

This mystery was expressed in the person, words, and works of Jesus Christ. Jesus revealed himself as the eternal and divine Son of God; more fully revealed the Father; and made known a third divine Person, the Holy Spirit, whom the Father and he, as risen Lord, sent to his Church.

Thus, the Divine Teacher gives his disciples authoritative knowledge of the true God, and calls them to become sons of God through the gift of the Spirit which he bestows on them.[12]

Catechetical instruction should foster an ever-increasing awareness of the Triune God. It should enable students to grasp, through faith, the great truth that beginning at Baptism, they are called to a lifelong developing intimacy with the three divine Persons.[13]

2. TRUE WORSHIP OF GOD IN A WORLD WHICH IGNORES HIM

Religious education must stimulate an unshakable belief that God is all-good. "The living God" (Matthew 16:16) is holy, just, and merciful. Infinitely wise and perfect, he has made firm commitments to men and bound them to himself by solemn covenants. He has each of us always in view. He frees us, saves us, and loves us with the love of a father, the love of a spouse. Instruction about God's goodness should awaken joy in the God who is the cause of our eternal hope[14] and should prompt us to worship him.

We worship God especially in the sacred liturgy, offering ourselves to him through our Lord Jesus Christ. We commit ourselves to carrying out his will in our every activity, and to use and increase the talents he has given us.[15] And from his goodness we receive the graces needed to profess the truth in love[16] and to bring forth the fruits of love, justice and peace, all to his glory.

The sad fact is that many people today pay little or no attention to God, while others are persuaded that God is distant, indifferent, or altogether absent.

That is because modern life is man-centered, not God-centered. Its climate is unfavorable to faith. Yet, no matter how hidden, some desire for God is lodged in every man.[17]

3. KNOWLEDGE OF GOD AND THE WITNESS OF CHRISTIAN LOVE

Sacred Scripture testifies that man can come to know God through the things God has made.[18] The Church holds and teaches that from reflection on created things human reason can come to a knowledge of God as the beginning and end of all that is.[19]

Yet unbelievers need help to find God. They ask, "Show us a sign." We who are committed to Christ can do so, as the first generation Christians did.[20] How? By the compelling witness of a life which shows a steadfast and mature faith in God, which is lived in personal love of Christ, and which carries out works of justice and charity.[21]

True, our final goal is in eternity. But faith in God and union with Christ also entail an obligation to work at solving the problems which beset men here and now.[22] And so Christians must show by their actions that faith in God, far from freeing them of concern for the world's troubles, impels them to be involved and to press for their solution.[23]

4. JESUS CHRIST, SON OF GOD, THE FIRSTBORN OF ALL CREATION, AND SAVIOR

The greatest of God's works is the taking on of human flesh (incarnation) by his Son, Jesus Christ. The Son came on earth and entered human history so as to renew the world from within and be for it an abiding source of supernatural life and salvation from sin.

He is the Firstborn of all creation. He is before all. All things hold together in him,[24] just as all have been created in him, through him, and for him.[25]

Obedient unto death, he was exalted as Lord of all, and through the reality of his resurrection was made known to us as God's Son in power.[26] Being the Firstborn of the dead, he gives eternal life to all.[27] In him we are created new men.[28] Through him all creatures will be saved from the slavery of corruption.[29] "There is no salvation in anyone else" (Acts 4:12). Nor has there ever been, from the very beginning.[30]

5. CREATION, THE BEGINNING OF THE HISTORY OF MAN'S SALVATION

The entire universe was created out of nothing. This includes our world in which salvation and redemption are in fact accomplished through Jesus Christ.

In the Old Testament, God's creative action showed his power and proved that he is always with his people.[31] The creation of angels and of the world is the beginning of the mystery of salvation.[32] And the creation of man[33] is the first gift leading to Christ. In Christ's resurrection from the dead the same all-powerful action of God stands out splendidly.[34]

For this reason, creation is to be presented not in isolation, but as directly relating to the salvation accomplished by Jesus Christ. So, too, when a Christian considers the doctrine of creation, he must not only recall the first action by which God "created the heavens and the earth," but should also remember God's continuing activity as he works out the salvation of men.

God is actively and lovingly present in human history from start to finish, using his limitless power in our behalf. Just as his presence shines forth in the history of Israel, just as he was so powerfully at work in the life, death, and resurrection of his Incarnate Son, so is he present among us today and will be for all generations. He will bring his saving work to final completion only at the end of the world, when there will be "new heavens and a new earth."[35]

6. JESUS CHRIST, THE CENTER OF ALL GOD'S SAVING WORKS

The Christian knows that in Jesus Christ he is joined to all history and all men. The story of man's salvation, set in the midst of the ongoing history of the world, is the carrying out of God's plan for us. Its aim is to form his people into "the whole Christ . . . that perfect man who is Christ come to full stature" (Ephesians 4:13).

Realizing this, the Christian addresses himself to his appointed task of making creation give glory to God. He does so to the full extent of his abilities and opportunities, through the power of Jesus the Savior.[36]

7. JESUS CHRIST, TRUE MAN AND TRUE GOD IN THE UNITY OF THE DIVINE PERSON

Head and Lord of the universe, the Son of God was "manifested in the flesh" (1 Timothy 3:16). This is "a wonderful mystery of our faith" (ibid.).

The man, Jesus Christ, lived among men. As man, he thought with a human mind, acted with a human will, loved with a human heart. By becoming man, he joined himself in a real way with every human being except in sin.[37] He accorded the human person a degree of respect and concern such as no one before had done.

He lived among men, was close to them, reached out to all — the virtuous and sinners, the poor and the rich, fellow-citizens and foreigners, and was especially solicitous for the suffering and the rejected. In him, God's love for man is seen.

And well it might be. For Jesus is also truly divine. He is not only the perfect man, but God's only-begotten Son:[38] "God from God, light from light, true God from true God, begotten not made, of one substance with the Father" (Nicene Creed).

In explaining the incarnation and the divinity of Christ, the teacher must take care to follow Christian tradition as expressed in Sacred Scripture and by the Fathers and Councils of the Church. The instruction should convey the age-old witness of Christian life about this truth: in Christ there is all fullness of divinity.[39]

8. JESUS CHRIST, SAVIOR AND REDEEMER OF THE WORLD

Christ appeared in the history of man and the world, a history subject to sin. Christ steps into the world as God made man, to be its Savior and Redeemer. God so loved sinners that he gave his Son, reconciling the world to himself.[40] It was by the obedience of the Son to the will and command of his Father that all men were saved (cf. Romans 5:19).

As the Messiah fulfilling Old Testament prophecy and history, Jesus carried out his earthly mission. He preached the Gospel of the Kingdom of God and summoned men to interior conversion and faith.[41] He persisted in his ministry despite the resistance of religious leaders of his day and their threats to his life.

Out of filial love for his Father[42] and redemptive love of us,[43] he gave himself up to death, and passed through it to the glory of the Father.[44]

By his death and resurrection he redeemed mankind from slavery to sin and to the devil. Risen truly and literally, the Lord became the unfailing source of life and of the outpouring of the Holy Spirit upon the human race.[45] He is the Firstborn among many brethren,[46] and created in himself a new humanity.[47]

9. THE HOLY SPIRIT IN THE CHURCH AND IN THE LIFE OF THE CHRISTIAN

The Holy Spirit carries out Christ's work in the world. As Christ is present where a human being is in need (Matthew 25:31ff.), so the Spirit is at work when persons answer God's invitation to love him and one another. The coming of the consoling Paraclete was promised by Christ.[48] He pledged that the Spirit or Truth would be within us and remain with us.[49] And the Holy Spirit did come at Pentecost,[50] never to depart. The Spirit is present in a special way in the community of those who acknowledge Christ as Lord, the Church. The Church then, is enlivened by the Spirit. Our lives also are to be guided by that same Holy Spirit, the third Person of the Trinity.

Catechetical instruction must underscore the importance and the work of the abiding Spirit of Truth in the Church and in our lives. For this the teachings of the Second Vatican Council will be useful.[51]

10. THE SACRAMENTS, ACTIONS OF CHRIST IN THE CHURCH
(THE UNIVERSAL SACRAMENT)

The saving work of Christ is continued in the Church. Through the gift of the Holy Spirit, the Church enjoys the presence of Christ and carries on his ministry and saving mission.

The Church has been entrusted with special means for carrying on Christ's works: namely, the sacraments which he instituted. They are outward signs both of God's grace and man's faith. They effectively show God's intention to sanctify man and man's willingness to receive this sanctification. In this way they bring us God's grace.[52]

The Church itself is in a true sense the universal sacrament. The Church is not only the People of God, but "by her relationship with Christ, the Church is, as it were, a sacrament (or sign and instrument) of intimate union with God and of the unity of all mankind."[53]

Sacraments are the principal actions through which Christ gives his Spirit to Christians and makes them a holy people. He has entrusted the sacraments to the Church, but they are always to be thought of as actions of Christ himself, from whom they get their power. Thus, it is Christ who baptizes, Christ who offers himself in the Sacrifice of the Mass through the ministry of the priests, and Christ who forgives sins in the Sacrament of Penance.

"The purpose of the sacraments is to sanctify men, to build up the body of Christ, and finally to give worship to God. Because they are signs, they also instruct . . . the very act of celebrating them disposes the faithful more effectively to receive the grace in a fruitful manner, to worship God duly, and to practice charity. It is therefore of capital importance that the faithful easily understand the sacramental signs, and with great eagerness have frequent recourse to the sacraments, instituted to nourish Christian life."[54]

Catechetical instruction, then, must teach the seven sacraments, according to this full meaning. Since they are sacraments of faith, the right attitude of with must be encouraged, as well as the sincerity and generosity required for celebrating and receiving them worthily.

The sacraments must be seen as sources of grace for individuals and communities, in addition to being remedies for sin and the effects of sin. Therefore, the Christian's union with God in grace is to be presented as in an important measure connected with the sacraments.[55]

11. RELIGIOUS INSTRUCTION ON THE SACRAMENTS

In religious education each sacrament is to be taught, with careful attention to its individual nature. The instructor should carefully explain the external ritual, or the "sign" for each, and should explain that sacraments, when worthily received, bring God's grace. The teacher should help the student appreciate the lifelong human and ecclesial goal of sacramental living. Such instruction will encourage the students to think about the meaning of the visible signs, as well as the invisible reality of God's saving love which these signs express.

Here, in broad outline, we note:

Baptism is the sacrament of rebirth as a child of God sanctified by the Spirit, of unity with Jesus in his death and resurrection, of cleansing from original sin and personal sins, and of welcome into the community of the Church. It permanently relates him to God with a relationship that can never be erased. It joins him to the priestly, prophetic, and kingly works of Christ.

Confirmation is the sacrament by which those born anew in baptism now receive the seal of the Holy Spirit, the gift of the Father and the Son. Confirmation, as the sealing of the candidate with the Spirit, is linked with the other sacraments of Christian initiation, baptism and the Eucharist. Religious instruction should emphasize the idea of initiation and explain the sealing of the Spirit as preparation for the witness of a mature Christian life, and for the apostolate of living in the world and extending and defending the faith.[56]

Penance brings to the Christian God's merciful forgiveness for sins committed after baptism. Sacramental absolution, which follows upon sincere confession of sin, true sorrow, and resolution not to sin again, is a means of obtaining pardon from God. Usually given to the individual, it also brings about a reconciliation with the faith community, the Church, which is wounded by our sins. Religious instruction should teach this sacrament as bringing individualized direction towards spiritual growth, towards eliminating habits of sin and working for perfection. Confession is for the Catholic the sacramental way of obtaining pardon for sins, of submitting his offenses to the mercy and forgiving grace of God. If one has fallen into serious sin, sacramental confession is the ordinary way established in the Church to reconcile the sinner with Christ and with his Church. It is also true that a sinner can be restored to grace by perfect sorrow or perfect contrition in the sense of the Church's Tradition. Therefore every Catholic, from his early years, should be instructed how to receive and best profit from the regular reception of this sacrament.[57]

Holy Orders in a special way conforms certain members of the People of God to Christ the Mediator. It puts them in positions of special service for building up the Body of Christ[58] and gives them a sacred power to fulfill that ministry of service. Through this sacrament Christ bestows a permanent charism of the Holy Spirit enabling the recipients to guide and shepherd the faith community, proclaim and explain the Gospel, and guide and sanctify God's people. Representing Christ, they primarily offer the Sacrifice of the Mass. Also as his representatives, they administer the Sacrament of Penance for the forgiveness of sins, and the Sacrament of the Anointing of the Sick.[59]

The Anointing of the Sick is the sacrament for the seriously ill, infirm and aged. It is best received as soon as the danger of death begins, from either sickness or old age. By this anointing and the accompanying prayers for the restoration of health, the entire Church through the priests asks the Lord to lighten their sufferings, forgive their sins, and bring them to eternal salvation. The Church encourages the sick to contribute to the spiritual good of the entire People of God by associating themselves freely to the sufferings and death of Christ.[60]

12. THE EUCHARIST, CENTER OF ALL SACRAMENTAL LIFE

The Eucharist has primacy among the sacraments. It is of the greatest importance for uniting and strengthening of the Church.[61] The Eucharistic celebration is carried out in obedience to the words of Jesus at the Last Supper: "Do this in memory of me."

When a priest pronounces the words of Eucharistic consecration, the underlying reality of bread and wine is changed into the body and blood of Christ, given for us in sacrifice. That change has been given the name "transubstantiation." This means that Christ himself, true God and true Man, is really and substantially present, in a mysterious way, under the appearances of bread and wine.

This sacrifice (of the Mass) is not merely a ritual which commemorates a past sacrifice. In it, through the ministry of priests, Christ perpetuates the sacrifice of the cross in an unbloody manner.[62] At the same time, the Eucharist is a meal which recalls the Last Supper, celebrates our unity together in Christ, and anticipates the messianic banquet of the kingdom. In the Eucharist Jesus nourishes Christians with his own self, the Bread of Life, so that they may become a people more acceptable to God and filled with greater love of God and neighbor.

To receive the Eucharist worthily the Christian must be in the state of grace (cf. 1 Corinthians 11:27–28).

Having been nourished by the Lord himself, the Christian should with active love eliminate all prejudices and all barriers to brotherly cooperation with others. The Eucharist is a sacrament of unity. It is meant to unite the faithful more closely each day with God and with one another.

The Eucharist, reserved in our churches, is a powerful help to prayer and service of others. Religious instruction should stress the gratitude, adoration and devotion due to the real presence of Christ in the Blessed Sacrament reserved.[63]

13. THE SACRAMENT OF MATRIMONY

Particular attention must be given to religious education concerning matrimony. In modern society it is necessary to emphasize that marriage was instituted by the Creator himself and given by him certain purposes, laws, and blessings. Students are to be acquainted with the vision and teaching of the Second Vatican Council concerning marriage and the family, concerning the indissolubility of marriage and the evil of divorce.[64]

Christ raised marriage of the baptized to the dignity of a Sacrament. The spouses, expressing their personal and irrevocable consent, are the ministers of the sacrament. Therefore they live together in Christ's grace. They imitate — and in a way represent — Christ's own love for his Church.[65] By this sacrament Christian spouses are as it were consecrated to uphold the dignity of matrimony and to carry out its duties. It should be made clear that the Church discourages the contracting of mixed marriages in order to encourage a full union of mind and life in matrimony.[66]

Following the Second Vatican Council, the religion teacher should show that marriage is the basis of family life. Special attention should be given to the unity and unbreakable quality of matrimony, as decreed by God. The purposes of marriage should be explained in accord with the teachings of the Second Vatican Council:

> "Marriage and conjugal love are by their nature ordained toward the begetting and education of children. . . . Hence, while not making the other purposes of matrimony of less account, the true practice of conjugal love, and the whole meaning of the family life which results from it, have this aim: that the couple be ready with stout hearts to cooperate with the love of the Creator and the Savior, who through them will enlarge and enrich His own family day by day. . . . Marriage to be sure is not instituted solely for procreation [but also that] the mutual love of the spouses, too, be embodied in a rightly ordered manner, that it grow and ripen."[67]

Similarly, there must be a clear presentation of the Church's teaching concerning chastity in marriage, moral methods of regulating births, and the protection due to human life once a child has been conceived.[68]

The teacher should explain the vocation of every family to function perfectly as a Community — that is, a group of persons sharing life together at a deep, personal level. Each member of the family has this obligation. Such a community will reach out to affect constructively the Church, the civic and the world community.[69]

14. THE NEW MAN IN THE SPIRIT

When man accepts the Spirit of Christ, God introduces him to a way of life completely new. It empowers a man to share in God's own life. He is joined to the Father and to Christ in a vital union which not even death can break.[70]

The indwelling Holy Spirit gives a man hope and courage, heals his weakness of soul, enables him to master passion and selfishness. The Spirit prompts man to pursue what is good and to advance in such virtues as charity, joy, peace, patience, kindness, longanimity, humility, fidelity, modesty, continence, and chastity.[71] The presence of the Holy Spirit makes prayer possible and effective.

God's dwelling in the soul is a matchless grace and manifold gift. Its effects have been expressed in many ways. Thus, a sinner is said to be "justified by God" or "given new life by the Holy Spirit," or "given a share in Christ's life in himself," or to receive grace. The root meaning is that a person dies to sin, shares in the divinity of the Son through the Spirit of adoption, and enters into close communion with the Most Holy Trinity.

In the history of salvation, it is divinely appointed that man is to receive this sanctifying grace of adoption as God's child and to inherit eternal life. Because of the grace of Christ the Savior, man is given supernatural life, meaning and dignity far beyond what his own nature confers.[72]

15. HUMAN AND CHRISTIAN FREEDOM

God's plan is that man, united with Jesus Christ, should give a free answer to God's call. At the outset, God endowed human nature with freedom. But this has been badly impaired by the sin of humanity, original sin. The resultant weakness is overcome by grace, so that man can live with holiness in the faith of Jesus Christ.[73]

The Church knows that, because of psychological difficulties or external conditions, freedom can be reduced slightly or considerably or altogether. Hence conditions most favorable to the exercise of genuine human freedom must be promoted, not only for man's temporal welfare but also for the higher good of grace and eternal salvation. Accordingly, the Church will seek to communicate a true sense and appreciation of freedom, will defend freedom against unjust force of every kind, and will summon Christians to work together with all men of good will to safeguard freedom.[74]

16. THE SINS OF MAN

In working out his salvation, man finds that the greatest problem is sin.

Original sin is his first obstacle. How does it affect him?

"Although he was made by God in a state of holiness, from the very dawn of history man abused his liberty, at the urging of the Evil One. Man set himself against God and sought to find fulfillment apart from God."[75]

"Through one man sin entered the world, and with sin death, death thus coming to all men inasmuch as all sinned" (Romans 5:12).

"It is human nature so fallen, stripped of the grace that clothed it, injured in its own natural powers and subjected to the dominion of death, that is transmitted to all men — and it is in this sense that every man is born in sin."[76] This sin of mankind is multitudinous, has caused incalculable sorrow and ruin, and weighs down on every man.

In addition to the effects of original sin, there is personal sin, that committed by the individual. By it a person, acting knowingly and deliberately, violates the moral law. The sinner fails in love of God. He turns away from, or even back from his lifetime goal of doing God's Will. He may even, by serious offense (mortal sin), rupture his relationship with the Father.

It is important that the awareness of sin not be lost or lessened. The Christian must have clear knowledge of right and wrong, so as to be able to choose with an informed conscience to love God and avoid offending him.

Religious instruction must not be silent about the reality of sin, the kinds of sin and the degree of gravity and personal wilfulness which indicate mortal sin. Instruction must remind the student of the sufferings and the death on the cross which Christ endured to destroy the effects of sin.[77]

But it must go on to speak eloquently of Gods forgiveness. Even though a man sins, he can be pardoned. The power of grace is greater than that of sin. The superabundant love of God restores the penitent and draws him toward salvation.[78]

17. THE MORAL LIFE OF CHRISTIANS

Christ directed his apostles to teach the observance of everything that he had commanded.[79] Catechetical instruction must include both the things which are to be believed and those which are to be done or avoided if we are to respond generously to God's love.

Christian morality defines a way of living worthy of a human being and of an adopted son of God. It is a positive response to God, by growing in the new life given through Jesus Christ. It is supported and guided by the grace and gifts of the Holy Spirit.[80]

Christian freedom needs to be guided in questions of day-to-day living. Each person must have a right conscience and follow it. Conscience is not feeling nor self-will, although these may affect the degree of culpability. Conscience is a personal judgment that something is right or wrong because of the will and law of God.

So the conscience of the Catholic Christian must pay respectful and obedient attention to the teaching authority of God's Church.[81] It is the duty of this teaching authority, or Magisterium, to give guidance for applying the enduring norms and values of Christian morality to specific situations of everyday life.

The Christian must know that there are moral values which are absolute and never to be disregarded or violated by anyone in any situation. Fidelity to them may require heroism of the sort which we see in the lives of the saints and the deaths of the martyrs.

Obedience to the Holy Spirit includes a faithful observance of the commandments of God, the laws of the Church, and just civil laws. All civil laws are not necessarily just, because at times civil laws permit what God forbids. "Better for us to obey God than men!" (Acts 5:29). Christian witness is especially powerful when it defends the values of God rather than those of the world.[82]

18. THE PERFECTION OF CHRISTIAN LOVE

The special characteristic of Christian moral teaching is its total relationship to the love of God, or charity. All commandments and norms for this moral teaching are summed up in faith working through charity.[83] Love of God is the soul of morality. God is love, and in God's plan that love reaches out in Jesus Christ, to unite men in mutual love.

It follows, then, that responding freely and perfectly to God and God's Will means keeping his commandments and living in his love. It means accepting and practicing the "new commandment" of charity.

Sustained by faith, man is to live a life of love of God and of his fellow men. This is his greatest responsibility, and the source of his greatest dignity. A man's holiness, whatever his vocation or state of life may be, is the perfection of love of God.[84]

Following the Second Vatican Council,[85] religious instruction should speak of the importance for humanity and for the Church of those women and men who, accepting a religious vocation, show in this special and needed way their love of God and true service to mankind. Such instruction should acknowledge the excellence which the Christian message gives to virginity consecrated in Christ.[86]

19. SPECIFICS IN THE TEACHING OF MORALITY

The duties and obligations flowing from love of God and man are to be taught in specific, practical fashion. The follower of Christ is to know the Christian response to the challenges and temptations of contemporary living. The Church has a duty to apply moral principles to current problems, personal and social.

The specifics of morality are to be taught within the overall framework of the Ten Commandments of God and the Sermon on the Mount, especially the Beatitudes (see Appendix A). Also included should be the spiritual and corporal works of mercy, the theological and moral virtues, the seven capital sins, etc. Whatever approach is used, the student should know the Ten Commandments as part of his religious heritage (see Appendix A). Teaching morality also should include instruction on the laws of the Church (see Appendix B). The Bible and the lives of the saints supply concrete examples of moral living.

Towards God the Christian has a lifelong obligation of love and service. The Will of God must be put first in the scale of personal values, and must be kept there throughout life. One must have toward God the attitude of a son to an all-good, all-loving Father, and must never think or live as if independent of God. He must gladly give to God genuine worship and true prayer, both liturgical and private.

Man must not put anyone or anything in place of God. This is idolatry, which has its variations in superstition, witchcraft, occultism. Honoring God, man is never to blaspheme nor perjure himself. Honoring God, one is to show respect for persons, places and things related specially to God.

Atheism, heresy, and schism are to be rejected in the light of man's duties to God.

Towards his fellow man the Christian has specific obligations in love. Like Christ, he will show that love by concern for the rights of his fellow man — his freedom, his housing, his food, his health, his right to work, etc. The Christian is to show to all others the justice and charity of Christ — to reach out in the spirit of the beatitudes to help all others, to build up a better society in the local community and justice and peace throughout the world. His judgment and speech concerning others are to be ruled by the charity due all sons of God. He will respect and obey all lawful authority in the home, in civil society, and in the Church.

Many are the sins against neighbor. It is sinful to be selfishly apathetic towards others in their needs. It is sinful to violate the rights of others — to steal, deliberately damage another's good name or property, cheat, not to pay one's debts. Respecting God's gift of life, the Christian cannot be anti-life and must avoid sins of murder, abortion, euthanasia, genocide, indiscriminate acts of war. He must not use immoral methods of family limitation. Sins of lying, detraction and calumny are forbidden, as are anger, hatred, racism and discrimination. In the area of sexuality, the Christian is to be modest in behavior and dress. In a sex-saturated society, the follower of Christ must be different. For the Christian there can be no premarital sex, fornication, adultery, or other acts of impurity or scandal to others. He must remain chaste, repelling lustful desires and temptations, self-abuse, pornography and indecent entertainment of every description.

Towards self the follower of Christ has certain duties. He must be another Christ in the world of his own day, a living example of Christian goodness. He must be humble and patient in the face of his own imperfections, as well as those of others. He must show a Christlike simplicity towards material things and the affluence of our society. The follower of Christ must be pure in words and actions even in the midst of corruption.

To be guarded against is the capital sin of price, with its many manifestations. So too with sloth — spiritual, intellectual and physical. The Christian must resist envy of others' success and of their financial and material possessions. He is not to surrender self-control and abuse his bodily health by intemperance in drugs, alcohol, food.

Obviously this listing does not cover all morality or all immorality. But it indicates the practical approach which will help the Christian to form a right conscience, choose always what is right, avoid sin and the occasions of sin, and live in this world according to the Spirit of Christ in love of God.

20. THE CHURCH, PEOPLE OF GOD AND INSTITUTION FOR SALVATION

The Church, founded by Christ, had its origin in his death and resurrection. It is the new People of God, prepared for in the Old Testament and given life, growth, and direction by Christ in the Holy Spirit. It is the work of God's saving love in Christ.

In the Catholic Church are found the deposit of faith, the sacraments, and the ministries inherited from the apostles. Through these gifts of God, the Church is able to act and grow as a community in Christ, serving mankind and giving men his saving word and activity.

The Church shares in the prophetic office of Christ.[87] Assembled by God's Word, it accepts that Word and witnesses to it in every quarter of the globe. So the Church is missionary by its very nature, and every member of the Church shares the command from Christ to carry the Good News to all mankind.[88]

The Church is also a priestly people.[89]

By God's design, it is a society with leaders—i.e., with a hierarchy. As such, it is a people guided by its bishops, who are in union with the Pope, the Bishop of Rome, the Vicar of Christ. He has succeeded to the office of Peter in his care and guidance of the whole flock of Christ[90] and is the head of the college of bishops. To them the community of faith owes respect and obedience, for "in exercising his office of father and pastor, a bishop should stand as one who serves."[91]

Religious instruction should treat the role of the Pope and of the bishops in their office of teaching, sanctifying and governing the Church. It should explain the gift of infallibility in the Church,[92] and the way and manner in which the teaching authority of the Church guides the faithful in truth.

The Holy Spirit preserves the Church as the body of Christ and his bride, so that—despite the sins of its members—it will never fail in faithfulness to him and will meet him in holiness at the end of the world. The Spirit also helps the Church constantly to purify and renew itself and its members. To help its members, the Spirit-guided Church can modernize in those areas that permit change.[93]

21. THE CHURCH AS A COMMUNITY

The Church is a community sharing together the life of Christ, a people assembled by God. Within this assembly there is a basic equality of all persons. There are different responsibilities in the Church. For example, the ministerial priesthood is essentially different from the "priesthood of the people." But all are united and equal as the one People of God.[94]

In the Church every individual has a call from God, a vocation to holiness. Each deserves respect, since all join in the one cause of Christ. The Pope and the bishops coordinate this work, in every rite, diocese, parish, and mission. In each, no matter how small or poor or isolated, "Christ is present, and by his power the one, holy, Catholic and Apostolic Church is gathered together."[95]

22. THE QUEST FOR UNITY

Christ willed that all who believe in him be one, so that the world might know that he was sent by the Father.[96] Christian unity, then, in faith and love, is God's Will. Prayer and work for Christian unity are essential to Catholic life, and religious education must bring this out. Catholics should be deeply, personally concerned over the present, sad divisions of Christians. Catholics should take the first steps in ecumenical dialogue and should try to make the Church more faithful to Christ and to its heritage from the apostles.[97]

We recognize the unique fullness of the Catholic Church which we believe to be the ordinary means of salvation, and which we desire to share with all men.

But we also recognize that Catholics can be enriched by the authentic insights into the Gospel as witnessed by other religious traditions.[98]

A still wider unity must be a concern of Catholic life and education: the unity of all men under God. Following the Second Vatican Council, religious education must show Christlike respect for all men of good will, beginning with our elder brothers in faith, the Jewish people, and reaching out to those others who with us believe in God.[99]

Religious instruction is, then, to show a sensitive appreciation of the dignity and unique value of every human being. The Church rejects as un-Christian any unjust discrimination or injustice because of race, national origin, ethnic origin, color, sex, class, or religion. God has given to every man intrinsic dignity, freedom and eternal importance. "If anyone says, 'My love is fixed on God,' yet hates his brother, he is a liar. One who has no love for the brother he has seen cannot love the God he has not seen" (1 John 4:20).

23. THE CHURCH AS THE INSTITUTION FOR SALVATION

The Church is a community of the People of God with Christ as leader and head. It is a structured institution to which Christ has given the mission of bringing the message of salvation to all men.[100] "Established by Christ as a fellowship of life, charity and truth, this messianic people is also used by him as an instrument for the redemption of all, and is sent forth into the whole world as the light of the world and the salt of the earth."[101]

The Church is not of this world, and can never conform itself to this world. But it both speaks and listens to the world, and strives to be seen by the world as faithful to the Gospel. So "Christians cannot yearn for anything more ardently than to serve the men of the modern world ever more generously and effectively. Therefore, holding faithfully to the Gospel and benefiting from its resources, and united with every man who loves and practices justice, Christians have shouldered a gigantic task demanding fulfillment in this world. Concerning this task they must give a reckoning to Him who will judge every man on the last day.[102]

In, but not of this world, the Church is "inspired by no earthly ambition."[103] Only in heaven will it be perfect. Engaged in the world, it always has heaven in view, toward which the People of God are journeying.[104]

24. MARY, MOTHER OF GOD, MOTHER AND MODEL OF THE CHURCH

The Gospel of Luke gives us Mary's words: "My Spirit finds joy in God my savior, for he has looked upon his servant in her lowliness; all ages to come shall call me blessed" (Luke 1:47–48).

Religious instruction should lead students to see Mary as singularly blessed and relevant to their own lives and needs. Following venerable Christian tradition as continued in the Second Vatican Council, the teacher should explain the special place of the Virgin Mary in the history of salvation and in the Church.[105]

The "ever-virgin mother of Jesus Christ our Lord and God,"[106] she is in the Church in a place highest after Christ, and also is very close to us as our spiritual Mother. In religious instruction there should be explanations of her special gifts from God (being Mother of God, being preserved from all stain of original sin, being assumed body and soul to heaven). The special veneration due to Mary—Mother of Christ, Mother of the Church, our spiritual Mother—should be taught by word and example.

The Church likewise honors the other saints who are already with the Lord in heaven. They inspire us by the heroic example of their lives. To them we pray, asking their intercession with God for us.[107]

The teacher should remind students of reverence towards the bodies of those who have gone before us in death, and our duty of praying for deceased relatives, friends and all the faithful departed.[108]

25. FINAL REUNION WITH GOD

During this earthly life, Christians look forward to their final reunion with God. They long for the coming of "our Lord Jesus Christ, who will give a new form to this lowly body of ours and remake it according to the pattern of his glorified body" (Philippians 3:21).[109]

But the final realities will come about only when Christ returns with power to bring history to its appointed end. Then as Judge of the living and the dead he will hand over his people to the Father. Then only will the Church reach perfection and enter into the fullness of God. Until the Lord's arrival in majesty, "some of his disciples are pilgrims on earth, some have finished this life and are being purified, and others are in glory, beholding clearly God himself three and one, as He is."[110]

Religious instruction on death, judgment, and eternity should be given in a spirit of consoling hope, as well as salutary fear (cf. Thessalonians 4:18). The Lord's resurrection means that death has been conquered. So we have reason to live, and to face death, with courage and joy. The renewed funeral liturgy sets the tone for religious instruction on death. In the risen Christ we live, we die, and we shall live again. We look ahead to a homecoming with God our loving Father.[111]

Religious instructions should treat seriously the awesome responsibility which each person has about his eternal destiny. The importance of the individual judgment after death, of the refining and purifying punishments of Purgatory, of the dreadful possibility of the eternal death of hell, and of the last judgment should be taught in the light of Christian hope.

On the day of the last judgment each person will fully reach his eternal destiny. Then all of us will be revealed "before the judgment place of Christ, so that each one may receive what he deserves, according to what he has done, good or bad, in his bodily life" (2 Corinthians 5:10). Then "the evildoers shall rise to be damned," and "those who have done right shall rise to live" (cf. John 5:29)—to a life eternally with God beyond what the heart of man can imagine, to receive the good things that God has prepared for those who love him.[112]

APPENDIX A

The Ten Commandments of God are of special importance in teaching specifics of morality. The Old Testament,[113] the New Testament[114] and the long use of the Church testify to this. A summary presentation of the Ten Commandments of God taken from the *New American Bible* translation[115] is:

1. I, the Lord, am your God. You shall not have other gods besides me.

2. You shall not take the name of the Lord, your God, in vain.

3. Remember to keep holy the sabbath day.

4. Honor your father and your mother.

5. You shall not kill.

6. You shall not commit adultery.

7. You shall not steal.

8. You shall not bear false witness against your neighbor.

9. You shall not covet your neighbor's wife.

10. You shall not covet anything that belongs to your neighbor.

The Beatitudes are likewise of particular importance in teaching specifics of morality. The traditional listing of the Beatitudes, as taken from the *New American Bible* translation, is:

1. Blest are the poor in spirit: the reign of God is theirs.

2. Blest are the sorrowing: they shall be consoled.

3. Blest are the lowly: they shall inherit the land.

4. Blest are they who hunger and thirst for holiness: they shall have their fill.

5. Blest are they who show mercy: mercy shall be theirs.

6. Blest are the single-hearted: for they shall see God.

7. Blest are the peacemakers: they shall be called sons of God.

8. Blest are those persecuted for holiness' sake: the reign of God is theirs. (Matthew 5:3 – 10)

APPENDIX B

From time to time the Church has listed certain specific duties of Catholics. Some duties expected of Catholic Christians today including the following. (Those traditional mentioned as Precepts of the Church[116] are marked with an asterisk.)

1. To keep holy the day of the Lord's Resurrection: to worship God by participating in Mass every Sunday and Holy Day of Obligation:* to avoid those activities that would hinder renewal of soul and body, e.g., needless work and business activities, unnecessary shopping, etc.

2. To lead a sacramental life: to receive Holy Communion frequently and the Sacrament of Penance regularly —

   — minimally, to receive the Sacrament of Penance at least once a year (annual confession is obligatory only if serious sin is involved).*

   — minimally, to receive Holy Communion at least once a year, between the First Sundays of Lent and Trinity Sunday.*

3. To study Catholic teaching in preparation for the Sacrament of Confirmation, to be Confirmed and then to continue to study and advance the cause of Christ.

4. To observe the marriage laws of the Church:* to give religious training (by example and word) to one's children; to use parish schools and religious education programs.

5. To strengthen and support the Church:* one's own parish community and parish priests; the worldwide Church and the Holy Father.

6. To do penance, including abstaining from meat and fasting from food on the appointed days.*

7. To join in the missionary spirit and apostolate of the Church.

NOTES

1. CD, 14.

2. LG, 25: "Among the principal duties of bishops, the preaching of the gospel occupies an eminent place. . . . They are authentic teachers, that is, teachers endowed with the authority of Christ, who preach to the people committed to them the faith they must believe and put into practice."

3. Cf. GCD, 70–76.

4. CD, 14.

5. IM, 118. Cf. *Apostolic Exhortation of Pope Paul VI to all Bishops* (December 8, 1970): Part II.

6. *Present Position of Catholics in England*, by Cardinal Newman (1852).

7. Cf. GCD, 22, 25.

8. Cf. entire DV. Note also the way in which the Second Vatican Council, in all its decrees, demonstrates the importance of the Sacred Scriptures.

9. DV, 12.

10. DV, 10.

11. DV, 8.

12. Cf. John 1:12 and Romans 8:15.

13. For this entire section, cf. GCD, 47.

14. Cf. 1 Peter 1:3–4.

15. Cf. Matthew 25:14 and following.

16. Cf. Ephesians 4:15.

17. For this entire section, cf. GCD, 48.

18. Cf. Romans 1:20; Acts 15:17; Psalm 19:1; Wisdom 13:1–9.

19. Cf. *Dogmatic Constitution Dei Filius* of the First Vatican Council.

20. Cf. Acts 2:42–47.

21. Cf. GS, 21.

22. Cf. John 4:20–21.

23. For this entire section, cf. GCD, 49.

24. Cf. Colossians 1:15–17.

25. Cf. Colossians 1:15 and following.

26. Cf. Romans 1:4.

27. Cf. 1 Corinthians 15:22.

28. Cf. Ephesians 2:10.

29. Cf. Romans 8:19–21.

30. For this entire section, cf. GCD, 50.

31. Isaiah 40:27–28; 51:9–19.

32. Cf. DV, 3.

33. Cf. Encyclical *Humani Generis* (1950) of Pope Pius XII, AAS 42:575–6. Cf. GS, 12, 14.

34. Ephesians 1:19–20.

35. Cf. 2 Peter 3:13. For this entire section, cf. GCD, 51.

36. Cf. 1 Corinthians 15:28. For this entire section, cf. GCD, 52.

37. Cf. GS, 22.

38. Cf. John 1:18.

39. Cf. *Declaration for Safeguarding the Belief in the Mysteries of the Incarnation and of the Most Holy Trinity against Some Recent Errors* (February 21, 1972), by the Sacred Congregation for the Doctrine of Faith. For this entire section, cf. GCD, 53.

40. Cf. 2 Corinthians 5:19.

41. Cf. Mark 1:15.

42. Cf. John 14:31.

43. Cf. Galatians 2:20; 1 John 3:16.

44. Cf. Philippians 2:9–11; Ephesians 1:20.

45. Cf. John 7:39; Acts 2:33; Romans 4:25; 8:11; 1 Corinthians 15:45; Hebrews 5:9.

46. Cf. Romans 8:29.

47. For this entire section, cf. GCD, 54.

48. John 14:16; 15:26.

49. John 14:17.

50. Cf. Acts 2:1–14 and following.

51. Cf. LG, 4.

52. Cf. *Decree on the Sacraments* of the Council of Trent: DS 1601, 1606.

53. Cf. LG, 1.

54. Cf. SC, 59.

55. For this entire section, cf. GCD, 55.

56. Cf. *Apostolic Constitution on the Sacrament of Confirmation* by Pope Paul VI (August 15, 1971).

57. Cf. *Addendum* of the GCD: "The special task of catechesis here is to explain in a suitable way that sacramental Confession is a means offered children of the Church to obtain pardon for sin, and furthermore that it is even necessary *per se* if one has fallen into serious sin. To be sure, Christian parents and religious educators ought to teach the child in such a way that above all he will strive to advance to a more intimate love of the Lord Jesus and to genuine love of neighbor. The doctrine on the sacrament of Penance is to be presented in a broad framework of attaining purification and spiritual growth with great confidence in the mercy and love of God." . . . "One should also keep in mind the usefulness of Confession, which retains its efficacy even when only venial sins are in question, and which gives an increase of grace and of charity, increases the child's good dispositions for receiving the Eucharist, and also helps to perfect the Christian life."

58. Cf. Ephesians 4:12.

59. Cf. PO, 13.

60. Cf. James 5:14–16; cf. LG, 11. For this entire section, cf. GCD, 56–57.

61. Cf. LG, 11, 17.

62. Cf. SC, 47.

63. For this entire section, cf. GCD, 58.

64. Cf. LG, 11, 35, 41; cf. GS, 48.

65. Cf. Ephesians 5:25.

66. Cf. *Motu Proprio* "Determining Norms for Mixed Marriages" of Pope Paul VI (1970).

67. Cf. GS, 49–50.

68. Cf. GS, 51; cf. *Encyclical On Human Life* of Pope Paul VI (1968), 10–17.

69. For this entire section, cf. GCD, 59.

70. Cf. John 14:23.

71. Cf. Galatians 5:22–23.

72. For this entire section, cf. GCD, 60.

73. Cf. Galatians 2:20.

74. For this entire section, cf. GCD, 61.

75. GS, 13.

76. *Credo of the People of God* of Pope Paul VI (1968), 16.

77. Cf. Romans 5.

78. For this entire section, cf. GCD, 62.

79. Cf. Matthew 28:20.

80. Cf. Romans 5:5.

81. Cf. DH, 8–9; cf. LG, 25: "In matters of faith and morals, the bishops speak in the name of Christ and the faithful are to accept their teaching and adhere to it with a religious assent of soul. This religious submission of will and of mind must be shown in a special way to the authentic teaching authority of the Roman Pontiff, even when he is not speaking *ex cathedra*. . . . "

82. For this entire section, cf. GCD, 63.

83. Cf. Romans 13:8–10; Galatians 5:6.

84. Cf. LG, 39–42.

85. Cf. LG, 43–44.

86. For this entire section, cf. GCD, 64.

87. Cf. LG, 12.

88. Cf. AG, 1–2.

89. Cf. Revelation 1:6; cf. LG, 10.

90. Cf. John 21:15–17.

91. Cf. CD, 16.

92. Cf. LG, 25.

93. For this entire section, cf. GCD, 65.

94. Cf. Ephesians 4:4–6; cf. LG, 32.

95. Cf. LG, 25. For this entire section, cf. GCD, 66.

96. Cf. John 17:20–21.

97. Cf. UR, 4–5.

98. Cf. LG, 8, 14–16; cf. DH, 1; cf. entire DH; cf. GCD, 27.

99. Cf. LG, 15–16; cf. entire NA.

100. Cf. Matthew 28:16–20.

101. LG, 9. Cf. entire AG.

102. GS, 93.

103. GS, 3.

104. For this entire section, cf. GCD, 67.

105. Cf. LG, 52–69.

106. First Eucharistic Prayer of the Mass.

107. Cf. LG, 49–50.

108. For this entire section, cf. GCD, 68.

109. Cf. 1 Corinthians 15.

110. LG, 49.

111. Cf. Luke 15.

112. Cf. LG, 48. For this entire section, cf. GCD, 69.

113. Cf. *Jerome Biblical Commentary*, 1:5; 1:23; 3:48–50; 6:20; 20:8.

114. Cf. Matthew 19:16–19; Mark 10:17–20; Luke 18:18–22.

115. Cf. Exodus 20:2–17 and Deuteronomy 5:6–21.

116. The traditionally listed chief Precepts of the Church are the following six:
    1. To assist at Mass on all Sundays and holy days of obligation.
    2. To fast and abstain on the days appointed.
    3. To confess our sins at least once a year.
    4. To receive Holy communion during the Easter time.
    5. To contribute to the support of the Church.
    6. To observe the laws of the Church concerning marriage.

ON
EVANGELIZATION
IN THE
MODERN WORLD

EVANGELII NUNTIANDI
1975

OVERVIEW OF *ON EVANGELIZATION IN THE MODERN WORLD*

by Thomas P. Walters

Catechesis is a form of the ministry of the word that initiates church members into the meaning of Christian signs and symbols. It is a ministry based on the assumption that the persons being catechized have already accepted the proclamation of Jesus Christ and are gathered by it into community. In practice, this generally is not the case. Too often, parish catechesis is directed toward individuals who have not consciously accepted the gospel proclamation. It is an attempt to catechize church members still in need of evangelization. It was this very concern that prompted Pope Paul VI to address the need for the church to proclaim more intentionally and more forcefully the love of God to all—both those outside and those within the Catholic community. The apostolic exhortation *On Evangelization in the Modern World* was the result.

On Evangelization in the Modern World (EN) was promulgated by Pope Paul VI on December 8, 1975, the tenth anniversary of the closing of the Second Vatican Council and one year after he had convoked a synod of bishops to deal specifically with the topic of evangelization.

The Second Vatican Council (1962–1965) laid the foundation for Catholic evangelization by speaking of the church community as the people of God, by giving a new understanding of and a sensitivity to ecumenism and by renewing a sense of the mission to share the gospel of Jesus Christ. The 1974 Synod of Bishops, while it dealt in depth with the topic of evangelization, provided the church with no written guidelines. Rather, the bishops chose to encourage Pope Paul VI to reflect on the Synod's deliberations and to provide the needed theological and pastoral direction. *On Evangelization in the Modern World* was the result.

This 20,000-word exhortation is the first church document devoted entirely to the topic of evangelization and is considered by some to be one of the most important and far-reaching documents issued since Vatican II. It was offered by Paul VI as a meditation on the concerns that flowed from the Council and created the context for the 1974 Synod, concerns that are just as relevant today. These concerns are captured by Pope Paul in the following question: "At this turning point of history, does the church or does she not find herself better equipped to proclaim the gospel and to put it into people's hearts with conviction, freedom of spirit and effectiveness?" (4).

Paul VI's response to this question is provided reflectively in five concise chapters. *On Evangelization in the Modern World* begins by centering evangelization in Christ and in the church. This is followed by chapters devoted to the concept of evangelization, the essential content of the evangelization process, methods of evangelization, the beneficiaries, the evangelizers and, finally, the very spirit of evangelization.

Pope Paul stresses the reciprocal link between the church and evangelization. Those who accept the proclamation of Jesus are gathered by it into community and bear the concomitant responsibility of sharing this good news with others both within the community and outside its boundaries (13,15). Evangelization cannot be understood without reference to the Christ of the New Testament nor can it be understood or undertaken apart from the church because it is the essential mission of the church.

In the words of Jesus, the first evangelizer (7), "I must proclaim the good news of the kingdom of God" (Luke 4:43). Pope Paul emphasizes that Jesus' life and his untiring preaching of the word illustrate the fact that at the center of the gospel message is the paradoxical kingdom, a kingdom that not only stresses liberation from those bounds that oppress humankind as well as from sin and evil but a kingdom made up of those things that the world rejects (8, 9).

EVANGELIZATION

In Paul VI's words, cultures "have to be regenerated by an encounter with the gospel" (20). Every task and every ministry within the church is to be concerned with communication of the gospel of Jesus Christ to all peoples through the preaching of the word of God, the celebration of the sacraments and the living out of a life of love in the Holy Spirit under the guidance of the church. None of this is new to those who have been involved actively in the church's catechetical ministry for the past 20 years. However, the force of the call to both implicit proclamation (the personal witness of one's life) and explicit proclamation (publicly evangelizing others) is as strong today as it was when the document was first published. The goal of evangelization is conversion, that is, the *metanoia* of embracing Jesus and his message and sharing this message with others.

In addition, Pope Paul emphasizes that evangelization cannot be reduced to any single element. It is multidimensional. It is to be reflected in the interplay of personal witness, explicit proclamation, inner-adherence, entry into an ecclesial community, reception of the sacraments and apostolic action.

It should be pointed out that evangelization as described in EN with its stress on the role of the hierarchical church with its sacramental and magisterial life as well as its social witness, should not be confused with the evangelism of eighteenth-century European pietism or American Protestant Revivalism.

THE CONTENT OF EVANGELIZATION

Evangelization demands a fidelity to the *message* being proclaimed and to the *people* who are to receive it. In this document, Pope Paul states continually that the true meaning of evangelization is the proclamation of the love of God that comes to us through Christ Jesus in such a manner that humankind, through the grace of God, accepts it with a free and firm commitment. He states also that this proclamation would be incomplete "if it did not take account of the unceasing interplay of the gospel and of man's concrete life, both personal and social"

(29). Human liberation and salvation in Jesus Christ are linked. And while temporal and political liberation can never be considered the goal of evangelization, Pope Paul stresses the necessity of the church always striving "to insert the Christian struggle for liberation into the universal plan of salvation which she herself proclaims" (38). Pope Paul stresses continually the need for constant and deep renewal and reform both within the church and in society-at-large.

METHOD

For the catechetically minded, the inclusion of this chapter is particularly satisfying because it addresses the issue of how to evangelize. And how one evangelizes is "permanently relevant," according to Pope Paul, "because the methods of evangelizing vary according to the different circumstances of time, place and culture and because they thereby present a certain challenge to our capacity for discovery and adaptation" (40).

And while the chapter is somewhat repetitious with its emphasis on the witness of life and verbal proclamation, Pope Paul does highlight three areas of concern that are particularly apt for today's church as it draws closer to the opening days of the twenty-first century. His observations center on preaching, mass media and the relationship between content and method in the church's evangelization efforts. With regard to preaching, Pope Paul stresses that faith comes from what is heard. Thus, the verbal proclamation remains perennially valid. The section of the exhortation that centers on the homily (43) will be of particular value to priests.

Pope Paul's emphasis on the use of the mass media is surprisingly positive. He indicates that in the mass media the church "finds a modern and effective version of the pulpit" and that through the media the church can succeed in "speaking to the multitudes" (45).

Finally, there is a word of caution to be found in this section for today's church. In light of the *Catechism of the Catholic Church*, Pope Paul's observation that "the content of evangelization must not overshadow the importance of the ways and means" (40) gives some pause for reflection.

THE BENEFICIARIES

In this section of his exhortation, Pope Paul focuses on the church's mission to "proclaim the good news to all creation" (Mark 16:15) despite many obstacles. The sections "Non-believers" and "The non-practicing" are of particular interest to those whose evangelizing efforts take place in the United States. One of the greatest dangers facing Catholics is the dilemma of knowing where and how their Catholic beliefs are to influence their public actions. Where and how are public beliefs to intersect with national policy in a secular society? Catholics in the United States live in a society that has experienced a shift from a view of religion as *the* view of life to religion as *a* view or, even worse, a society "without any need for recourse to God, who thus becomes superfluous and an encumbrance" (55).

Likewise, in growing numbers Catholics no longer stand over and against the secular culture; they have become the culture. Too many Catholics have grown indifferent to their baptismal call. Pope Paul encourages the church to "constantly seek the proper means and language for presenting, or representing, to them God's revelation and faith in Jesus Christ" (56).

EVANGELISTS

Evangelization begins with the coming of the Holy Spirit to the evangelist. It is only from this "pentecostal" experience that true evangelization takes place. The evangelist serves as God's instrument in transmitting the good news to others. In order that the evangelist be this instrument and evangelize faithfully and effectively, Pope Paul insists that the following two principles be kept in mind: (1) the evangelizer must not undertake this mission on his or her own initiative or authority because evangelization is at root an ecclesial task, and (2) the evangelizer must act "in communion with the church and her pastors" (60).

Pope Paul concludes this section by stressing the need for serious preparation for all who have devoted themselves to the ministry of the word from catechists to the heads of small communities. In a present-day church that too often finds itself dependent on the ministerial services of the untrained volunteer, Pope Paul's call to "be vigilant concerning the adequate formation of all the ministers of the word" (73) continues to challenge the church's resolve in this matter.

THE SPIRIT

In this final chapter, Pope Paul explains evangelization in terms of the Holy Spirit. It is only through the power of the Holy Spirit that one becomes worthy of the charism of the evangelizer and that the evangelical mission is carried out. Pope Paul writes, "It is the Holy Spirit who, today just as at the beginning of the church, acts in every evangelizer who allows himself to be possessed and led by him. The Holy Spirit places on his lips the words which he could not find by himself, and at the same time, the Holy Spirit predisposes the soul of the hearer to be open and receptive to the good news and to the kingdom being proclaimed" (75). Just as the work of evangelization was begun by the Holy Spirit at Pentecost, it is the same Spirit that continues the work today.

IN CONCLUSION

On Evangelization in the Modern World was written reflectively to give encouragement and confidence to all with regard to the church's central task of evangelization. In a pastoral and meditative way, Pope Paul highlights the hopes and addresses the fears regarding evangelization raised by the 1974 Synod of Bishops. The hope of Pope Paul both before and following the publication of this exhortation was to reawaken interest in and enthusiasm for the work of evangelization, so that

> the world of our time, which is searching, sometimes with anguish, sometimes with hope, be enabled to receive the good news not from evangelizers who are dejected, discouraged, impatient or anxious but from ministers of the gospel whose lives glow with fervor, who have first received the joy of

Christ and who are willing to risk their lives so that the kingdom may be proclaimed and the church established in the midst of the world (80).

On Evangelization in the Modern World stands as a present-day challenge to all Catholics to develop an evangelizing attitude that moves them beyond what has become an all too comfortable "personal salvation mindset" to one of being willing witnesses of the risen Lord—Catholics with a renewed sense of their mission to share the gospel of Jesus Christ.

OUTLINE

ON EVANGELIZATION IN THE MODERN WORLD

SPECIAL COMMITMENT TO EVANGELIZATION

1.   There is no doubt that the effort to proclaim the Gospel to the people of today, who are buoyed up by hope but at the same time often oppressed by fear and distress, is a service rendered to the Christian community and also to the whole of humanity.

For this reason the duty of confirming the brethren—a duty which with the office of being the Successor of Peter[1] we have received from the Lord, and which is for us a "daily preoccupation,"[2] a program of life and action, and a fundamental commitment of our Pontificate—seems to us all the more noble and necessary when it is a matter of encouraging our brethren in their mission as evangelizers, in order that, in this time of uncertainty and confusion, they may accomplish this task with ever increasing love, zeal and joy.

ON THE OCCASION OF THREE EVENTS

2.   This is precisely what we wish to do here, at the end of this Holy Year during which the Church, "striving to proclaim the Gospel to all people,"[3] has had the single aim of fulfilling her duty of being the messenger of the Good News of Jesus Christ—the Good News proclaimed through two fundamental commands: "Put on the new self"[4] and "Be reconciled to God."[5]

We wish to do so on this tenth anniversary of the closing of the Second Vatican Council, the objectives of which are definitively summed up in this single one: to make the Church of the twentieth century ever better fitted for proclaiming the Gospel to the people of the twentieth century.

We wish to do so one year after the Third General Assembly of the Synod of Bishops, which, as is well known, was devoted to evangelization; and we do so all the more willingly because it has been asked of us by the Synod Fathers themselves. In fact, at the end of that memorable Assembly, the Fathers decided to remit to the Pastor of the universal Church, with great trust and simplicity, the fruits of all their labors, stating that they awaited from him a fresh forward impulse, capable of creating within a Church still more firmly rooted in the undying power and strength of Pentecost a new period of evangelization.[6]

THEME FREQUENTLY EMPHASIZED IN THE COURSE OF OUR PONTIFICATE

3.   We have stressed the importance of this theme of evangelization on many occasions, well before the Synod took place. On 22 June 1973, we said to the Sacred College of Cardinals: "The conditions of the society in which we live

oblige all of us therefore to revise methods, to seek by every means to study how we can bring the Christian message to modern man. For it is only in the Christian message that modern man can find the answer to his questions and the energy for his commitment of human solidarity."[7] And we added that in order to give a valid answer to the demands of the Council which call for our attention, it is absolutely necessary for us to take into account a heritage of faith that the Church has the duty of preserving in its untouchable purity, and of presenting it to the people of our time, in a way that is as understandable and persuasive as possible.

4.   This fidelity both to a message whose servants we are and to the people to whom we must transmit it living and intact is the central axis of evangelization. It poses three burning questions, which the 1974 Synod kept constantly in mind:

—In our day, what has happened to that hidden energy of the Good News, which is able to have a powerful effect on man's conscience?

—To what extent and in what way is that evangelical force capable of really transforming the people of this century?

—What methods should be followed in order that the power of the Gospel may have its effect?

Basically, these inquiries make explicit the fundamental question that the Church is asking herself today and which may be expressed in the following terms: after the Council and thanks to the Council, which was a time given her by God, at this turning-point of history, does the Church or does she not find herself better equipped to proclaim the Gospel and to put it into people's hearts with conviction, freedom of spirit and effectiveness?

5.   We can all see the urgency of giving a loyal, humble and courageous answer to this question, and of acting accordingly.

In our "anxiety for all the Churches,"[8] we would like to help our Brethren and sons and daughters to reply to these inquiries. Our words come from the wealth of the Synod and are meant to be a meditation on evangelization. May they succeed in inviting the whole People of God assembled in the Church to make the same meditation; and may they give a fresh impulse to everyone, especially those "who are assiduous in preaching and teaching,"[9] so that each one of them may follow "a straight course in the message of the truth,"[10] and may work as a preacher of the Gospel and acquit himself perfectly of his ministry.

Such an exhortation seems to us to be of capital importance, for the presentation of the Gospel message is not an optional contribution for the Church. It is the duty incumbent on her by the command of the Lord Jesus, so that people can believe and be saved. This message is indeed necessary. It is unique. It cannot be replaced. It does not permit either indifference, syncretism or accommodation. It is a question of people's salvation. It is the beauty of the Revelation that it represents. It brings with it a wisdom that is not of this world. It is able to stir up by itself faith — faith that rests on the power of God.[11] It is truth. It merits having the apostle consecrate to it all his time and all his energies, and to sacrifice for it, if necessary, his own life.

I
FROM CHRIST THE EVANGELIZER
TO THE EVANGELIZING CHURCH

WITNESS AND MISSION OF JESUS

6.   The witness that the Lord gives of himself and that Saint Luke gathered together in his Gospel — "I must proclaim the Good News of the kingdom of God"[12] — without doubt has enormous consequences, for it sums up the whole mission of Jesus: "That is what I was sent to do."[13] These words take on their full significance if one links them with the previous verses, in which Christ has just applied to himself the words of the Prophet Isaiah: "The Spirit of the Lord has been given to me, for he has anointed me. He has sent me to bring the good news to the poor."[14]

Going from town to town, preaching to the poorest — and frequently the most receptive — the joyful news of the fulfillment of the promises and of the Covenant offered by God is the mission for which Jesus declares that he is sent by the Father. And all the aspects of his mystery — the Incarnation itself, his miracles, his teaching, the gathering together of the disciples, the sending out of the Twelve, the Cross and the Resurrection, the permanence of his presence in the midst of his own — were components of his evangelizing activity.

JESUS, THE FIRST EVANGELIZER

7.   During the Synod, the Bishops very frequently referred to this truth: Jesus himself, the Good News of God,[15] was the very first and the greatest evangelizer; he was so through and through: to perfection and to the point of the sacrifice of his early life.

To evangelize: what meaning did this imperative have for Christ? It is certainly not easy to express in a complete synthesis the meaning, the content and the modes of evangelization as Jesus conceived it and put it into practice. In any case the attempt to make such a synthesis will never end. Let it suffice for us to recall a few essential aspects.

PROCLAMATION OF THE KINGDOM OF GOD

8.   As an evangelizer, Christ first of all proclaims a kingdom, the Kingdom of God; and this is so important that, by comparison, everything else becomes "the rest," which is "given in addition."[16] Only the Kingdom therefore is absolute, and it makes everything else relative. The Lord will delight in describing in many

ways the happiness of belonging to this Kingdom (a paradoxical happiness which is made up of things that the world rejects),[17] the demands of the Kingdom and its Magna Charta,[18] the heralds of the Kingdom,[19] its mysteries,[20] its children,[21] the vigilance and fidelity demanded of whoever awaits its definitive coming.[22]

PROCLAMATION OF LIBERATING SALVATION

9. As the kernel and center of his Good News, Christ proclaims salvation, this great gift of God which is liberation from everything that oppresses man but which is above all liberation from sin and the Evil One, in the joy of knowing God and being known by him, of seeing him, and of being given over to him. All of this is begun during the life of Christ and definitively accomplished by his death and Resurrection. But it must be patiently carried on during the course of history, in order to be realized fully on the day of the final coming of Christ, whose date is known to no one except the Father.[23]

AT THE PRICE OF CRUCIFYING EFFORT

10. This Kingdom and this salvation, which are the key words of Jesus Christ's evangelization, are available to every human being as grace and mercy, and yet at the same time each individual must gain them by force — they belong to the violent, says the Lord,[24] through toil and suffering, through a life lived according to the Gospel, through abnegation and the Cross, through the spirit of the beatitudes. But above all each individual gains them through a total interior renewal which the Gospel calls *metanoia;* it is a radical conversion, a profound change of mind and heart.[25]

TIRELESS PREACHING

11. Christ accomplished this proclamation of the Kingdom of God through the untiring preaching of a word which, it will be said, has no equal elsewhere: "Here is a teaching that is new, and with authority behind it."[26] "And he won the approval of all, and they were astonished by the gracious words that came from his lips."[27] "There has never been anybody who has spoken like him."[28] His words reveal the secret of God, his plan and his promise, and thereby change the heart of man and his destiny.

WITH EVANGELICAL SIGNS

12. But Christ also carries out this proclamation by innumerable signs, which amaze the crowds and at the same time draw them to him in order to see him, listen to him and allow themselves to be transformed by him: the sick are cured, water is changed into wine, bread is multiplied, the dead come back to life. And among all these signs there is the one to which he attaches great importance: the humble and the poor are evangelized, become his disciples and gather together "in his name" in the great community of those who believe in him. For this Jesus who declared, "I must preach the Good News of the Kingdom of God,"[29] is the same Jesus of whom John the Evangelist said that he had come and was to die "to gather together in unity the scattered children of God."[30] Thus he accomplishes his revelation, completing it and confirming it by the

entire revelation that he makes of himself, by words and deeds, by signs and miracles, and more especially by his death, by his Resurrection and by the sending of the Spirit of Truth.[31]

FOR AN EVANGELIZED AND EVANGELIZING COMMUNITY

13.   Those who sincerely accept the Good News, through the power of this acceptance and of shared faith, therefore gather together in Jesus' name in order to seek together the Kingdom, build it up and live it. They make up a community which is in its turn evangelizing. The command to the Twelve to go out and proclaim the Good News is also valid for all Christians, though in a different way. It is precisely for this reason that Peter calls Christians "a people set apart to sing the praises of God,"[32] those marvelous things that each one was able to hear in his own language.[33] Moreover, the Good News of the Kingdom which is coming and which has begun is meant for all people of all times. Those who have received the Good News and who have been gathered by it into the community of salvation can and must communicate and spread it.

EVANGELIZATION: VOCATION PROPER TO THE CHURCH

14.   The Church knows this. She has a vivid awareness of the fact that the Savior's words, "I must proclaim the Good News of the kingdom of God,"[34] apply in all truth to herself. She willingly adds with Saint Paul: "Not that I boast of preaching the gospel, since it is a duty that has been laid on me; I should be punished if I did not preach it!"[35] It is with joy and consolation that at the end of the great Assembly of 1974 we heard these illuminating words: "We wish to confirm once more that the task of evangelizing all people constitutes the essential mission of the Church."[36] It is a task and mission which the vast and profound changes of present-day society make all the more urgent. Evangelizing is in fact the grace and vocation proper to the Church, her deepest identity. She exists in order to evangelize, that is to say in order to preach and teach, to be the channel of the gift of grace, to reconcile sinners with God, and to perpetuate Christ's sacrifice in the Mass, which is the memorial of his death and glorious Resurrection.

RECIPROCAL LINKS BETWEEN THE CHURCH AND EVANGELIZATION

15.   Anyone who re-reads in the New Testament the origins of the Church, follows her history step by step and watches her live and act, sees that she is linked to evangelization in her most intimate being:

— The Church is born of the evangelizing activity of Jesus and the Twelve. She is the normal, desired, most immediate and most visible fruit of this activity: "Go, therefore, make disciples of all the nations."[37] Now, "they accepted what he said and were baptized. That very day about three thousand were added to their number. . . . Day by day the Lord added to their community those destined to be saved."[38]

—Having been born consequently out of being sent, the Church in her turn is sent by Jesus. The Church remains in the world when the Lord of glory returns to the Father. She remains as a sign — simultaneously obscure and luminous — of a new presence of Jesus, of his departure and of his permanent presence. She prolongs and continues him. And it is above all his mission and his condition of being an evangelizer that she is called upon to continue.[39] For the Christian community is never closed in upon itself. The intimate life of this community — the life of listening to the Word and the Apostles' teaching, charity lived in a fraternal way, the sharing of bread[40] — this intimate life only acquires its full meaning when it becomes a witness, when it evokes admiration and conversion, and when it becomes the preaching and proclamation of the Good News. Thus it is the whole Church that receives the mission to evangelize, and the work of each individual member is important for the whole.

—The Church is an evangelizer, but she begins by being evangelized herself. She is the community of believers, the community of hope lived and communicated, the community of brotherly love; and she needs to listen unceasingly to what she must believe, to her reasons for hoping, to the new commandment of love. She is the People of God immersed in the world, and often tempted by idols, and she always needs to hear the proclamation of the "mighty works of God"[41] which converted her to the Lord; she always needs to be called together afresh by him and reunited. In brief, this means that she has a constant need of being evangelized, if she wishes to retain freshness, vigor and strength in order to proclaim the Gospel. The Second Vatican Council recalled[42] and the 1974 Synod vigorously took up again this theme of the Church which is evangelized by constant conversion and renewal, in order to evangelize the world with credibility.

—The Church is the depositary of the Good News to be proclaimed. The promises of the New Alliance in Jesus Christ, the teaching of the Lord and the Apostles, the Word of life, the sources of grace and of God's loving kindness, the path of salvation — all these things have been entrusted to her. It is the content of the gospel, and therefore of evangelization, that she preserves as a precious living heritage, not in order to keep it hidden but to communicate it.

—Having been sent and evangelized, the Church herself sends out evangelizers. She puts on their lips the saving Word, she explains to them the message of which she herself is the depositary, she gives them the mandate which she herself has received and she sends them out to preach. To preach not their own selves or their personal ideas,[43] but a Gospel of which neither she nor they are the absolute masters and owners, to dispose of it as they wish, but a Gospel of which they are the ministers, in order to pass it on with complete fidelity.

THE CHURCH, INSEPARABLE FROM CHRIST

16. There is thus a profound link between Christ, the Church and evangelization. During the period of the Church that we are living in, it is she who has the task of evangelizing. This mandate is not accomplished without her, and still less against her.

It is certainly fitting to recall this fact at a moment like the present one when it happens that not without sorrow we can hear people—whom we wish to believe are well-intentioned but who are certainly misguided in their attitude—continually claiming to love Christ but without the Church, to listen to Christ but not the Church, to belong to Christ but outside the Church. The absurdity of this dichotomy is clearly evident in this phrase of the Gospel: "Anyone who rejects you rejects me."[44] And how can one wish to love Christ without loving the Church, if the finest witness to Christ is that of Saint Paul: "Christ loved the Church and sacrificed himself for her"?[45]

II
WHAT IS EVANGELIZATION?

COMPLEXITY OF EVANGELIZING ACTION

17.   In the Church's evangelizing activity there are of course certain elements and aspects to be specially insisted on. Some of them are so important that there will be a tendency simply to identify them with evangelization. Thus it has been possible to define evangelization in terms of proclaiming Christ to these who do not know him, of preaching, of catechesis, of conferring Baptism and the other Sacraments.

Any partial and fragmentary definition which attempts to render the reality of evangelization in all its richness, complexity and dynamism does so only at the risk of impoverishing it and even of distorting it. It is impossible to grasp the concept of evangelization unless one tries to keep in view all its essential elements.

These elements were strongly emphasized at the last Synod, and are still the subject of frequent study, as a result of the Synod's work. We rejoice in the fact that these elements basically follow the lines of those transmitted to us by the Second Vatican Council, especially in *Lumen Gentium, Gaudium et Spes* and *Ad Gentes.*

RENEWAL OF HUMANITY

18.   For the Church, evangelizing means bringing the Good News into all the strata of humanity, and through its influence transforming humanity from within and making it new: "Now I am making the whole of creation new."[46] But there is no new humanity if there are not first of all new persons renewed by Baptism[47] and by lives lived according to the Gospel.[48] The purpose of evangelization is therefore precisely this interior change, and if it had to be expressed in one sentence the best way of stating it would be to say that the Church evangelizes when she seeks to convert,[49] solely through the divine power of the Message she proclaims, both the personal and collective consciences of people, the activities in which they engage, and the lives and concrete milieus which are theirs.

19.   Strata of humanity which are transformed: for the Church it is a question not only of preaching the Gospel in ever wider geographic areas or to ever greater numbers of people, but also of affecting and as it were upsetting, through the power of the Gospel, mankind's criteria of judgment, determining values, points of interest, lines of thought, sources of inspiration and models of life, which are in contrast with the Word of God and the plan of salvation.

EVANGELIZATION OF CULTURES

20.   All this could be expressed in the following words: what matters is to evangelize man's culture and cultures (not in a purely decorative way as it were by applying a thin veneer, but in a vital way, in depth and right to their very roots), in the wide and rich sense which these terms have in *Gaudium et Spes*,[50] always taking the person as one's starting-point and always coming back to the relationships of people among themselves and with God.

The Gospel, and therefore evangelization, are certainly not identical with culture, and they are independent in regard to all cultures. Nevertheless, the Kingdom which the Gospel proclaims is lived by men who are profoundly linked to a culture, and the building up of the Kingdom cannot avoid borrowing the elements of human culture or cultures. Though independent of cultures, the Gospel and evangelization are not necessarily incompatible with them; rather they are capable of permeating them all without becoming subject to any one of them.

The split between the Gospel and culture is without a doubt the drama of our time, just as it was of other times. Therefore every effort must be made to ensure a full evangelization of culture, or more correctly of cultures. They have to be regenerated by an encounter with the Gospel. But this encounter will not take place if the Gospel is not proclaimed.

PRIMARY IMPORTANCE OF WITNESS OF LIFE

21.   Above all the Gospel must be proclaimed by witness. Take a Christian or a handful of Christians who, in the midst of their own community, show their capacity for understanding and acceptance, their sharing of life and destiny with other people, their solidarity with the efforts of all for whatever is noble and good. Let us suppose that, in addition, they radiate in an altogether simple and unaffected way their faith in values that go beyond current values, and their hope in something that is not seen and that one would not dare to imagine. Through this wordless witness these Christians stir up irresistible questions in the hearts of those who see how they live: Why are they like this? Why do they live in this way? What or who is it that inspires them? Why are they in our midst? Such a witness is already a silent proclamation of the Good News and a very powerful and effective one. Here we have an initial act of evangelization. The above questions will perhaps be the first that many non-Christians will ask, whether they are people to whom Christ has never been proclaimed, or baptized

people who do not practice, or people who live as nominal Christians but according to principles that are in no way Christian, or people who are seeking, and not without suffering, something or someone whom they sense but cannot name. Other questions will arise, deeper and more demanding ones, questions evoked by this witness which involves presence, sharing, solidarity, and which is an essential element, and generally the first one, in evangelization.[51]

All Christians are called to this witness, and in this way they can be real evangelizers. We are thinking especially of the responsibility incumbent on immigrants in the country that receives them.

NEED OF EXPLICIT PROCLAMATION

22.   Nevertheless this always remains insufficient, because even the finest witness will prove ineffective in the long run if it is not explained, justified—what Peter called always having "your answer ready for people who ask you the reason for the hope that you all have"[52]—and made explicit by a clear and unequivocal proclamation of the Lord Jesus. The Good News proclaimed by the witness of life sooner or later has to be proclaimed by the word of life. There is no true evangelization if the name, the teaching, the life, the promises, the Kingdom and the mystery of Jesus of Nazareth, the Son of God are not proclaimed. The history of the Church, from the discourse of Peter on the morning of Pentecost onwards, has been intermingled and identified with the history of this proclamation. At every new phase of human history, the Church, constantly gripped by the desire to evangelize, has but one preoccupation: whom to send to proclaim the mystery of Jesus? In what way is this mystery to be proclaimed? How can one ensure that it will resound and reach all those who should hear it? This proclamation—*kerygma*, preaching or catechesis—occupies such an important place in evangelization that it has often become synonymous with it; and yet it is only one aspect of evangelization.

FOR A VITAL AND COMMUNITY ACCEPTANCE

23.   In fact the proclamation only reaches full development when it is listened to, accepted and assimilated, and when it arouses a genuine adherence in the one who has thus received it. An adherence to the truths which the Lord in his mercy has revealed; still more, an adherence to a program of life—a life henceforth transformed—which he proposes. In a word, adherence to the Kingdom, that is to say the "new world," to the new state of things, to the new manner of being, of living, of living in community, which the Gospel inaugurates. Such an adherence, which cannot remain abstract and unincarnated, reveals itself concretely by a visible entry into a community of believers. Thus those whose life has been transformed enter a community which is itself a sign of transformation, a sign of newness of life: it is the Church, the visible sacrament of salvation.[53] But entry into the ecclesial community will in its turn be expressed through many other signs which prolong and unfold the sign of the Church. In the dynamism of evangelization, a person who accepts the Church as the Word

which saves[54] normally translates it into the following sacramental acts: adherence to the Church, and acceptance of the Sacraments, which manifest and support this adherence through the grace which they confer.

24.   Finally: the person who has been evangelized goes on to evangelize others. Here lies the test of truth, the touchstone of evangelization: it is unthinkable that a person should accept the Word and give himself to the Kingdom without becoming a person who bears witness to it and proclaims it in his turn.

To complete these considerations on the meaning of evangelization, a final observation must be made, one which we consider will help to clarify the reflections that follow.

Evangelization, as we have said, is a complex process made up of varied elements: the renewal of humanity, witness, explicit proclamation, inner adherence, entry into the community, acceptance of signs, apostolic initiative. These elements may appear to be contradictory, indeed mutually exclusive. In fact they are complementary and mutually enriching. Each one must always be seen in relationship with the others. The value of the last Synod was to have constantly invited us to relate these elements rather than to place them in opposition one to the other, in order to reach a full understanding of the Church's evangelizing activity.

It is this global vision which we now wish to outline, by examining the content of evangelization and the methods of evangelizing and by clarifying to whom the Gospel message is addressed and who today is responsible for it.

III
THE CONTENT OF EVANGELIZATION

ESSENTIAL CONTENT AND SECONDARY ELEMENTS

25.   In the message which the Church proclaims there are certainly many secondary elements. Their presentation depends greatly on changing circumstances. They themselves also change. But there is the essential content, the living substance, which cannot be modified or ignored without seriously diluting the nature of evangelization itself.

WITNESS GIVEN TO THE FATHER'S LOVE

26.   It is not superfluous to recall the following points: to evangelize is first of all to bear witness, in a simple and direct way, to God revealed by Jesus Christ, in the Holy Spirit; to bear witness that in his Son God has loved the world— that in his Incarnate Word he has given being to all things and has called men to eternal life. Perhaps this attestation of God will be for many people the unknown God[55] whom they adore without giving him a name, or whom they

seek by a secret call of the heart when they experience the emptiness of all idols. But it is fully evangelizing in manifesting the fact that for man the Creator is not an anonymous and remote power; he is the Father: " . . . that we should be called children of God; and so we are."[56] And thus we are one another's brothers and sisters in God.

AT THE CENTER OF THE MESSAGE: SALVATION IN JESUS CHRIST

27.   Evangelization will also always contain — as the foundation, center and at the same time summit of its dynamism — a clear proclamation that, in Jesus Christ, the Son of God made man, who died and rose from the dead, salvation is offered to all men, as a gift of God's grace and mercy.[57] And not an immanent salvation, meeting material or even spiritual needs, restricted to the framework of temporal existence and completely identified with temporal desires, hopes, affairs and struggles, but a salvation which exceeds all these limits in order to reach fulfillment in a communion with the one and only divine Absolute: a transcendent and eschatological salvation, which indeed has its beginning in this life but which is fulfilled in eternity.

UNDER THE SIGN OF HOPE

28.   Consequently evangelization cannot but include the prophetic proclamation of a hereafter, man's profound and definitive calling, in both continuity and discontinuity with the present situation: beyond time and history, beyond the transient reality of this world, and beyond the things of this world, of which a hidden dimension will one day be revealed — beyond man himself, whose true destiny is not restricted to his temporal aspect but will be revealed in the future life.[58] Evangelization therefore also includes the preaching of hope in the promises made by God in the new Covenant in Jesus Christ, the preaching of God's love for us and of our love for God; the preaching of brotherly love for all men — the capacity of giving and forgiving, of self-denial, of helping one's brother and sister — which, springing from the love of God, is the kernel of the Gospel; the preaching of the mystery of evil and of the active search for good. The preaching likewise — and this is always urgent — of the search for God himself through prayer which is principally that of adoration and thanksgiving, but also through communion with the visible sign of the encounter with God which is the Church of Jesus Christ; and this communion in its turn is expressed by the application of those other signs of Christ living and acting in the Church which are the Sacraments. To live the Sacraments in this way, bringing their celebration to a true fullness, is not, as some would claim, to impede or to accept a distortion of evangelization: it is rather to complete it. For in its totality, evangelization — over and above the preaching of a message — consists in the implantation of the Church, which does not exist without the driving force which is the sacramental life culminating in the Eucharist.[59]

MESSAGE TOUCHING LIFE AS A WHOLE

29.   But evangelization would not be complete if it did not take account of the unceasing interplay of the Gospel and of man's concrete life, both personal and

social. This is why evangelization evolves an explicit message adapted to the different situations constantly being realized, about the rights and duties of every human being, about family life without which personal growth and development is hardly possible,[60] about life in society, about international life, peace, justice and development—a message especially energetic today about liberation.

A MESSAGE OF LIBERATION

30.   It is well known in what terms numerous Bishops from all the continents spoke of this at the last Synod, especially the Bishops from the Third World, with a pastoral accent resonant with the voice of the millions of sons and daughters of the Church who make up these peoples. Peoples, as we know, engaged with all their energy in the effort and struggle to overcome everything which condemns them to remain on the margin of life: famine, chronic disease, illiteracy, poverty, injustices in international relations and especially in commercial exchanges, situations of economic and cultural neo-colonialism sometimes as cruel as the old political colonialism. The Church, as the Bishops repeated, has the duty to proclaim the liberation of millions of human beings, many of whom are her own children—the duty of assisting the birth of this liberation, of giving witness to it, of ensuring that it is complete. This is not foreign to evangelization.

NECESSARILY LINKED TO HUMAN ADVANCEMENT

31.   Between evangelization and human advancement—development and liberation—there are in fact profound links. These include links of an anthropological order, because the man who is to be evangelized is not an abstract being but is subject to social and economic questions. They also include links in the theological order, since one cannot dissociate the plan of creation from the plan of Redemption. The latter plan touches the very concrete situations of injustice to be combatted and of justice to be restored. They include links of the eminently evangelical order, which is that of charity: how in fact can one proclaim the new Commandment without promoting in justice and in peace the true, authentic advancement of man? We ourself have taken care to point this out, by recalling that it is impossible to accept "that in evangelization one could or should ignore the importance of the problems so much discussed today, concerning justice, liberation, development and peace in the world. This would be to forget the lesson which comes to us from the Gospel concerning love of our neighbor who is suffering and in need."[61]

The same voices which during the Synod touched on this burning theme with zeal, intelligence and courage have, to our great joy, furnished the enlightening principles for a proper understanding of the importance and profound meaning of liberation, such as it was proclaimed and achieved by Jesus of Nazareth and such as it is preached by the Church.

WITHOUT REDUCTION OR AMBIGUITY

32.   We must not ignore the fact that many, even generous Christians who are sensitive to the dramatic questions involved in the problem of liberation, in their wish to commit the Church to the liberation effort are frequently tempted to

reduce her mission to the dimensions of a simply temporal project. They would reduce her aims to a man-centered goal; the salvation of which she is the messenger would be reduced to material well-being. Her activity, forgetful of all spiritual and religious preoccupation, would become initiatives of the political or social order. But if this were so, the Church would lose her fundamental meaning. Her message of liberation would no longer have any originality and would easily be open to monopolization and manipulation by ideological systems and political parties. She would have no more authority to proclaim freedom as in the name of God. This is why we have wished to emphasize, in the same address at the opening of the Synod, "the need to restate clearly the specifically religious finality of evangelization. This latter would lose its reason for existence if it were to diverge from the religious axis that guides it: the Kingdom of God, before anything else, in its fully theological meaning. . . ."[62]

EVANGELICAL LIBERATION

33.   With regard to the liberation which evangelization proclaims and strives to put into practice one should rather say this:

— it cannot be contained in the simple and restricted dimension of economics, politics, social or cultural life; it must envisage the whole man, in all his aspects, right up to and including his openness to the absolute, even the divine Absolute;

— it is therefore attached to a certain concept of man, to a view of man which it can never sacrifice to the needs of any strategy, practice or short term efficiency.

CENTERED ON THE KINGDOM OF GOD

34.   Hence, when preaching liberation and associating herself with those who are working and suffering for it, the Church is certainly not willing to restrict her mission only to the religious field and dissociate herself from man's temporal problems. Nevertheless she reaffirms the primacy of her spiritual vocation and refuses to replace the proclamation of the Kingdom by the proclamation of forms of human liberation; she even states that her contribution to liberation is incomplete if she neglects to proclaim salvation in Jesus Christ.

ON AN EVANGELICAL CONCEPT OF MAN

35.   The Church links human liberation and salvation in Jesus Christ, but she never identifies them, because she knows through revelation, historical experience and the reflection of faith that not every notion of liberation is necessarily consistent and compatible with an evangelical vision of man, of things and of events; she knows too that in order that God's Kingdom should come it is not enough to establish liberation and to create well-being and development.

And what is more, the Church has the firm conviction that all temporal liberation, all political liberation — even if it endeavors to find its justification in such or such a page of the Old or New Testament, even if it claims for its ideological postulates and its norms of action theological data and conclusions, even if it pretends to be today's theology—carries within itself the germ of its own negation and fails to reach the ideal that it proposes for itself, whenever its profound motives are not those of justice in charity, whenever its zeal lacks a truly spiritual dimension and whenever its final goal is not salvation and happiness in God.

INVOLVING A NECESSARY CONVERSION

36.   The Church considers it to be undoubtedly important to build up structures which are more human, more just, more respectful of the rights of the person and less oppressive and less enslaving, but she is conscious that the best structures and the most idealized systems soon become inhuman if the inhuman inclinations of the human heart are not made wholesome, if those who live in these structures or who rule them do not undergo a conversion of heart and of outlook.

EXCLUDING VIOLENCE

37.   The Church cannot accept violence, especially the force of arms—which is uncontrollable once it is let loose—and indiscriminate death as the path to liberation, because she knows that violence always provokes violence and irresistibly engenders new forms of oppression and enslavement which are often harder to bear than those from which they claimed to bring freedom. We said this clearly during our journey in Colombia: "We exhort you not to place your trust in violence and revolution: that is contrary to the Christian spirit, and it can also delay instead of advancing that social uplifting to which you lawfully aspire."[63] "We must say and reaffirm that violence is not in accord with the Gospel, that it is not Christian; and that sudden or violent changes of structures would be deceitful, ineffective of themselves, and certainly not in conformity with the dignity of the people."[64]

SPECIFIC CONTRIBUTION OF THE CHURCH

38.   Having said this, we rejoice that the Church is becoming ever more conscious of the proper manner and strictly evangelical means that she possesses in order to collaborate in the liberation of many. And what is she doing? She is trying more and more to encourage large numbers of Christians to devote themselves to the liberation of men. She is providing these Christian "liberators" with the inspiration of faith, the motivation of fraternal love, a social teaching which the true Christian cannot ignore and which he must make the foundation of his wisdom and of his experience in order to translate it concretely into forms of action, participation and commitment. All this must characterize the spirit of a committed Christian, without confusion with tactical attitudes or with the service of a political system. The Church strives always to insert the Christian struggle for liberation into the universal plan of salvation which she herself proclaims.

What we have just recalled comes out more than once in the Synod debates. In fact we devoted to this theme a few clarifying words in our address to the Fathers at the end of the Assembly.[65]

It is to be hoped that all these considerations will help to remove the ambiguity which the word "liberation" very often takes on in ideologies, political systems or groups. The liberation which evangelization proclaims and prepares is the one which Christ himself announced and gave to man by his sacrifice.

RELIGIOUS LIBERTY

39. The necessity of ensuring fundamental human rights cannot be separated from this just liberation which is bound up with evangelization and which endeavors to secure structures safeguarding human freedoms. Among these fundamental human rights, religious liberty occupies a place of primary importance. We recently spoke of the relevance of this matter, emphasizing "how many Christians still today, because they are Christians, because they are Catholics, live oppressed by systematic persecution! The drama of fidelity to Christ and of the freedom of religion continues, even if it is disguised by categorical declarations in favor of the rights of the person and of life in society!"[66]

IV
THE METHODS OF EVANGELIZATION

SEARCH FOR SUITABLE MEANS

40. The obvious importance of the content of evangelization must not overshadow the importance of the ways and means.

This question of "how to evangelize" is permanently relevant, because the methods of evangelizing vary according to the different circumstances of time, place and culture, and because they thereby present a certain challenge to our capacity for discovery and adaptation.

On us particularly, the pastors of the Church, rests the responsibility for reshaping with boldness and wisdom, but in complete fidelity to the content of evangelization, the means that are most suitable and effective for communicating the Gospel message to the men and women of our times.

Let it suffice, in this meditation, to mention a number of methods which, for one reason or another, have a fundamental importance.

THE WITNESS OF LIFE

41. Without repeating everything that we have already mentioned, it is appropriate first of all to emphasize the following point: for the Church, the first means of evangelization is the witness of an authentically Christian life, given over to God in a communion that nothing should destroy and at the same time given to one's neighbor with limitless zeal. As we said recently to a group of lay people, "Modern man listens more willingly to witnesses than to teachers, and if he does

listen to teachers, it is because they are witnesses."[67] Saint Peter expressed this well when he held up the example of a reverent and chaste life that wins over even without a word those who refuse to obey the word.[68] It is therefore primarily by her conduct and by her life that the Church will evangelize the world, in other words, by her living witness of fidelity to the Lord Jesus — the witness of poverty and detachment, of freedom in the face of the powers of this world, in short, the witness of sanctity.

A LIVING PREACHING

42.   Secondly, it is not superfluous to emphasize the importance and necessity of preaching. "And how are they to believe in him of whom they have never heard? And how are they to hear without a preacher? . . . So faith comes from what is heard and what is heard comes by the preaching of Christ."[69] This law once laid down by the Apostle Paul maintains its full force today.

Preaching, the verbal proclamation of a message, is indeed always indispensable. We are well aware that modern man is sated by talk; he is obviously often tired of listening and, what is worse, impervious to words. We are also aware that many psychologists and sociologists express the view that modern man has passed beyond the civilization of the word, which is now ineffective and useless, and that today he lives in the civilization of the image. These facts should certainly impel us to employ, for the purpose of transmitting the Gospel message, the modern means which this civilization has produced. Very positive efforts have in fact already been made in this sphere. We cannot but praise them and encourage their further development. The fatigue produced these days by so much empty talk and the relevance of many other forms of communication must not however diminish the permanent power of the word, or cause a loss of confidence in it. The word remains ever relevant, especially when it is the bearer of the power of God.[70] This is why Saint Paul's axiom, "Faith comes from what is heard,"[71] also retains its relevance: it is the Word that is heard which leads to belief.

LITURGY OF THE WORD

43.   This evangelizing preaching takes on many forms, and zeal will inspire the reshaping of them almost indefinitely. In fact there are innumerable events in life and human situations which offer the opportunity for a discreet but incisive statement of what the Lord has to say in this or that particular circumstance. It suffices to have true spiritual sensitivity for reading God's message in events. But at a time when the liturgy renewed by the Council has given greatly increased value to the Liturgy of the Word, it would be a mistake not to see in the homily an important and very adaptable instrument of evangelization. Of course it is necessary to know and put to good use the exigencies and the possibilities of the homily, so that it can acquire all its pastoral effectiveness. But above all it is necessary to be convinced of this and to devote oneself to it with love. This preaching, inserted in a unique way into the Eucharistic celebration, from which it receives special force and vigor, certainly has a particular role in evangelization, to the extent that it expresses the profound faith of the sacred

minister and is impregnated with love. The faithful assembled as a Paschal Church, celebrating the feast of the Lord present in their midst, expect much from this preaching, and will greatly benefit from it provided that it is simple, clear, direct, well-adapted, profoundly dependent on Gospel teaching and faithful to the Magisterium, animated by a balanced apostolic ardor coming from its own characteristic nature, full of hope, fostering belief, and productive of peace and unity. Many parochial or other communities live and are held together thanks to the Sunday homily, when it possesses these qualities.

Let us add that, thanks to the same liturgical renewal, the Eucharistic celebration is not the only appropriate moment for the homily. The homily has a place and must not be neglected in the celebration of all the Sacraments at paraliturgies, and in assemblies of the faithful. It will always be a privileged occasion for communicating the Word of the Lord.

CATECHETICS

44. A means of evangelization that must not be neglected is that of catechetical instruction. The intelligence, especially that of children and young people, needs to learn through systematic religious instruction the fundamental teachings, the living content of the truth which God has wished to convey to us and which the Church has sought to express in an ever richer fashion during the course of her long history. No one will deny that this instruction must be given to form patterns of Christian living and not to remain only notional. Truly the effort for evangelization will profit greatly — at the level of catechetical instruction given at church, in the schools, where this is possible, and in every case in Christian homes — if those giving catechetical instruction have suitable texts, updated with wisdom and competence, under the authority of the Bishops. The methods must be adapted to the age, culture and aptitude of the persons concerned; they must seek always to fix in the memory, intelligence and heart the essential truths that must impregnate all of life. It is necessary above all to prepare good instructors — parochial catechists, teachers, parents — who are desirous of perfecting themselves in this superior art, which is indispensable and requires religious instruction. Moreover, without neglecting in any way the training of children, one sees that present conditions render ever more urgent catechetical instruction, under the form of the catechumenate, for innumerable young people and adults who, touched by grace, discover little by little the face of Christ and feel the need of giving themselves to him.

UTILIZATION OF THE MASS MEDIA

45. Our century is characterized by the mass media or means of social communication, and the first proclamation, catechesis or the further deepening of faith cannot do without these means, as we have already emphasized.

When they are put at the service of the Gospel, they are capable of increasing almost indefinitely the area in which the Word of God is heard; they enable the Good News to reach millions of people. The Church would feel guilty before the Lord if she did not utilize these powerful means that human skill is daily rendering more perfect. It is through them that she proclaims "from the house-tops"[72] the message of which she is the depositary. In them she finds a modern and effective version of the pulpit. Thanks to them she succeeds in speaking to the multitudes.

Nevertheless the use of the means of social communication for evangelization presents a challenge: through them the evangelical message should reach vast numbers of people, but with the capacity of piercing the conscience of each individual, of implanting itself in his heart as though he were the only person being addressed, with all his most individual and personal qualities, and evoke an entirely personal adherence and commitment.

INDISPENSABLE PERSONAL CONTACT

46.   For this reason, side-by-side with the collective proclamation of the Gospel, the other form of transmission, the person-to-person one, remains valid and important. The Lord often used it (for example with Nicodemus, Zacchaeus, the Samaritan woman, Simon the Pharisee), and so did the Apostles. In the long run, is there any other way of handing on the Gospel than by transmitting to another person one's personal experience of faith? It must not happen that the pressing need to proclaim the Good News to the multitudes should cause us to forget this form of proclamation whereby an individual's personal conscience is reached and touched by an entirely unique word that he receives from someone else. We can never sufficiently praise those priests who through the Sacrament of Penance or through pastoral dialogue show their readiness to guide people in the ways of the Gospel, to support them in their efforts, to raise them up if they have fallen, and always to assist them with discernment and availability.

ROLE OF THE SACRAMENTS

47.   Yet, one can never sufficiently stress the fact that evangelization does not consist only of the preaching and teaching of a doctrine. For evangelization must touch life: the natural life to which it gives a new meaning, thanks to the evangelical perspectives that it reveals; and the supernatural life, which is not the negation but the purification and elevation of the natural life.

This supernatural life finds its living expression in the seven Sacraments and in the admirable radiation of grace and holiness which they possess.

Evangelization thus exercises its full capacity when it achieves the most intimate relationship, or better still a permanent and unbroken intercommunication, between the Word and the Sacraments. In a certain sense it is a mistake to make a contrast between evangelization and sacramentalization, as is sometimes done. It is indeed true that a certain way of administering the Sacraments, without the solid support of catechesis regarding these same Sacraments and a global catechesis, could end up by depriving them of their effectiveness to a great extent. The role of evangelization is precisely to educate people in the faith in such a way as to lead each individual Christian to live the Sacraments as true Sacraments of faith — and not to receive them passively or to undergo them.

48.   Here we touch upon an aspect of evangelization which cannot leave us insensitive. We wish to speak about what today is often called popular religiosity.

One finds among the people particular expressions of the search for God and for faith, both in the regions where the Church has been established for centuries and where she is in the course of becoming established. These expressions were for a long time regarded as less pure and were sometimes despised, but today they are almost everywhere being rediscovered. During the last Synod the Bishops studied their significance with remarkable pastoral realism and zeal.

Popular religiosity of course certainly has its limits. It is often subject to penetration by many distortions of religion and even superstitions. It frequently remains at the level of forms of worship not involving a true acceptance by faith. It can even lead to the creation of sects and endanger the true ecclesial community.

But if it is well oriented, above all by a pedagogy of evangelization, it is rich in values. It manifests a thirst for God which only the simple and poor can know. It makes people capable of generosity and sacrifice even to the point of heroism, when it is a question of manifesting belief. It involves an acute awareness of profound attributes of God: fatherhood, providence, loving and constant presence. It engenders interior attitudes rarely observed to the same degree elsewhere: patience, the sense of the Cross in daily life, detachment, openness to others, devotion. By reason of these aspects, we readily call it "popular piety," that is, religion of the people, rather than religiosity.

Pastoral charity must dictate to all those whom the Lord has placed as leaders of the ecclesial communities the proper attitude in regard to this reality, which is at the same time so rich and so vulnerable. Above all one must be sensitive to it, know how to perceive its interior dimensions and undeniable values, be ready to help it to overcome its risks of deviation. When it is well oriented, this popular religiosity can be more and more for multitudes of our people a true encounter with God in Jesus Christ.

V
THE BENEFICIARIES OF EVANGELIZATION

ADDRESSED TO EVERYONE

49.   Jesus' last words in Saint Mark's Gospel confer on the evangelization which the Lord entrusts to his Apostles a limitless universality: "Go out to the whole world; proclaim the Good News to all creation."[73]

The Twelve and the first generation of Christians understood well the lesson of this text and other similar ones; they made them into a program of action. Even persecution, by scattering the Apostles, helped to spread the Word and to establish the Church in ever more distant regions. The admission of Paul to the rank of the Apostles and his charism as the preacher to the pagans (the non-Jews) of Jesus' Coming underlined this universality still more.

50.   In the course of twenty centuries of history, the generations of Christians have periodically faced various obstacles to this universal mission. On the one hand, on the part of the evangelizers themselves, there has been the temptation for various reasons to narrow down the field of their missionary activity. On the other hand, there has been the often humanly insurmountable resistance of the people being addressed by the evangelizer. Furthermore, we must note with sadness that the evangelizing work of the Church is strongly opposed, if not prevented, by certain public powers. Even in our own day it happens that preachers of God's Word are deprived of their rights, persecuted, threatened or eliminated solely for preaching Jesus Christ and his Gospel. But we are confident that despite these painful trials the activity of these apostles will never meet final failure in any part of the world.

Despite such adversities the Church constantly renews her deepest inspiration, that which comes to her directly from the Lord: To the whole world! To all creation! Right to the ends of the earth! She did this once more at the last Synod, as an appeal not to imprison the proclamation of the Gospel by limiting it to one sector of mankind or to one class of people or to a single type of civilization. Some examples are revealing.

FIRST PROCLAMATION TO THOSE WHO ARE FAR OFF

51.   To reveal Jesus Christ and his Gospel to those who do not know them has been, ever since the morning of Pentecost, the fundamental program which the Church has taken on as received from her Founder. The whole of the New Testament, and in a special way the Acts of the Apostles, bears witness to a privileged and in a sense exemplary moment of this missionary effort which will subsequently leave its mark on the whole history of the Church.

She carries out this first proclamation of Jesus Christ by a complex and diversified activity which is sometimes termed "pre-evangelization" but which is already evangelization in a true sense, although at its initial and still incomplete stage. An almost indefinite range of means can be used for this purpose: explicit preaching, of course, but also art, the scientific approach, philosophical research and legitimate recourse to the sentiments of the human heart.

RENEWED PROCLAMATION TO A DECHRISTIANIZED WORLD

52.   This first proclamation is addressed especially to those who have never heard the Good News of Jesus, or to children. But, as a result of the frequent situations of dechristianization in our day, it also proves equally necessary for innumerable people who have been baptized but who live quite outside Christian life, for simple people who have a certain faith but an imperfect knowledge of the foundations of that faith, for intellectuals who feel the need to know Jesus Christ in a light different from the instruction they received as children, and for many others.

53.   This first proclamation is also addressed to the immense sections of mankind who practice non-Christian religions. The Church respects and esteems these non-Christian religions because they are the living expression of the soul of vast groups of people. They carry within them the echo of thousands of years of searching for God, a quest which is incomplete but often made with great sincerity and righteousness of heart. They possess an impressive patrimony of deeply religious texts. They have taught generations of people how to pray. They are all impregnated with innumerable "seeds of the Word"[74] and can constitute a true "preparation for the Gospel."[75] to quote a felicitous term used by the Second Vatican Council and borrowed from Eusebius of Caesarea.

Such a situation certainly raises complex and delicate questions that must be studied in the light of Christian Tradition and the Church's Magisterium, in order to offer to the missionaries of today and of tomorrow new horizons in their contacts with non-Christian religions. We wish to point out, above all today, that neither respect and esteem for these religions nor the complexity of the questions raised is an invitation to the Church to withhold from these non-Christians the proclamation of Jesus Christ. On the contrary the Church holds that these multitudes have the right to know the riches of the mystery of Christ[76] — riches in which we believe that the whole of humanity can find, in unsuspected fullness, everything that it is gropingly searching for concerning God, man and his destiny, life and death, and truth. Even in the face of natural religious expressions most worthy of esteem, the Church finds support in the fact that the religion of Jesus, which she proclaims through evangelization, objectively places man in relation with the plan of God, with his living presence and with his action; she thus causes an encounter with the mystery of divine paternity that bends over towards humanity. In other words, our religion effectively establishes with God an authentic and living relationship which the other religions do not succeed in doing, even though they have, as it were, their arms stretched out towards heaven.

This is why the Church keeps her missionary spirit alive, and even wishes to intensify it in the moment of history in which we are living. She feels responsible before entire peoples. She has no rest so long as she has not done her best to proclaim the Good News of Jesus the Savior. She is always preparing new generations of apostles. Let us state this fact with joy at a time when there are not lacking those who think and even say that ardor and the apostolic spirit are exhausted, and that the time of the missions is now past. The Synod has replied that the missionary proclamation never ceases and that the Church will always be striving for the fulfillment of this proclamation.

54.   Nevertheless the Church does not feel dispensed from paying unflagging attention also to those who have received the faith and who have been in contact with the Gospel often for generations. Thus she seeks to deepen, consolidate, nourish and make ever more mature the faith of those who are already called the faithful or believers, in order that they may be so still more.

This faith is nearly always today exposed to secularism, even to militant atheism. It is a faith exposed to trials and threats, and even more, a faith besieged and actively opposed. It runs the risk of perishing from suffocation or starvation if it is not fed and sustained each day. To evangelize must therefore very often be to give this necessary food and sustenance to the faith of believers, especially through a catechesis full of Gospel vitality and in a language suited to people and circumstances.

The Church also has a lively solicitude for the Christians who are not in full communion with her. While preparing with them the unity willed by Christ, and precisely in order to realize unity in truth, she has the consciousness that she would be gravely lacking in her duty if she did not give witness before them of the fullness of the revelation whose deposit she guards.

NON-BELIEVERS

55. Also significant is the preoccupation of the last Synod in regard to two spheres which are very different from one another but which at the same time are very close by reason of the challenge which they make to evangelization, each in its own way.

The first sphere is the one which can be called the increase of unbelief in the modern world. The Synod endeavored to describe this modern world: how many currents of thought, values and countervalues, latent aspirations or seeds of destruction, old convictions which disappear and new convictions which arise are covered by this generic name!

From the spiritual point of view, the modern world seems to be for ever immersed in what a modern author has termed "the drama of atheistic humanism."[77]

On the one hand one is forced to note in the very heart of this contemporary world the phenomenon which is becoming almost its most striking characteristic: secularism. We are not speaking of secularization, which is the effort, in itself just and legitimate and in no way incompatible with faith or religion, to discover in creation, in each thing or each happening in the universe, the laws which regulate them with a certain autonomy, but with the inner conviction that the Creator has placed these laws there. The last Council has in this sense affirmed the legitimate autonomy of culture and particularly of the sciences.[78] Here we are thinking of a true secularism: a concept of the world according to which the latter is self-explanatory, without any need for recourse to God, who thus becomes superfluous and an encumbrance. This sort of secularism, in order to recognize the power of man, therefore ends up by doing without God and even by denying him.

New forms of atheism seem to flow from it: a man-centered atheism, no longer abstract and metaphysical but pragmatic, systematic and militant. Hand in hand with this atheistic secularism, we are daily faced, under the most diverse forms, with a consumer society, the pursuit of pleasure set up as the supreme value, a desire for power and domination, and discrimination of every kind: the inhuman tendencies of this "humanism."

In this same modern world, on the other hand, and this is a paradox, one cannot deny the existence of real stepping-stones to Christianity, and of evangelical values at least in the form of a sense of emptiness or nostalgia. It would not be an exaggeration to say that there exists a powerful and tragic appeal to be evangelized.

56.   The second sphere is that of those who do not practice. Today there is a very large number of baptized people who for the most part have not formally renounced their Baptism but who are entirely indifferent to it and not living in accordance with it. The phenomenon of the non-practicing is a very ancient one in the history of Christianity; it is the result of a natural weakness, a profound inconsistency which we unfortunately bear deep within us. Today, however it shows certain new characteristics. It is often the result of the uprooting typical of our time. It also springs from the fact that Christians live in close proximity with non-believers and constantly experience the effects of unbelief. Furthermore, the non-practicing Christians of today, more so than those of previous periods, seek to explain and justify their position in the name of an interior region, of personal independence or authenticity.

Thus we have atheists and unbelievers on the one side and those who do not practice on the other, and both groups put up a considerable resistance to evangelization. The resistance of the former takes the form of a certain refusal and an inability to grasp the new order of things, the new meaning of the world, of life and of history; such is not possible if one does not start from a divine absolute. The resistance of the second group takes the form of inertia and the slightly hostile attitude of the person who feels that he is one of the family, who claims to know it all and to have tried it all and who no longer believes it.

Atheistic secularism and the absence of religious practice are found among adults and among the young, among the leaders of society and among the ordinary people, at all levels of education, and in both the old Churches and the young ones. The Church's evangelizing action cannot ignore these two worlds, nor must it come to a standstill when faced with them; it must constantly seek the proper means and language for presenting, or re-presenting, to them God's revelation and faith in Jesus Christ.

PROCLAMATION TO THE MULTITUDES

57.   Like Christ during the time of his preaching, like the Twelve on the morning of Pentecost, the Church too sees before her an immense multitude of people who need the Gospel and have a right to it, for God "wants everyone to be saved and reach full knowledge of the truth."[79]

The Church is deeply aware of her duty to preach salvation to all. Knowing that the Gospel message is not reserved to a small group of the initiated, the privileged or the elect but is destined for everyone, she shares Christ's anguish at the sight of the wandering and exhausted crowds "like sheep without a shepherd" and she often repeats his words: "I feel sorry for all these people."[80] But the Church is also conscious of the fact that, if the preaching of the Gospel is to be effective, she must address her message to the heart of the multitudes, to communities of the faithful whose action can and must reach others.

ECCLESIAL COMMUNAUTÉS DE BASE

58.   The last Synod devoted considerable attention to these "small communities," or *communautés de base*, because they are often talked about in the Church today. What are they, and why should they be the special beneficiaries of evangelization and at the same time evangelizers themselves?

According to the various statements heard in the Synod, such communities flourish more or less throughout the Church. They differ greatly among themselves, both within the same region and even more so from one region to another.

In some regions they appear and develop, almost without exception, within the Church, having solidarity with her life, being nourished by her teaching and united with her pastors. In these cases, they spring from the need to live the Church's life more intensely, or from the desire and quest for a more human dimension such as larger ecclesial communities can only offer with difficulty, especially in the big modern cities which lend themselves both to life in the mass and to anonymity. Such communities can quite simply be in their own way an extension on the spiritual and religious level — worship, deepening of faith, fraternal charity, prayer, contact with pastors — of the small sociological community such as the village, etc. Or again their aim may be to bring together, for the purpose of listening to and meditating on the Word, for the Sacraments and the bond of the agape, groups of people who are linked by age, culture, civil state or social situation: married couples, young people, professional people, etc., people who already happen to be united in the struggle for justice, brotherly aid to the poor, human advancement. In still other cases they bring Christians together in places where the shortage of priests does not favor the normal life of a parish community. This is all presupposed within communities constituted by the Church, especially individual Churches and parishes.

In other regions, on the other hand, *communautés de base* come together in a spirit of bitter criticism of the Church, which they are quick to stigmatize as "institutional" and to which they set themselves up in opposition as charismatic communities, free from structures and inspired only by the Gospel. Thus their obvious characteristic is an attitude of fault-finding and of rejection with regard to the Church's outward manifestations: her hierarchy, her signs. They are radically opposed to the Church. By following these lines their main inspiration very quickly becomes ideological, and it rarely happens that they do not quickly fall victim to some political option or current of thought, and then to a system, even a party, with all the attendant risks of becoming its instrument.

The difference is already notable: the communities which by their spirit of opposition cut themselves off from the Church, and whose unity they wound, can well be called *communautés de base*, but in this case it is a strictly sociological name. They could not, without a misuse of terms, be called ecclesial *communautés de base*, even if, while being hostile to the hierarchy, they claim to remain within the unity of the Church. This name belongs to the other groups, those which come together within the Church in order to unite themselves to the Church and to cause the Church to grow.

These latter communities will be a place of evangelization, for the benefit of the bigger communities, especially the individual Churches. And, as we said at the end of the last Synod, they will be a hope for the universal Church to the extent:

— that they seek their nourishment in the Word of God and do not allow themselves to be ensnared by political polarization or fashionable ideologies, which are ready to exploit their immense human potential;

— that they avoid the ever present temptation of systematic protest and a hypercritical attitude, under the pretext of authenticity and a spirit of collaboration;

— that they remain firmly attached to the local Church in which they are inserted, and to the universal Church, thus avoiding the very real danger of becoming isolated within themselves, then of believing themselves to be the only authentic Church of Christ, and hence of condemning the other ecclesial communities;

— that they maintain a sincere communion with the pastors whom the Lord gives to his Church and with the Magisterium which the spirit of Christ has entrusted to these pastors;

— that they never look on themselves as the sole beneficiaries or sole agents of evangelization — or even the only depositaries of the Gospel — but, being aware that the Church is much more vast and diversified, accept the fact that this Church becomes incarnate in other ways than through themselves;

— that they constantly grow in missionary consciousness, fervor, commitment and zeal;

— that they show themselves to be universal in all things and never sectarian.

On these conditions, which are certainly demanding but also uplifting, the ecclesial *communautés de base* will correspond to their most fundamental vocation: as hearers of the Gospel which is proclaimed to them and privileged beneficiaries of evangelization, they will soon become proclaimers of the Gospel themselves.

VI

THE WORKERS FOR EVANGELIZATION

THE CHURCH: MISSIONARY IN HER ENTIRETY

59.   If people proclaim in the world the Gospel of salvation, they do so by the command of, in the name of and with the grace of Christ the Savior. "They will

never have a preacher unless one is sent,"[81] wrote he who was without doubt one of the greatest evangelizers. No one can do it without having been sent.

But who then has the mission of evangelizing?

The Second Vatican Council gave a clear reply to this question: it is upon the Church that "there rests, by divine mandate, the duty of going out into the whole world and preaching the Gospel to every creature."[82] And in another text: " . . . the whole Church is missionary, and the work of evangelization is a basic duty of the People of God."[83]

We have already mentioned this intimate connection between the Church and evangelization. While the Church is proclaiming the Kingdom of God and building it up, she is establishing herself in the midst of the world as the sign and instrument of this Kingdom which is and which is to come. The Council repeats the following expression of Saint Augustine on the missionary activity of the Twelve: "They preached the word of truth and brought forth Churches."[84]

AN ECCLESIAL ACT

60.   The observation that the Church has been sent out and given a mandate to evangelize the world should awaken in us two convictions.

The first is this: evangelization is for no one an individual and isolated act; it is one that is deeply ecclesial. When the most obscure preacher, catechist or pastor in the most distant land preaches the Gospel, gathers his little community together or administers a Sacrament, even alone, he is carrying out an ecclesial act, and his action is certainly attached to the evangelizing activity of the whole Church by institutional relationships, but also by profound invisible links in the order of grace. This presupposes that he acts not in virtue of a mission which he attributes to himself or by a personal inspiration, but in union with the mission of the Church and in her name.

From this flows the second conviction: if each individual evangelizes in the name of the Church, who herself does so by virtue of a mandate from the Lord, no evangelizer is the absolute master of his evangelizing action, with a discretionary power to carry it out in accordance with individualistic criteria and perspectives; he acts in communion with the Church and her pastors.

We have remarked that the Church is entirely and completely evangelizing. This means that, in the whole world and in each part of the world where she is present, the Church feels responsible for the task of spreading the Gospel.

THE PERSPECTIVE OF THE UNIVERSAL CHURCH

61.   Brothers and sons and daughters, at this stage of our reflection, we wish to pause with you at a question which is particularly important at the present time. In the celebration of the liturgy, in their witness before judges and executioners and in their apologetical texts, the first Christians readily expressed their deep faith in the Church by describing her as being spread throughout the universe. They were fully conscious of belonging to a large community which neither

space nor time can limit: "From the just Abel right to the last of the elect,"[85] "indeed to the ends of the earth,"[86] "to the end of time."[87]

This is how the Lord wanted his Church to be: universal, a great tree whose branches shelter the birds of the air,[88] a net which catches fish of every kind[89] or which Peter drew in filled with one hundred and fifty-three big fish,[90] a flock which a single shepherd pastures.[91] A universal Church without boundaries or frontiers except, alas, those of the heart and mind of sinful man.

THE PERSPECTIVE OF THE INDIVIDUAL CHURCH

62. Nevertheless this universal Church is in practice incarnate in the individual Churches made up of such or such an actual part of mankind, speaking such and such a language, heirs of a cultural patrimony, of a vision of the world, of an historical past, of a particular human substratum. Receptivity to the wealth of the individual Church corresponds to a special sensitivity of modern man.

Let us be very careful not to conceive of the universal Church as the sum, or, if one can say so, the more or less anomalous federation of essentially different individual Churches. In the mind of the Lord the Church is universal by vocation and mission, but when she puts down her roots in a variety of cultural, social and human terrains, she takes on different external expressions and appearances in each part of the world.

Thus each individual Church that would voluntarily cut itself off from the universal Church would lose its relationship to God's plan and would be impoverished in its ecclesial dimension. But, at the same time, a Church *toto orbe diffusa* would become an abstraction if she did not take body and life precisely through the individual Churches. Only continual attention to these two poles of the Church will enable us to perceive the richness of this relationship between the universal Church and the individual Churches.

ADAPTATION AND FIDELITY IN EXPRESSION

63. The individual Churches, intimately built up not only of people but also of aspirations, of riches and limitations, of ways of praying, of loving, of looking at life and the world which distinguish this or that human gathering, have the task of assimilating the essence of the Gospel message and of transposing it, without the slightest betrayal of its essential truth, into the language that these particular people understand, then of proclaiming it in this language.

The transposition has to be done with the discernment, seriousness, respect and competence which the matter calls for in the field of liturgical expression,[92] and in the areas of catechesis, theological formulation, secondary ecclesial structures, and ministries. And the word "language" should be understood here less in the semantic or literary sense than in the sense which one may call anthropological and cultural.

The question is undoubtedly a delicate one. Evangelization loses much of its force and effectiveness if it does not take into consideration the actual people to whom it is addressed, if it does not use their language, their signs and symbols, if it does not answer the questions they ask, and if it does not have an impact on their concrete life. But on the other hand evangelization risks losing its power and disappearing altogether if one empties or adulterates its content under the pretext of translating it; if, in other words, one sacrifices this reality and destroys the unity without which there is no universality, out of a wish to adapt a universal reality to a local situation. Now, only a Church which preserves the awareness of her universality and shows that she is in fact universal is capable of having a message which can be heard by all, regardless of regional frontiers.

Legitimate attention to individual Churches cannot fail to enrich the Church. Such attention is indispensable and urgent. It responds to the very deep aspirations of peoples and human communities to find their own identity ever more clearly.

OPENNESS TO THE UNIVERSAL CHURCH

64.   But this enrichment requires that the individual Churches should keep their profound openness towards the universal Church. It is quite remarkable, moreover, that the most simple Christians, the ones who are most faithful to the Gospel and most open to the true meaning of the Church, have a completely spontaneous sensitivity to this universal dimension. They instinctively and very strongly feel the need for it, they easily recognize themselves in such a dimension. They feel with it and suffer very deeply within themselves when, in the name of theories which they do not understand, they are forced to accept a Church deprived of this universality, a regionalist Church, with no horizon.

As history in fact shows, whenever an individual Church has cut itself off from the universal Church and from its living and visible center—sometimes with the best of intentions, with theological, sociological, political or pastoral arguments, or even in the desire for a certain freedom of movement or action—it has escaped only with great difficulty (if indeed it has escaped) from two equally serious dangers. The first danger is that of a withering isolationism, and then, before long, of a crumbling away, with each of its cells breaking away from it just as it itself has broken away from the central nucleus. The second danger is that of losing its freedom when, being cut off from the center and from the other Churches which gave it strength and energy, it finds itself all alone and a prey to the most varied forces of enslavery and exploitation.

The more an individual Church is attached to the universal Church by solid bonds of communion, in charity and loyalty, in receptiveness to the Magisterium of Peter, in the unity of the *lex orandi* which is also the *lex credendi*, in the desire for unity with all the other Churches which make up the whole—the more such a Church will be capable of translating the treasure of faith into the legitimate variety of expressions of the profession of faith, of prayer and worship, of Christian life and conduct and of the spiritual influence on the people among which it dwells. The more will it also be truly evangelizing, that is to say capable of drawing upon the universal patrimony in order to enable its own people to profit from it, and capable too of communicating to the universal Church the experience and the life of this people, for the benefit of all.

65.   It was precisely in this sense that at the end of the last Synod we spoke clear words full of paternal affection, insisting on the role of Peter's Successor as a visible, living and dynamic principle of the unity between the Churches and thus of the universality of the one Church.[93] We also insisted on the grave responsibility incumbent upon us, but which we share with our Brothers in the Episcopate, of preserving unaltered the content of the Catholic faith which the Lord entrusted to the Apostles. While being translated into all expressions, this content must be neither impaired nor mutilated. While being clothed with the outward forms proper to each people, and made explicit by theological expression which takes account of differing cultural, social and even racial milieux, it must remain the content of the Catholic faith just exactly as the ecclesial Magisterium has received it and transmits it.

DIFFERING TASKS

66.   The whole Church therefore is called upon to evangelize, and yet within her we have different evangelizing tasks to accomplish. This diversity of services in the unity of the same mission makes up the richness and beauty of evangelization. We shall briefly recall these tasks.

First, we would point out in the pages of the Gospel the insistence with which the Lord entrusts to the Apostles the task of proclaiming the Word. He chose them,[94] trained them during several years of intimate company,[95] constituted[96] and sent them out[97] as authorized witnesses and teachers of the message of salvation. And the Twelve in their turn sent out their successors who, in the apostolic line, continue to preach the Good News.

THE SUCCESSOR OF PETER

67.   The Successor of Peter is thus, by the will of Christ, entrusted with the preeminent ministry of teaching the revealed truth. The New Testament often shows Peter "filled with the Holy Spirit" speaking in the name of all.[98] It is precisely for this reason that Saint Leo the Great describes him as he who has merited the primacy of the apostolate.[99] This is also why the voice of the Church shows the Pope "at the highest point — *in apice, in specula* — of the apostolate."[100] The Second Vatican Council wished to reaffirm this when it declared that "Christ's mandate to preach the Gospel to every creature (cf. Mark 16:15) primarily and immediately concerns the Bishops with Peter and under Peter."[101]

The full, supreme and universal power[102] which Christ gives to his Vicar for the pastoral government of his Church is thus specially exercised by the Pope in the activity of preaching and causing to be preached the Good News of salvation.

68.   In union with the Successor of Peter, the Bishops, who are successors of the Apostles, receive through the power of their episcopal ordination the authority to teach the revealed truth in the Church. They are teachers of the faith.

Associated with the Bishops in the ministry of evangelization and responsible by a special title are those who through priestly ordination "act in the person of Christ."[103] They are educators of the People of God in the faith and preachers, while at the same time being ministers of the Eucharist and of the other Sacraments.

We pastors are therefore invited to take note of this duty, more than any other members of the Church. What identifies our priestly service, gives a profound unity to the thousand and one tasks which claim our attention day by day and throughout our lives, and confers a distinct character on our activities, is this aim, ever present in all our action: to proclaim the Gospel of God.[104]

A mark of our identity which no doubts ought to encroach upon and no objection eclipse is this: as pastors, we have been chosen by the mercy of the Supreme Pastor,[105] in spite of our inadequacy, to proclaim with authority the Word of God, to assemble the scattered People of God, to feed this People with the signs of the action of Christ which are the Sacraments, to set this People on the road to salvation, to maintain it in that unity of which we are, at different levels, active and living instruments, and unceasingly to keep this community gathered around Christ faithful to its deepest vocation. And when we do all these things, within our human limits and by the grace of God, it is a work of evangelization that we are carrying out. This includes ourself as Pastor of the universal Church, our Brother Bishops at the head of the individual Churches, priests and deacons united with their Bishops and whose assistants they are, by a communion which has its source in the Sacrament of Orders and in the charity of the Church.

RELIGIOUS

69.   Religious, for their part, find in their consecrated life a privileged means of effective evangelization. At the deepest level of their being they are caught up in the dynamism of the Church's life, which is thirsty for the divine Absolute and called to holiness. It is to this holiness that they bear witness. They embody the Church in her desire to give herself completely to the radical demands of the beatitudes. By their lives they and a sign of total availability to God, the Church and the brethren.

As such they have a special importance in the context of the witness which, as we have said, is of prime importance in evangelization. At the same time as being a challenge to the world and to the Church herself, this silent witness of poverty and abnegation, of purity and sincerity, of self-sacrifice in obedience, can become an eloquent witness capable of touching also non-Christians who have good will and are sensitive to certain values.

In this perspective one perceives the role played in evangelization by religious men and women consecrated to prayer, silence, penance and sacrifice. Other religious, in great numbers, give themselves directly to the proclamation of Christ. Their missionary activity depends clearly on the hierarchy and must be coordinated with the pastoral plan which the latter adopts. But who does not see the immense contribution that these religious have brought and continue to bring to evangelization? Thanks to their consecration they are eminently willing and free to leave everything and to go and proclaim the Gospel even to the ends of the earth. They are enterprising and their apostolate is often marked by an originality, by a genius that demands admiration. They are generous: often they are found at the outposts of the mission, and they take the greatest of risks for their health and their very lives. Truly the Church owes them much.

THE LAITY

70. Lay people, whose particular vocation places them in the midst of the world and in charge of the most varied temporal tasks, must for this very reason exercise a very special form of evangelization.

Their primary and immediate task is not to establish and develop the ecclesial community—this is the specific role of the pastors—but to put to use every Christian and evangelical possibility latent but already present and active in the affairs of the world. Their own field of evangelizing activity is the vast and complicated world of politics, society and economics, but also the world of culture, of the sciences and the arts, of international life, of the mass media. It also includes other realities which are open to evangelization, such as human love, the family, the education of children and adolescents, professional work, suffering. The more Gospel-inspired lay people there are engaged in these realities, clearly involved in them, competent to promote them and conscious that they must exercise to the full their Christian powers which are often buried and suffocated, the more these realities will be at the service of the Kingdom of God and therefore of salvation in Jesus Christ, without in any way losing or sacrificing their human content but rather pointing to a transcendent dimension which is often disregarded.

THE FAMILY

71. One cannot fail to stress the evangelizing action of the family in the evangelizing apostolate of the laity.

At different moments in the Church's history and also in the Second Vatican Council, the family has well deserved the beautiful name of "domestic Church."[106] This means that there should be found in every Christian family the various aspects of the entire Church. Furthermore, the family, like the Church, ought to be a place where the Gospel is transmitted and from which the Gospel radiates.

In a family which is conscious of this mission, all the members evangelize and are evangelized. The parents not only communicate the Gospel to their children, but from their children they can themselves receive the same Gospel as deeply lived by them.

And such a family becomes the evangelizer of many other families, and of the neighborhood of which it forms part. Families resulting from a mixed marriage also have the duty of proclaiming Christ to the children in the fullness of the consequences of a common Baptism; they have moreover the difficult task of becoming builders of unity.

YOUNG PEOPLE

72. Circumstances invite us to make special mention of the young. Their increasing number and growing presence in society and likewise the problems assailing them should awaken in every one the desire to offer them with zeal and intelligence the Gospel ideal as something to be known and lived. And on the other hand, young people who are well trained in faith and prayer must become more and more the apostles of youth. The Church counts greatly on their contribution, and we ourself have often manifested our full confidence in them.

DIVERSIFIED MINISTRIES

73. Hence the active presence of the laity in the temporal realities takes on all its importance. One cannot, however, neglect or forget the other dimension: the laity can also feel themselves called, or be called, to work with their pastors in the service of the ecclesial community, for its growth and life, by exercising a great variety of ministries according to the grace and charisms which the Lord is pleased to give them.

We cannot but experience a great inner joy when we see so many pastors, religious and lay people, fired with their mission to evangelize, seeking ever more suitable ways of proclaiming the Gospel effectively. We encourage the openness which the Church is showing today in this direction and with this solicitude. It is an openness to meditation first of all, and then to ecclesial ministries capable of renewing and strengthening the evangelizing vigor of the Church.

It is certain that, side-by-side with the ordained ministries, whereby certain people are appointed pastors and consecrate themselves in a special way to the service of the community, the Church recognizes the place of non-ordained ministries which are able to offer a particular service to the Church.

A glance at the origins of the Church is very illuminating, and gives the benefit of an early experience in the matter of ministries. It was an experience which was all the more valuable in that it enabled the Church to consolidate herself and to grow and spread. Attention to the sources however has to be complemented by attention to the present needs of mankind and of the Church. To drink at these ever inspiring sources without sacrificing anything of their values, and at the same time to know how to adapt oneself to the demands and needs of today—these are the criteria which will make it possible to seek wisely and to discover the ministries which the Church needs and which many of her members will gladly embrace for the sake of ensuring greater vitality in the ecclesial community. These ministries will have a real pastoral value to the extent that they are established with absolute respect for unity and adhering to the directives of the pastors, who are the ones who are responsible for the Church's unity and the builders thereof.

These ministries, apparently new but closely tied up with the Church's living experience down the centuries — such as catechists, directors of prayer and chant, Christians devoted to the service of God's Word or to assisting their brethren in need, the heads of small communities, or other persons charged with the responsibility of apostolic movements — these ministries are valuable for the establishment, life, and growth of the Church, and for her capacity to influence her surroundings and to reach those who are remote from her. We owe also our special esteem to all the laypeople who accept to consecrate a part of their time, their energies, and sometimes their entire lives, to the service of the missions.

A serious preparation is needed for all workers for evangelization. Such preparation is all the more necessary for those who devote themselves to the ministry of the Word. Being animated by the conviction, ceaselessly deepened, of the greatness and riches of the Word of God, those who have the mission of transmitting it must give the maximum attention to the dignity, precision and adaptation of their language. Everyone knows that the art of speaking takes on today a very great importance. How would preachers and catechists be able to neglect this?

We earnestly desire that in each individual Church the Bishops should be vigilant concerning the adequate formation of all the ministers of the Word. This serious preparation will increase in them the indispensable assurance and also the enthusiasm to proclaim today Jesus Christ.

VII
THE SPIRIT OF EVANGELIZATION

PRESSING APPEAL

74. We would not wish to end this encounter with our beloved Brethren and sons and daughters without a pressing appeal concerning the interior attitudes which must animate those who work for evangelization.

In the name of the Lord Jesus Christ, and in the name of the Apostles Peter and Paul, we wish to exhort all those who, thanks to the charisms of the Holy Spirit and to the mandate of the Church, are true evangelizers, to be worthy of this vocation, to exercise it without the reticence of doubt or fear, and not to neglect the conditions that will make this evangelization not only possible but also active and fruitful. These, among many others, are the fundamental conditions which we consider it important to emphasize.

UNDER THE ACTION OF THE HOLY SPIRIT

75. Evangelization will never be possible without the action of the Holy Spirit. The Spirit descends on Jesus of Nazareth at the moment of his baptism when the

voice of the Father—"This is my beloved Son with whom I am well pleased"[107]—manifests in an external way the election of Jesus and his mission. Jesus is "led by the Spirit" to experience in the desert the decisive combat and the supreme test before beginning this mission.[108] It is "in the power of the Spirit"[109] that he returns to Galilee and begins his preaching at Nazareth, applying to himself the passage of Isaiah: "The Spirit of the Lord is upon me." And he proclaims: "Today this Scripture has been fulfilled."[110] To the disciples whom he was about to send forth he says, breathing on them: "Receive the Holy Spirit."[111]

In fact, it is only after the coming of the Holy Spirit on the day of Pentecost that the Apostles depart to all the ends of the earth in order to begin the great work of the Church's evangelization. Peter explains this event as the fulfillment of the prophecy of Joel: "I will pour out my Spirit."[112] Peter is filled with the Holy Spirit so that he can speak to the people about Jesus, the Son of God.[113] Paul too is filled with the Holy Spirit[114] before dedicating himself to his apostolic ministry, as is Stephen when he is chosen for the ministry of service and later on for the witness of blood.[115] The Spirit, who causes Peter, Paul and the Twelve to speak, and who inspires the words that they are to utter, also comes down "on those who heard the Word."[116]

It is in the "consolation of the Holy Spirit" that the Church increases.[117] The Holy Spirit is the soul of the Church. It is he who explains to the faithful the deep meaning of the teaching of Jesus and of his mystery. It is the Holy Spirit who, today just as at the beginning of the Church, acts in every evangelizer who allows himself to be possessed and led by him. The Holy Spirit places on his lips the words which he could not find by himself, and at the same time the Holy Spirit predisposes the soul of the hearer to be open and receptive to the Good News and to the Kingdom being proclaimed.

Techniques of evangelization are good, but even the most advanced ones could not replace the gentle action of the Spirit. The most perfect preparation of the evangelizer has no effect without the Holy Spirit. Without the Holy Spirit the most convincing dialectic has no power over the heart of man. Without him the most highly developed schemas resting on a sociological or psychological basis are quickly seen to be quite valueless.

We live in the Church at a privileged moment of the Spirit. Everywhere people are trying to know him better, as the Scripture reveals him. They are happy to place themselves under his inspiration. They are gathering about him; they want to let themselves be led by him. Now if the Spirit of God has a pre-eminent place in the whole life of the Church, it is in her evangelizing mission that he is most active. It is not by chance that the great inauguration of evangelization took place on the morning of Pentecost, under the inspiration of the Spirit.

It must be said that the Holy Spirit is the principal agent of evangelization: it is he who impels each individual to proclaim the Gospel, and it is he who in the depths of consciences causes the word of salvation to be accepted and understood.[118] But it can equally be said that he is the goal of evangelization: he alone stirs up the new creation, the new humanity of which evangelization is to be the result, with that unity in variety which evangelization wishes to achieve within the Christian community. Through the Holy Spirit the Gospel penetrates to the heart of the world, for it is he who causes people to discern the signs of the times — signs willed by God — which evangelization reveals and puts to use within history.

The Bishops' Synod of 1974, which insisted strongly on the place of the Holy Spirit in evangelization, also expressed the desire that pastors and theologians — and we would also say the faithful marked by the seal of the Spirit by Baptism — should study more thoroughly the nature and manner of the Holy Spirit's action in evangelization today. This is our desire too, and we exhort all evangelizers, whoever they may be, to pray without ceasing to the Holy Spirit with faith and fervor and to let themselves prudently be guided by him as the decisive inspirer of their plans, their initiatives and their evangelizing activity.

AUTHENTIC WITNESSES OF LIFE

76.   Let us now consider the very persons of the evangelizers.

It is often said nowadays that the present century thirsts for authenticity. Especially in regard to young people it is said that they have a horror of the artificial or false and that they are searching above all for truth and honesty.

These "signs of the times" should find us vigilant. Either tacitly or aloud — but always forcefully — we are being asked: Do you really believe what you are proclaiming? Do you live what you believe? Do you really preach what you live? The witness of life has become more than ever an essential condition for real effectiveness in preaching. Precisely because of this we are, to a certain extent, responsible for the progress of the Gospel that we proclaim.

"What is the state of the Church ten years after the Council?" we asked at the beginning of this meditation. Is she firmly established in the midst of the world and yet free and independent enough to call for the world's attention? Does she testify to solidarity with people and at the same time to the divine Absolute? Is she more ardent in contemplation and adoration and more zealous in missionary, charitable and liberating action? Is she ever more committed to the effort to search for the restoration of the complete unity of Christians, a unity that makes more effective the common witness, "so that the world may believe"?[119] We are all responsible for the answers that could be given to these questions.

We therefore address our exhortation to our brethren in the Episcopate, placed by the Holy Spirit to govern the Church.[120] We exhort the priests and deacons, the Bishops' collaborators in assembling the People of God and in animating spiritually the local communities. We exhort the religious, witnesses of a Church called to holiness and hence themselves invited to a life that bears testimony to the beatitudes of the Gospel. We exhort the laity: Christian families, youth, adults, all those who exercise a trade or profession, leaders, without forgetting the poor who are often rich in faith and hope — all lay people who are conscious of their evangelizing role in the service of their Church or in the midst of society and the world. We say to all of them: our evangelizing zeal must spring from true holiness of life, and, as the Second Vatican Council suggests, preaching must in its turn make the preacher grow in holiness, which is nourished by prayer and above all by love for the Eucharist.[121]

The world which, paradoxically, despite innumerable signs of the denial of God, is nevertheless searching for him in unexpected ways and painfully experiencing the need of him — the world is calling for evangelizers to speak to it of a God whom the evangelists themselves should know and be familiar with as if they could see the invisible.[122] The world calls for and expects from us simplicity of life, the spirit of prayer, charity towards all, especially towards the lowly and the poor, obedience and humility, detachment and self-sacrifice. Without this mark of holiness, our word will have difficulty in touching the heart of modern man. It risks being vain and sterile.

THE SEARCH FOR UNITY

77.   The power of evangelization will find itself considerably diminished if those who proclaim the Gospel are divided among themselves in all sorts of ways. Is this not perhaps one of the great sicknesses of evangelization today? Indeed, if the Gospel that we proclaim is seen to be rent by doctrinal disputes, ideological polarizations or mutual condemnations among Christians, at the mercy of the latters' differing views on Christ and the Church and even because of their different concepts of society and human institutions, how can those to whom we address our preaching fail to be disturbed, disoriented, even scandalized?

The Lord's spiritual testament tells us that unity among his followers is not only the proof that we are his but also the proof that he is sent by the Father. It is the test of the credibility of Christians and of Christ himself. As evangelizers, we must offer Christ's faithful not the image of people divided and separated by unedifying quarrels, but the image of people who are mature in faith and capable of finding a meeting-point beyond the real tensions, thanks to a shared, sincere and disinterested search for truth. Yes, the destiny of evangelization is certainly bound up with the witness of unity given by the Church. This is a source of responsibility and also of comfort.

At this point we wish to emphasize the sign of unity among all Christians as the way and instrument of evangelization. The division among Christians is a serious reality which impedes the very work of Christ. The Second Vatican Council states clearly and emphatically that this division "damages the most holy cause of preaching the Gospel to all men, and it impedes many from embracing the faith."[123] For this reason, in proclaiming the Holy Year we considered it necessary to recall to all the faithful of the Catholic world that "before all men can be brought together and restored to the grace of God our Father, communion must be re-established between those who by faith have acknowledged and accepted Jesus Christ as the Lord of mercy who sets men free and unites them in the Spirit of love and truth."[124]

And it is with a strong feeling of Christian hope that we look to the efforts being made in the Christian world for this restoration of the full unity willed by Christ. Saint Paul assures us that "hope does not disappoint us."[125] While we still work to obtain full unity from the Lord, we wish to see prayer intensified. Moreover we make our own the desire of the Fathers of the Third General Assembly of the Synod of Bishops, for a collaboration marked by greater commitment with the Christian brethren with whom we are not yet united in perfect unity, taking as a basis the foundation of Baptism and the patrimony of faith which is common to us. By doing this we can already give a greater common witness to Christ before the world in the very work of evangelization. Christ's command urges us to do this; the duty of preaching and of giving witness to the Gospel requires this.

SERVANTS OF THE TRUTH

78.   The Gospel entrusted to us is also the word of truth. A truth which liberates[126] and which alone gives peace of heart is what people are looking for when we proclaim the Good News to them. The truth about God, about man and his mysterious destiny, about the world; the difficult truth that we seek in the Word of God and of which, we repeat, we are neither the masters nor the owners, but the depositaries, the heralds and the servants.

Every evangelizer is expected to have a reverence for truth, especially since the truth that he studies and communicates is none other than revealed truth and hence, more than any other, a sharing in the first truth which is God himself. The preacher of the Gospel will therefore be a person who even at the price of personal renunciation and suffering always seeks the truth that he must transmit to others. He never betrays or hides truth out of a desire to please men, in order to astonish or to shock, nor for the sake of originality or a desire to make an impression. He does not refuse truth. He does not obscure revealed truth by being too idle to search for it, or for the sake of his own comfort, or out of fear. He does not neglect to study it. He serves it generously, without making it serve him.

We are the pastors of the faithful people, and our pastoral service impels us to preserve, defend, and to communicate the truth regardless of the sacrifices that this involves. So many eminent and holy pastors have left us the example of this love of truth. In many cases it was an heroic love. The God of truth expects us to be the vigilant defenders and devoted preachers of truth.

Men of learning—whether you be theologians, exegetes or historians— the work of evangelization needs your tireless work of research, and also care and tact in transmitting the truth to which your studies lead you but which is always greater than the heart of men, being the very truth of God.

Parents and teachers, your task—and the many conflicts of the present day do not make it an easy one—is to help your children and your students to discover truth, including religious and spiritual truth.

79. The work of evangelization presupposes in the evangelizer an ever increasing love for those whom he is evangelizing. That model evangelizer, the Apostle Paul, wrote these words to the Thessalonians, and they are a program for us all: "With such yearning love we chose to impart to you not only the gospel of God but our very selves, so dear had you become to us."[127] What is this love? It is much more than that of a teacher; it is the love of a father; and again, it is the love of mother.[128] It is this love that the Lord expects from every preacher of the Gospel, from every builder of the Church. A sign of love will be the concern to give the truth and to bring people into unity. Another sign of love will be a devotion to the proclamation of Jesus Christ, without reservation or turning back. Let us add some other signs of this love.

The first is respect for the religious and spiritual situation of those being evangelized. Respect for their tempo and pace; no one has the right to force them excessively. Respect for their conscience and convictions, which are not to be treated in a harsh manner.

Another sign of this love is concern not to wound the other person, especially if he or she is weak in faith,[129] with statements that may be clear for those who are already initiated but which for the faithful can be a source of bewilderment and scandal, like a wound in the soul.

Yet another sign of love will be the effort to transmit to Christians, not doubts and uncertainties born of an erudition poorly assimilated but certainties that are solid because they are anchored in the Word of God. The faithful need these certainties for their Christian life; they have a right to them, as children of God who abandon themselves entirely into his arms and to the exigencies of love.

WITH THE FERVOR OF THE SAINTS

80. Our appeal here is inspired by the fervor of the greatest preachers and evangelizers, whose lives were devoted to the apostolate. Among these we are glad to point out those whom we have proposed to the veneration of the faithful during the course of the Holy Year. They have known how to overcome many obstacles to evangelization.

Such obstacles are also present today, and we shall limit ourself to mentioning the lack of fervor. It is all the more serious because it comes from within. It is manifested in fatigue, disenchantment, compromise, lack of interest and above all lack of joy and hope. We exhort all those who have the task of evangelizing, by whatever title and at whatever level, always to nourish spiritual fervor.[130]

This fervor demands first of all that we should know how to put aside the excuses which would impede evangelization. The most insidious of these excuses are certainly the ones which people claim to find support for in such and such a teaching of the Council.

Thus one too frequently hears it said, in various terms, that to impose a truth, be it that of the Gospel, or to impose a way, be it that of salvation, cannot but be a violation of religious liberty. Besides, it is added, why proclaim the Gospel when the whole world is saved by uprightness of heart? We know likewise that the world and history are filled with "seeds of the Word"; is it not therefore an illusion to claim to bring the Gospel where it already exists in the seeds that the Lord himself has sown?

Anyone who takes the trouble to study in the Council's documents the questions upon which these excuses draw too superficially will find quite a different view.

It would certainly be an error to impose something on the consciences of our brethren. But to propose to their consciences the truth of the Gospel and salvation in Jesus Christ, with complete clarity and with a total respect for the free options which it presents — "without coercion, or dishonorable or unworthy pressure"[131] — far from being an attack on religious liberty is fully to respect that liberty, which is offered the choice of a way that even nonbelievers consider noble and uplifting. Is it then a crime against others' freedom to proclaim with joy a Good News which one has come to know through the Lord's mercy?[132] And why should only falsehood and error, debasement and pornography have the right to be put before people and often unfortunately imposed on them by the destructive propaganda of the mass media, by the tolerance of legislation, the timidity of the good and the impudence of the wicked? The respectful presentation of Christ and his Kingdom is more than the evangelizer's right; it is his duty. It is likewise the right of his fellowmen to receive from him the proclamation of the Good News of salvation. God can accomplish this salvation in whomsoever he wishes by ways which he alone knows.[133] And yet, if his Son came, it was precisely in order to reveal to us, by his word and by his life, the ordinary paths of salvation. And he has commanded us to transmit this revelation to others with his own authority. It would be useful if every Christian and every evangelizer were to pray about the following thought: men can gain salvation also in other ways, by God's mercy, even though we do not preach the Gospel to them; but as for us, can we gain salvation if through negligence or fear or shame — what Saint Paul called "blushing for the Gospel"[134] — or as a result of false ideas we fail to preach it? For that would be to betray the call of God, who wishes the seed to bear fruit through the voice of the ministers of the Gospel; and it will depend on us whether this grows into trees and produces its full fruit.

Let us therefore preserve our fervor of spirit. Let us preserve the delightful and comforting joy of evangelizing, even when it is in tears that we must sow. May it mean for us — as it did for John the Baptist, for Peter and Paul, for the other Apostles and for a multitude of splendid evangelizers all through the Church's history — an interior enthusiasm that nobody and nothing can quench. May it be the great joy of our consecrated lives. And may the world of our time, which is searching, sometimes with anguish, sometimes with hope, be enabled to receive the Good News not from evangelizers who are dejected, discouraged, impatient or anxious, but from ministers of the Gospel whose lives glow with fervor, who have first received the joy of Christ, and who are willing to risk their lives so that the Kingdom may be proclaimed and the Church established in the midst of the world.

CONCLUSION

HERITAGE OF THE HOLY YEAR

81.   This then, Brothers and sons and daughters, is our heartfelt plea. It echoes the voice of our Brethren assembled for the Third General Assembly of the Synod of Bishops. This is the task we have wished to give you at the close of a Holy Year which has enabled us to see better than ever the needs and the appeals of a multitude of brethren, both Christians and non-Christians, who await from the Church the Word of salvation.

May the light of the Holy Year, which has shone in the local Churches and in Rome for millions of consciences reconciled with God, continue to shine in the same way after the Jubilee through a program of pastoral action with evangelization as its basic feature, for these years which mark the eve of a new century, the eve also of the third millennium of Christianity.

MARY, STAR OF EVANGELIZATION

82.   This is the desire that we rejoice to entrust to the hands and the heart of the Immaculate Blessed Virgin Mary, on this day which is especially consecrated to her and which is also the tenth anniversary of the close of the Second Vatican Council. On the morning of Pentecost she watched over with her prayer the beginning of evangelization prompted by the Holy Spirit: may she be the Star of the evangelization ever renewed which the Church, docile to her Lord's command, must promote and accomplish, especially in these times which are difficult but full of hope!

In the name of Christ we bless you, your communities, your families, all those who are dear to you, in the words which Paul addressed to the Philippians: "I give thanks to my God every time I think of you—which is constantly, in every prayer I utter—rejoicing, as I plead on your behalf, at the way you have all continually helped to promote the gospel . . . I hold all of you dear—you who . . . are sharers of my gracious lot . . . to defend the solid grounds on which the gospel rests. God himself can testify how much I long for each of you with the affection of Christ Jesus!"[135]

Given in Rome, at Saint Peter's, on the Solemnity of the Immaculate Conception of the Blessed Virgin Mary, December 8, 1975, the thirteenth year of our Pontificate.

NOTES

1. Cf. Luke 22:32.

2. 2 Corinthians 11:28.

3. Cf. AG, 1.

4. Cf. Ephesians 4:24; 2:15; Colossians 3:10; Galatians 3:27; Romans 13:14; 2 Corinthians 5:17.

5. 2 Corinthians 5:20.

6. Cf. Paul VI, Address for the closing of the Third General Assembly of the Synod of Bishops (October 26, 1974): AAS 66 (1974): 634–635; 637.

7. Paul VI, Address to the College of Cardinals (June 22, 1973): AAS 65 (1973): 383.

8. 2 Corinthians 11:28.

9. 1 Timothy 5:17.

10. 2 Timothy 2:15.

11. Cf. 1 Corinthians 2:5.

12. Luke 4:43.

13. Luke 4:43.

14. Luke 4:18; cf. Isaiah 61:1.

15. Cf. Mark 1:1; Romans 1:1–3.

16. Cf. Matthew 6:33.

17. Cf. Matthew 5:3–12.

18. Cf. Matthew 5–7.

19. Cf. Matthew 10.

20. Cf. Matthew 13.

21. Cf. Matthew 18.

22. Cf. Matthew 24–25.

23. Cf. Matthew 24:36; Acts 1:7; 1 Thessalonians 5:1–2.

24. Cf. Matthew 11:12; Luke 16:16.

25. Cf. Matthew 4:17.

26. Mark 1:27.

27. Luke 4:22.

28. John 7:46.

29. Luke 4:43.

30. John 11:52.

31. Cf. DV, 4.

32. 1 Peter 2:9.

33. Cf. Acts 2:11.

34. Luke 4:43.

35. 1 Corinthians 9:16.

36. "Declaration of the Synod Fathers," 4: L'Osservatore Romano (October 27, 1974): 6.

37. Matthew 28:19.

38. Acts 2:41, 47.

39. Cf. LG, 8; AG, 5.

40. Cf. Acts 2:42–46; 4:32–35; 5:12–16.

41. Cf. Acts 2:11; 1 Peter 2:9.

42. Cf. AG, 5, 11–12.

43. Cf. 2 Corinthians 4:5; Saint Augustine, Sermo XLVI, De Pastoribus: CCL 41: 529–530.

44. Luke 10:16; cf. Saint Cyprian, De Unitate Ecclesiae, 14: PL 4:527; Saint Augustine, Enarrat. 88, Sermo, 2, 14: PL 37:1140; Saint John Chrysostom, Hom. de capto Eutropio, 6: PG 52:402.

45. Ephesians 5:25.

46. Revelation 21:5, cf. 2 Corinthians 5:17; Galatians 6:16.

47. Cf. Romans 6:4.

48. Cf. Ephesians 4:23–24; Colossians 3:9–10.

49. Cf. Romans 1:16; 1 Corinthians 1:18, 2:4.

50. Cf. 53: AAS 58 (1966):1075.

51. Cf. Tertullian, Apologeticum, 39: CCL 1:150–153; Minucius Felix, Octavius 9 and 31: CSLP (Turin, 1962): 11–13, 47–48.

52. 1 Peter 3:15.

53. Cf. LG, 1, 9, 48; GS, 42, 45; AG, 1, 5.

54. Cf. Romans 1:16; 1 Corinthians 1:18.

55. Cf. Acts 17:22–23.

56. 1 John 3:1; cf. Romans 8:14–17.

57. Cf. Ephesians 2:8; Romans 1:16. Cf. Sacred Congregation for the Doctrine of the Faith, *Declaratio ad fidem tuendam in mysteria Incarnationis et SS. Trinitaties e quibusdam recentibus erroribus* (February 21, 1972): AAS 64 (1972): 237–241.

58. Cf. 1 John 3:2; Romans 8:29; Philippians 3:20–21; LG, 48–51.

59. Cf. Sacred Congregation for the Doctrine of the Faith, *Declaratio circa Catholicam Doctrinam de Ecclesia contra nonnullos errores hodiernos tuendam* (June 24, 1973): AAS 65 (1973): 396–408.

60. Cf. GS, 47–52; Paul VI, Encyclical Letter *Humanae Vitae:* AAS 60 (1968): 481–503.

61. Paul VI, Address for the opening of the Third General Assembly of the Synod of Bishops (September 27, 1974): AAS 66 (1974): 562.

62. AAS 66 (1974): 562.

63. Paul VI, Address to the *Campesinos* of Colombia (August 23, 1968): AAS 60 (1968): 623.

64. Paul VI, Address for the "Day of Development" at Bogotá (August 23, 1968): AAS 60 (1968): 627; cf. Saint Augustine, *Epistola* 229, 2: PL 33: 1020.

65. Paul VI, Address for the closing of the Third General Assembly of the Synod of Bishops (October 26, 1974): AAS 66 (1974): 637.

66. Address given on October 15, 1975: *L'Osservatore Romano* (October 17, 1975).

67. Pope Paul VI, Address to the Members of the *Concilium de Laicis* (October 2, 1974): AAS 66 (1974): 568.

68. Cf. 1 Peter 3:1.

69. Romans 10:14, 17.

70. Cf. 1 Corinthians 2:1–5.

71. Romans 10:17.

72. Cf. Matthew 10:27; Luke 12:3.

73. Mark 16:15.

74. Cf. Saint Justin, *I Apol.* 46, 1–4; II *Apol.* 7 (8) 1–4; 10, 1–3; 13, 3–4; Clement of Alexandria, *Stromata* I, 19, 91, 94; AG, 11; LG, 17.

75. Eusebius of Caesarea, *Praeparatio Evangelica* I, 1; cf. LG, 16.

76. Cf. Ephesians 3:8.

77. Cf. Henri de Lubac, *Le drame de l'humanisme athée*, Paris, 1945.

78. Cf. GS, 59.

79. 1 Timothy 2:4.

80. Matthew 9:36; 15:32.

81. Romans 10:15.

82. DH, 13; LG, 5; AG, 1.

83. AG, 35.

84. Saint Augustine, *Enarratio in Psalmis* 44: 23, CCL 38: 510; cf. AG, 1.

85. Saint Gregory the Great, *Homil. in Evangelia* 19, 1: PL 76: 1154.

86. Acts 1:8; cf. *Didache* 9, 1.

87. Matthew 28:20.

88. Cf. Matthew 13:32.

89. Cf. Matthew 13:47.

90. Cf. John 21:11.

91. Cf. John 10:1–16.

92. Cf. SC, 37–38; cf. also the liturgical books and other documents subsequently issued by the Holy See for the putting into practice of the liturgical reform desired by the same Council.

93. Paul VI, Address for the closing of the Third General Assembly of the Synod of Bishops (October 26, 1974): AAS 66 (1974): 636.

94. Cf. John 15:16; Mark 3:13–19; Luke 6:13–16.

95. Cf. Acts 1:21–22.

96. Cf. Mark 3:14.

97. Cf. Mark 3:14–15; Luke 9:2.

98. Acts 4:8; cf. 2:14; 3:12.

99. Cf. St. Leo the Great, *Sermo* 69, 3; *Sermo* 70, 1–3; *Sermo* 94, 3; *Sermo* 95, 2: SC 200: 50–52; 58–66; 258–260; 268.

100. Cf. First Ecumenical Council of Lyons, Constitution *Ad apostolicae dignitatis: Conciliorum Oecumenicorum Decreta;* Ecumenical Council of Vienne, Constitution *Ad providam Christi;* Fifth Lateran Ecumenical Council, Constitution *In apostolici culminis, ed cit.*, 608; Constitution *Postquam ad universalis;* Constitution *Supernae dispositionis;* Constitution *Divina disponente clementia.*

101. AG, 38.

102. LG, 22.

103. LG, 10, 37; AG, 39; PO, 2, 12, 13.

104. Cf. 1 Thessalonians 2:9.

105. Cf. 1 Peter 5:4.

106. LG, 11; AA, 11; Saint John Chrysostom,
     In Genesim Serm. vi, 2; vii, 1: PG 54:
     607–608.

107. Matthew 3:17.

108. Matthew 4:1.

109. Luke 4:14.

110. Luke 4:18, 21; cf. Isaiah 61:1.

111. John 20:22.

112. Acts 2:17.

113. Cf. Acts 4:8.

114. Cf. Acts 9:17.

115. Cf. Acts 6:5, 10; 7:55.

116. Acts 10:44.

117. Acts 9:31.

118. AG, 4.

119. John 17:21.

120. Cf. Acts 20:28.

121. PO, 13.

122. Cf. Hebrews 11:27.

123. AG, 6; UR, 1.

124. Bull *Apostolorum Limina*, vii: AAS 66
     (1974): 305.

125. Romans 5:5.

126. Cf. John 8:32.

127. 1 Thessalonians 2:8; cf. Philippians 1:8.

128. Cf. 1 Thessalonians 2:7–11; 1 Corinthians
     4:15; Galatians 4:19.

129. Cf. 1 Corinthians 8:9–13; Romans 14:15.

130. Cf. Romans 12:11.

131. DH, 4.

132. DH, 9–14.

133. AG, 7.

134. Cf. Romans 1:16.

135. Philippians 1:3–4, 7–8.

SHARING
THE
LIGHT OF FAITH

NATIONAL CATECHETICAL DIRECTORY
FOR
CATHOLICS OF THE UNITED STATES
1978

OVERVIEW OF *SHARING THE LIGHT OF FAITH: NATIONAL CATECHETICAL DIRECTORY FOR CATHOLICS OF THE UNITED STATES*

by John R. Zaums

Since the Second Vatican Council (1962–1965), the Catholic Church throughout the world has found itself immersed in a turmoil of rapid change. Certain modes of thinking and acting in many areas of church life have given way to, or have been tempered by, somewhat different patterns of thought and expression. Obviously such transitions, especially in the area of catechesis, have not occurred without a great deal of controversy, confusion and tension.

In 1971, the Catholic bishops of the United States undertook a major project with the hope of adding more clarity and direction for those who were confused or uncertain about answers to the questions of "what," "where," "when," and "how" related to catechesis. The project culminated in the 1979 publication of *Sharing the Light of Faith: National Catechetical Directory for Catholics of the United States* (NCD). This text, which was designed to speak to the pastoral, religious and sociocultural needs of Catholics today, is a pastoral and practical document containing norms and guidelines for teaching religion to U.S. Catholics of all ages and circumstances. It was prepared for a wide audience involved in catechesis, including parents and guardians, professional and paraprofessional catechists, religious, deacons and priests, diocesan and parish committees and boards, and writers and publishers of catechetical material.

HISTORICAL ROOTS

The NCD needs to be understood against the backdrop of discussions that took place during the Second Vatican Council regarding the publication of a *universal* catechism, something that both the Councils of Trent and Vatican I had mandated. Of all the bishops and others who sent proposals for the agenda of Vatican II, only one, Bishop Pierre Marie Locionte of France, argued against the production of one catechism and formally recommended the composition of a "directory," a text that would provide directives for the catechesis of persons of differing ages and circumstances. After much debate, the Council fathers adopted Locionte's vision of a general directory and approved article 44 of the *Decree on the Bishops' Pastoral Office*, which states that "another directory should be composed with respect to the catechetical instruction of the Christian people and should deal with the fundamental principles of such instruction, its arrangement and the composition of books on the subject." In opting for a directory instead of a single universal catechism, the fathers of Vatican II officially adopted a policy of catechetical pluralism. Because of differing conditions throughout the world, they were saying, catechesis, of necessity, needs to be approached differently from place to place.

Once Vatican II had concluded, it fell to the Sacred Congregation for the Clergy to implement the Council's directive to compose a directory. In 1971, five years from the time it began its task, the Congregation approved the final text of the *General Catechetical Directory* (GCD).

As stated in its foreword, "The immediate purpose of the Directory is to provide assistance in the production of catechetical directories and catechisms." The GCD, therefore, was to be an intermediate document, its purpose being to encourage conferences of bishops to produce national directories to reflect the pastoral needs and cultural concerns of their regions. The NCD is the response of the U.S. Catholic Church.

DEVELOPING THE NATIONAL CATECHETICAL DIRECTORY

In the same year during which the GCD was published, the American bishops began the process that would lead ultimately to the production of America's national directory. Responsibility for producing the document was given to two bodies: a seven-member Bishops' Committee of Policy and Review, whose function it was to set policy and to review the development of the document, and a twelve-member Directory Committee selected from 300 candidates. This committee was composed of four bishops, two priests, two religious, one brother, one layman and two laywomen—together representing major geographical areas of the United States and a wide spectrum of theological views and cultural groups. It was primarily a decision-making body in all aspects of the preparation of the NCD, under the policy and review authority of the Bishops' Committee. According to Wilfrid H. Paradis, NCD project director, this was the first time in the history of the U.S. Catholic Church that decision-making authority in matters of catechesis was shared by bishops with representatives of the laity, religious and clergy.

What also was unique about the NCD was that every American Catholic who so chose was free to participate in its preparation. The first of four drafts that appeared in 1974 was drawn up in light of over 17,400 recommendations made by thousands of individuals and groups from across the nation regarding what they felt were the major catechetical concerns of the day. This first draft, in turn, was submitted to American Catholics for criticism and, in light of 76,335 recommendations made by over 70,000 respondents, a second draft was drawn up and published in 1976. From the recommendations received, a third draft was prepared and submitted for criticism to the American bishops in the summer of 1977. From their recommendations a fourth draft was brought before the National Conference of Catholic Bishops during their November 1977 meeting held in Washington, D.C. After four days of discussion and the passage of approximately 75 amendments to the fourth draft, the American bishops accepted the amended fourth draft by a vote of 216 to 12. This draft was approved by Rome and finally published in 1979.

For a number of reasons, the entire process, which culminated in the publication of the NCD, is one of the most significant developments in the history of American Catholic catechesis. First, it provided the occasion for a vast nationwide program of education in the field of catechesis that extended through three consultations over a period of four years. Second, it represented, up to that time, the broadest and most successful in-depth consultation with the church at large ever attempted by the U.S. Catholic Church. Because it proved to be so effective, the consultation process employed in developing the NCD has provided the church with a viable model for conducting consultations on a range of other key issues. And third, the NCD has proven to be one of the most practical and pastoral catechetical resources ever produced by the Catholic Church in the United States, and, two decades later, it continues to exercise tremendous influence.

THE TEXT ITSELF

In 11 chapters, the NCD presents a comprehensive picture of the U.S. Catholic Church's understanding of catechetical theory and practice. Chapter I highlights major aspects of contemporary culture as they relate to catechesis, including issues of diversity, technology, communications and family. Chapter II looks at the catechetical ministry of the church that encompasses the ministries of word, worship and service—all of which are directed toward fostering mature faith. Also treated in this chapter are the biblical, liturgical, ecclesial and natural sources or "signs" of catechesis. Chapter III relates the concepts of faith and revelation to catechesis. Chapter IV discusses the meaning of church and the church's relationship to other Christian communities, other major religions and those who profess no religion. Chapter V presents, in summary form, the principal elements of the Christian message. Chapter VI looks at the close relationship between liturgy and catechesis and offers a catechetical perspective on sacraments, prayer and sacramentals. Chapter VII describes the basis of the church's social ministry and offers guidance for the development of catechesis on behalf of justice, mercy and peace. Chapter VIII considers the relationship between the life of faith and human development, and offers specific guidelines for catechesis for persons at different stages of development. Chapter IX considers the ideal qualities that catechists ought to possess, as well as various catechetical roles and the preparation needed for each role. Chapter X describes organizational structures such as the parish, diocese and national offices that, in their catechetical efforts, help to ensure opportunities for growth in faith. And, finally, chapter XI discusses a number of useful catechetical resources, including media, textbooks and audio-visual materials.

SPECIFIC STRENGTHS

Although the NCD embodies many strengths, only the eight most significant are highlighted here. First, the NCD is a readable and helpful resource that provides a clear vision of, and comprehensive approach to, catechesis for the U.S. Catholic Church. Second, by stressing the four major components of catechesis— namely, message, community, worship and service—the document argues throughout for an approach to catechesis that is holistic. Third, because of its many practical norms and guidelines, and also because of the solid overview of Catholic belief and practice that it provides, the NCD gives some much needed clarity and direction to catechetical practice, and, consequently, helped to address some of the painful polarization in the area of catechesis that occurred in the years since Vatican II. Fourth, the NCD approaches faith from a developmental and formative perspective, thus underscoring the importance of lifelong learning and growth in faith. Fifth, the document develops the many forms that catechesis takes at different stages of human development, and it repeatedly stresses the need to adapt the message to the specific ages, experiences, cultures, circumstances and needs of individuals and communities. Sixth, it provides an extensive treatment of Catholic social teaching and emphasizes the need to catechize intentionally for a more just and peaceful world. Seventh, priority is given to the catechesis of adults, including parents who are the primary educators of their children. And finally the NCD identifies those specific qualities that ought to characterize catechists and other catechetical personnel, and it argues strongly for the presence of trained catechetical personnel within parishes and dioceses and at the national level.

A NEEDED REVISION

Five years after its publication, as called for in paragraph 7, the document was evaluated and it was determined that it did not need to be revised. Five years later it was reviewed for a second time, and again it was decided that a revision was not warranted. In 1993, the question of revision was revisited, this time by the Subcommittee on Catechesis, a body of the United States Catholic Conference's Committee on Education. After studying the results of a field survey conducted by Eugene Hemrick, a survey that focused on whether or not the NCD should be revised, subcommittee members determined that a minor revision of the NCD was indeed called for. The process for doing so is being worked out as of this writing, but no revision is expected until 1996 or later because the GCD, the document on which national directories are based, is itself just now being revised—a task that will not be completed until 1996 at the earliest.

Much has happened within both the United States and the Catholic Church since the NCD was first published; this changing situation will have to be considered carefully in any revision, no matter how minor. For example, the social context, as described throughout the text, needs to be rewritten in a way that responds to contemporary issues concerning women, cultural diversity, sexuality, persons with disabilities, and families. Also, the many catechetical and related church documents that have appeared since 1979, especially the *Catechism of the Catholic Church*, will have to be taken into account. Very focused attention will need to be given to emerging areas of catechetical practice, including lectionary- and family-based catechesis, sacramental preparation and reception— particularly regarding confirmation and reconciliation, the order of Christian initiation of adults, multicultural catechesis, the use of media and new technologies, and the relationship of evangelization to catechesis. As to the text itself, issues concerning tone, style, format and the use of inclusive language also will have to be addressed.

Given the climate of our times, those who will be revising the NCD will have to struggle mightily to preserve some of its many strengths. Yes, the document needs to be revised in light of the *Catechism of the Catholic Church*. Content is of paramount importance but so also is process. The "what" of catechesis needs to be stressed but so also do the "why," "how," "when" and "where" questions affecting catechetical practice. The NCD is a landmark document that can benefit greatly from some revision. It is my hope that those charged with the task, while doing so, can own the same vision and spirit of Vatican II shared by those who originally developed *Sharing the Light of Faith*.

OUTLINE

PREFACE

PART A: BACKGROUND INFORMATION ON THIS DIRECTORY

PART B: OVERVIEW OF CATECHESIS

CHAPTER I: SOME CULTURAL AND RELIGIOUS CHARACTERISTICS AFFECTING CATECHESIS IN THE UNITED STATES
    Part A: Diversity
    Part B: Science and Technology
    Part C: Profile of United States Catholics
    Part D: Family and Home in the United States

CHAPTER II: THE CATECHETICAL MINISTRY OF THE CHURCH
    Part A: Catechesis — A Form of Ministry of the Word
    Part B: Forms of Catechesis
    Part C: Source and Signs of Catechesis
    Part D: Catechetical Criteria

CHAPTER III: REVELATION, FAITH AND CATECHESIS
    Part A: God's Self-revelation
    Part B: Revelation Calls for Response in Faith
    Part C: A Catechetical Approach to Revelation and Faith

CHAPTER IV: THE CHURCH AND CATECHESIS
    Part A: Meaning of Church
    Part B: The Church in Dialogue

CHAPTER V: PRINCIPAL ELEMENTS OF THE CHRISTIAN MESSAGE FOR CATECHESIS
    Part A: The Mystery of the One God
    Part B: Creation
    Part C: Jesus Christ
    Part D: The Holy Spirit
    Part E: The Church
    Part F: The Sacraments
    Part G: The Life of Grace
    Part H: The Moral Life
    Part I: Mary and the Saints
    Part J: Death, Judgment, Eternity

CHAPTER VI: CATECHESIS FOR A WORSHIPING COMMUNITY
    Part A: Liturgy and Catechesis

Part B: Sacraments/Mysteries
  Section I: Sacraments — Mysteries of Initiation
  Section II: Sacraments — Mysteries of Reconciliation and Healing
  Section III: Sacraments — Mysteries of Commitment
  Section IV: The Eucharistic Liturgy for Groups with Special Needs

Part C: Prayer

Part D: Sacred Art and Sacramentals

CHAPTER VII: CATECHESIS FOR SOCIAL MINISTRY

Part A: Foundations of Catholic Social Teaching
  Section I: The Biblical Base
  Section II: The Moral Basis
  Section III: Relationship of the Social Ministry to the Mission of the Church

Part B: A Brief Overview of the Development of Catholic Social Teaching

Part C: Facing Contemporary Social Issues
  Section I: Major Concepts
  Section II: Some Contemporary Problems

CHAPTER VIII: CATECHESIS TOWARD MATURITY IN FAITH

Part A: Faith and Human Development

Part B: Catechesis and Human Development
  Section I: The Stages of Human Development
  Section II: Conscience Formation
  Section III: Sexuality and Catechesis

Part C: Catechesis for Persons with Special Needs

Part D: Some Significant Factors Affecting Catechesis in the United States

CHAPTER IX: CATECHETICAL PERSONNEL

Part A: Ideal Qualities of Catechists

Part B: Catechetical Roles and Preparation

CHAPTER X: ORGANIZATION FOR CATECHESIS

Part A: General Organizational Guidelines

Part B: The Parish

Part C: The Diocese

Part D: Provinces, Regions, the National Office

Part E: Higher Education

Part F: Other Catechetical Settings

CHAPTER XI: CATECHETICAL RESOURCES

Part A: Resources in General

Part B: Radio and Television

Part C: The Press

Part D: Media Literacy

Part E: Other Catechetical Materials
  Section I: Textbooks
  Section II: Other Instructional Materials
  Section III: Preparation and Evaluation of Catechetical Materials

PREFACE

1. INTRODUCTION

Jesus Christ lives and, with His Father, unceasingly sends forth the Holy Spirit, who abides in believers' hearts as the source of light and love. No one walks in darkness who possesses the life-giving Spirit.

In the 1960s the Second Vatican Council gave testimony to the presence of Christ, the light of nations, within His Church. It reaffirmed the Church's mission to lead people to God, heal human anxieties, uphold human dignity, and bear witness as a community united through the bond of love. Recognizing that many people see Christ's light only in the lives of Christians, the Council called upon the members of the Church to make this light shine more brightly by their words and deeds and so lead others to Christ.

PART A: BACKGROUND INFORMATION ON THIS DIRECTORY

2. MANDATE

The Council called for the renewal of catechetics.[1] To assist this renewal, it prescribed that a directory be prepared dealing with fundamental principles of catechesis, organizations, and the composition of books on the subject.[2]

The *General Catechetical Directory*, prepared by the Sacred Congregation for the Clergy, after consultation with conferences of bishops around the world, was approved by Pope Paul VI on March 18, 1971. It draws together and organizes principles and guidelines for catechesis for the universal Church. It emphasizes the Church's concern that the faith of Catholics be informed and living. It urges bishops' conferences to prepare national directories applying its principles and guidelines. *Sharing the Light of Faith, National Catechetical Directory for Catholics of the United States* (NCD) has been prepared in response.

3. COLLABORATION OF THE EASTERN AND WESTERN CATHOLIC CHURCHES

This document has been developed jointly by members of Eastern and Western Churches of the Catholic Church with jurisdictions in the United States, and has been approved by the bishops of all these Churches. Though it is written largely from the perspective of the Western Church, special effort has been made to inform and interest all Catholics concerning the rich diversity found within Catholic unity. It is hoped that, while respecting the integrity and proper traditions of the Eastern and Western Churches, it will assist all Catholics in certain aspects of catechesis.

4. CONSULTATION PROCESS

The NCD has been prepared in dialogue with large numbers of Catholics and other interested persons in the United States. This was done in response to the bishops' desire for dialogue: within the Catholic community; between the Catholic Church and the other Christian churches, as well as with representatives of other religions; and between the Church and the human family.[3]

The process of dialogue included three extensive consultations with the Church at large and with scholars, involving hundreds of thousands of people and resulting in tens of thousands of recommendations. The NCD was the subject of regional meetings of the bishops in the spring of 1975, during which laity, religious, and clergy joined with them in discussing catechetical needs. The NCD also reflects the deliberations and conclusions of the Fourth General Assembly of the Synod of Bishops convened at the Vatican in 1977 to discuss "Catechesis in Our Time, With Special Reference to the Catechesis of Children and Young People."

5. SOURCES

It is appropriate at the outset to say something about the term "catechetical" in this document's title. It comes from the ancient word "catechesis," which appears often in the documents of the Church. Catechesis refers to efforts which help individuals and communities acquire and deepen Christian faith and identity through initiation rites, instruction, and formation of conscience. It includes both the message presented and the way in which it is presented. The NCD therefore draws upon the Church's biblical, patristic, historical, liturgical, theological, missiological, and catechetical heritages. It also makes use of sound contemporary developments in the sacred and human sciences, as well as the "signs of the times" — the contemporary cultural situation. Another source is the wisdom of God's people, united with their bishops under the guidance of the Holy Spirit.

6. AUDIENCE

This NCD has been prepared particularly for those responsible for catechesis in the United States. Among those who will benefit, directly or indirectly, are parents and guardians exercising their responsibilities as the primary educators of children; professional and paraprofessional catechists at all levels; men and women religious; deacons and priests involved in this ministry; and members of diocesan and parish council education committees or boards with catechetical duties. The NCD is also of basic importance to writers and publishers of catechetical texts and other materials for catechesis.

7. AUTHORITY

This NCD is an official statement of the National Conference of Catholic Bishops of the United States and has been reviewed and approved by the Sacred Congregation for the Clergy according to established norms.[4]

Not all parts of this document are of equal importance. The teaching of the Church in regard to revelation and the Christian message is to be held by all; the norms or criteria identified in article 47 pertaining to all catechesis must be observed.[5] The other portions of the NCD are also important, but the treatment of such matters as stages of human development, methodology, catechetical roles and training, organization and structures, resources, etc. is subject to change in light of new knowledge or different circumstances.

Because the methods and cultural context of catechesis are very likely to change and new Church documents on the subject will be published, this document will be reviewed periodically for updating and improvement. Approximately five years after its approval by the Holy See, it will be submitted to an extensive evaluation, in a manner to be determined by the National Conference of Catholic Bishops.

PART B: OVERVIEW OF CATECHESIS

8. A BRIEF BACKGROUND TO CONTEMPORARY CATECHESIS

The Church continues the mission of Jesus, whose teaching has come down to us through the apostles. The ministry of catechesis serves the Church in that mission. Great importance has always been attached to catechesis, but its methods and emphases have varied in different times and places, from apostolic times to the present, according to changing circumstances and needs. Such differences appear in the catechetical traditions and histories of the Eastern and Western Churches or, as they are also called, the Oriental and Occidental Churches.

Historical records indicate that catechesis was introduced into what is now the United States during the late 16th and early 17th centuries by Spanish and French missionaries in their ministry to the American Indians. Archbishop John Carroll of Baltimore, the first Catholic bishop in the United States (1789–1815), had a strong interest in religious instruction. Later generations of Catholics have consistently manifested the same concern.

In the United States during the 19th century many catechisms and other instructional materials for catechizing were published in English as well as virtually all the other languages spoken by the Catholic immigrants. The *Baltimore Catechism* (published 1885; revised 1941) became the dominant text in Catholic religious education in the United States until shortly before the Second Vatican Council (1962–1965). Also of critical importance was the decision of the Third Plenary Council of Baltimore that parish schools be built near all churches and that, except in unusual circumstances, parents be required to send their children to these schools. This policy gave great impetus to the growth of the parochial schools, in which millions of Catholic children and youth have received, and continue to receive, extensive religious education.

The 20th century has been especially eventful for catechesis in the United States. Some developments are mentioned in the next article. Many others are cited throughout this NCD as accepted elements of contemporary catechesis.

The Confraternity of Christian Doctrine (CCD) has played a major role in the development of catechetics in the United States during this century. First established here in 1902, the CCD developed especially under the leadership of Bishop Edwin V. O'Hara. In 1934 the bishops set up a national office of the confraternity, with Bishop O'Hara as first chairman. Within a few years the CCD spread into virtually every part of the country.

Extensive immigration of Eastern Rite Catholics occurred mainly from the end of the 19th century to the early 1920s. Most came from the Middle East or from Central and Eastern Europe. There are now more than one million in this country. During the 1940s and 1950s, many members of these Churches began to rediscover their religious and cultural traditions; they have developed instructional texts and materials to meet their unique needs.

9. HOPEFUL SIGNS IN CATECHETICS IN THE UNITED STATES

While catechetical ministry in the United States faces many problems, there are also many hopeful signs and trends. These will be discussed before some of the contemporary problems.

Increasingly, catechetics is taking into account significant contemporary developments in the sacred and human sciences. For some time it has also given particular attention to social justice, prompted by scripture and the papal social encyclicals, especially since Leo XIII.

Catechesis is recognizing the contemporary concern for education in morality and values, encouraging this within the framework of the teaching of Jesus and His Church, the influence of God's Spirit, and parental guidance.

In many places, lay people are assuming increasing responsibility and leadership in catechetical work. Women, especially women religious, have for a long time made impressive contributions to catechetics. Now the role of the laity, both men and women, is expanding further, as they assume new responsibilities involving greater leadership in the Church.

Lay involvement is receiving a significant impetus from representative and advisory bodies developed since the Second Vatican Council. Among the promising new instruments of shared responsibility are pastoral councils, boards of education committees responsible for comprehensive catechetical programs, councils of the laity, and boards of education at the diocesan, interparochial, and parochial levels. Such new structures have led to a marked increase in comprehensive catechetical planning and the skills related to it. Planning has fostered prudent use of time, resources, and personnel. It has also contributed to the understanding and observance of the principles of subsidiary and accountability.

Adult catechesis, including parent and family education and allied programs for the enrichment of married life, has become more prominent. The rite of the Christian initiation of adults is being introduced for both the catechumenate and adult catechesis. Of particular interest are small Christian communities which provide an atmosphere for more effective catechesis, including the *comunidad de base* found especially in the Hispanic community.[6]

Among other positive developments are the growing tendency in youth ministry to include catechesis within a total ministry to this age group; greater commitment to serving the needs of the mentally, emotionally, and physically handicapped; heightened awareness of the needs of racial, ethnic, and cultural groups, as well as their special contributions to the Church; and the expansion of programs for the continuing education of the clergy.

It is also widely recognized that Catholic schools are to be communities of faith in which the Christian message, the experience of community, worship, and social concern are integrated in the total experience of students, their parents, and members of the faculty.

Aided by the spread of graduate schools and programs of religious education, as well as summer schools, seminars, institutes, and a wide assortment of professional publications and texts, Catholic catechists and catechetical administrators now enjoy greater opportunities for professional growth than in the past. At the same time, attention is also given to the centrality for their ministry of their personal faith commitment in and to Christ.

Modern technology — records, audio cassettes, filmstrips, films, video cassettes, video discs, instructional, cable, public and commercial television, with satellite transmission — contributes much to catechetical efforts. It is important for communicating Christ's message to people for whom media other than the printed word are an increasingly significant part of learning and growth.

The most heartening development has been the renewed interest of many Catholics in the Bible, liturgy, and prayer. A new spiritual maturity exists in many sectors of the Catholic community in the United States today.

10. CONTEMPORARY PROBLEMS IN CATECHETICS IN THE UNITED STATES

Because catechesis is concerned with applying the certain, timeless teachings of faith to the uncertain, changing conditions of each generation, some errors of judgment, misplaced emphasis, and ill-timed innovations are likely. Recent difficulties and disagreements revolve largely around the orthodoxy and adequacy of doctrinal content in contemporary catechetical methodology. This NCD gives serious attention to these questions. No small part of the difficulty arises from the fact that today most children are catechized in a way which bears little resemblance to the ways in which their parents received religious instruction.

Contemporary catechesis also confronts a variety of problems arising from social conditions. Some of these are described in Chapter 1 and elsewhere in this document.

11. CONCLUSION

This NCD seeks to help the entire Catholic community grow in unity, love, and peace. Its purpose is correspondingly evangelical and missionary, looking toward an increase in the vitality and holiness of Christ's body which is the Church.

Though "the Church is more than ever alive," yet "it seems good to consider that everything still remains to be done; the work begins today and never comes to an end."[7] This document is presented to the Catholic community in the confidence that, as in the past, the Holy Spirit will guide the Church in our land in its catechetical ministry both now and in the future.

CHAPTER I
SOME CULTURAL AND RELIGIOUS CHARACTERISTICS AFFECTING CATECHESIS IN THE UNITED STATES

12. APPLYING GENERAL PRINCIPLES

It is a complex task to apply the principles and guidelines of the *General Catechetical Directory* to Catholic catechesis in the United States, a nation of well over 200 million people of many different racial, ethnic, and cultural backgrounds. The difficulty is increased by differences related to region, age, style of life, temperament, and other factors. While the NCD seeks to be responsive to all conditions and catechetical needs in this country, only some major aspects of contemporary culture, with special relevance to catechesis, will be noted here.

These phenomena are grouped under four headings: diversity, the influence of science and technology, a brief profile of United States Catholics, and the importance of family and home.

PART A: DIVERSITY

13. RACE, ETHNICITY, AND CULTURE

Nearly every race and ethnic group on earth is represented in the population of the United States. Relatively recent immigrations have greatly increased the Catholic population.[8] Here the oppressed and needy from many nations have sought a haven and a land of opportunity. The Church from the beginning sheltered and fostered these cultural, racial, and ethnic groups as they strove to find their way in a strange new country. Yet local churches did at times fail to appreciate, refuse to try to understand, and neglect to welcome the newcomers. Some, in fact, have left the Church and either joined other existing denominations, established their own, or joined the ranks of the unchurched.

Today, however, the United States appears to be growing in appreciation of cultural diversity, recognizing the splendid beauty of all races, cultures, and ethnic groups. At the same time, peoples throughout the world look to this country for support in their struggle for human rights.

14. THE MANY RELIGIONS

The United States has from the beginning been a refuge for those fleeing religious persecution. Many new religions have also been founded here. Yet at present nearly 40 percent of the people are not formally affiliated with any religion. The unchurched in the United States now are estimated to number 81 million.[9]

The great religious diversity of the United States and the very large number of unchurched persons, including lapsed Catholics, together point to the need both for ecumenical activities and for continuing efforts directed to the evangelization of all.

The number and percentage of Catholics in a given area also have an obvious practical bearing on catechesis. The figures vary greatly: for example, from a high of nearly two-thirds in Rhode Island to below 2 percent in North and South Carolina. In the nation as a whole, roughly one person in every four has been baptized as a Catholic.

15. CHURCH AND CHURCHES

The Catholic Church in the United States is quite diverse. It includes the Catholic Church of the West and the Catholic Churches of the East. The former is sometimes called the Latin Church. The latter have their origins in the Apostolic Churches of the East — Constantinople, Alexandria, Antioch, and Jerusalem — and are usually organized according to the major traditions: Byzantine, Antiochene, Chaldean, Armenian, and Alexandrian. Those with established hierarchies in the United States are the Ukrainians, Ruthenians, and Melkites, all of the Byzantine tradition, and the Maronites of the Antiochene tradition. Those without their own hierarchies here include the Romanians, Russians, Byelorussians, Italo-Albanians, and Italo-Greeks of the Byzantine tradition, and the Armenians, Syrians, Chaldeans, and Malankarese.

Over the centuries the Eastern and Western Churches have developed diverse traditions, theologies, liturgies, and forms of spirituality, all faithful expressions of the teaching of Christ. Representing cultures and world views with which most Catholics in this country are not familiar, the Eastern Churches provide significant alternative resources for catechesis. The insights of all the traditions are needed to deal with the varieties of pluralism in the United States.

16. UNITY OF THE FAITH AND THEOLOGICAL PLURALISM[10]

Pluralism in theological expression of faith, common today, is not new in the history of the Church. Found in the New Testament and present in the early centuries in the great theological currents of the West and the East, pluralism in the course of time grew and manifested itself in a variety of theological schools.

Theological reflection is integral to the Church's life and thought. In the past, the Church not only tolerated but encouraged a pluralism of theological tendencies, reflecting attempts to provide better explanations of themes and problems addressed under different aspects. Today the Church continues to encourage pluralism for pastoral and evangelical reasons, provided always that the pluralism in question contributes to a genuine enrichment of the doctrine of the faith and is in constant fidelity to it. Theological expression also takes into account different cultural, social, and even racial and ethnic contexts, while at the same time remaining faithful to the content of the Catholic faith as received and handed on by the magisterium of the Church.[11]

Catechists must be sensitive to the distinction between faith and theology. There is one faith, but there can be many theologies. Yet in regard even to matters which admit of a legitimate variety of theological opinions, the common doctrine of the Church is to be taught and the belief of the faithful respected. The unequal value of various theological systems should also be recognized. Which particular theological opinions should be raised in catechesis, and when they should be raised, are to be determined by the readiness of the learners and the preparation of the teacher. When catechists are engaged in the teaching dimension of their ministry, they teach not in their own names but in the name of the Church: from it they receive a commission, and under the direction of its hierarchy they are to carry out their ministry.

PART B: SCIENCE AND TECHNOLOGY

17. SCIENCE AND TECHNOLOGY

The rapid progress of science and technology in the United States has put into human hands unprecedented power to reap great benefit for the human race or sow disaster upon the earth. Men and women have new capacities to attempt to solve some of the persistent problems confronting the people of the entire world; but, they also have new power to deny human dignity and even survival to much of humanity.

Science and technology hold out the promise of improving the world food supply, curing diseases and plagues, and distributing the world's goods more equitably. They can also be used to violate human freedom, curtail human rights, and kill vast numbers of people.

18. THE ARMS RACE

The greatest threat to human survival lies in the awesome power of modern weaponry. Warfare and the arms race menace civilization: atomic devices including hydrogen and neutron bombs; biological weapons capable of spreading disease and plagues to human and animal life; and chemical projectiles, with deadly gases and liquids. Furthermore, the arms race is a colossal waste of God-given resources.

Disarmament is a critical and fundamental issue. The Second Vatican Council placed the problem in perspective when it declared that people, especially leaders and rulers, must "make a true beginning of disarmament, not indeed a unilateral disarmament, but one proceeding at an equal pace according to agreement, and backed up by authentic and workable safeguards."[12]

19. LIFE SCIENCES

Similarly, the unprecedented progress in life sciences, especially in the field of biology and allied disciplines, has generated new moral problems while calling into being a new specialty called bioethics, which deals with human life in all its stages.

Awareness of the intrinsic value of life and respect for human dignity are fundamental to any consideration of the problems of abortion, infanticide, the care of those who are severely handicapped, infirm, or aged, the definition of death and euthanasia, behavior control through surgery and drug therapy, genetic engineering, and population control.

20. TECHNOLOGY

Technological progress has had contradictory effects on life in this country. In becoming highly mobile and migratory, people, especially families, have been drawn further apart; yet, in another sense, the almost universal coverage of modern communications media has brought people into increasingly constant and immediate contact.

21. MOBILITY

Mobility is a characteristic of life in the United States. Almost one person out of five changes residence annually (though most moves are for short distances, and two people out of three live in the state in which they were born). Movers tend to be younger, better educated, and male. The majority of people, including Catholics (about three out of four), live in metropolitan areas.[13]

The breakdown of family ties and community identity along with intensified loneliness are among the negative results of this mobility. Except perhaps in rural areas and surviving ethnic neighborhoods, Church leaders can no longer take for granted a sense of community; often they must instead work to develop and sustain it.

22. COMMUNICATIONS

The impact of the communications revolution, especially television, is very powerful in the United States. The influx of information is overwhelming. A person living in the United States today is said to be exposed to more information in a week than his or her counterpart of two centuries ago was in a year.

Many find that they are given more information than they can assimilate or evaluate. People need to acquire "literacy" in relation to the new media — that is, they need to grow in their ability to evaluate television and other contemporary media by critical standards which include gospel values.

Yet another threat to human dignity and privacy is posed by the enormous capacity of computers and data banks to store billions of data indefinitely and retrieve them readily. All manner of records, medical, personal, educational, financial, have now become available to government and even private agencies. Such records can be helpful in many ways and can work to the advantage of many people; yet at the same time the invasion of personal, corporate, and institutional privacy can pose a very real threat to human rights. Solutions lie not only in the physical protection of data banks and in legal sanctions, but also in the moral order of justice.

PART C: PROFILE OF UNITED STATES CATHOLICS

23. POSITIVE ELEMENTS

While no brief description can adequately portray Catholicism in this country, it is possible to sketch some elements of the total picture.

Most Catholics approve the changes initiated by the Second Vatican Council, despite differences concerning the implementation of its documents. There has been an increase in the weekly reception of Holy Communion. New religious forms have emerged, such as the Cursillo, charismatic renewal, prayer groups, Marriage Encounter, youth retreats, home liturgies, and parish renewal programs. Among members of the Eastern Catholic Churches there is a resurgence of interest in their Eastern traditions. Various aspects and programs of catechesis have flourished. There is continued generosity in giving time and money to worthy causes at home and abroad. Numerous examples of Christian witness exist.

24. PROBLEMS

There are also serious problems. Many Catholics express little or no confidence in organized religion, say their religious beliefs are of limited or no importance to them, and are registered in no parish.[14] Surveys indicate that, with respect to doctrine, many Catholics are poorly informed about their faith or have deliberately rejected parts of it. For example, many express doubt that the pope is infallible when he teaches solemnly in matters of faith and morals; that there can be such a thing as eternal punishment for evil; that the devil exists; that the Church has a right to teach on racial integration. There is widespread acceptance of remarriage after divorce; of sexual relations between engaged persons; of artificial birth control; of legal abortion in certain cases.[15] Even many church-affiliated people, Catholics and others, make no conscious connection between their religious beliefs and their moral choices.

Although new forms of devotion have emerged and grown in popularity, traditional religious practice—notably including Sunday Mass attendance—has declined since the early 1960s.[16] Uncertainty, confusion, and apathy are widespread. Large numbers are Christian in name only: they have never really responded with a mature faith to the Lord and His Church. Long-term trends are not clear, but recent developments are a cause of concern even while they contain elements of hope.

While most Catholics have not seriously thought of leaving the Church,[17] a growing number have abandoned active membership. This phenomenon varies considerably with age and education, generally decreasing with age and increasing with the level of education. People under 30 who have attended college have been most affected.[18]

Atheism, however, does not appear to be a major problem. Very few (3 percent) of the people of the United States deny that there is a personal God or a higher power of some kind.[19]

Clearly, evangelization and catechesis are needed to solve some of these problems. The sophistication, self-awareness, and maturity with which different people approach doctrinal and moral issues vary greatly, for a variety of reasons. It is necessary to present and give witness to the Church's authentic teaching in a way which respects the sincerity of those who are seeking to know what is true and do what is right.[20] Many persons need a gradual integration into the community of believers. Assistance in this regard is offered in the pertinent sections of this NCD.

PART D: FAMILY AND HOME IN THE UNITED STATES

25. IMPORTANCE OF THE HOME AND COMMUNITY IN CATECHESIS

Education, broadly defined, includes the entire process by which culture is transmitted from one generation to the next. Educational research supports the view that the home is the critical educational institution. Study after study identifies home and family as vital forces strongly affecting school achievement. Throughout the world the home is the crucial factor in determining children's overall performance. Behavioral disorders and social pathology in children and youth frequently begin in family disorganization: arising not only from within the family itself, but from the circumstances in which the family finds itself and from the way of life which results.

Family and community are also extremely important in the catechetical process. While other factors are involved (e.g., age, sex, size of community, present study of religion, parental approval of the friends of their children, etc.), the impact of parents is primary among the human factors which influence this process. This is the principal reason for the current emphasis on preparation for parenthood and parent education, as well as a subsidiary motive for adult education.[21]

The vital influence of parents on the social and religious development of their children must be more widely recognized. Family life needs to be strengthened so that children and youth will derive their values from the home, rather than from potentially undesirable sources outside the home. The Church, especially through the parish, should provide an intensified support system for family life.

26. CHANGES IN FAMILIES

In the past quarter-century in the United States the family has experienced progressive fragmentation and isolation, along with changes in its structure and child-bearing role. Catholic families have been affected together with the rest. Changes are more rapid among younger families with young children, increase with economic deprivation and industrialization, and reach a peak among low-income families living in the central core of larger cities.

27. ILLUSTRATIONS OF CHANGE IN FAMILIES

a) Divorce

There are now over one million divorces a year in the United States. Millions of children and young people under 18 have experienced family breakup on account of divorce. Nearly one-third of all school-age children are not living with both natural parents.

b) One-parent families

The number of one-parent families has risen with the increased rate of divorce, desertion, and births outside of marriage. Currently about one family in every five with school-age children is headed by one parent.

One-parent households are much more common in large cities and among younger families. They occur least often in rural and suburban areas. However, patterns of fragmentation found a few years ago only in major metropolitan centers are now also present in smaller urban areas. Families in similar circumstances (as to age, region, education, income, etc.) now tend to be affected in much the same way.

c) Unwed mothers

After families divided by divorce, the most rapidly growing category of one parent families is that of families headed by unwed mothers.

The number of live births out of wedlock tripled between 1960 and the mid-1970s. A preponderant number of women who become pregnant out of wedlock and give birth to their children do not place them for adoption. The overwhelming proportion of out-of-wedlock births occur to women under 25.

d) Families where both parents work

In more than half of the families with school-age children both parents work outside the home or are seeking such work. Most have full-time jobs. In about one-third of the families with preschool children, both parents work. Needless to say, extensive parental absence from the home is more likely in one-parent families.

The great increase in the number of working mothers has been a major factor in the expansion of nursery schools, day care centers of all kinds, and ordinary babysitting. Millions of school-age youngsters ("latchkey children") return from school to empty homes. They contribute, at a rate far out of proportion to their numbers, to the ranks of those with academic difficulties or behavioral problems.

e) Family size

The average size of households in the United States has dropped significantly in recent years. A dramatic decline in childbearing has been a major factor.

f) Delay of marriage

People are marrying later now than in the past; and more and more persons of both sexes choose to remain single. Many postpone or refrain from marriage for career or vocational reasons. At the same time, a substantial number of men and women are living together without marriage and, generally, without having children.

28. EFFECTS OF CHANGE ON FAMILIES

These trends appear to be nationwide and are having profound effects on society and religion. They underline the fact that the members of many families need extensive support if they are to grow in faith and live according to the example of Christ and the teaching of His Church.

29. CONCLUSION

This overview has presented some contemporary cultural and religious factors confronting catechesis in the United States. Many more could be mentioned (e.g., the special characteristics of children and youth, young adults, and the elderly; the special obstacles to catechesis presented by illiteracy, extreme poverty, drug abuse, alcoholism, etc.).

Continuing research is needed so that those engaged in catechesis will understand contemporary social phenomena and be better equipped to bring people to Christian maturity by means which take these phenomena into realistic account. There is a particularly urgent need for analysis of the current status of the family, the roles of men and women within the family and society generally, and the alterations brought about by social and economic changes.

The picture presented here and elsewhere in this NCD is a sober one. Two points need to be borne in mind: first, because catechesis occurs in a cultural and social context, the catechist must take the negative as well as the positive aspects of the situation into account; second, God's kingdom has already been established, and Christ's followers are called to manifest and work for the ever fuller realization of that kingdom in all areas of life.

CHAPTER II
THE CATECHETICAL MINISTRY OF THE CHURCH

30. MISSION OF THE CHURCH

The Church continues the mission of Jesus, prophet, priest, and servant king. Its mission, like His, is essentially one—to bring about God's kingdom —but this one mission has three aspects: proclaiming and teaching God's word, celebrating the sacred mysteries, and serving the people of the world. Corresponding to the three aspects of the Church's mission and existing to serve it are three ministries: the ministry of the word, the ministry of worship, and the ministry of service. In saying this, however, it is important to bear in mind that the several elements of the Church's mission are inseparably linked in reality (each includes and implies the others), even though it is possible to study and discuss them separately.

PART A: CATECHESIS—A FORM OF MINISTRY OF THE WORD

31. FORMS OF MINISTRY OF THE WORD

The ministry of the word takes different forms, depending on circumstances and on the particular ends in view.[22] Proclamation and teaching of God's word are present in evangelization, catechesis, liturgy, and theology, in a manner appropriate to each.

32. CATECHETICAL MINISTRY

Like other pastoral activities, catechetical ministry must be understood in relation to Jesus' threefold mission. It is a form of the ministry of the word, which proclaims and teaches.[23] It leads to and flows from the ministry of worship, which sanctifies through prayer and sacrament.[24] It supports the ministry of service, which is linked to efforts to achieve social justice and has traditionally been expressed in spiritual and corporal works of mercy.[25]

Catechesis is an esteemed term in Christian tradition. Its purpose is to make a person's "faith become living, conscious, and active, through the light of instruction."[26] While aiming to enrich the faith life of individuals at their particular stages of development, every form of catechesis is oriented in some way to the catechesis of adults, who are capable of a full response to God's word.[27] Catechesis is a lifelong process for the individual and a constant and concerted pastoral activity of the Christian community.

33. TASK OF CATECHESIS: TO FOSTER MATURE FAITH

Faith grows and matures. People of mature faith recognize the real and lasting value of human activity in this world, while also directing their "thoughts and desires to the full consummation of the kingdom in eternal life."[28] They "constantly [strive] for conversion and renewal, and [give] diligent ear to what the Spirit says to the Church."[29] They live in communion with God and other people, willingly accepting the responsibilities which arise from these relationships.[30] Maturity of faith implies that one "knows the mystery of salvation revealed in Christ, and the divine signs and works which are witnesses to the fact that this mystery is being carried out in human history."[31] A mature Christian has an active sacramental and prayer life.[32] Such a person tests and interprets human events, "especially the signs of the times," in a wholly Christian spirit,[33] and is zealous to spread the gospel in order to make the Church known as the sign and instrument of the salvation and unity of the human race.[34]

Such faith is a grace, a gift of God. Growth in faith is intimately related to one's response to this gift. (Cf. Colossians 2:6f) So "the life of faith admits of various degrees," both in acceptance of God's word and in the ability to explain and apply it.[35] (The act of faith is considered at greater length in Chapter III, while the stages on the way to mature faith are examined in Chapter VIII.)

34. CATECHESIS AND PRE-EVANGELIZATION

Catechesis presupposes prior pre-evangelization and evangelization. These are likely to be most successful when they build on basic human needs — for security, affection, acceptance, growth, and intellectual development — showing how these include a need, a hunger, for God and His word.

Often, however, catechesis is directed to individuals and communities who, in fact, have not experienced pre-evangelization and evangelization, and have not made acts of faith corresponding to those stages. Taking people as they are, catechesis attempts to dispose them to respond to the message of revelation in an authentic, personal way.

There is a great need in the United States today to prepare the ground for the gospel message. Many people have no religious affiliation. Many others have not committed their lives to Christ and His Church, even though they are church members. Radical questioning of values, rapid social change, pluralism, cultural influences, and population mobility — these and other factors underline the need for pre-evangelization.

35. CATECHESIS AND EVANGELIZATION

Although evangelization and catechesis are distinct forms of the ministry of the word, they are closely linked in practice. Evangelization "has as its purpose the arousing of the beginnings of faith."[36] It seeks to bring the good news "into all the strata of humanity," in this way "transforming humanity from within and making it new."[37] It aims at interior change, conversion of "the personal and collective conscience of people, the activities in which they engage, and the lives and concrete milieux which are theirs."[38]

Such change and renewal are also goals of catechesis, which disposes people "to receive the action of the Holy Spirit and to deepen conversion," and does so "through the word, to which are joined the witness of life and prayer."[39]

To consider evangelization only as a verbal proclamation of the gospel robs it of much of its richness; just as it does not do justice to catechesis to think of it as instruction alone. Like evangelization, catechesis is incomplete if it does not take into account the constant interplay between gospel teaching and human experience — individual and social, personal and institutional, sacred and secular.

36. CATECHESIS AND LITURGY

From its earliest days the Church has recognized that liturgy and catechesis support each other. Prayer and the sacraments call for informed participants; fruitful participation in catechesis calls for the spiritual enrichment that comes from liturgical participation.

While every liturgical celebration has educative and formative value, liturgy should not be treated as subservient to catechesis. On the contrary, catechesis should "promote an active, conscious, genuine participation in the liturgy of the Church, not merely by explaining the meaning of the ceremonies, but also by forming the minds of the faithful for prayer, for thanksgiving, for repentance, for praying with confidence, for a community spirit, and for understanding correctly the meaning of the creeds."[40]

Sacramental catechesis has traditionally been of two kinds: preparation for the initial celebration of the sacraments and continued enrichment following their first reception. The first is elementary or general in nature; it aims to introduce catechumens to the teaching of scripture and the creed. The second reflects on the meaning of the Christian mysteries and explores their consequences for Christian witness. Preparatory sacramental catechesis can be for a specified period of time — some weeks or months; the catechesis which follows is a lifelong matter. In the early Church sacramental catechesis focused on the Sacraments of Initiation: Baptism, Confirmation, and Eucharist. Over the course of time similar catecheses have been developed for the other sacraments: Reconciliation, Matrimony, Holy Orders, and the Anointing of the Sick.

37. CATECHESIS AND THEOLOGY

Catechesis draws on theology, and theology draws in turn on the richness of the Church's catechetical experience. Both must be at the service of the Church. Though intimately related, they are distinguishable in practice by their goals, methods, and criteria.

Theology seeks fuller understanding of the gospel message through reflection on the life of Christians and the formal teachings of the Church. It employs systematic and critical methods. It uses philosophy, history, linguistics, and other disciplines in attempting to understand and express Christian truth more clearly.

Catechesis also makes use of the sacred and human sciences. It does this not as theology does — for systematic study and analyses of the faith — but in order to better proclaim the faith and, in cooperation with the Holy Spirit, lead individual Christians and the community to maturity of faith, a richer living of the fullness of the gospel message.

38. CATECHESIS IN MORALITY

Catechesis in morality is an essential element of catechetical ministry.

The Gospels contain Jesus' moral teaching as transmitted by the apostolic Church. The epistles, especially those of St. Paul, denounce conduct unbecoming to Christians and specify the behavior expected of those who have been baptized into Christ. (Cf., e.g., Ephesians 4:17–32; Colossians 3:5–11)

Through the ages moral teaching has been an integral part of the Catholic message, and an upright life has been a hallmark of a mature Christian. Catechisms have traditionally emphasized a code of Christian conduct, sometimes summarized under three headings: a sense of personal integrity; social justice and love of neighbor; and accountability to God as a loving Father who is also Lord of all.

Catechesis therefore includes the Church's moral teaching, showing clearly its relevance to both individual ethics and current public issues. It takes into account the stages through which individuals and communities pass as they grow in ability to make moral judgments and to act in a responsible, Christian manner. Catechesis expresses the Church's moral teaching clearly and emphasizes the faithful acceptance of this teaching—an acceptance which carries a twofold responsibility on the part of individuals and the community: to strive for perfection and give witness to Christian beliefs and values and to seek to correct conditions in society and the Church which hinder authentic human development and the flourishing of Christian values.

PART B: FORMS OF CATECHESIS

39. GENERAL DIVERSITY OF CATECHETICAL ACTIVITY

Conducted in a variety of circumstances and directed to widely diverse audiences, catechetical activity takes many forms. There is catechesis for different age levels—children, pre-adolescents and adolescents, young adults and adults—and for different groups (e.g., the non-English speaking, members of particular cultural, racial, and ethnic groups, the handicapped, etc.) within each age category. It will also vary in form according to the language, vocation, abilities, and geographical location of those catechized. Its components include sharing faith life, experiencing liturgical worship, taking part in Christian service, and participating in religious instruction. Programs should be designed to take into account participants' experiences and circumstances. As far as possible, catechesis should be adapted to the needs of each individual.

Furthermore, although the initiation, education, and formation of individuals and the faith community pertain especially to catechesis,[41] every pastoral activity has a catechetical dimension.

For the past century Catholic catechetical effort in the United States has focused primarily upon children and adolescents. Much of this effort has been carried on in Catholic schools. Other major catechetical programs for children and adolescents who do not attend Catholic schools have been and are being developed under the auspices of national and diocesan offices and in parishes.

40. ADULT CATECHESIS

Without neglecting its commitment to children, catechesis needs to give more attention to adults than it has been accustomed to do. It should not be thought that adult catechesis is important only by reason of its relationship to the catechesis of children (i.e., adults must be catechized so that they can catechize the young) or that parent and teacher education are the whole of adult catechesis—though they are certainly forms of it. Rather, the primary reason for adult catechesis—its first and essential objective—is to help adults themselves grow to maturity of faith as members of the Church and society. The *General Catechetical Directory* views adult catechesis as the summit of the entire catechetical enterprise[42] (cf. Colossians 1:28); while, from another perspective, it stands at the center of the Church's educational mission.[43]

It is adult Christians who are capable of mature faith, and whose lives exemplify gospel values to the young members of the Christian community and the rest of society. They strongly influence the way in which children and catechumens perceive faith. It is essential that they express gospel values by living with the hope and joy that come with faith. The Church, for its part, must encourage its adult members to grow in faith and give them opportunities to do so.

PART C: SOURCE AND SIGNS OF CATECHESIS

41. SOURCE OF CATECHESIS

The source of catechesis, which is also its content, is one: God's word, fully revealed in Jesus Christ and at work in the lives of people exercising their faith under the guidance of the magisterium, which alone teaches authentically.[44] God's word deposited in scripture and tradition is manifested and celebrated in many ways: in the liturgy and "in the life of the Church, especially in the just and in the saints"; moreover, "in some way it is known too from those genuine moral values which, by divine providence, are found in human society."[45] Indeed, potentially at least, every instance of God's presence in the world is a source of catechesis.

42. SIGNS: MANIFESTATIONS OF THE SOURCE

The various manifestations of the source of catechesis are called signs because they point to a deeper reality: God's self-communication in the world. Drawing upon the words and deeds of revelation to express a vision of God's love and saving power, catechesis recalls the revelation brought to perfection in Christ and "interprets human life in our age, the signs of the times, and the things of this world."[46] The signs of God's saving activity have come to be classified under four general headings: biblical signs, liturgical signs, ecclesial signs, and natural signs. Though closely related, signs of each kind have special characteristics.

43. BIBLICAL SIGNS

Catechesis studies scripture as a source inseparable from the Christian message. It seeks ways to make the biblical signs better understood, so that people may more fully live the message of the Bible. (Cf. 2 Timothy 3:14–17)

Catechesis encourages people to use the Bible as a source and inspiration for prayer. It fosters informed participation in the liturgy by helping people recognize biblical themes and language which are part of the readings and sacramental rites. It reflects constantly on the biblical signs in order to penetrate their meaning more deeply.

The term "biblical signs" refers to the varied and wonderful ways, recorded in scripture, by which God reveals Himself. Among the chief signs, to be emphasized in all catechesis, are: the creation account, which culminates in the establishment of God's kingdom; the covenant made by God with Abraham and his descendants and God's new covenant in Jesus Christ which is extended to all people; the exodus from bondage to freedom and the parallel, but far more profound, passage from death to life accomplished by Christ's paschal mystery. Underlying all as an authentic biblical sign is the community of believers—the People of Israel, the Church—from among whom, under the inspiration of the Holy Spirit, certain individuals composed and assembled these holy writings and transmitted them to future generations as testimony to their beliefs and their experience of grace.

44. LITURGICAL SIGNS

As explained above, catechesis has the task of preparing individuals and communities for knowing, active, and fruitful liturgical and sacramental celebration and for profound reflection upon it. How this is done is discussed in Chapter VI. Here we wish only to note that the celebration of the liturgy, the sacramental rites, and the Church Year are important sources for catechesis.

The liturgy and sacraments are the supreme celebration of the paschal mystery. They express the sanctification of human life. As efficacious signs which mediate God's saving, loving power, they accomplish the saving acts which they symbolize. In and through the sacramental rites above all, Christ communicates the Holy Spirit to the Church. "In the earthly liturgy, by way of foretaste, we share in that heavenly liturgy which is celebrated in the holy city of Jerusalem toward which we journey as pilgrims."[47]

45. ECCLESIAL SIGNS

Other aspects of the Church's life besides liturgy are important for catechesis. In general, these ecclesial signs are grouped under two headings: doctrine or creedal formulations and the witness of Christian living.

Creeds and formulas which state the Church's belief are expressions of the living tradition which, from the time of the apostles, has developed "in the Church with the help of the Holy Spirit."[48] They are formulated to meet particular liturgical needs (e.g., the Apostles' Creed), to counteract specific errors (e.g., the Nicene Creed), or simply to express the common beliefs of the Church (e.g., the Credo of the People of God). "The integral, vital substance handed down through the creed provides the fundamental nucleus of the mystery of the One and Triune God as it was revealed to us through the mystery of God's Son, the Incarnate Savior living always in his Church."[49]

Human language is limited, however, especially when it comes to expressing transcendent mysteries. Therefore it is valid to distinguish between the truth itself and the language or words in which it is expressed. One and the same truth may be expressed in a variety of ways. Catechesis must nevertheless recognize creedal statements and doctrinal formulas as indispensable instruments for handing on the faith.

The Church also gives witness to its faith through its way of life, its manner of worship, and the service it renders. The lives of heroic Christians, the saints of past and present, show how people are transformed when they come to know Jesus Christ in the Spirit. The forgiveness and reconciliation experienced by repentant sinners are signs of the Church as a healing community. Concern for and ministry to the poor, disadvantaged, helpless, and hopeless are signs that the Church is a servant. Uniting in love and mutual respect people from every corner of the earth, every racial and ethnic background, all socioeconomic strata, the Church is a sign of our union with God and one another effected in Jesus Christ. Every Christian community, characterized by its stewardship, is meant to be a sign of that assembly of believers which will reach fulfillment in the heavenly kingdom. Such a community catechizes its members by its very life and work, giving witness in a multitude of ways to God's love as revealed and communicated to us in Christ.

46. NATURAL SIGNS

Its prophetic mission requires that the Church, in communion with all people of good will, examine the signs of the times and interpret them in light of the gospel.[50] Catechesis seeks to teach the faithful to test and interpret all things, including natural signs, in a wholly Christian spirit.[51]

Central human values are expressed in the arts, science, and technology; in family, culture, economic, and social life; in politics and international relations. Catechesis for adults should therefore teach them to evaluate correctly, in light of faith, contemporary cultural and sociological developments, new questions of a religious and moral nature, and the interplay between temporal responsibilities and the Church's mission to the world. It must give an intellectually satisfying demonstration of the gospel's relevance to life.[52] In short, it has the task of examining at the most profound level the meaning and value of everything created, including the products of human effort, in order to show how all creation sheds light on the mystery of God's saving power and is in turn illuminated by it.

PART D: CATECHETICAL CRITERIA

47. NORMS OF CATECHESIS[53]

While it is neither possible nor desirable to establish a rigid order to dictate a uniform method for the exposition of content, certain norms or criteria guide all sound catechesis. These are developed further throughout this NCD.

First and foremost, catechesis is trinitarian and christocentric in scope and spirit, consciously emphasizing the mystery of God and the plan of salvation, which leads to the Father, through the Son, in the Holy Spirit. (Cf. Ephesians 1:3–14) Catechesis is centered in the mystery of Christ. The center of the message should be Christ, true God and true man, His saving work carried out in His incarnation, life, death, and resurrection.[54]

Since catechesis seeks to foster mature faith in individuals and communities, it is careful to present the Christian message in its entirety. It does so in such a way that the interrelationship of the elements of this message is apparent, together with the fact that they form a kind of organic whole. Thus their significance in relation to God's mystery and saving works is best communicated.

In practice, this means recognizing a certain hierarchy of truths. "These truths may be grouped under four basic heads: the mystery of God the Father, the Son, and the Holy Spirit, Creator of all things; the mystery of Christ the incarnate Word, who was born of the Virgin Mary, and who suffered, died, and rose for our salvation; the mystery of the Holy Spirit, who is present in the Church, sanctifying it and guiding it until the glorious coming of Christ, our Savior and Judge; and the mystery of the Church, which is Christ's Mystical Body, in which the Virgin Mary holds the pre-eminent place."[55] This hierarchy of truths does not mean that some truths pertain less to faith itself than others do, but rather that some truths of faith enjoy a higher priority inasmuch as other truths are based on and illumined by them. In presenting the truths of faith, catechesis must foster close contact with the various forms of life in the ecclesial community.[56] Sound catechesis also recognizes the circumstances—cultural, linguistic, etc.—of those being catechized. Finally, while interpreting the present life in the light of revelation, catechesis seeks to dispose people "to hope in the future life that is the consummation of the whole history of salvation."[57] (Cf. Colossians 1:23)

"This task of catechesis, not an easy one, must be carried out under the guidance of the magisterium of the Church, whose duty it is to safeguard the truth of the divine message, and to watch that the ministry of the word uses appropriate forms of speaking, and prudently considers the help which theological research and human sciences can give."[58] Thus, the bishop holds the primary position of authority over programs of catechesis. Under him the pastor holds the office of direct responsibility in the local Church. The teaching of what is opposed to the faith of the Catholic Church, its doctrinal and moral positions, its laws, discipline, and practice should in no way be allowed or countenanced in catechetical programs on any level.

Catechesis strives to express and foster a profound dialogue, which arises from God's loving self-communication and the trusting response of human beings in faith, under the guidance of the Spirit. The next chapter considers in greater detail this dialogue.

CHAPTER III
REVELATION, FAITH AND CATECHESIS

48. INTRODUCTION

Christ gave the Church the mission of proclaiming the message of salvation and unfolding its mystery among all peoples. (Cf. Matthew 28:19f) In doing this the Church is guided by God's own way of revealing Himself. From the beginning He has gradually made known the inexhaustible mystery of His love in words and deeds and, in so doing, summoned a response in faith from His people. The loving self-revelation of God and the response of humankind together constitute a profound dialogue.

PART A: GOD'S SELF-REVELATION

49. THE ART OF REVELATION, A MYSTERY OF LOVE

God's inner life is a deep mystery, for He is "great beyond our knowledge" (Job 36:26). The Word, however, fully comprehends the Father, and God reveals Himself through His Word. "The Word became flesh and made his dwelling among us, and we have seen his glory: The glory of an only Son coming from the Father, filled with an enduring love." (John 1:14)

The term "revelation" has both a general and a strict sense. It has been applied to the constant evidence which God provides of Himself "in created realities."[59] This manifestation of God is available to all human beings, even in the present condition of the human race.[60] Strictly speaking, however, revelation designates that communication of God which is in no way deserved by us, for it has as its aim our participation in the life of the Trinity, a share in divine life itself. This revelation is a gift of God upon which no one has a claim. Because it goes beyond anything which we can dare imagine, the proper response to this revelation is that self-surrender known as the obedience of faith. (Cf. Romans 16:26)

50. USE OF THE WORD "REVELATION" IN THIS DOCUMENT

The word "revelation" is used in this document to refer to that divine public revelation which closed at the end of the Apostolic Age. The terms "manifestation" and "communication" are used for the other modes by which God continues to make Himself known and share Himself with human beings through His presence in the Church and the world.

51. GOD'S SELF-MANIFESTATION THROUGH CREATION

God manifests Himself through creation. "Since the creation of the world, invisible realities, God's external power and divinity, have become visible, recognized through the things he has made." (Romans 1:20)

The first chapter of Genesis tells us that God spoke and created all things. Because it is "spoken" by God, creation is a great symbol of Him.[61]

Because human beings are created in God's image and likeness (cf. Genesis 1:27), they are most capable of making God manifest in their lives. The more fully people live in fidelity to the image of God in them, the more clearly perceptible is the divine in human life.

Human cultures also mirror divine attributes in various ways. The religions of humanity, especially, give a certain perception "of that hidden power which hovers over the course of things and over the events of human life, at times, indeed, recognition can be found of a Supreme Divinity and of a Supreme Father too. Such a perception and such a recognition instill the lives of these peoples with a profound religious sense."[62] These are concrete examples and expressions of what can be termed God's natural revelation.[63]

52. GOD'S REVELATION THROUGH ISRAEL

Sin and its effects have been part of the human condition ever since our first parents sinned. (Cf. Romans 5:12) But God, intending our redemption, called Abraham to be the father of a people (cf. Genesis 12:1 ff.)—a people with whom God entered into a loving relationship through the Sinai covenant: "I will dwell in the midst of the Israelites and will be their God." (Exodus 29:45)

God spoke to His people through judges and kings, priests and prophets, sages and biblical writers. He fed His people, protected them, liberated them, loved them, corrected, punished, and forgave them. He taught them that He alone is God, compassionate and true to His promises. He invited their free response.

God inspired men and women like Moses, Miriam, Joshua, Deborah, and David to act on His behalf and interpret to others the meaning of His deeds. He inspired authors to record the words and deeds of revelation for the benefit of future generations, and to bring forth from the community the Old Testament accounts which best express His love.

53. GOD'S REVELATION THROUGH HIS SON, JESUS CHRIST

Thus the stage was set for a broader and deeper covenant, God's fullest self-revelation in Jesus Christ. "God so loved the world that he gave his only Son, that whoever believes in him may not die but may have eternal life." (John 3:16)

St. Ephrem, in the Eastern tradition, said God imprinted upon nature and in sacred scripture symbols and figures which would manifest Him, as a preparation for revealing Himself in the humanity of Jesus. The purpose of the created universe was to manifest the Son of God and prepare humanity for His coming.[64]

God's revelation reached its supreme expression in the incarnation, life, death, burial, and resurrection of Jesus Christ, by the power of the Spirit. Jesus inaugurated God's kingdom among human beings. He confronted the sinful, dehumanizing forces which alienate people from God, from other human beings, and, indeed, from basic elements of their own personhood. Coming among us as a servant, Jesus expressed His love for the Father and for us by obediently accepting suffering and death, and so reconciling us with God. (Cf. Philippians 2:6ff)

The apostles were privileged eyewitnesses of God's self-revelation in Christ both before and after His resurrection. (Cf. John 21:24) Jesus promised to send them the Holy Spirit, who would enable them to bear witness to Him. (Cf. John 14:26) This apostolic witness is normative for the faith of the Church. The Church is thus convinced that "the Christian dispensation . . . as the new and definitive covenant, will never pass away, and we now await no further new public revelation before the glorious manifestation of our Lord Jesus Christ."[65] (Cf. 1 Timothy 6:14; Titus 2:13)

God's revelation in and through Jesus Christ, proclaimed by the apostles, is thus unique, irrevocable, and definitive. Still, the Church does not simply possess the memory of something that happened long ago. Rather "God, who spoke of old, uninterruptedly converses with the Bride of His beloved Son; and the Holy Spirit, through whom the living voice of the gospel resounds in the

Church, and through her, in the world, leads unto all truth those who believe and makes the word of Christ dwell abundantly in them."[66] (Cf. Colossians 3:16)

"The Roman Pontiff and the bishops, in view of their office and of the importance of the matter, strive painstakingly and by appropriate means to inquire properly into that revelation and to give apt expression to its contents. But they do not allow that there could be any new public revelation pertaining to the divine deposit of faith."[67] Pope Paul VI reiterates this teaching: "Revelation is inserted in time, in history, at a precise date, on the occasion of a specific event, and it must be regarded as concluded and complete for us with the death of the Apostles."[68]

54. GOD'S MANIFESTATION THROUGH THE HOLY SPIRIT

God continues to manifest Himself through the Holy Spirit at work in the world and, especially, in the Church. Christ, risen and living, is present to believers through the power of the Spirit, who has united Christians since Pentecost, awakening in them the memory of the Lord's life, death, and resurrection, and making these acts present, especially through scripture and the sacraments. The Spirit's action also makes believers sensitive to God's promptings in their hearts, moving them to respond and bear witness to Him so that others, too, may come to know the Lord. (Cf. 1 Corinthians 2:12ff)

Finally, the Spirit helps believers perceive the divine presence in history and interpret human experiences in the light of faith. As the word of the Lord helped the prophets see the divine plan in the signs of their times, so today the Spirit helps the people of the Church interpret the signs of these times and carry out their prophetic tasks.

55. GOD'S MANIFESTATION THROUGH THE DAILY LIVES OF BELIEVERS

Because Christ's revelation is inexhaustible, we can always know more about it and understand it better. (Cf. Ephesians 3:18f) We grow in such knowledge and understanding when we respond to God manifesting Himself through creation, the events of daily life, the triumphs and tragedies of history. God speaks to us in a special manner in His word—sacred scripture—and through prayer, communicating His love and beauty to us through the Holy Spirit. Above all, He communicates Himself through the sacraments, through the witness of the faithful, and through the full life and teaching of the Church."[69]

But even as He manifests Himself, God remains a mystery. "How deep are the riches and the wisdom and the knowledge of God! How inscrutable his judgments, how unsearchable his ways! For 'who has known the mind of the Lord? Or who has been his counselor?'" (Romans 11:33f) Beyond a certain point we must rely on love, expressed in contemplative prayer and lives of charity, for further growth in knowledge and experience of God.

PART B: REVELATION CALLS FOR RESPONSE IN FAITH

56. REVELATION CALLS FOR RESPONSE

Though the response to God's revelation and love will vary according to one's background and circumstances, the act of faith involves "total adherence . . . under the influence of grace to God revealing himself."[70] This is the faith *by which* one believes. Total adherence includes not only the mind but also the will and emotions; it is the response of the whole person, including belief in the "content of revelation and of the Christian message."[71] This latter is the faith *which* one believes. Thus faith involves both a relationship and its expression.

57. FAITH AND GRACE

The interior help of the Holy Spirit must "precede and assist" faith, "moving the heart and turning it to God, opening the eyes of the mind and giving 'joy and ease to everyone in assenting to the truth and believing it.'"[72] (Cf. Romans 1:16f) Thus one believes in response to grace.

Faith calls for responses of assent, trust, surrender, and obedience to God. Thus faith means commitment, and in this sense it is a deep personal relationship with the Lord. Moments of doubt and anxiety, arising from our weakness, can be expected in the life of faith. Nevertheless, God is faithful. The Lord Jesus reminds us: "Have faith in God and faith in me. . . . I am the way, the truth and the life." (John 14:1 – 6)

58. FAITH AS A FREE RESPONSE

Faith is a free response to God revealing. This is "one of the major tenets of Catholic doctrine. . . . Man, redeemed by Christ the Savior and through Christ Jesus called to be God's adopted son, cannot give his adherence to God revealing Himself unless the Father draw him to offer to God the reasonable and free submission of faith."[73] At the same time, faith is also obligatory, in the sense that one who violates conscience by refusing to believe "will be condemned." (Mark 16:16)

59. FAITH EXPRESSED IN WORDS AND DEEDS

Faith is expressed in words and deeds.

What we are to believe is found in tradition and scripture, which together "form one sacred deposit of the word of God which is committed to the Church."[74] "Scripture is the word of God inasmuch as it is consigned to writing under the inspiration of the divine Spirit. To the successors of the apostles, sacred tradition hands on in its full purity God's word. . . . Thus, led by the light of the Spirit of truth, these successors can in their preaching preserve this word of God faithfully, explain it, and make it more widely known."[75]

The tradition which comes from the apostles is unfolded in and by the Church with the help of the Holy Spirit. (Cf. 1 Corinthians 12:2f) Believers grow in insight through study and contemplation. Such growth comes about "through the intimate understanding of spiritual things they experience, and through the preaching of those who have received through episcopal succession the sure gift of truth."[76]

As the community of believers grows in understanding, its faith is expressed in creeds, dogmas, and moral principles and teachings. The meaning of dogmatic formulas "remains ever true and constant in the Church, even when it is expressed with greater clarity or more developed."[77] Because they are expressed in the language of a particular time and place, however, these formulations sometimes give way to new ones, proposed and approved by the magisterium of the Church, which express the same meaning more clearly or completely.[78]

What we believe is also expressed in the deeds of the Church community. The "deeds" in question are worship — especially the celebration of the Eucharist, in which the risen Christ speaks to His Church and continues His saving work — and acts performed to build up Christ's body through service to the community of faith or voluntary service in the universal mission of the Church. (Cf. Ephesians 4:11f) While it is true that our actions establish the sincerity of our words, it is equally true that our words must be able to explain our actions. In catechesis Catholics are taught a facility in talking about their faith, lest they be silent when it comes to explaining what they are doing and why.

Belief can also be expressed in the visual arts, in poetry and literature, in music and architecture, in philosophy, and scientific or technological achievements. These, too, can be signs of God's presence, continuations of His creative activity, instruments by which believers glorify Him and give witness to the world concerning the faith that is in them.

PART C: A CATECHETICAL APPROACH TO REVELATION AND FAITH

60. CATECHETICAL GUIDELINES CONCERNING REVELATION AND FAITH

These general guidelines for catechesis arise from what has been said.

a) Catechists should draw upon all the sources: biblical, liturgical, ecclesial, and natural.

i) Biblical, liturgical, and ecclesial sources

Catechists have vast resources available to them in the Church. These include the Bible, liturgical rites, the Church Year, dogma, doctrines, moral principles and laws, Church history, and theological insights, both ancient and modern. (For liturgical and ecclesial sources, cf. articles 44 and 45.)

The Bible has an essential and indispensable role to play in Christian catechesis. "Ignorance of the scriptures is ignorance of Christ."[79] Catechesis keeps ever in mind the vision of the Second Vatican Council: every Catholic reading, knowing, understanding, and loving the sacred scriptures. The Bible is not just a book to be read and studied. It contains God's word, which should be the object of our prayerful meditation. As a source of inspiration and spiritual nourishment, the Bible ought to be a constant companion.

Catechists will be thoroughly familiar with both the New and Old Testaments. Hearing scripture read in the liturgy and reading it privately deepen their understanding of the Christian message. Courses in scripture are imperative in preparing catechists to make better use of God's word as a major catechetical source.

Homes, classrooms, and other places of catechesis should have an approved[80] edition of the Bible. In time, students should have and use their own copies of the scriptures.

Catechesis explains the number and structure of the books of the Old and New Testaments, speaks of them as God's inspired word, and treats their major themes, such as creation, salvation, and final fulfillment. The Bible is presented as a collection of divinely inspired books, each with its human author or authors, history of composition, and literary form or forms. Such information helps one understand "what meaning the sacred writers really intended, and what God wanted to manifest by means of their words."[81]

The books of the New Testament, especially the Gospels, enjoy preeminence as principal witness of the life and teachings of Jesus, the Incarnate Word. Everyone, according to ability, should become acquainted with the infancy narratives, the miracles and parables of Jesus' public life, and the accounts of His passion, death, and resurrection. Catechesis also develops the principal themes found in the epistles, and gives some attention to the literary characteristics of all the New Testament books, besides providing an introduction to critical exegesis. Major themes of the Old Testament are also to be known as preparing for Christ: creation and redemption, sin and grace, the covenant with Abraham and the chosen people, the exodus from Egypt and the Sinai covenant, the Babylonian captivity and the return, the Emmanuel and suffering servant passages in Isaiah, etc. Individuals are encouraged to meditate on the meaning of the scriptures for their lives. There is value in committing particular passages to memory.

In adult catechesis the work of biblical scholars is studied as a means to achieving "deeper insight into the sense intended by God speaking through the sacred writer."[82] However, critical scholarship of itself is not the ultimate source of the full interpretation of the sacred texts. This interpretation is the gift of the Holy Spirit given to the Church and guarded by the magisterium.

ii) Natural sources

As Jesus often used the experiences of His listeners as the starting point of His parables, catechists should use examples from daily life, the arts, and the sciences to draw out the meaning of God's revelation and show its relevance for contemporary life.

b) Catechists note the historical character of revelation and faith.

God's revelation occurred through a process of unfolding. "In times past, God spoke in fragmentary and varied ways to our fathers through the prophets;

in this, the final age, he has spoken to us through his Son." (Hebrews 1:1) The Fathers of the Church, especially in their baptismal catechesis, took note of the historical dimension of the drama of salvation. So, in catechesis, "memory of the past, awareness of the present, and hope of the future ought to be evident."[83]

c) Catechists need to understand the development of doctrine.

Catechists need to have a clear understanding of what is meant by the development of doctrine, namely: (1) that new and deeper insights into the meanings and applications of doctrines can occur;[84] (2) that new terminology can emerge for the expression of doctrine; and (3) that, through its magisterium, the Church can define doctrines whose status as part of divine revelation and the Church's tradition is, in the absence of such definition, not explicitly evident.

Catechists teach as authentic doctrines only those truths which the magisterium teaches. When referring to speculative matters, they identify them as such.

d) Catechists situate catechesis within the community of believers.

The Church, the Body of Christ, is always the context for catechesis. The meaning and vitality of catechesis grow especially in the parish — the praying, believing, and serving community of faith. The parish gives spiritual, moral, and material support to regular, continuing catechesis.

e) Catechists pray for discernment of the Spirit.

In those with whom they come in contact catechists will encounter a variety of gifts suited to the service of the Church and the world. The First Epistle to the Corinthians (chapters 12 – 14) offers classic guidance for perceiving and evaluating the Spirit's gifts. Catechists pray for discernment, which will enable them to be open to the authentic call of the Spirit and to help others be open.[85]

f) Catechists emphasize God's living presence.

In order to speak convincingly of revelation and faith one must be alert to God's living presence. Christ is uniquely present in the Eucharist. He is also present in the other sacraments and in prayer, as well as in other people, in daily life, the signs of the times, and occasions of service: "I assure you, as often as you did it for one of my least brothers, you did it for me." (Matthew 25:40)

g) Catechists give guidance on private revelation.

Divine public revelation is the basis of Catholic faith. While some private manifestations (also called private revelations) can occur, claims of these are to be approached with caution. Catechesis stresses that alleged heavenly messages or miraculous events must be investigated and approved by the local bishop before being given any credence.

61. CONCLUSION

In speaking of God's self-revelation and of our grace-inspired response of faith, our consequent belief in the truth of what God has revealed, our assent to this truth and trusting surrender, this chapter has referred to the profound dialogue between God and humankind. Catechesis draws attention to this dialogue and seeks to shed light upon it. The next chapter considers the Church: the assembly of believers who respond to God's self-giving by forming and sustaining a community of faith, hope, and love.

CHAPTER IV
THE CHURCH AND CATECHESIS

62. INTRODUCTION

This chapter discusses the meaning of church. It provides catechetical principles and guidance concerning the Catholic Church's mission and concerning its relationship to other Christian churches and communities, the Jewish people, other major religions, and those who profess no religion.

PART A: MEANING OF CHURCH

63. MYSTERY OF DIVINE LOVE

"The Church is a mystery. It is a reality imbued with the hidden presence of God."[86] Born of the Father's love, Christ's redeeming act, and the outpouring of the Holy Spirit, it reflects the very mystery of God.

As a divine reality inserted into human history, the Church is a kind of sacrament. Its unique relationship with Christ makes it both sign and instrument of God's unfathomable union with humanity and of the unity of human beings among themselves. Part of the Church's mission is to lead people to a deeper understanding of human nature and destiny and to provide them with more profound experiences of God's presence in human affairs.

As a mystery, the Church cannot be totally understood or fully defined. Its nature and mission are best captured in scriptural parables and images, taken from ordinary life, which not only express truth about its nature but challenge the Church: for example, to become more a People of God, a better servant, more faithful and holy, more united around the teaching authority of the hierarchy.

64. PEOPLE OF GOD

The Church is also a human reality, a community of believers, the People of God. Jesus called men and women to become free from the slavery of sin, to pass through the saving waters of Baptism, to believe, worship, and witness to all He said and did. The first letter of Peter calls this new people "a chosen race, a royal priesthood, a holy nation, a people he claims for his own to proclaim the glorious works of the One who called you from darkness into his marvelous light." (1 Peter 2:9)

65. ONE BODY IN CHRIST

This new People of God is "one Body in Christ." (Romans 12:5) Through His death and resurrection the Son redeemed humankind, overcoming sin and division. (Cf. 2 Corinthians 5:15) Although glorified now at the right hand of the

Father, the Lord Jesus remains incarnate in the world through the Church, His body. Through the Spirit we are vivified and made one in Christ, the head of this body of which we are members.

The Church expresses and celebrates its identity above all in the Eucharist. St. Paul, who often[87] refers to the Church as the Body of Christ, brings together the meaning of the Eucharist and the Church in his first letter to the Corinthians: "Is not the cup of blessing we bless a sharing in the blood of Christ? And is not the bread we break a sharing in the body of Christ? Because the loaf of bread is one, we, many though we are, are one body, for we all partake of one loaf." (1 Corinthians 10:16f)

Christ unceasingly bestows the Spirit on the members of the Church, thus joining them with Himself in His continuing mission in and to the world. St. Paul pleads with the members of Christ's body to live in a manner worthy of their calling. (Cf. Ephesians 4:1) They are to grow to "form that perfect man who is Christ come to full stature." (Ephesians 4:13) They are to build the body which is the Church in love and unity. (Cf. Ephesians 4:16)

66. THE CHURCH AS SERVANT

Like Christ, who came into the world "not to be served by others but to serve" (Matthew 20:28), the Church seeks to minister to all peoples. It has a mission to heal and reconcile as its founder did. (Cf. 2 Corinthians 5:18f) It must perform the corporal and spiritual works of mercy, assisting the needy, whatever their condition. (Cf. Matthew 25:35–40) The good and faithful servant acts out of concern and love, not for personal gain or glory. (Cf. Luke 22:27) One way in which the Church fulfills its role as servant is its teaching ministry: in today's world one of its chief forms of service is its witness to a transcendent God, to unchanging truths, and to the gospel message.

67. THE CHURCH AS SIGN OF THE KINGDOM

The Church — that community of loving believers in the risen Lord — is called to be a sign of God's kingdom already in our midst. It is called to serve the kingdom and to advance it among all peoples of the world. In seeing the Church, people should have at least a glimpse of the kingdom, a glimpse of what it will be like to be united in love and glory with one another in Christ the Lord, king of heaven and earth.

To be a sign of the kingdom already here, the Church on every level — most immediately on the parish level — must be committed to justice, love, and peace, to grace and holiness, truth and life, for these are the hallmarks of the kingdom of God. (Cf. Roman Missal, Preface for the Feast of Christ the King)

68. THE PILGRIM CHURCH

The Church on earth represents the initial manifestation of the kingdom of God. Like pilgrims on a long, hard journey to a holy place, the Church's members have to bear the burden of their own sins, weakness, and frailty on the way to God's eternal city. Along the way they amend their sinful habits and resume their quest for union with God. The power of the risen Lord gives this pilgrim Church "strength to overcome patiently and lovingly the afflictions and hardships which assail her from within and without, and to show forth in the world the mystery of the Lord in a faithful though shadowed way, until at last it will be revealed in total splendor."[88]

As mystery, people, one body in Christ, servant, sign of the kingdom, and pilgrim, the Church is conceived as God's family, whose members are united to Christ and led by the Spirit in their journey to the Father. The Church merits our prayerful reflection and wholehearted response.

69. THE CHURCH AS A HIERARCHICAL SOCIETY

At the same time, as the Second Vatican Council teaches, the Church is also a visible society established by Christ with ordained ministers to serve its members.

The pope, Christ's vicar on earth, is the chief shepherd and supreme authority. Patriarchs[89] and other bishops join with the pope in service to the whole membership of the Church through the faithful performance of their Christ-given roles as teachers, sanctifiers, and rulers. The body of bishops united with the Roman pontiff, and never apart from him, has supreme and full authority over the universal Church.[90] Priests and deacons collaborate intimately with their bishops in the service of God's people.

The clergy serve the Church through authentic Christian teaching, sacramental ministry, and direction in various organizations and activities for God's kingdom. Of special importance for unity of faith are the Church's official teachings on matters of faith and morals authoritatively promulgated by the pope and bishops. These teachings give the faithful assurance of truth in their profession of faith and their adherence to moral standards and ideals.

70. THE CALL OF CHRISTIANS TO COMMUNITY

Under the impulse of the Spirit, the Church from its very beginning has been a community of believers. "Those who believed shared all things in common." (Acts 2:44)

"Community" involves a sharing of beliefs, experiences, ideals, and values. Christian community leads one to put aside selfish goals and private interest for the sake of a common good. It is based on the willingness of all community members, as good stewards, to accept responsibility, individually and corporately, for the way each lives, uses his or her time, talent, and treasure, and responds to the needs and rights of others. (Cf. Galatians 6:2)

The early Christians celebrated their identity as a worshiping community in word and sacrament. "They devoted themselves to the apostles' instruction and communal life, to the breaking of the bread and prayers." (Acts 2:42)

Now, as then, the Church is called to hear and proclaim Jesus' saving gospel. At worship the community again hears in faith Christ's living message and is reminded of how to live in obedience to His law of love. In the breaking of the bread, God's people experience the risen Christ: their hope of salvation is reaffirmed. With the great "Amen" of faith after the eucharistic prayer, the Church acknowledges Christ as the source of its communal identity and pledges to live out that grace by visible witness.

71. MISSIONARY NATURE OF THE CHURCH

Because the Church is "missionary by her very nature,"[91] all Christians, in obedience to the mandate of the Church's founder, are called to proclaim the gospel "to the whole of creation." (Matthew 16:15) They do this in various ways. Some — ordained ministers, professed religious, and lay persons — serve in foreign countries, among other cultures, or among the unchurched or non-practicing in the United States — wherever there are people to be evangelized. Others do so by their generosity and support of home and foreign missionary societies. All have an obligation to promote the growth of the kingdom by constant prayer and personal sacrifice.

72. MARKS OF THE CHURCH

Certain signs or marks identify this community of faith. In the Creed Christians confess their belief in the one, holy, catholic, and apostolic Church. These four marks simultaneously describe the Church and identify its mission. They are gifts bestowed upon the Church by the Lord — but gifts which the Church must also strive to realize ever more fully in its life.

a) One

At the Last Supper Jesus prayed for the Church's unity, "That all may be one, as you, Father are in me, and I in you." (John 17:21) How is this unity to be perceived?

First, in the celebration of the Eucharist, which is both a sign and a cause of unity. Second, in the affirmation by the Church's members that there is but "one Lord, one faith, one baptism, one God and Father of all" (Ephesians 4:5), which reminds us of the unity yet to be achieved among Christians and among all people. (Cf. Ephesians 4:13) Third, in explicit efforts by the members of the Church to become a community of deeper faith, hope, and love, where Christ's peace reigns. (Cf. Colossians 3:15) Finally, in the fact that, while the Holy Spirit is the Church's principle of unity, the pope, patriarchs, and bishops embody that principle in a special way. "The Roman Pontiff, as the successor of Peter, is the perpetual and visible source and foundation of the unity of the bishops and of the multitude of the faithful. The individual bishop . . . is the visible principle and foundation of unity in his particular church."[92]

b) Holy

Its union with Christ gives the Church a holiness which can never fail and empowers it to foster holiness in its members. This holiness, engendered by the Spirit, is expressed in the lives of Christians who strive to grow in charity and to help others do the same. (1 Corinthians 3:16f) The lives of saintly men and women, and the rich tradition of prayer and mysticism, remind us that holiness resides in the following of Christ. Pilgrim and sinful people that they are, the members of the Church nevertheless give visible evidence of God's holiness through acts of repentance and conversion, and through striving daily for holiness.

c) Catholic

Jesus commissioned the Church to carry the gospel to all nations. The catholicity or universality of the Church rests on the fact that the gospel message is capable of being integrated with all cultures. It corresponds to all that is authentically human. Potentially, therefore, according to the mind of its founder, the community of believers embraces an exceptionally broad range of authentic religious expressions and a membership as diverse as the human race.

But catholicity resides also in the fraternal diversity of the Churches within the Catholic communion—in the variety of rites and the multiplicity of local dioceses. Moreover it is manifested by the presence of this one, same society throughout the world.

d) Apostolic

This sign has both a historical and dynamic significance.

Historically, it means that the Church traces itself back to Christ and the apostles. "You form a building which rises on the foundation of the apostles and prophets, with Christ Jesus himself as the capstone." (Ephesians 2:20) As successors of the apostles, bishops "receive from Him the mission to teach all nations and to preach the gospel to every creature."[93]

Dynamically, the apostolic sign refers to continuing fidelity to Christ's loving and saving work and message, to ministry and service inspired by the evangelical vision and teaching of the original apostles.

73. THE CHURCH AND THE CHURCHES

God's Church is a community of baptized persons of all nations and cultures and also a communion of local Churches. St. Paul addressed and sent greetings to "the Church of God which is in Corinth" (1 Corinthians 1:2), "to the churches in Galatia" (Galatians 1:2), and to "the Church of the Thessalonians"(2 Thessalonians 1:1). These local Churches later became dioceses, as we understand that term today, each expressing the totality of the Catholic Church. In Europe these local Churches—dioceses—were organized under the bishop of Rome, the patriarch of the West, and followed in their liturgical practices what came to be known as the Latin Rite. In the East several patriarchates came into being, each with its distinct institutions, liturgical rites, and Christian way of life. Their presence in the United States is described in article 15.

The Second Vatican Council recognized this diversity as a positive reality. "That Church, Holy and Catholic, which is the Mystical Body of Christ, is made up of the faithful who are organically united in the Holy Spirit through the same faith, the same sacraments, and the same government and who, combining into various groups held together by a hierarchy, form separate Churches or rites. Between these, there flourishes such an admirable brotherhood that this variety within the Church in no way harms her unity, but rather manifests it. For it is the mind of the Catholic Church that each individual Church or rite retain its traditions whole and entire, while adjusting its way of life to the various needs of time and place."[94]

The Eastern and Western Churches in communion with the bishop of Rome as supreme head of the universal Church (cf. Matthew 16:17ff) perform a special ministry in making their unity visible in the world. At the same time, each particular Church has its own identity and traditions, which are to be respected. Each should govern itself according to its own proper procedures.[95]

The universal Church needs the witness which the particular Churches can give one another; for no one theology or liturgical tradition can exhaust the richness of Christ's message and His love. To carry out its mission to preach the gospel to all peoples, the Church must always strive more fully to understand and practice catholicity, that wholeness of the gospel message which characterizes the Church in its fullness. In fostering the expression of all the traditions which comprise the universal Church, it will be clear that the Church's unity is not based on a particular language, rite, spiritual tradition, or theological school, but upon the one cornerstone, Jesus Christ. (Cf. 1 Peter 2:4 – 8)

74. CATECHETICAL GUIDELINES

One of the principal tasks of catechesis is to witness to the Church as a sign and instrument of intimate union with God and the unity of humankind. The following guidelines, in addition to those suggested by the text, are relevant.

a) The Church's inner reality as mystery and its outward reality as a human community should both be emphasized.

b) Biblical images are selected which shed light on the Church's nature and mission.

c) Emphasis should be given to those common beliefs and experiences, especially the Eucharist, those ideals and values which are the basis of shared life and unity in the Catholic community.

d) People should be encouraged to reflect the marks of the Church in their lives by working for unity, striving to grow in holiness, participating in the missionary efforts of the Church, and increasing their understanding of and loyalty to the Church's apostolic nature.

e) Catechists, including clergy, religious, and especially parents, should encourage young men and women to consider missionary careers at home and abroad.

f) Emphasis should be placed on the need for fidelity to Christ's preaching and mission. (Cf. Mark 16:15f) The special role of the magisterium in guaranteeing the authentic teaching of the gospel should be explained. (Cf. Ephesians 2:20)

g) Catechists should foster understanding and unity among Catholics by accurately presenting the history and practices of each Church tradition in the context of the universal Church. The following principles are pertinent in this regard.

i) The Catholic Church is manifest and recognizable in the local Churches which express and celebrate the authentic faith.

ii) The communion of local Churches witnesses to the catholicity of the Church and to legitimate diversity in the profession of the one faith in Jesus Christ as Lord.

PART B: THE CHURCH IN DIALOGUE

75. OTHER CHRISTIAN CHURCHES

The Catholic Church perceives itself to have a special relationship with those Eastern Churches which are not in full communion within it. This relationship arises from the fact that these Eastern Churches possess "true sacraments, above all—by apostolic succession—the priesthood, and the Eucharist."[96] The "entire heritage of spirituality and liturgy, of discipline and theology, in their various traditions, belongs to the full Catholic and apostolic character of the Church."[97]

In a very positive way the Catholic Church also recognizes the separate churches and ecclesial communities in the West with which it has a special affinity and close relationship arising from the long span of earlier centuries when Christians lived in ecclesiastical communion.[98] Several among these have maintained Catholic traditions and institutions, and are in closer relationship to the Catholic Church.

In our times Christians have become more eager for the restoration of unity, in response to Jesus' prayer that His followers might be one. (Cf. John 17:20f) Many are striving to discern and obey God's will in this matter. The quest for unity has led the Catholic Church to engage in ecumenical dialogue with other Christian churches and has made it more aware of the common witness to the Lord already given to the world by Christians. The religious pluralism of the United States offers an important opportunity to advance ecumenism.

Catholics pray that Christ's Spirit will draw us to unity, so that all may worship Father, Son, and Holy Spirit with one voice and one heart. Urged by the divine call, catechesis has an important role in creating an environment for the growth of Christian unity.

76. CATECHETICAL GUIDELINES FOR ECUMENISM

While Christians are called to support and encourage ecumenism, catechesis should point out that human efforts alone cannot restore Christian unity. Catechesis can, however, foster ecumenism in a variety of ways: by clearly explaining Catholic doctrine in its entirety and working for the renewal of the Church and its members; by presenting information about other Christians honestly and accurately, avoiding words, judgments, and actions which misrepresent their beliefs and practices; by communicating the divine truths and values Catholics share with other Christians and promoting cooperation in projects for the common good. Ecumenical dialogue and common prayer, especially public and private petitions for unity, are to be encouraged. Catechetical textbooks should conform to the guidelines found here and in the *Directory for Ecumenism* according to the age and readiness of learners.[99] When circumstances seem to call for teaching religion to children and youth in an ecumenical setting, this should be done only with the knowledge and guidance of the local ordinary.

Catechesis should be especially sensitive in dealing with the Orthodox Churches which have so much in common with the Catholic tradition. Dialogue and collaboration should be as extensive and cordial as possible.[100] Members of the Eastern Churches in communion with Rome make a unique contribution to the ecumenical movement by remaining faithful to their Eastern heritage.

Catechesis should also be sensitive in dealing with the separated churches and ecclesial communities of the West, many of which share much in common with Catholic tradition. The numerous bilateral studies and proposed agreements should be suitably presented.

77. THE JEWISH PEOPLE

There are several reasons why Catholics in the United States should be especially sensitive to relationships with the Jewish people. First, Catholics and Jews share a common heritage—a heritage not only of biblical revelation rooted in faith in the one true God and the liberation of the exodus event, but also in the family origins of Jesus, Mary, and the apostles. Second, the members of the largest Jewish population in the world are our fellow citizens. Finally, the tragic, scandalous, centuries-long persecution of the Jewish people, including the terrible holocaust in Central Europe and active persecution up to this day, calls for the specific and direct repudiation of anti-Semitism in any form and for determination to resist anti-Semitism and its causes.

Christ's passion and death "cannot be blamed on all the Jews then living, without distinction, nor upon the Jews of today." The Church "deplores the hatred, persecutions, and displays of anti-Semitism directed against the Jews at any time and from any source."[101]

In seeking together to grow in appreciation of one another's heritages, Catholics and Jews should cooperate in scholarship, particularly in reference to sacred scripture, and in social action programs, and should promote a mutual understanding of the Christian and Jewish traditions as they address political, moral, and religious problems in the United States.[102]

78. THE MOSLEM PEOPLE

The Catholic Church esteems the people of Islam. Catholics share with Moslems certain beliefs; in God as creator of the human race and all-powerful maker of heaven and earth; in Abraham as a pre-eminent patriarch in the history of salvation; in Jesus Christ as God's prophet; in Mary as the virgin mother. Catholics and Moslems also share a deep reverence for the worship of God through prayer, fasting, and almsgiving.

Familiarity with the history of Islam, especially the centuries-old quarrels and hostilities between Christians and Moslems, is basic to mutual understanding. Collaboration in promoting spiritual and moral values in society, common to both Catholic and Moslem traditions, is an obligation for Catholics. The safeguarding and fostering of social justice, moral values, freedom, and world peace based on belief in God challenges both Catholics and Moslems.[103]

79. OTHER RELIGIONS

God's Word "gives light to every man." (John 1:9) Almost all religions strive to answer the restless searchings of the human heart through teachings, rules of life, and sacred ceremonies.[104]

Millions of people around the globe follow traditional religions, handed down from time immemorial, whose rites and mores generate among them a sense of solidarity. Students and teachers should learn about these religions in order to aid the Church's missionary endeavor, which seeks to reach these people and incorporate them into its worship, belief, and life for the sake of Christ Jesus while redeeming those elements of their religious and cultural traditions which can become part of ecclesial life.

The Catholic Church regards the positive and enriching aspects of these religions with honor and reverence. In particular it searches for common bonds with religions such as Hinduism and Buddhism.

This interest should spur catechists to:

1) Present an accurate account of the essential elements of traditional non-Christian religious beliefs, as perceived by their adherents in the light of their own religious experience.

2) Develop an appreciation of their insights and contributions to humanity.

3) Promote joint projects in the cause of justice and peace.

80. RELATIONSHIP TO THOSE WHO PROFESS NO RELIGION

There are many varieties and degrees of religious skepticism and disbelief. Some who profess no formal religion nevertheless believe in God and base their lives on this belief. Others, doubting God's existence, do not regard the question of whether He does or does not exist as important or relevant in their lives. Still others profess not to believe in God at all.

Whether they are believers or non-believers, however, all people are created in God's image and likeness and are, therefore, worthy of respect and esteem. The Catholic Church champions the dignity of the human vocation—a calling to union with God—and holds out lasting hope to those who do not expect to enjoy any destiny higher than earthly existence.

In supporting and working for human rights and freedom, the Church is confident that its message is in harmony with the most authentic and profound desires of the human heart. Further, it is the mission of the Church to evangelize so that all people may see Christ as both the perfect human being and "the image of the invisible God." (Colossians 1:15)

Catholics must strive to understand those who profess no faith and to collaborate with all persons of good will in promoting the human values common to all.[105]

Ecumenical activity with other Christians and with non-Christians aims at growth in mutual understanding. Catechesis must, however, present ecumenism in such a way as to guard against the danger of religious indifferentism. Indifferentism would be expressed, for instance, in the idea that it makes no difference whether one believes in Christ or not as long as one follows one's conscience and is sincere.

81. CONCLUSION

Arising from an outpouring of the Spirit, the Church is a divine mystery; but as People of God and pilgrim, it is also a human reality. These themes come together in the image of the Body of Christ, especially when the Church celebrates its identity in word and sacrament. The Church's communal beauty is seen in the visible signs of unity, holiness, catholicity, and apostolicity. Committed to service and to dialogue with all people of good will, the Church seeks to extend the fruits of Christ's saving death and joyful resurrection to each individual and all peoples.

This chapter has referred to the teaching authority of the hierarchy as an instrument of service for the preservation of the unity of Catholic belief. Next we turn to the more outstanding elements of this Catholic belief.

CHAPTER V
PRINCIPAL ELEMENTS OF THE CHRISTIAN MESSAGE FOR CATECHESIS

82. INTRODUCTION

Having spoken of the Church, we now consider the more outstanding elements of the message of salvation, which Christ commissioned the Catholic Church to proclaim and teach to all nations and peoples.[106]

Certain duplications with other sections of the NCD are necessary here in order to present in sequence the elements of the Christian message which catechesis highlights in relation to the one God; creation; Jesus Christ; the Holy Spirit; the Church; the sacraments; the life of grace; the moral life; Mary and the saints; and death, judgment, and eternity.

PART A: THE MYSTERY OF THE ONE GOD

83. THE MYSTERY OF THE TRINITY

The history of salvation is the story of God's entry into human affairs to save human beings from sin and bring them to Himself.

In the Old Testament God revealed Himself as the one, true, personal God, creator of heaven and earth (cf. Isaiah 42:5), who transcends this world. By words and actions God prepared for the ultimate disclosure of Himself as a Trinity: Father, Son, and Holy Spirit. (Cf. Matthew 3:16; 28:19; John 14:23, 26)

The mystery of the Holy Trinity was revealed in the person, words, and works of Jesus Christ. He revealed His Father as "our" Father and Himself as God's eternal and divine Son. He also made known a third divine person, the Holy Spirit, the lord and giver of life, whom the Father and He, as risen Lord, send to His Church. He calls His disciples to become God's children through the gift of the Spirit which He bestows on them. (Cf. John 1:12; Romans 8:15)

84. TRUE WORSHIP OF GOD IN THE MODERN WORLD

God is all-good, holy, just and merciful, infinitely wise and perfect. He has made firm commitments to human beings and bound them to Himself by solemn covenants. He has each individual always in view. He frees, saves, and loves His people with the love of a father and spouse. His goodness is the source of our eternal hope (cf. 1 Peter 1:3f) and should prompt us to worship Him.

God is worshiped in the sacred liturgy, in which people offer themselves to Him through Christ in and by the power of the Holy Spirit. People also worship God in individual and community prayer. Those who wish to love and obey God seek to carry out His will in their every activity and to use rightly and increase the talents He has given them. (Cf. Matthew 25:14ff) From His goodness He bestows on people the grace which they need to "profess the truth in love" (Ephesians 4:15) and to bring forth the fruits of love, justice, and peace, all to His glory.

Many people today pay little or no attention to God. Others are persuaded that God is distant, indifferent, or altogether absent. Because modern life tends to focus on the tangible rather than on the transcendent, it cannot be said to offer a climate favorable to faith. Yet desire for God, no matter how hidden and unconscious, is present in every human being.

PART B: CREATION

85. THE BEGINNING OF THE HISTORY OF SALVATION

The entire universe was created out of nothing. The Old Testament treats God's creative action as a sign of His power and love, proving that He is always with His people. (Cf. Isaiah 40:27f; 51:9–16) The creation of visible and invisible things, of the world and of angels, is the beginning of the mystery of salvation.[107] Our creation by God[108] is His first gift and call to us—a gift and call meant ultimately to lead to our final glorification in Christ. In Christ's resurrection from the dead, God's same all-powerful action stands out splendidly. (Cf. Ephesians 1:19f) The unity of soul and body which constitutes the human person is disrupted by death but will be restored to us by God in our resurrection.

The creation of the human person is the climax of God's creative activity in this world. Made in God's likeness, each person possesses a capacity for knowledge that is transcendent, love that is unselfish, and freedom for self-direction. Inherent in each unique human person called into existence by God, these qualities reflect the essential immortality of the human spirit.

Creation should be presented as directly related to the salvation accomplished by Jesus Christ. In reflecting on the doctrine of creation, one should be mindful not only of God's first action creating the heavens and the earth, but of His continuing activity in sustaining creation and working out human salvation.

Actively and lovingly present on behalf of human beings, throughout human history, God is present among us today and will remain present for all generations. Only at the end of the world, when there will be "new heavens and a new earth" (2 Peter 3:13), will His saving work come to final completion.

86. KNOWLEDGE OF GOD AND THE WITNESS OF CHRISTIAN LOVE

As scripture testifies, we can come to know God through the things He has made.[109] Reason, reflecting on created things, can come to a knowledge of God as the beginning and end of all that is.[110]

Yet unbelievers commonly need the help of other people to find God. To their plea—"Show us a sign"—Christ's followers today can respond as did the first generation Christians (cf. Acts 2:42–47): by the compelling witness of lives which manifest steadfast and mature faith in God, express personal love of Christ, and include works of justice and charity.[111]

Though our final goal is in eternity, faith in God and union with Christ entail an obligation to seek solutions for human problems here and now.

PART C: JESUS CHRIST

87. SON OF GOD, THE FIRSTBORN OF ALL CREATION, AND SAVIOR

In taking on human flesh through the ever-virgin Mary and entering human history, God's Son, Jesus Christ, renewed the world from within and became for it an abiding source of supernatural life and salvation from sin.

He is the firstborn of all creation. He is before all. All things hold together in Him; all have been created in Him, through Him, and for Him. (Cf. Colossians 1:15f)

Obedient unto death, even to death on a cross, He was exalted as Lord of all, and through His resurrection (cf. Philippians 2:5 – 11) was made known to us as God's Son in power. (Cf. Romans 1:4) He is the "firstborn of the dead" (Colossians 1:18); He gives eternal life to all. (Cf. 1 Colossians 15:22) In Him we are created new. (Cf. 2 Corinthians 5:17) Through Him all creatures are saved from the slavery of corruption. (Cf. Romans 8:20f) "There is no salvation in anyone else" (Acts 4:12) nor has there ever been.

88. JESUS, CENTER OF ALL GOD'S SAVING WORKS

In Jesus Christ the Christian is joined to all history and all human beings. The story of salvation, set in the midst of human history, is no less than the working out of God's plan for humankind: to form His people into the whole Christ, "that perfect man who is Christ come to full stature." (Ephesians 4:13)

Realizing this, Christians address themselves to their fundamental task: to the full extent of their abilities and opportunities, through the power of Jesus the savior (cf. 1 Corinthians 15:28), to bring creation to give the greatest possible glory to God.

89. TRUE GOD AND TRUE MAN IN THE UNITY OF THE DIVINE PERSON

Jesus Christ is truly divine, God's only-begotten Son (cf. John 1:18): "God from God, light from light, true God begotten not made, of one substance with the Father" (Nicene Creed).

Jesus is also truly human. As such, He thinks with a human mind, acts with a human will, loves with a human heart. He was made truly one of us, like us in all things except sin.[112] He accorded unparalleled respect and concern to the human person, reaching out to all—virtuous and sinners, poor and the rich, fellow-citizens and foreigners—and showing special solicitude for the suffering and rejected.

90. CHRIST, SAVIOR AND REDEEMER OF THE WORLD

God so loved sinners that He gave His Son to reconcile the world to Himself. (Cf. John 3:16f; 2 Corinthians 5:19) All people have been saved by the Son's obedience to His Father's will. (Cf. Romans 5:19)

In carrying out His earthly mission as the Messiah, Jesus fulfilled Old Testament prophecy and history. He preached the gospel of the kingdom of God and summoned people to interior conversion and faith. (Cf. Mark 1:15) He persisted in His ministry despite resistance, threats, and apparent failure.

Out of filial love for His Father (cf. John 14:31) and redemptive love for us, He gave Himself up to death (cf. Galatians 2:20; 1 John 3:16) and passed through death to the glory of the Father. (Cf. Philippians 2:9ff; Ephesians 1:20)

By His life, death, and resurrection He redeemed humankind from slavery to sin and the devil. Truly risen, the Lord is the unfailing source of life and of the outpouring of the Holy Spirit upon the human race.[113] He is the firstborn among many brothers and sisters (cf. Romans 8:29), and creates in Himself a new humanity.

91. CHRIST, OUR LIFE

Thus the meaning and destiny of human life are most fully revealed in Jesus Christ. He tells us that God, whom we are to love and serve above all else (cf. Deuteronomy 6:5; Matthew 22:37), loves us more than we can hope to understand, and offers us His love irrevocably. "Neither death nor life, neither angels nor principalities, neither the present nor the future, nor powers, neither height nor depth nor any other creature, will be able to separate us from the love of God that comes to us in Christ Jesus, our Lord." (Romans 8:38f) Jesus is the new covenant, the sacred and enduring bond, between God and humankind.[114]

"Whatever came to be in him, found life . . . any who did accept him he empowered to become children of God." (John 1:4, 12) Christ, in whom the divine and the human are most perfectly one, manifests in the world God's hidden plan to share His life with us, to pour out His own Spirit upon all flesh (cf. Acts 2:17), so that we who were formed in His image should be called, and be, His children (cf. 1 John 3:1; Galatians 4:5ff), addressing Him in truth as "our Father."

Christ also reveals the response we are to make to our calling and gives us the power to make it. This is the power of God's own Spirit. "All who are led by the Spirit of God are sons of God." (Romans 8:14) The indwelling Holy Spirit gives hope and courage, heals weakness of soul, and enables one to master passion and selfishness. The Spirit prompts people to seek what is good and helps them to advance in such virtues as charity, joy, peace, patience, kindness, forbearance, humility, fidelity, modesty, continence, and chastity. (Cf. Galatians 5:22f)

Christ teaches that love of God and love of neighbor spring from the same Spirit and are inseparable. (Cf. 1 John 4:12f, 20f) We are to love all human beings, even enemies, as we love ourselves;[115] even more, we are to obey Christ's new command to love all others as He has loved us. (Cf. John 13:34; 15:12f)

By this command Christ tells us something new — about God, about love, and about ourselves. His commandment to love is "new" not simply because of the scope and unselfishness of the love involved, but because it summons human beings to love with a divine love called charity, as the Father, Son, and Spirit do. This call carries with it the inner gift of their life and the power of their love, for Christ does not command what is impossible.

Christ's life is one of total obedience to the Father in the Spirit. His obedience entailed hunger and thirst and weariness, obscurity and rejection, suffering and death. By accepting the suffering which came to Him as He walked the way of loving obedience, Jesus did not deny His humanity but realized it perfectly. In giving His Son the glorious victory over death, the Father showed His pleasure with the Son's loving obedience. (Cf. Philippians 2:8–11)

St. Paul tells us to "put on the Lord Jesus Christ." (Romans 13:14) This means imitating Christ in our daily lives—loving, forgiving, healing, reconciling—living as He lived.

PART D: THE HOLY SPIRIT

92. THE HOLY SPIRIT IN THE CHURCH AND IN THE LIFE OF THE CHRISTIAN

The Holy Spirit continues Christ's work in the world. Christ promised the coming of the consoling Paraclete. (Cf. John 14:16; 15:26) He pledged that the Spirit of truth would be within us and remain with His Church. (Cf. John 14:17) And the Holy Spirit came at Pentecost (cf. Acts 2:1–4), never to depart. As Christ is present where a human being is in need (cf. Matthew 25:31–40), so the Spirit is at work where people answer God's invitation to believe in Him and to love Him and one another. While the Spirit animates the whole of creation and permeates the lives of human beings, He is present in a special way in the Church, the community of those who acknowledge Christ as Lord. Our lives are to be guided by the same Holy Spirit, the third person of the Trinity.

"The Lord Jesus so arranged the ministry of the apostles and so promised to send the Holy Spirit, that both they and the Spirit were to be associated in effecting the work of salvation always and everywhere. . . . He vivifies ecclesiastical institutions as a kind of soul and instills into the hearts of the faithful the same mission spirit which motivated Christ Himself."[116]

PART E: THE CHURCH

93. PEOPLE OF GOD

The Church, founded by Christ, had its origin in His death and resurrection. It is the new People of God, prepared for in the Old Testament and given life, growth, and direction by Christ in the Holy Spirit. It is the work of God's saving love in Christ.

In the Catholic Church are found the deposit of faith, the sacraments, and the ministries inherited from the apostles. Through these gifts of God, the Church is able to act and grow as a community in Christ, serving human beings and mediating to them His saving word and activity.

The Church shares in Christ's prophetic office.[117] Assembled by God's word, it accepts that word and witnesses to it in every quarter of the globe. So the Church is missionary by its very nature, and all its members share responsibility for responding to Christ's command to carry the good news to all humanity.[118]

The Church is also a priestly people.[119] (Cf. Revelation 1:6) All of its members share in Christ's priestly ministry. By regeneration and the anointing of the Holy Spirit, the baptized are consecrated as a priestly people. Though the ministerial or hierarchical priesthood differs, not only in degree, but in essence from the priesthood of the faithful, nevertheless, they are interrelated.[120] "At a lower level of the hierarchy are deacons, upon whom hands are imposed 'not unto the priesthood, but unto a ministry of service.'"[121]

By God's design the Church is a society with leaders—i.e., with a hierarchy. As such, it is a people guided by its bishops, who are in union with the pope, the bishop of Rome, the vicar of Christ. The pope has succeeded to the office of Peter, with its responsibility for care and guidance of the whole flock of Christ (cf. John 21:15ff), and is the head of the college of bishops. The community of faith owes respect and obedience to its bishops; while "exercising his office of father and pastor, a bishop should stand as one who serves."[122]

The pope and the bishops have the office of teaching, sanctifying, and governing the Church, and enjoy the gift of infallibility in guiding the Church when they exercise supreme teaching authority.[123]

The pope, in virtue of his office, enjoys infallibility when, as the supreme shepherd and teacher of all the faithful, he defines a doctrine of faith or morals. Therefore his definitions of themselves, and not from the consent of the Church, are correctly called irreformable. Even when he is not speaking *ex cathedra* his teachings in matters of faith and morals demand religious submission of will and of mind.[124]

"Bishops, teaching in communion with the Roman pontiff, are to be respected by all as witnesses to divine and Catholic truth. In matters of faith and morals, the bishops speak in the name of Christ and the faithful are to accept their teaching and adhere to it with a religious assent of soul."[125]

Priests and deacons share in a special way in the teaching role of their bishops. Within the local community they are called to be special signs of unity with the bishop and with the whole Church.

At the same time, "the body of the faithful as a whole, anointed as they are by the Holy One (cf. John 2:20, 27), cannot err in matters of belief. Thanks to a supernatural sense of the faith which characterizes the people as a whole, it manifests this unerring quality when, from the bishops to the entire laity, it shows universal agreement in matters of faith and morals."[126]

The Holy Spirit preserves the Church as Christ's body and bride, so that, despite the sinfulness of its members, it will never fail in faithfulness to Him and will meet Him in holiness at the end of the world. The Spirit also helps the Church constantly to purify and renew itself and its members, for whose sake the Church, guided by the Spirit, can update itself in those areas where change is permitted.

94. THE CHURCH AS COMMUNITY

The Church is a community of people assembled by God, whose members share the life of Christ. Within this assembly all enjoy a basic equality. All are called to holiness. All are united by close spiritual bonds. All share "one Lord, one faith, one baptism." (Ephesians 4:5)

In the Church every vocation is worthy of honor. Every gift is given for the good of all. All are called to build up the Body of Christ.[127] All share in the dignity of being Christian.

Throughout the history of the Church some of its members have devoted themselves to the service of God and the Christian community through commitment to an evangelical form of life based on vows of chastity, poverty, and obedience. Today such men and women serve the Church in a wide variety of ministries.

All members of the Church should seek to foster vocations to the religious life and secular institutes. The rich vision of Christian life lived out in chastity, poverty, and obedience is of benefit to all the faithful, who should offer prayers and encouragement for the growth of religious communities and secular institutes.

95. THE QUEST FOR UNITY

Christ willed the unity of all who believe in Him; thus the world would know that He was sent by the Father. (Cf. John 17:20f) Catholics should be deeply, personally concerned about the present sad divisions which separate Christians. It is essential that they pray and work for Christian unity, with full communion and organic unity as the goal. Catholics should take the first steps in ecumenical dialogue, while working also to make the Church more faithful to Christ and its apostolic heritage.[128]

Catholics are aware of the uniqueness of the Catholic Church which possesses the fullness of the ordinary means of salvation—a fullness in which they desire all people to share. At the same time, they also recognize that they can be enriched by the authentic insights of other religious traditions.[129]

Catholic life and education must also be concerned with a still wider unity: the unity of all persons under God. The Church rejects as un-Christian any discrimination because of race, national or ethnic origin, color, sex, class, or religion. God has given every human being intrinsic dignity, freedom, and eternal importance. "If anyone says, 'My love is fixed on God,' yet hates his brother, he is a liar. One who has no love for the brother he has seen cannot love the God he has not seen." (1 John 4:20)

96. THE CHURCH AS INSTITUTION FOR SALVATION

The Church is a structured institution whose Christ-given mission is to bring the message of salvation to all people.[130] (Cf. Matthew 28:16–20) Though it is not of the world and can never conform itself to the world, the Church does engage in dialogue with the world and strives to be seen by it as faithful to the gospel. Christians should therefore seek "to serve the men and women of the modern world ever more generously," aware that in committing themselves to the pursuit of justice they "have shouldered a gigantic task demanding fulfillment in this world," but one concerning which they "must give a reckoning to Him who will judge every man on the last day."[131]

Yet the Church is "inspired by no earthly ambition."[132] It will be perfect only in heaven, and it is heaven, toward which God's people are journeying, that the Church has always in view.

PART F: THE SACRAMENTS

97. ACTIONS OF CHRIST IN THE CHURCH (THE UNIVERSAL SACRAMENT)

Christ's saving work is continued in the Church through the power of the Holy Spirit.

The Church has been entrusted with special means for this purpose: the sacraments which Christ instituted. They are outward signs of God's grace and humankind's faith. They effectively show God's intention to sanctify us and our willingness to grow in sanctity. In this way they bring us God's grace.[133]

The Church itself is in Christ like a sacrament, or sign and instrument of intimate union with God, and of the unity of the whole human race.[134]

It is principally through these actions—His actions—called sacraments that Christ becomes present to His people, conferring His Spirit on them and making them holy by drawing them into union with Himself. Though entrusted to the Church, the sacraments are always to be thought of as actions of Christ, from whom they receive their power. It is Christ who baptizes, Christ who offers Himself in the sacrifice of the Mass, Christ who forgives sins in the Sacrament of Reconciliation.

The purpose of the sacraments is to sanctify humankind, build up the Body of Christ, and give worship to God. As signs, they also instruct: the very act of celebrating them disposes people more effectively to receive and grow in the life of grace, to worship God, and to practice charity. It is therefore of capital importance that people be thoroughly familiar with the sacramental signs and turn often to them for nourishment in the Christian life.[135] The sacraments are treated in detail in Chapter VI, Parts A and B.

PART G: THE LIFE OF GRACE

98. SIN AND GRACE

Sin is the greatest obstacle human beings face in their efforts to love God and their brothers and sisters and work out their salvation.

Original sin is the first obstacle. Made by God in the state of holiness, human beings from the dawn of history abused their liberty at the devil's urging. They set themselves against God and sought fulfillment apart from Him.[136] "Through one man sin entered the world and with sin death, death thus coming to all men inasmuch as all sinned." (Romans 5:12) Every human being is "born in sin" in the sense that "it is human nature . . . fallen, stripped of the grace that clothed it, injured in its own natural powers and subjected to the dominion of death, that is transmitted to all."[137]

In addition to the effects of original sin, there is personal sin, committed by the individual. Such sin is different from unavoidable failure or limitation. It is willful rejection, either partial or total, of one's role as a child of God and a member of His people. By it sinners knowingly and deliberately disobey God's command to love Him, other people, and themselves in a morally right way. They turn aside or even away from their lifetime goal of doing God's will. This they do either by sins of commission or sins of omission — i.e., not doing what one is morally obliged to do in a particular circumstance. (Classic illustrations are found in the story of the good Samaritan: cf. Luke 10:25–37 and Matthew 25:41–46.)

Personal sin resides essentially in interior rejection of God's commands of love, but this rejection is commonly expressed in exterior acts contrary to God's law. A grave offense (mortal sin) radically disrupts the sinner's relationship with the Father and places him or her in danger of everlasting loss.[138] Even lesser offenses (venial sins) impair this relationship and can pave the way for the commission of grave sins.

Sin and its effects are visible everywhere: in exploitative relationships, loveless families, unjust social structures and policies, crimes by and against individuals and against creation, the oppression of the weak and the manipulation of the vulnerable, explosive tensions among nations and among ideological, racial and religious groups, and social classes, the scandalous gulf between those who waste goods and resources, and those who live and die amid deprivation and underdevelopment, wars and preparations for war. Sin is a reality in the world.

"But despite the increase of sin, grace has far surpassed it." (Romans 5:20) Grace is God's generous and free gift to His people. It is union with God, a sharing in His life, the state of having been forgiven one's sins, of being adopted as God's own child and sustained by God's unfailing love. Grace is possible for us because of Christ's redemptive sacrifice.

God remained faithful to His love for us, sending His own Son "in the likeness of sinful flesh" (Romans 8:3) into the midst of this sinful world. Because of sin human beings are helpless if left to themselves, unable even to do the good they know and truly wish to do. (Cf. Romans 7:14f) But God has saved us from sin through Jesus. So that by His obedience many might be made righteous (cf. Romans 5:19), He was faithful unto death. This was His final, irrevocable act of absolute self-giving in love to God and to human beings.

Christ's offer of grace, love, and life is valid forever. Transcending space and time, He is present to all and offers to each person the life that is His. Christ ardently desires that all receive His gift and share His life. It is freely offered, there for the taking, unless in their freedom people reject His call and choose not to be united with Him.

The sacraments are important means for bringing about the Christian's union with God in grace. They are sources of grace for individuals and communities, as well as remedies for sin and its effects.

We who have been baptized in Christ are to consider ourselves "dead to sin but alive for God in Christ Jesus." (Romans 6:11) "Since we live by the Spirit, let us follow the Spirit's lead." (Galatians 5:25)

Even so, achieving the final triumph over sin is a lifelong task. Christ's call to conversion is ever timely, for sin remains in the world and its power is strong in human beings. "My inner self agrees with the law of God, but I see in my body's members another law at war with the law of my mind; this makes me the prisoner of the law of sin in my members." (Romans 7:22f)

Disciples of Jesus who accept Him as their way and desire to love God and one another as they have been loved must acknowledge their sinfulness and undergo conversion: "a profound change of the whole person by which one begins to consider, judge, and arrange his life according to the holiness and love of God."[139] In a special way Christians engage in a continuing process of conversion through the Sacrament of Penance, in which sins are forgiven and we are reconciled with God and with the community of faith. Christ's followers are to live the paschal mystery proclaimed at Mass: "Dying, you destroyed our death, rising you restored our life."[140] Central to Christ's life and mission, this paschal mystery must have an equally central place in the life and mission of one who aspires to be Christ's disciple.

Living in His spirit, therefore, Christians are to deny themselves, take up the cross each day, and follow in His steps. (Cf. Luke 9:23f) Christ's atoning sacrifice is "the vital principle in which the Christian lives, and without which Christianity is not."[141] As brothers and sisters of Jesus who are also His followers and members of His body, Christians must accept suffering and death as He did, and in so accepting them share His life. "If we have been united with Him through likeness to His death," so also "through a like resurrection" we shall be raised from the dead by the glory of the Father. (Romans 6:4f) By union with Christ one has already begun to share the risen life here on earth. (Cf. 2 Peter 1:4)

100. FULFILLMENT IN AND THROUGH CHRIST

All people seek happiness: life, peace, joy, wholeness and wholesomeness of being. The happiness human beings seek and for which they are fashioned is given in Jesus, God's supreme gift of love. He comes in the Father's name to bring the fulfillment promised to the Hebrew people and, through them, to all people everywhere. He is Himself our happiness and peace, our joy and beatitude.

Of old the divine pattern for human existence was set forth in the decalogue. In the new covenant Jesus said: "He who obeys the commandments he has from me is the man who loves me; and he who loves me will be loved by my Father." (John 14:21; cf. 15:14) In the beatitudes (Matthew 5:3–12; Luke 6:20–23), Jesus, our brother, promises us the dignity of life as God's sons and daughters, the eternal enjoyment of a destiny which, now glimpsed imperfectly, has yet to appear in its glorious fullness. Through these beatitudes Jesus also teaches values to be cherished and qualities to be cultivated by those who wish to follow Him.

Living according to these values by the grace of Christ, one even now possesses the promised fulfillment in some measure. As God's reign takes root within us we become "gentle and humble of heart" like Jesus (Matthew 11:29) through deeds done in holiness, and thus "a kingdom of justice, love, and peace"[142] is furthered in this world.

PART H: THE MORAL LIFE

101. HUMAN AND CHRISTIAN FREEDOM

God reveals to us in Jesus who we are and how we are to live. It is His plan that we freely respond, making concrete in the particular circumstances of our lives what the call to holiness and the commandment of love require of us. This is not easy. Nor may our decisions be arbitrary, for "good" and "bad," "right" and "wrong" are not simply whatever we choose to make them. On the contrary, there are moral values and norms which are absolute and never to be disregarded or violated by anyone in any situation. Fidelity to moral values and norms of this kind can require the heroism seen in the lives of the saints and the deaths of martyrs. This heroism is the result of Christ's redemptive love, accepted and shared.

Psychological difficulties or external conditions can diminish the exercise of freedom slightly, considerably, or almost to the vanishing point. Therefore conditions favorable to the exercise of genuine human freedom must be promoted, not only for the sake of our temporal welfare but also for the sake of considerations bearing upon grace and eternal salvation.

102. GUIDANCE OF THE NATURAL MORAL LAW

God's guidance for the making of moral decisions is given us in manifold forms. The human heart is alive with desire for created goods, and behind this desire is longing for God. "Athirst is my soul for God, the living God." (Psalm 42:3) Desire for created goods and longing for the uncreated good are not in contradiction, since Christ came to perfect human nature, not to destroy it. He is the goal to whom all creatures tend, for whom all creatures long, in whom all hold together. (Cf. Colossians 1:15–20) Everything good and worthwhile in the adventure of a human life is such because it shows forth in some way the glory of God and points back to Him. Though all other goods draw people in part to their perfection as individuals, members of human communities, and stewards of the world, union with God is the supreme and only perfect fulfillment. Created goods and loves are His gifts, and they tell us of their giver and His will for humanity. Those who follow Christ will value all that is truly human and be reminded by it of His call.

Human beings rejoice in friends, in being alive, in being treated as persons rather than things, in knowing the truth. In doing so they are rejoicing in being themselves—images of God called to be His children. Truth and life, love and peace, justice and friendship go into what it means to be human. True morality, then, is not something imposed from without; rather it is the way people accept their humanity as restored to them in Christ.

In giving these material and spiritual goods and the desire for them, God wills that human beings be open to them and eager to foster them in themselves and others. All these goods form a starting point for reflecting upon the meaning and purpose of life. In the life of every person are reflected many elements of the "divine law — eternal, objective and universal — whereby God orders, directs, and governs the entire universe and all the ways of the human community."[143] All these goods together bear witness to the existence of what is often called the natural moral law. No disciple of Christ will neglect these goods. One is not possessed of His Spirit if one tosses them aside with contempt, spurning the loving gifts of the Father, grasps at them selfishly and denies them to others, or acts as if they, not their giver, were the ultimate end and meaning of life.[144]

103. CONSCIENCE AND PERSONAL RESPONSIBILITY

Even when people have become conscious of these fundamental goods and have cultivated an attitude of cherishing them in themselves and others, more remains to be done. It is still necessary to decide how to realize and affirm them in concrete circumstances. Such decisions are called judgments of conscience. In the final analysis, they take place in the "most secret core and sanctuary" of the person, where one "is alone with God."[145]

We live in good faith if we act in accord with conscience. Nevertheless moral decisions still require much effort. Decisions of conscience must be based upon prayer, study, consultation, and an understanding of the teachings of the Church. One must have a rightly formed conscience and follow it. But one's judgments are human and can be mistaken; one may be blinded by the power of sin or misled by the strength of desire. "Beloved, do not trust every spirit, but put the spirits to a test to see if they belong to God." (1 John 4:1; cf. 1 Corinthians 12:10)

Clearly, then, it is necessary to do everything possible to see to it that judgments of conscience are informed and in accord with the moral order of which God is creator. Common sense requires that conscientious people be open and humble, ready to learn from the experience and insight of others, willing to acknowledge prejudices and even change their judgments in light of better instruction. Above and beyond this, followers of Jesus will have a realistic approach to conscience which leads them to accept what He taught and judge things as He judges them.

104. GUIDANCE OF THE CHURCH

Where are we to look for the teachings of Jesus, hear His voice, and discern His will?

In scripture, whose books were written under the inspiration of the Holy Spirit. In prayer, where people grow in knowledge and love of Christ and in commitment to His service. In the events of human life and history, where Christ and His Spirit are at work. In the Church, where all these things converge. This is why the Second Vatican Council said: "In the formation of their consciences, the Christian faithful ought carefully to attend to the sacred and certain doctrine of the Church."[146]

There are many instruments and agents of teaching in the Church. All have roles in drawing out the richness of Christ's message and proclaiming it, each according to his or her gift.

The pope and the bishops in communion with him have been anointed by the Holy Spirit to be the official and authentic teachers of Christian life. For Jesus "established His holy Church by sending forth the apostles as He Himself had been sent by the Father. (Cf. John 20:21) He willed that their successors, namely the bishops, should be shepherds in His Church even to the consummation of the world."[147] It is their office and duty to express Christ's teaching on moral questions and matters of belief. This special teaching office within the Catholic Church is a gift of the Lord Jesus for the benefit of all His followers in their efforts to know what He teaches, value as He values, and live as free, responsible, loving, and holy persons. (Cf. Luke 10:16) The authoritative moral teachings of the Church enlighten personal conscience and are to be regarded as certain and binding norms of morality.

Following Christ's teaching and example in the family of the Church, people become more like Him and more perfect as the Father's children. Christ brings the life of the Father and fills His followers' lives with His Spirit. In face of the challenges encountered in living the Christian life the best answer is this: "In him who is the source of my strength, I have strength for everything." (Philippians 4:13)

105. SPECIFICS IN THE TEACHING OF MORALITY

The obligations which flow from love of God and human beings should be taught in a specific practical way. The Church has a duty to apply moral principles to current problems, personal and social. Catechesis should therefore include the Christian response not only to perennial challenges and temptations but to those which are typically contemporary.

The specifics of morality should be taught in light of the Ten Commandments (cf. Appendix A), the Sermon on the Mount, especially the beatitudes, and Christ's discourse at the Last Supper. Whatever approach is used, students should know the decalogue as part of their religious heritage. Among the matters to be treated are the spiritual and corporal works of mercy, the theological and moral virtues, the seven capital sins, and traditional formulations concerning the Christian moral life which express the wisdom, drawn from experience and reflection, of those who have gone before us in the faith. Catechesis in Christian living should also include instruction in the laws of the Church, among which should be included what are called the "Precepts of the Church." (Cf. Appendix B) The Bible and the lives of the saints provide concrete examples of moral living.

What follows is by no means intended to cover all areas and issues of morality. The purpose is simply to indicate the practical approach which catechesis should take.

a) Duties toward God

Toward God, a Christian has a lifelong obligation of love and service. Christ is the model, and His life was, above all, a life of total obedience to the Father. For us, too, God's will must be first in our scale of personal values.

One's attitude toward God should be that of a son or daughter toward an all-good, all-loving Father—never judging and acting as if one were independent of Him, gladly making Him the object of worship and prayer, both liturgical and private.

For the follower of Christ the first day of every week, commemorating the resurrection, is a special day, the Lord's day. Catechesis on the resurrection calls attention to the special significance of Sunday. Each Sunday should be kept as a day for special personal renewal, free from work and everyday business. It is both a privilege and a serious duty of the individual Catholic, as well as the Catholic faith community, to assemble on Sunday in order to recall the Lord Jesus and His acts, hear the word of God, and offer the sacrifice of His body and blood in the eucharistic celebration. This is, in fact, a precept of the Church following the commandment of God.

No one and nothing should occupy God's place in one's life. Otherwise one's attitude and behavior are idolatrous. (Superstition, witchcraft, and occultism are specific examples of idolatry, while such things as excessive love of money and material possessions, pride, and arrogance can be called "idolatrous" in the sense that they, too, reflect the attitude of one who gives to something else the place in his or her life which should be reserved for God.) People who seek to honor God will not blaspheme or commit perjury. They will show respect for persons, places, and things related to God. Clearly, obligations to God rule out atheism, heresy, and schism.

b) Duties toward other people

Toward other people, the Christian has specific obligations in justice and in charity. Every human being is of priceless value: made in God's image, redeemed by Christ, and called to an eternal destiny. That is why we are to recognize all human beings as our neighbors and love them with the love of Christ. We must be concerned both for the spiritual condition of others and for their temporal condition. Our concern will therefore extend to their authentic freedom, their spiritual and moral well-being, their intellectual and cultural welfare, their material and physical needs (e.g., housing, food, health, employment, etc.). Such concern will be expressed in action, including efforts to build a cultural, social, and political order based on peace and justice—locally, nationally, and internationally.

A Christian's manner of judging and speaking about others should reflect the justice and charity due persons whom God has created and made His adopted children. He or she will respect and obey all lawfully exercised authority in the home, in civil society, and in the Church. A Christian will practice good manners and courtesy which, though not necessarily signs of moral goodness, are appropriate expressions of respect for others and tend to create an environment in which it is easier to be morally good.

There are many ways of sinning against one's neighbors. One can do so by being selfishly apathetic toward their real needs or by actively violating their rights: for example, by stealing, deliberately damaging their good names or property, cheating, not paying debts.

Respect for life, and for what is associated with life's transmission and preservation, enjoys a special priority in the Christian scale of moral values. Clearly Christians cannot be anti-life, cannot commit or condone the sins of murder, abortion, euthanasia, genocide, and indiscriminate acts of war. They also have a duty to work to bring about conditions in which such anti-life acts are less likely, as, for example, by supporting the responsible efforts to achieve arms control and disarmament. In view of the present tragic reality of legalized abortion practiced on a massive scale in our country, followers of Christ are obliged not only to be personally opposed to abortion, but to seek to remove circumstances which influence some to turn to abortion as a solution to their problems, and also to work for the restoration of a climate of opinion and a legal order which respect the value of unborn human life. The Church proclaims the value of the life-giving meaning of marital intercourse. It rejects the ideology of artificial contraception. The Church forbids methods of family limitation directed against the life-giving meaning of sexual intercourse. It condemns the view that sterilization and artificial contraception are morally legitimate means of family limitation.[148]

One who seeks to follow Christ does not adopt the values and practices of a sexually permissive society. The Christian tradition holds the sexual union between husband and wife in high honor, regarding it as a special expression of their convenanted love which mirrors God's love for His people and Christ's love for the Church. But like many things human, the use of sex can be either creative or destructive. Sexual intercourse is a moral and human good only within marriage; outside marriage it is wrong. For a Christian, therefore, premarital sex, extramarital sex, adultery, homosexual behavior, or other acts of impurity or scandal to others are forbidden. A Christian practices the virtue of chastity by cultivating modesty in behavior, dress, and speech, resisting lustful desires and temptations, rejecting masturbation, avoiding pornography and indecent entertainment of every kind, and encouraging responsible social and legal policies which accord respect to human sexuality.[149]

Obligations toward neighbor also embrace many contemporary issues in the field of social justice.

c) Duties toward self

Toward self, too, the follower of Christ has moral duties. He or she must be another Christ in the world, a living example of Christian goodness. Among the characteristics of such a person are humility and patience in the face of one's own imperfections, as well as those of others; Christ-like simplicity with respect to material things and the affluence typical of our society; and purity of word and action even in the midst of corruption.

It is critically important to guard against the capital sin of pride, which manifests itself in many ways. The same is true of sloth — spiritual, intellectual, and physical. Christians may not envy others their success, their innate or acquired qualities, their wealth or material possessions. Nor may they violate the requirements of self-control and abuse bodily health by intemperate use of drugs, alcohol, tobacco, or food.

Catechesis seeks to help people form right consciences, choose what is morally right, avoid sin and its occasions, and live in this world according to the Spirit of Christ, in love of God and neighbor. To do this requires self-discipline and self-sacrifice. It is not easy, but, in the strength which comes from the gifts of Christ and His Spirit, it is possible for sincere followers of Christ.

PART I: MARY AND THE SAINTS

106. MARY, MOTHER OF GOD, MOTHER AND MODEL OF THE CHURCH

The Gospel of Luke gives us Mary's words: "My spirit finds joy in God my savior, for he has looked upon his servant in her lowliness; all ages to come shall call me blessed." (Luke 1:47f) The "ever-virgin mother of Jesus Christ our Lord and God"[150] occupies a place in the Church second only to that of Christ. Mary is close to us as our spiritual mother.

Singularly blessed, Mary speaks significantly to our lives and needs in the sinlessness of her total love. Following venerable Christian tradition continued in the Second Vatican Council, the Church recognizes her as loving mother,[151] its "model and excellent exemplar in faith and charity."[152]

The special gifts bestowed on her by God include her vocation as mother of God, her immaculate conception (her preservation from original sin), and her entry into Christ's resurrection in being assumed body and soul to heaven. The special love and veneration due her as mother of Christ, mother of the Church, and our spiritual mother should be taught by word and example.[153]

107. OTHER SAINTS

The Church also honors the other saints who are already with the Lord in heaven. We who come after them draw inspiration from their heroic example, look for fellowship in their communion, and in prayer seek their intercession with God on our behalf.[154] Associated with the Communion of Saints, the traditional value of indulgences may be explained.

PART J: DEATH, JUDGMENT, ETERNITY

108. DEATH

Christians have a duty to pray for deceased relatives, friends, and all the faithful departed. They also reverence the bodies of those who have preceded them in death. The renewed funeral liturgy sets the tone for catechesis concerning death: we live, die and shall live again in the risen Christ; we look forward to a homecoming with God our loving Father. (Cf. Luke 15)

109. JUDGMENT

Each individual has an awesome responsibility for his or her eternal destiny. The importance of the individual judgment after death, of the refining and purifying passage through purgatory, of the dreadful possibility of the eternal death which is hell, of the last judgment — all should be understood in light of Christian hope.

At the last judgment all people will fully reach their eternal destiny. The lives of all are to be revealed before the tribunal of Christ so that "each one may receive his recompense, good or bad, according to his life in the body." (2 Corinthians 5:10) Then "the evildoers shall rise to be damned," and "those who have done right shall rise to live" (John 5:29): a life eternally with God beyond what the human heart can imagine, a life of eternal enjoyment of the good things God has prepared for those who love Him.[155]

110. FINAL UNION WITH GOD

During their earthly lives Christians look forward to final union with God in heaven. They long for Christ's coming. "He will give a new form to this lowly body of ours and remake it according to the pattern of his glorified body." (Philippians 3:21; cf. also 1 Corinthians 15)

The final realities will come about only when Christ returns with power to bring history to its appointed end. Then, as judge of the living and the dead, He will hand over His people to the Father. Only then will the Church reach perfection. Until that comes to pass, "some of His disciples are exiles on earth. Some have finished with this life and are being purified. Others are in glory, beholding clearly God Himself triune and one, as He is."[156]

Consoling hope, as well as salutary fear, should color one's attitude toward death, judgment, and eternity. (Cf. 1 Thessalonians 4:13f) The Lord's resurrection signals the conquest of death, thus we have reason to live and face death with courage and joy.

111. CONCLUSION

This chapter has set forth the more outstanding elements of belief which the Church has received, serves, and teaches. Next we shall consider the liturgical expression of this same faith.

CHAPTER VI
CATECHESIS FOR A WORSHIPING COMMUNITY
PART A: LITURGY AND CATECHESIS

112. INTRODUCTION

The Church is a worshiping community. In worship it praises God for His goodness and glory. It also acknowledges its total dependence on God, the Father, and accepts the gift of divine life which He wishes to share with us in the Son, through the outpouring of the Spirit. Worship creates, expresses, and fulfills the Church. It is the action in and by which men and women are drawn into the mystery of the glorified Christ.

Faith and worship are intimately related. Faith brings the community together to worship; and in worship faith is renewed. The Church celebrates Christ's life, death, resurrection in its liturgy; it proclaims its faith in His presence in the Church, in His word, in the sacramental celebrations; it gives praise and thanks, asks for the things it needs, and strengthens itself to carry out its commission to give witness and service.

Different ecclesial and liturgical traditions within the Catholic Church have different ways of celebrating faith in worship. While this chapter is concerned mainly with the liturgy of the Western Church, an attempt has also been made to introduce certain perspectives of the Eastern Churches.

113. THE RELATIONSHIP OF LITURGY AND CATECHESIS

There is a close relationship between catechesis and liturgy. Both are rooted in the Church's faith, and both strengthen faith and summon Christians to conversion, although they do so in different ways. In the liturgy the Church is at prayer, offering adoration, praise, and thanksgiving to God, and seeking and celebrating reconciliation: here one finds both an expression of faith and a means for deepening it. As for catechesis, it prepares people for full and active participation in liturgy (by helping them understand its nature, rituals, and symbols) and at the same time flows from liturgy, inasmuch as, reflecting upon the community's experiences of worship, it seeks to relate them to daily life and to growth in faith.

PART B: SACRAMENTS/MYSTERIES

114. THE SACRAMENTS/MYSTERIES AS SYMBOL

"The mystery of Christ is continued in the Church . . . in a specific way through the signs that Christ instituted, which signify the gift of grace and produce it, and are properly called sacraments."[157]

The Word of God is the full manifestation of the Father; thus He may be called a symbol, an icon, an image of the Father. Created through the Word, the world is in its very reality a symbol of its creator.

Because they have been created by His Word and in His image, human beings have the greatest capacity for symbolizing God. Jesus Christ, the Word incarnate, was the perfect symbol or sacrament of God on earth. The community of faith, which strives to follow Christ's example and live by His teachings, is the symbol or sacrament of His continued presence among us.

The sacraments, symbolic actions which effect what they symbolize, celebrate the coming of the Spirit at special moments in the life of the community of faith and its members, and express the Church's faith and interaction with Christ. The Church celebrates the mysteries of God's presence through word, bread, wine, water, oil, and the actions of the ordained ministers and the people.

The Eastern Churches call the sacraments "mysteries." The mysteries of Baptism, Chrismation (which the Western Church calls Confirmation), the Eucharist, and the other sacraments are understood as bringing the recipients into an experience of the holy. The Eastern Fathers draw an analogy between the presence of the Father in creation, the Son in the word (that is, revelation), and the Spirit in the waters of Baptism, the oil of chrism, and the Eucharist, as well as in the recipients of these mysteries. Creation viewed as a symbol, the humanity of Christ, and the tangible mysteries or sacraments—all reveal the reality of God.

Christians attribute all God's divinizing action to the Holy Spirit, God's power dwelling in creation. For example, the gesture of imposing hands in Holy Orders and the Rite of Reconciliation is meant to express the invoking of the Spirit. For this reason, too, the Eastern Churches especially highlight the calling down of the Holy Spirit (Epiklesis) in the celebration of the eucharistic liturgy.

Section I: Sacraments—Mysteries of Initiation

115. INTRODUCTION

Christian initiation is celebrated in Baptism, Confirmation or Chrismation, and Eucharist. Through these visible actions a person is incorporated into the Church and shares its mission in the world. Baptism and Confirmation (Chrismation) enable recipients, through sharing in Christ's priestly office, to be intimately associated in the offering of the sacrifice of the Eucharist.

Full initiation into the Church occurs by stages. The *Rite of Christian Initiation of Adults* (Roman) provides a norm for catechetical as well as liturgical practice in this regard. The intimate relationship of the sacraments of Baptism, Confirmation, and Eucharist should be emphasized in the catechesis of both adults and children. Such catechesis will involve many members of the parish community who support and pray with the catechized, besides instructing them so that they may grow in understanding of the Christian message.

116. BAPTISM

Baptism cleanses people from original sin and from all personal sins, gives them rebirth as children of God, incorporates them into the Church, sanctifies them with the gifts of the Holy Spirit, and, impressing on their souls an indelible character, initiates them in Christ's priestly, prophetic, and kingly roles.[158] Furthermore, the Church has always taught that Baptism is necessary for salvation.[159]

By accepting Baptism into Christ's death and resurrection, people affirm their faith and are initiated and welcomed into the community of faith. Dedicated to and enlightened by the Spirit, made sons and daughters of God with a permanent relationship in Christ, and cleansed from sin through water and the Holy Spirit, they become a new creation.

In response to their call to share in Christ's priesthood, the baptized are to minister both to the community of faith and to the whole world. Single life, married life, the life of the evangelical counsels, and the ordained ministry are all suitable contexts for such service.

117. CATECHESIS FOR BAPTISM

Catechesis for Baptism is directed primarily to adults—adult candidates for Baptism and the parents and godparents of infants who are to be baptized. According to the *Rite of Christian Initiation of Adults*, catechumens proceed through the stages of evangelization, catechumenate, purification and enlightenment, and post-baptismal catechesis.[160] This process also provides helpful guidelines for the catechesis of parents and godparents. Authentic understanding of the significance of Baptism naturally leads to continuing catechesis.

Baptismal catechesis involves the community of the faithful, who share their faith with those being catechized. Adult catechumens and the parents of children to be baptized alike need the community's prayers, witness, and support. Pre- and post-baptismal catechesis may take many forms, such as prayer, fasting, service, and instruction.

Baptismal catechesis centers on the Father's love; the life, death, and resurrection of Jesus the Son; the cleansing of original and personal sin; and the gift of the Spirit to the Church. It includes proclaiming God's word, so that those called may respond in faith.

Immediate preparation includes catechesis concerning the baptismal ritual and symbols: i.e., water as life-giving and cleansing, oil as strengthening and healing, light as driving out darkness, the community as the setting in which Christ is present.

Preparation for the Baptism of infants[161] is a "teachable" moment, when the parish community can encourage parents to reexamine the meaning which faith has in their lives. In offering catechesis to parents and sponsors, the Church shows its love for and eagerness to support them as well as their children.

Children should not be deprived of Baptism. "An infant should be baptized within the first weeks after birth. If the child is in danger of death, it is to be baptized without delay."[162]

118. CONFIRMATION/CHRISMATION

As a Sacrament of Initiation, Confirmation (Chrismation) is intimately related to Baptism and the Eucharist. Christians are reborn in Baptism, strengthened by Confirmation, and sustained by the food of Eucharist. Specifically, in Confirmation/Chrismation they are signed with the gift of the Spirit and become more perfect images of their Lord. Confirmation renews and strengthens the Christian's baptismal call to bear witness to Christ before the world and work eagerly for the building up of His body.

Confirmation emphasizes the transformation of life by the outpouring of the Holy Spirit in His fullness. Confirmed Christians claim as fully their own the new life into which they were first initiated at Baptism. The Church community expresses its continued support and concern for the spiritual growth of those confirmed, while the latter promise in turn to help others grow and mature in the Christian life.

119. CATECHESIS FOR CONFIRMATION

In the Eastern Churches, Baptism and Chrismation are celebrated together in infancy, and their intimate relationship is apparent. Though the Western Church has for many centuries generally separated the celebration of Baptism from Confirmation, it also recognized that they are intimately related. By emphasizing this relationship in the *Rite of Christian Initiation of Adults,* the Western Church has once again made clear how these two sacramental moments are parts of a unified process of initiation.

Catechesis for adults preparing for Confirmation follows the pattern recommended in the *Rite of Christian Initiation of Adults.*

The revised Rite of Confirmation[163] says episcopal conferences may designate the appropriate age for Confirmation. Practice in this matter now varies so much among the dioceses of the United States, that it is impossible to prescribe a single catechesis for this sacrament. A few years ago young people were generally confirmed around the age of 10 or 12. More recently, emphasis upon Confirmation as the sacrament of Christian commitment has led to postponement until the recipients are 12, 14, or, in some dioceses, 17 or older. Appropriate catechesis for these ages is being given. Among the elements of such catechesis in various places are performance standards for Church membership and community service; requiring a specified minimum number of hours of service to qualify for Confirmation; a letter of request for Confirmation; formational programs of catechesis extending over two or three years; and the use of adult advisors.

As with Baptism, catechesis for this sacrament takes place within the parish community, which has an obligation to participate in the catechetical preparation of those to be confirmed. The parish is the faith community into whose life of prayer and worship they will be more fully initiated. It also embodies the message to which they are to respond and gives witness, in service, to the faith they profess. The parish should strive to catechize on behalf of "obedience to Christ" and "loyal testimony to him" through the power of the Spirit.[164]

As the primary educators of their children, parents, along with sponsors, are to be intimately involved in catechesis for Confirmation. This will help them renew and strengthen their own faith, besides enabling them to set a better example for their children or godchildren. The parental program is an important element in planning for Confirmation for children and young people.

120. THE EUCHARIST[165]

Initiated into the Christian mystery by Baptism and Confirmation (Chrismation), Christians are fully joined to the Body of Christ in the Eucharist. The Eucharist is the center and heart of Christian life for both the universal and local Church and for each Christian. All that belongs to Christian life leads to the eucharistic celebration or flows from it.

It is a traditional theme of both the Eastern and Western Churches that Eucharist forms Church. Eucharist and Church are the basic realities, bearing the same names: communion and Body of Christ. The Eucharist increases charity within the visible community. The other mysteries (sacraments) dispose people to participate fruitfully in the central mystery of the Eucharist. The Eucharist is also seen as the chief source of divinization and maintains the pledge of immortality.

The Eucharist is a memorial of the Lord's passion, death, and resurrection. This holy sacrifice is both a commemoration of a past event and a celebration of it here and now. Through, with, and in the Church, Christ's sacrifice on the cross and the victory of His resurrection become present in every celebration.

The eucharistic celebration is a holy meal which recalls the Last Supper, reminds us of our unity with one another in Christ, and anticipates the banquet of God's kingdom. In the Eucharist, Christ the Lord nourishes Christians, not only with His word but especially with His body and blood, effecting a transformation which impels them toward greater love of God and neighbor.

"By means of the homily the mysteries of the faith and the guiding principles of the Christian life are expounded from the sacred text during the course of the liturgical year. The homily, therefore, is to be highly esteemed as part of the liturgy itself."[166]

The Eucharist is also a Sacrament of Reconciliation, completing and fulfilling the Sacraments of Initiation. In each Eucharist we reaffirm our conversion from sin, a conversion already real but not yet complete. The Eucharist proclaims and effects our reconciliation with the Father. "Look with favor on your Church's offering, and see the Victim whose death has reconciled us to yourself."[167]

121. CATECHESIS FOR THE EUCHARIST[168]

Catechesis recognizes the Eucharist as the heart of Christian life. It helps people understand that celebration of the Eucharist nourishes the faithful with Christ, the Bread of Life, in order that, filled with the love of God and neighbor, they may become more and more a people acceptable to God and build up the Christian community with the works of charity, service, missionary activity, and witness.[169]

Reflecting upon Christ's life as proclaimed in the Gospels, catechesis considers the Last Supper and the Jewish roots of this covenant meal. It expresses the Church's faith that Christ is present not only in the Christian assembly and in the reading of His word, but in a unique and most excellent way in this sacrament; that the bread and wine are changed, a change traditionally and appropriately expressed by the word transubstantiation, so that, while the appearances of bread and wine remain, the reality is the body and blood of Christ.

Catechesis should also help people understand the importance and significance of the liturgy of the word in the eucharistic celebration.

To encourage reverent and informed participation in the Sacrament of the Eucharist, catechesis gives instruction about the meaning of the ritual, symbols, and parts of the Mass. It also includes instruction and practice in the prayers and rubrics for the laity at Mass.[170] If possible, those catechized should learn to plan eucharistic liturgies, to serve as gift bearers, readers, ushers, etc. Catechesis should make people aware of their obligation to be free of serious sin before receiving Holy Communion. It should also instruct them concerning the time of the eucharistic fast and the conditions under which Holy Communion may be received more than once a day.

Catechesis speaks of the Lord's real and abiding presence in the Blessed Sacrament, and encourages visits and eucharistic devotions. Among the latter is devotion to the Eucharistic Heart of Jesus, a devotion which has among its objectives to call particular attention to Jesus' love in instituting the Eucharist.[171] Catechesis also includes conduct in Church, including appropriate devotional gestures and postures, and how to visit and pray to the eucharistic Lord apart from Mass.

122. CATECHESIS FOR FIRST COMMUNION

The preparation of adults for first reception of the Eucharist is an integral part of the catechumenate process.

As for children, their parents, catechists, and pastors are responsible for determining when they are ready to receive First Communion.

Parents have a right and duty to be intimately involved in preparing their children for First Communion. Catechesis aims to help parents grow in understanding and appreciation of the Eucharist and participate readily in catechizing their children.

Catechesis for children seeks to strengthen their awareness of the Father's love, of the call to participate in Christ's sacrifice, and of the gift of the Spirit. Children should be taught that the Holy Eucharist is the real body and blood of Christ, and what appear to be bread and wine are actually His living body. Children around the age of seven tend to think concretely; they grasp concepts like "unity" and "belonging" from experiences, such as sharing, listening, eating, conversing, giving, thanking, and celebrating. Such experiences, coupled with explanations of the Eucharist adapted to their intellectual capacity and with further efforts to familiarize them with the main events of Jesus' life, help them to participate more meaningfully in the action of the Mass and to receive Christ's body and blood in communion in an informed and reverent manner.

Catechesis for First Communion is conducted separately from introductory catechesis for the Sacrament of Reconciliation, since each sacrament deserves its own concentrated preparation. Continued catechesis is given yearly in all catechetical programs for children, inasmuch as the sacraments require lifelong participation and study.

In some Eastern Churches in the United States, First Communion completes an infant's reception of the Sacraments of Initiation and is celebrated in conjunction with Baptism and Chrismation. In this context, eucharistic catechesis follows reception of the sacrament and supports the young Christian's growth into the mystery.

Section II: Sacraments — Mysteries of Reconciliation and Healing

123. INTRODUCTION

We are incorporated into Christ's body, the Church, through the Sacraments of Initiation. When we have been weakened by sin or sickness, we are healed and strengthened within that body through the sacraments of Reconciliation and Anointing of the Sick.

124. THE SACRAMENT OF RECONCILIATION

Jesus began His work on earth by calling people to repentance and faith: "Reform your lives and believe in the gospel." (Mark 1:15) Conversion means turning from sin toward Him — present in His Church, in the Eucharist, in His work, and in our neighbor — with love and a desire for reconciliation.

Jesus began His risen life by giving His apostles power to forgive sins. (Cf. John 20:23) The Sacrament of Reconciliation continues His work of forgiving and reconciling. It celebrates the prodigal's return to the eternally merciful Father, renewing the sinner's union with God — and also with the community, inasmuch as our sins harm our brothers and sisters.

The revised ritual offers various forms and options for celebrating this sacrament. Among these are communal celebrations, which more clearly show its ecclesial nature. Penitents have a choice of the customary anonymity or a setting face-to-face with the confessor. A choice is also offered among various prayers and readings.

The sacrament's traditional and essential elements are contrition, confession, absolution, and satisfaction. Contrition is heartfelt sorrow and aversion from sin as an offense against God, with the firm intention of sinning no more. It expresses a conversion, "a profound change of the whole person by which one begins to consider, judge and arrange" one's whole life to conform more with Christ's values.[172] Following the revised rite, the penitent, as a sign of conversion, first listens to the priest proclaim God's word calling to conversion. Having earlier reviewed his or her sins, attitudes, failures, etc., the penitent confesses sins, makes an appropriate expression of sorrow, and receives forgiveness and reconciliation from the priest in Christ's name. Afterward the penitent performs the agreed-upon act of satisfaction (penance).

The Sacrament of Reconciliation, including individual and complete confession and absolution, remains the ordinary way of reconciling the faithful with God and with the Church. The Church holds and teaches that this method of receiving the sacrament is necessary and willed by Christ. Individual confession and absolution cannot be easily or ordinarily set aside. Particular, occasional circumstances may render it lawful and even necessary to give general absolution to a number of penitents without their previous individual confession, though the obligation to confess serious sin still remains. The existence of these serious circumstances is identified by the local bishop in consultation with other bishops according to articles 31 and 32 of the Rite of Penance.[173]

Secrecy is essential for safeguarding the sacrament; both penitent and sacrament are protected by the priest's obligation to maintain secrecy. The penitent ought to exercise prudent care in speaking about his or her own confession.

Frequent participation in this sacrament, even though one has not committed a serious sin, is a highly desirable way of celebrating ongoing conversion and making progress in holiness.

125. CATECHESIS FOR THE SACRAMENT OF RECONCILIATION

An understanding of sin, of oneself as a sinner, and of the conditions requisite for a serious sin are necessary preliminaries in catechesis for this sacrament.

The catechesis itself emphasizes God's mercy and loving forgiveness. It also emphasizes that faith, a gift of God, is a call to conversion from sin.

Catechesis for Reconciliation challenges people to acknowledge the difference between good and evil in the social order, to measure their values and priorities against those of the gospel and the Church, to accept individual and corporate responsibility for their decisions and the consequences of those decisions, and to repent of their participation in evil. A formal examination of conscience, like the one printed in the addenda to the revised ritual, can be useful.

Catechesis prepares the community to celebrate in ritual the realities of repentance, conversion, and reconciliation. Everyone needs this sacrament, for we are all sinners, not just those seriously estranged from God and the Church, and we all find here an opportunity to confront our sinfulness, acknowledge our need for conversion, seek pardon and peace, and celebrate our union with the healing, merciful Christ and His Church. Similarly, we all need to grow in our ability to celebrate this sacrament fruitfully and make good use of the options which are available.

Catechesis calls attention to the obligation to celebrate the sacrament whenever one is in mortal sin and, minimally, to confess such sin within a year. It also notes that, in a world where alienation and loneliness seem to be the norm, it is an expression of one's Christian faith to forgive others and seek forgiveness when necessary.

126. CATECHESIS OF CHILDREN FOR RECONCILIATION

Catechesis for children must always respect the natural disposition, ability, age, and circumstances of individuals. It seeks, first, to make clear the relationship of the sacrament to the child's life; second, to help the child recognize moral good and evil, repent of wrongdoing, and turn for forgiveness to Christ and the Church; third, to encourage the child to see that, in this sacrament, faith is expressed by being forgiven and forgiving; fourth, to encourage the child to approach the sacrament freely and regularly.

Parents should be involved in the preparation of children for this sacrament.

Catechesis for the Sacrament of reconciliation is to precede First Communion and must be kept distinct by a clear and unhurried separation. This is to be done so that the specific identity of each sacrament is apparent and so that, before receiving First Communion, the child will be familiar with the revised Rite of Reconciliation and will be at ease with the reception of the sacrament. The Sacrament of Reconciliation normally should be celebrated prior to the reception of First Communion.[174]

Because continuing, lifelong conversion is part of what it means to grow in faith, catechesis for the Sacrament of Reconciliation is ongoing. Children have a right to a fuller catechesis each year. Adults also have a right to continuing catechesis concerning the sacrament. Lent is an especially appropriate season for this.

127. THE ANOINTING OF THE SICK

Jesus' care and concern for the sick permeate the Gospels. Though primarily concerned with spiritual sickness, He was not indifferent to bodily afflictions and seemed often to point to the relationship between the two. To be faithful to Him, the Church must care for those who are sick in body as well as spirit.

The Anointing of the Sick is the special sacrament for Christians dangerously ill as a result of sickness or old age. "As soon as any one of the faithful begins to be in danger of death from sickness or old age, the appropriate time for him to receive this sacrament has certainly already arrived."[175]

The discouragement and anxiety which often accompany illness and suffering can weaken faith; but the Church invites the sick to come to Christ to be healed, to be made whole, to receive peace. (Cf. James 5:14f) The Church commends those receiving the sacrament "to the suffering and glorified Lord, that He may raise them up and save them."[176] If physical health is beneficial to salvation, it may be restored. If the sick need forgiveness, their sins will be pardoned.

Communal celebrations of the Anointing of the Sick are recommended. On such occasions the sick, surrounded by the Church in the person of their family and friends, can receive special support and encouragement from the faith community.

While the revised rite for this sacrament emphasizes ministry to the sick, it also treats ministry to the dying. The continuous Rite of Reconciliation, Anointing, and Viaticum (receiving the Eucharist) is provided for the dying.

128. CATECHESIS FOR THE ANOINTING OF THE SICK

Both catechesis for this sacrament and pastoral care of the sick should examine the meaning of sickness, healing, suffering, and death in the light of faith.

The sacrament is intended for those dangerously ill because of sickness or old age, for patients undergoing surgery on account of dangerous illness, for elderly persons who are in a weak condition, even if they are not dangerously ill, for children who are seriously ill and have sufficient understanding to be comforted by its reception.[177] Since this is a departure in many respects from the Church's practice in the immediate past, catechesis is imperative concerning the Christian interpretation of sickness and healing.

Catechesis encourages the faithful to ask for the anointing and receive it with complete faith and devotion, not delaying its reception. All who care for the sick should be taught the meaning and purpose of anointing.

Catechesis encourages the members of the local parish to visit the sick and express love and concern for them. The faith community should seek out those of its members who have been cut off from it and confined by illness, offering them love and support, praying with them, ministering to their needs. Catechesis points out and provides opportunities for service to the sick, and includes prayer for and with them.

Together with Reconciliation and Viaticum, this sacrament prepares the Christian for death. Catechesis notes that Christians should do more for the dying than wait passively with them. It encourages listening, praying, sharing the word of God, as well as simply being present, or whatever else may make their passage to eternal life peaceful.

Section III: Sacraments — Mysteries of Commitment

129. INTRODUCTION

Every Christian's ultimate commitment is to love and serve God revealed in Jesus Christ present in His Church. But individual Christians are called to live out this commitment in various ways. Most do so in the context of marriage and family life, some by serving the faith community as ordained ministers. The sacraments of Matrimony and Holy Orders celebrate these callings, and sanctify and strengthen those who commit themselves to them.

130. THE SACRAMENT OF MATRIMONY

Christian marriage is the union of a baptized man and woman who freely enter into a loving covenant with each other in Christ. The self-giving love of bride and bridegroom is sealed and strengthened by the Lord; the married couple imitates, and in a way represents, Christ's faithful love for His bride, the Church.

Thus husbands and wives become signs, in and to the world, of God's steadfast love for His people.

The steadfast and selfless love of husband and wife is beautifully expressed and symbolized in the Eastern tradition by the crowning of the newly married; the marriage ceremony itself is called the "crowning." The ceremony signals the establishment of a new "kingdom," based on mutual love, as a witness to Christ's love for His Church.

The Church proclaims the permanent, exclusive, and binding nature of this loving covenant. In the case of Christian marriage, the man and the woman are themselves the ministers of the sacrament. When either partner in a marriage is Catholic, the couple should be aware of and follow the norms and laws of the Church governing Christian marriage.

Marriage and conjugal love are naturally oriented toward the begetting and education of children. The unitive goal of marriage is also important, for "marriage . . . is not instituted solely for procreation. Rather, its very nature as an unbreakable compact between persons, and the welfare of the children, both demand that the mutual love of the spouses, too, be embodied in a rightly ordered manner, that it grow and ripen. Therefore, marriage persists as a whole manner and communion of life, and maintains its value and indissolubility even when offspring are lacking—despite, rather often, the very intense desire of the couple.[178]

131. CATECHESIS FOR MATRIMONY

The parish community helps people preparing for marriage by providing thorough premarital instructions in which they have opportunity to reflect on the nature of the marriage relationship, the joys and problems of married life, and the responsibilities they will assume toward each other and their children.

Catechesis helps couples understand marriage as a holy relationship, blessed and supported by God for the duration of life itself. Through the Sacrament of Matrimony His grace is constantly available to them.

Catechesis seeks to help couples recognize that only people courageous enough to make promises for life have the love and strength to surmount the inevitable challenges of marriage. Such unselfish love, rooted in faith, is ready to forgive when need arises, and to make the sacrifices demanded to foster the precious and holy marriage relationship. Catechesis stresses that one of the purposes of marriage is this mutual support and growth of love of husband and wife.

Catechesis calls attention to the fact that openness to the procreation and education of children must always be present and is vitally linked to growth in marital and family love.[179]

Catechesis also includes a clear presentation of the Church's teaching concerning moral methods of regulating births, the evil of artificial birth control and of sterilization for that purpose, and the crime of abortion; it should stress the protection due to human life once conceived.

Shared faith is a positive, strengthening element in marriage. While recognizing the sacramental character of interdenominational Christian marriages between the baptized, the Church encourages marriages within the Catholic faith. A Catholic must request a canonical dispensation for an interfaith marriage. Catechesis for those preparing for such marriages should encourage them to engage in honest, open reflection on the special difficulties they will face. The basic unity of belief among Christians should be recognized, along with the differences which will affect the way the couple live out their married life.

Catechesis for Matrimony is not limited to the period immediately before marriage. People begin to learn the meaning of married love and to acquire reverence for married life very early in childhood; parents are the primary catechists of their children with respect to such matters. Catechesis on Matrimony, married life, and Christian "parenting" should be given to young people of high school age; and relevant catechesis for adults should be available at all stages of married life. Whenever possible, married couples should be involved in giving catechesis concerning Matrimony.

At the core of Christian marriage are a radical, permanent commitment and a high ideal of loving fidelity, marital chastity, mutual generosity, fecundity, and personal and social growth. Living up to these demands can be difficult in a secularized, hedonistic, and pluralistic culture in which divorce and remarriage are generally accepted. Concern for those who have suffered the trauma of divorce should be integral to the Catholic community. Spiritual and psychological counseling, in an atmosphere of understanding, is vital for those who have experienced marital failure. Divorced persons and their children should be welcomed by the parish community and made to feel truly a part of parish life. Catechesis on the Church's teaching concerning the consequences of remarriage after divorce is not only necessary but will be supportive for the divorced.

Parish and diocesan catechetical programs which foster supportive interaction between spouses and among couples should be encouraged and made available to all married couples.

132. THE SACRAMENT OF HOLY ORDERS

Jesus Christ, the supreme high priest, exercises His salvific work today by extending to all persons the fruits of His death and resurrection, particularly, and in a unique way, in the sacred mystery of the Eucharist. In Holy Orders one is called apart to share in an active and intimate manner the priestly saving action of Jesus Christ in a ministry of sanctifying, teaching, and building the Christian community.[180] All the faithful are participants in this mystery of redemption as they share in Christ's work. Yet ordained priesthood confers the power to act in the person of Christ and in His name and with His power to renew these mysteries, especially the mystery of the eucharistic sacrifice.

Bishops are the successors of the apostles as pastors of souls. Episcopal ordination confers the fullness of the Sacrament of Orders. In the person of the bishop Christ is present in the midst of His people, proclaiming the gospel and preaching the faith to all who believe. During the ceremony of episcopal ordination in the Byzantine rite, the bishop is called to be an imitator of Christ, the true shepherd, who laid down His life for His sheep.[181]

Priests are Christ's ministers. The Church is built up and grows through their ordination to public ministry. In the Byzantine rite, this charge is expressed by the prayer, addressed to Christ, that the new minister may "announce the gospel of your kingdom . . . sanctify the word of your truth . . . offer spiritual sacrifices to you, and . . . renew your people by the washing of rebirth."[182]

Deacons are also called, in Holy Orders, to minister to the Church. They are ordained to serve all people through a threefold ministry "of the Word, of the liturgy and of charity."[183]

133. CATECHESIS FOR HOLY ORDERS

Catechesis concerning ordained ministry must be given to all members of the faith community, so that all may share a common vision of the task of these ministers, ordained to the priestly orders.

Catechesis makes it clear that in a special way bishops, priests, and deacons are called—and through ordination empowered—to minister in Christ's name and that of the Church. They do this by proclaiming the word, embodying the gospel in the community of believers, leading the community in worship, healing its divisions, and summoning its members to reconciliation. Public celebration of ordinations and installations calls attention to the intimate link between the community and its ordained members.

Catechesis encourages the people to support bishops, priests, and deacons in their efforts to be faithful to their call and in the exercise of their ministry. It encourages prayer for the Church's ministers and for new vocations to the ordained ministry. It provides opportunities for people to consider the call to ordained ministry as a possible way for them to live out the Christian commitment.

Section IV: The Eucharistic Liturgy for Groups with Special Needs

134. INTRODUCTION

The eucharistic liturgy is the community's central act of worship. Ordinarily, the parish Sunday Mass is the community celebration which reflects and shapes the lives of parishioners.

Occasionally, however, the Eucharist is celebrated by smaller groups whose members are joined by special ties. Masses for such groups can further their growth in faith and in understanding of the Eucharist, by encouraging them to reflect not only upon the particular bonds which bring them together but upon the unity symbolized and effected by eucharistic celebration in the larger community.

Catechists are frequently asked to assist such groups in preparing for their Masses. In doing so, they should take into consideration the nature of the liturgical celebration.[184]

135. MASSES FOR CHILDREN

Children often cannot participate fully in adult liturgies because they do not understand the words and symbols used or understand them only imperfectly.[185] Recognizing this, the Sacred Congregation for Divine Worship issued a *Directory for Masses with Children* in 1973. It sets the framework for catechizing children for eucharistic celebration.

The directory emphasizes the need to integrate liturgical and eucharistic formation with the overall educational experience of children. Catechists should work and plan together to ensure that the children, besides having some idea of God and the supernatural, also have some experience of the human values involved in eucharistic celebration: e.g., acting together as a community, exchanging greetings, the capacity to listen, to forgive and to ask forgiveness, the expression of gratitude, the experience of symbolic actions.[186] Family participation in Masses for children is encouraged on occasion in order to encourage family unity.

136. MASSES FOR YOUTH

For young people to be able to prepare and plan Masses which reflect their faith and feelings, catechesis is needed. It should include study of the Gospels, of the nature of the Church and liturgy, of the way in which the Church celebrates its union with Christ in the Eucharist, and the liturgy's intimate relationship to life, faith, doctrine, and the Church. The meaning of the symbols, of bread, wine, and faith community, is probed. Youth are gradually introduced to the rich liturgical and musical traditions of the Church.

While young people are encouraged to participate actively in celebrating the Mass and to accept the roles open to them, the value of family worship and worship with the larger parish community should also be recognized.

137. MASSES FOR CULTURAL GROUPS

In planning Masses for particular cultural, racial, and ethnic groups it is important to take their needs, preferences, and gifts into account. Preparation for intergroup celebrations should involve mutual planning and effort, so that all may profit from the diverse liturgical heritages.

In liturgical celebrations, homogeneous cultural, racial, or ethnic communities have the right to use their own language and cultural expressions of faith in ritual, music, art. However, while diversity enriches the Church and makes it possible for the participants to experience worship more deeply, adaptations must respect the nature of liturgy as the worship of the Church. Not every cultural adaptation will be possible or suitable for liturgical use. More research is needed in this area.

138. MASSES FOR THOSE WITH HANDICAPPING CONDITIONS

Masses (and all other sacramental celebrations) for handicapped persons require special adaptations. Each handicapping condition calls for a different approach.

Many mentally handicapped persons, for example, respond profoundly to concrete visual symbols and gesture. Their liturgical celebrations should use color, art, and music, with less emphasis on verbal expressions of faith. Abstract symbols are generally avoided.

To take another example, it should be borne in mind that because most people who are deaf or have severe hearing disabilities live otherwise normal lives, their special needs may go unnoticed. However, provision should be made for Masses and other sacramental celebrations in sign language. If the celebrant himself cannot use this language, qualified interpreters should translate the liturgy into sign language. The use of amplification, good lighting for effective speechreading, and audio-visuals, all in accordance with the specific needs of hearing-impaired persons, should be encouraged.

All adaptations should be designed by qualified specialists and persons who work with the handicapped persons, in consultation, as far as possible, with the handicapped persons themselves. However, specialized liturgies should never entirely replace the integration of handicapped people into the larger worshiping community.

139. CATECHETICAL GUIDELINES FOR EUCHARISTIC CELEBRATIONS

Since catechists are often called on to prepare people to participate in the liturgy or to direct them in studying and reflecting on it, they themselves should have adequate liturgical preparation, both theoretical and practical. Also, whenever possible, catechists should seek the advice and collaboration of pastors or priests with pastoral experience in addition to formally trained liturgists.

At every level, particularly the national, dialogue between catechists and liturgists should be pursued in order to clarify the relationship between catechesis and liturgy, and to identify areas for cooperation and mutual assistance.

Liturgies for special groups point to the celebration of the parish and the wider Catholic community. Adaptations can be made according to age, maturity, race, cultural or ethnic group, and handicap. Members of the particular group can be involved in liturgical planning and celebration in ways that take the same factors into account. However, the norms and guidelines in the official liturgical books are to be observed.

PART C: PRAYER

140. INTRODUCTION

At the very heart of the Christian life lies free self-surrender to the unutterable mystery of God. Prayer, for both individuals and communities, means a deepening awareness of covenanted relationship with God, coupled with the effort to live in total harmony with His will. Private prayer permeates the daily life of the Christian and helps the individual to enter into communal or public prayer. There are four general purposes of prayer: adoration, thanksgiving, petition, and contrition. As a life of prayer matures it becomes more simple, and adoration, thanksgiving, and contrition tend to predominate.

Individuals and communities also pray in word and ritual. This prayer helps people achieve and express the reality of internal self-surrender to God, which lives in the depths of consciousness and flows out into life. Sacramental celebrations are the prayer of the Church, as also is the Liturgy of the Hours.

Whether communal or individual, all strivings in prayer are efforts to associate ourselves as consciously and consistently as possible with the constant activity of the Spirit dwelling within us. He calls us to be open to His inspirations, to cooperate with His initiatives, to remove obstacles to our becoming other Christs. Acknowledging the Spirit's initiative, catechists call upon Him when planning group expressions of prayer and open themselves to His promptings.

141. THE LITURGY OF THE HOURS

Since apostolic times, the Christian community has prayed at least twice daily in a structured, public way. Realizing the need for a prayer form transcending the needs and insights of individuals and expressing the worship of the community, the Church turned to the scriptures as the source of its Liturgy of the Hours. This communal prayer is made up of psalms, canticles, readings from scripture and selected Christian writers, hymns, responsories, and intercessory prayers. Its essential pattern is that of a dialogue between God and His people. Through it, local Churches unite themselves with the universal Church to praise God unceasingly with one voice.

The revision of the Liturgy of the Hours has made this prayer accessible once again to the whole People of God. It can be adapted for families, parish groups, and special occasions.

Catechists need to experience the richness and beauty of this prayer in order to appreciate it and be able to introduce it to others. Whenever possible, therefore, leaders in the parish community should provide opportunities for celebration of morning and/or evening prayer.

142. PARALITURGIES OR SCRIPTURAL CELEBRATIONS

Paraliturgies or scriptural celebrations are forms of prayer which appeal to many Catholics today. Generally based on the pattern of the Liturgy of the Hours, they include hymns or songs, psalms, scripture readings, intercessions, responsories or acclamations, and opportunities for silent prayer and reflection.

Because they are flexible in structure, paraliturgies can be designed for special occasions and oriented to particular themes. Although not substitutes for the official liturgy of the Church, they can deepen faith, strengthen community, foster Christian love, lead to more ardent and fruitful participation in sacramental celebration, and intensify the community's commitment to social justice. They offer opportunities for broad participation in planning and leadership. Catechists can foster appreciation of scriptural prayer by planning paraliturgies with those they catechize and providing frequent opportunities for such prayer.

143. DEVOTIONS AND OTHER FORMS OF PRAYER

It is difficult to imagine a strong Catholic spiritual life without devotion to particular mysteries or saints. Both the Eastern and the Western Churches have a rich tradition of devotions. Whether private or public, these should harmonize with the liturgy, be in some way derived from it, and lead people toward it.

In the Western Church devotion to the Blessed Sacrament reserved for adoration has a special place. Holy hours, Benediction, visits of adoration, the 40 Hours Devotions, Corpus Christi processions are all in the Church's tradition. First Friday eucharistic devotions, associated also with the devotion to the Sacred Heart of Jesus, invite many to share in the abiding love of God's presence among His people.

The venerable devotion to the Sacred Heart, based on the symbol of the human heart as a center of love and on the reality of God's love (1 John 4:7), considers the heart of Christ as the special meeting place of the divine and the human. Encouraged by several papal documents in this century,[187] devotion to the Sacred Heart has inspired many to respond to Jesus' invitation: "Learn from me, for I am gentle and humble of heart." (Matthew 11:29)

Among other devotions, the Way of the Cross is associated especially with the Lenten season, and the rosary of the Blessed Virgin Mary with the months of May and October. In fact, with the multiplicity of ethnic and cultural backgrounds, devotions to the Lord, the virgin and the saints provide a rich tapestry on which is woven the many threads of our ancestry in the faith.

Among the devotions celebrated in Eastern Catholic communities are the Akathistos (praises to our Lord or the Mother of God) and Paraklesis (office of consolation), and Molebens (prayer services), Supplication–Benediction, Lenten services and rosary (privately) in the Byzantine Church, and the Christmas novena, devotion to the cross on the Fridays of Lent, and offices to the saints in the Maronite Church.

Biblical prayer, involving reading scripture and meditating on it, is highly attractive to many today. Some learn favorite psalms and canticles by heart and base private prayer on them. Others repeat the name of Jesus, either by itself or inserted in brief phrases, such as "Lord Jesus Christ, Son of the living God, have mercy on me a sinner." Intercessory prayer—for oneself, one's family and friends, for the Church and the world—is another way of expressing one's love and confidence toward God. In seeking intimacy with God, silence is necessary; for prayer is a conversation, in which one must listen as well as speak. Meditation and contemplation are highly recommended.

Another contemporary phenomenon is the spread of prayer groups, either in homes or in churches and church-related facilities. Their chief purposes are to praise and thank God for all He has accomplished for us through Jesus in the power of the Holy Spirit, and to lead participants to live more deeply in the presence and power of the Spirit. Catechesis should familiarize people of all ages with this "prayer movement" and may properly encourage and foster participation in these groups.

Singing hymns and religious songs is also a form of prayer. (Cf. Ephesians 5:19f) Parishes should provide opportunities for people to learn hymns. The rich musical heritage of the Church, including Gregorian chant, should be preserved and made part of the parish musical repertoire.

Sharing common prayers helps people pray together as a community. Thus the great traditional prayers of the Church—such as the Apostles' Creed, the Sign of the Cross, the Lord's Prayer, the Hail Mary, and the Glory to the Father—should be known by all. Everyone should know some form of an act of contrition.

144. THE LITURGICAL YEAR

The Fathers and the tradition of the Catholic Church teach that the historical events by which Christ Jesus won our salvation through His passover are not merely commemorated or recalled in the course of the liturgical year; rather the celebration of the liturgical year exerts "a special sacramental power and influence which strengthens Christian life."[188] "We ourselves believe and profess this same truth."[189]

"The Church celebrates the memory of Christ's saving work on appointed days in the course of the year. Every week the Church celebrates the memorial of the resurrection on Sunday, which is called the Lord's day. This is also celebrated, together with the passion of Jesus, on the great feast of Easter once a year. Throughout the year the entire mystery of Christ is unfolded, and the birthdays (days of death) of the saints are commemorated."[190] "Each day is made holy through the liturgical celebrations of God's people, especially the eucharistic sacrifice and the divine office."[191]

a) Sunday

The Church celebrates the paschal mystery on the first day of the week, the Lord's day or Sunday. "This follows a tradition handed down from the Apostles, which took its origin from the day of Christ's resurrection. Thus Sunday should be considered the original feast day."[192]

b) Other days

The weekdays extend and develop the Sunday celebration. Often "in the course of the year, as the Church celebrates the mystery of Christ, Mary, the Mother of God, is especially honored, and the martyrs and the other saints are proposed as examples for the faithful."[193]

c) The liturgical seasons

The Easter Triduum of the passion and the resurrection of Christ is the "culmination of the entire liturgical year. What Sunday is to the week, the solemnity of Easter is to the year."[194] The fifty days from Easter Sunday to Pentecost are one long feast day, sometimes called "the great Sunday."[195]

The season of Lent is a preparation for Easter. The liturgy prepares adult catechumens "for the celebration of the paschal mystery by the several stages of Christian initiation; it also prepares the faithful, who recall their baptism and do penance."[196]

The Church considers the Christmas season, which celebrates the birth of our Lord and His epiphanies (Magi, Cana, Baptism), "second only to the annual celebration of the Easter mystery."[197]

"The season of Advent has a two-fold character. It is a time of preparation for Christmas when the first coming of God's son to men is recalled." Also it is the "season when minds are directed to Christ's second coming at the end of time. It is thus a season of joyful and spiritual expectation" for the day of the Lord.[198]

"Apart from the seasons of Easter, Lent, Christmas, and Advent . . . there are thirty-three or thirty-four weeks in the course of the year which celebrate no particular aspect of the mystery of Christ. Instead, especially on the last Sundays, the mystery of Christ in all its fullness is celebrated. This period is known as Ordinary Time."[199]

d) Catechesis for the liturgical year

Catechesis for keeping time holy in prayer and the liturgical year is directed to every Christian. "By means of devotional exercises, instruction, prayer, and works of penance and mercy, the Church, according to traditional practices, completes the formation of the faithful during the various seasons of the Church year."[200]

The Commentary on the Revised Liturgical Year and *The General Norms for the Liturgical Year and the Calendar*[201] themselves provide an ample model for catechesis. The many local customs and the multiple ethnic heritages of our people, if properly directed, offer an immense reservoir for parents, teachers, and children to understand better the great loving work of God in Christ.

145. CATECHESIS FOR PRAYER

Inasmuch as it seeks to lead individuals and communities to deeper faith, all catechesis is oriented to prayer and worship. The deepening of faith strengthens the covenant relationship with God and calls Christians to respond in worship and ritual. By the nature of their ministry, catechists are often called to lead the community to prayer.

Catechesis promotes active, conscious participation in the liturgy, helps the faithful to meditate on God's word, and provides opportunities for praying.

Catechesis for prayer begins very early in childhood by hearing others pray; even small children can learn to call upon the Father, Jesus, and the Holy Spirit. In time, the child will become familiar with the various prayers and prayer forms mentioned earlier and make them part of his or her life. Catechesis encourages daily prayer, family prayer, and prayer at special times, e.g., before and after meals.

Building upon the sense of wonder, catechesis leads people to a sense of the sacred and to recognition of God's presence in their lives. This is the source of both spontaneous and formal prayer.

To lead others to pray, the catechist must be a prayerful person. To lead others to participate fully in liturgical worship, the catechist should have experienced full participation and be familiar with sacramental theology and the principles of liturgical celebration. Whenever possible, dioceses and parishes should provide opportunities for such liturgical catechesis.

PART D: SACRED ART AND SACRAMENTALS

146. SACRED ART

The fine arts are among the noblest products of human genius. Ideally, their highest manifestation is sacred art. Things used in divine worship "should be truly worthy, becoming, and beautiful, signs and symbols of heavenly realities."[202]

The Western Church has never adopted a particular style or school of art as peculiarly its own, finding virtually all to be suitable instruments for expressing Christian values and truth. "She has admitted fashions from every period according to the talents and circumstances of peoples, and the needs of the various rites."[203] Catechesis should include an introduction to the religious art of the past, such as music, painting, sculpture, mosaics, and frescoes.

In expressing their faith, the Eastern Churches have developed and found great significance in the traditional forms of icons (images). Iconography views redeemed creation as a manifestation of the creator. This art form seeks to express in painting what is divinely mysterious in reality. The composition, perspective, color, and lighting, and the decorative elements of icons all take on a religious sense.

Contemporary art is as suitable for the service of religious worship as the art of past ages, provided it expresses the reverence and honor which are due the sacred. Within the limits set down by the liturgical law of the Church, catechists may make appropriate use of modern literature, dance, drama, mime, music, paintings, sculpture, banners, and audio-visual media in small liturgies, home Masses, and paraliturgies. Catechists should therefore familiarize themselves with liturgical law and official guidelines relating to the liturgy.

147. SACRAMENTALS

Sacramentals are sacred signs which bear a resemblance to the sacraments:[204] they signify effects, particularly of a spiritual kind, which are obtained through the Church's intercession. They remind us of the symbolic nature of all creation, and encourage prayer and attitudes of reverence. Examples of sacramentals are baptismal water, holy oils, blessed ashes, candles, palms, crucifixes, and medals.

In introducing the sacramentals, catechists should discuss their relationship to faith and their function in the Church and in the lives of individuals.

148. CONCLUSION

Gathered to offer thanks to the Father in Christ through the Holy Spirit, the faith community grows in its sense of unity and its awareness of the Church's mission to the world. The liturgy, heart of the Church's life, leads its members to seek justice, charity, and peace. Both liturgy and catechists call the attention of Christians to what the Lord, the apostles, and the prophets taught concerning these matters. In the next chapter we shall consider the sources and content of catechesis for social ministry directed to the goals of justice, mercy, and peace.

CHAPTER VII
CATECHESIS FOR SOCIAL MINISTRY

149. INTRODUCTION

Building on what has been said about Christian life, community, doctrine, and worship, this chapter describes the bases of the Church's social ministry; briefly sketches the development of Catholic social teaching and identifies some of its principal themes; and offers guidance for the continued development of a catechesis on behalf of justice, mercy, and peace.

PART A: FOUNDATIONS OF CATHOLIC SOCIAL TEACHING

150. BASES IN SCRIPTURE, MORAL DOCTRINE, AND THE MISSION OF THE CHURCH

Catholic social teaching is based upon scripture, upon the development of moral doctrine in light of scripture, upon the centuries-old tradition of social teaching and practice, and upon efforts to work out the relationship of social ministry to the Church's overall mission. Catholic social teaching has also been enriched by the contributions of philosophers and thinkers of all ages, including some who predate Christianity itself. With regard to social ministry, the words of the Second Vatican Council should always be kept in mind: "While helping the world and receiving many benefits from it, the Church has a single intention: that God's kingdom may come, and that the salvation of the whole human race may come to pass."[205]

Section I: The Biblical Base

151. INTRODUCTION

One finds powerful and compelling bases for the Church's social ministry throughout the Bible, especially in the Old Testament covenants and prophets, and in the Gospels and some epistles in the New Testament. The brief treatment which follows is meant to illustrate these rich sources and their implications with respect to the obligations inherent in the pursuit of justice, mercy, and peace.

152. OLD TESTAMENT

The Old Testament contains an urgent, recurring summons to practice justice and mercy—a divine summons based on the precept of love: "You shall love your neighbor as yourself." (Leviticus 19:18) Love is to lead to justice, equity, and charity. (Cf. Deuteronomy 24:6–22)

The Israelites are commanded to respond to the problems of the needy (cf. Deuteronomy 15:11), of orphans, widows, and aliens (cf. Deuteronomy 10:17ff; 24:17), poor neighbors (cf. Exodus 22:20–26), debtors, and the enslaved (cf. Deuteronomy 15:12–15; Isaiah 58:6). They are admonished to share bread with the hungry, shelter the oppressed and homeless, and clothe the naked (cf. Isaiah 58:7); to be honest "in using measures of length or weight or capacity" (Leviticus 19:35f; cf. Deuteronomy 25:13–16); to refrain from coveting or seizing fields or houses or cheating people of their inheritance (cf. Micah 2:1–13).

Through the prophet Isaiah the Lord commanded His people to pursue justice: "Put away your misdeeds from before my eyes . . . make justice your aim." (Isaiah 1:16f) Through Amos He commanded: "Let justice surge like water, and goodness like an unfailing stream." (Amos 5:24) Earnest conformity to God's moral will is especially incumbent upon leaders and public figures. (Cf. Jeremiah 22:13–16; Proverbs 8:15; Ecclesiastes 5:7f)

The Old Testament is very explicit in warning against mere lip service (cf. Isaiah 29:13f) and indicating the punishment of evildoers (cf., e.g., Micah 2:1–10). Conversely, it assures the People of Israel that they will be rewarded for doing what is right: "A lasting covenant I will make with them." (Isaiah 61:8)

153. NEW TESTAMENT

The scope of social ministry is broadened and social teaching is refined in the New Testament, especially in the example and words of Jesus. The New Testament expresses the universal kinship of all people, who call on "Our Father in heaven." (Matthew 6:9) In God's eyes there does not exist Jew or Greek, slave or freeman, male or female. All are one in Christ Jesus. (Cf. Galatians 3:28) Universal human dignity is recalled in the story of Lazarus, the poor man to whom salvation is granted while the rich man who had no mercy on him in life is condemned. (Cf. Luke 16:19–31)

The obligations of charity are movingly described in the parable of the good Samaritan, who showed himself to be neighbor to the man who fell in with robbers (cf. Luke 10:36f), thus doing what was required "to inherit everlasting life" (Luke 10:25). Another dramatic illustration of the need for compassion is the biblical description of the last judgment, at which, we are told, the heirs to the kingdom will be identified as those who showed compassion to the hungry, the thirsty, the stranger, the naked, the ill, and the prisoner: "I assure you, as often as you did it for one of my least brothers, you did it for me." (Matthew 25:40) The Gospel also enjoins us to love our enemies, to do good to those who hate us, and to give aid to all who seek it from us; conversely it reminds us that no special credit is to be claimed for doing good to those who do good to us. (Cf. Luke 6:27–34)

John admonishes us to love in deed and in truth "and not merely talk about it." (1 John 3:18) Faith without works is as dead as a body without breath (cf. James 2:26); it is "thoroughly lifeless" (James 2:17).

In fact, God's love cannot survive in people who, possessing a sufficiency of this world's goods, close their hearts to brothers or sisters in need. (Cf. 1 John 3:17) Looking after orphans and widows in their distress (and keeping oneself unspotted by the world) is equated with "pure worship." (James 1:27)

The New Testament arouses a spirit of mutual concern and formulates principles to insure that people respect one another's rights and perform their duties. It requires forgiveness (cf. Luke 6:37), patience (cf. Romans 2:7), justice (cf. Luke 11:42), and promises peace (cf. John 14:27), love (cf. 15:9, 12), and union with God (cf. 17:21ff).

154. EXAMPLE OF JESUS

Jesus' obedience to the Father led Him to give Himself fully for the salvation and liberation of others.[206] In the paschal mystery of His living, suffering, dying, and rising Catholic social teaching finds its ultimate ground and source.

Jesus identified Himself as the one who had come to serve, not to be served. He cited His ministry of service as the key to His identity and mission (cf. Luke 4:16ff) and clearly stated that anyone who aspires to follow Him must likewise serve the needs of all (cf. Matthew 20:26f; Luke 22:26f).

Jesus not only affirmed the second great commandment—"You shall love your neighbor as yourself" (Leviticus 19:18; cf. Mark 12: 33)—but further specified that this love be like His own: "Love one another as I have loved you." (John 15:12) His was an unconditional giving of self to and for others.

Jesus' birth was heralded by the song of angels: "Peace on earth to those on whom his [God's] favor rests." (Luke 2:14) Christ said: "Peace is my farewell to you, my peace is my gift to you; I do not give it to you as the world gives peace." (John 14:27) His coming inaugurated the messianic era of the prince of peace, foretold by Isaiah in the often quoted text, "They shall beat their swords into plowshares and their spears into pruning hooks; One nation shall not raise the sword against another, nor shall they train for war again." (Isaiah 2:4f)

Jesus gave many precepts and counsels which teach us how to love in Him and be like Him. Several times He summarized His law in two great commandments of love of God and love of neighbor, and on several occasions He reaffirmed the Ten Commandments. (Cf. Matthew 19:17ff; Mark 10:17ff; Luke 18:18ff) He gave us the Sermon on the Mount (cf. Matthew 5—7), His discourse at the Last Supper (cf. John 14—17), and numerous other indications, in word and example, of how He expects us to live — in Him, for the Father, by the power of the Holy Spirit.

Section II: The Moral Basis

155. NEED FOR SYSTEMATIC DEVELOPMENT

While the scriptures set forth specific content for social morality in certain instances, for the most part the Bible provides a series of themes which identify social responsibility as an element in Christian life without going into specifics. The systematic investigation and explanation of the meaning of social responsibility in Christian life has been the work of Catholic social teaching.

156. DIGNITY OF THE HUMAN PERSON

The fundamental concept in Catholic social teaching is the dignity of the human person. Human dignity and sacredness, present from the moment of conception, are rooted in the fact that every human being is created directly by God in His image and likeness (cf. Genesis 1:26) and is destined to be with Him forever. The psalmist of the Old Testament and the evangelists of the New reflect the biblical belief that the person is the pinnacle of God's visible creation, set apart from, and over, the rest of the created order. The same theme is reflected in Preface v for the Sundays in the Ordinary Time of the year (Roman Missal): "All things are of your making, all times and seasons obey your laws, but you chose to create man in your own image, setting him over the whole world in all its wonder."

In Catholic teaching the concept of human dignity implies not only that the person is the steward of creation and cooperates with the creator to perfect it,[207] but that the rest of creation, in its material, social, technological, and economic aspects, should be at the service of the person. Human dignity is secure only when the spiritual, psychological, emotional, and bodily integrity of the person is respected as a fundamental value.

157. SPECTRUM OF HUMAN RIGHTS

Flowing directly from our humanity are certain rights and duties which safeguard and promote human dignity. All human beings have these basic rights and duties, regardless of intelligence, background, contribution to society, race, sex, class, vocation, or nationality. Pope John XXIII gave a systematic catalogue of basic rights in his encyclical *Peace on Earth* (1963).[208] These should be an integral part of catechesis on social ministry.

Rights and duties are complementary: if one person has a right, others have a duty to respect it. The goal is to enable all people more clearly to manifest the divine image present in them.

158. PERSONS ARE SOCIAL BY NATURE

Human beings are social by nature. This means that family, state, and society are natural contexts for human life. They are essential for personal development, including the religious dimension.

This emphasis on the social nature of human beings and its implications is a critically important aspect of Catholic social teaching. Since societies are essential to human development, their organization and functioning—legal, political, economic, cultural—raise vitally important moral issues. Catholic social teaching provides principles by which the Church as an institution, and Christians as individuals, can evaluate political, economic, social, and legal structures. As the Church's teaching on personal morality establishes norms of conscience which help us assess issues pertaining to personal character and interpersonal relationships, so its teaching concerning social morality provides norms of conscience for judging social structures and institutional relationships.

159. RELATIONSHIP OF PERSONAL AND SOCIAL MORALITY

The personal and social spheres of morality are distinct but not separate. All personal actions and human institutions are subject to the judgment of the moral law. Social morality is, however, characterized by the exceptional diversity and complexity of the situations encountered. The Church provides broad guidelines for Christian conscience which must be carefully applied to particular situations, with due recognition given to regional, sociopolitical, and cultural differences. "In the face of such widely varying situations it is difficult for us to utter a unified message and to put forth a solution which has universal validity. . . . It is up to the Christian communities to analyze with objectivity the situation which is proper to their own country, to shed on it the light of the Gospel's unalterable words and to draw principles of reflection, norms of judgment and directives for action from the social teaching of the Church."[209]

Since people of discernment and good will can come to different conclusions in applying principles to particular complex social situations, catechesis should help people anticipate this eventuality and should explain it in a way that avoids reducing social morality to a kind of pragmatism or relativism.

Because of the pressing nature of numerous unresolved social problems today, all the members of the Catholic community are urged to study the Church's teaching and to become actively involved in seeking solutions according to their roles and responsibilities in society.

Section III: Relationship of the Social Ministry to the Mission of the Church

160. SOCIAL MINISTRY WITHIN THE MISSION OF THE CHURCH

Before examining the general development of social teaching and some of its specific content, it is important to specify how social ministry relates to the Church's total mission.

Christ gave His Church no distinct mission in the political, economic, or social order. Rather, its activities in these areas derive from its religious mission. This religious mission is, however, a source of insights and spiritual motivation which can serve to structure and consolidate the human community according to divine law.[210]

The Church shares responsibility for the promotion of justice in the world with many other agencies in society and is to cooperate with people of good will who esteem human values and seek justice, freedom, and the development of peoples.[211]

Throughout its history the Church has catechized concerning the corporal works of mercy. The practice of these corporal works of mercy by Catholics has made the Church more Christlike, more credible before the world. For the past century, furthermore, the systematic development of the Church's moral teaching on social issues has been pursued with particular diligence. Much less systematic attention, however, has been given to the relationship of social ministry to the Church's nature and mission as sign and servant of God's kingdom. How important is social ministry in the mission of the Church?

Building on its teaching in *The Dogmatic Constitution on the Church*, the Second Vatican Council examined, in *The Pastoral Constitution on the Church in the Modern World*, the role and value of Church presence and Christian action in the social, political, economic, and cultural spheres. The treatment of the Church in these two documents taken together points to the conclusion that a rounded view of the Church requires an understanding both of its inner life and of its ministry of service to society. "The expectation of a new earth must not weaken but rather stimulate our concern for cultivating this one."[212]

The Second General Assembly of the Synod of Bishops in 1971[213] further expanded the understanding of the Church's ministry in society. In *Justice in the World*, the bishops said: "Action on behalf of justice and participation in the transformation of the world fully appear to us as a constitutive dimension of the preaching of the Gospel, or, in other words, of the Church's mission for the redemption of the human race and its liberation from every oppressive situation."[214] At the same time, "The Church links human liberation and salvation in Jesus Christ, but she never identifies them."[215] Pope Paul VI has called "the cause of human dignity and of human rights the cause of Christ and his Gospel."[216]

Action on behalf of justice is a significant criterion of the Church's fidelity to its missions. It is not optional, nor is it the work of only a few in the Church. It is something to which all Christians are called according to their vocations, talents, and situations in life.

Any group or institution which ventures to speak to others about justice should itself be just, and should be seen as such. The Church must therefore submit its own policies, programs, and manner of life to continuing review. For example, faith demands a certain frugality in the use of temporal possessions and the Church is obliged to live and to administer its goods in such a way that it can authentically proclaim the gospel to the poor; yet the plight of the many millions of hungry people in our world today calls seriously into question the morality of typical life styles and patterns of consumption in our affluent society.[217] We are all — bishops, priests, religious, and — laity—called to an ongoing examination of conscience on such matters.

PART B: A BRIEF OVERVIEW OF THE DEVELOPMENT OF CATHOLIC SOCIAL TEACHING

161. IMPORTANCE OF A HISTORICAL PERSPECTIVE

The Church's understanding of and involvement in social ministry have evolved over the centuries. Catechesis should indicate this at the proper time, in a manner suited to the abilities and needs of those being catechized.

162. MINISTRY OF MERCY AND CHARITY

Even as its social teaching was developing, the Church was giving major emphasis to the practice of mercy and charity. (The relationship between charity and justice is described below.) Early writers, such as St. Basil, St. Clement of Alexandria, St. Ambrose, and others,[218] discoursed with eloquence and passion upon the obligations of charity and the rights of the poor. Pope St. Leo the Great (+461) noted in one of his sermons that "where he [God] finds charity with its loving concern, there he recognizes the reflection of his own fatherly care."[219]

The early monastic orders strove to give Christlike love and attention to the poor, the sick, the traveler, the pilgrim, and others in need. Many saints, canonized men and women, and countless others whose names are not recorded in history, devoted their lives to serving the poor and the needy.

Works of mercy and charity are always incumbent upon the Church and its members, and should involve more than just disbursing superfluous goods.[220] They are carried on with great vitality today by the Catholic Church in the United States and throughout the world. In this country, the Church has founded and maintains many charitable and social service programs and institutions — hospitals, homes for the aged, children's institutions, treatment centers for drug addicts and alcoholics, community houses, refuges for the homeless, recreation programs, and many others. Catholic Charities organizations and similar agencies, as well as volunteer associations (St. Vincent de Paul Society, Ladies of Charity, etc.) have donated hundreds of millions of dollars and hours to the relief of fellow human beings.

The works of charity performed by the Catholic Church in the United States reach beyond this country. Supported by the generosity of the faithful, missionaries have alleviated all forms of need while proclaiming the good news in other lands. Catholic Relief Services and other agencies have assisted millions throughout the world.

For two millennia, as Pope John XXIII remarked, by teaching and example the Church has held aloft the torch of charity, as Christ instructed it to do.[221] Catechesis relates this story of generosity, identifies its sources, and encourages people to respond generously to Christ's mandate.

163. DEVELOPMENT THROUGH THE FIRST NINETEEN CENTURIES

It was understood from the earliest days that the gospel had social implications. In the Acts of the Apostles we find the Christian community deciding how property should be administered and how "widows and orphans" should be cared for. (Acts 2:44f; 6:1–4)

As the Church grew from a small community living on the edge of the Roman Empire to the principal social institution of medieval Europe, the social implications of the gospel became increasingly imperative in shaping its life. Central to this process were the teachings of the Church Fathers, the writings of medieval canonists and theologians, and the pastoral leadership of bishops and popes.

The development of social teaching was spurred by the great voyages of discovery and subsequent colonization of the New World; by European colonialism in other parts of the globe; by the dislocations and serious human and economic problems created by the Industrial Revolution which began in the 18th century; and by the monumental social problems created by the mass migration of the mid-19th century and later.

It is beyond the scope of this NCD to trace in further detail the development of social teaching from the early Church, through the Middle Ages and the post-Reformation period. More important to understanding Catholic social thought today are developments during the past century.

164. SINCE THE END OF THE NINETEENTH CENTURY

Since the late 19th century a systematic and organized body of social teaching has developed in the Church, relating gospel teaching and the Catholic tradition to the conditions of modern life. Of central importance are the papal encyclicals, pastoral letters, and conciliar documents, from Pope Leo XIII (*On the Condition of Labor*, 1891) through the writings of Pope Paul VI.[222] Around this central core have developed extensive commentary, preaching, and catechesis.

This social teaching touches upon a wide variety of topics: education; social and economic justice within nations; the moral analysis of social structures; world order, international justice and peace, and the complex obstacles to their achievement; problems typical of societies with high levels of industrial development and extensive urbanization (e.g., the role of women, the alienation of youth, the impact of the media, labor relations); models of social and economic development and their evaluation; and the political vocation as part of the Christian vocation.

PART C: FACING CONTEMPORARY SOCIAL ISSUES
Section I: Major Concepts

165. SOCIAL DIMENSION OF MORALITY

It is impossible to grasp or communicate the content of Catholic social teaching without a clear understanding of the social dimension of morality. Here we shall analyze three concepts: social justice, the social consequences of sin, and the relationship of justice and charity. *The Pastoral Constitution on the Church in the Modern World* provides the context: "Let everyone consider it his sacred obligation to count social necessities among the primary duties of modern man, and to pay heed to them. For the more unified the world becomes, the more plainly do the offices of men extend beyond particular groups and spread by degrees to the whole world. But this challenge cannot be met unless individual men and their associations cultivate in themselves the moral and social virtues, and promote them in society."[223]

a) Social justice

This general description of social morality is made more specific in Pope John's teaching that society should be organized and directed by four values: truth, justice, freedom, and love.[224] Each exists and is easily recognized in personal relationships; but, as *Peace on Earth* sought to demonstrate, each also has a social dimension.

Social justice focuses not only on personal relationships but on institutions, structures, and systems of social organization (keeping in mind, however, that these are composed of persons) which foster or impede the common good at the local, national, and international levels. Social justice is the concept by which one evaluates the organization and functioning of the political, economic, social, and cultural life of society. Positively, the Church's social teaching seeks to apply the gospel command of love to and within social systems, structures, and institutions.

The complexity and scope of structural or institutional injustices are commonly such that isolated individuals cannot remedy them by themselves. Some form of political participation, such as voting for candidates who support just laws and policies, is usually required. The close link between political participation (by citizens, groups, and public authority) and social justice is one reason why Paul VI so strongly emphasized the political vocation as part of the Christian vocation today.

Catholic social teaching affirms as fundamental the right of all people to form their own associations, such as labor unions, employer groups, societies for the promotion of culture, recreation, and the like. The Church supports the rights not only of individuals but of groups organized for the pursuit of legitimate ends. It holds that persons should be free to assemble and act peaceably on behalf of human rights.

In summary, social justice affects our personal relations with others; it does so *through* the structures of society; it helps us evaluate our responsibility for the kind of society we are willing to support and share in. The agents of social justice are normally groups working to shape social institutions in the direction of justice, love, truth, and freedom for all.

b) Social consequences of sin

The development of the concept of "social sin"[225] is another example of how the Church seeks to highlight the social dimension of Christian morality. Speaking of how "unjust systems and structures" oppress people, the bishops of the 1971 Synod said: "The hopes and forces which are moving the world in its very foundations are not foreign to the dynamism of the Gospel, which through the power of the Holy Spirit frees men from personal sin and from its consequences in social life."[226]

The choice of sin occurs in the human heart, and sin is expressed through personal choices and actions. But it has social consequences. Sin is expressed in some of the structures of human communities. Sinful structures are not simply imperfect human organizations; rather, such structures involve a systematic abuse of the rights of certain groups or individuals. The sinfulness lies in the unjust way in which social relationships are organized. An extreme example is institutionalized racial or ethnic segregation; a less striking example is the absence or inadequacy of minimum wage laws. A very contemporary example is the imbalance in the distribution of the world's goods, which calls for a new international economic order.

Responsibility for correcting a situation of "social sin" rests upon all who participate in the society in question: those whose rights are being systematically denied are called to assert them; others are called to seek to change existing patterns of social relationships.[227]

"Social sin" can affect such large numbers of people that it is almost impossible to identify its causes. It can be so deeply rooted as almost to defy eradication. It can be the fault of so many that no one in particular can be held to blame. But precisely because social injustices are so complex, one must resist the temptation to think that there is no remedy for them.

c) Relationship of justice and charity

Some discussions of the social responsibility of Christians tend to set justice and charity in opposition: justice is regarded as a secular idea and obligatory, charity as a Christian concept and optional. In fact, both are part of Christian social responsibility and are complementary.

"Love implies an absolute demand for justice, namely a recognition of the dignity and rights of one's neighbor."[228] Justice is therefore the foundation of charity: i.e., if I love my neighbor, it is absolutely required that I respect his or her rights and meet his or her needs. It is impossible to give of oneself in love without first sharing with others what is due them in justice. This can be expressed very succinctly by saying that justice is love's absolute minimum.

Conversely, justice reaches its fulfillment in charity; once the demands of justice are met, there is still room, in a Christian view of human relationships, to go beyond what is due others by right and share with them in the self-giving manner of Christ. Charity excuses from none of the demands of justice; it calls one to go beyond justice and engage in sacrificial service of others in imitation of Christ, the suffering servant.

Section II: Some Contemporary Problems

166. INTRODUCTION

In view of the vast problems facing contemporary society and the speed with which problems and priorities can change, Catholic organizations and institutions at all levels must be constantly alert to society's current and foreseeable needs.

In order to suggest the scope and content of catechesis for social justice, we shall mention here a variety of issues currently of particular concern to the United States, grouping them under three general headings: respect for human life, national problems, and international problems. In categorizing social issues, however, it is important to be aware of their often complex interrelationships in actuality: catechists should avoid treating in isolation social problems which are in fact related.

Since the Catholic Church is concerned with and regularly addresses many social issues, those involved in catechesis for social ministry should keep abreast of the pronouncements of the Holy See, the United States bishops, and other sources in the Church.[229]

167. RESPECT FOR HUMAN LIFE

As we have seen, respect and reverence for human life arise from the dignity of the human person made in God's image and likeness. Life is a precious gift from the creator. Through its laws and institutions, society must respect the life of every human being from conception to natural death. Direct attacks on human life—such as abortion, infanticide, euthanasia, and certain forms of fetal experimentation[230]—are gravely immoral.

The right of life touches also upon life's quality. The respect due life is, for example, violated in attempts to hamper another's capacity to live as fully as possible, or to reduce a person to a state of dependency. The authentic meaning of "quality of life" is seriously misconstrued when it is taken to justify such things as the destruction of lives deemed defective because of mental, physical, or social handicaps.

Respect for life should also underlie one's assessment of issues pertaining to warfare and defense policy, as well as the question of capital punishment. These topics have been addressed by the bishops of the United States.

168. NATIONAL PROBLEMS

Many other social problems face the United States today. Among the more pressing are: racism; other forms of discrimination, including discrimination against women; encroachments on basic rights by the federal and state governments and courts, reflected in such issues as abortion, pornography, school prayer, etc.; questions of economic justice, including poverty, unemployment, a just price for basic economic goods, and a living wage; problems of refugees and immigrants, particularly those without documentation; various questions pertaining to unionization; farm labor; land ownership; agricultural policy; population issues; bioethical questions arising from the revolution in life sciences; energy policy; ecology; defense policy, military expenditures, and conscientious objection; food and nutrition; housing; health care; the abuse and other problems of the aged and of handicapped persons; family policy and child abuse; alcoholism and drug abuse; capital punishment; inadequacies and abuses in the judicial and prison systems; political and governmental corruption; and threats to personal and corporate privacy and freedom.

In the field of education it is necessary to affirm and vindicate the right of all children and youth to a suitable education free from unjust segregation and unequal treatment; the right of parents to enjoy true freedom in the choice of schools for their children and freedom from unjust financial burdens; and the clear rights of children to their fair share of support by the state.[231]

Many of these questions have been addressed by the bishops of the United States and, in a more global manner, by papal and Roman documents. This body of teaching deserves close study by Catholics actively seeking solutions to contemporary social problems in collaboration with their fellow citizens.

169. INTERNATIONAL ISSUES

International issues have received increasing attention from the Church during the pontificates of Popes Pius XII, John XXIII and Paul VI. On a number of occasions the bishops of the United States have addressed such issues as peace; prisoners of war; immigration; communism; international order and justice; the United Nations; human rights in general and their violation in particular countries and areas of the world; religious persecution; world population; the world food crisis; and social reconstruction.

170. CATECHETICAL GUIDELINES FOR JUSTICE, MERCY AND PEACE

Catechesis concerning justice, mercy, and peace should be part of the catechetical process. It should include efforts to motivate people to act on behalf of these values.

1. Catechesis recognizes that the root cause of social injustice, selfishness, and violence reside within the human person: the imbalances of the modern world are linked to a more basic imbalance in the human heart.[232] Injustice, greed, lack of mercy, violence, and war are social consequences of sin.

2. Catechesis for justice, mercy, and peace calls for a renewal of heart based on the recognition of sin in its individual and social manifestations.[233] It seeks to bring people to recognize their individual and collective obligations to strive to overcome the grave injustices in the world, as well as their inability to do so by their own strength. It points out that all must listen with humble and open hearts to God's word calling attention to new paths of action on behalf of justice, mercy, and peace.

3. Catechesis explains the relationship of personal morality to social morality. It makes clear that the Church provides principles which Christians have a duty to apply carefully to particular situations. Catechists must be careful not to confuse their personal or political opinions with the explicit teaching of the Church on social issues.

4. Catechesis strives to awaken a critical sense, leading to reflection on society and its values and to assessment of the social structures and economic systems which shape human lives.

5. Each Catholic has a responsibility for social action according to his or her circumstances. Because social and economic questions are generally decided in the political order, Catholics should play a responsible role in politics, including fulfilling the duties of informed citizenship and seeking public office.

6. Effective catechesis is based on the sources of the Church's social teaching. Rooted in the Old and New Testaments and uniquely expressed in the ministry of Jesus, social teaching has developed throughout the Church's history. Papal, conciliar, and episcopal documents should be consulted and made part of the content of catechesis, as should the "signs of the times," including manifestations of the interdependence of the world community.

Catechesis also points out that the effectiveness of the Church's social ministry depends largely on the witness which its members give to justice, mercy, and peace in their relationships with one another, as well as upon the witness of the Church's corporate and institutional life.

7. The fundamental concept underlying the social teaching of the Church is the dignity of the person, a dignity rooted in likeness to God and the call to communion with Him. Human rights and the value of human life, from conception to natural death, are emphasized in catechesis. Respect for human life includes appropriate concern for life's quality, as well as its existence and preservation.

8. Catechesis speaks of the works of charity performed by the Church and its members throughout history. It stresses that these works are essential and motivate people—beginning with the very young according to their level of understanding—to give of their time, talents, and earthly goods, even to the point of sacrifice. Catechists also present the lives of saints and other outstanding Catholics who have exemplified the Church's social awareness and desire to help.

9. Catechesis seeks to move people to live justly, mercifully, and peacefully as individuals, to act as the leaven of the gospel in family, school, work, social, and civic life, and to work for appropriate social change.

10. Catechesis includes activities (involving vital contact with the reality of injustice)[234] which empower people to exercise more control over their destinies and bring into being communities where human values are fully respected and fostered.

11. Catechesis for justice, mercy, and peace is a continuing process[235] which concerns every person and every age. It first occurs in the family by word and by example. It is continued in a systematic way by Church institutions, parishes, schools, trade unions, political parties, and the like. This catechesis is an integral part of parish catechetical programs. It should also be an integral part of the curriculum and environment of Catholic schools. It is desirable that courses for children and youth be complemented by programs for parents.

12. The Church and its institutions should seek out and listen to different points of view on complex social situations. Catechetical materials can reflect different perspectives with respect to justice and peace, showing how these agree with or differ from the Church's teaching.

13. Adult catechesis on social justice and the total biblical concept of stewardship is much needed and should be given priority.

14. Social ministry should be identified as a valid and necessary ministry in the Church and proposed as a possible vocation to those being catechized. Conscious efforts are required to develop leadership in this ministry.

15. Catechists should point out the harm which can be done to children's values, attitudes, and behavior by toys and games which make war and its weapons seem glamorous. They should call attention to the damage which excessive exposure to violence and immorality in the mass media, especially television, can do to children and adults.

171. CONCLUSION

So far this NCD has considered some characteristics of Catholicism in the United States; revelation and the response of faith; the meaning of Church, along with some outstanding elements of its message and its mission to others; the fundamental need for worship and prayer; and social ministry. Next we shall turn to those to be catechized.

CHAPTER VIII
CATECHESIS TOWARD MATURITY IN FAITH

172. INTRODUCTION

This chapter considers the relationship between the life of faith and human development; how people grow in their ability to recognize and respond to God's revelation; conscience formation; sexuality and catechesis; the catechesis of persons with special needs; and certain factors which currently affect the handing-on of the faith in the United States. Revelation, faith, grace, and related matters pertaining to faith are discussed in their own right in Chapter III.

PART A: FAITH AND HUMAN DEVELOPMENT

173. THE DEVELOPMENTAL CHARACTER OF THE LIFE OF FAITH

Jesus' words, "You are my friends if you do what I command you" (John 15:14), point to the fact that the life of faith involves a relationship, a friendship, between persons. As the quality of a friendship between human beings is affected by such things as their maturity and freedom, their knowledge of each other, and the manner and frequency of their communication, so the quality of a friendship with God is affected by the characteristics of the human party. Because people are capable of continual development, so are their relationships with God. Essentially, development in faith is the process by which one's relationship with the Father becomes more like Jesus' (cf. John 14:6f): it means becoming more Christlike. This is not just a matter of subjective, psychological change, but involves establishing and nurturing a real relationship to Jesus and the Father in the Holy Spirit, through a vigorous sacramental life, prayer, study, and serving others.

174. THE RELATIONSHIP OF GROWTH IN FAITH TO HUMAN DEVELOPMENT

Because the life of faith is related to human development, it passes through stages or levels; furthermore, different people possess aspects of faith to different degrees. This is true, for example, of the comprehensiveness and intensity with which they accept God's word, of their ability to explain it, and of their ability to apply it to life.[236] Catechesis is meant to help at each stage of human development and lead ultimately to full identification with Jesus.

175. THE ROLE OF THE BEHAVIORAL SCIENCES

The Church encourages the use of the biological, social, and psychological sciences in pastoral care.[237] "The catechetical movement will in no way be able to advance without scientific study."[238] Manuals for catechists should take into account psychological and pedagogical insights, as well as suggestions about methods.[239]

The behavioral sciences cause neither faith nor growth in faith; but for that matter, neither does the catechist. Faith is from God: "This is not your own doing, it is God's gift." (Ephesians 2:8)

These sciences do, however, help us understand how people grow in their capacity for responding in faith to God's grace. They can, therefore, make a significant contribution to catechesis. At the same time, catechists should not be uncritical in their approach to these sciences, in which new discoveries are constantly being made while old theories are frequently modified or even discarded. There are different schools of psychology and sociology which do not agree in all respects; nor are all developments of equal merit. Catechists should not imagine that any one school or theory has all the answers. Finally, behavioral sciences do not supply the doctrinal and moral content of catechetical programs. Their discoveries and developments must be constantly and carefully evaluated by competent persons before being integrated into catechetics.

The framework used here to describe the stages of human development is one of a number that could be used. Other models offer valuable insights. One's understanding of catechesis should not be linked exclusively to a single explanation of the stages of human development and its implications for growth in faith.

176. ELEMENTS OF METHODOLOGY

a) A new methodology

In the covenant of the Old Testament, God announced His plan of salvation prophetically and by means of types. He revealed the truth about Himself gradually over centuries.

Now, in the fullness of time when revelation has been consummated in Christ, the Church uses a pedagogy adapted to the final age of salvation history, one in which the message is presented in its entirety while also being expressed according to the circumstances and ability of those being catechized. The principal elements of the Christian message (cf. Chapter v) must be central in all Catholic catechesis; they must never be overlooked or minimized, and must receive adequate and frequent emphasis.

b) No single methodology

Catechesis is not limited to one methodology. Although certain norms or criteria apply to all catechesis, they do not determine a fixed methodology, nor even an order for presenting the truths of faith. For instance, catechesis can begin with God and proceed to Christ, or do the reverse; it can proceed from God to humanity, or from humanity to God; and so on.

Whatever the method, catechists are responsible for choosing and creating conditions which will encourage people to seek and accept the Christian message and integrate it more fully in their living out of the faith.

c) Induction and deduction

All methods used in catechesis employ both induction and deduction, each with a different emphasis. The inductive approach proceeds from the sensible, visible, tangible experiences of the person, and leads, with the help of the Holy Spirit, to more general conclusions and principles. The deductive approach proceeds in the opposite manner, beginning with general principles, such as a commandment, whether from the decalogue or the Sermon on the Mount, and applying it to the real world of the person being catechized. The deductive approach produces its fullest impact when preceded by the inductive.[240]

d) Experience

Experience is of great importance in catechesis. Experiential learning, which can be considered a form of inductive methodology, gives rise to concerns and questions, hopes and anxieties, reflections and judgments, which increase one's desire to penetrate more deeply into life's meaning. Experience can also increase the intelligibility of the Christian message, by providing illustrations and examples which shed light on the truths of revelation. At the same time, experience itself should be interpreted in the light of revelation.

The experiential approach is not easy, but it can be of considerable value to catechesis.[241] Catechists should encourage people to reflect on their significant experiences and respond to God's presence there. Sometimes they will provide appropriate experiences. They should seek to reach the whole person, using both cognitive (intellectual) and affective (emotional) techniques.

e) Formulations[242]

In every age and culture Christianity has commended certain prayers, formulas, and practices to all members of the faith community, even the youngest. While catechesis cannot be limited to the repetition of formulas and it is essential that formulas and facts pertaining to faith be understood, memorization has nevertheless had a special place in the handing-on of the faith throughout the ages and should continue to have such a place today, especially in catechetical programs for the young. It should be adapted to the level and ability of the child and introduced in a gradual manner, through a process which, begun early, continues gradually, flexibly, and never slavishly. In this way certain elements of Catholic faith, tradition, and practice are learned for a lifetime and can contribute to the individual's continued growth in understanding and living the faith.

Among these are the following:

1. Prayers such as the Sign of the Cross, Lord's Prayer, Hail Mary, Apostles' Creed, Acts of Faith, Hope and Charity, Act of Contrition.

2. Factual information contributing to an appreciation of the place of the word of God in the Church and the life of the Christian through an awareness and understanding of: the key themes of the history of salvation; the major personalities of the Old and New Testaments; and certain biblical texts expressive of God's love and care.

3. Formulas providing factual information regarding worship, the Church Year, and major practices in the devotional life of Christians including the parts of the Mass, the list of the sacraments, the liturgical seasons, the holy days of obligation, the major feasts of our Lord and our Lady, the various eucharistic devotions, the mysteries of the rosary of the Blessed Virgin Mary, and the Stations of the Cross.

4. Formulas and practices dealing with the moral life of Christians including the commandments, the beatitudes, the gifts of the Holy Spirit, the theological and moral virtues, the precepts of the Church, and the examination of conscience.

PART B: CATECHESIS AND HUMAN DEVELOPMENT
Section I: The Stages of Human Development

177. INFANCY AND EARLY CHILDHOOD (BIRTH TO AGE 5)[243]

Life's beginning stages are of critical importance to individual growth and development. Here foundations are laid which influence the ability to accept self, relate to others, and respond effectively to the environment. Upon these foundations rests the formation of the basic human and Christian personality — and so also one's human capacity for relating to God.

Healthy growth is most likely in a positive, nurturing environment — normally, the immediate family. Family relationships and interaction provide young children with their most powerful models for developing attitudes, values, and ways of responding to external influences which foster or hinder Christian and human growth.

God's love is communicated to infants and young children primarily through parents. Their faith, their confidence in human potential, and their loving and trusting attitude toward God and human beings strongly influence the child's faith. Parents are best prepared for this role by prior education for parenthood and by prenatal and pre-baptismal catechesis concerning the religious upbringing of children. During this stage in the lives of children, catechesis is directed primarily to their parents, to help them in their task. This also contributes to strengthening the conjugal bond and deepening their Christian commitment.

Parents and others in intimate contact with infants and small children should speak naturally and simply about God and their faith, as they do about other matters they want the children to understand and appreciate. Catechesis for prayer, accommodated to age and understanding, is part of this religious formation; it encourages the child to call upon God who loves and protects us, upon Jesus, God's Son and our brother, who leads us to the Father, and upon the Holy Spirit who dwells in our hearts. The child is also encouraged to pray to Mary, Jesus' mother and ours, and to the saints.[244] Parental example, including the practice of prayer, is particularly important.

Catechetical programs for preschool children seek to foster their growth in a wider faith community. While they should build upon and reinforce everything positive in the family and home environment, they can also be of particular importance for children who lack certain opportunities at home, children in one-parent families, and those whose parents do not spend much time with them, either because they both work outside the home or for some other reason.

Early childhood catechetical programs allow 3- to 5-year-olds to develop at their own pace, in ways suited to their age, circumstances, and learning abilities. They encourage appropriate attitudes toward worship and provide occasions of natural celebration with other children and adults, including religious and clergy. They seek, by deepening the child's sense of wonder and awe, to develop the capacity for spontaneous prayer and prayerful silence.

In formal catechetical programs for young children, groups should be small and at least one adult should work with the children of each level. The staff should be composed of parents and other adults, and should include persons with training in such areas as theology, scripture, early childhood growth and development, and methodology.

The learning of young children can also be fostered through coordinated courses for the entire family, which help parents become active, confident, and competent in encouraging their children's emerging faith.

178. CHILDHOOD (AGES 6 – 10)

Emotional development at this age is mainly a matter of growing in the capacity for satisfactory relationships with a wider circle of children and adults. Self-acceptance, trust, and personal freedom undergo significant changes, with acceptance of self coming to involve an awareness of specific talents (or their absence), unqualified trust of others giving way to a qualified trust which excludes some people and situations, and the expression of personal freedom being modified by recognition that other people, too, have rights and freedom.

Intellectual capacity gradually expands. Before, the world was viewed in very concrete terms drawn from direct personal experiences; now, the ability to form abstract ideas or concepts based on experience increases.

Catechesis calls attention to God's self-revelation and His invitation to us to be His children and friends; it points out that the revelation, the invitation, and the capacity to respond are all supernatural gifts. How children understand these realities still depends largely on analogous experiences in their relationships with other people. But "other people" now include a community much larger than the immediate family, notably the community to which children are exposed through media, particularly television which occupies so much of most children's time. TV should be evaluated in relation not only to the behavior it may encourage but that which it prevents — for instance, conversations, games, family festivities, and other activities which foster learning and character development.

The immediate environment, normally the home, remains the principal setting in which children experience a relationship with God. But now the support of the larger community becomes highly important to education in the faith, and its absence a more serious matter. Children accustomed to seeing others give witness to their faith are more likely to be ready for a fuller, more systematic presentation of concepts, forms of liturgical expression, and religious practices.

The child's first serious experience of work, usually in school, is relevant to catechesis. It serves as an introduction to values important in both the secular and religious spheres of life: the joy of doing things well, cooperation with others, and discipline experienced as something understandable and reasonable.[245]

Catechesis seeks to help children make an increasingly personal response to God's word and gifts. This response is not just a matter of external expressions, however useful they may be, but is truly heartfelt and prayerful. Catechesis approaches young persons with reverence and aids them in discovering and developing their unique, God-given gifts with the help of the gospel.

In presenting the values and teachings of Jesus, catechesis takes note of children's experience and encourages them to apply the same teachings and values to their lives.

At this stage significant changes occur in the ability to learn and understand. Certain prayer formulas become more intelligible. Stories like the parables take on deeper meaning. Practices like sharing and helping others make a great deal more sense. Memorization can be used very effectively, provided the child has a clear understanding of what is memorized and it is expressed in familiar language.

In the Western Church and in most Eastern Churches in the United States, catechesis is ordinarily provided at this stage for the sacraments of Reconciliation and Eucharist. Preparation for the reception of these sacraments is discussed in articles 122 and 126.

179. PRE-ADOLESCENCE AND PUBERTY (AGES 10–13)

Important physical changes have a direct bearing on how pre-adolescents perceive other people and relate to them. Young people at this stage face the task of coming to terms with themselves and others as sexual beings. While the foundations for doing so are laid in infancy, the effort now becomes conscious. They need to accept themselves precisely as male or female and to acquire a whole new way of relating to others. Usually, too, this involves some confusion, uncertainty, curiosity, awkwardness, and experimentation, as young people "try on" different patterns of behavior while searching for their unique identity. Puberty also adds a new dimension to the practice of personal freedom: increased responsibility for directing one's actions, together with increased readiness to accept their consequences.

Now more than ever interests extend beyond the home to the peer group, which exercises an increasing influence on attitudes, values, and behavior. Sensitivity toward others is growing, and efforts to develop a sense of community and of membership in the Church should continue.

While each child develops at his or her own rate, girls are generally more advanced than boys of the same age. The characteristics typical of this stage will be more or less intense according to an individual's physical and emotional attributes, home influences, previous experiences, and cultural background.

Catechesis should make use of all aspects of the pre-adolescent's experience, including the needs generated by rapid, radical change. The example of living faith given by others — at home and in the larger community — remains highly important and catechetically effective.

Topics like the nature of scripture, the Church, the sacraments, and the reasons which underlie moral norms can be discussed in greater depth than before. Reading and lectures can be used more effectively. But the life of faith is still best presented through concrete experiences which afford the pre-adolescent opportunities to incorporate Christian values into his or her life. These experiences are a point of departure for presenting the deeper aspects of the faith and its mysteries. Audio-visuals, projects, and field trips can be effective catechetical tools for this purpose. This is the age of hero worship, and it is helpful to present—in a manner which appeals to contemporary youth—the lives and deeds of the saints and other outstanding persons,[246] and especially the words and example of Jesus.

Growing more aware of themselves as individuals, pre-adolescents become better able to experience faith as a personal relationship with God. Prayer and service to others can become more meaningful. However, while it is possible for pre-adolescents, with the help of grace, to commit themselves to God, their faith is not that of fully mature persons.

Participation in the Mass, sacraments, and other rituals of the adult community can also become more meaningful. Young people can take a greater part in planning, preparing, and celebrating the liturgy.

As the sense of personal responsibility for behavior comes into sharper focus, specific Christian principles of conduct become more important, and the Sacrament of Reconciliation takes on deeper meaning.

Crises of faith, particularly relating to identification with the Church, occur among some pre-adolescents today. It is therefore extremely important that catechists with appropriate theoretical and practical expertise design catechetical programs which anticipate and ease such crises.

180. ADOLESCENCE

a) No specific age bracket

There are generally accepted age brackets for earlier stages, but not for adolescence. Different cultural, racial, and ethnic groups have their own standards for determining the length of time between puberty and adulthood.

b) Development of conscious spiritual life

The transition from childhood can be marked by an experience of emptiness. The self-awareness, relationship with others, sense of personal freedom, and intellectual understanding of reality achieved in childhood no longer suffice, but there is often nothing at hand to take their place. Now—and later, too—many have profound lack of self-confidence, magnified by life's complexity and ambiguity. The Church's ministry of service and healing richly equips it to respond to their need for interior reconciliation.

Interior turmoil and self-doubt are often expressed in external symptoms popularly associated with adolescence: boredom, frustration, sharp changes in mood, withdrawal, rebelliousness, apathy toward religion. Adolescents should be encouraged to understand that these symptoms are typical of many maturing persons and to be patient with themselves even while seeking to acquire the skills which will enable them to deal with their problems. Unfortunately, at precisely this time many experience difficulty in articulating their feelings, particularly to their parents.

Yet adolescents also commonly manifest increasing spiritual insight into themselves, other people, and life in general. A growing self-awareness and self-acceptance and a resultant greater capacity for authentic love of others begin to emerge, as well as increasing ability to respond with a mature faith.

A new sense of responsibility matching their expanded capacity for independent action often leads adolescents to reject, or seem to reject, laws and rules which they regard as arbitrary, external restrictions on their personal freedom. Many substitute a kind of inner law or norm of behavior based on personal ideals.

As idealism grows, so does the desire for continuous growth, even perfection, in the life of faith—or at least the ability to appreciate its value. Adolescents are increasingly critical of real or imagined imperfections in the Church and the adult faith community. The example of the adult community is extremely important at this time, although the direct influence of family and parents generally declines. For good or evil, peers exert the strongest influence of all; thus the need for developing strong youth ministry programs. School and media, especially television, also exert strong influences.

As they become more intellectually competent, adolescents need more intellectual stimulation and growth. At this time catechesis seeks to make clear the inner coherence of the truths of faith, their relation to one another and to humanity's final end. Careful attention must be given to the rational bases for faith; the intellectual investigation and articulation of religious belief are not "merely a kind of addition," but should be "counted as an essential need for the life of faith."[247] Appropriate experiences, involving participation by adolescents, provide a context in which doctrine can be systematically presented and reflected upon most effectively.

While the foundations of vocations—to marriage, the single life, priesthood and religious life, etc.—are laid and nurtured from early childhood on, vocational choices are imminent in adolescence. Now is the time to address the question directly and study the possibilities open to individuals, taking into account such things as youthful idealism, God's call, and the grace of the Holy Spirit. Catechists should be aware, however, that more and more young people are today delaying vocational and career choices until later in life.

Private prayer tends to become more personal and reflective now, while ritualized prayer often loses its attraction. Young people who see no point to prayer and meditation should be introduced—or reintroduced—to the idea that it is personal communication with Jesus and, through and in Him, with the Father. This can help make prayer an attractive reality in their lives. Prayer in all forms should be an integral and appealing part of catechesis for this age group.

Most people pass through adolescence during their teens, but in some cases the transition is delayed. The awakening of a conscious spiritual life is normally an impetus to move to the next stage of development, adulthood.

181. SOME GUIDELINES FOR THE CATECHESIS OF CHILDREN AND YOUTH

Norms and guidelines for the catechesis of children and youth are indicated throughout this chapter, as well as in other parts of the NCD. The most important task of such catechesis is to provide, through the witness of adults, an environment in which young people can grow in faith.

The following guidelines offer supplementary assistance to catechists.

1. In order to understand children and youth and communicate with them one must listen to them with respect, be sensitive to their circumstances, and be aware of their current values.

2. Both in the Church and in human society, children and young people have a dignity of their own. They are important not only for what they will do in the future, but for what they are here and now—for their intrinsic value and their value in relation to the common good.

3. Through catechesis all should be encouraged to know and respect other cultural, racial, and ethnic groups. Catechetical materials should be adapted to accommodate cultural, racial, and ethnic pluralism, the concerns of particular groups, and persons with special needs, as described in Part C of this chapter.

4. Effective catechesis takes into account the fact that the child's comprehension and other powers develop gradually. Religious truths are presented in greater depth, and more mature challenges are proposed, as the capacity for understanding and growth in faith increases.

5. Catechesis also provides experiences to live faith and apply the message of salvation to real-life situations. It encourages the use of imagination, as well as intelligence and memory. It stimulates not only exterior but interior activity—a prayerful response from the heart. Fostering a sense of community is also an important part of education for social life.

6. As children mature, catechesis does more to help them observe, explore, interpret, and judge their experiences, ascribe a Christian meaning to their lives, and act according to the norms of faith and love.[248] The presence in today's society of many conflicting values makes it all the more important to help young people to interiorize authentic values.

7. Catechesis emphasizes that growth in faith includes growth in the desire for a deeper, more mature knowledge of the truths of faith.

8. Private prayer is presented as an instrument of individual reflection and personal communication with God.

9. As the adolescent grows in intellectual ability, catechesis fosters insight into the interrelationship of religious truths and their relationship to the individual's final end. Especially in view of the contemporary emphasis on scientific criteria and methods, it also carefully establishes the rational foundations of faith.

10. Because adolescents are better able to reason deductively, it is possible to make more use of systematic, formal methods of instruction and study. However, deductive reasoning and methodology are more effective when preceded by induction. Sound methodology therefore includes providing continued opportunities for concrete experiences of lived faith, in which the message of salvation is applied to specific situations. Such things as field trips, meaningful social action, weekend retreats and programs, group dynamics of a sound and tested nature, simulation games, audio-visuals, and similar techniques can be very helpful. Constructive interaction and personal involvement are extremely important, and are present in gospel-based value clarification, group discussions, programs for the development of communication skills, and group prayer.

11. A correct understanding of experiential learning includes recognition that the entire faith community is an important part of the experience of children and youth: parents, catechists, and community all have roles in the catechesis of the young.

12. Catechetical materials are adapted to the stages of intellectual, spiritual, emotional, and physical development. Properly sequenced programs present the Christian message, and the history of the Church's response to it, in a manner appropriate to each age level. Particular truths receive the emphasis appropriate to their significance in the total body of revealed truth. Multi-year programs are best evaluated in their totality. Using appropriate media and methodology, these programs should give satisfactory emphasis to doctrine and moral content, to efforts to develop community, to worship, and to service of the faith community and society at large.

13. Research, experimentation, and professional competence are required in the continued development of catechetical programs which respect the developmental character of human maturation and growth in faith. Ideally, national, regional, and diocesan agencies and private institutions should cooperate with one another and with publishers of catechetical materials to produce such programs.

182. EARLY ADULTHOOD

The point of transition from adolescence to early adulthood varies considerably from one individual to another. Here we are considering young adults as those between the ages of 18 and 35, although not everyone has reached psychological, emotional, and spiritual maturity even by the latter age.

There are many subgroups with overlapping membership within the young adult population (e.g., high school students, members of the military, veterans, college, university, and technical school students, blue-collar workers and professionals, unemployed persons, members of particular cultural, racial, and ethnic groups). Young adults may be single, married with children, unmarried with children, married without children, separated, divorced, or widowed. Some are physically handicapped, emotionally disturbed, or mentally retarded. Obviously, no single catechetical approach will suffice for all.

Young adults are among the most likely to sever contact with organized religion.[249] This is unfortunate for many reasons, not least because this is the period during which critical decisions are generally made concerning state of life, choice of partner, and career.[250] It must be recognized that many in this age group are alienated from the institutional Church and may be lost if greater emphasis is not placed on their evangelization and catechesis.

183. THE MAKING OF LIFE DECISIONS

Near the end of adolescence or in early adulthood it becomes necessary to translate one's ideals into a personal way of life. Long-term choices and decisions must be made concerning vocation, career, and even religious affiliation. Such choices condition future growth. Prolonged unwillingness to make any choices of this kind prevents continued growth and is usually a sign that, regardless of age, the individual is still at an earlier stage of maturity.

Catechesis seeks to help people make the crucial decisions of this period in accord with God's will. It invites young adults to commit themselves to the living of full Christian lives and to engage in ministry within and for the Church community.

Catechesis also continues to present scripture and encourage reflection on it. While experience and personal interaction remain helpful for learning, reading and disciplined study are even more important than before. Catechesis seeks to encourage faith-inspired decisions and close identification with the adult faith community, including its liturgical life and mission. At this age level, catechesis, particularly of those continuing their education in college, will include courses in Christian philosophy and theology.

184. MIDDLE ADULTHOOD

At present there is no generally accepted theory of life stages in adulthood that satisfies stringent scientific criteria. The middle years seem to resist categories. In fact, middle age itself is a relatively new concept: before 1900, when average life expectancy in the United States was less than 50, old age was thought to set in around 40. Catechists, nevertheless, will find many helpful insights in the new and increasingly numerous studies on the stages of adult life.

Typically, an individual enters the adult years with optimism and enthusiasm. Ideals are dominant. High goals are set. Ambition is strong. Challenges are eagerly accepted. Self-confidence is undimmed.

Crises of limits arise when people are defeated and disappointed in their efforts to achieve major goals in life: for example, through the experience of incompatibility and disillusionment in marriage; divorce; job dissatisfaction or job loss; the uncertainties associated with deciding on a second career; severe financial problems; difficulty in maintaining friendships; inability to undertake or sustain commitments; severe illness; the death of a loved one and its consequences; serious problems with offspring; inability to express deep emotions; profound loss of self-esteem; fear of failure; fear of success.

As a result, many people experience increasing boredom and loneliness, a sense of routine, fatigue, discouragement in facing decisions and their consequences. Ideals suffer in confrontation with hard reality. Hopes for ultimate success are dimmed by failure and the experience of personal weakness. The first signs of physical aging begin to appear. Eventually, a kind of spiritual crisis is likely. Before, the limitations of being human were to a great extent either not apparent or not part of one's personal experience; now they are inescapable realities in one's own life.

Several options are possible: escape—literal, physical flight or retreat into fantasies; change—new life decisions which may or may not succeed; rebellion, resentment, and hostility; or acceptance of one's limitations and, thereby, of one's humanity. Escape delays or prevents further growth; change may further growth or be another kind of escape; hostility is generally self-destructive. Positive acceptance means moving to a new stage of maturity, which can be a basis for spiritual growth. With grace and the use of Christian wisdom,[251] it is possible to deepen one's relationship with God and other people. One can also exercise a more truly personal freedom, for many obstacles to the exercise of responsible freedom have been removed and one is better able to place oneself wholly at God's disposal and to love without expecting anything in return, either from God or other people.

Catechesis can help adults live out their life decisions; prepare them for the crises of life; and assist them through these crises.

185. SOME GUIDELINES FOR THE CATECHESIS OF ADULTS

A number of catechetical norms and guidelines for adult catechesis have already been mentioned in this chapter. Others are noted elsewhere. What follows is intended to offer further assistance with regard to the Christian message as it pertains to adults, as well as to methodology.

a) The Christian message

The content of adult catechesis is as comprehensive and diverse as the Church's mission. It should include those universally relevant elements which are basic to the formation of an intelligent and active Catholic Christian and also catechesis pertaining to the particular needs which adults identify themselves as having.

The following description of content is not exhaustive.[252] Its elements have been selected either because of their relationship to the fundamental objectives of catechesis or their relevance to the present social scene in the United States.

Adult catechesis includes the study of scripture, tradition, liturgy, theology, morality, and the Church's teaching authority and life.[253] Church history is important for placing events in proper perspective.

Adult catechesis seeks to present the Church in all its dimensions, including its missionary nature, its role as sign or sacrament of Christ's presence in the world, its ecumenical commitment, and its mandate to communicate the whole truth of Christ to all persons in all times. (Cf. Matthew 28:20)

Because Christ commissioned the apostles to teach people to observe everything He had commanded (cf. Matthew 28:20), catechesis includes "not only those things which are to be believed, but also those things which are to be done."[254] Adult catechesis seeks to make adults keenly aware that an authentically Christian moral life is one guided and informed by the grace and gifts of the Holy Spirit, and that decisions of conscience should be based on study, consultation, prayer, and understanding of the Church's teaching.

Adult catechesis gives parents and guardians additional instruction to help them in carrying out their particular responsibilities. It also provides similar instruction, at least of a general kind, to all adults, since the entire community has obligations toward the young.

It addresses the Church's mission to promote justice, mercy, and peace, including the vindication of religious, human, and civil rights which are violated.

Adult catechesis offers education for change, including the skills essential for dealing with the rapid changes typical of life today.

Adult catechesis gives special attention to spiritual life and prayer.

b) The methods

Adults should play a central role in their own education. They should identify their needs, plan ways to meet them, and take part in the evaluation of programs and activities.

Catechesis for adults respects and makes use of their experiences, their cultural, racial, and ethnic heritages, their personal skills, and the other resources they bring to catechetical programs. Whenever possible, adults should teach and learn from one another.

Much effective learning comes from reflecting upon one's experiences in the light of faith. Adults must be helped to translate such reflection into practical steps to meet their responsibilities in a Christian manner. Where appropriate experiences have not been part of a person's life, the catechetical process attempts to provide them, to the extent possible. This suggests the use of discussion techniques, especially in small groups, and the cultivation of communication skills.

Other methods of adult catechesis include reading, lectures, workshops, seminars, the use of the media, the Catholic press and other publications, and audio-visuals: in fact, all methods available to sound secular education. Specifically religious experiences — retreats, prayer meetings, and the like — provide extremely valuable opportunities for people to pause and reflect on their lives.

All catechetical programs, including those for adults, should be evaluated periodically.

186. LATER ADULTHOOD

As people mature, their increased knowledge and proper love of self make it possible for them to enter more readily into self-giving relationships with others. Their courage, honesty, and concern increase. Their practical experience grows. They come to enjoy higher levels of personal freedom. Properly used, these can be the most creative and fruitful years. The attitudes, example, and experience of mature persons make them invaluable educators in and of the faith community.

It would be a mistake, however, to suppose that as people grow older they automatically grow more religious or more mature in their faith. Generally speaking, pastoral ministry has paid too little attention to old age.[255] The needs of this age group have seldom been addressed by catechesis. Everyone needs to be confirmed in supernatural hope and prepared for the coming passage from this life to eternal happiness with God.

Death should be depicted for what it is, the final opportunity to assent to the divine will and give oneself freely to God. Several stages have been identified in the process by which an individual typically comes to terms with the fact that he or she will die: denial, anger, bargaining with God, depression, and finally acceptance. Impending or anticipated death provides an opportunity to catechize the elderly and their families on the meaning of Christian death as a sharing in the paschal mystery, a personal sharing in Christ's death so that one may share also in His resurrection, as well as on the steps by which one prepares oneself spiritually for death. So the aged become signs of God's presence, of the sacredness of earthly life, of eternal life, and of the resurrection to come.[256]

187. SOME RECOMMENDATIONS FOR CATECHESIS IN LATER ADULTHOOD

Aging is a natural process with positive and negative aspects. Besides continuing the emphases of adult catechesis, catechesis for the aging seeks to give them physical, emotional, intellectual, and spiritual support so that they can make fruitful use of leisure time, understand and accept the increasing limitations imposed by age, and grow in faith even as they grow in years.

Catechesis notes the significant contributions which the aged make to the entire community through their work and witness.

Catechists and all others who deal with the aged should make use of the growing body of research in geriatrics and related subjects. This area, relatively unexplored, is one where the Church could usefully initiate research, develop creative new programs, and disseminate information about effective programs which already exist.

Elderly people themselves can provide some of the most effective catechesis for the aged. They should receive preparation for this work and should have the opportunity not only to participate in programs but direct them.

188. THE IMPORTANCE OF ADULT CATECHESIS

The act of faith is a free response to God's grace; and maximum human freedom only comes with the self-possession and responsibility of adulthood. This is one of the principal reasons for regarding adult catechesis as the chief form of catechesis. To assign primacy to adult catechesis does not mean sacrificing catechesis at other age levels; it means making sure that what is done earlier is carried to its culmination in adulthood.

Rapid changes in society and the Church make adult catechesis especially important today. Adults need help in dealing with their problems and communicating their faith to the young. Adult catechesis is also relevant to the Church's mission on behalf of justice, mercy, peace, and respect for human life — a mission which depends heavily upon informed and motivated lay people.[257] Adults need to learn and practice the gospel demands of stewardship: God gives everyone a measure of personal time, talent, and treasure to use for His glory and the service of neighbor.

Because of its importance and because all other forms of catechesis are oriented in some way to it, the catechesis of adults must have high priority at all levels of the Church. The success of programs for children and youth depends to a significant extent upon the words, attitudes, and actions of the adult community, especially parents, family, and guardians.

189. MOTIVATION FOR ADULT CATECHESIS

There are many ways of motivating people to become involved in adult catechesis; here we shall mention only a few. Today, when perhaps more adults than ever before are participating in continuing education courses of all kinds, there is every reason to think many can be attracted to appealing catechetical programs.

The best inducement to participate is an excellent program. People are drawn by the testimony of satisfied participants, as well as by personal invitations from friends and Church leaders.

The total learning environment of the parish is also an important factor in motivating adults. This includes the quality of the liturgies, the extent of shared decision making, the priorities in the parish budget, the degree of commitment to social justice, the quality of the other catechetical programs. Programs for adults should confront people's real questions and problems honestly and openly. As far as possible, they should offer positive reinforcements and rewards; the learning environment should be attractive and comfortable; adults should be encouraged to realize their potential for becoming religiously mature — or more mature — persons. Good publicity in the media, religious and secular, is also very helpful.

Section II: Conscience Formation

190. THE PROCESS OF CONSCIENCE FORMATION

Conscience is discussed in articles 101–105. Here we consider formation of conscience. Both sections should be consulted in catechesis dealing with conscience.[258]

An individual's conscience should develop as he or she matures. Many psychologists trace a series of stages of growth in the faculty and process by which moral judgments are made. Knowledge of these stages can be helpful when interpreted in a Christian context.

Conscience formation is influenced by such human factors as level of education, emotional stability, self-knowledge, and the ability for clear objective judgment. It is also influenced by external factors: attitudes in the communities to which an individual belongs and cultural and social conditions, particularly as reflected in parents and family.

The central factor in the formation of conscience and sound moral judgment should be Christ's role in one's life. (Cf. John 14:6ff; 12:46–50) His ideals, precepts, and example are present and accessible in scripture and the tradition of the Church. To have a truly Christian conscience, one must faithfully communicate with the Lord in every phase of one's life, above all through personal prayer and through participation in the sacramental life and prayer of the Church. All other aspects of conscience formation are based on this.

Catholics should always measure their moral judgments by the magisterium, given by Christ and the Holy Spirit to express Christ's teaching on moral questions and matters of belief and so enlighten personal conscience.[259]

The process of conscience formation should be adapted to age, understanding, and circumstances of life. People should not only be taught Christian moral principles and norms, but encouraged and supported in making responsible decisions consistent with them. The community's example of Christian love is one of the best sources of such encouragement and support.

The Church is "a force for freedom and is freedom's home."[260] Taking into account the age and maturity of the learner, freedom must be respected in conscience formation as in all catechesis. "When grace infuses human liberty, it makes freedom fully free and raises it to its highest perfection in the freedom of the Spirit."[261]

It is a task of catechesis to elicit assent to all that the Church teaches, for the Church is the indispensable guide to the complete richness of what Jesus teaches. When faced with questions which pertain to dissent from non-infallible teachings of the Church, it is important for catechists to keep in mind that the presumption is always in favor of the magisterium.[262]

Conscience, though inviolable, is not a law unto itself; it is a practical dictate, not a teacher of doctrine. Doctrine is taught by the Church, whose members have a serious obligation to know what it teaches and adhere to it loyally.

In performing their catechetical functions, catechists should present the authentic teaching of the Church.

Section III: Sexuality and Catechesis

191. SEXUALITY AND CATECHESIS[263]

According to the Second Vatican Council, "As they [children and young people] advance in years, they should be given positive and prudent sexual education."[264] Education in sexuality includes all dimensions of the topic: moral, spiritual, psychological, emotional, and physical. Its goal is training in chastity in accord with the teaching of Christ and the Church, to be lived in a wholesome manner in marriage, the single state, the priesthood, and religious life. Sexuality is an important element of the human personality, an integral part of one's overall consciousness. It is both a central aspect of one's self-understanding (i.e., as male or female) and a crucial factor in one's relationships with others.

Many experiences have some potential bearing, positive or negative, upon education in sexuality; and virtually all catechists and educators have at least some potential responsibility in this regard, whether or not they ever deal directly with the matter.

Education in sexuality must always be given with reverence and respect, which extend to the language used. More than that, all have a need for catechesis in sexuality in the context of religious values. The God-given dignity and beauty of sex and the sanctity of marriage and family life should be emphasized. Christ's love for the Church is the model for the love between husband and wife. (Cf. Ephesians 5:25) To abuse the sanctity of love and marriage is anti-sexual, contrary to a proper understanding of sexuality, and in violation of God's will and command. Catechesis calls particular attention to the role of self-control, self-discipline, prayer, the reception of the sacraments, and devotion to the Blessed Mother, model of chastity, as elements in developing a Christian approach to sexuality.

Catechesis should call attention simultaneously to the essential equality of men and women and to the respect due the uniqueness and complementarity of the two sexes.

Education which helps people understand and accept their sexuality begins in infancy and continues in adulthood. The best catechesis for children comes from the wholesome example of their parents and other adults.

However, many parents need assistance in catechizing their children on this subject.[265] The Church can be of great help in this matter. Parents will find help in suitable reading materials and audio-visuals, in family life education and other instructional programs. Appropriate materials can be used by parents in giving instruction to their children. Catechesis should help parents in giving instruction to their children. Catechesis should help parents be competent and at ease with respect to content and methodology. Catechists themselves need suitable preparation.

In recent years education in sexuality has been introduced under different titles into public school systems as well as many Catholic schools and parish catechetical programs. Some courses and programs treat sexuality in a comprehensive manner, including its physical aspects along with the rest; but others deal almost exclusively with physical aspects without reference to values or ethics. This is unfortunate, for human sexuality involves much more besides the physical. Education in sexuality should be given in an integral manner.

The primacy of the parental right in education obviously extends to children's formation in relation to sexuality. Blessed with the grace of their state in life, parents are presumed to know and understand their children better than anyone else. Parents—especially those with some special familiarity with education in sexuality—should be invited to take part in planning, presenting, and evaluating programs. They should be involved in developing or assessing the philosophy and objectives of such courses and should have opportunities to examine proposed curricula and materials before they are introduced into the classroom.

It is helpful for parents to become acquainted with the teachers who will instruct their children. Also, when possible, parents themselves should participate in the instruction, either regularly or occasionally.

Parents have a right and duty to protest programs which violate their moral and religious convictions. If protests based on well-founded convictions and accurate information are unsuccessful, they have a right to remove their children from the classes, taking care to cause as little embarrassment to the children as possible.

Even after their reasonable requirements and specifications have been met, however, some parents may remain anxious about education in sexuality. They should not let their feelings express themselves in indiscriminate opposition to all classroom instruction in sexuality, for that would not be consistent with the position of the Second Vatican Council[266] and the bishops of the United States. Furthermore, to the extent such opposition might impede or disrupt responsible efforts along these lines, it would violate the rights of other, no less conscientious parents who desire such instruction for their children.[267]

PART C: CATECHESIS FOR PERSONS WITH SPECIAL NEEDS

192. INTRODUCTION

Articles 134–139 consider the liturgical needs of various special groups. Now we consider their catechetical needs.

193. ADAPTING CATECHESIS TO A PLURALISTIC SOCIETY

Catechesis is prepared to accommodate all social and cultural differences in harmony with the message of salvation. Within the fundamental unity of faith, the Church recognizes diversity, the essential equality of all, and the need for charity and mutual respect among all groups in a pluralistic Church and society.

Guidelines for catechesis by geographical area can easily be inferred from what follows concerning the catechesis of cultural, racial, and ethnic groups. Catechetical guidelines concerning the Catholic Church's relationship to other religious traditions are discussed in articles 75–79.

194. CATECHESIS OF CULTURAL, RACIAL, AND ETHNIC GROUPS

At one time or another almost every cultural, racial, and ethnic group in the United States has held minority status in society and in the Church. Many still do. "Minority" can be understood either numerically or as referring to a group whose members are hindered in their efforts to obtain, keep, or exercise their rights.

In some cases, it is important that catechesis distinguish among subgroups within larger groups. For example, the Spanish-speaking, while sharing a common language, include Mexican-Americans, Puerto Ricans, Cubans, and others, each group with its distinct cultural characteristics, customs, needs, and potential. The same is true of various tribes and nations of Native Americans, Afro-Americans, and others.

The preparation of catechists is of the greatest importance. Ideally, the catechist will be a member of the particular racial, cultural, or ethnic group. Those who are not should understand and empathize with the group, besides having adequate catechetical formation.

The language of the particular group should be used in the catechesis of its members: not just its vocabulary, but its thought patterns, cultural idioms, customs, and symbols. Catechetical materials should suit its characteristics and needs. Rather than simply translating or adapting materials prepared for others, it is generally necessary to develop new materials. To be appropriate, even adaptations must involve more than translations and picture changes. Catechetical materials should affirm the identity and dignity of the members of the particular group, using findings of the behavioral sciences for this purpose.

Catechesis takes into account the educational and economic circumstances of diverse groups, avoiding unrealistic demands on time, physical resources, and finances and making adjustments which correspond to the educational level of those being catechized.

Catechesis takes into account a group's special needs in relation to justice and peace, and prepares its members to assume their responsibility for achieving its just goals.

Even in culturally homogeneous areas and parishes catechesis should be multi-cultural, in the sense that all should be educated to know and respect other cultural, racial, and ethnic groups. Minority group members should be invited and encouraged to participate in religious and social functions.

The Church at all levels must make a special commitment to provide funds, research, materials, and personnel for catechesis directed to minority groups. Parishes in which there are no members of such groups have an obligation to help provide funds and personnel. Dioceses with many minority group members should be assisted by dioceses in which there are few or none. Parochial, regional, and national leadership and coordination are needed.

At the same time, the leaders of minority groups should support catechesis, especially by engaging in broad consultation to ascertain their people's catechetical needs. Community leaders can stimulate catechetical research, planning, and promotion, and participate in actual catechesis.

At all times catechesis must respect the personal dignity of minority group members, avoiding condescension and patronizing attitudes. The ultimate goal is that minority groups be able to provide for their own catechetical needs, while remaining closely united in faith and charity with the rest of the Church. This unity can be fostered in many ways, including the educational and informational efforts of mission agencies and missionaries.

195. PERSONS WITH HANDICAPPING CONDITIONS

Handicapped persons, approximately 12.5 percent of the total population of the United States, include the mentally retarded, those with learning disabilities, the emotionally disturbed, the physically handicapped, the hard of hearing, the deaf, the visually impaired, the blind, and others. Many handicapped persons are in isolating conditions which tend to cut them off from learning. Each handicapped person has special needs — including a need for catechesis — which must be recognized and met.

Catechetical programs should not segregate the handicapped from the rest of the community excessively or unnecessarily.

Catechesis for certain groups (e.g., the deaf, the blind, the mentally retarded) often requires specialized materials, training, and skills (such as the ability to sign). The entire Church has a responsibility for providing training and research; leadership preparation and funding are needed at the national, diocesan, and local levels. On the diocesan and parish levels, sharing of resources and personnel and collaboration in the preparation and sponsorship of programs are appropriate; the possibility of ecumenically sponsored and conducted programs should also be investigated.

It is particularly important for the families of the handicapped persons to be involved in their catechesis. Supportive participation by family members helps them better understand handicapped individuals.

The goal is to present Christ's love and teaching to each handicapped person in as full and rich a manner as he or she can assimilate.

196. OTHER PERSONS WITH SPECIAL NEEDS

The list of groups with special needs is almost endless: the aged — often among the socially and economically disadvantaged; the illiterate and educationally deprived; young single people in college or vocational programs; young single workers; military personnel; unmarried people with children; young married couples with or without children; couples in mixed marriages; the divorced; the divorced and remarried; middle-aged singles; the widowed; the imprisoned; persons with a homosexual orientation; etc.

Catechesis is also needed by people in the "caring" professions—such as doctors, nurses, and social workers—who have their own special requirements along with many opportunities for witness and for catechizing in their dealings with the deprived, the sick, and the dying.

The Church is seriously obliged to provide catechesis suited to the special needs of these and other groups. Some were overlooked in the past, but in several cases these special needs are of relatively recent origin: for example, those of the aged, whose current difficulties are largely associated with increased longevity and the decline of the extended family; and those of young single people, whose needs are related to the recent emergence of new life styles.

Catechesis is part of a total pastoral ministry to people with special needs. It emphasizes aspects of the Church's teaching and practice which will help them make personal, faith-filled responses to their special circumstances. Sensitivity and careful planning are essential.

Catechetical programs should, whenever possible, be developed in consultation with representatives of those for whom they are intended. The aim should be to help them overcome the obstacles they face and achieve as much integration as they can into the larger community of faith.

PART D: SOME SIGNIFICANT FACTORS AFFECTING CATECHESIS IN THE UNITED STATES

197. ISOLATION OF INFANTS, CHILDREN, AND YOUTH

Interaction between parents and children in all spheres has decreased significantly in the United States in the past twenty-five years. (This is caused, to a considerable extent, by factors mentioned in articles 24–28.) Children begin to be segregated from their parents in the first years of life, and this isolation continues through preschool, elementary school, high school, and college.

As adults give less time to parenting, young people respond by creating a youth subculture, whose values and attitudes are dictated largely by television and peers instead of by parents and teachers.

In view of the intrinsic importance of parents and family in transmitting cultural and religious attitudes and values, this isolation of infants, children, and youth poses major problems for catechesis. Comprehensive solutions require a major reorganization of social institutions, beyond the scope of this NCD to prescribe. Catechists can, however, at least make parents aware of the problem and its consequences, and encourage as much interaction as possible between them and their children. Of special importance is family catechesis, where young people can spend "quality time" with parents or guardians.

198. CHILDREN AND YOUTH NOT ATTENDING SCHOOL

According to census figures, nearly 3 percent of the children aged 7 to 10 in the United States and over 10 percent of those 16 and 17 receive no formal schooling. Migration is one of the causes of nonattendance at school. Efforts are needed to locate these children and youth and persuade them to participate in catechetical programs. Their nonattendance may also reflect other problems — e.g., illiteracy, a handicap — which must be dealt with before formal catechesis is possible. Parental involvement is extremely important.

199. CHILDREN AND YOUTH FROM RELIGIOUSLY INDIFFERENT FAMILIES

As noted in article 24 and elsewhere, the number of religiously indifferent parents seems to have grown in the United States in recent years. The causes of this phenomenon must be identified if catechetical programs oriented to evangelization are to have an impact on them and their children.

Parish members should seek out such families and invite them to take part in parish activities: e.g., services for the sick, the elderly, the poor, and others who are in need. Efforts should be made to include them in such things as weekend retreats and days of prayer. Home visitations by parishioners and priests may also help motivate them to become religiously active.

200. SOME CHARACTERISTICS OF YOUTH

Although contemporary youth culture changes rapidly, it is helpful to describe some of its current traits with particular significance for catechesis.

a) Population trends

Over the next several years the number of school-age children and youth in the United States will decrease, while the proportion belonging to racial, cultural, and ethnic minorities increases.

The number of children and youth in Catholic elementary and secondary schools has been declining since 1965, although there have been recent signs of stabilization. At the same time, large numbers of young Catholics receive no formal catechesis.[268] Research into this problem, particularly its causes and effects, is badly needed.

b) Age of religious crisis

Between 12 and 18 many young people either begin to abandon the faith of their childhood or become more deeply committed to it.

There is a tendency for young people around age 13 to regard much previous teaching about religion as childish, in the erroneous belief that there is no coherent and mature explanation for what they have learned earlier. Resolution of the conflict between faith and reason, formerly thought to take place by age 20, now appears to be occurring earlier.[269] These developments must be taken into account in preparing catechetical programs and materials for young people facing or about to face a crisis of faith.

c) Traditional beliefs and religious practice[270]

There is ample evidence of a contemporary decline in traditional beliefs and religious practices. For instance, fewer youths than in the past believe in a personal God, divine revelation, life after death, and the Bible as God's word. Sunday and holy day Mass attendance has decreased, as has the practice of daily prayer.

There is a more permissive attitude with regard to sexual morality and greater use of alcohol, marijuana, and other drugs. While crimes of assault have declined, truancy, running away from home, and theft have increased. The suicide rate among young people rose 250 percent between 1954 and 1973 (10.9 per 100,000); in a recent poll 23 percent said they believe that in some circumstances it is not wrong to take one's life.

Many experts attribute these phenomena to isolation and loneliness. Others hold that society burdens young people with awesome pressures and responsibilities which they are not ready to handle alone.

d) Positive aspects

While some young people are moving away from organized religion, others remain firmly committed. A few never attend religious services or say prayer is of little importance to them. But a clear majority of those 13 to 18 believe that, in some way, the Church and religious authorities represent God, and about one-fourth of Catholic youth claim to be active in Church-sponsored activities. For the most part, young people are searching for direction to help them become what God has created them to be. A large majority are satisfied with their country, families, and schools. Adolescents are also strongly interested in the practical dimensions of life.

In general, young people mirror the values and standards of society. Their problems tend to be essentially symptoms of malaise in the larger community; they are more the victims than the source of religious and social ills. Most are conscientious persons growing toward maturity, really concerned about their mistakes and interested in their fellow human beings. Such qualities offer a starting point for effective catechesis.

e) Some observations and recommendations

The "personal-experiential" dimension of religion (closeness to God, frequency of prayer, and the importance of religion in one's life) is least affected as the person grows older. This indicates that for many adolescents a personal relationship with Jesus Christ is not bound up with formal religious practice or traditional beliefs.

Thus there seems to be no inherent reason why young people should become more prone to lose their faith as they grow older. They are more exposed to competing world views and value systems, but catechesis can and should be adapted to mental age and to the social context and other circumstances.

It is significant that many adolescents apparently stop thinking about religion long before they consciously reject it. Various reasons are suggested: boredom with religion as they know it; the association of religion with fairy tales ("science has proved religion isn't true"); religion's apparent remoteness from life; confusion concerning the language and thought of the Bible. To the extent that these explanations are valid, the answer seems to lie in adapting catechesis to the mental age of young people, and allowing them to question, discuss, and explore religious beliefs. The young insist on dialogue, as opposed to what they consider religious indoctrination. If such steps as these are taken; if young people are provided with models of faith which they perceive as credible and relevant; if they are challenged to confront the fullness of religious truth—then there is reason to hope that, as they grow older, adolescents will progress in faith and religious practice and suffer no delay in the process of religious maturation.

All this indicates that adolescents are more like adults than children in relation to faith. Catechesis must reflect this fact.

Catechists should be aware that, with God's grace, many factors can help foster religiousness in youth. Operating in varying ways and to varying degrees are age, sex, social class, city size, parental education, parental religious practice, parental affection-support, parent approval of friends, attendance at religion classes, etc. The two most important factors are parental religious practice and the current study of religion. In addition, parental affection and support have a positive effect, especially on social morality.[271] These considerations point to priorities in youth catechesis, including the active involvement of parents. Furthermore, by creating a sense of community, religion can probably help relieve some of the tensions created by changing attitudes toward sex, religion, politics, and social relationships.

201. SOME CHARACTERISTICS OF YOUNG ADULTS

a) College students[272]

College students, close to half of the 18 to 21 age group, differ in many respects from other young adults.

Many studies have been made of their religious attitudes and values. Because of rapid changes, it is quite possible that data gathered a few years ago no longer reflect current attitudes. However, there are certain long-term trends of which catechists and campus ministers should be aware.

Research on college students over the past fifty years shows that: they now have more freedom and personal responsibility than ever before; there have been changes in moral orientations, including greater tolerance regarding the specifics of moral codes; a distinct conscious youth culture has emerged.

In recent years, living a moral life, the importance of religion, and patriotism have all receded in importance for students. In all areas related to sexual morality (premarital and extramarital sex, relations between consenting homosexuals, having an abortion, etc.) deviations from traditional norms find greater acceptance. Along with the desire for greater sexual freedom, there is less regard for authority and for hard work.

Many conclude that the emphasis on individualism, autonomy, and personal fulfillment will continue in the years ahead, while positive attitudes toward authority, personal sacrifice, and traditional sexual morality will grow progressively weaker. It has been observed that there is even a considerable difference in religious beliefs and practices between freshmen and seniors, with first-year students more traditional than fourth-year ones.

Religious belief and practice have declined among Catholics on both secular and Catholic campuses. While more trend studies are needed to ascertain the current situation, it appears that students in some Catholic colleges are becoming increasingly like students in other colleges in the United States as far as religion is concerned.

Further study is also needed concerning the finding that, between 1948 and 1974, the percentage of college students reacting wholly or partly against beliefs taught them at home rose from 57 percent to 79 percent. At the same time, the median age for the onset of doubt fell to 14.4 (from 16.4 in 1948), indicating that the crucial time for religious development is in high school, not college. Another part of the picture is the alarming rate at which college-educated persons leave the Church (discussed in article 24).

Several factors appear to have influenced religious changes among students. For example, the surveys reflect some rural-urban difference; and students who are more "cosmopolitan" (acquainted with and accepting of different cultural settings) tend to be a bit weaker in religious commitment. The most important factor, however, seems to be the amount of religious influence in the home. Students who are closer to their parents have more ties to traditional religion and the Church. To a large extent, attitudes toward the Church seem to be extensions of attitudes toward the family and thus to reflect interpersonal and social factors.

There is some evidence that, while the roles of both mother and father are important, they are different. For example, conflict with the mother appears to contribute more to later rejection of her religious values.

b) Non-college young adults[273]

While in the past college education generally tended to exert a secularizing influence on religious practice and belief, among Catholics it was related positively to orthodoxy and religious practice. In regard to both orthodoxy and moral values, however, the difference has been narrowing in recent years.

College youth attend Mass more frequently and appear to be more orthodox in doctrinal matters, but non-college youth are more traditional on moral issues (e.g., sexual freedom, abortion, the need to live a moral life). On the specific issue of acceptance of papal authority, the decline has been greatest among college males and the least among non-college males. Women experienced an intermediate degree of impact, with the college-educated reporting more questioning than non-college women.

Non-college youth pray more frequently and are more inclined to regard religion as an important value in life. The apostasy rate (leaving the Church) is also somewhat lower among youth under 30 who did not attend college.

c) Some observations and recommendations

The younger, more affluent, and more closely aligned with the national culture a person is, the more subject he or she is to short-range changes in religious commitment.

Religious disaffection may be linked to a general mentality of independence; sociopolitical changes have apparently been accompanied by disillusionment with many social institutions, including organized religion. Religious commitments are closely related to other important commitments, and when social changes take place, religious commitments also change. Apparently religious commitment is determined not only by clergy, church, and school, but even more by family, community, and nation. The extensive social changes in the United States in recent years must be taken seriously into account in preparing catechetical programs for college students and all others.[274]

The general decline in orthodoxy, moral values, religious devotion, and acceptance of ecclesiastical authority has been most precipitous among young people. But the majority have not defected from the Church, even though their participation is sometimes peripheral. This strongly suggests that the young generation, including young adults, are waiting for the Church to address itself more specifically and forcefully to the new forces and values shaping society.

202. SOME CHARACTERISTICS OF LATER ADULTHOOD

The number of persons 65 or older is increasing rather rapidly in the United States. It is expected to rise from 22.8 million in 1976 to approximately 30 million in 1990.

Because women tend to live longer than men, there are now 143 women for every 100 men over 65 in this country. Women, on the average, can expect to live more than 20 years with their husbands after the children leave home, and about eight years as widows.

The vast majority of persons over 65 are not employed, but are in good health (although perhaps with some chronic, non-disabling condition). Perhaps no more than 10 percent need nursing home care, and half of these are receiving such care.

Pastoral ministers should know how many elderly people are present within parish or diocesan boundaries. This information is needed in developing catechetical programs.

203. CONCLUSION

We have described in broad terms how a human being grows and changes from birth to death, and pointed to the relationship between this process and growth in the life of faith. Catechists recognize, however, that another, mysterious, uniquely powerful action is taking place: the work of the Holy Spirit in each person, in the Church, and in the world.

Having considered those who are catechized, we shall next consider those who do the catechizing—catechetical personnel.

CHAPTER IX
CATECHETICAL PERSONNEL

204. INTRODUCTION

In this NCD the term catechist is used in a broad sense to designate anyone who participates formally or informally in catechetical ministry. All members of a community of believers are called to share in this ministry by being witnesses to the faith. Some, however, are called to more specific catechetical roles. Parents, teachers, and principals in Catholic schools, parish catechists, coordinators or directors of religious education, those who work in diocesan and national catechetical offices, deacons, priests, and bishops—all are catechists with distinct roles. Here we shall describe ideal qualities, for which all catechists should strive, and discuss the various roles and the educational preparation required for them.

PART A: IDEAL QUALITIES OF CATECHISTS

205. AN IDEAL AND A CHALLENGE

Because it points to an ideal, what follows is meant to be a challenge as well as a guide. This ideal should not discourage present or prospective catechists. On the contrary, as they participate in the catechetical ministry their religious lives will be intensified and they will find themselves growing in the qualities needed for successful ministry to others. It is these human and Christian qualities of catechists, more than their methods and tools, upon which the success of catechesis depends.

206. RESPONSE TO A CALL

As important as it is that a catechist have a clear understanding of the teaching of Christ and His Church, this is not enough. He or she must also receive and respond to a ministerial call, which comes from the Lord and is articulated in the local Church by the bishop. The response to this call includes willingness to give time and talent, not only to catechizing others, but to one's own continued growth in faith and understanding.

207. WITNESS TO THE GOSPEL

For catechesis to be effective, the catechist must be fully committed to Jesus Christ. Faith must be shared with conviction, joy, love, enthusiasm, and hope. "The summit and center of catechetical formation lies in an aptitude and ability to communicate the Gospel message."[275] This is possible only when the catechist believes in the gospel and its power to transform lives. To give witness to the gospel, the catechist must establish a living, ever-deepening relationship with the Lord. He or she must be a person of prayer, one who frequently reflects on the scriptures and whose Christlike living testifies to deep faith. Only men and women of faith can share faith with others, preparing the setting within which people can respond in faith to God's grace.

208. COMMITMENT TO THE CHURCH

One who exercises the ministry of the word represents the Church, to which the word has been entrusted. The catechist believes in the Church and is aware that, as a pilgrim people, it is in constant need of renewal. Committed to this visible community, the catechist strives to be an instrument of the Lord's power and a sign of the Spirit's presence.

The catechist realizes that it is Christ's message which he or she is called to proclaim. To insure fidelity to that message, catechists test and validate their understanding and insights in the light of the gospel message as presented by the teaching authority of the Church.

209. SHARER IN COMMUNITY

The catechist is called to foster community as one who has "learned the meaning of community by experiencing it."[276] Community is formed in many ways. Beginning with acceptance of individual strengths and weaknesses, it progresses to relationships based on shared goals and values. It grows through discussion, recreation, cooperation on projects, and the like.

Yet it does not always grow easily; patience and skill are frequently required. Even conflict, if creatively handled, can be growth-producing, and Christian reconciliation is an effective means of fostering community. Many people have had little experience of parish community and must be gradually prepared for it.

Christian community is fostered especially by the Eucharist, "which is at once sign of community and cause of its growth."[277] The catechist needs to experience this unity through frequent participation in the celebration of the Eucharist with other catechists and with those being catechized. Awareness of membership in a Christian community leads to awareness of the many other communities in the world which stand in need of service. The catechist seeks to cooperate with other parish leaders in making the parish a focal point of community in the Church.

210. SERVANT OF THE COMMUNITY

Authentic experience of Christian community leads one to the service of others. The catechist is committed to serving the Christian community, particularly in the parish, and the community-at-large. Such service means not only responding to needs when asked, but taking the initiative in seeking out the needs of individuals and communities, and encouraging students to do the same.

Sensitive to the community's efforts to find solutions to "a host of complex problems such as war, poverty, racism, and environmental pollution, which undermine community within and among nations,"[278] the catechist educates to peace and justice, and supports social action when appropriate. The Church often becomes involved in efforts to solve global problems through missionaries, who also carry out in a special way its mission of universal evangelization. The catechist should show how support for missionary endeavors is not only required by the Church's missionary nature but is an expression of solidarity within the human community.

211. KNOWLEDGE, SKILLS, AND ABILITIES

Although even the best preparation for catechetical ministry will have little effect without the action of the Holy Spirit in the hearts of catechists and those being catechized, catechists should certainly seek to acquire the knowledge, skills, and abilities needed to communicate the gospel message effectively. They must have a solid grasp of Catholic doctrine and worship; familiarity with scripture; communication skills; the ability to use various methodologies; understanding of how people grow and mature and of how persons of different ages and circumstances learn.

PART B: CATECHETICAL ROLES AND PREPARATION

212. PARENTS AS CATECHISTS

Parents are the first and foremost catechists of their children.[279] They catechize informally but powerfully by example and instruction. They communicate values and attitudes by showing love for Christ and His Church and for each other, by reverently receiving the Eucharist and living in its spirit, and by fostering justice and love in all their relationships. Their active involvement in the parish, their readiness to seek opportunities to serve others, and their practice of frequent and spontaneous prayer, all make meaningful their professions of belief. Parents nurture faith in their children by showing them the richness and beauty of lived faith. Parents should frequently be reminded of their obligation to see to it that their children participate in catechetical programs sponsored by the Church.

When children are baptized the Church community promises to help parents foster their faith. It keeps this promise, first of all, by its own witness as a worshiping, believing, serving community; and also by providing formal catechesis for adults, youth, and children. Adult catechesis, which deepens the faith of parents, helps them nurture faith in their children.

The Church community also keeps its promise to parents by providing programs intended specifically to help them in their catechetical role. Such programs focus on the task of parents in relation to particular moments or issues in the child's religious life, such as sacramental preparation and moral development. They also seek to familiarize parents with the stages in children's growth and the relevance these have for catechesis.

When formally participating in the catechesis of their children, parents must be mindful of the pre-eminent right of the Church to specify the content of authentic catechesis. They always have an obligation to catechize according to the teaching authority of the Church.[280]

Parish and diocesan personnel should collaborate in planning and presenting programs for parents, including the parents of handicapped children. Parents themselves should have a direct role in planning such programs.

213. PARISH CATECHISTS

Parish catechists, many of whom are volunteers, may be engaged in catechizing adults, young people, children, or those with special needs. Theirs is a particular way of carrying out the promise which the Church makes at every Baptism: to support, pray for, and instruct the baptized and foster their growth in faith.

The fundamental tasks of catechists are to proclaim Christ's message, to participate in efforts to develop community, to lead people to worship and prayer, and to motivate them to serve others. To accomplish all this, catechists must identify and create "suitable conditions which are necessary for the Christian message to be sought, accepted, and more profoundly investigated."[281] They recognize, however, that faith is a gift and that it is not ultimately their efforts but the interaction of God's grace and human freedom which lead people to accept faith and respond to it.

Parish and diocesan personnel and others involved in catechetical ministry should help catechists develop the qualities outlined here. Because catechists approach their task with varying degrees of competence, programs should be designed to help individuals acquire the particular knowledge and skills they need. Catechists typically participate in a variety of teaching and learning programs, liturgical experiences, classes, retreats, service programs, study clubs, and similar activities. They carry on their ministry in parish catechetical programs, Catholic schools, and other settings. Their training should equip them to make effective use of the resources available for catechesis and to adapt materials to the age, capacity, and culture of those they seek to reach.

Men and women from all walks of life volunteer for parish catechetical programs. Parish and diocesan programs for the preparation and in-service training of volunteers should include the following elements.

1. Basic orientation and preparation, including instruction in theology, scripture, psychology, and catechetical techniques. They should be shown how to identify goals and achieve them in their particular circumstances.

2. Opportunities for liturgical celebrations, prayer, retreats, and other experiences of Christian community with others engaged in this ministry.

3. Continuing in-service educational opportunities.

4. Regular assistance, from more experienced persons, in planning and evaluating their performance.

5. Opportunities to evaluate not only their performance but the programs in which they are involved.

6. More specialized training for those who will work with physically or mentally handicapped persons.

7. Cultivation of a sense of community among the catechists during the entire formation process.

8. Some form of commissioning ceremony which expresses the faith community's call and the catechists' dedicated response.

214. DIRECTORS AND COORDINATORS OF RELIGIOUS EDUCATION

As awareness has grown of the need for continuing, comprehensive catechesis for all, an increasing number of men and women have assumed positions as parish or inter-parish directors and coordinators of religious education. Such positions vary in their specific functions, depending on factors like size of staff, scope of program, and parish size.

Two basic roles seem to be emerging, together with variations on them. In one, the individual is responsible for overall direction of the parish's catechetical programs. This includes working with the pastor, other ministers, and appropriate committees, boards, or councils involved in setting policy and planning; designing catechetical programs; assisting in liturgical planning; conducting sacramental preparation workshops; and providing opportunities for staff development. Appropriate preparation includes studies in theology, scripture, liturgy, psychology, educational theory, and administration, as well as practical experience with children and adults.

The other role involves responsibility for administration of a parish's catechetical program on a particular level or for a particular group or groups. Functions include working with the pastor, the director, and other staff members in recruiting catechists; and being responsible for the general day-to-day operation of the program. For this work, a good background in catechetics, administration, and communication skills is needed, together with parish experience.

Both roles are generally designated by the title Director, Minister, or Coordinator of Religious Education; but the title varies from place to place.

People who hold such positions need to continue their education in order to bring fresh insights to their ministry. They should participate in diocesan programs of in-service education. Parishes are encouraged to provide funds to help them attend catechetical institutes, conventions, retreats, and accredited summer school programs.

Pastors or parish boards which hire directors or coordinators must formulate clear and specific agreements with them concerning their duties, in line with diocesan policies. These agreements should also specify the spiritual, psychological, and financial support to be provided by the parish.

215. SCHOOL PRINCIPALS

The Catholic school principal plays a critical role in realizing the goals of Catholic education. While specifics of this role vary according to circumstances, certain functions relating to catechesis are basic.

Recognizing that all faculty members share in catechetical ministry,[282] principals recruit teachers with appropriate qualifications in view of the Catholic school's apostolic goals and character. They provide opportunities for ongoing catechesis for faculty members by which they can deepen their faith and grow in the ability to integrate in their teaching the fourfold dimensions of Catholic education: message, community, worship, and service. In collaboration with the faculty, principals see to it that the curriculum reflects these dimensions.

Principals foster community among faculty and students. They understand the Catholic school as a part of larger communities, religious and secular. They collaborate with parish, area, or diocesan personnel in planning and implementing programs for a total, integrated approach to catechesis. They also establish norms and procedures of accountability and evaluation within the school, and in relation to the larger community.

216. PERMANENT DEACONS

Permanent deacons are ordained to a ministry of service and participate in the catechetical ministry of the Church. Commissioned as ministers of word as well as sacrament, they exercise this ministry in teaching and preaching. Among their duties are preparing others for the sacraments; ministering in hospitals, prisons, and other institutions; directing or participating in parish or diocesan catechetical programs; serving as campus ministers.

The preparation of permanent deacons should include studies in theology, scripture, communication skills, and catechetical formation for their particular area of catechetical ministry. As part of their training, candidates for the diaconate and the priesthood should have supervised catechetical experiences in parishes, hospitals, or other institutional settings.

217. PASTORS AND PRIEST ASSOCIATES

Priests exercise a uniquely important role and have a special responsibility for the success of the catechetical ministry. They are a source of leadership, cooperation, and support for all involved in this ministry. As leaders in developing a faith community under the guidance of the Holy Spirit, they perform indispensable catechetical functions: encouraging catechists, praying with them, teaching and learning with them, supporting them. The preaching ministry of the priest is one of his most important catechetical functions. His liturgical sacramental ministry is also a central factor in the catechesis of the Christian community. The priest gives active support to catechetical programs by participating in planning, by catechizing, by providing liturgical celebrations for classes or groups, and by other expressions of interest and concern.

The pastor is primarily responsible for seeing to it that the catechetical needs, goals, and priorities of the parish are identified, articulated, and met. In planning and carrying out the catechetical ministry, he works with his priest associates, parish council, board of education or analogous body, directors and coordinators, principals, teachers, parents, and others. He respects the organizational principles mentioned in articles 221–223 and attempts to make as much use as possible of team ministry in catechetical efforts.

It is imperative that priests continue their education after ordination. This can be done to some degree through reading, participating in discussions, and attending lectures. However, dioceses, in collaboration with colleges, universities, and seminaries, should provide ongoing clergy education programs, in theology, scripture, and other subjects according to need. This is particularly important because of the rapid changes in society and in many fields of knowledge. By study, reading, and prayer a priest enriches his ministry and also encourages parishioners to take seriously their own obligation to grow in faith.

218. DIOCESAN CATECHETICAL PERSONNEL

a) The bishop

The bishop, chief catechist in the diocese (cf. Acts 20:28), is responsible for seeing to it that sound catechesis is provided for all its people. He should not only "devote himself personally to the work of the Gospel," but should "supervise the entire ministry of the word in regards to the flock committed to his care."[283]

In carrying out his responsibility the bishop ensures that catechetical goals and priorities are established by the Christian community, that the necessary structures exist, and that appropriate programs are designed, carried out, and evaluated. He takes every opportunity to preach and teach personally. He summons his people to faith and strengthens them in it, using such means as parish visits, pastoral letters, and the communications media.

The bishop does not work alone. He is assisted by parents, catechists, director and coordinators, religious, deacons, and priests. He is responsible for choosing qualified leaders for the catechetical ministry; for ensuring that catechists are adequately prepared for their work; and for seeing to it that all involved in this ministry receive continuing catechetical formation. He is also mindful of his own need for continuing education.

b) Diocesan staff

The bishop directs catechesis through the diocesan offices responsible for catechetical activities. These serve parishes in many ways.

"The extent and diversity of the problems which must be handled demand that the responsibilities be divided among a number of truly skilled people."[284]

Although catechetical needs and priorities vary from one diocese to another, diocesan offices should in general perform the following functions.

1. Encourage and motivate catechists on every level by visits, in-service training, newsletters, diocesan institutes, etc.

2. Propose alternative models of educational priorities which can be adapted to the needs of particular areas, parishes, or schools.

3. Supply guidelines for parish organization, programs of sacramental preparation, and other programs to help parishes provide comprehensive catechesis.

4. Recommend catechetical curricula and textbooks.

5. Provide in-service training and formation opportunities for parish and regional catechetical leaders.

6. Provide prior training and continuing education for catechists, by establishing permanent centers for catechetical training or cooperating with Catholic colleges or universities in setting up such programs.

7. Keep catechetical personnel informed concerning important Church documents and recommendations which pertain to catechesis.

8. Provide access to catechetical resources, including textbooks and instructional aids.

9. Provide personnel and resources to meet the needs of the physically and mentally handicapped.

10. Conduct regular surveys to determine the number of adults, youth, children, preschoolers, physically or mentally handicapped persons, etc. receiving formal catechetical instruction; the number who are not receiving instruction at each level; the availability of training and continuing education of personnel; the kinds of programs in use and their effectiveness; the number of hours of instruction being given; the service and worship components of programs; costs; etc.

11. Establish norms for accrediting catechists, including directors and coordinators, catechists in parish programs, Catholic school personnel, etc. These norms should require demonstrated competence and should not be based solely on "paper credentials."

12. Integrate catechesis with the diocese's total plan for Catholic education and prepare parish catechetical personnel to do the same.

13. Establish and provide instruments for evaluating programs, including both their cognitive and affective dimensions.

14. Keep the diocese mindful of its mission to evangelize.

Diocesan personnel should have previous catechetical experience in parishes or schools, as well as formation comparable to that required for parish directors, coordinators, and teachers in Catholic schools.

Frequent participation in celebrating the Eucharist together is highly desirable for the staff members of diocesan offices. In this way they foster community among themselves, grow in their ability to proclaim the message in truth, intensify their prayer life, and make their work truly a service of the Lord.

219. CONCLUSION

This chapter has discussed the ideal personal qualities of catechists, as well as the training and skills required by particular catechetical roles. Next we turn to organizational principles and structure.

CHAPTER X
ORGANIZATION FOR CATECHESIS

220. INTRODUCTION

One can hardly emphasize too strongly the catechetical importance of the witness to faith given by individuals living according to their Christian beliefs and values. But organizational structures are also needed to achieve the goals and ideals set forth in this NCD. Appropriate structures can help ensure opportunities for the entire Christian community to grow in faith.

Some topics treated in this chapter have already been discussed in Chapter VIII in relation to faith and human development; here they are examined from the point of view of organization.

PART A: GENERAL ORGANIZATIONAL GUIDELINES

221. ORGANIZATIONAL PRINCIPLES

The following principles are important to catechetical organization.

a) Effective planning is person-centered. It does not propose structures without reference to the people involved. It sets growth in faith as the goal and recognizes the Christian family as the basic community within which faith is nurtured.

b) Each of its members has a responsibility for the whole Church. Each has a duty to foster a living, conscious, active faith community. Laity, religious, and clergy alike are called to participate in those aspects of catechesis — organization, implementation, evaluation — with respect to which they are interested and qualified. Recognizing that they are stewards of God's gifts, they should be generous in supporting the catechetical effort. Shared responsibility implies the development and use of such structures as councils and boards.

c) Planning groups should make a clear statement of their philosophy, their goals, and the basic beliefs underlying the goals. (Cf. next article.)

d) Higher-level planning groups should not try to do what can be done as well, or better, by groups at lower levels. For example, diocesan bodies ought not to set policies or make decisions which deprive parishes of authority concerning matters they are able to handle. Respect for local decision making encourages initiative, while freeing larger units to concentrate on needs which only they can meet, or which require coordination or a common approach. Groups should seek outside help only when needs clearly exceed local capabilities.

e) At all levels it is essential that overall plans make provision for communication and accountability.

f) Administrators in each local community are responsible for the equitable allocation of available services, opportunities, and resources. Strong central leadership is needed to ensure that resources are used for the good of all. Communities in need should have opportunities equal to those enjoyed by more favored communities.

g) Structures should flow from need and be suited to the achievement of the stated goals.

h) Goal setting, planning, implementation, accountability, and evaluation are continuing processes.

222. PLANNING AND EVALUATION

a) Planning

Planning is an essential part of any serious organizational effort. There are many planning processes; catechists involved in organization should be exposed to several and familiar with at least one.

Certain elements are common to all planning systems:

i) a clear understanding of the essential mission and major objectives;

ii) assessment of needs, as well as current and potential resources;

iii) identification of long- and short-range goals;

iv) identification of concrete activities to reach the goals, rated according to priority;

v) establishment of a budget which reflects available resources;

vi) establishment of favorable conditions for carrying out the activities which have been decided upon;

vii) periodic review and evaluation;

viii) restatement of goals and activities when necessary.

It is important that planning for catechetical programs at the parish, diocesan, and national levels be part of a total pastoral plan. Such a plan, which takes into consideration the Church's entire mission, is best developed by representatives of the various ministries in the Church.[285] Urgent demands upon limited resources require cooperation among all pastoral ministries.

Planning is a continuous process. The associated skills develop with experience. Good planning enriches decision making and forestalls crisis-oriented decisions.

b) Evaluation

Catechetical programs should be subjected to regular evaluation. The evaluation should be made in light of established goals and objectives, which themselves should be evaluated periodically.

There is a need to develop instruments for evaluating catechetical programs. The United States Catholic Conference, National Conference of Diocesan Directors of Religious Education-CCD, National Catholic Educational Association, and other representative agencies should collaborate in meeting this need. The norms and guidelines set forth throughout this NCD provide criteria for evaluation.

223. RESEARCH

Rapid developments in the Church, society, and education underline the great need for research related to catechesis. Wherever possible, dioceses and parishes ought to examine themselves in order to ascertain their requirements and make plans for meeting them.

Diocesan, regional, and national groups are responsible for developing research instruments and projecting and testing models for local use. It is the responsibility of the religious education representative of the USCC Department of Education to coordinate efforts on the various levels and disseminate the results of research to diocesan offices and other interested parties. The other offices of the Department of Education, the departments of the United States Catholic Conference, and the agencies of the National Conference of Catholic Bishops provide the same services to their constituents, with regard to the catechetical components of their ministries.

The Office of Research, Policy and Program Development of the USCC Department of Education has the following functions: to maintain a listing of current and completed research in Catholic education, including catechetics; to help identify present and future research needs; to make a continuing study of trends in Catholic education, including projections for the immediate and distant futures. The staff works closely with Catholic colleges, universities, learned societies, and research groups in performing these functions.

Associated with the Office of Research, Policy and Program Development is the United States Center for the Catholic Biblical Apostolate. In relation to catechesis its pastoral purpose is to ascertain the needs of the dioceses with respect to Bible study programs, especially in adult education, and to promote popular biblical publications as well as wide distribution of the scriptures.[286]

It is highly desirable that catechists at all levels know and use the results of research. Useful research at any level should be shared as widely as possible with the rest of the Church.

PART B: THE PARISH

224. THE PARISH COMMUNITY

The parish is the basic structure within which most Catholics express and experience faith. Ordinarily, a parish is made up of the people within a defined territorial area, for whose care and service a priest has been assigned by the bishop. There are other parishes for Catholics of a particular ethnic group or particular rite; and there are some parishes which do not have fixed boundaries but are made up of persons linked by common social bonds.[287]

Catholics have a right to look to their parishes to carry out Christ's mission by being centers of worship, preaching, witness, community, and service. At the same time, parishioners have reciprocal duties of involvement and support toward their parishes. Maturity of faith obviously rules out the neglect of one's duties as a parish member.

Every parish needs a coherent, well-integrated catechetical plan which provides opportunities for all parishioners to encounter the gospel message and respond by fostering community and giving service.

The parish and its catechetical program take into account that the whole Church is missionary and that evangelization is a basic duty of God's people.[288]

A single representative board, responsible for the total educational program, should be involved in catechetical planning in every parish. Different circumstances will require different organizational forms. The board can be a separate body, a committee of the parish council, or some other entity, elected or appointed. Its members should receive training and pastoral formation to help them share a vision of the Church's global mission, of the overall parish goals, and of catechetical priorities in the context of those goals.

As far as possible, parish catechetical programs are to be established, financed, staffed, and evaluated in light of the goal of meeting the needs of everyone in the parish. Particular concern will be directed to the handicapped, the neglected, those unable to speak up effectively on behalf of their own rights and interests, and minority cultural, racial, and ethnic groups.

Parish catechetical efforts should be related to the catechetical undertakings of neighboring parishes and other religious groups. They should take into account the schedules and programs of public and parochial schools. Interparochial cooperation is particularly necessary to make resources available to poor or otherwise disadvantaged communities.

Parish bulletins and other publications should be utilized in catechesis.

225. ADULTS

Through a parish catechetical board, a committee, or a chairperson of adult catechesis, the pastor should see to it that catechetical programs are available for adults as part of the total catechetical program.

The form adult catechesis takes will depend on a variety of factors: size and makeup of parish, community stability, cultural and educational background of parishioners, etc. There are a number of appropriate models: small group discussions, lectures with questions and discussion, retreat programs, sacramental programs, dialogues between adults and young people, adult catechumenate.

Parish planning groups should be creative in designing ways to reach and motivate adults to participate.

Priests should be mindful that the Sunday homily, based on the scriptures of the day, is a notable opportunity to nurture the faith of the adult community through the ministry of the word.

226. FAMILY MINISTRY

Family ministry involves announcing the good news to those within the immediate family circle first of all. However, family members should in turn be aware of the Christian family's authentic mission to evangelize the wider community. "In a family which is conscious of this mission, all the members evangelize and are evangelized. The parents not only communicate the Gospel to their children, but from their children they can themselves receive the same Gospel as deeply lived by them. And such a family becomes the evangelizer of many other families, and of the neighborhood of which it forms part."[289]

As the Church in miniature, the family is called to serve the needs of its own members, other persons and families, and the larger community. In it evangelization, worship, catechesis, and Christian service are vitally present.

Many parishes offer family-centered catechetical programs. These are intended to bring families together—to learn, experience, and celebrate some aspect of Catholic belief or living—and help them carry out their responsibilities in and to the Church's catechetical mission.

Some family programs center upon the liturgy, using themes of the liturgical year as the starting point. Participants separate according to age (preschool, primary, intermediate, junior and senior high school, and adult levels) to discuss the theme and then come back together for a common activity and celebration. Suggestions for home activities may also be given. Other programs, such as "family evenings," focus on the family in the home setting. Each family examines the designated theme in relation to its own circumstances, in order better to understand and carry out its mission in the world. Some family programs have a more elaborate design and aim at total catechesis.

While family-centered catechesis is to be encouraged, peer group catechetical experience should also be part of a total catechetical program.

Within families there is need and opportunity for spouses to catechize each other and for parents to catechize children. There are several possibilities: e.g., parents can catechize their children directly, which is the ideal; they can participate in parish catechetical programs which serve their children; spouses can catechize each other by trustingly and openly sharing their insights concerning the gospel's relevance to their lives.

Since the Christian family is a "domestic Church," prayer and worship are central to it. Christian family life involves prayerful celebration within the family, as well as liturgical celebration in the parish community of which it is an integral, active part.

Another component of authentic family ministry and an important goal of family catechesis is the rendering of Christlike service. Sensitized to others' needs by the imperatives of Christian love and justice, the individual family seeks, according to its ability and opportunities, to minister to the spiritual, psychological, and physical needs of the whole human family.

Family ministry is a vital source of strength for the catechetical process in the home and in the parish.

More research is needed concerning the influence of the home on family members. This would help catechists and people engaged in family ministries to develop more effective forms of home- and family-oriented catechesis.

227. YOUNG ADULT MINISTRY

This is a "catechetical moment of the gospel" with respect to young adults (18–35), for all practical purposes a newly identified population in U.S. society, many of whose members are engaged in an intense search for spirituality and values.

Church-sponsored young adult programs should respond to the expressed needs of participants while reflecting the four interrelated purposes of catechesis: to proclaim the mysteries of the faith; to foster community; to encourage worship and prayer; and to motivate service to others.

The gradual manner of God's self-revelation, manifested in scripture, provides a model for catechetical efforts directed to young adults, as does the catechesis recommended in the revised *Rite of Christian Initiation of Adults*. Program content includes psychological and sociological matters considered in the light of faith, questions of faith and moral issues, and similar matters pertaining to human experience.

Catechists not only instruct young adults but learn from them; they will be heard by young adults only if they listen to them. Young adult ministries must be developed and conducted in ways which emphasize self-direction, dialogue, and mutual responsibility. The Church should encourage young adults to minister to one another, to listen to God's word in community, and to serve other members of the faith community and the world community. It should offer leadership in developing new ministries, alternative community experiences, and instruments of effective catechesis, for this purpose using the talents of young adults who are willing to collaborate.

a) Description of youth ministry

Youth catechesis is most effective within a total youth ministry. Such ministry requires the collaboration of many people with different kinds of expertise.

It is *to* youth that it seeks to respond to adolescents' unique needs. It is *with* youth in that it is shared. It is *by* youth in that they participate in directing it. It is *for* youth in that it attempts to interpret the concerns of youth and be an advocate for them.

Total ministry to youth includes catechetical activities in which the message is proclaimed, community is fostered, service is offered, and worship is celebrated. There is need for a variety of models integrating message, community, service, and worship and corresponding to the stages of development and levels of perception of the young. Guidance and healing, involvement of youth in ministry, and interpretation and advocacy of their legitimate interests and concerns also have catechetical dimensions.

The need for a variety of approaches should be taken into consideration in preparing social, recreational, and apostolic programs, as well as retreats and other spiritual development activities.

b) Parish catechetical programs for youth

Parish and community programs designed to meet the needs of Catholic students who do not attend Catholic high schools provide settings for formal catechesis for many Catholic young people in the United States. Participation in such programs is voluntary, and they are usually less structured than school programs and open to a number of alternative models.

Professional advice, local initiative, and consultation with young people themselves should all go into the planning of these programs. Local circumstances should determine such decisions as whether to make them parish or home-centered, whether they should have a formal "classroom" or informal "group" format, whether they should be scheduled weekly over an extended period of time or concentrated in a shorter time span, or whether some particular mixture of formats and schedules should be employed.

Catechetical planners should know the number of young people of high school age in the community and how many are not being reached by the catechetical ministry of school or parish.

Adequate personnel, professional services, and budget are essential. Programs broad enough to appeal to all the young people of a community are usually most effective.

The study of scripture, the Church, the sacraments, and morality should be part of the overall program. In a comprehensive ministerial program such instruction will flow from and lead to service, liturgy, and community.

The community dimension will usually be expressed in a preference for small groups within which relationships can develop. Weekend prayer, "search," encounter, or retreat experiences provide liturgical experiences in a communal setting of acceptance and exchange.

Service opportunities (e.g., visiting the aged or shut-ins, assisting catechists who teach handicapped children, working with community action programs) should also be part of programs for youth. They help develop lasting motivation for service to others.

Catechesis consistently speaks of the Church's missionary nature and the obligation of all its members to share in some way in its missionary activity. It discusses religious vocations (priesthood, diaconate, brotherhood, and sisterhood) and encourages students to be open to the call of the Holy Spirit. Lay ministries are also presented as a form of direct involvement in the mission of the Church. In particular, catechesis should remind parents of the need to extend a prudent but positive invitation to their children to consider a religious vocation as a way of living out their Christian commitment.

229. CATECHETICAL PROGRAMS FOR CHILDREN

While giving increased emphasis to adult catechesis, the faith community must also strive continually to provide parish programs of high quality for children.

Primary, intermediate, and junior high school catechesis are specialized fields requiring specialized training. They are grouped here to emphasize the need for sequence and coordination.

Though the influence of peers and of adult catechists is important, catechetical programs are not intended to supplant parents as the primary educators of their children. Parental involvement in catechetical programs is essential.

Adequately staffed and budgeted parish catechetical programs at every level should be provided for children who do not attend Catholic schools. The limited time available for these programs makes it absolutely necessary to set priorities and to give them active support.

Curricula should be properly sequenced, presenting essential truths in a manner appropriate to the abilities of the age group. Whether a curriculum's content is sufficiently comprehensive is determined by judging the curriculum as a whole. As the ability to understand develops, more important truths should be reinforced and treated in greater depth. Religious learning should relate to the child's general experience of learning.

It is essential that a parish elementary catechetical program include opportunities for participants to experience community. Children grow in their understanding and appreciation of what a worshiping community is through participating in class or group prayer and in liturgies which have been carefully planned together by students and teachers.

The concept of service has limited application on the elementary level, especially in the early years. Parents play an important role in its development by sensitively prompting their children to perform acts of kindness and compassion in the home and neighborhood. Service-oriented class projects can be introduced in the intermediate grades. By junior high school, service projects similar to those mentioned above in the discussion of youth ministry are appropriate.

Catechesis introduces children to the idea that the Church's mission is the mission of Jesus and of the Holy Spirit. It describes this work of the Church and explains the notion of vocation.

230. CATECHESIS FOR PRESCHOOL CHILDREN

Preschool programs should focus mainly on parents, providing them with opportunities to deepen their faith and become more adept at helping their children "form a foundation of that life of faith which will gradually develop and manifest itself."[290] However, programs for preschool children themselves are also desirable, in accordance with the guidance given in article 177.

231. SPECIAL CATECHESIS

Catechetical programs for people with mental, emotional, or physical handicaps should be provided on the parochial, regional, or diocesan level. Each handicap requires its own approach, and separate programs are therefore required for each category of handicapped persons. Those involved in special catechetical programs should receive the training needed to perform their particular duties.

The parish community should be informed about the needs of its handicapped members and encouraged to support them with love and concern. The faith witness of handicapped persons can be a model and stimulus to growth in faith on the part of parishioners generally.

The families of the handicapped also need care and concern, including assistance directed to helping them participate with competence and confidence in the catechesis of their handicapped members.

232. CATHOLIC SCHOOLS

Catholic schools are unique expressions of the Church's effort to achieve the purposes of Catholic education among the young. They "are the most effective means available to the Church for the education of children and young people."[291]

Catholic schools may be part of the parish structure, interparochial or regional, diocesan or private. Growth in faith is central to their purpose.

As a community and an institution, the school necessarily has an independent life of its own. But a parochial school is also a community within the wider community, contributing to the parish upon which it depends and integrated into its life. Integration and interdependence are major matters of parish concern; each program in a total catechetical effort should complement the others.[292]

Similarly, regional, diocesan, and private schools should work in close collaboration with neighboring parishes. The experience of community in the schools can benefit and be benefitted by the parishes.

Teachers in Catholic schools are expected to accept and live the Christian message and to strive to instill a Christian spirit in their students. As catechists, they will meet standards equivalent to those set for other disciplines and possess the qualities described in Chapter IX, Part A.

The school should have a set religion curriculum, with established goals and objectives, open to review and evaluation by parish boards and diocesan supervisory teams. It is recommended that an integrated curriculum provide options for catechists and students by offering electives along with the core curriculum.

It is desirable that Catholic high schools in a diocese work together to share resources, provide opportunities for teacher training and development, and cooperate in establishing program guidelines.

The school's principal and faculty are responsible for making clear the importance of religion. The quality of the catechetical experience in the school and the importance attached to religious instruction, including the amount of time spent on it, can influence students to perceive religion as either highly important or of little importance.

Its nature as a Christian educational community, the scope of its teaching, and the effort to integrate all learning with faith distinguish the Catholic school from other forms of the Church's educational ministry to youth and give it special impact. In Catholic schools children and young people "can experience learning and living fully integrated in the light of faith,"[293] because such schools strive "to relate all human culture eventually to the news of salvation, so that the life of faith will illumine the knowledge which students gradually gain of the world, of life and of mankind."[294] Cooperative teaching which cuts across the lines of particular disciplines, interdisciplinary curricula, team teaching, and the like help to foster these goals of Catholic education.

"Building and living community must be prime, explicit goals of the contemporary Catholic school."[295] Principal and faculty members have a responsibility to help foster community among themselves and the students. Creative paraliturgies and sacramental celebrations for particular age groups can strengthen the faith community within the school.

Catholic school students should be introduced gradually to the idea and practice of Christian service. In early years, efforts to instill a sense of mission and concern for others help lay a foundation for later service projects, as does study of the lives of the saints and outstanding contemporaries.

Junior and senior high school programs should foster a social conscience sensitive to the needs of all. Familiarity with the Church's social encyclicals and its teaching on respect for human life will be part of this formation. (Cf. Chapter VII) Opportunities for field and community experiences are highly desirable. Teachers, administrators, parents, and students should be involved in planning service projects. One measure of a school's success is its ability to foster a sense of vocation, of eagerness to live out the basic baptismal commitment to service, whether this is done as a lay person, religious, deacon, or priest.

Catechesis speaks of the missionary nature of the Church. It points out that all Christians are responsible for missionary activity by reason of the love of God, which prompts in them a desire to share with everyone the spiritual goods of this life and the life to come. Catholic schools provide opportunities for participation in missionary projects through the Holy Childhood Association, the Society for the Propagation of the Faith, etc. They also provide students with opportunities to search for the gifts that the Holy Spirit offers them for this ministry.

Through a carefully planned process, the entire school community — parents, students, faculty, administrators, pastors, and others — needs to be involved in the development of its goals, philosophy, and programs.

233. CATHOLIC SCHOOLS AND THE DISADVANTAGED

The Second Vatican Council urged bishops and all Catholics to "spare no sacrifice" in helping Catholic schools to fulfill their functions more perfectly, and especially to care for "the needs of those who are poor in the goods of this world or who are deprived of the assistance and affection of a family or who are strangers to the gift of faith."[296]

In many places in the United States the Church has responded with an extremely large human and economic investment in schools whose pupils are for the most part disadvantaged children in the poverty areas of large cities. An increasing number of parents in poverty areas are making heroic personal sacrifices to send their children to Catholic schools, convinced that the education provided there affords a realistic and hopeful opportunity for breaking out of "the hellish cycle of poverty"[297] and moving into the social and economic mainstream. These schools serve a critical human and social need, while also providing a complete education which includes catechesis and guidance. In urban areas the Catholic school has a special role of giving witness and fostering evangelization.

234. RELIGION AND PUBLIC EDUCATION

In a series of decisions concerning prayer and Bible reading during the 1960s, the United States Supreme Court in effect excluded specific efforts to inculcate religious values from the public schools.[298]

Efforts have been made to fill the vacuum created by these decisions by introducing into public schools courses and programs which in one way or another bear upon religion and values. The objective study of religion, whatever form it takes, seeks to convey information about religion or to foster appreciation of its nonreligious contributions, but not to advocate religious belief and values; while courses in sex education, psychology, and sociology, along with "sensitivity" and value clarification programs, deal directly with values.

Many believe it is not possible to produce neutral textbooks on religion and values, much less to teach in a truly neutral way about such matters. Some ask whether "neutrality" about religion and values is appropriate, even supposing it were possible. Many, particularly parents and Church leaders, believe so-called neutrality of this kind weakens young people's religious and moral beliefs and leads to relativism and indifference.

In order to remedy the situation, parents and community leaders, including representatives of churches and synagogues, should become involved in the planning, development, implementation, and evaluation of courses and programs dealing with religion and values. Issues of a highly controversial nature should be treated with extreme sensitivity. Teachers and administrators should be conscious of their responsibility to deal respectfully with pupils from diverse backgrounds and value systems, and should be adequately trained to do so. When young people or their parents object to a program on religious or moral grounds, the public schools should exempt such pupils from participation without embarrassing them.

It is important that parish planners be aware of such courses and programs in public schools and be prepared to address the issues and questions they raise in parish catechetical programs.

235. RELEASED TIME

The laws of some states provide for releasing students from public school during regular school hours so that they can attend catechetical programs off the school premises.[299]

Some states make an hour or more available each week for catechetical instruction. Others provide for "staggered" time, releasing students on an individual or group basis at different hours and days throughout the week. While a number of places have reported good success with these forms of released time, others have complained that scheduling and transportation present serious practical difficulties; they have also noted the bad effect of compartmentalizing religion and relegating catechesis to a small and inadequate portion of the child's or youth's total school time.

More satisfactory results have been reported in a few places which make available a block of time for catechesis—several hours, a whole day, or even several consecutive days.

Good results have been achieved in both released time programs and after-school catechesis by catechetical centers established adjacent to public schools.

Released time programs are more effective when part of a broader parish catechetical program.

Dioceses and state Catholic conferences will find it helpful to appraise the local situation and seek viable released time programs, if these are desired. As this is an issue that interests many, a cooperative approach with other churches is advantageous.

Parishes, individually or collectively, should seek out viable alternatives to released time in cooperation with educational administrators in the public sector.

236. ETHNIC PARISHES

Revived interest in ethnicity, based on recognition of the major contribution made by ethnic groups to the nation's cultural richness, has stimulated interest in ethnic parishes. They provide significant liturgical and cultural experiences for many people. While "ethnic" forms of religious expression are to be encouraged, means should also be sought for sharing their values with the Church at large, including neighboring geographical parishes.

Representatives of national parishes and of cultural and ethnic groups should be the prime movers in planning and organizing catechetical programs for themselves.

237. MILITARY PARISHES

The special needs of military personnel and their families must be recognized by both diocesan and military chaplaincy administrators. Military and diocesan parishes should cooperate. Diocesan catechetical offices should relate to and serve military parishes.

Because of the mobility and, at times, the isolation of military life, it is important to give priority to standard procedures for procuring catechetical materials, and to the development of parental and lay leadership. The need for professional catechists and coordinators, especially on large bases or posts, is as urgent as in any civilian parish.

Military parishes provide good opportunities for ecumenical efforts, since places of worship and educational facilities are frequently shared by all denominations.

PART C: THE DIOCESE

238. DIOCESAN STRUCTURES

The chief elements of the diocesan administrative structure directly related to catechesis are as follows:

a) Diocesan pastoral council

In fulfilling his duties as pastor and chief teacher of the diocese, the bishop consults with the diocesan pastoral council where one exists.[300] Its consultative function extends to everything which is part of the bishop's pastoral responsibility.

The council assists in establishing a broad pastoral plan for the diocese. In relation to catechesis, it works with the bishop to identify the values, philosophy, needs, and goals of the Christian community, both in general and with specific reference to catechesis. It also consults with other diocesan bodies, such as the diocesan council of the laity, priests' senate, sisters' council, etc.

b) Diocesan catechetical/education board

The diocesan board has the responsibility of developing policy, thus giving unified leadership to the various concerns reflected in the total catechetical ministry.

Its tasks are to identify, define, and set priorities among catechetical/educational objectives related to the goals specified by the pastoral council; to specify broad programs to achieve the goals; and to make decisions concerning implementation. Periodically the board should evaluate itself and its performance. A diocesan board is most effective when it is broadly representative of all the people of the diocese. In choosing members, cultural, racial, and ethnic groups, geographic regions, and the like should be considered. Its members should include people of faith active in catechesis and related educational and pastoral fields. When possible, it is advantageous for the membership to include specialists of various kinds, parents, youth, and public educators. The board should seek advice from other boards and similar bodies in the local Church and from individuals who can assist the catechetical ministry.

c) Diocesan catechetical office

The *General Catechetical Directory* refers to the "Catechetical Office" which is "part of the diocesan curia" and "the means which the bishop as head of the community and teacher of doctrine utilizes to direct and moderate all of the catechetical activities of the diocese."[301]

No single model can be recommended here for a diocesan administrative structure to direct catechetical activities. The size, needs, administrative style, and resources of a particular diocese affect this decision. However, a number of workable models or structures have been developed during the past decade.

In large dioceses with complex problems, a chief diocesan administrator of Catholic education, representing the bishop, is responsible for and coordinates the entire catechetical/educational mission through a Department of Education. All offices — which may include a School Office, Office of Religious Education (CCD), Adult Education Office, Campus and Young Adult Ministry Office, and Family Life Ministry Office — report directly to this chief administrator. Frequent collaboration among staff of the various offices fosters the coordination of catechetical efforts and facilitates interdisciplinary projects and programs.

In some dioceses, the Office of Religious Education is responsible for administering diocesan catechetical policy. Where this structure exists as the "catechetical office," personnel should be available to administer and service adult, youth, elementary, preschool, and special catechetical programs.

In other dioceses there is an Office for Christian Formation, with a vicar or secretary responsible for administering catechetical policy and coordinating the catechetical functions with other aspects of pastoral ministry: education, liturgy, ecumenism, etc.

Whatever its structure, the Diocesan Catechetical Office should have sufficient professional personnel to serve as resources to parishes, areas, or regions in relation to all aspects of catechesis. It should engage in regular collaboration and cooperation with other diocesan offices which have a catechetical dimension: i.e., offices for continuing education of the clergy, liturgy, ecumenism, communications, social justice, etc.

PART D: PROVINCES, REGIONS, THE NATIONAL OFFICE

239. REGIONAL AND PROVINCIAL COOPERATION

Regional and provincial cooperation is desirable to coordinate diocesan efforts, provide a common voice in consultation, and broaden the insights and experiences of all involved. Such cooperation should involve bishops, diocesan catechetical personnel, pastors, priests, deacons, religious, and laity, especially parents. Planned coordination promotes mutual assistance and the sharing of programs and personnel, and fosters people's growth in faith through action. Liaison should be established and maintained with state Catholic conferences, where they exist, and with ecumenical groups involved in catechetical or religious education work.

240. NATIONAL CATECHETICAL OFFICE

The *General Catechetical Directory* states that a conference of bishops should have a permanent structure to promote catechetics on the national level.[302] The Department of Education of the United States Catholic Conference, through its religious education component, has the mission of carrying out the catechetical policies of the bishops of the United States.

Through its coordinator and specialists in catechetics, the department is to keep informed of catechetical developments, evaluate them, identify needs, specify directions for the future, and determine strategies of implementation. It is to disseminate information and provide consultation, especially with regional groupings, while undertaking only those activities that cannot be done, or done as well, at the local, diocesan, or regional levels. The department also is to collaborate with national professional associations.

It is desirable that the United States Catholic Conference include specialists from the Eastern Churches on the staff of its Department of Education or, at least, establish liaison with the corresponding entities of the Eastern Churches in order to insure catholicity in catechetical programs.

Before national policy decisions are made, the department is to consult with various advocacy groups and with the USCC Committee on Education, which is a representative group responsible for formulating and recommending policy. Policy itself is established by the USCC Administrative Board and the General Assembly of Bishops.

To the extent possible, the Department of Education is to maintain liaison and exchange information with the national catechetical offices of other countries.

PART E: HIGHER EDUCATION

241. SEMINARIES

Seminarians in college or the theologate need a clear understanding of the roles they will have in the catechetical programs of the parishes and institutions to which they will be assigned as priests.

"In addition to having an accurate knowledge of Sacred Scripture and systematic theology, the seminarian should learn those special skills of pedagogy needed to communicate the Gospel message in a clear, precise and well-organized way."[303] It is also necessary that seminarians come to understand the process of human growth and development so that they can give catechesis adapted to the age and ability of those being catechized. They should have an opportunity to acquire the skills necessary to organize and direct a catechetical program on the parish level.

The catechetical preparation of seminarians should be carried on in collaboration with the personnel of the diocesan catechetical office. Training includes in-service experiences, catechetical workshops, and congresses.

Seminaries serve the local Church by making their faculties and facilities as available as far as possible to the diocese and the community-at-large.

242. COLLEGES AND UNIVERSITIES

a) Graduate programs in religious studies

Graduate departments of religious education offer a variety of programs for people preparing for professional careers in catechetical ministry. Such programs establish academic qualifications for professional leadership, serve as centers for research and development, and convene appropriate seminars. They should be interdisciplinary, offering advanced courses in theology, scripture, liturgy, catechetics, communications, parish administration, and related sacred and human sciences.

Graduate schools of religious studies, through their own national organizations and in cooperation with the USCC Department of Education, are invited to establish uniform standards for candidates for advanced degrees in catechetics.

Graduate programs should make special provisions to meet the needs of cultural, racial, and ethnic groups or individuals with special catechetical requirements: for example, through research, placement of student catechists, and pilot programs directed to such groups.

Graduate schools are encouraged to offer courses and programs in the theologies, liturgies, and forms of spirituality of the Eastern Churches. In doing so, they will be taking advantage of and helping to make more widely known an often neglected source of enrichment for the Church.

Within their financial means, graduate schools can meet a great need by providing scholarships to poor but talented persons, representatives of minority groups, and those who wish to dedicate themselves to some aspect of special education but are unable to pay for their training.

Graduate departments should seek to know and collaborate with local pastoral personnel. Whenever possible, they should cooperate with diocesan catechetical offices in arranging field experiences for their students in local pastoral settings (parishes, schools, institutions, etc.). Catechetical offices and graduate schools can also serve the Church by cooperating in other training efforts related to adult catechesis.

b) Undergraduate programs

Catholic colleges are encouraged to offer undergraduate degree programs in catechetics and theology, both for those who wish to pursue graduate studies and become full-time catechetical workers and for those who may assume other leadership roles in the Church. The requirements for such degrees should be as demanding as those for any other academic discipline.

It is important that Catholic institutions of higher learning maintain strong programs in theology and religious studies. Besides being centers of authentic Catholic theology, they should, as far as possible, offer courses in other theologies to meet the needs of an ecumenical age.

The cooperation of Catholic colleges with diocesan catechetical offices, neighboring parishes, and other institutions which require the services of catechists is highly desirable. The college faculty should be available to help ascertain local pastoral needs and provide supervised in-service training in catechetics or theology programs.

243. CAMPUS MINISTRY

Campus ministry is the Church's presence on the college and university campus. It views the milieu of post-secondary education as a creative center of society, where ideas germinate and are tested, leadership is formed, and the future of society is often determined.

Campus ministry involves pastoral service to the entire campus community: students, administrators, faculty, and staff. In every institution, regardless of size and character, campus ministry confronts a range of concerns which reflect in microcosm the catechetical concerns facing the entire Church.

Especially on the nonsectarian, non-Catholic campus, today's student often receives uncritical exposure to modern ideologies and philosophies, to crucial questions concerning faith, ethical behavior, and human life, and to a multiplicity of cults and new religious movements. Campus ministry must create, in an atmosphere of freedom and reverence, an alternative forum for theological and philosophical inquiry. This includes classes on Catholic thought, scripture seminars, opportunities for different forms of prayer, workshops or lectures in social justice, and opportunities to share on various levels with other recognized religious groups. Formal and informal counseling relating to spiritual, social, and psychological concerns should also be offered to help people integrate the gospel into their lives.

Pastoral service on the campus is to emphasize worship, community, and tradition through the development of a community of faith. It should offer enriching exposure to modern and traditional liturgical forms, not only in the liturgy itself but through paraliturgical services emphasizing the communal aspects of sacramental life.

Finally, campus ministry should seek to serve the university institution itself. It should work for responsible governance on the part of the academic institution and for the maintenance of high standards and values. Campus ministers must be concerned with the institution's programs, policies, and research, and with how these promote or hinder human development. This affords them opportunities to deepen understanding of social justice and be of service to the broader community.

Since these various modes of service are expanding and becoming more complex, campus ministry must have adequate personnel. Today's ministry staff is, typically, composed not only of priests, but increasingly of religious and lay persons, faculty, and graduate students, each with special areas of concern and often working as a team to develop a community of faith. As part of the diocese's mission and responsibility, campus ministry should be carried on in cooperation with local parish communities.

PART F: OTHER CATECHETICAL SETTINGS

244. RESIDENTIAL FACILITIES

Catechesis takes place in a variety of comprehensive but specialized settings, such as convalescent or nursing homes, child-care institutions, residential facilities for the mentally handicapped, and schools for the deaf. People in such facilities have a right to live as normally as possible.

Chaplains in such facilities should be trained for their specific tasks, including catechetical approaches suited to particular groups.

Professional or nonprofessional catechists with appropriate experience work with chaplains by visiting the residents regularly and catechizing, either formally or informally.

Parish, diocesan, and other Church structures and agencies must take the needs of persons in residential facilities into consideration in their planning. As far as possible, they should be incorporated into the life of the parish community, with steps taken to accommodate their special needs.

245. SPECIALIZED GROUPINGS

A number of movements in the United States bring together men and women who are seeking to deepen their faith. Groups which join for prayer, worship, and the sharing of insights provide catechetical settings. Their members should be encouraged to participate actively in their parishes. Priests, religious, and lay people need to become involved with such groups, and diocesan and parish catechetical offices should assist them as much as possible.

246. CHAPLAINCIES

Hospitals, professional groups, police and fire departments, fraternities, prisons, and juvenile homes provide settings for adult catechesis and reflection. Chaplains to such groups and institutions should take advantage of these opportunities. Diocesan and parish catechetical personnel should assist the chaplains as much as possible, particularly by offering standards for catechesis in these settings.

247. OTHER MINISTERIAL TRAINING CENTERS

Ministerial training centers, such as formation centers for religious men and women or lay people, should provide quality programs in catechesis, appropriate to the particular ministry for which the students are preparing.

Catechesis encourages the development of new ministries in and for the life of the Church. The concept of the priesthood of the laity calls for the development of new ministries to supplement the pastoral office in the Church. This would include ministries in the liturgical, catechetical, teaching, service, and administrative fields.

248. CONCLUSION

At all levels high priority must be given to providing structures within and through which the total catechesis of God's people can be accomplished. In providing such structures, national, regional, diocesan, and parish planning groups should apply the principles set forth in this chapter. Next we turn to the resources which catechists have available for their work.

CHAPTER XI
CATECHETICAL RESOURCES

249. INTRODUCTION

The quality of catechists is more important than the quality of their tools. But good tools in the hands of skilled catechists can do much to foster growth in faith. Catechetical "tools" are many and varied. They include human and organizational resources, the communications media, textbooks, and audiovisual materials.

PART A: RESOURCES IN GENERAL

250. ORGANIZATIONAL RESOURCES

There are many organizational resources which provide catechetical information and services. A partial list includes the committees and offices of the National Conference of Catholic Bishops, the United States Catholic Conference, and related bodies (e.g., the NCCB Committee for Pro-Life Activities, the Campaign for Human Development, etc.); the National Conference of Diocesan Directors of Religious Education-CCD (NCDD); the National Catholic Educational Association (NCEA); other national Catholic organizations; colleges and universities, catechetical institutes and schools; publishers; diocesan offices; professional organizations associated with other churches; the educational components of local, state, and federal agencies; libraries and data banks; religious orders; and retreat houses. Catechetical agencies are encouraged to compile and maintain inventories of such resources, lest valuable sources of assistance be overlooked.

251. HISTORICAL USE OF COMMUNICATIONS MEDIA IN CATECHESIS

The collaboration of catechesis and the arts and media deserves close attention and encouragement. From the very beginning, the Church has used the arts to communicate Christ's message and fix it in people's minds and hearts. Biblical stories, saints' lives, and religious themes of all sorts have been depicted in stained glass, mosaics, painting, and sculpture. Music, poetry, dance, drama, architecture, and other art forms have also served catechetical purposes. Contemporary media such as television, films, photography, filmstrips, slides, and tapes do so today.

252. IMPACT OF COMMUNICATIONS MEDIA IN CATECHESIS

The communications revolution has had a profound impact on our world, with implications as great for religion as for any other area of life. Contemporary media offer marvelous new opportunities for catechesis, but they also present serious challenges and problems. They can unite people, foster the sharing of ideas, promote mutual help, justice, and peace, and carry the gospel to those who otherwise might never hear it.

There are at least three different ways of thinking of the communications media in relation to catechesis: as shapers of the environment in which it takes place; as useful catechetical tools; and as appropriate subject matter. Not all catechists can or need be media specialists, but all should have some understanding of the implications of media for their work. The media are relevant to every level of catechesis; they help foster human development and are capable of contributing to growth in theological understanding and to faith experience itself.

Although media are instruments for transmitting messages, they also possess inherent capabilities and potentialities.[304] Every medium has its own integrity and special genius requiring specific skills of interpretation on the part of both communicators and audiences. There is an intrinsic connection between medium and message, between the "how" and "what" of communication. In using and evaluating media, catechists should be aware that a concept concretized in a medium is no longer simply an abstract idea but an event. Communication is not just the delivering of messages but an experience of sharing among human beings.

PART B: RADIO AND TELEVISION

253. INSTRUMENTS OF CATECHESIS

Broadcast media present special opportunities and challenges to the creativity of catechists. Radio and television can be direct instruments of catechesis. Catechists who plan to use them for this purpose should either acquire specialized media training or collaborate with others experienced in broadcast production. It may be appropriate for them to seek positions as consultants or advisors to producers of programs dealing with religious matters within their competence.

254. ACCOUNTABILITY OF BROADCAST MEDIA

The broadcast media should be encouraged and supported when they promote human values and called to task when they air unworthy, degrading presentations. This points to the need to make people familiar with the criteria and procedures which local television and radio stations are legally required to observe in order to obtain and keep their operating licenses. Individuals should be made aware that they have a right and duty to state their views to broadcasters.

255. AUDIENCE

Knowledge of the audience is as important to successful broadcast production as familiarity with media technology. Producers must understand people's attitudes and values. Religious and catechetical programming should be professionally excellent and responsive to the interests and needs of viewers and listeners.

Broadcast media can be particularly helpful in meeting special catechetical needs and problems. They can, for instance, be the most effective means of communicating with people in isolated and rural areas, as well as with such groups as the aged and shut-ins. Radio and television also offer opportunities for ecumenical collaboration and so, potentially, for reaching larger audiences.

256. AIR TIME

As a condition of licensing, local radio and television stations are required to make public service time available free of charge to eligible groups. Catechists, generally in cooperation with diocesan communications offices, should investigate the possibility of applying for this air time to present programs. They should realize, though, that public service time is generally not available at peak viewing and listening hours. Free air time is also offered (often at better hours) for TV and radio spot announcements; and many excellent spots of a religious or value-oriented nature are available from Catholic and other religious producers. Though cost and other factors may generally rule out the purchase of air time, the possibility is worth investigating in particular situations.

257. COLLABORATION IN USE OF RESOURCES

More pooling of local, diocesan, and national talent and funds is essential to upgrade the amount and quality of religious and catechetical programming. The Catholic Television Network (CTN), an organization formed by the U.S.

dioceses with their own instructional television capabilities, is one such effort. The Office of Film and Broadcasting and the Office of Promotion and Training in the United States Catholic Conference's Department of Communication are also sources of information about the electronic media and of material of possible use to catechists.

258. ONGOING TECHNOLOGICAL DEVELOPMENTS

People concerned with the religious and catechetical potential of media need to be alert to significant changes in technology, organizational structure, and policy now occurring or anticipated in the broadcasting industry. Cable television, for example, may bring about major changes in the foreseeable future, including a great increase in the number and variety of programs. Catechists and Church-related communicators at the diocesan and national levels should be informed participants in these developments. It is important that the Church have an active role in the planning and licensing process which precedes the inauguration of cable TV in a community, besides monitoring and taking early advantage of other media developments as they occur.

PART C: THE PRESS

259. CATHOLIC PRESS

Despite the emergence of electronic data, print media of many different kinds continue to reach daily into virtually every home and place of work in the country.

The Catholic press has long been central to the Church's communication effort in the United States. It is the least expensive way of regularly bringing comprehensive religious news and instructional features to a large number of Catholics. It helps foster the sense of Christian community among its readers. It serves as a forum, providing the people of the Church with opportunities for discussion and the exchange of ideas.

Catholic newspapers, magazines, books, pamphlets, and parish bulletins can be useful catechetical tools, especially in adult programs. Editors and publishers should provide appealing publications which help contemporary Catholics evaluate their experience in the light of Christian values, foster their growth in faith, and promote community among them. Minority cultural, racial, and ethnic groups should have access to and make use of Catholic publications which are in their languages and reflect their special cultural values and concerns.

There is need for continuing dialogue and cooperation between catechetical leaders and the editors and publishers of Catholic publications at the diocesan and national levels. The aim is to exchange ideas and information about catechetical needs and about the effective use of the Catholic press for catechetical purposes. Catechists and catechetical offices at all levels should provide the Catholic press with news releases and photographs which reflect newsworthy aspects of catechesis—trends, programs, meetings, personalities. They should also offer suggestions for interpretive features and columns of a catechetical nature, and should be prepared to supply these when asked. As opportunities arise, they should collaborate with the Catholic press as planners, consultants, and writers.

260. SECULAR PRESS

The secular press also offers opportunities to catechists, although it would generally be unrealistic to consider it a vehicle for direct catechesis.

Either through a diocesan (or other) communications office or directly, catechists should provide secular publications with accurate and interesting information on catechetical matters. Typically, this is done by news releases. Catechesis ought to be prepared to respond to press inquiries and to spend time when necessary discussing questions and issues with journalists. Secular publications are usually willing to entertain suggestions for articles and features on catechetical topics, provided these are of general interest. Community-oriented newspapers, many of them published weekly or biweekly, offer perhaps the best opportunities; but there may also be occasional opportunities in large daily newspapers and even national publications. Particularly when approaching the secular press on the latter levels, catechists are advised to work with diocesan or national communications offices.

PART D: MEDIA LITERACY

261. TRAINING MEDIA PRODUCERS

All who use the communications media in their work "have a duty in conscience to make themselves competent in the art of social communication,"[305] and this applies in particular to people with educational responsibilities, including catechists. Theory, technique, and research are part of media training. In line with what has been said above, catechists should learn how to take media into account as a crucial part of the cultural background and experience of those being catechized; how to use media in catechesis; and how to help their students understand and evaluate media in the light of religious values.

262. TRAINING MEDIA USERS

Catechetical instruction concerning media should help people become knowledgeable viewers, listeners, and readers. Such training is necessary for them "to benefit to the full from what the instruments of social communications have to offer."[306] It is also required if they are to seek to improve the quality of media, either by advocacy directed at professional communicators, or by pursuing careers in media.

Because television occupies so much of the time of so many people in the United States, catechesis should seek to foster critical understanding of this medium in particular. Viewers need to know, for example, how programs are planned and produced; techniques used by advertisers and others to influence and persuade; whether and to what degree TV gives a true picture of life or distorts reality; and the role of profit motives in determining policy in commercial television.

Because people grow in maturity and because there are frequent changes in the media, continuing education is necessary to keep abreast of the changes.

PART E: OTHER CATECHETICAL MATERIALS

263. INTRODUCTION

Designers of catechetical curricula should take written materials and materials in other media into consideration as elements in a total plan. The classroom learning situation itself is only one element in total catechesis.

Section I: Textbooks

264. TEXTBOOKS

Textbooks are guides for learning, summary statements of course content, and ready instruments of review. They must present the authentic and complete message of Christ and His Church, adapted to the capacity of the learners, with balanced emphasis proportionate to the importance of particular truths. Modern texts do more than present information. Their graphics, for example, can foster learning and stimulate — or discourage — interest. The graphics in catechetical texts must be in the best tradition of Christian art, chosen with sensitivity to the age, psychological development, intellectual capacity, and background of learners.

Teachers' manuals are essential components of any textbook series. They should contain "an explanation of the message of salvation (constant references must be made to the sources, and a clear distinction must be kept between those things which pertain to faith and to the doctrine that must be held, and those things which are mere opinions of theologians); psychological and pedagogical advice; suggestions about methods."[307] Manuals or developed notes for parents should accompany any materials designed for children. Wherever possible, special manuals for use in catechesis of the handicapped should be developed, by professionals in special education.

Textbooks must avoid racism, sexism, and narrow provincialism of all kinds, and must take special care to represent other religious traditions fairly. They should provide for variety in worship and service. In catechizing older children, youth, and adults, the Bible should be used as a text for study along with other textbooks.

The various regional, cultural, economic, and religious characteristics in the United States are to be taken into account in the preparation and evaluation of textbooks and other materials. Some of these are identified in Chapter I and Chapter VIII, Part D.

Section II: Other Instructional Materials

265. OTHER INSTRUCTIONAL MATERIALS

a) Correspondence courses

Correspondence courses, using print or electronic media, can be helpful in supplementing catechetical programs for everyone. They are of particular importance in the catechesis of families and individuals in isolated areas, the sick, the elderly, people with irregular working hours, those who wish to study the faith privately, and any others who find it difficult to participate in organized catechetical programs. In special circumstances, correspondence courses can be used for training teachers, helping parents in the catechesis of their children, etc.

b) Other media

Today most people, especially the young, are accustomed and even expect to experience much of their learning through sophisticated media presentations. The Church needs to make creative use of these tools in communicating with them.

Instructional media are of many kinds, both print and nonprint, and include activities such as arts, crafts, dramatics, mime, dance, role playing, simulation or instructional games, music, storytelling, visuals such as posters and charts, videotapes, films, filmstrips, slides, cassette tapes, and overhead transparencies. All instructional materials used in catechesis should be artistically sensitive and technically competent. They should also be theologically accurate and should reflect the insights derived from good catechetical research.

It is essential that all catechists be trained in the use of media. Training will cover such things as the language of film and television and the characteristics of different media,[308] and will include opportunities to learn how to operate audio-visual equipment.

Media centers, established on a diocesan or regional basis, can provide consulting services for catechists in the use of media. Typically, these centers will include libraries of media materials available free or on a rental basis, provide in-service training programs, and offer production facilities to supplement those available from commercial sources. In some areas bookmobiles can provide an extension of the services of the media center.

Section III: Preparation and Evaluation of Catechetical Materials

266. PREPARATION AND EVALUATION

All catechetical textbooks and other materials are to be prepared according to the criteria and guidelines contained in this NCD. It is also fully expected that all such texts and materials will be evaluated by those responsible for catechesis in light of these criteria and guidelines. The appropriate offices of the United States Catholic Conference will assist publishers, producers, and others in this regard.

CONCLUSION

Effective catechesis is always a gift of God. "I planted the seed and Apollos watered it, but God made it grow." (1 Corinthians 3:6) It is important, therefore, to pray for this gift. Catechesis goes forward in the light of the risen Christ, energized by the love of the Holy Spirit, drawing creativity from the power of the Father.

Yet effective catechesis also depends a great deal on human effort: on planning, performance, and evaluation, on personal qualities and commitment. Especially does it depend upon the faith, hope, and love of catechists, responding to God's grace by growing in these virtues and ministering to others. The person of the catechist is the medium in which the message of the faith is incarnated. Whether catechists be parents, teachers, religious, priests, bishops, or any other of God's people, their witness to faith plays a pivotal role in catechesis.

St. Frances Xavier Cabrini, St. Elizabeth Ann Seton, and St. John Neumann are luminous figures in the history of the Catholic Church in the United States who exercised fruitful ministries because they were heroic in their goodness. Their example should be imitated and their intercession sought by those striving, like them, to share with others the light of faith and the love of Christ.

Finally, therefore, the guidelines in this NCD are meant not simply to provide a framework for programs and activities, but to foster hope and confidence in the work of catechesis. Writing under the sign of the rainbow and in the spirit of the brightening dawn of Easter, we seek to lead people, and to be led, ever more fully into the light.

APPENDIX A

The Ten Commandments of God are of special importance in teaching specifics of morality. The Old Testament, the New Testament, and the long tradition of the Church testify to this. A summary presentation of the Ten Commandments of God taken from the New American Bible translation[309] is:

1. I, the Lord, am your God. You shall not have other gods besides me.

2. You shall not take the name of the Lord, your God, in vain.

3. Remember to keep holy the sabbath day.

4. Honor your father and your mother.

5. You shall not kill.

6. You shall not commit adultery.

7. You shall not steal.

8. You shall not bear false witness against your neighbor.

9. You shall not covet your neighbor's wife.

10. You shall not covet anything that belongs to your neighbor.

APPENDIX B

From time to time the Church has listed certain specific duties of Catholics.[310] Among those expected of Catholic Christians today are the following:

1. To keep holy the day of the Lord's resurrection; to worship God by participating in Mass every Sunday and holy day of obligation; to avoid those activities that would hinder renewal of soul and body on the sabbath (e.g., needless work and business activities, unnecessary shopping, etc.).

2. To lead a sacramental life; to receive Holy Communion frequently and the Sacrament of Reconciliation regularly—minimally, to receive the Sacrament of Reconciliation at least once a year (annual confession is obligatory only if serious sin is involved); minimally also, to receive Holy Communion at least once a year, between the First Sunday of Lent and Trinity Sunday.

3. To study Catholic teaching in preparation for the Sacrament of Confirmation, to be confirmed, and then to continue to study and advance the cause of Christ.

4. To observe the marriage laws of the Church; to give religious training, by example and word, to one's children; to use parish schools and catechetical programs.

5. To strengthen and support the Church—one's own parish community and parish priests, the worldwide Church and the pope.

6. To do penance, including abstaining from meat and fasting from food on the appointed days.

7. To join in the missionary spirit and apostolate of the Church.

NOTES

1. Cf. CD, 14. Chapter II discusses catechetics.

2. CD, 44.

3. Cf. *Paths of the Church* (Paul VI, 1964), 113–114, 78–112; cf. UR and NA.

4. Cf. GCD, 134.

5. Cf. GCD, foreword.

6. Such small communities exist more or less everywhere throughout the Church. They often spring from a desire to live the Church's life more intensely, or from the desire and search for religious experience on a more "human" scale than some feel large ecclesial communities can easily offer. Cf. EN, 58.

7. *Paths of the Church* (Paul VI, 1964): 117.

8. In 1973–74, 15% of Catholics in the United States had been born outside the United States; 39% had fathers born outside the United States; 36% had mothers who were not native-born; 55% had all grandparents born abroad. Only 20% had all grandparents born in this country. Cf. *Catholic Schools in a Declining Church* (1976): 40.

9. Cf. "Evangelizing the 80,000,000 Unchurched Americans," George Gallup Jr., report given at the Marriottsville Spiritual Center, Marriottsville MD (November 12, 1975): 2.

10. This section reflects the text of *The Theological Formation of Future Priests*. Sacred Congregation for Catholic Education, February 22, 1976. United States Catholic Conference, (1976): 64–68. Cf. UR, 4.

11. Cf. EN, 65.

12. GS, 82.

13. There are 276 such metropolitan areas in the United States. They are found in every state except Vermont and Wyoming.

14. Cf. Gallup: 2–3.

15. Cf. *Catholic Schools in a Declining Church* (1976): 32, 35–36. Similar results have been obtained in other surveys.

16. Cf. Catholic Schools: 29–30.

17. Cf. Catholic Schools: 32.

18. Cf. Catholic Schools: 145–146.

19. Cf. *Religion in America*, 1976. The Gallup Poll Opinion Index, Report 130: 14.

20. In this connection, the words of Pope Paul VI need to be kept in mind: "While being clothed with the outward forms proper to each people, and made explicit by theological expression which takes account of different cultural, social and even racial milieux, it must remain the content of the Catholic faith just exactly as the ecclesial magisterium has received it and transmits it." EN, 65.

21. The principal goal of adult catechesis is growth in the faith of the adult.

22. Cf. GCD, 17.

23. Cf. Luke 1:2; Acts 6:4; Romans 12:7; Ephesians 4:11f.

24. Cf. Romans 15:16; Hebrews 8:1f–6; 1 Peter 2:5–9.

25. Cf. Matthew 25:33–40; Romans 12:6ff; 2 Corinthians 9:12f; 1 Peter 4:10f.

26. CD, 14.

27. Cf. GCD, 20.

28. GCD, 29.

29. GCD, 22.

30. GCD, 23.

31. GCD, 24; Ephesians 1:9f.

32. Cf. GCD, 25.

33. GCD, 26; GS, 62.

34. Cf. GCD, 28; LG, 1.

35. GCD, 30.

36. GCD, 17.

37. EN, 18.

38. EN; cf. Romans 12:2.

39. GCD, 22.

40. GCD, 25.

41. Cf. GCD, 31.

42. Cf. GCD, 20.

43. Cf. TJD, 43.

44. Cf. GCD, 45.

45. GCD, 45.

46. GCD, 11.

47. SC, 8.

48. GCD, 13; DV, 8.

49. "A Message to the People of God," Fourth General Assembly of the Synod of Bishops (October 29, 1977): 8.

50. GS, 4.

51. Cf. GCD, 26; GS, 62.

52. Cf. GCD, 97.

53. Cf. GCD, 37–44.

54. "A Message to the People of God," 7.

55. GCD, 43.

56. Cf. GCD, 43.

57. GCD, 44.

58. GCD, 38.

59. DV, 3.

60. Cf. DV, 3.

61. God's self-manifestation through creation is often referred to as natural revelation.

62. NA, 2.

63. Cf. NA, 2; GS, 58.

64. St. Ephrem, *Nisibene Hymns*, 3, 3; 48, 7, etc.

65. DV, 4.

66. DV, 8.

67. LG, 25.

68. General audience, January 19, 1972. Cf. DS, 3421.

69. Cf. DS 3421; GCD 11, 13, 26, 44.

70. GCD, 36.

71. GCD, 36.

72. DV, 5; Second Council of Orange, DS 377; First Vatican Council, DS 3010.

73. DH, 10.

74. DV, 10.

75. DV, 9.

76. DV, 8.

77. Cf. *Declaration in Defense of the Catholic Doctrine on the Church Against Certain Errors of the Present Day.* Sacred Congregation for the Doctrine of the Faith, (June 24, 1973): 5.

78. *In Defense of Catholic Doctrine*, 5.

79. St. Jerome, *Commentary on Isaiah, Prol.*, quoted in DV, 25.

80. The sign that a Bible has been approved for Catholic use is the "imprimatur" or preliminary statement that the translation has been checked for accuracy and authorized by a Catholic bishop.

81. DV, 12.

82. "Instruction on the Historical Truth of the Gospels." Pontifical Biblical Commission, 1964. In *Catholic Biblical Quarterly*: 26 (July 1964): 299–304.

83. GCD, 44.

84. An example of doctrinal development is noted in DH, 1: "In taking up the matter of religious freedom this sacred Synod intends to develop the doctrine of recent Popes on the inviolable rights of the human person and on the constitutional order of society."

85. "Judgment as to their [charisms'] genuineness and proper use belongs to those who preside over the Church, and to whose special competence it belongs, not indeed to extinguish the Spirit, but to test all things and hold fast to that which is good." (Cf. 1 Thessalonians 5:12–19ff); LG, 12.

86. From Pope Paul VI's opening allocution at the second session (September 19, 1963).

87. For example, Romans 12:5; 1 Corinthians 12:13; 1 Corinthians 12:27; Ephesians 4:4; Colossians 1:18.

88. LG, 8.

89. Cf. OE, 9.

90. Cf. LG, 22.

91. AG, 2.

92. LG, 23.

93. LG, 24.

94. OE, 2.

95. Cf. OE, 5.

96. UR, 15.

97. UR, 17.

98. Cf. UR, 19.

99. In addition to UR, cf. *Directory Concerning Ecumenical Matters: Part One* (May 14, 1967), and *Part Two: Ecumenism in Higher Education* (April 16, 1970), Secretariat for Promoting Christian Unity.

100. Cf. UR, 14–18.

101. NA, 4.

102. In addition to NA, 4, cf. *Guidelines on Religious Relations with the Jews* (December 1, 1974), Commission for Religious Relations with the Jews; and *Statement on Catholic-Jewish Relations on the Occasion of the Celebration of the Tenth Anniversary of Nostra Aetate* (November 20, 1975), National Conference of Catholic Bishops. Additional information may be obtained from the Secretariat for Catholic-Jewish Relations, National Conference of Catholic Bishops, 3211 Fourth St., N. E., Washington, D.C. 20017-1194.

103. Cf. NA, 3.

104. Cf. NA, 2.

105. Cf. NA, 5; GS, 21.

106. This text is based on BT, a document approved by the bishops of the United States in November 1972, and subsequently reviewed and approved by the Holy See. *Basic Teachings* was largely inspired by the GCD, 47–69. It has been modified to take into account some major documents published since 1972. Articles 14 through 19, on morality, have been revised, largely in the light of two documents: To Live in Christ Jesus, a collective pastoral approved by the bishops of the United States in November 1976; and *Declaration on Certain Questions Concerning Sexual Ethics*, issued by the Sacred Congregation for the Doctrine of the Faith in December 1975. The discussion of the sacraments has been placed in Parts A and B of Chapter VI, "Catechesis for a Worshiping Community," and articles 11–13 have been replaced with materials from the revised instructions and rituals.

Also, of the topics discussed in the Introduction to BT, the importance of prayer is treated in Part C of Chapter VI, participation in the liturgy is dealt with throughout that chapter; familiarity with the Bible appears in several articles: 43, 52–53, 60a)i, 143, 179, 185, 190, 207, 223. Knowing and observing the Ten Commandments, the Beatitudes and the Precepts of the Church are mentioned in articles 100, 105, 154. The Ten Commandments and the precepts are in the Appendices.

107. Cf. DV, 3; GCD, 51.

108. Cf. Pope Pius XII, *Humani Generis;* GS, 12, 14.

109. Cf. Romans 20; Acts 15:17; Psalm 19:1; Wisdom 13:1–9.

110. Cf. Dogmatic Constitution *Dei Filius* of the First Vatican Council.

111. Cf. GS, 21.

112. Cf. GS, 22.

113. Cf. John 7:39; Acts 2:,33; Romans 4:25; 8:11; 1 Corinthians 15:45; Hebrews 5:6.

114. Cf. Words of institution, eucharistic prayers.

115. Cf. Leviticus 19:18; Matthew 5:44–48; 22:37–40; Luke 10:25–28.

116. AG, 4.

117. Cf. LG, 12.

118. Cf. AG, 1–2.

119. Cf. LG, 10.

120. LG, 10.

121. LG, 29.

122. CD, 16.

123. Cf. LG, 25. "Magisterium" is the teaching of the bishops, successors of the apostles, in union with and never apart from the teaching of the successor of St. Peter, the pope, as well as the official teaching of the pope alone.

124. LG, 25.

125. LG, , 25.

126. LG, 12.

127. Cf. LG, 32.

128. Cf. UR, 4–5.

129. Cf. LG, 8, 14–16; cf. DH, 1; cf. entire UR; cf. GCD, 27.

130. Cf. LG, 9; entire AG.

131. GS, 93.

132. GS, 3.

133. Decree on the Sacraments of the Council of Trent, DS 1601, 1606.

134. Cf. LG, 1.

135. Cf. SC, 59.

136. Cf. GS, 13.

137. Pope Paul VI, *Credo of the People of God*, (June 30, 1968).

138. The Holy See has rejected the opinion that mortal sin exists only "in the formal refusal directly opposed to God's will, or in that selfishness which completely and deliberately closes itself to the love of neighbor." It is not only in such cases that there comes into play the "fundamental option," i.e., the decision which is necessary for mortal sin to exist. On the contrary, mortal sin is found "in every deliberate transgression in serious matter, of each of the moral laws," and not only in formal and direct resistance to the commandment of charity. Cf. *Sexual Ethics* (Doctrine of the Faith, 1975), 10.

139. Pope Paul VI, *Paenitemini*, Apostolic Constitution of February 17, 1966.

140. Cf. Roman Missal, Memorial Acclamation.

141. John Henry Newman, *Parochial and Plain Sermons*, V, 7.

142. Roman Missal, Preface for the Feast of Christ the King.

143. DH, 3; cf. St. Thomas Aquinas, *Summa Theologiae*, 1–2. 91, 1 and 2; 94, 1.

144. Cf. GS, 16.

145. GS, 16.

146. DH, 14.

147. LG, 18.

148. Cf. GS, 51; Pope Paul VI, *On the Regulation of Birth (Humanae Vitae)* (July 25, 1968); *Human Life in Our Day*, a collective pastoral of the American hierarchy issued November 15, 1968.

149. For a discussion of premarital sex, homosexuality, and masturbation, cf. *Sexual Ethics* (Doctrine of the Faith, 1975).

150. Roman Ritual, First Eucharistic Prayer of the Mass.

151. Cf. LG, 52–59.

152. LG, 53.

153. The bishops' pastoral letter, *Behold Your Mother, Woman of Faith*, published in 1973, can be very helpful in catechizing on this subject. Cf. also *Devotion to the Blessed Virgin Mary (Marialis Cultus)*, an Apostolic Exhortation of His Holiness, Pope Paul VI (February 2, 1974).

In 1859, at the request of the bishops of the United States, Pope Pius IX placed the nation under the protection of Mary's Immaculate Conception.

154. Cf. LG, 49–51.

155. Cf. LG, 48.

156. LG, 49.

157. GCD, 55.

158. Cf. GCD, 57.

159. Cf. LG, 14.

160. The Roman Ritual, *Rite of Christian Initiation of Adults*. Sacred Congregation for Divine Worship, 1972.

161. The Roman Ritual, *Rite of Baptism for Children*. Sacred Congregation for Divine Worship, 1969.

162. Rule of Baptism, 8.

163. The Roman Pontifical, *Rite of Confirmation*, Apostolic Constitution on the Sacrament of Confirmation, Pope Paul VI, 1971.

164. Rite of Confirmation, 11.

165. The Congregation of Rites published a very important *Instruction on Eucharistic Worship* on May 25, 1967. In that *Instruction* there is a seven-part article (3) that deals specifically with "The Principal Points of Doctrine."

166. CS, 52.

167. Roman Ritual, Eucharistic Prayer III.

168. In the *Instruction on Eucharistic Worship*, there are eleven articles (5–15) under the title "Some General Principles of Particular Importance in the Catechesis of the People on the Mystery of the Eucharist." These principles should be a guideline for all catechists, writers, and publishers.

169. GCD, 58.

170. *The General Instruction of the Roman Missal* gives full information concerning the prayers and actions at Mass proper to the laity.

171. "[It will not] be easy to grasp the force of that love by which Christ was impelled to give us himself as our spiritual food except by fostering a special devotion to the Eucharistic Heart of Jesus." Pius xii, *Haurietis Aquas* (1956), 185.

172. The Roman Ritual, *Rite of Penance.* Sacred Congregation for Divine Worship, 1973, 6a).

173. Cf. Rite of Penance, 32.

174. *Quam Singulari,* decree of the Congregation for the Discipline of the Sacraments, 1910; letter (Prot. N. 2/76) of the Sacred Congregation for the Sacraments and Divine Worship and the Sacred Congregation for the Clergy, March 31, 1977, to Archbishop Joseph L. Bernardin, president of nccb/uscc, signed by James Cardinal Knox and John Cardinal Wright. Cf. also GCD, Addendum.

175. SC, 73.

176. The Roman Ritual, *Rite of Anointing and Pastoral Care of the Sick.* Sacred Congregation for Divine Worship, 1972, 5.

177. Cf. Rite of Anointing, 8, 10–12.

178. GS, 50.

179. Cf. Pope Paul vi, *On the Regulation of Birth (Humanae Vitae).*

180. Cf. *The Ministerial Priesthood,* Second General Assembly of the Synod of Bishops, 1971.

181. Cf. also, the Roman Pontifical, *The Ordination of Bishops.* Sacred Congregation for Divine Worship, 1972.

182. Cf. The Roman Pontifical, *The Ordination of Priests.*

183. The Roman Pontifical, *The Ordination of Deacons.*

184. It should be recalled, as the Second Vatican Council stated, and as the pope has many times confirmed, that regulation of the sacred liturgy depends on ecclesiastical authority. "Therefore no other person, not even a priest, may add, remove or change anything in the liturgy on his own authority." SC, 22.

185. DMC, 2.

186. DMC, 9.

187. Pius xii, in his encyclical *Haurietis Aquas* (1956), states: "If the evidence on which devotion to the Wounded Heart of

Jesus rests is rightly weighed, it is clear to all that we are dealing here, not with an ordinary form of piety which anyone may at his discretion slight in favor of other devotions, or esteem lightly, but with a duty of religion most conducive to Christian perfection," 150. Cf. also *Annum Sacrum,* Leo xiii (1899); *Miserentissimus Redemptor,* Pius xi (1928).

188. General Decree and Instruction, *Maxima Redemptions Nostrae Mysteriis,* Sacred Congregation of Rites (November 16, 1955), AAS 47.

189. Pope Paul vi, Moto Proprio, *Approval of the General Norms for the Liturgical Year and the New General Roman Calendar* (February 14, 1969).

190. GNLY, 1.

191. GNLY, 3.

192. GNLY, 4.

193. GNLY, 8.

194. GNLY, 18.

195. GNLY, 22.

196. GNLY, 27.

197. GNLY, 32.

198. GNLY, 39.

199. GNLY, 43.

200. GNLY, 1.

201. *Roman Calendar, Text and Commentary,* United States Catholic Conference, 1976.

202. SC, 122.

203. SC, 123; cf. EN, 62; Paul vi, discourse to the artists of Rome, AAS 56 (1964): 439–442.

204. Cf. SC, 60–63.

205. GS, 45.

206. Cf. JW, Introduction.

207. Paul vi, On the *Development of Peoples* (1967), 27.

208. John xxiii, *Peace on Earth* (1963), 8–33.

209. Paul vi, *The Eightieth Anniversary of Rerum Novarum (Octogesima Adveniens,* 1971), 4.

210. Cf. GS, 42.

211. Cf. JW, II. The Gospel Message and the Mission of the Church, The Mission of the Church, Hierarchy and Christians;

III. The Practice of Justice, Cooperation Between Local Churches; Ecumenical Collaboration.

212. GS, 39.

213. Synodal documents do not have the same teaching authority as the documents of ecumenical councils, but they are certainly of great weight and stature in the Church.

214. JW, Introduction.

215. Paul VI, *On Evangelization* (1975), 35.

216. Message to the United States bishops' "Call to Action" convocation, October 1976.

217. Cf. JW, III, The Practice of Justice, The Church's Witness.

218. Cf. GS, 69.

219. *Sermo 10, In Quadragesima*, 3–5: PL 54: 299–301.

220. Cf. GS, 69.

221. Cf. Pope John XXIII, *Christianity and Social Progress (Mater et Magistra)* (May 15, 1961), 6.

222. The specific papal, conciliar and synodal documents which embody much of the teaching include: Leo XIII's *On the Condition of Labor (Rerum Novarum*, 1891); Pius XI's *Reconstruction of the Social Order (Quadragesimo Anno*, 1931); Pius XII's Christmas Messages (1939–1957), his Radio Messages (1939–1957), and his Radio Message of Pentecost (1941); John XXIII's *Christianity and Social Progress (Mater et Magistra*, 1961) and *Peace on Earth (Pacem in Terris*, 1963); GS (1965) and DH (1965); Paul VI's *On the Development of Peoples (Populorum Progressio*, 1967), and the Apostolic Letter, *The Eightieth Anniversary of Rerum Novarum (Octogesima Adveniens*, 1971); the Second General Assembly of the Synod of Bishops, *Justice in the World* (1971).

223. GS, 30.

224. Cf. John XXIII, *Peace on Earth* (1963), 35–38.

225. Sin is personal though it has social consequences.

226. JW, Introduction.

227. Cf. John XXIII, *Peace on Earth* (1963), 30.

228. JW, II, The Gospel Message and the Mission of the Church, The Saving Justice of God Through Christ.

229. Major documents of the Holy See and the bishops are available from the Publications Office, United States Catholic Conference (3211 Fourth St., N. E., Washington, D.C. 20017-1194), soon after they appear. Papal and other Roman documents are printed in *The Pope Speaks* published by Our Sunday Visitor, Inc. (P.O. Box 920, Huntington, IN 46750).

230. Among the numerous documents on abortion and related topics, cf. *Declaration on Procured Abortion*, Sacred Congregation for the Doctrine of the Faith, 1974. Documentation and information on abortion and the right to life may be obtained from the Publications Office, United States Catholic Conference (3211 Fourth St., N.E., Washington, D.C. 20017-1194).

231. Cf. DH, 5; GE, 6.

232. Cf. GS, 10.

233. Cf. JW, III, The Practice of Justice, Educating for Justice.

234. Cf. JW, III.

235. Cf. JW, III.

236. Cf. GCD, 30, 38.

237. For the use of the social and psychological sciences in pastoral care, cf. GS, 52, 62.

238. GCD, 131; cf. GE, 1.

239. Cf. GCD, 121.

240. Cf. GCD, 72.

241. Cf. GCD, 74.

242. Cf. GCD, 73.

243. Cf. GCD, 78.

244. Cf. GCD, 78.

245. Cf. GCD, 79.

246. Cf. GCD, 83.

247. GCD, 88.

248. One method of discernment has been described as operating on three levels; the sociological (empirical reality—what is going on in society); anthropological (within the mind and heart—what is happening to men and women); theological (the acting out of God's designs—how do I act in the light of the gospel?).

249. Cf. *Catholic Schools in a Declining Church* (1976): 148.

250. Cf. GCD, 83, which invites study of the stage of young adulthood.

251. Cf. GCD, 94.

252. Cf. GCD, 97, for a treatment of the special functions of catechesis for adults.

253. Cf. LG, 14.

254. GCD, 63.

255. GCD, 95.

256. Cf. GCD, 95.

257. Cf. AA, 2, 7.

258. The catechist should always keep in mind that "the conscience of the faithful, even when informed by the virtue of prudence, must be subject to the magisterium of the Church, whose duty it is to explain the whole moral law authoritatively, in order that it may rightly and correctly express the objective moral order." GCD, 63.

259. Cf. TLCJ, 1; LG.

260. *The Church in Our Day*, National Conference of Catholic Bishops. United States Catholic Conference, November 1967, p. 64.

261. *The Catholic School*, Sacred Congregation for Catholic Education. United States Catholic Conference, 1977, 84.

262. Cf. *Human Life in Our Day*, A Collective Pastoral of the American Hierarchy. United States Catholic Conference, 1968, p. 18.

263. For more on this subject, cf. *Sexual Ethics* (Doctrine of the Faith, 1975).

264. GE, 1.

265. In one study, it was found that only 12 percent of young people are taught about sex by their parents. Most learn from their peers. *Adolescent Appraisals and Selected Institutions (Home, Church, School, Youth Organizations)*, Calderwood, Deryck. Oregon State University, 1970.

266. Cf. GE, 1.

267. Cf. TJD, 57.

268. Cf. *Where Are the 6.6 Million? A Statistical Survey of Catholic Elementary and Secondary Formal Religious Education 1965–1974*, Paradis, Wilfrid H., Thompson, Andrew D. United States Catholic Conference, 1976; cf. also update for 1975 by the same authors.

269. Cf. *Religion and American Youth* (1976): 8–9.

270. Cf. *Religion and American Youth*: 18–21.

271. Cf. *Religion and American Youth*: 11–21.

272. Cf. *Religion and American Youth*: 22–43.

273. Cf. *Religion and American Youth*: 43–49.

274. Cf. *Religion and American Youth*: 24.

275. GCD, 111.

276. TJD, 23.

277. TJD, 24.

278. TJD, 29.

279. Cf. GE, 3; AA, 11.

280. Cf. AA, 24.

281. GCD, 71.

282. *Teach Them*, A Statement of the Catholic Bishops. United States Catholic Conference, May 6, 1976. United States Catholic Conference, 1976, p. 7.

283. *Directory on the Pastoral Ministry of Bishops*, Sacred Congregation for Bishops, February 22, 1973. Publications Service, Canadian Catholic Conference, 65.

284. GCD, 126.

285. Cf. GCD, 129; TJD, 142.

286. Cf. DV, 22.

287. Cf. *Directory on the Pastoral Ministry of Bishops*, Sacred Congregation for Bishops, February 22, 1973. Publications Service, Canadian Catholic Conference, 174.

288. AG, 35–38; LG, chapters i and ii.

289. EN (Paul vi, 1975), 71.

290. GCD, 78.

291. TJD, 118; cf. also, *The Catholic School*, Sacred Congregation for Catholic Education. United States Catholic Conference, 1977.

292. Cf. TJD, 92.

293. TJD, 103.

294. GE, 8.

295. TJD, 108.

296. GE, 9.

297. Letter of Pope Paul VI to French social action groups meeting in France, July 1, 1970.

298. *Engel v. Vitale*, 370. U.S. 421 (1961); *School District of Abington Township v. Schempp, Murray v. Curlett*, 374 U.S. 203 (1963).

299. Cf. *Illinois ex. rel. McCallum, Board of Education*, 333 U.S. 203, 227 (1948); and *Zorach v. Clauson*, 343 U.S. 306 (1952).

300. Cf. CD, 27; for the desirability of such councils, cf. *Directory on the Pastoral Ministry of Bishops*, 204.

301. GCD, 126.

302. Cf. GCD, 128.

303. *Program of Priestly Formation*, 151.

304. Cf. IM, 14; EN, 45.

305. EN, 15.

306. EN, 65.

307. GCD, 121.

308. Cf. GCD, 122.

309. Cf. Exodus 20:2–17; Deuteronomy 5:6–21.

310. Cf. BT, 28.

ON
CATECHESIS
IN OUR
TIME

CATECHESI TRADENDAE
1979

OVERVIEW OF *ON CATECHESIS IN OUR TIME*

by Jane E. Regan

The International Synod of Bishops meeting in Rome in October 1977 had catechesis as its focus, with particular emphasis on children and youth. This month-long meeting attended to the variety of catechetical issues present in the church throughout the world. It had been more than a decade since the conclusion of the Second Vatican Council; the time seemed right for a consideration of the way in which the whole of the Christian message is conveyed and passed on to the present generation of believers. At the conclusion of the Synod, the bishops issued a message to the people of God that summarized the central themes discussed at the meeting. They also addressed a set of resolutions to Pope Paul VI.[1] In October 1979, Pope John Paul II issued the apostolic exhortation *Catechesi Tradendae* (CT), which reflected the discussion and documentation of the 1977 Synod. Building on the work completed earlier by Paul VI, John Paul II set out a vision of catechesis for the universal church and the place of this activity in the pastoral life of the church.

The document's nine chapters present in a fairly methodical fashion the central components of an understanding of catechesis. The first two chapters establish the foundations for catechesis: It is essentially christocentric (chapter 1) and rooted in the church's historical tradition (chapter 2). The next two chapters define the place of catechesis within the life of the church: Catechesis is seen as a dimension of evangelization (chapter 3) with scripture and tradition as its main source (chapter 4). Attention is given next to the practical realities of the catechetical enterprise, with an examination of the participants (chapter 5), the methods (chapter 6) and the process for imparting catechesis (chapter 7). The final two chapters emphasize again the importance of catechesis in establishing a Christian's identity and the necessity that all Christians be involved in the catechetical endeavor.

CENTRAL THEMES

In the Synod of 1974, the meeting just prior to the meeting on catechesis in 1977, the focus was evangelization. In *On Evangelization in the Modern World* (1975), Pope Paul VI had set out the description, content and expression of evangelization. He articulated the complexity of evangelization and its multifaceted nature: "Evangelization, as we have said, is a complex process made up of varied elements: the renewal of humanity, witness, explicit proclamation, inner adherence, entry into the community, acceptance of signs, [and] apostolic initiative."[2] In CT, catechesis is described as one moment in the process of evangelization; this serves as a central theme in the document.

It is in situating catechesis within the context of evangelization that the core objectives of catechesis are made clear. While recognizing that the initial proclamation that leads to conversion might not have taken place or might not have been completed adequately, CT delineates the focus of catechesis as building the initial faith (CT, 19–20). In light of this, catechesis is defined as "an education of children, young people and adults in the faith, which includes especially the teaching of Christian doctrine imparted, generally speaking in an organic and systematic way, with a view to initiating the hearers into the fullness of Christian life" (CT, 18).[3] This description of catechesis introduces another central theme of CT: the concept of "systematic catechesis."

The relationship and possible tension between a focus on the kerygma, with its emphasis on doctrine and salvation history, and a focus on the life experience and cultural context of the learner was one of the concerns raised at the Synod and reflected both in the message to the people of God that was issued by the bishops at the conclusion of the Synod of 1977 and in the propositions sent to Pope Paul VI. The terms "systematic" and "systematic catechesis" serve as a way of addressing this possible tension.[4] According to CT, systematic catechesis is not improvised; deals with the essentials; is sufficiently complete, extending beyond an initial proclamation; and initiates the learner into the fullness of Christian life (CT, 21). The document argues that one cannot cast off orderly, systematic study of the Christian message and concentrate instead on life experience. Throughout the document, regular reference is made to the relationship between life experience and the Christian message, between culture and tradition. While CT does not fully address the relationship, it does acknowledge that catechesis must give expression to the active living tradition that is to be interpreted for today.

Present throughout CT is a third theme that gives shape to the understanding of catechesis reflected in the document: catechesis as an essential ecclesial action. In the opening paragraphs of CT, the historical foundation of catechesis is stated briefly (10–13). Drawing insights from early periods, CT concludes that "[c]atechesis is intimately bound up with the whole of the church's life" (13). It is seen as a fundamental source of the church's internal strength and external activity (15). It is seen as the duty and right of the whole church, an activity "for which the whole church must feel responsible and must wish to be responsible" (16). *On Catechesis in our Time* makes clear that everyone is in need of catechesis (chapter 5) and that all are called to participate in this task (chapter 9).

Of particular interest in light of contemporary catechetical conversation are the discussions of the roles of the parish (64) and of the family (68) in the catechetical task. In both discussions, emphasis is placed on the parish and family as the primary settings for catechesis and on the importance of forming parish leaders and parents to teach in ways appropriate to the situation. It is clear that the primary interest is in instruction. For example, in discussing the role of catechesis in the family, CT recommends that parents go beyond simply explaining the religious dimension of the events that mark the regular cycle of family life. They are encouraged to "follow and repeat, within the setting of family life, the more methodical teaching received elsewhere" (68). While the emphasis is on instruction within these two crucial settings, there also is the recognition that catechesis takes place within these settings not just as formal instruction but in the very life of the parish and the family. In that sense, catechesis is an ecclesial activity not only because each member of the church has a specific role and responsibility but also because all members contribute to the life of the parish and of the family, which is itself faith formative. Further attention is given to this theme in subsequent catechetical writings and in the apostolic exhortation on the family, *Familiaris Consortio*, the document flowing from the Synod of 1980.

AREAS FOR DEVELOPMENT

Like all documents, CT is a product of its time. The broader catechetical conversations, the ecclesial realities and the episcopal concerns of the mid-1970s color the content and emphases of the text. While recognizing the continuing applicability of the insights set out in CT for catechesis at the end of the twentieth century, there are topics that, as presented in the document, warrant further development. Two such topics are sacramental (or liturgical) catechesis and adult catechesis.

The discussion of sacramental catechesis receives scant attention in CT. The essential relationship between catechesis and sacraments is set out in chapter 3, and it is mentioned in passing in the examination of the catechesis of children (37). In both contexts, the emphasis is on catechesis as preparation for and as instruction about the sacraments. The discussion in chapter 3 affirms the complementarity of good catechesis and good liturgy; however, the implication is that catechesis is exclusively didactic and even propositional while liturgy is experiential. Catechesis is spoken about only as preparation for liturgical participation.

In a church formed and transformed by the implementation of the order of Christian initiation of adults, this understanding of the role of catechesis and the relationship between catechesis and liturgy is inadequate. The insights from the order of Christian initiation of adults have helped us to name that sacramental catechesis is not primarily about instruction in one sacrament but about forming us into a people aware of God's sacramental presence. Liturgical catechesis is not primarily a preparation for liturgical celebrations but an ongoing reflection on the mystery of Christ celebrated through the liturgy.[5] This developed understanding is an essential component of contemporary catechesis.

A second topic that has undergone significant development in the years since the presentation of CT is that of adult catechesis. While this area of the catechetical enterprise is always in need of development in the parish setting, theoretical conversations about the place of adults in the faith formation process have matured significantly since the mid-1970s.

As set out in the introductory paragraphs of CT, the topic of the Synod of 1977 was catechesis, with particular emphasis on children and youth. Thus, the lack of attention to the catechesis and faith formation of adults is somewhat understandable. However, the understanding of adult catechesis that is present in the document is inadequate. Adult catechesis is described as a "central problem" (43) and seems to be understood primarily as a way of "catching up" those adults who did not receive adequate catechesis in childhood (44). While acknowledgment is given to the centrality of adult catechesis, little attention is given to the means by which such catechesis is to take place. In the final analysis, the focus of the Synod and CT on the catechesis of children and adults belies the essential nature of adult catechesis as stated in the document. To say, as the *General Catechetical Directory* and the *National Catechetical Directory* of the United States do, that all catechesis is oriented toward adults does not diminish the importance of the catechesis of children and adults; it simply sets that activity within the broader context. This context is not developed adequately in CT.

IN CONTEXT

On Catechesis in our Time is best understood when read within its historical context. It is beyond this introductory essay to provide a snapshot of the ecclesial and catechetical perspective of the late 1970s. However, it is worth noting that the character of CT as a document flowing from a universal synod of bishops provides an important contextual element for CT and for catechesis in general. The topics addressed by the synods of the 1970s give us a view of the nature of the church and its internal and external relationships. These synods begin with the meeting in 1971, with its focus on the mission of the people of God to further justice in the world, and they continue that conversation with the synod on evangelization of 1974. The broader questions of the church's relationship with the world and its responsibility to convey the gospel message in word and action provides the framework for the discussion of catechesis in the Synod of 1977. The importance of initiating persons into the Christian life and the process of maturing faith, which are at the heart of CT, are brought closer to home in the synod of 1980, with its focus on the family.

As we read CT and consider its significance and implications for catechesis today, we would be well reminded of this more comprehensive context for understanding and engaging in catechesis. It is in fact an expression of the reality of the church and an activity essential to the health and growth of the people of God.

NOTES

1. "Message to the People of God: Synod 1977," *Origins* (November 10, 1977): 321–28. For a summary and discussion of the documentation of the 1977 Synod, including the 34 propositions submitted to the pope, see *The Living Light* 15 (1978): 1–128.

2. EN, 24.

3. It is interesting to note that this is the definition or description of catechesis that is presented in the *Catechism of the Catholic Church*. See the prologue of the *Catechism*, 5.

4. For a detailed discussion of the concept of systematic catechesis as used in CT, see Anne Campbell, "Toward a Systematic Catechesis: An Interpretation of *Catechesi Tradendae*," *The Living Light* 17 (1980): 311–20.

5. It is interesting to note that the discussion of liturgical catechesis in the *Catechism of the Catholic Church* develops this understanding of catechesis quite effectively. Although beginning with a citation of CT, the *Catechism* then enhances the understanding in the earlier document with this statement: "Liturgical catechesis aims to initiate people into the mystery of Christ (It is 'mystagogy.') by proceeding from the visible to the invisible, from the sign to the thing signified, from the 'sacraments' to the 'mysteries'" (1075).

OUTLINE

INTRODUCTION

1.   The Church has always considered catechesis one of her primary tasks, for, before Christ ascended to his Father after his Resurrection, he gave the Apostles a final command—to make disciples of all nations and to teach them to observe all that he had commanded.[1] He thus entrusted them with the mission and power to proclaim to humanity what they had heard, what they had seen with their eyes, what they had looked upon and touched with their hands, concerning the Word of Life.[2] He also entrusted them with the mission and power to explain with authority what he had taught them, his words and actions, his signs and commandments. And he gave them the Spirit to fulfil this mission.

Very soon the name of catechesis was given to the whole of the efforts within the Church to make disciples, to help people to believe that Jesus is the Son of God, so that believing they might have live in his name,[3] and to educate and instruct them in this life and thus build up the Body of Christ. The Church has not ceased to devote her energy to this task.

PAUL VI'S SOLICITUDE

2.   The most recent Popes gave catechesis a place of eminence in their pastoral solicitude. Through his gestures, his preaching, his authoritative interpretation of the Second Vatican Council (considered by him the great catechism of modern times), and through the whole of his life, my venerated predecessor Paul VI served the Church's catechesis in a particularly exemplary fashion. On 18 March 1971, he approved the *General Catechetical Directory* prepared by the Sacred Congregation for the Clergy, a directory that is still the basic document for encouraging and guiding catechetical renewal throughout the Church. He set up the International Council for Catechesis in 1975. He defined in masterly fashion the role and significance of catechesis in the life and mission of the Church when he addressed the participants in the First International Catechetical Congress on 25 September 1971,[4] and he returned explicitly to the subject in his Apostolic Exhortation *Evangelii Nuntiandi*.[5] He decided that catechesis, especially that meant for children and young people, should be the theme of the Fourth General Assembly of the Synod of Bishops,[6] which was held in October 1977 and which I myself had the joy of taking part in.

A FRUITFUL SYNOD

3.   At the end of that Synod the Fathers presented the Pope with a very rich documentation, consisting of the various interventions during the Assembly,

the conclusions of the working groups, the Message that they had with his consent sent to the people of God,[7] and especially the imposing list of "Propositions" in which they expressed their views on a very large number of aspects of present-day catechesis.

The Synod worked in an exceptional atmosphere of thanksgiving and hope. It saw in catechetical renewal a precious gift from the Holy Spirit to the Church of today, a gift to which the Christian communities at all levels throughout the world are responding with a generosity and inventive dedication that win admiration. The requisite discernment could then be brought to bear on a reality that is very much alive and it could benefit from great openness among the people of God to the grace of the Lord and the directives of the Magisterium.

PURPOSE OF THIS EXHORTATION

4.   It is in the same climate of faith and hope that I am today addressing this Apostolic Exhortation to you, Venerable Brothers and dear sons and daughters. The theme is extremely vast and the Exhortation will keep to a few only of the most topical and decisive aspects of it, as an affirmation of the happy results of the Synod. In essence, the Exhortation takes up again the reflections that were prepared by Pope Paul VI, making abundant use of the documents left by the Synod. Pope John Paul I, whose zeal and gifts as a catechist amazed us all, had taken them in hand and was preparing to publish them when he was suddenly called to God. To all of us he gave an example of catechesis at once popular and concentrated on the essential, one made up of simple words and actions that were able to touch the heart. I am therefore taking up the inheritance of these two Popes in response to the request which was expressly formulated by the Bishops at the end of the Fourth General Assembly of the Synod and which was welcomed by Pope Paul VI in his closing speech.[8] I am also doing so in order to fulfil one of the chief duties of my apostolic charge. Catechesis has always been a central care in my ministry as a priest and as a bishop.

I ardently desire that this Apostolic Exhortation to the whole Church should strengthen the solidity of the faith and of Christian living, should give fresh vigor to the initiatives in hand, should stimulate creativity — with the required vigilance — and should help to spread among the communities the joy of bringing the mystery of Christ to the world.

I
WE HAVE BUT ONE TEACHER, JESUS CHRIST

PUTTING INTO COMMUNION WITH THE PERSON OF CHRIST

5.   The Fourth General Assembly of the Synod of Bishops often stressed the Christocentricity of all authentic catechesis. We can here use the word "Christocentricity" in both its meanings, which are not opposed to each other or mutually exclusive, but each of which rather demands and completes the other.

In the first place, it is intended to stress that at the heart of catechesis we find, in essence, a Person, the Person of Jesus of Nazareth, "the only Son from the Father . . . full of grace and truth,"[9] who suffered and died for us and who now after rising, is living with us forever. It is Jesus who is "the way, and the truth, and the life,"[10] and Christian living consists in following Christ, the *sequela Christi*.

The primary and essential object of catechesis is, to use an expression dear to Saint Paul and also to contemporary theology, "the mystery of Christ." Catechizing is in a way to lead a person to study this Mystery in all its dimensions: "To make all men see what is the plan of the mystery . . . comprehend with all the saints what is the breadth and length and height and depth . . . know the love of Christ which surpasses knowledge . . . (and be filled) with all the fullness of God."[11] It is therefore to reveal in the Person of Christ the whole of God's eternal design reaching fulfillment in that Person. It is to seek to understand the meaning of Christ's actions and words and of the signs worked by him, for they simultaneously hide and reveal his mystery. Accordingly, the definitive aim of catechesis is to put people not only in touch but in communion, in intimacy, with Jesus Christ: only he can lead us to the love of the Father in the Spirit and make us share in the life of the Holy Trinity.

TRANSMITTING CHRIST'S TEACHING

6.   Christocentricity in catechesis also means the intention to transmit not one's own teaching or that of some other master, but the teaching of Jesus Christ, the Truth that he communicates or, to put it more precisely, the Truth that he is.[12] We must therefore say that in catechesis it is Christ, the Incarnate Word and Son of God, who is taught—everything else is taught with reference to him—and it is Christ alone who teaches—anyone else teaches to the extent that he is Christ's spokesman, enabling Christ to teach with his lips. Whatever be the level of his responsibility in the Church, every catechist must constantly endeavor to transmit by his teaching and behavior the teaching and life of Jesus. He will not seek to keep directed towards himself and his personal opinions and attitudes the attention and the consent of the mind and heart of the person he is catechizing. Above all, he will not try to inculcate his personal opinions and options as if they expressed Christ's teaching and the lessons of his life. Every catechist should be able to apply to himself the mysterious words of Jesus: "My teaching is not mine, but his who sent me."[13] Saint Paul did this when he was dealing with a question of prime importance: "I received from the Lord what I also delivered to you."[14] What assiduous study of the word of God transmitted by the Church's Magisterium, what profound familiarity with Christ and with the Father, what a spirit of prayer, what detachment from self must a catechist have in order that he can say: "My teaching is not mine"!

CHRIST THE TEACHER

7.   This teaching is not a body of abstract truths. It is the communication of the living mystery of God. The person teaching it in the Gospel is altogether superior in excellence to the "masters" in Israel, and the nature of his doctrine

surpasses theirs in every way because of the unique link between what he says, what he does and what he is. Nevertheless, the Gospels clearly relate occasions when Jesus "taught." "Jesus began to do and teach"[15] — with these two verbs, placed at the beginning of the book of the Acts, Saint Luke links and at the same time distinguishes two poles in Christ's mission.

Jesus taught. It is the witness that he gives of himself: "Day after day I sat in the Temple teaching."[16] It is the admiring observation of the evangelists, surprised to see him teaching everywhere and at all times, teaching in a manner and with an authority previously unknown: "Crowds gathered to him again; and again, as his custom was, he taught them;"[17] "and they were astonished at his teaching, for he taught them as one who had authority."[18] It is also what his enemies note for the purpose of drawing from it grounds for accusation and condemnation: "He stirs up the people, teaching throughout all Judaea, from Galilee even to this place."[19]

THE ONE "TEACHER"

8.   One who teaches in this way has a unique title to the name of "Teacher." Throughout the New Testament, especially in the Gospels, how many times is he given this title of Teacher![20] Of course the Twelve, the other disciples, and the crowds of listeners call him "Teacher" in tones of admiration, trust and tenderness.[21] Even the Pharisees and the Sadducees, the Doctors of the Law, and the Jews in general do not refuse him the title: "Teacher, we wish to see a sign from you";[22] "Teacher, what shall I do to inherit eternal life?"[23] But above all, Jesus himself at particularly solemn and highly significant moments calls himself Teacher: "You call me Teacher and Lord; and you are right, for so I am";[24] and he proclaims the singularity, the uniqueness of his character as Teacher: "You have one teacher,"[25] the Christ. One can understand why people of every kind, race and nation have for two thousand years in all the languages of the earth given him this title with veneration, repeating in their own ways the exclamation of Nicodemus: "We know that you are a teacher come from God."[26]

This image of Christ the Teacher is at once majestic and familiar, impressive ant reassuring. It comes from the pen of the evangelists and it has often been evoked subsequently in iconography since earliest Christian times,[27] so captivating is it. And I am pleased to evoke it in my turn at the beginning of these considerations on catechesis in the modern world.

TEACHING THROUGH HIS LIFE AS A WHOLE

9.   In doing so, I am not forgetful that the majesty of Christ the Teacher and the unique consistency and persuasiveness of his teaching can only be explained by the fact that his words, his parables and his arguments are never separable from his life and his very being. Accordingly, the whole of Christ's life was a continual teaching: his silences, his miracles, his gestures, his prayer, his love for people, his special affection for the little and the poor, his acceptance of the total sacrifice on the Cross for he redemption of the world, and his Resurrection are the actualization of his word and the fulfillment of revelation. Hence

for Christians the crucifix is one of the most sublime and popular images of Christ the Teacher.

These consideration follow in the wake of the great traditions of the Church and they all strengthen our fervor with regard to Christ, the Teacher who reveals God to man and man to himself, the Teacher who saves, sanctifies and guides, who lives, who speaks, rouses, moves, redresses, judges, forgives, and goes with us day by day on the path of history, the Teacher who comes and will come in glory.

Only in deep communion with him will catechists find light and strength for an authentic, desirable renewal of catechesis.

II
AN EXPERIENCE AS OLD AS THE CHURCH

THE MISSION OF THE APOSTLES

10.   The image of Christ the Teacher was stamped on the spirit of the Twelve and of the first disciples, and the command" Go . . . and make disciples of all nations"[28] set the course for the whole of their lives. Saint John bears witness to this in his Gospel when he reports the words of Jesus: "No longer do I call you servants, for the servant does not know what his master is doing; but I have called you friends, for all that I have heard from my Father I have made known to you."[29] It was not they who chose to follow Jesus; it was Jesus who chose them, kept them with him, and appointed them even before his Passover, that they should go and bear fruit and that their fruit should remain.[30] For this reason he formally conferred on them after the Resurrection the mission of making disciples of all nations.

The whole of the book of the Acts of the Apostles is a witness that they were faithful to their vocation and to the mission they had received. The members of the first Christian community are seen in it as "devoted to the apostles' teaching and fellowship, to the breaking of bread and the prayers."[31] Without any doubt we find in that a lasting image of the Church being born of and continually nourished by the word of the Lord, thanks to the teaching of the Apostles, celebrating that word in the Eucharistic Sacrifice and bearing witness to it before the world in the sign of charity.

When those who opposed the Apostles took offence at their activity, it was because they were "annoyed because (the Apostles) were teaching the people"[32] and the order they gave them was not to teach at all in the name of Jesus.[33] But we know that the Apostles considered it right to listen to God rather than to men on this very matter.[34]

CATECHESIS IN THE APOSTOLIC AGE

11.   The Apostles were not slow to share with others the ministry of apostleship.[35] They transmitted to their successors the task of teaching. They entrusted it also to the deacons from the moment of their institution: Stephen, "full of

grace and power," taught unceasingly, moved by the wisdom of the Spirit.[36] The Apostles associated "many others" with themselves in the task of teaching,[37] and even simple Christians scattered by persecution "went about preaching the word."[38] Saint Paul was in a pre-eminent way the herald of this preaching, from Antioch to Rome, where the last picture of him that we have in Acts is that of a person "teaching about the Lord Jesus Christ quite openly."[39] His numerous letters continue and give greater depth to his teaching. The letters of Peter, John, James and Jude are also, in every case, evidence of catechesis in the apostolic age.

Before being written down, the Gospels were the expression of an oral teaching passed on to the Christian communities, and they display with varying degrees of clarity a catechetical structure. Saint Matthew's account has indeed been called the catechist's gospel, and Saint Mark's the catechumen's gospel.

THE FATHERS OF THE CHURCH

12. This mission of teaching that belonged to the Apostles and their first fellow workers was continued by the Church. Making herself day after day a disciple of the Lord, she earned the title of "Mother and Teacher."[40] From Clement of Rome to Origen,[41] the post-apostolic age saw the birth of remarkable works. Next we see a striking fact: some of the most impressive Bishops and pastors, especially in the third and fourth centuries, considered it an important part of their episcopal ministry to deliver catechetical instructions and write treatises. It was the age of Cyril of Jerusalem and John Chrysostom, of Ambrose and Augustine, the age that saw the flowering, from the pen of numerous Fathers of the Church, of works that are still models for us.

It would be impossible here to recall, even very briefly, the catechesis that gave support to the spread and advance of the Church in the various periods of history, in every continent, and in the widest variety of social and cultural contexts. There was indeed no lack of difficulties. But the word of the Lord completed its course down the centuries; it sped on and triumphed, to use the words of the Apostle Paul.[42]

COUNCILS AND MISSIONARY ACTIVITY

13. The ministry of catechesis draws ever fresh energy from the Councils. The Council of Trent is a noteworthy example of this. It gave catechesis priority in its constitutions and decrees. It lies at the origin of the Roman Catechism, which is also known by the name of that Council and which is a work of the first rank as a summary of Christian teaching and traditional theology for use by priests. It gave rise to a remarkable organization of catechesis in the Church. It aroused the clergy to their duty of giving catechetical instruction. Thanks to the work of holy theologians such as Saint Charles Borromeo, Saint Robert Bellarmine and Saint Peter Canisius, it involved the publication of catechisms that were real models for that period. May the Second Vatican Council stir up in our time a like enthusiasm and similar activity.

The missions are also a special area for the application of catechesis. The people of God have thus continued for almost two thousand years to educate themselves in the faith in ways adapted to the various situations of believers and the many different circumstances in which the Church finds herself.

Catechesis is intimately bound up with the whole of the Church's life. Not only her geographical extension and numerical increase but even more her inner growth and correspondence with God's plan depend essentially on catechesis. It is worthwhile pointing out some of the many lessons to be drawn from the experiences in Church history that we have just recalled.

CATECHESIS AS THE CHURCH'S RIGHT AND DUTY

14. To begin with, it is clear that the Church has always looked on catechesis as a sacred duty and an inalienable right. On the one hand, it is certainly a duty springing from a command given by the Lord and resting above all on those who in the New Covenant receive the call to the ministry of being pastors. On the other hand, one can likewise speak of a right: from the theological point of view every baptized person, precisely by reason of being baptized, has the right to receive from the Church instruction and education enabling him or her to enter on a truly Christian life; and from the viewpoint of human rights, every human being has the right to seek religious truth and adhere to it freely, that is to say "without coercion on the part of individuals or of social groups and any human power," in such a way that in this matter of religion, "no one is to be forced to act against his or her conscience or prevented from acting in conformity to it."[43]

That is why catechetical activity should be able to be carried out in favorable circumstances of time and place, and should have access to the mass media and suitable equipment, without discrimination against parents, those receiving catechesis or those imparting it. At present this right is admittedly being given growing recognition, at least on the level of its main principles, as is shown by international declarations and conventions in which, whatever their limitations, one can recognize the desires of the consciences of many people today.[44] But the right is being violated by many States, even to the point that imparting catechesis, having it imparted, and receiving it become punishable offenses. I vigorously raise my voice in union with the Synod Fathers against all discrimination in the field of catechesis, and at the same time I again make a pressing appeal to those in authority to put a complete end to these constraints on human freedom in general and on religious freedom in particular .

PRIORITY OF THIS TASK

15. The second lesson concerns the place of catechesis in the Church's pastoral programs. The more the Church, whether on the local or the universal level, gives catechesis priority over other works and undertakings the results of which would be more spectacular, the more she finds in catechesis a strengthening of her internal life as a community of believers and of her external activity as a missionary Church. As the twentieth century draws to a close, the Church is bidden by God and by events — each of them a call from him — to

renew her trust in catechetical activity as a prime aspect of her mission. She is bidden to offer catechesis her best resources in people and energy, without sparing effort, toil or material means, in order to organize it better and to train qualified personnel. This is no mere human calculation; it is an attitude of faith. And an attitude of faith always has reference to the faithfulness of God, who never fails to respond.

SHARED BUT DIFFERENTIATED RESPONSIBILITY

16.   The third lesson is that catechesis always has been and always will be a work for which the whole Church must feel responsible and must wish to be responsible. But the Church's members have different responsibilities, derived from each one's mission. Because of their charge, pastors have, at differing levels, the chief responsibility for fostering, guiding and coordinating catechesis. For his part, the Pope has a lively awareness of the primary responsibility that rests on him in this field: in this he finds reasons for pastoral concern but principally a source of joy and hope. Priests and religious have in catechesis a pre-eminent field for their apostolate. On another level, parents have a unique responsibility. Teachers, the various ministers of the Church, catechists, and also organizers of social communications, all have in various degrees very precise responsibilities in this education of the believing conscience, an education that is important for the life of the Church and affects the life of society as such. It would be one of the best results of the General Assembly of the Synod that was entirely devoted to catechesis if it stirred up in the Church as a whole and in each sector of the Church a lively and active awareness of this differentiated but shared responsibility.

CONTINUAL BALANCED RENEWAL

17.   Finally, catechesis needs to be continually renewed by a certain broadening of its concept, by the revision of its methods, by the search for suitable language, and by the utilization of new means of transmitting the message. Renewal is sometimes unequal in value; the Synod Fathers realistically recognized not only an undeniable advance in the vitality of catechetical activity and promising initiatives but also the limitations or even "deficiencies" in what has been achieved to date.[45] These limitations are particularly serious when they endanger integrity of content. The Message to the People of God rightly stressed that "routine, with its refusal to accept any change, and improvisation, with its readiness for any ventures, are equally dangerous" for catechesis.[46] Routine leads to stagnation, lethargy and eventual paralysis. Improvisation begets confusion on the part of those being given catechesis and, when these are children, on the part of their parents; it also begets all kinds of deviations, and the fracturing and eventually the complete destruction of unity. It is important for the Church to give proof today, as she has done at other periods of her history, of evangelical wisdom, courage and fidelity in seeking out and putting into operation new methods and new prospects for catechetical instruction.

III
CATECHESIS IN THE CHURCH'S PASTORAL AND MISSIONARY ACTIVITY

18. Catechesis cannot be dissociated from the Church's pastoral and missionary activity as a whole. Nevertheless it has a specific character which was repeatedly the object of inquiry during the preparatory work and throughout the course of the Fourth General Assembly of the Synod of Bishops. The question also interests the public both within and outside the Church.

This is not the place for giving a rigorous formal definition of catechesis, which has been sufficiently explained in the *General Catechetical Directory*.[47] It is for specialists to clarify more and more its concept and divisions.

In view of uncertainties in practice, let us simply recall the essential landmarks — they are already solidly established in Church documents — that are essential for an exact understanding of catechesis and without which there is a risk of failing to grasp its full meaning and import.

All in all, it can be taken here that catechesis is an education of children, young people and adults in the faith, which includes especially the teaching of Christian doctrine imparted, generally speaking, in an organic and systematic way, with a view to initiating the hearers into the fullness of Christian life. Accordingly, while not being formally identified with them, catechesis is built on a certain number of elements of the Church's pastoral mission that have a catechetical aspect, that prepare for catechesis, or that spring from it. These elements are: the initial proclamation of the Gospel or missionary preaching through the *kerygma* to arouse faith, apologetics or examination of the reasons for belief, experience of Christian living, celebration of the sacraments, integration into the ecclesial community, and apostolic and missionary witness.

Let us first of all recall that there is no separation or opposition between catechesis and evangelization. Nor can the two be simply identified with each other. Instead, they have close links whereby they integrate and complement each other.

The Apostolic Exhortation *Evangelii Nuntiandi* of 8 December 1975, on evangelization in the modern world, rightly stressed that evangelization — which has the aim of bringing the Good News to the whole of humanity, so that all may live by it — is a rich, complex and dynamic reality, made up of elements, or one would say moments, that are essential and different from each other, and that must all be kept in view simultaneously.[48] Catechesis is one of these moments — a very remarkable one — in the whole process of evangelization.

CATECHESIS AND THE INITIAL PROCLAMATION OF THE GOSPEL

19. The specific character of catechesis, as distinct from the initial conversion — bringing proclamation of the Gospel, has the twofold Objective of maturing the initial faith and of educating the true disciple of Christ by means of a deeper

and more systematic knowledge of the person and the message of our Lord Jesus Christ.[49]

But in catechetical practice, this model order must allow for the fact that the initial evangelization has often not taken place. A certain number of children baptized in infancy come for catechesis in the parish without receiving any other initiation into the faith and still without any explicit personal attachment to Jesus Christ; they only have the capacity to believe placed within them by baptism and the presence of the Holy Spirit; and opposition is quickly created by the prejudices of their non-Christian family background or of the positivist spirit of their education. In addition, there are other children who have not been baptized and whose parents agree only at a later date to religious education: for practical reasons, the catechumenal stage of these children will often be carried out largely in the course of the ordinary catechesis. Again, many preadolescents and adolescents who have been baptized and been given a systematic catechesis and the sacraments still remain hesitant for a long time about committing their whole lives to Jesus Christ, even though they do not actually try to avoid religious instruction in the name of their freedom. Finally, even adults are not safe from temptations to doubt or to abandon their faith, especially as a result of their unbelieving surroundings. This means that "catechesis" must often concern itself not only with nourishing and teaching the faith but also with arousing it unceasingly with the help of grace, with opening the heart, with converting, and with preparing total adherence to Jesus Christ on the part of those who are still on the threshold of faith. This concern will in part decide the tone, the language and the method of catechesis.

SPECIFIC AIM OF CATECHESIS

20. Nevertheless, the specific aim of catechesis is to develop, with God's help, an as yet initial faith, and to advance in fullness and to nourish day by day the Christian life of the faithful, young and old. It is in fact a matter of giving growth, at the level of knowledge and in life, to the seed of faith sown by the Holy Spirit with the initial proclamation and effectively transmitted by baptism.

Catechesis aims therefore at developing understanding of the mystery of Christ in the light of God's word, so that the whole of a person's humanity is impregnated by that word. Changed by the working of grace into a new creature, the Christian thus gets himself to follow Christ and learns more and more within the Church to think like him, to judge like him, to act in conformity with his commandments, and to hope as he invites us to.

To put it more precisely: within the whole process of evangelization, the aim of catechesis is to be the teaching and maturation stage, that is to say, the period in which the Christian, having accepted by faith the person of Jesus Christ as the one Lord and having given him complete adherence by sincere conversion of heart, endeavors to know better this Jesus to whom he has entrusted himself: to know his "mystery," the Kingdom of God proclaimed by him, the requirements and promises contained in his Gospel message, and the paths that he has laid down for any one who wishes to follow him.

It is true that being a Christian means saying "yes" to Jesus Christ, but let us remember that this "yes" has two levels: it consists in surrendering to the word of God and relying on it, but it also means, at a later stage, endeavoring to know better and better the profound meaning of this word.

NEED FOR SYSTEMATIC CATECHESIS

21.   In his closing speech at the Fourth General Assembly of the Synod, Pope Paul VI rejoiced "to see how everyone drew attention to the absolute need for systematic catechesis, precisely because it is this reflective study of the Christian mystery that fundamentally distinguishes catechesis from all other ways of presenting the word of God."[50]

In view of practical difficulties, attention must be drawn to some of the characteristics of this instruction:

—it must be systematic, not improvised but programmed to reach a precise goal;

—it must deal with essentials, without any claim to tackle all disputed questions or to transform itself into theological research or scientific exegesis;

—it must nevertheless be sufficiently complete, not stopping short at the initial proclamation of the Christian mystery such as we have in the *kerygma*;

—it must be an integral Christian initiation, open to all the other factors of Christian life.

I am not forgetting the interest of the many different occasions for catechesis connected with personal, family, social and ecclesial life—these occasions must be utilized and I shall return to them in Chapter VI—but I am stressing the need for organic and systematic Christian instruction, because of the tendency in various quarters to minimize its importance.

CATECHESIS AND LIFE EXPERIENCE

22.   It is useless to play off orthopraxis against orthodoxy: Christianity is inseparably both. Firm and well-thought-out convictions lead to courageous and upright action; the endeavor to educate the faithful to live as disciples of Christ today calls for and facilitates a discovery in depth of the mystery of Christ in the history of salvation.

It is also quite useless to campaign for the abandonment of serious and orderly study of the message of Christ in the name of a method concentrating on life experience. "No one can arrive at the whole truth on the basis solely of some simple private experience, that is to say without an adequate explanation of the message of Christ, who is 'the way, and the truth, and the life' (John 14:6)."[51]

Nor is any opposition to be set up between a catechesis taking life as its point of departure and a traditional, doctrinal and systematic catechesis.[52] Authentic catechesis is always an orderly and systematic initiation into the revelation that God has given of himself to humanity in Christ Jesus, a revelation stored in the depths of the Church's memory and in Sacred Scripture, and constantly communicated from one generation to the next by a living active *traditio.* This revelation is not however isolated from life or artificially juxtaposed to it. It is concerned with the ultimate meaning of life and it illumines the whole of life with the light of the Gospel, to inspire it or to question it.

That is why we can apply to catechists an expression used by the Second Vatican Council with special reference to priests: "instructors (of the human being and his life) in the faith."[53]

CATECHESIS AND SACRAMENTS

23.   Catechesis is intrinsically linked with the whole of liturgical and sacramental activity for it is in the sacraments, especially in the Eucharist, that Christ Jesus works in fullness for the transformation of human beings.

In the early Church, the catechumenate and preparation for the sacraments of baptism and the Eucharist were the same thing. Although in the countries that have long been Christian the Church has changed her practice in this field, the catechumenate has never been abolished; on the contrary it is experiencing a renewal in those countries[54] and is abundantly practiced in the young missionary Churches. In any case, catechesis always has reference to the sacraments. On the one hand, the catechesis that prepares for the sacraments is an eminent kind, and every form of catechesis necessarily leads to the sacraments of faith. On the other hand, authentic practice of the sacraments is bound to have a catechetical aspect. In other words, sacramental life is impoverished and very soon turns into hollow ritualism if it is not based on serious knowledge of the meaning of the sacraments, and catechesis becomes intellectualized if it fails to come alive in sacramental practice.

CATECHESIS AND ECCLESIAL COMMUNITY

24.   Finally, catechesis is closely linked with the responsible activity of the Church and of Christians in the world. A person who has given adherence to Jesus Christ by faith and is endeavoring to consolidate that faith by catechesis needs to live in communion with those who have taken the same step. Catechesis runs the risk of becoming barren if no community of faith and Christian life takes the catechumen in at a certain stage of his catechesis. That is why the ecclesial community at all levels has a twofold responsibility with regard to catechesis: it has the responsibility of providing for the training of its members, but it also has the responsibility of welcoming them into an environment where they can live as fully as possible what they have learned.

Catechesis is likewise open to missionary dynamism. If catechesis is done well, Christians will be eager to bear witness to their faith, to hand it on to their children, to make it known to others, and to serve the human community in every way.

25.   Thus through catechesis the gospel *kerygma* (the initial ardent proclamation by which a person is one day overwhelmed and brought to the decision to entrust himself to Jesus Christ by faith) is gradually deepened, developed in its implicit consequences, explained in language that includes an appeal to reason, and channelled towards Christian practice in the Church and the world. All this is no less evangelical than the *kerygma*, in spite of what is said by certain people who consider that catechesis necessarily rationalizes, dries up and eventually kills all that is living, spontaneous and vibrant in the *kerygma*. The truths studied in catechesis are the same truths that touched the person's heart when he heard them for the first time. Far from blunting or exhausting them, the fact of knowing them better should make them even more challenging and decisive for one's life.

In the understanding expounded here, catechesis keeps the entirely pastoral perspective with which the Synod viewed it. This broad meaning of catechesis in no way contradicts but rather includes and goes beyond a narrower meaning which was once commonly given to catechesis in didactic expositions, namely the simple teaching of the formulas that express faith.

In the final analysis, catechesis is necessary both for the maturation of the faith of Christians and for their witness in the world: it is aimed at bringing Christians to "attain to the unity of the faith and of the knowledge of the Son of God, to mature manhood, to the measure of the stature of the fullness of Christ";[55] it is also aimed at making them prepared to make a defence to any one who calls them to account for the hope that is in them.[56]

IV
THE WHOLE OF THE GOOD NEWS DRAWN
FROM ITS SOURCE

CONTENT OF THE MESSAGE

26.   Since catechesis is a moment or aspect of evangelization, its convent cannot be anything else but the content of evangelization as a whole. The one message—the Good News of salvation—that has been heard once or hundreds of times and has been accepted with the heart, is in catechesis probed unceasingly by reflection and systematic study, by awareness of its repercussions on one's personal life—an awareness calling for ever greater commitment—and by inserting it into an organic and harmonious whole, namely Christian living in society and the world.

THE SOURCE

27.   Catechesis will always draw its content from the living source of the word of God transmitted in Tradition and the Scriptures, for "sacred Tradition and sacred Scripture make up a single sacred deposit of the word of God, which is

entrusted to the Church," as was recalled by the Second Vatican Council, which desired that "the ministry of the word—pastoral preaching, catechetics and all forms of Christian instruction . . . —(should be) healthily nourished and (should) thrive in holiness through the word of Scripture."[57]

To speak of Tradition and Scripture as the source of catechesis is to draw attention to the fact that catechesis must be impregnated and penetrated by the thought, the spirit and the outlook of the Bible and the Gospels through assiduous contact with the texts themselves; but it is also a reminder that catechesis will be all the richer and more effective for reading the texts with the intelligence and the heart of the Church and for drawing inspiration from the two thousand years of the Church's reflection and life.

The Church's teaching, liturgy and life spring from this source and lead back to it, under the guidance of the pastors and, in particular, of the doctrinal Magisterium entrusted to them by the Lord.

THE CREED AN EXCEPTIONALLY IMPORTANT EXPRESSION OF DOCTRINE

28. An exceptionally important expression of the living heritage placed in the custody of the pastors is found in the Creed or, to put it more concretely, in the Creeds that at crucial moments have summed up the Church's faith in felicitous syntheses. In the course of the centuries an important element of catechesis was constituted by the *traditio Symboli* (transmission of the summary of the faith), followed by the transmission of the Lord's prayer. This expressive rite has in our time been reintroduced into the initiation of catechumens.[58] Should not greater use be made of an adapted form of it to mark that most important stage at which a new disciple of Jesus Christ accepts with full awareness and courage the content of what will from then on be the object of his earnest study?

In the Creed of the People of God, proclaimed at the close of the nineteenth centenary of the martyrdom of the Apostles Peter and Paul, my predecessor Paul VI decided to bring together the essential elements of the Catholic faith, especially those that presented greater difficulty or risked being ignored.[59] This is a sure point of reference for the content of catechesis.

FACTORS THAT MUST NOT BE NEGLECTED

29. In the third chapter of his Apostolic Exhortation *Evangelii Nuntiandi*, the same Pope recalled "the essential content, the living substance" of evangelization.[60] Catechesis too must keep in mind each of these factors and also the living synthesis of which they are part.[61]

I shall therefore limit myself here simply to recalling one or two points.[62] Anyone can see, for instance, how important it is to make the child, the adolescent, the person advancing in faith understand "what can be known about God";[63] to be able in a way to tell them: "What you worship as unknown, this I proclaim to you";[64] to set forth briefly for them[65] the mystery of the Word of God become man and accomplishing man's salvation by his Passover, that is to say through his death and Resurrection, but also by his preaching, by the signs worked by him, and by the sacraments of his permanent presence in our midst.

The Synod Fathers were indeed inspired when they asked that care should be taken not to reduce Christ to his humanity alone or his message to a no more than earthly dimension, but that he should be recognized as the Son of God, the mediator giving us in the Spirit free access to the Father.[66]

It is important to display before the eyes of the intelligence and of the heart, in the light of faith, the sacrament of Christ's presence constituted by the mystery of the Church, which is an assembly of human beings who are sinners and yet have at the same time been sanctified and who make up the family of God gathered together by the Lord under the guidance of those whom "the Holy Spirit has made . . . guardians, to feed the Church of God."[67]

It is important to explain that the history of the human race, marked as it is by grace and sin, greatness and misery, is taken up by God in his Son Jesus, "foreshadowing in some way the age which is to come."[68]

Finally, it is important to reveal frankly the demands—demands that involve self-denial but also joy—made by what the Apostle Paul liked to call "newness of life,"[69] "a new creation,"[70] being in Christ,[71] and "eternal life in Christ Jesus,"[72] which is the same thing as life in the world but lived in accordance with the beatitudes and called to an extension and transfiguration hereafter.

Hence the importance in catechesis of personal moral commitments in keeping with the Gospel and of Christian attitudes, whether heroic or very simple, to life and the world—what we call the Christian or evangelical virtues. Hence also, in its endeavor to educate faith, the concern of catechesis not to omit but to clarify properly realities such as man's activity for his integral liberation,[73] the search for a society with greater solidarity and fraternity, the fight for justice and the building of peace.

Besides, it is not to be thought that this dimension of catechesis is altogether new. As early as the patristic age, Saint Ambrose and Saint John Chrysostom—to quote only them—gave prominence to the social consequences of the demands made by the Gospel. Close to our own time, the catechism of Saint Pius x explicitly listed oppressing the poor and depriving workers of their just wages among the sins that cry to God for vengeance.[74] Since *Rerum Novarum* especially, social concern has been actively present in the catechetical teaching of the Popes and the bishops. Many Synod Fathers rightly insisted that the rich heritage of the Church's social teaching should, in appropriate forms, find a place in the general catechetical education of the faithful.

INTEGRITY OF CONTENT

30. With regard to the content of catechesis, three important points deserve special attention today.

The first point concerns the integrity of the content. In order that the sacrificial offering of his of her faith[75] should be perfect, the person who becomes a disciple of Christ has the right to receive "the word of faith"[76] not in mutilated, falsified or diminished form but whole and entire, in all its rigor and vigor.

Unfaithfulness on some point to the integrity of the message means a dangerous weakening of catechesis and putting at risk the results that Christ and the ecclesial community have a right to expect from it. It is certainly not by chance that the final command of Jesus in Matthew's Gospel bears the mark of a certain entireness: "All authority . . . has been given to me . . . make disciples of all nations . . . teaching them to observe all . . . I am with you always." This is why, when a person first becomes aware of "the surpassing worth of knowing Christ Jesus,"[77] whom he has encountered by faith, and has the perhaps unconscious desire to know him more extensively and better, "hearing about him and being taught in him, as the truth is in Jesus,"[78] there is no valid pretext for refusing him any part whatever of that knowledge. What kind of catechesis would it be that failed to give their full place to man's creation and sin, to God's plan of redemption and its long, loving preparation and realization, to the Incarnation of the Son of God, to Mary, the Immaculate One, the Mother of God, ever Virgin, raised body and soul to the glory of heaven, and to her role in the mystery of salvation, to the mystery of lawlessness at work in our lives [79] and the power of God freeing us from it, to the need for penance and asceticism, to the sacramental and liturgical actions, to the reality of the Eucharistic presence, to participation in divine life here and hereafter, and so on? Thus, no true catechist can lawfully, on his own initiative, make a selection of what he considers important in the deposit of faith as opposed to what he considers unimportant, so as to teach the one and reject the other.

BY MEANS OF SUITABLE PEDAGOGICAL METHODS

31.   This gives rise to a second remark. It can happen that in the present situation of catechesis reasons of method or pedagogy suggest that the communication of the riches of the content of catechesis should be organized in one way rather than another. Besides, integrity does not dispense from balance and from the organic hierarchical character through which the truths to be taught, the norms to be transmitted, and the ways of Christian life to be indicated will be given the proper importance due to each. It can also happen that a particular sort of language proves preferable for transmitting this content to a particular individual or group. The choice made will be a valid one to the extent that, far from being dictated by more or less subjective theories or prejudices stamped with a certain ideology, it is inspired by the humble concern to stay closer to a content that must remain intact. The method and language used must truly be means for communicating the whole and not just a part of "the words of eternal life"[80] and "the ways of life."[81]

ECUMENICAL DIMENSION OF CATECHESIS

32.   The great movement, one certainly inspired by the Spirit of Jesus, that has for some years been causing the Catholic Church to seek with other Christian Churches or confessions the restoration of the perfect unity willed by the Lord, brings me to the question of the ecumenical character of catechesis. This movement reached its full prominence in the Second Vatican Council[82] and since then has taken on a new extension within the Church, as is shown concretely by the impressive series of events and initiatives with which everyone is now familiar.

Catechesis cannot remain aloof from this ecumenical dimension, since all the faithful are called to share, according to their capacity and place in the Church, in the movement towards unity.[83]

Catechesis will have an ecumenical dimension if, while not ceasing to teach that the fullness of the revealed truths and of the means of salvation instituted by Christ is found in the Catholic Church,[84] it does so with sincere respect, in words and in deeds, for the ecclesial communities that are not in perfect communion with this Church.

In this context, it is extremely important to give a correct and fair presentation of the other Churches and ecclesial communities that the Spirit of Christ does not refrain from using as means of salvation; "moreover, some, even very many, of the outstanding elements and endowments which together go to build up and give life to the Church herself, can exist outside the visible boundaries of the Catholic Church."[85] Among other things, this presentation will help Catholics to have both a deeper understanding of their own faith and a better acquaintance with and esteem for their other Christian brethren, thus facilitating the shared search for the way towards full unity in the whole truth. It should also help non-Catholics to have a better knowledge and appreciation of the Catholic Church and her conviction of being the "universal help towards salvation."

Catechesis will have an ecumenical dimension if, in addition, it creates and fosters a true desire for unity. This will be true all the more if it inspires serious efforts—including the effort of self-purification in the humility and the fervor of the Spirit in order to clear the ways—with a view not to facile irenics made up of omissions and concessions on the level of doctrine, but to perfect unity, when and by what means the Lord will wish.

Finally, catechesis will have an ecumenical dimension if it tries to prepare Catholic children and young people, as well as adults, for living in contact with non-Catholics, affirming their Catholic identity while respecting the faith of others.

ECUMENICAL COLLABORATION IN THE FIELD OF CATECHESIS

33. In situations of religious plurality, the Bishops can consider it opportune or even necessary to have certain experiences of collaboration in the field of catechesis between Catholics and other Christians, complementing the normal catechesis that must in any case be given to Catholics. Such experiences have a theological foundation in the elements shared by all Christians.[86] But the communion of faith between Catholics and other Christians is not complete and perfect; in certain cases there are even profound divergences. Consequently, this ecumenical collaboration is by its very nature limited: it must never mean a "reduction" to a common minimum. Furthermore, catechesis does not consist merely in the teaching of doctrine: it also means initiating into the whole of Christian life, bringing full participation in the sacraments of the Church. Therefore, where there is an experience of ecumenical collaboration in the field of catechesis, care must be taken that the education of Catholics in the Catholic Church should be well ensured in matters of doctrine and of Christian living.

During the Synod, a certain number of Bishops drew attention to what they referred to as the increasingly frequent cases in which the civil authority or other circumstances impose on the schools in some countries a common instruction in the Christian religion, with common textbooks, class periods, etc., for Catholics and non-Catholics alike. Needless to say, this is not true catechesis. But this teaching also has ecumenical importance when it presents Christian doctrine fairly and honestly. In cases where circumstances impose it, it is important that in addition a specifically Catholic catechesis should be ensured with all the greater care.

THE QUESTION OF TEXTBOOKS DEALING WITH THE VARIOUS RELIGIONS

34.   At this point another observation must be made of the same lines but from a different point of view. State schools sometimes provide their pupils with books that for cultural reasons (history, morals or literature) present the various religions, including the Catholic religion. An objective presentation of historical events, of the different religions and of the various Christian confessions can make a contribution here to better mutual understanding. Care will then be taken that every effort is made to ensure that the presentation is truly objective and free from the distorting influence of ideological and political systems or of prejudices with claims to be scientific. In any case, such schoolbooks can obviously not be considered catechetical works: they lack both the witness of believers stating their faith to other believers and an understanding of the Christian mysteries and of what is specific about Catholicism, as these are understood within the faith.

V
EVERYBODY NEEDS TO BE CATECHIZED

THE IMPORTANCE OF CHILDREN AND THE YOUNG

35.   The theme designated by my predecessor Paul VI for the Fourth General Assembly of the Synod of Bishops was: "Catechesis in our time, with special reference to the catechesis of children and young people." The increase in the number of young people is without doubt a fact charged with hope and at the same time with anxiety for a large part of the contemporary world. In certain countries, especially those of the Third World, more than half of the population is under twenty-five or thirty years of age. This means millions and millions of children and young people preparing for their adult future. And there is more than just the factor of numbers: recent events, as well as the daily news, tell us that, although this countless multitude of young people is here and there dominated by uncertainty and fear, seduced by the escapism of indifference or drugs, or tempted by nihilism and violence, nevertheless it constitutes in its major part the great force that amid many hazards is set on building the civilization of the future.

In our pastoral care we ask ourselves: How are we to reveal Jesus Christ, God made man, to this multitude of children and young people, reveal him not just in the fascination of a first fleeting encounter but through an acquaintance, growing deeper and clearer daily, with him, his message, the plan of God that he has revealed, the call he addresses to each person, and the Kingdom that he wishes to establish in this world with the "little flock"[87] of those who believe in him, a Kingdom that will be complete only in eternity? How are we to enable them to know the meaning, the import, the fundamental requirements, the law of love, the promises and the hopes of this Kingdom?

There are many observations that could be made about the special characteristics that catechesis assumes at the different stages of life.

INFANTS

36. One moment that is often decisive is the one at which the very young child receives the first elements of catechesis from its parents and the family surroundings. These elements will perhaps be no more than a simple revelation of a good and provident Father in heaven to whom the child learns to turn its heart. The very short prayers that the child learns to lisp will be the start of a loving dialogue with this hidden God whose word it will then begin to hear. I cannot insist too strongly on this early initiation by Christian parents in which the child's faculties are integrated into a living relationship with God. It is a work of prime importance. It demands great love and profound respect for the child who has a right to a simple and true presentation of the Christian faith.

CHILDREN

37. For the child there comes soon, at school and in church, in institutions connected with the parish or with the spiritual care of the Catholic or State school not only an introduction into a wider social circle, but also the moment for a catechesis aimed at inserting him or her organically into the life of the Church, a moment that includes an immediate preparation for the celebration of the sacraments. This catechesis is didactic in character, but is directed towards the giving of witness in the faith. It is an initial catechesis but not a fragmentary one, since it will have to reveal, although in an elementary way, all the principal mysteries of faith and their effects on the child's moral and religious life. It is a catechesis that gives meaning to the sacraments, but at the same time it receives from the experience of the sacraments a living dimension that keeps it from remaining merely doctrinal, and it communicates to the child the joy of being a witness to Christ in ordinary life.

ADOLESCENTS

38. Next comes puberty and adolescence, with all the greatness and dangers which that age brings. It is the time of discovering oneself and one's own inner world, the time of generous plans, the time when the feeling of love awakens, with the biological impulses of sexuality, the time of the desire to be together, the time of a particularly intense joy connected with the exhilarating discovery of life. But often it is also the age of deeper questioning, of anguished or even

frustrating searching, of a certain mistrust of others and dangerous introspection, and the age sometimes of the first experiences of setbacks and of disappointments. Catechesis cannot ignore these changeable aspects of this delicate period of life. A catechesis capable of leading the adolescent to reexamine his or her life and to engage in dialogue, a catechesis that does not ignore the adolescent's great questions — self-giving, belief, love and the means of expressing it constituted by sexuality — such a catechesis can be decisive. The revelation of Jesus Christ as a friend, guide and model, capable of being admired but also imitated; the revelation of his message which provides an answer to the fundamental questions; the revelation of the loving plan of Christ the Savior as the incarnation of the only authentic love and as the possibility of uniting the human race — all this can provide the basis for genuine education in faith. Above all, the mysteries of the Passion and death of Jesus, through which, according to Saint Paul, he merited his glorious Resurrection, can speak eloquently to the adolescent's conscience and heart and cast light on his first sufferings and on the sufferings of the world that he is discovering.

THE YOUNG

39. With youth comes the moment of the first great decisions. Although the young may enjoy the support of the members of their family and their friends, they have to rely on themselves and their own conscience and must ever more frequently and decisively assume responsibility for their destiny. Good and evil, grace and sin, life and death will more and more confront one another within them, not just as moral categories but chiefly as fundamental options which they must accept or reject lucidly, conscious of their own responsibility. It is obvious that a catechesis which denounces selfishness in the name of generosity, and which without any illusory over-simplification presents the Christian meaning of work, of the common good, of justice and charity, a catechesis on international peace and on the advancement of human dignity, on development, and on liberation, as these are presented in recent documents of the Church,[88] fittingly completes in the minds of the young the good catechesis on strictly religious realities which is never to be neglected. Catechesis then takes on considerable importance, since it is the time when the Gospel can be presented, understood and accepted as capable of giving meaning to life and thus of inspiring attitudes that would have no other explanation, such as self-sacrifice, detachment, forbearance, justice, commitment, reconciliation, a sense of the Absolute and the unseen. All these are traits that distinguish a young person from his or her companions as a disciple of Jesus Christ.

Catechesis thus prepares for the important Christian commitments of adult life. For example, it is certain that many vocations to the priesthood and religious life have their origin during a well imparted catechesis in infancy and adolescence.

From infancy until the threshold of maturity catechesis is thus a permanent school of the faith and follows the major stages of life, like a beacon lighting the path of the child, the adolescent and the young person.

40.   It is reassuring to note that, during the Fourth General Assembly of the Synod and the following years, the Church has widely shared in concern about how to impart catechesis to children and young people. God grant that the attention thus aroused will long endure in the Church's consciousness. In this way the Synod has been valuable for the whole Church by seeking to trace with the greatest possible precision the complex characteristics of present-day youth; by showing that these young persons speak a language into which the message of Jesus must be translated with patience and wisdom and without betrayal; by demonstrating that, in spite of appearances, these young people have within them, even though often in a confused way, not just a readiness or openness, but rather a real desire to know "Jesus . . . who is called Christ";[89] and by indicating that if the work of catechesis is to be carried out rigorously and seriously, it is today more difficult and tiring than ever before, because of the obstacles and difficulties of all kinds that it meets; but it is also more consoling, because of the depth of the response it receives from children and young people. This is a treasure which the Church can and should count on in the years ahead.

Some categories of young people to whom catechesis is directed call for special attention because of their particular situation.

THE HANDICAPPED

41.   Children and young people who are physically or mentally handicapped come first to mind. They have a right, like others of their age, to know "the mystery of faith." The greater difficulties that they encounter give greater merit to their efforts and to those of their teachers. It is pleasant to see that Catholic organizations especially dedicated to young handicapped people contributed to the Synod their experience in this matter, and drew from the Synod a renewed desire to deal better with this important problem. They deserve to be given warm encouragement in this endeavor.

YOUNG PEOPLE WITHOUT RELIGIOUS SUPPORT

42.   My thoughts turn next to the ever increasing number of children and young people born and brought up in a non-Christian or at least non-practicing home but who wish to know the Christian faith. They must be ensured a catechesis attuned to them, so that they will be able to grow in faith and live by it more and more, in spite of the lack of support or even the opposition they meet in their surroundings.

ADULTS

43.   To continue the series of receivers of catechesis, I cannot fail to emphasize now one of the most constant concerns of the Synod Fathers, a concern imposed with vigor and urgency by present experiences throughout the world: I am referring to the central problem of the catechesis of adults. This is the principal form of catechesis, because it is addressed to persons who have the greatest responsibilities and the capacity to live the Christian message in its

fully developed form.[90] The Christian community cannot carry out a permanent catechesis without the direct and skilled participation of adults, whether as receivers or as promoters of catechetical activity. The world in which the young are called to live and gives witness to the faith which catechesis seeks to deepen and strengthen is governed by adults: the faith of these adults too should continually be enlightened, stimulated and renewed, so that it may pervade the temporal realities in their charge. Thus, for catechesis to be effective, it must be permanent, and it would be quite useless if it stopped short just at the threshold of maturity, since catechesis, admittedly under another form, proves no less necessary for adults.

QUASI-CATECHUMENS

44.   Among the adults who need catechesis, our pastoral missionary concern is directed to those who were born and reared in areas not yet Christianized, and who have never been able to study deeply the Christian teaching that the circumstances of life have at a certain moment caused them to come across. It is also directed to those who in childhood received a catechesis suited to their age but who later drifted away from all religious practice and all adults find themselves with religious knowledge of a rather childish kind. It is likewise directed lo those who feel the effects of a catechesis received early in life but badly imparted or badly assimilated. It is directed to those who, although they were born in a Christian country or in sociologically Christian surroundings, have never been educated in their faith and, as adults, are really catechumens.

DIVERSIFIED AND COMPLEMENTARY FORMS OF CATECHESIS

45.   Catechesis is therefore for adults of every age, including the elderly — persons who deserve particular attention in view of their experience and their problems — no less than for children, adolescents and the young. We should also mention migrants, those who are by-passed by modern developments, those who live in areas of large cities which are often without churches, buildings and suitable organization, and other such groups. It is desirable that initiatives meant to give all these groups a Christian formation, with appropriate means (audio-visual aids, booklets, discussions, lectures), should increase in number, enabling many adults to fill the gap left by an insufficient or deficient catechesis, to complete harmoniously at a higher level their childhood catechesis, or even to prepare themselves enough in this field to be able to help others in a more serious way.

It is important also that the catechesis of children and young people, permanent catechesis, and the catechesis of adults should not be separate watertight compartments. It is even more important that there should be no break between them. On the contrary, their perfect complementarity must be fostered: adults have much to give to young people and children in the field of catechesis, but they can also receive much from them for the growth of their own Christian lives.

It must be restated that nobody in the Church of Jesus Christ should feel excused from receiving catechesis. This is true even of young seminarians and young religious, and of all those called to the task of being pastors and catechists. They will fulfil this task all the better if they are humble pupils of the Church, the great giver as well as the great receiver of catechesis.

VI
SOME WAYS AND MEANS OF CATECHESIS

COMMUNICATIONS MEDIA

46. From the oral teaching by the Apostles and the letters circulating among the Churches down to the most modern means, catechesis has not ceased to look for the most suitable ways and means for its mission, with the active participation of the communities and at the urging of the pastors. This effort must continue.

I think immediately of the great possibilities offered by the means of social communication and the means of group communication: television, radio, the press, records, tape-recordings — the whole series of audio-visual means. The achievements in these spheres are such as to encourage the greatest hope. Experience shows, for example, the effect had by instruction given on radio or television, when it combines a high aesthetic level and rigorous fidelity to the Magisterium. The Church now has many opportunities for considering these questions — as, for instance, on Social Communications Days — and it is not necessary to speak of them at length here, in spite of their prime importance.

UTILIZATION OF VARIOUS PLACES, OCCASIONS AND GATHERINGS

47. I am also thinking of various occasions of special value which are exactly suitable for catechesis: for example, diocesan, regional or national pilgrimages, which gain from being centered on some judiciously chosen theme based on the life of Christ, of the Blessed Virgin or of the Saints. Then there are the traditional missions, often too hastily dropped but irreplaceable for the periodic and vigorous renewal of Christian life — they should be revived and brought up to date. Again, there are Bible-study groups, which ought to go beyond exegesis and lead their members to live by the word of God. Yet other instances are the meetings of ecclesial basic communities, insofar as they correspond to the criteria laid down in the Apostolic Exhortation *Evangelii Nuntiandi*.[91] I may also mention the youth groups that, under varying names and forms but always with the purpose of making Jesus Christ known and of living by the Gospel, are in some areas multiplying and flourishing in a sort of springtime that is very comforting for the Church: these include Catholic Action groups, charitable groups, prayer groups and Christian meditation groups. These groups are a source of great hope for the Church of tomorrow. But, in the name of Jesus, I exhort the young people who belong to them, their leaders, and the priests who devote the best part of their ministry to them: No matter what it costs, do not allow these groups — which are exceptional occasions for meeting others, and which are blessed with such riches of friendship and solidarity among the young, of joy and enthusiasm, of reflection on events and facts — do not allow them to lack

serious study of Christian doctrine. If they do, they will be in danger—a danger that has unfortunately proved only too real of disappointing their members and also the Church.

The catechetical endeavor that is possible in these various surroundings, and in many others besides, will have all the greater chance of being accepted and bearing fruit if it respects their individual nature. By becoming part of them in the right way, it will achieve the diversity and complementarity of approach that will enable it to develop all the riches of its concept, with its three dimensions of word, memorial and witness —doctrine, celebration and commitment in living—which the Synod message to the People of God emphasized.[92]

THE HOMILY

48.   This remark is even more valid for the catechesis given in the setting of the liturgy especially at the Eucharistic assembly. Respecting the specific nature and proper cadence of this setting, the homily takes up again the journey of faith put forward by catechesis, and brings it to its natural fulfillment. At the same time it encourages the Lord's disciples to begin anew each day their spiritual journey in truth, adoration and thanksgiving. Accordingly, one can say that catechetical teaching too finds its source and its fulfillment in the Eucharist, within the whole circle of the liturgical year. Preaching, centered upon the Bible texts, must then in its own way make it possible to familiarize the faithful with the whole of the mysteries of the faith and with the norms of Christian living. Much attention must be given to the homily: it should be neither too long nor too short; it should always be carefully prepared, rich in substance and adapted to the hearers and reserved to ordained ministers. The homily should have its place not only in every Sunday and feast-day Eucharist, but also in the celebration of baptisms, penitential liturgies, marriages and funerals. This is one of the benefits of the liturgical renewal.

CATECHETICAL LITERATURE

49.   Among these various ways and means—all the Church's activities have a catechetical dimension—catechetical works, far from losing their essential importance, acquire fresh significance. One of the major features of the renewal of catechetics today is the rewriting and multiplication of catechetical books taking place in many parts of the Church. Numerous very successful works have been produced and are a real treasure in the service of catechetical instruction. But it must be humbly and honestly recognized that this rich flowering has brought with it articles and publications which are ambiguous and harmful to young people and to the life of the Church. In certain places, the desire to find the best forms of expression or to keep up with fashions in pedagogical methods has often enough resulted in certain catechetical works which bewilder the young and even adults, either by deliberately or unconsciously omitting elements essential to the Church's faith, or by attributing excessive importance to certain themes at the expense of others, or, chiefly, by a rather horizontalist over-all view out of keeping with the teaching of the Church's Magisterium.

Therefore, it is not enough to multiply catechetical work. In order that these works may correspond with their aim, several conditions are essential:

a) they must be linked with the real life of the generation to which they are addressed, showing close acquaintance with its anxieties and questionings, struggles and hopes;

b) they must try to speak a language comprehensible to the generation in question;

c) they must make a point of giving the whole message of Christ and his Church, without neglecting or distorting anything, and in expounding it they will follow a line and structure that highlights what is essential;

d) they must really aim to give to those who use them a better knowledge of the mysteries of Christ, aimed at true conversion and a life more in conformity with God's will.

CATECHISMS

50. All those who take on the heavy task of preparing these catechetical tools, especially catechism texts, can do so only with the approval of the pastors who have the authority to give it, and taking their inspiration as closely as possible from the *General Catechetical Directory*, which remains the standard of reference.[93]

In this regard, I must warmly encourage the Episcopal Conferences of the whole world to undertake, patiently but resolutely, the considerable work to be accomplished in agreement with the Apostolic See in order to prepare genuine catechisms which will be faithful to the essential content of Revelation and up to date in method, and which will be capable of educating the Christian generations of the future to a sturdy faith.

This brief mention of ways and means of modern catechetics does not exhaust the wealth of suggestions worked out by the Synod Fathers. It is comforting to think that at the present time every country is seeing valuable collaboration for a more organic and more secure renewal of these aspects of catechetics. There can be no doubt that the Church will find the experts and the right means for responding, with God's grace, to the complex requirements of communicating with the people of today.

VII
HOW TO IMPART CATECHESIS

DIVERSITY OF METHODS

51. The age and the intellectual development of Christians, their degree of ecclesial and spiritual maturity and many other personal circumstances demand that catechesis should adopt widely differing methods for the attainment of its specific aim: education in the faith. On a more general level, this variety is also

demanded by the social and cultural surroundings in which the Church carries out her catechetical work.

The variety in the methods used is a sign of life and a resource. That is how it was considered by the Fathers of the Fourth General Assembly of the Synod, although they also drew attention to the conditions necessary for that variety to be useful and not harmful to the unity of the teaching of the one faith.

AT THE SERVICE OF REVELATION AND CONVERSION

52.   The first question of a general kind that presents itself here concerns the danger and the temptation to mix catechetical teaching unduly with overt or masked ideological views, especially political and social ones, or with personal political options. When such views get the better of the central message to be transmitted, to the point of obscuring it and putting it in second place or even using it to further their own ends, catechesis then becomes radically distorted. The Synod rightly insisted on the need for catechesis to remain above one-sided divergent trends — to avoid "dichotomies" — even in the field of theological interpretation of such questions. It is on the basis of Revelation that catechesis will try to set its course, Revelation as transmitted by the universal Magisterium of the Church, in its solemn or ordinary form. This Revelation tells of a creating and redeeming God, whose Son has come among us in our flesh and enters not only into each individual's personal history but into human history itself, becoming its center. Accordingly, this Revelation tells of the radical change of man and the universe, of all that makes up the web of human life under the influence of the Good News of Jesus Christ. If conceived in this way, catechesis goes beyond every form of formalistic moralism, although it will include true Christian moral teaching. Chiefly, it goes beyond any kind of temporal, social or political "messianism." It seeks to arrive at man's innermost being.

THE MESSAGE EMBODIED IN CULTURES

53.   Now a second question. As I said recently to the members of the Biblical Commission: "The term 'acculturation' or 'inculturation' may be a neologism, but it expresses very well one factor of the great mystery of the Incarnation."[94] We can say of catechesis, as well as of evangelization in general, that it is called to bring the power of the Gospel into the very heart of culture and cultures. For this purpose, catechesis will seek to know these cultures and their essential components; it will learn their most significant expressions; it will respect their particular values and riches. In this manner it will be able to offer these cultures the knowledge of the hidden mystery[95] and help them to bring forth from their own living tradition original expressions of Christian life, celebration and thought. Two things must however be kept in mind.

On the one hand the Gospel message cannot be purely and simply isolated from the culture in which it was first inserted (the Biblical world or, more concretely, the cultural milieu in which Jesus of Nazareth lived), nor, without serious loss, from the cultures in which it has already been expressed down the centuries; it does not spring spontaneously from any cultural soil; it has always been transmitted by means of an apostolic dialogue which inevitably becomes part of a certain dialogue of cultures.

On the other hand, the power of the Gospel everywhere transforms and regenerates. When that power enters into a culture, it is no surprise that it rectifies many of its elements. There would be no catechesis if it were the Gospel that had to change when it came into contact with the cultures.

To forget this would simply amount to what Saint Paul very forcefully calls "emptying the cross of Christ of its power."[96]

It is a different matter to take, with wise discernment, certain elements, religious or otherwise, that form part of the cultural heritage of a human group and use them to help its members to understand better the whole of the Christian mystery. Genuine catechists know that catechesis "takes flesh" in the various cultures and milieus: one has only to think of the peoples with their great differences, of modern youth, of the great variety of circumstances in which people find themselves today. But they refuse to accept an impoverishment of catechesis through a renunciation or obscuring of its message, by adaptations, even in language, that would endanger the "precious deposit" of the faith,[97] or by concessions in matters of faith or morals. They are convinced that true catechesis eventually enriches these cultures by helping them to go beyond the defective or even inhuman features in them, and by communicating to their legitimate values the fullness of Christ.[98]

THE CONTRIBUTION OF POPULAR DEVOTION

54. Another question of method concerns the utilization in catechetical instruction of valid elements in popular piety. I have in mind devotions practiced by the faithful in certain regions with moving fervor and purity of intention, even if the faith underlining them needs to be purified or rectified in many aspects. I have in mind certain easily understood prayers that many simple people are fond of repeating. I have in mind certain acts of piety practiced with a sincere desire to do penance or to please the Lord. Underlying most of these prayers and practices, besides elements that should be discarded, there are other elements which, if they were properly used, could serve very well to help people advance towards knowledge of the mystery of Christ and of his message: the love and mercy of God, the Incarnation of Christ, his redeeming Cross and Resurrection, the activity of the Spirit in each Christian and in the Church, the mystery of the hereafter, the evangelical virtues to be practiced, the presence of the Christian in the world, etc. And why should we appeal to non-Christian or even anti-Christian elements, refusing to build on elements which, even if they need to be revised and improved, have something Christian at their root?

MEMORIZATION

55. The final methodological question the importance of which should at least be referred to — one that was debated several times in the Synod — is that

of memorization. In the beginnings of Christian catechesis, which coincided with a civilization that was mainly oral, recourse was had very freely to memorization. Catechesis has since then known a long tradition of learning the principal truths by memorizing. We are all aware that this method can present certain disadvantages, not the least of which is that it lends itself to insufficient or at times almost non-existent assimilation, reducing all knowledge to formulas that are repeated without being properly understood. These disadvantages and the different characteristics of our own civilization have in some places led to the almost complete suppression—according to some, alas, the definitive suppression—of memorization in catechesis. And yet certain very authoritative voices made themselves heard on the occasion of the Fourth General Assembly of the Synods calling for the restoration of a judicious balance between reflection and spontaneity, between dialogue and silence, between written work and memory work. Moreover certain cultures still set great value on memorization.

At a time when, in non-religious teaching in certain countries, more and more complaints are being made about the unfortunate consequences of disregarding the human faculty of memory, should we not attempt to put this faculty back into use in an in intelligent and even an original way in catechesis, all the more since the celebration or "memorial" of the great events of the history of salvation require a precise knowledge of them? A certain memorization of the words of Jesus, of important Bible passages, of the Ten Commandments, of the formulas of profession of the faith, of the liturgical texts, of the essential prayers, of key doctrinal ideas, etc., far from being opposed to the dignity of young Christians, or constituting an obstacle to personal dialogue with the Lord, is a real need, as the Synod Fathers forcefully recalled. We must be realists. The blossoms, if we may call them that, of faith and piety do not grow in the desert places of a memory-less catechesis. What is essential is that the texts that are memorized must at the same time be taken in and gradually understood in depth, in order to become a source of Christian life on the personal level and the community level.

The plurality of methods in contemporary catechesis can be a sign of vitality and ingenuity. In any case, the method chosen must ultimately be referred to a law that is fundamental for the whole of the Church's life: the law of fidelity to God and of fidelity to man in a single loving attitude.

VIII
THE JOY OF FAITH IN A TROUBLED WORLD

AFFIRMING CHRISTIAN IDENTITY

56.   We live in a difficult world in which the anguish of seeing the best creations of man slip away from him and turn against him creates a climate of uncertainty.[99] In this world catechesis should help Christians to be, for their own joy and the service of all, "light" and "salt."[100] Undoubtedly this demands

that catechesis should strengthen them in their identity and that it should continually separate itself from the surrounding atmosphere of hesitation, uncertainty and insipidity. Among the many difficulties, each of them a challenge for faith, I shall indicate a few in order to assist catechesis in overcoming them.

IN AN INDIFFERENT WORLD

57. A few years ago, there was much talk of the secularized world, the post-Christian era. Fashion changes, but a profound reality remains. Christians today must be formed to live in a world which largely ignores God or which, in religious matters, in place of an exacting and fraternal dialogue, stimulating for all, too often flounders in a debasing indifferentism, if it does not remain in a scornful attitude of "suspicion" in the name of the progress it has made in the field of scientific "explanations." To "hold on" in this world, to offer to all a "dialogue of salvation"[101] in which each person feels respected in his or her most basic dignity, the dignity of one who is seeking God, we need a catechesis which trains the young people and adults of our communities to remain clear and consistent in their faith, to affirm serenely their Christian and Catholic identity, to "see him who is invisible"[102] and to adhere so firmly to the absoluteness of God that they can be witnesses to him in a materialistic civilization that denies him.

WITH THE ORIGINAL PEDAGOGY OF THE FAITH

58. The irreducible originality of Christian identity has for corollary and condition no less original a pedagogy of the faith. Among the many prestigious sciences of man that are nowadays making immense advances, pedagogy is certainly one of the most important. The attainments of the other sciences — biology, psychology, sociology — are providing it with valuable elements. The science of education and the art of teaching are continually being subjected to review, with a view to making them better adapted or more effective, with varying degrees of success.

There is also a pedagogy of faith, and the good that it can do for catechesis cannot be overstated. In fact, it is natural that techniques perfected and tested for education in general should be adapted for the service of education in the faith. However, account must always be taken of the absolute originality of faith. Pedagogy of faith is not a question of transmitting human knowledge, even of the highest kind; it is a question of communicating God's Revelation in its entirety. Throughout sacred history, especially in the Gospel, God himself used a pedagogy that must continue to be a model for the pedagogy of faith. A technique is of value in catechesis only to the extent that it serves the faith that is to be transmitted and learned; otherwise it is of no value.

LANGUAGE SUITED TO THE SERVICE OF THE CREDO

59. A problem very close to the preceding one is that of language. This is obviously a burning question today. It is paradoxical to see that, while modern studies, for instance in the field of communication, semantics and symbolology, attribute extraordinary importance to language, nevertheless language is being

misused today for ideological mystification, for mass conformity in thought and for reducing man to the level of an object.

All this has extensive influence in the field of catechesis. For catechesis has a pressing obligation to speak a language suited to today's children and young people in general and to many other categories of people — the language of students, intellectuals and scientists; the language of the illiterate or of people of simple culture; the language of the handicapped, and so on. Saint Augustine encountered this same problem and contributed to its solution for his own time with his well-known work *De Catechizandis Rudibus*. In catechesis as in theology, there is no doubt that the question of language is of the first order. But there is good reason for recalling here that catechesis cannot admit any language that would result in altering the substance of the content of the Creed, under any pretext whatever, even a pretended scientific one. Deceitful or beguiling language is no better. On the contrary, the supreme rule is that the great advances in the science of language must be capable of being placed at the service of catechesis so as to enable it really to "tell" or "communicate" to the child, the adolescent, the young people and adults of today the whole content of doctrine without distortion.

RESEARCH AND CERTAINTY OF FAITH

60. A more subtle challenge occasionally comes from the very way of conceiving faith. Certain contemporary philosophical schools, which seem to be exercising a strong influence on some theological currents and, through them, on pastoral practice, like to emphasize that the fundamental human attitude is that of seeking the infinite, a seeking that never attains its object. In theology, this view of things will state very categorically that faith is not certainty but questioning, not clarity but a leap in the dark.

These currents of thought certainly have the advantage of reminding us that faith concerns things not yet in our possession, since they are hoped for; that as yet we see only "in a mirror dimly";[103] and that God dwells always in inaccessible light.[104] They help us to make the Christian faith not the attitude of one who has already arrived, but a journey forward as with Abraham. For all the more reason one must avoid presenting as certain things which are not.

However, we must not fall into the opposite extreme, as too often happens. The Letter to the Hebrews says that "faith is the assurance of things hoped for, the conviction of things not seen."[105] Although we are not in full possession, we do have an assurance and a conviction. When educating children, adolescents and young people, let us not give them too negative an idea of faith — as if it were absolute non-knowing, a kind of blindness, a world of darkness — but let us show them that the humble yet courageous seeking of the believer, far from having its starting point in nothingness, in plain self-deception, in fallible opinions or in uncertainty, is based on the word of God who cannot deceive or be deceived, and is unceasingly built on the immovable rock of this word. It is the search of the Magi under the guidance of a star,[106] the search of which Pascal, taking up a phrase of Saint Augustine, wrote so profoundly: "You would not be searching for me, if you had not found me."[107]

It is also one of the aims of catechesis to give young catechumens the simple but solid certainties that will help them to seek to know the Lord more and better.

61.   In this context, it seems important to me that the connection between catechesis and theology should be well understood.

Obviously this connection is profound and vital for those who understand the irreplaceable mission of theology in the service of faith. Thus it is no surprise that every stirring in the field of theology also has repercussions in that of catechesis. In this period immediately after the Council, the Church is living through an important but hazardous time of theological research. The same must be said of hermeneutics with respect to exegesis.

Synod Fathers from all continents dealt with this question in very frank terms: they spoke of the danger of an "unstable balance" passing from theology to catechesis and they stressed the need to do something about this difficulty. Pope Paul VI himself had dealt with the problem in no less frank terms in the introduction to his Solemn Profession of Faith[108] and in the Apostolic Exhortation marking the fifth anniversary of the close of the Second Vatican Council.[109]

This point must again be insisted on. Aware of the influence that their research and their statements have on catechetical instruction, theologians and exegetes have a duty to take great care that people do not take for a certainty what on the contrary belongs to the area of questions of opinion or of discussion among experts. Catechists for their part must have the wisdom to pick from the field of theological research those points that can provide light for their own reflection and their teaching, drawing, like the theologians, from the true sources, in the light of the Magisterium. They must refuse to trouble the minds of the children and young people, at this stage of their catechesis, with outlandish theories, useless questions and unproductive discussions, things that Saint Paul often condemned in his pastoral letters.[110]

The most valuable gift that the Church can offer to the bewildered and restless world of our time is to form within it Christians who are confirmed in what is essential and who are humbly joyful in their faith. Catechesis will teach this to them, and it will itself be the first to benefit from it: "The man who wishes to understand himself thoroughly—and not just in accordance with immediate, partial, often superficial, and even illusory standards and measures of his being—must come to Christ with his unrest and uncertainty, and even his weakness and sinfulness, his life and death. He must, so to speak, enter into Christ with all his own self, he must 'appropriate' Christ and assimilate the whole of the reality of the Incarnation and Redemption in order to find himself."[111]

IX
THE TASK CONCERNS US ALL

62.   Now, beloved Brothers and sons and daughters, I would like my words, which are intended as a serious and heartfelt exhortation from me in my ministry as pastor of the universal Church, to set your hearts aflame, like the letters of Saint Paul to his companions in the Gospel, Titus and Timothy, or like Saint Augustine writing for the deacon Deogratias, when the latter lost heart before his task as a catechist, a real little treatise on the joy of catechizing.[112] Yes, I wish to sow courage, hope and enthusiasm abundantly in the hearts of all those many diverse people who are in charge of religious instruction and training for life in keeping with the Gospel.

BISHOPS

63.   To begin with, I turn to my brother Bishops: The Second Vatican Council has already explicitly reminded you of your task in the catechetical area,[113] and the Fathers of the Fourth General Assembly of the Synod have also strongly underlined it.

Dearly beloved Brothers, you have here a special mission within your Churches: you are beyond all others the ones primarily responsible for catechesis, the catechists par excellence. Together with the Pope, in the spirit of episcopal collegiality, you too have charge of catechesis throughout the Church. Accept therefore what I say to you from my heart.

I know that your ministry as Bishops is growing daily more complex and overwhelming. A thousand duties call you: from the training of new priests to being actively present within the lay communities, from the living, worthy celebration of the sacraments and acts of worship to concern for human advancement and the defence of human rights. But let the concern to foster active and effective catechesis yield to no other care whatever in any way. This concern will lead you to transmit personally to your faithful the doctrine of life. But it should also lead you to take on in your diocese, in accordance with the plans of the Episcopal Conference to which you belong, the chief management of catechesis, while at the same time surrounding yourselves with competent and trustworthy assistants. Your principal role will be to bring about and maintain in your Churches a real passion for catechesis, a passion embodied in a pertinent and effective organization, putting into operation the necessary personnel, means and equipment, and also financial resources. You can be sure that if catechesis is done well in your local Churches, everything else will be easier to do. And needless to say, although your zeal must sometimes impose upon you the thankless task of denouncing deviations and correcting errors, it will much more often win for you the joy and consolation of seeing your Churches flourishing because catechesis is given in them as the Lord wishes.

64.   For your part, priests, here you have a field in which you are the immediate assistants of your Bishops. The Council has called you "instructors in the faith";[114] there is no better way for you to be such instructors than by devoting your best efforts to the growth of your communities in the faith. Whether you are in charge of a parish, or are chaplains to primary or secondary schools or universities, or have responsibility for pastoral activity at any level, or are leaders of large or small communities, especially youth groups, the Church expects you to neglect nothing with a view to a well-organized and well-oriented catechetical effort. The deacons and other ministers that you may have the good fortune to have with you are your natural assistants in this. All believers have a right to catechesis; all pastors have the duty to provide it. I shall always ask civil leaders to respect the freedom of catechetical teaching; but with all my strength I beg you ministers of Jesus Christ: Do not, for lack of zeal or because of some unfortunate preconceived idea, leave the faithful without catechesis. Let it not be said that "the children beg for food, but no one gives to them."[115]

MEN AND WOMEN RELIGIOUS

65.   Many religious institutes for men add women came into being for the purpose of giving Christian education to children and young people, especially the most abandoned. Throughout history, men and women religious have been deeply committed to the Church's catechetical activity, doing particularly apposite and effective work. At a time when it is desired that he links between religious and pastors should be accentuated and consequently the active presence of religious communities and their members in the pastoral projects of the local Churches, I wholeheartedly exhort you whose religious consecration should make you even more readily available for the Church's service to prepare as well as possible for the task of catechesis according to the differing vocations of your institutes and the missions entrusted to you, and to carry this concern everywhere. Let the communities dedicate as much as possible of what ability and means they have to the specific work of catechesis.

LAY CATECHISTS

66.   I am anxious to give thanks in the Church's name to all of you, lay teachers of catechesis in the parishes, the men and the still more numerous women throughout the world, who are devoting yourselves to the religious education of many generations. Your work is often lowly and hidden but it is carried out with ardent and generous zeal, and it is an eminent form of the lay apostolate, a form that is particularly important where for various reasons children and young people do not receive suitable religious training in the home. How many of us have received from people like you our first notions of catechism and our preparation for the sacrament of penance, for our first communion and confirmation! The Fourth General Assembly of the Synod did not forget you. I join with it in encouraging you to continue your collaboration for the life of the Church.

But the term "catechists" belongs above all to the catechists in mission lands. Born of families that are already Christian or converted at some time to

Christianity and instructed by missionaries or by another catechist, they then consecrate their lives, year after year, to catechizing children and adults in their own country. Churches that are flourishing today would not have been built up without them. I rejoice at the efforts made by the Sacred Congregation for the Evangelization of Peoples to improve more and more the training of these catechists. I gratefully recall the memory of those whom the Lord has already called to himself. I beg the intercession of those whom my predecessors have raised to the glory of the altars. I wholeheartedly encourage these engaged in the work. I express the wish that many others may succeed them and that they may increase in numbers for a task so necessary for the missions.

IN THE PARISH

67.   I now wish to speak of the actual setting in which all these catechists normally work. I am returning this time, taking a more overall view, to the "places" for catechesis, some of which have already been mentioned in Chapter VI: the parish, the family, the school, organizations.

It is true that catechesis can be given anywhere, but I wish to stress, in accordance with the desire of very many Bishops, that the parish community must continue to be the prime mover and pre-eminent place for catechesis. Admittedly, in many countries the parish has been as it were shaken by the phenomenon of urbanization. Perhaps some have too easily accepted that the parish should be considered old-fashioned, if not doomed to disappear, in favor of more pertinent and effective small communities. Whatever one may think, the parish is still a major point of reference for the Christian people, even for the non-practicing. Accordingly, realism and wisdom demand that we continue along the path aiming to restore to the parish, as needed, more adequate structures and, above all, a new impetus through the increasing integration into it of qualified, responsible and generous members. This being said, and taking into account the necessary diversity of places for catechesis (the parish as such, families taking in children and adolescents, chaplaincies for State schools, Catholic educational establishments, apostolic movements that give periods of catechesis, clubs open to youth in general, spiritual formation weekends, etc.), it is supremely important that all these catechetical channels should really converge on the same confession of faith, on the same membership of the Church, and on commitments in society lived in the same Gospel spirit: "one Lord, one faith, one baptism, one God and Father."[116] That is why every big parish or every group of parishes with small numbers has the serious duty to train people completely dedicated to providing catechetical leadership (priests, men and women religious, and lay people), to provide the equipment needed for catechesis under all aspects, to increase and adapt the places for catechesis to the extent that it is possible and useful to do so, and to be watchful about the quality of the religious formation of the various groups and their integration into the ecclesial community.

In short, without monopolizing or enforcing uniformity, the parish remains, as I have said, the pre-eminent place for catechesis. It must rediscover its vocation, which is to be a fraternal and welcoming family home, where those who have been baptized and confirmed become aware of forming the People of God. In that home, the bread of good doctrine and the Eucharistic Bread are broken for them in abundance, in the setting of the one act of worship;[117] from that home they are sent out day by day to their apostolic mission in all the centers of activity of the life of the world.

IN THE FAMILY

68.   The family's catechetical activity has a special character, which is in a sense irreplaceable. This special character has been rightly stressed by the Church, particularly by the Second Vatican Council.[118] Education in the faith by parents, which should begin from the children's tenderest age,[119] is already being given when the members of a family help each other to grow in faith through the witness of their Christian lives, a witness that is often without words but which perseveres throughout a day-to-day life lived in accordance with the Gospel. This catechesis is more incisive when, in the course or family events (such as the reception of the sacraments, the celebration of great liturgical feasts, the birth of a child, a bereavement) care is taken to explain in the home the Christian or religious content of these events. But that is not enough: Christian parents must strive to follow and repeat, within the setting of family life, the more methodical teaching received elsewhere. The fact that these truths about the main questions of faith and Christian living are thus repeated within a family setting impregnated with love and respect will often make it possible to influence the children in a decisive way for life. The parents themselves profit from the effort that this demands of them, for in a catechetical dialogue of this sort each individual both receives and gives.

Family catechesis therefore precedes, accompanies and enriches all other forms of catechesis. Furthermore, in places where anti-religious legislation endeavors even to prevent education in the faith, and in places where widespread unbelief or invasive secularism makes the religious growth practically impossible, "the Church of the home"[120] remains the one place where children and young people can receive an authentic catechesis. Thus there cannot be too great an effort on the part of Christian parents to prepare for this ministry of being their own children's catechists and to carry it out with tireless zeal. Encouragement must also be given to the individuals or institutions that, through person-to-person contacts, through meetings, and through all kinds of pedagogical means, help parents to perform their task: the service they are doing to catechesis is beyond price.

AT SCHOOL

69.   Together with and in connection with the family, the school provides catechesis with possibilities that are not to be neglected. In the unfortunately decreasing number of countries in which it is possible to give education in the faith within the school framework, the Church has the duty to do so as well as possible. This of course concerns first and foremost the Catholic school: it would no longer deserve this title if, no matter how much it shone for its high

level of teaching in non-religious matters, there were justification for reproaching it for negligence or deviation in strictly religious education. Let it not be said that such education will always be given implicitly and indirectly. The special character of the Catholic school, the underlying reason for it, the reason why Catholic parents should prefer it, is precisely the quality of the religious instruction integrated into the education of the pupils. While Catholic establishments should respect freedom of conscience, that is to say avoid burdening consciences from without by exerting physical or moral pressure, especially in the case of the religious activity of adolescents, they still have a grave duty to offer a religious training suited to the often widely varying religious situations of the pupils. They also have a duty to make them understand that, although God's call to serve him in spirit and truth, in accordance with the commandments of God and the precepts of the Church, does not apply constraint, it is nevertheless binding in conscience.

But I am also thinking of non-confessional and public schools. I express the fervent wish that, in response to a very clear right of the human person and of the family, and out of respect for everyone's religious freedom, all Catholic pupils may be enabled to advance in their spiritual formation with the aid of a religious instruction dependent or the Church, but which, according to the circumstances of different countries, can be offered either by the school or in the setting of the school, or again within the framework of an agreement with the public authorities regarding school timetables, if catechesis takes place only in the parish or in another pastoral center. In fact, even in places where objective difficulties exist, it should be possible to arrange school timetables in such a way as to enable the Catholics to deepen their faith and religious experience, with qualified teachers, whether priests or lay people.

Admittedly, apart rom the school, many other elements of life help in influencing the mentality of the young, for instance, recreation, social background and work surroundings. But those who study are bound to bear the stamp of their studies, to be introduced to cultural or moral values within the atmosphere of the establishment in which they are taught, and to be faced with many ideas met with in school. It is important for catechesis to take full account of this effect of the school on the pupils, if it is to keep in touch with the other elements of the pupils' knowledge and education; thus the Gospel will impregnate the mentality of the pupils in the field of their learning, and the harmonization of their culture will be achieved in the light of faith. Accordingly I give encouragement to the priests, religious and lay people who are devoting themselves to sustaining these pupils' faith. This is moreover an occasion for me to reaffirm my firm conviction that to show respect for the Catholic faith of the young to the extent of facilitating its education, its implantation, its consolidation, its free profession and practice would certainly be to the honor of any Government, whatever be the system on which it is based or the ideology from which it draws its inspiration.

70. Lastly, encouragement must be given to the lay associations, movements and groups, whether their aim is the practice of piety, the direct apostolate, charity and relief work, or a Christian presence in temporal matters. They will all accomplish their objectives better, and serve the Church better, if they give an important place in their internal organization and their method of action to the serious religious training of their members. In this way every association of the faithful in the Church has by definition the duty to educate in the faith.

This makes more evident the role given to the laity in catechesis today, always under the pastoral direction of their Bishops, as the Propositions left by the Synod stressed several times.

TRAINING INSTITUTES

71. We must be grateful to the Lord for this contribution by the laity, but it is also a challenge to our responsibility as Pastors, since these lay catechists must be carefully prepared for what is, if not a formally instituted ministry, at the very least a function of great importance in the Church. Their preparation calls on us to organize special Centers and Institutes, which are to be given assiduous attention by the Bishops. This is a field in which diocesan, interdiocesan or national cooperation proves fertile and fruitful. Here also the material aid provided by the richer Churches to their poorer sisters can show the greatest effectiveness, for what better assistance can one Church give to another than to help it to grow as a Church with its own strength?

I would like to recall to all those who are working generously in the service of the Gospel, and to whom I have expressed here my lively encouragement, the instruction given by my venerated predecessor Paul VI: "As evangelizers, we must offer . . . the image of people who are mature in faith and capable of finding a meeting-point beyond the real tensions, thanks to a shared, sincere and disinterested search for truth. Yes, the destiny of evangelization is certainly bound up with the witness of unity given by the Church. This is a source of responsibility and also of comfort."[121]

CONCLUSION

THE HOLY SPIRIT, THE TEACHER WITHIN

72. At the end of this Apostolic Exhortation, the gaze of my heart turns to him who is the principle inspiring all catechetical work and all who do this work — the Spirit of the Father and of the Son, the Holy Spirit.

In describing the mission that this Spirit would have in the Church, Christ used the significant words: "He will teach you all things, and bring to your remembrance all that I have said to you."[122] And he added: "When the Spirit of truth comes, he will guide you into all the truth . . . he will declare to you the things that are to come."[123]

The Spirit is thus promised to the Church and to each Christian as a Teacher within, who, in the secret of the conscience and the heart, makes one understand what one has heard but was not capable of grasping: "Even now the Holy Spirit teaches the faithful," said Saint Augustine in this regard, "in accordance with each one's spiritual capacity. And he sets their hearts aflame with greater desire according as each one progresses in the charity that makes him love what he already knows and desire what he has yet to know."[124]

Furthermore, the Spirit's mission is also to transform the disciples into witnesses to Christ: "He will bear witness to me; and you also are witnesses."[125]

But this is not all. For Saint Paul, who on this matter synthesizes a theology that is latent throughout the New Testament, it is the whole of one's "being a Christian," the whole of the Christian life, the new life of the children of God, that constitutes a life in accordance with the Spirit.[126] Only the Spirit enables us to say to God: "Abba, Father."[127] Without the Spirit we cannot say: "Jesus is Lord."[128] From the Spirit come all the charisms that build up the Church, the community of Christians.[129] In keeping with this, Saint Paul gives each disciple of Christ the instruction: "Be filled with the Spirit."[130] Saint Augustine is very explicit: "Both (our believing and our doing good) are ours because of the choice of our will, and yet both are gifts from the Spirit of faith and charity."[131]

Catechesis, which is growth in faith and the maturing of Christian life towards its fullness, is consequently a work of the Holy Spirit, a work that he alone can initiate and sustain in the Church.

This realization, based on the text quoted above and on many other passages of the New Testament, convinces us of two things.

To begin with, it is clear that, when carrying out her mission of giving catechesis, the Church—and also every individual Christian devoting himself to that mission within the Church and in her name—must be very much aware of acting as a living pliant instrument of the Holy Spirit. To invoke this Spirit constantly, to be in communion with him, to endeavor to know his authentic inspirations must be the attitude of the teaching Church and of every catechist.

Secondly, the deep desire to understand better the Spirit's action and to entrust oneself to him more fully—at a time when "in the Church we are living an exceptionally favorable season of the Spirit," as my Predecessor Paul VI remarked in his Apostolic Exhortation *Evangelii Nuntiandi*[132]—must bring about a catechetical awakening. For "renewal in the Spirit" will be authentic and will have real fruitfulness in the Church, not so much according as it gives rise to extra-ordinary charisms, but according as it leads the greatest possible number of the faithful, as they travel their daily paths, to make a humble, patient and persevering effort to know the mystery of Christ better and better, and to bear witness to it.

I invoke on the catechizing Church this Spirit of the Father and the Son, and I beg him to renew catechetical dynamism in the Church.

73.   May the Virgin of Pentecost obtain this for us through her intercession. By a unique vocation, she saw her Son Jesus "increase in wisdom and in stature, and in favor."[133] As he sat on her lap and later as he listened to her throughout the hidden life at Nazareth, this Son, who was "the only Son from the Father," "full of grace and truth," was formed by her in human knowledge of the Scriptures and of the history of God's plan for his people, and in adoration of the Father.[134] She in turn was the first of his disciples. She was the first in time, because even when she found her adolescent son in the Temple she received from him lessons that she kept in her heart.[135] She was the first disciple above all else because no one has been "taught by God"[136] to such depth. She was "both mother and disciple," as Saint Augustine said of her, venturing to add that her discipleship was more important for her than her motherhood.[137] There are good grounds for the statement made in the Synod Hall that Mary is "a living catechism" and "the mother and model of catechists."

May the presence of the Holy Spirit, through the prayers of Mary, grant the Church unprecedented enthusiasm in the catechetical work that is essential for her. Thus will she effectively carry out, at this moment of grace, her inalienable and universal mission, the mission given her by her Teacher: "Go therefore and make disciples of all nations."[138]

With my Apostolic Blessing.

Given in Rome, at Saint Peter's, on 16 October 1979, the second year of my pontificate.

NOTES

1. Cf. Matthew 28:19–20.

2. Cf. 1 John 1:1.

3. Cf. John 20:31.

4. Cf. AAS 63 (1971): 758–764.

5. Cf. 44; cf. also 45–48 and 54: AAS 68 (1976): 34–35; 35–38; 43.

6. According to the Motu Proprio *Apostolica Sollicitudo* of 15 September 1965, the Synod of Bishops can come together in General Assembly, in Extraordinary Assembly or in Special Assembly. In the present Apostolic Exhortation the words "Synod," "Synod Fathers" and "Synod Hall" always refer, unless otherwise indicated, to the Fourth General Assembly of the Synod of Bishops on catechesis, held in Rome in October 1977.

7. Cf. *Synodus Episcoporum, De catechesi hoc nostro tempore tradenda praesertim pueris atque iuvenibus, Ad Populum Dei Nuntius*, e Civitate Vaticana, 28-x-1977; cf. "L'Osservatore Romano," (30 October 1977): 3–4.

8. Cf. AAS 69 (1977): 633.

9. John 1:14.

10. John 14:6.

11. Ephesians 3:9, 18–19.

12. Cf. John 14:6.

13. John 7:16. This is a theme dear to the Fourth Gospel: cf. John 3:34; 8:28; 12:49–50; 14:24; 17:8, 14.

14. 1 Corinthians 11:23: the word "deliver" employed here by St. Paul was frequently repeated in EN to describe the evangelizing activity of the Church, for example, 4, 15, 78, 79.

15. Acts 1:1.

16. Matthew 26:55; cf. John 18:20.

17. Mark 10:1.

18. Mark 1:22; cf. also Matthew 5:2; 11:1; 13:54; 22:16; Mark 2:13; 4:1, 6:2, 6; Luke 5:3, 17; John 7:14; 8:2, etc.

19. Luke 23:5.

20. In nearly fifty places in the four Gospels, this title, inherited from the whole Jewish tradition but here given a new meaning that Christ himself often seeks to emphasize, is attributed to Jesus.

21. Cf., among others, Matthew 8:19; Mark 4:38, 9:38; 10:35; 13:1; John 11:28.

22. Matthew 12:38

23. Luke 10:25; cf. Matthew 22:16.

24. John 13:13–14; cf. also Matthew 10:25; 26:18 and parallel passages.

25. Matthew 23:8. Saint Ignatius of Antioch takes up this affirmation and comments as follows: "We have received the faith; this is why we hold fast, in order to be recognized as disciples of Jesus Christ, our only Teacher" (*Epistola ad Magnesios*, IX, 2).

26. John 3:2.

27. The portrayal of Christ as Teacher goes back as far as the Roman Catacombs. It is frequently used in the mosaics of Romano-Byzantine art of the third and fourth centuries. It was to form a predominant artistic motif in the sculptures of the great Romanesque and Gothic cathedrals of the Middle Ages.

28. Matthew 28:19.

29. John 15:15.

30. Cf. John 15:16.

31. Acts 2:42.

32. Acts 4:2.

33. Cf. Acts 4:18; 5:28.

34. Cf. Acts 4:19.

35. Cf. Acts 1:25.

36. Cf. Acts 6:8 ff.; cf. also Philip catechizing the minister of the Queen of the Ethiopians: Acts 8:26 ff.

37. Cf. Acts 15:35.

38. Acts 8:4.

39. Acts 28:31.

40. Cf. Pope John XXIII, *Mater et Magistra* (AAS 53 [1961]: 401): the Church is "mother" because by baptism she unceasingly begets new children and increases God's family; she is "teacher" because she makes her children grow in the grace of their baptism by nourishing their *sensus fidei* through instruction in the truths of faith.

41. Cf., for example, the letter of Clement of Rome to the Church of Corinth, the *Didache*, the *Epistola Apostolorum*, the writings of Irenaeus of Lyons *(Demonstratio Apostolicae Praedictionis and Adversus Haereses)*, of Tertullian *(De Baptismo)*, of Clement of Alexandria *(Paedagogus)*, of Cyprian *(Testimonia ad Quirinum)*, of Origen *(Contra Celsum)*, etc.

42. Cf. 2 Thessalonians 3:1.

43. DH, 2.

44. Cf. The Universal Declaration of Human Rights (UNO), 10 December 1948, art. 18; The International Pact on Civil and Political Rights (UNO) 16 December 1966, art. 4; Final Act of the Conference on European Security and Cooperation, para. VII.

45. Cf. *Synodus Episcoporum, De catechesi hoc nostro tempore tradenda praesertim pueris atque iuvenibus, Ad Populum Dei Nuntius, 1.*

46. *Ad Populum Dei Nuntius, 6.*

47. GCD, 17–35.

48. Cf. 17–24.

49. Cf. *Synodus Episcoporum, De catechesi hoc nostro tempore tradenda praesertim pueris atque iuvenibus, Ad Populum Dei Nuntius, 1.*

50. Concluding Address to the Synod, 29 October 1977.

51. Concluding Address to the Synod, 29 October 1977.

52. GCD, 40, 46.

53. Cf. PO, 6.

54. Cf. *Ordo Initiationis Christianae Adultorum.*

55. Ephesians 4:13.

56. Cf. 1 Peter 3;15.

57. DV, 10, 24; cf. GCD, 45 where the principal and complementary sources of catechesis are well set out.

58. Cf. *Ordo Initiationis Christianae Adultorum*, 25–26; 183–187.

59. Cf. AAS 60 (1968): 436–445. Besides these great professions of faith of the Magisterium, note also the popular professions of faith, rooted in the traditional Christian culture of certain countries; cf. what I said to the young people at Gniezno, 3 June 1979, regarding the Bogurodzica song-message: "This is not only a song: it is also a profession of faith, a symbol of the Polish Credo, it is a catechesis and also a document of Christian education. The principal truths of faith and the principles of morality are contained here. This is not only a historical object. It is a document of life. (It has even been called) 'the Polish catechism'" (AAS 71 [1979]): 754.

60. EN, 25.

61. EN, especially 26–39; the "principal elements of the Christian message" are presented in a more systematic fashion in the GCD, 47–69, where one also finds the norm for the essential doctrinal content of catechesis.

62. GCD, 37–46.

63. Romans 1:19.

64. Acts 17:23.

65. Cf. Ephesians 3:3.

66. Cf. Ephesians 2:18.

67. Acts 20:28.

68. GS, 39

69. Romans 6:4.

70. 2 Corinthians 5:17.

71. Cf. 2 Corinthians 5:17.

72. Romans 6:23.

73. Cf. EN, 36–38.

74. Cf. *Catechismo maggiore*, Fifth part, chap. 6, 965–966.

75. Cf. Philippians 2:17.

76. Romans 10:8.

77. Philippians 3:8.

78. Cf. Ephesians 4:20–21.

79. Cf. 2 Thessalonians 2:7.

80. John 6:69; cf. Acts 5:20; 7:38.

81. Acts 2:28, quoting Psalm 16:11.

82. Cf. entire UR.

83. Cf. UR, 5; cf. AG, 15; GCD, 27.

84. Cf. UR, 3, 4.

85. UR, 3.

86. Cf. UR; cf. LG, 15.

87. Luke 12:32.

88. Cf., for example, GS; Pope Paul VI, Encyclical *Populorum Progressio*: AAS 59 (1967): 257–299; Apostolic Letter *Octogesima Adveniens*: AAS 63 (1971): 401–441; EN.

89. Matthew 1:16.

90. Cf. CD, 14; AG; GCD, 20; cf. also *Ordo Initiationis Christianae Adultorum*.

91. EN, 58.

92. Cf. *Synodus Episcoporum, De catechesi hoc nostro tempore tradenda praesertim pueris atque iuvenibus, Ad Populum Dei Nuntius*, 7–10.

93. Cf. GCD, 119–121.

94. Cf. AAS 71 (1979): 607.

95. Cf. Romans 16:25; Ephesians 3:5.

96. 1 Corinthians 1:17.

97. Cf. 2 Timothy 1:14.

98. Cf. John 1:16; Ephesians 1:10.

99. Cf. Encyclical *Redemptor Hominis*, 15–16.

100. Cf. Matthew 5:13–16.

101. Cf. Pope Paul VI, Encyclical *Ecclesiam Suam*, Part Three.

102. Cf. Hebrews 11:27.

103. 1 Corinthians 13:12.

104. Cf. 1 Timothy 6:16.

105. Hebrews 11:1.

106. Cf. Matthew 2:1 ff.

107. Blaise Pascal, *Le mystère de Jésus: Pensées*, 553.

108. Pope Paul VI, *Sollemnis Professio Fidei*, 4.

109. Pope Paul VI, Apostolic Exhortation *Quinque Iam Anni*.

110. Cf. 1 Timothy 1:3 ff; 4:1 ff; 2 Timothy 2:14 ff; 4:1–5; Titus 1:10–12; EN, 78.

111. Encyclical *Redemptor Hominis*, 10.

112. *De Catechizandis Rudibus*, PL 40: 310–347.

113. CD, 14.

114. PO, 6.

115. Lamentations 4:4.

116. Ephesians 4:5–6.

117. Cf. SC, 35, 52; cf. also *Institutio Generalis Missalis Romani*, promulgated by a Decree of the Sacred Congregation of Rites on 6 April 1969, 33, and what has been said above in Chapter VI concerning the homily.

118. Since the High Middle Ages, provincial councils have insisted on the responsibility of parents in regard to education in the faith: cf. Sixth Council of Arles (813), Canon 19; Council of Mainz (813), Canons 45, 47; Sixth Council of Paris (829), Book 1, Chapter 7: Mansi *Sacrorum Conciliorum Nova et Amplissima Collectio*, XIV, 62, 74, 542. Among the more recent documents of the Magisterium, note the Encyclical *Divini Illius Magistri* of Pius XI, 31 December 1929: AAS 22 (1930): 49–86; the many discourses and messages of Pius XII; and above all the texts of the Second Vatican Council: LG, 11, 35; AA, 11, 30; GS, 52; GE, 3.

119. GE, 3.

120. LG, 11; AA, 11.

121. EN, 77.

122. John 14:26.

123. John 16:13.

124. *In Ioannis Evangelium Tractatus*, 97, 1: PL 35: 1877.

125. John 15:26–27.

126. Cf. Romans 8:14–17; Galatians 4:6.

127. Romans 8:15.

128. 1 Corinthians 12:3.

129. Cf. 1 Corinthians 12:4–11.

130. Ephesians 5:18.

131. *Retractationum Liber I*, 23, 2: PL 32: 621.

132. EN, 75.

133. Cf Luke 2:52.

134. Cf. John 1:14; Hebrews 10:5; Summa theologicae III, Q. 12, a. 2; a. 3, ad 3.

135. Cf. Luke 2:51.

136. Cf. John 6:45.

137. Cf. *Sermo 25*, 7: PL 46: 937–938.

138. Matthew 28:19.

RITE

OF

CHRISTIAN INITIATION

OF

ADULTS

1988

Unlike the other documents in this volume, which are presented in full, the *Rite of Christian Initiation of Adults* as presented here is not complete. Presented are the General Introduction to the Rite and the introductions to each stage of the process of initiation.

The restoration of the process of initiation has itself prompted Christians to recognize what had been dormant for a long time: that initiation is not something that is merely learned. Its fullness comes from the *experience* of becoming a Christian in all aspects of human life. The introductions to the stages of the rite are included in order to highlight the connection between liturgy and catechesis, yet the experience of the RCIA in a worshiping community is itself the best teacher of this connection.

OVERVIEW OF THE *RITE OF CHRISTIAN INITIATION OF ADULTS*

by Anne Marie Mongoven, OP

INTRODUCTION

The Second Vatican Council called for a revision of the rite of baptism for adults and a restoration of the catechumenate. This directive initiated a process of reform in the way adults become members of the Catholic Church. Before the Council, adults who wished to become Catholics received private instruction from their parish priest. Then, when the priest decided they were ready for membership, they were baptized in a private ceremony with a few friends or family members present.

Thirty years after the Council, an entirely new process of initiation is in place. On September 1, 1988, the restored initiation presented in the *Rite of Christian Initiation of Adults* became the mandatory process for initiating adults into the church in the United States. This rite offers a text which, when enacted by the community, leads adults to full membership in the Catholic Church. The text of a liturgical *rite* resembles the *libretto* of an opera. The opera does not come alive until it is performed. No liturgical rite comes alive in a book. The rite expresses life and faith when the community enacts it.

This rite of initiation, called the RCIA, presents the initiation of adults into the church as a public journey of conversion in the midst of the faith community. Conversion and initiation are not "private" affairs to be conducted by the priest and the "convert." They are public, community expressions of faith. When an adult enters the church today, he or she enters into the midst of a faith community that includes sponsors, godparents, catechists, priests, other parish ministers, family, friends and all parishioners. The rite urges all parishioners of the local church community to be "fully prepared . . . to give help to those who are searching for Christ" (9).

THE STRUCTURE OF THE RITE

The RCIA presumes a gradual process of initiation that moves through periods of conversion marked by rites that sometimes are called "steps" or "doorposts." The rites between the periods celebrate new stages of conversion. The structure of the RCIA sets forth four periods of conversion:

1. a period of inquiry that ends with the rite of acceptance into the order of catechumens;

2. the period of the catechumenate that begins with the rite of acceptance and continues with catechesis until the rite of election;

3. the period of enlightenment or election that begins with the lenten preparation for the Easter celebration and the sacraments of initiation; and

4. after initiation the final period extends through the whole of the Easter season with a mystagogical catechesis.

Conversion as the turning away from sin and a turning toward God happens, gradually, throughout the process of the RCIA. In conversion, the individual candidates and the community of candidates together turn toward the Light whom Christians name Christ. This turning cannot be hurried, timed or programmed so that the periods fit into an academic year schedule or even into the lenten season. The RCIA notes that "the duration of the catechumenate will depend on the grace of God and on various circumstances. Nothing . . . can be settled a priori" (76). When possible, the catechumens experience the rite of election in the lenten season and celebrate initiation at the Easter Vigil. When pastoral needs indicate this arrangement does not suit the catechumen, the schedule should change.

THE PROCESS OF CATECHESIS

Each of the four periods includes catechesis on the symbols, scriptures and prayer texts. Catechesis on moral issues, doctrine, justice, prayer, community and their relationship to daily living are woven into all four periods. The rite points out that this catechesis for catechumens should be gradual and complete, "accommodated to the liturgical year and solidly supported by celebrations of the word." The catechesis not only instructs candidates and catechumens about dogmas and precepts but ought to lead them "to a profound sense of the mystery of salvation in which they desire to participate" (75, 1).

In catechesis the community shares its *tradition*, that is, its heritage, its history, its rituals, its life, its meanings and its values, with those being initiated. During the third period, the period of enlightenment or election, the church acknowledges the significance of what it is handing on by celebrating the rite of the Presentation of the Creed. This rite proclaims the elects' ratification of the meaning of the Creed, which the catechists have taught. In this rite, they declare their allegiance, commitment and love for the God Christians call Trinity and their acceptance of the love and redemption that that God offers in an unconditional way to all humankind. In handing on the Creed, the celebrant says to the elect:

> My dear friends, listen carefully to the words of that faith by which you
> will be justified. The words are few, but the mysteries they contain are
> great (160).

It is the catechist who, in the name of the community, hands on the symbol of this mystery of salvation, the Creed, to the elect, so that it becomes for them not simply a doctrine to be learned but a proclamation of faith to be lived.

The RCIA calls for a catechesis that will help the catechumens "turn more readily to God in prayer"; one that is rich in the experience of the proclamation of the word, supported by "sponsors, godparents and the entire Christian community," with opportunities "to practice love of neighbor, even at the cost of self-renunciation." It recognizes that "it does not do justice to catechesis to think of it as instruction alone" (*Sharing the Light of Faith: National Catechectical Directory for Catholics of the United States*, 35) (NCD). Catechesis, while presenting Catholic teaching in its entirety, also "enlightens faith, directs the heart toward God, fosters participation in the liturgy, inspires apostolic activity and nurtures a life completely in accord with the spirit of Christ" (NCD, 78). This is the rich form of catechesis that emerges from renewal and that is integral to the RCIA.

Initiation revolves around conversion, and for Christians, conversion focuses on Jesus as the Christ, the one through whom God is made visible, tangible and audible to humanity. The living, dying, rising, loving Christ is the center, the heart of the initiation process. The local community embodies this dying-rising Lord for the candidates and catechumens. As the Body of Christ, the community dies to selfishness and sin and rises with love and hope for new life. This Body of Christ calls the candidates and catechumens to recognize Jesus as the center and core of their lives.

The whole of the initiation process has a paschal character. Every catechesis focuses on the paschal mystery in our lives, both as individuals and as a community of faith. The liturgical rites celebrate the paschal mystery through acceptance, election and initiation. Through the catechesis and liturgical rites, the community experiences a true dying to self and rising with Christ. The dying is to death through sin. The rising is to life with hope. Rising in faith is rising within the paschal mystery. Through initiation, all become one in Christ Jesus.

The rite points out the significance of the paschal character of initiation. It states that "the whole initiation must bear a markedly paschal character"(8). It recommends that as a "general rule," initiation should be celebrated in the paschal season, preferably at the Easter Vigil.

THE INITIATION

As the assembly gathers to celebrate the Easter Vigil, the community of the elect comes together with the assembly to celebrate the climax of the initiation process. This climax begins with the one great initiatory event (baptism/confirmation/eucharist) and continues for the 50 days of the Easter Season. The elect gather to listen to the story, to be bathed in the waters of redemption, to be anointed with the fragrant oils and to enter fully with the whole assembly into the proclamation of the eucharist and the sharing of the sacred Body and Blood of Christ in communion. As this event closes, the newly initiated neophytes are sent with the whole community to serve others.

This night is the beginning of 50 days of mystagogia. This is a time when the initiatory community gathers around its new members and leads them step-by-step into a fuller understanding of the mysteries of faith. The RCIA states that

> this is a time for the community and the neophytes together to grow in deepening their grasp of the paschal mystery and in making it part of their lives through meditation on the gospel, sharing in the eucharist and doing the works of charity (244).

During this period, the new members, led by their catechists and RCIA team members, enter more fully into the life of the parish community. It is imperative that the mystagogical period focuses on the lectionary reading and the proclamation of the Easter word. For as the word of God breathed new life into the initiates throughout the periods of inquiry, catechumenate and enlightenment, so now as the newly initiated take their places within the community the resurrection and postresurrection narratives proclaim the risen Christ and the renewed Christian community. The neophytes learn that the word is eternal, always proclaiming and giving new life, always challenging and renewing the church.

THE CATECHIST

While many ministers of the community participate in the initiation process, and while the local assembly is the primary minister to the candidates, the catechist has a significant role to play in the life of the initiating community. The RCIA states that the catechist "should, whenever possible, have an active part in the rites." Catechists also should see that the catechesis "is filled with the spirit of the gospel." They should adapt the catechesis to the liturgical signs and the cycle of the church's year. The catechesis ought to be "suited to the needs of the catechumens, and as far as possible enriched by local traditions" (16).

The church, as it always does, asks much from its catechists who are part of the RCIA. It asks that they be women and men of faith, filled with the spirit of the gospel, able to lead the community in prayer and free to encourage the community to serve those who are in need. It presumes that they are people of prayer, not only their own private prayer but also the world of ritual, bodily prayer. The rite asks the catechists to bless the people (96); to sign them with the cross on the forehead or on each of the senses (55b); and to proclaim the word within the assembly, to preach, to intercede and to exorcise (92).

Catechists and liturgists need to work together so that the catechist will learn from the liturgist what it means to preside and will know how to bless and anoint and sign. Liturgists, catechists, sponsors, godparents and the elect together can help the catechists or liturgists to prepare a homily for the liturgical gatherings. All members of the RCIA ministry team exist in order to serve those who are becoming members of the church.

A CATECHETICAL-LITURGICAL RITE

The RCIA is a unique rite in that it is the only rite that sets out both the catechetical and liturgical dimensions of the process of conversion. It demonstrates the intimate relationship between catechesis and liturgy through the structure of its catechetical-liturgical cycle. First, the catechists, through their ministry of reflection and interpretation of the word and life, lead the community to express its faith in liturgical ritual. Second, the liturgical ritual confirms the catechesis and expresses the faith of the community, bodily, in space and time. Third, this ritual then leads the community to regather, catechetically, to reflect again on the ritual through which the community expressed its faith. And the cycle begins again.

Sharing the Light of Faith: National Catechetical Directory for Catholics of the United States states that the RCIA is a model of catechesis and provides a norm for all catechesis (NCD, 115, 227). It is both model and norm because it takes the people where they are, as seekers, inquirers, candidates, catechumens or neophytes and leads them, with the local community through the liturgical rites, to embrace the paschal mystery as their own mystery.

OUTLINE

RITE OF CHRISTIAN INITIATION OF ADULTS

INTRODUCTION

1.   The rite of Christian initiation presented here is designed for adults who, after hearing the mystery of Christ proclaimed, consciously and freely seek the living God and enter the way of faith and conversion as the Holy Spirit opens their hearts. By God's help they will be strengthened spiritually during their preparation and at the proper time will receive the sacraments fruitfully.

2.   This rite includes not simply the celebration of the sacraments of baptism, confirmation, and eucharist, but also all the rites belonging to the catechumenate. Endorsed by the ancient practice of the Church, a catechumenate that would be suited to contemporary missionary activity in all regions was so widely requested that the Second Vatican Council decreed its restoration, revision, and adaptation to local traditions[1]

3.   So that the rite of initiation will be more useful for the work of the Church and for individual, parochial, and missionary circumstances, the rite is first presented in Part I of this book in its complete and usual form (nos. 36–251). This is designed for the preparation of a group of candidates, but by simple adaptation pastors can devise a form suited to one person.

Part II provides rites for special circumstances: the Christian initiation of children (nos. 252–330), a simple form of the rite for adults to be carried out in exceptional circumstances (nos. 331–369), and a short form of the rite for those in danger of death (nos. 370–399). Part II also includes guidelines for preparing uncatechized adults for confirmation and eucharist (nos. 400–410) along with four (4) optional rites which may be used with such candidates, and the rite of reception of baptized Christians into the full communion of the Catholic Church (nos. 473–504).

Rites for catechumens and baptized but previously uncatechized adults celebrated in combination, along with a rite combining the reception of baptized Christians into the full communion of the Catholic Church with the celebration of Christian initiation at the Easter Vigil (nos. 562–594), are contained in Appendix I. The two additional appendices contain acclamations, hymns, and songs, and the National Statutes for the Catechumenate in the Dioceses of the United States of America.

STRUCTURE OF THE INITIATION OF ADULTS

4.   The initiation of catechumens is a gradual process that takes place within the community of the faithful. By joining the catechumens in reflecting on the value of the paschal mystery and by renewing their own conversion, the faithful provide an example that will help the catechumens to obey the Holy Spirit more generously.

5.   The rite of initiation is suited to a spiritual journey of adults that varies according to the many forms of God's grace, the free cooperation of the individuals, the action of the Church, and the circumstances of time and place.

6.   This journey includes not only the periods for making inquiry and for maturing (see no. 7), but also the steps marking the catechumens' progress, as they pass, so to speak, through another doorway or ascend to the next level.

   1. The first step: reaching the point of initial conversion and wishing to become Christians, they are accepted as catechumens by the Church.

   2. The second step: having progressed in faith and nearly completed the catechumenate, they are accepted into a more intense preparation for the sacraments of initiation.

   3. The third step: having completed their spiritual preparation, they receive the sacraments of Christian initiation.

   These three steps are to be regarded as the major, more intense moments of initiation and are marked by three liturgical rites: the first by the rite of acceptance into the order of catechumens (nos. 41–74); the second by the rite of election or enrollment of names (nos. 118–137); and the third by the celebration of the sacraments of Christian initiation (nos. 206–243).

7.   The steps lead to periods of inquiry and growth; alternatively the periods may also be seen as preparing for the ensuing step.

   1. The first period consists of inquiry on the part of the candidates and of evangelization and the precatechumenate on the part of the Church. It ends with the rite of acceptance into the order of catechumens .

   2. The second period, which begins with the rite of acceptance into the order of catechumens and may last for several years, includes catechesis and the rites connected with catechesis. It comes to an end on the day of election.

   3. The third and much shorter period, which follows the rite of election, ordinarily coincides with the Lenten preparation for the Easter celebration and the sacraments of initiation. It is a time of purification and enlightenment and includes the celebration of the rites belonging to this period

   4. The final period extends through the whole Easter season and is devoted to the postbaptismal catechesis or mystagogy. It is a time for deepening

the Christian experience, for spiritual growth, and for entering more fully into the life and unity of the community.

Thus there are four continuous periods: the precatechumenate, the period for hearing the first preaching of the Gospel (nos. 36–40); the period of the catechumenate, set aside for a thorough catechesis and for the rites belonging to this period (nos. 75–117); the period of purification and enlightenment (Lenten preparation), designed for a more intense spiritual preparation, which is assisted by the celebration of the scrutinies and presentations (nos. 138–205); and the period of postbaptismal catechesis or mystagogy, marked by the new experience of sacraments and community (nos. 244–251).

8.   The whole initiation must bear a markedly paschal character, since the initiation of Christians is the first sacramental sharing in Christ's dying and rising and since, in addition, the period of purification and enlightenment ordinarily coincides with Lent[2] and the period of postbaptismal catechesis or mystagogy with the Easter season. All the resources of Lent should be brought to bear as a more intense preparation of the elect and the Easter Vigil should be regarded as the proper time for the sacraments of initiation. Because of pastoral needs, however, the sacraments of initiation may be celebrated at other times (see nos. 26–30).

MINISTRIES AND OFFICES

9.   In light of what is said in *Christian Initiation*, General Introduction (no. 7), the people of God, as represented by the local Church, should understand and show by their concern that the initiation of adults is the responsibility of all the baptized.[3] Therefore the community must always be fully prepared in the pursuit of its apostolic vocation to give help to those who are searching for Christ. In the various circumstances of daily life, even as in the apostolate, all the followers of Christ have the obligation of spreading the faith according to their abilities.[4] Hence, the entire community must help the candidates and the catechumens throughout the process of initiation: during the period of the precatechumenate, the period of the catechumenate, the period of purification and enlightenment, and the period of postbaptismal catechesis or mystagogy. In particular:

1. During the period of evangelization and precatechumenate, the faithful should remember that for the Church and its members the supreme purpose of the apostolate is that Christ's message is made known to the world by word and deed and that his grace is communicated.[5] They should therefore show themselves ready to give the candidates evidence of the spirit of the Christian community and to welcome them into their homes, into personal conversation, and into community gatherings.

2. At the celebrations belonging to the period of the catechumenate, the faithful should seek to be present whenever possible and should take an active part in the responses, prayers, singing, and acclamations.

3. On the day of election, because it is a day of growth for the community, the faithful, when called upon, should be sure to give honest and carefully considered testimony about the catechumens.

4. During Lent, the period of purification and enlightenment, the faithful should take care to participate in the rites of the scrutinies and presentations and give the elect the example of their own renewal in the spirit of penance, faith, and charity. At the Easter Vigil, they should attach great importance to renewing their own baptismal promises .

5. During the period immediately after baptism, the faithful should take part in the Masses for neophytes, that is, the Sunday Masses of the Easter season (see no. 25), welcome the neophytes with open arms in charity, and help them to feel more at home in the community of the baptized.

10. A sponsor accompanies any candidate seeking admission as a catechumen. Sponsors are persons who have known and assisted the candidates and stand as witnesses to the candidates' moral character, faith, and intention. It may happen that it is not the sponsor for the rite of acceptance and the period of the catechumenate but another person who serves as godparent for the periods of purification and enlightenment and of mystagogy.

11. Their godparents (for each a godmother or godfather, or both) accompany the candidates on the day of election, at the celebration of the sacraments of initiation, and during the period of mystagogy.[6] Godparents are persons chosen by the candidates on the basis of example, good qualities, and friendship, delegated by the local Christian community, and approved by the priest. It is the responsibility of godparents to show the candidates how to practice the Gospel in personal and social life, to sustain the candidates in moments of hesitancy and anxiety, to bear witness, and to guide the candidates' progress in the baptismal life. Chosen before the candidates' election, godparents fulfill this office publicly from the day of the rite of election, when they give testimony to the community about the candidates. They continue to be important during the time after reception of the sacraments when the neophytes need to be assisted so that they remain true to their baptismal promises.

12. The bishop,[7] in person or through his delegate, sets up, regulates, and promotes the program of pastoral formation for catechumens and admits the candidates to their election and to the sacraments. It is hoped that, presiding if possible at the Lenten liturgy, he will himself celebrate the rite of election and, at the Easter Vigil, the sacraments of initiation, at least for the initiation of those who are fourteen years old or older. Finally, when pastoral care requires, the bishop should depute catechists, truly worthy and properly prepared, to celebrate the minor exorcisms (nos. 90–94) and the blessings of the catechumens (nos. 95–97).

13. Priests, in addition to their usual ministry for any celebration of baptism, confirmation, and the eucharist,[8] have the responsibility of attending to the pastoral and personal care of the catechumens,[9] especially those who seem hesitant and discouraged. With the help of deacons and catechists, they are to provide

instruction for the catechumens; they are also to approve the choice of godparents and willingly listen to and help them; they are to be diligent in the correct celebration and adaptation of the rites throughout the entire course of Christian initiation (see no. 35).

14. The priest who baptizes an adult or a child of catechetical age should, when the bishop is absent, also confer confirmation,[10] unless this sacrament is to be given at another time (see no. 24). When there are a large number of candidates to be confirmed, the minister of confirmation may associate priests with himself to administer the sacrament. It is preferable that the priests who are so invited:

> 1. either have a particular function or office in the diocese, being, namely, either vicars general, episcopal vicars, or district or regional vicars;

> 2. or be the parish priests (pastors) of the places where confirmation is conferred, parish priests (pastors) of the places where the candidates belong, or priests who have had a special part in the catechetical preparation of the candidates.[11]

15. Deacons should be ready to assist in the ministry to catechumens. Conferences of bishops that have decided in favor of the permanent diaconate should ensure that the number and distribution of permanent deacons are adequate for the carrying out of the steps, periods, and formation programs of the catechumenate wherever pastoral needs require.[12]

16. Catechists, who have an important office for the progress of the catechumens and for the growth of the community, should, whenever possible, have an active part in the rites. When deputed by the bishop (see no. 12), they may perform the minor exorcisms and blessings contained in the ritual.[13] When they are teaching, catechists should see that their instruction is filled with the spirit of the Gospel, adapted to the liturgical signs and the cycle of the Church's year, suited to the needs of the catechumens, and as far as possible enriched by local traditions.

TIME AND PLACE OF INITIATION

17. As a general rule, parish priests (pastors) should make use of the rite of initiation in such a way that the sacraments themselves are celebrated at the Easter Vigil and the rite of election takes place on the First Sunday of Lent. The rest of the rites are spaced on the basis of the structure and arrangement of the catechumenate as described previously (nos. 6–8). For pastoral needs of a more serious nature, however, it is lawful to arrange the schedule for the entire rite of initiation differently, as will be detailed later (nos. 26–30).

PROPER OR USUAL TIMES

18. The following should be noted about the time of celebrating the rite of acceptance into the order of catechumens (nos. 41–74).

1. It should not be too early, but should be delayed until the candidates, according to their own dispositions and situation, have had sufficient time to conceive an initial faith and to show the first signs of conversion (see no. 42).

2. In places where the number of candidates is smaller than usual, the rite of acceptance should be delayed until a group is formed that is sufficiently large for catechesis and the liturgical rites.

3. Two dates in the year, or three if necessary, are to be fixed as the usual times for carrying out this rite.

19.   The rite of election or enrollment of names (nos. 118–137) should as a rule be celebrated on the First Sunday of Lent. As circumstances suggest or require, it may be anticipated somewhat or even celebrated on a weekday.

20.   The scrutinies (nos. 150–156, 164–177) should take place on the Third, Fourth, and Fifth Sundays of Lent, or, if necessary, on the other Sundays of Lent, or even on convenient weekdays. Three scrutinies should be celebrated. The bishop may dispense from one of them for serious reasons or, in extraordinary circumstances, even from two (see nos. 34.3, 331). When, for lack of time, the election is held early, the first scrutiny is also to be held early; but in this case care is to be taken not to prolong the period of purification and enlightenment beyond eight weeks.

21.   By ancient usage, the presentations, since they take place after the scrutinies, are part of the same period of purification and enlightenment. They are celebrated during the week. The presentation of the Creed to the catechumens (nos. 157–163) takes place during the week after the first scrutiny; the presentation of the Lord's Prayer (nos. 178–184) during the week after the third scrutiny. For pastoral reasons however, to enrich the liturgy in the period of the catechumenate, each presentation may be transferred and celebrated during the period of the catechumenate as a kind of "rite of passage" (see nos. 79, 104–105).

22.   On Holy Saturday, when the elect refrain from work and spend their time in recollection, the various preparation rites may be celebrated: the recitation or "return" of the Creed by the elect, the ephphetha rite, and the choosing of a Christian name (nos. 185–205).

23.   The celebration of the sacraments of Christian initiation (nos. 206–243) should take place at the Easter Vigil itself (see nos. 8, 17). But if there are a great many catechumens, the sacraments are given to the majority that night and reception of the sacraments by the rest may be transferred to days within the Easter octave, whether at the principal church or at a mission station. In this case either the Mass of the day or one of the ritual Masses "Christian Initiation: Baptism" may be used and the readings are chosen from those of the Easter Vigil.

24.   In certain cases when there is serious reason, confirmation may be postponed until near the end of the period of postbaptismal catechesis, for example, Pentecost Sunday (see no. 249).

25.   On all the Sundays of the Easter season after Easter Sunday, the so-called Masses for neophytes are to be scheduled. The entire community and the newly baptized with their godparents should be encouraged to participate (see nos. 247–248).

26.   The entire rite of Christian initiation is normally arranged so that the sacraments will he celebrated during the Easter Vigil. Because of unusual circumstances and pastoral needs, however, the rite of election and the rites belonging to the period of purification and enlightenment may be held outside Lent and the sacraments of initiation may be celebrated at a time other than the Easter Vigil or Easter Sunday.

Even when the usual time has otherwise been observed, it is permissible, but only for serious pastoral needs (for example, if there are a great many people to be baptized), to choose a day other than the Easter Vigil or Easter Sunday, but preferably one during the Easter season, to celebrate the sacraments of initiation; the program of initiation during Lent, however, must be maintained.

When the time is changed in either way, even though the rite of Christian initiation occurs at a different point in the liturgical year, the structure of the entire rite, with its properly spaced intervals, remains the same. But the following adjustments are made.

27.   As far as possible, the sacraments of initiation are to be celebrated on a Sunday, using, as occasion suggests, the Sunday Mass or one of the ritual Masses "Christian Initiation: Baptism" (see nos. 23, 208).

28.   The rite of acceptance into the order of catechumens is to take place when the time is right (see no. 18).

29.   The rite of election is to be celebrated about six weeks before the sacraments of initiation, so that there is sufficient time for the scrutinies and the presentations. Care should be taken not to schedule the celebration of the rite of election on a solemnity of the liturgical year.

30.   The scrutinies should not he celebrated on solemnities, but on Sundays or even on weekdays, with the usual intervals.

PLACE OF CELEBRATION

31.   The rites should be celebrated in the places appropriate to them as indicated in the ritual. Consideration should be given to special needs that arise in secondary stations or mission territories.

ADAPTATIONS BY THE CONFERENCES OF BISHOPS IN THE USE OF THE ROMAN RITUAL

32.   In addition to the adaptations envisioned in *Christian Initiation*, General Introduction (nos. 30–33), the rite of Christian initiation of adults allows for other adaptations that will be decided by the conference of bishops.

The conference of bishops has discretionary power to make the following decisions:

1. to establish for the precatechumenate, where it seems advisable, some way of receiving inquirers who are interested in the catechumenate (see no. 39);

2. to insert into the rite of acceptance into the order of catechumens a first exorcism and a renunciation of false worship, in regions where paganism is widespread (see nos. 69–72) [The National Conference of Catholic Bishops has approved leaving to the discretion of the diocesan bishop this inclusion of a first exorcism and a renunciation of false worship in the rite of acceptance into the order of catechumens];

3. to decide that in the same rite the tracing of the sign of the cross upon the forehead (nos. 54–55) be replaced by making that sign in front of the forehead, in regions where the act of touching may not seem proper [The National Conference of Catholic Bishops has established as the norm in the dioceses of the United States the tracing of the cross on the forehead. It leaves to the discretion of the diocesan bishop the substitution of making the sign of the cross in front of the forehead for those persons in whose culture the act of touching may not seem proper];

4. to decide that in the same rite candidates receive a new name in regions where it is the practice of non-Christian religions to give a new name to initiates immediately (no. 73) [The National Conference of Catholic Bishops establishes as the norm in the dioceses of the United States that there is to be no giving of a new name. It also approves leaving to the discretion of the diocesan bishop the giving of a new name to persons from those cultures in which it is the practice of non-Christian religions to give a new name];

5. to allow within the same rite, according to local customs, additional rites that symbolize reception into the community (no. 74) [The National Conference of Catholic Bishops has approved the inclusion of an optional presentation of a cross (no. 74) while leaving to the discretion of the diocesan bishop the inclusion of additional rites that symbolize reception into the community];

6. to establish during the period of the catechumenate, in addition to the usual rites (nos. 81–97), "rites of passage": for example, early celebration of the presentations (nos. 157–163, 178–184), the ephphetha rite, the catechumens' recitation of the Creed, or even an anointing of the catechumens (nos. 98–103) [The National Conference of Catholic Bishops approves the use of the anointing with the oil of catechumens during the period of

the catechumenate as a kind of "rite of passage" (see no. 33.7). In addition it approves when appropriate in the circumstances, the early celebration of the presentations (nos. 157–163, 178–184), the ephphetha rite (nos. 197–199), and the catechumens' recitation of the Creed (nos. 193–196)];

7. to decide on the omission of the anointing with the oil of catechumens or its transferral to the preparation rites for Holy Saturday or its use during the period of the catechumenate as a kind of "rite of passage" (nos. 98–103) [The National Conference of Catholic Bishops approves the omission of the anointing with the oil of catechumens both in the celebration of baptism and in the optional preparation rites for Holy Saturday. Thus, anointing with the oil of catechumens is reserved for use in the period of the catechumenate and in the period of purification and enlightenment and is not to be included in the preparation rites on Holy Saturday or in the celebration of initiation at the Easter Vigil or at another time];

8. to make more specific and detailed the formularies of renunciation for the rite of acceptance into the order of catechumens (nos. 70–72) and for the celebration of baptism (no. 224) [The National Conference of Catholic Bishops has established as the norm in the dioceses of the United States that the formularies of renunciation should not be adapted. But for those cases where certain catechumens may be from cultures in which false worship is widespread it has approved leaving to the discretion of the diocesan bishop this matter of making more specific and detailed the formularies of renunciation in the rite of acceptance into the order of catechumens and in the celebration of baptism].

ADAPTATIONS BY THE BISHOP

34. It pertains to the bishop for his own diocese:

1. to set up the formation program of the catechumenate and to lay down norms according to local needs (see no. 12);

2. to decide whether and when, as circumstances warrant, the entire rite of Christian initiation may be celebrated outside the usual times (see no. 26);

3. to dispense, on the basis of some serious obstacle, from one scrutiny or, in extraordinary circumstances, even from two (see no. 331);

4. to permit the simple rite to be used in whole or in part (see no. 331);

5. to depute catechists, truly worthy and properly prepared, to give the exorcisms and blessings (see nos. 12, 16);

6. to preside at the rite of election and to ratify, personally or through a delegate, the admission of the elect (see no. 12);

7. in keeping with the provisions of law,[14] to stipulate the requisite age for sponsors (see *Christian Initiation*, General Introduction, no. 10.2).

35.   Celebrants should make full and intelligent use of the freedom given to them either in *Christian Initiation*, General Introduction (no. 34) or in the rubrics of the rite itself. In many places the manner of acting or praying is intentionally left undetermined or two alternatives are offered, so that ministers, according to their prudent pastoral judgment, may accommodate the rite to the circumstances of the candidates and others who are present. In all the rites the greatest freedom is left in the invitations and instructions, and the intercessions may always be shortened, changed, or even expanded with new intentions, in order to fit the circumstances or special situation of the candidates (for example, a sad or joyful event occurring in a family) or of the others present (for example, sorrow or joy common to the parish or civic community).

The minister will also adapt the texts by changing the gender and number as required.

OUTLINE FOR CHRISTIAN INITIATION OF ADULTS

PERIOD OF EVANGELIZATION AND PRECATECHUMENATE

This is a time, of no fixed duration or structure, for inquiry and introduction to Gospel values, an opportunity for the beginnings of faith.

FIRST STEP: ACCEPTANCE INTO THE ORDER OF CATECHUMENS

This is the liturgical rite, usually celebrated on some annual date or dates, marking the beginning of the catechumenate proper, as the candidates express and the Church accepts their intention to respond to God's call to follow the way of Christ.

PERIOD OF THE CATECHUMENATE

This is the time, in duration corresponding to the progress of the individual, for the nurturing and growth of the catechumens' faith and conversion to God; celebrations of the word and prayers of exorcism and blessing are meant to assist the process.

SECOND STEP: ELECTION OR ENROLLMENT OF NAMES

This is the liturgical rite, usually celebrated on the First Sunday of Lent, by which the Church formally ratifies the catechumens' readiness for the sacraments of initiation and the catechumens, now the elect, express the will to receive these sacraments.

PERIOD OF PURIFICATION AND ENLIGHTENMENT

This is the time immediately preceding the elects' initiation, usually the Lenten season preceding the celebration of this initiation at the Easter Vigil; it is a time of reflection, intensely centered on conversion, marked by celebration of the scrutinies and presentations and of the preparation rites on Holy Saturday.

THIRD STEP: CELEBRATION OF THE SACRAMENTS OF INITIATION

This is the liturgical rite, usually integrated into the Easter Vigil, by which the elect are initiated through baptism, confirmation, and the eucharist.

PERIOD OF POSTBAPTISMAL CATECHESIS OR MYSTAGOGY

This is the time, usually the Easter season, following the celebration of initiation, during which the newly initiated experience being fully a part of the Christian community by means of pertinent catechesis and particularly by participation with all the faithful in the Sunday eucharistic celebration.

PERIOD OF EVANGELIZATION AND PRECATECHUMENATE

36.   Although the rite of initiation begins with admission to the catechumenate, the preceding period or precatechumenate is of great importance and as a rule should not be omitted. It is a time of evangelization: faithfully and constantly the living God is proclaimed and Jesus Christ whom he has sent for the salvation of all. Thus those who are not yet Christians, their hearts opened by the Holy Spirit, may believe and be freely converted to the Lord and commit themselves sincerely to him. For he who is the way, the truth, and the life fulfills all their spiritual expectations, indeed infinitely surpasses them.[15]

37.   From evangelization, completed with the help of God, come the faith and initial conversion that cause a person to feel called away from sin and drawn into the mystery of God's love. The whole period of the precatechumenate is set aside for this evangelization, so that the genuine will to follow Christ and seek baptism may mature.

38.   During this period, priests and deacons, catechists and other laypersons are to give the candidates a suitable explanation of the Gospel (see no. 42). The candidates are to receive help and attention so that with a purified and clearer intention they may cooperate with God's grace. Opportunities should be provided for them to meet families and other groups of Christians.

39.   It belongs to the conference of bishops to provide for the evangelization proper to this period. The conference may also provide, if circumstances suggest and in keeping with local custom, a preliminary manner of receiving those interested in the precatechumenate, that is, those inquirers who, even though they do not fully believe, show some leaning toward the Christian faith (and who may be called "sympathizers").

   1. Such a reception, if it takes place, will be carried out without any ritual celebration; it is the expression not yet of faith, but of a right intention.

   2. The reception will be adapted to local conditions and to the pastoral situation. Some candidates may need to see evidence of the spirit of Christians that they are striving to understand and experience. For others, however, whose catechumenate will be delayed for one reason or another, some initial act of the candidates or the community that expresses their reception may be appropriate.

   3. The reception will be held at a meeting or gathering of the local community, on an occasion that will permit friendly conversation. An inquirer or "sympathizer" is introduced by a friend and then welcomed and received by the priest or some other representative member of the community.

40.   During the precatechumenate period, parish priests (pastors) should help those taking part in it with prayers suited to them, for example, by celebrating for their spiritual well-being the prayers of exorcism and the blessings given in the ritual (nos. 94, 97).

FIRST STEP: ACCEPTANCE INTO THE ORDER OF CATECHUMENS

41. The rite that is called the rite of acceptance into the order of catechumens is of the utmost importance. Assembling publicly for the first time, the candidates who have completed the period of the precatechumenate declare their intention to the Church and the Church in turn, carrying out its apostolic mission, accepts them as persons who intend to become its members. God showers his grace on the candidates, since the celebration manifests their desire publicly and marks their reception and first consecration by the Church.

42. The prerequisite for making this first step is that the beginnings of the spiritual life and the fundamentals of Christian teaching have taken root in the candidates.[16] Thus there must be evidence of the first faith that was conceived during the period of evangelization and precatechumenate and of an initial conversion and intention to change their lives and to enter into a relationship with God in Christ. Consequently, there must also be evidence of the first stirrings of repentance, a start to the practice of calling upon God in prayer, a sense of the Church, and some experience of the company and spirit of Christians through contact with a priest or with members of the community. The candidates should also be instructed about the celebration of the liturgical rite of acceptance.

43. Before the rite is celebrated, therefore, sufficient and necessary time, as required in each case, should be set aside to evaluate and, if necessary, to purify the candidates' motives and dispositions. With the help of the sponsors (see no. 10), catechists, and deacons, parish priests (pastors) have the responsibility for judging the outward indications of such dispositions.[17] Because of the effect of baptism once validly received (see *Christian Initiation*, General Introduction, no. 4), it is the duty of parish priests (pastors) to see to it that no baptized person seeks for any reason whatever to be baptized a second time.

44. The rite will take place on specified days during the year (see no. 18) that are suited to local conditions. The rite consists in the reception of the candidates, the celebration of the word of God, and the dismissal of the candidates; celebration of the eucharist may follow.

By decision of the conference of bishops, the following may be incorporated into this rite: a first exorcism and renunciation of false worship (nos. 70–72), the giving of a new name (no. 73), and additional rites signifying reception into the community (no. 74). [See no. 33 for the decisions made by the National Conference of Catholic Bishops regarding these matters.]

45. It is desirable that the entire Christian community or some part of it, consisting of friends and acquaintances, catechists and priests, take an active part in the celebration. The presiding celebrant is a priest or a deacon. The sponsors should also attend in order to present to the Church the candidates they have brought.

46.   After the celebration of the rite of acceptance, the names of the catechumens are to be duly inscribed in the register of catechumens, along with the names of the sponsors and the minister and the date and place of the celebration.

47.   From this time on the Church embraces the catechumens as its own with a mother's love and concern. Joined to the Church, the catechumens are now part of the household of Christ,[18] since the Church nourishes them with the word of God and sustains them by means of liturgical celebrations. The catechumens should be eager, then, to take part in celebrations of the word of God and to receive blessings and other sacramentals. When two catechumens marry or when a catechumen marries an unbaptized person, the appropriate rite is to be used.[19] One who dies during the catechumenate receives a Christian burial.

PERIOD OF THE CATECHUMENATE

75.   The catechumenate is an extended period during which the candidates are given suitable pastoral formation and guidance, aimed at training them in the Christian life.[20] In this way, the dispositions manifested at their acceptance into the catechumenate are brought to maturity. This is achieved in four ways.

1. A suitable catechesis is provided by priests or deacons, or by catechists and others of the faithful, planned to be gradual and complete in its coverage, accommodated to the liturgical year, and solidly supported by celebrations of the word. This catechesis leads the catechumens not only to an appropriate acquaintance with dogmas and precepts but also to a profound sense of the mystery of salvation in which they desire to participate.

2. As they become familiar with the Christian way of life and are helped by the example and support of sponsors, godparents, and the entire Christian community, the catechumens learn to turn more readily to God in prayer, to bear witness to the faith, in all things to keep their hopes set on Christ, to follow supernatural inspiration in their deeds, and to practice love of neighbor, even at the cost of self-renunciation. Thus formed, "the newly converted set out on a spiritual journey. Already sharing through faith in the mystery of Christ's death and resurrection, they pass from the old to a new nature made perfect in Christ. Since this transition brings with it a progressive change of outlook and conduct, it should become manifest by means of its social consequences and it should develop gradually during the period of the catechumenate. Since the Lord in whom they believe is a sign of contradiction, the newly converted often experience divisions and separations, but they also taste the joy that God gives without measure."[21]

3. The Church, like a mother, helps the catechumens on their journey by means of suitable liturgical rites, which purify the catechumens little by little and strengthen them with God's blessing. Celebrations of the word of God are arranged for their benefit, and at Mass they may also take part

with the faithful in the liturgy of the word, thus better preparing themselves for their eventual participation in the liturgy of the eucharist. Ordinarily, however, when they are present in the assembly of the faithful they should be kindly dismissed before the liturgy of the eucharist begins (unless their dismissal would present practical or pastoral problems). For they must await their baptism, which will join them to God's priestly people and empower them to participate in Christ's new worship (see no. 67 for formularies of dismissal).

4. Since the Church's life is apostolic, catechumens should also learn how to work actively with others to spread the Gospel and build up the Church by the witness of their lives and by professing their faith.[22]

76.　The duration of the catechumenate will depend on the grace of God and on various circumstances, such as the program of instruction for the catechumenate, the number of catechists, deacons, and priests, the cooperation of the individual catechumens, the means necessary for them to come to the site of the catechumenate and spend time there, the help of the local community. Nothing, therefore, can be settled a priori.

The time spent in the catechumenate should be long enough — several years if necessary — for the conversion and faith of the catechumens to become strong. By their formation in the entire Christian life and a sufficiently prolonged probation the catechumens are properly initiated into the mysteries of salvation and the practice of an evangelical way of life. By means of sacred rites celebrated at successive times they are led into the life of faith, worship, and charity belonging to the people of God.

77.　It is the responsibility of the bishop to fix the duration and to direct the program of the catechumenate. The conference of bishops, after considering the conditions of its people and region,[23] may also wish to provide specific guidelines. At the discretion of the bishop, on the basis of the spiritual preparation of the candidate, the period of the catechumenate may in particular cases be shortened (see nos. 331–335); in altogether extraordinary cases the catechumenate may be completed all at once (see nos. 332, 336–369).

78.　The instruction that the catechumens receive during this period should be of a kind that while presenting Catholic teaching in its entirety also enlightens faith, directs the heart toward God, fosters participation in the liturgy, inspires apostolic activity, and nurtures a life completely in accord with the spirit of Christ.

79.　Among the rites belonging to the period of the catechumenate, then, celebrations of the word of God (nos. 81–89) are foremost. The minor exorcisms (nos. 90–94) and the blessings of the catechumens (nos. 95–97) are ordinarily celebrated in conjunction with a celebration of the word. In addition, other rites may be celebrated to mark the passage of the catechumens from one level of catechesis to another: for example, an anointing of the catechumens may be celebrated (nos. 98–103) and the presentations of the Creed and the Lord's Prayer may be anticipated (see nos. 104–105).

80. During the period of the catechumenate, the catechumens should give thought to choosing the godparents who will present them to the Church on the day of their election (see no. 11; also *Christian Initiation, General Introduction,* nos. 8–10).

Provision should also be made for the entire community involved in the formation of the catechumens — priests, deacons, catechists, sponsors, godparents, friends and neighbors — to participate in some of the celebrations belonging to the catechumenate, including any of the optional "rites of passage" (nos. 98–105).

SECOND STEP: ELECTION OR ENROLLMENT OF NAMES

118. The second step in Christian initiation is the liturgical rite called both election and the enrollment of names, which closes the period of the catechumenate proper, that is, the lengthy period of formation of the catechumens' minds and hearts. The celebration of the rite of election, which usually coincides with the opening of Lent, also marks the beginning of the period of final, more intense preparation for the sacraments of initiation, during which the elect will be encouraged to follow Christ with greater generosity.

119. At this second step, on the basis of the testimony of godparents and catechists and of the catechumens' reaffirmation of their intention, the Church judges their state of readiness and decides on their advancement toward the sacraments of initiation. Thus the Church makes its "election," that is, the choice and admission of those catechumens who have the dispositions that make them fit to take part, at the next major celebration, in the sacraments of initiation.

This step is called election because the acceptance made by the Church is founded on the election by God, in whose name the Church acts. The step is also called the enrollment of names because as a pledge of fidelity the candidates inscribe their names in the book that lists those who have been chosen for initiation.

120. Before the rite of election is celebrated, the catechumens are expected to have undergone a conversion in mind and in action and to have developed a sufficient acquaintance with Christian teaching as well as a spirit of faith and charity. With deliberate will and an enlightened faith they must have the intention to receive the sacraments of the Church, a resolve they will express publicly in the actual celebration of the rite.

121. The election, marked with a rite of such solemnity, is the focal point of the Church's concern for the catechumens. Admission to election therefore belongs

to the bishop, and the presiding celebrant for the rite of election is the bishop himself or a priest or a deacon who acts as the bishop's delegate (see no. 12).

Before the rite of election the bishop, priests, deacons, catechists, godparents, and the entire community, in accord with their respective responsibilities and in their own way, should, after considering the matter carefully, arrive at a judgment about the catechumens' state of formation and progress. After the election, they should surround the elect with prayer, so that the entire Church will accompany and lead them to encounter Christ.

122. Within the rite of election the bishop celebrant or his delegate declares in the presence of the community the Church's approval of the candidates. Therefore to exclude any semblance of mere formality from the rite, there should be a deliberation prior to its celebration to decide on the catechumens' suitableness. This deliberation is carried out by the priests, deacons, and catechists involved in the formation of the catechumens and by the godparents and representatives of the local community. If circumstances suggest, the group of catechumens may also take part. The deliberation may take various forms, depending on local conditions and pastoral needs. During the celebration of election, the assembly is informed of the decision approving the catechumens.

123. Before the rite of election godparents are chosen by the catechumens; the choice should be made with the consent of the priest, and the persons chosen should, as far as possible, be approved for their role by the local community (see no. 11). In the rite of election the godparents exercise their ministry publicly for the first time. They are called by name at the beginning of the rite to come forward with the catechumens (no. 130); they give testimony on behalf of the catechumens before the Community (no. 131); they may also write their names along with the catechumens in the book of the elect (no. 132).

124. From the day of their election and admission, the catechumens are called "the elect." They are also described as *competentes* ("co-petitioners"), because they are joined together in asking for and aspiring to receive the three sacraments of Christ and the gift of the Holy Spirit. They are also called *illuminandi* ("those who will be enlightened"), because baptism itself has been called *illuminatio* ("enlightenment") and it fills the newly baptized with the light of faith. In our own times, other names may be applied to the elect that, depending on regions and cultures, are better suited to the people's understanding and the idiom of the language.

125. The bishop celebrant or his delegate, however much or little he was involved in the deliberation prior to the rite, has the responsibility of showing in the homily or elsewhere during the celebration the religious and ecclesial significance of the election. The celebrant also declares before all present the Church's decision and, if appropriate in the circumstances, asks the community to express its approval of the candidates. He also asks the catechumens to give a personal expression of their intention and, in the name of the Church, he carries out the act of admitting them as elect. The celebrant should open to all the divine mystery expressed in the call of the Church and in the liturgical celebration of

this mystery. He should remind the faithful to give good example to the elect and along with the elect to prepare themselves for the Easter solemnities.

126. The sacraments of initiation are celebrated during the Easter solemnities, and preparation for these sacraments is part of the distinctive character of Lent. Accordingly, the rite of election should normally take place on the First Sunday of Lent and the period of final preparation of the elect should coincide with the Lenten season. The plan arranged for the Lenten season will benefit the elect by reason of both its liturgical structure and the participation of the community. For urgent pastoral reasons, especially in secondary mission stations, it is permitted to celebrate the rite of election during the week preceding or following the First Sunday of Lent.

When, because of unusual circumstances and pastoral needs, the rite of election is celebrated outside Lent, it is to be celebrated about six weeks before the sacraments of initiation, in order to allow sufficient time for the scrutinies and presentations. The rite is not to be celebrated on a solemnity of the liturgical year (see no. 29).

127. The rite should take place in the cathedral church, in a parish church or, if necessary, in some other suitable and fitting place.

128. The rite is celebrated within Mass, after the homily, and should be celebrated within the Mass of the First Sunday of Lent. If, for pastoral reasons, the rite is celebrated on a different day, the texts and the readings of the ritual Mass "Christian Initiation: Election or Enrollment of Names" may always be used. When the Mass of the day is celebrated and its readings are not suitable, the readings are those given for the First Sunday of Lent or others may be chosen from elsewhere in the Lectionary.

When celebrated outside Mass, the rite takes place after the readings and the homily and is concluded with the dismissal of both the elect and the faithful.

[An optional parish rite to send catechumens for election by the bishop precedes the rite of election and is found at no. 106.]

PERIOD OF PURIFICATION AND ENLIGHTENMENT

138. The period of purification and enlightenment, which the rite of election begins, customarily coincides with Lent. In the liturgy and liturgical catechesis of Lent the reminder of baptism already received or the preparation for its reception, as well as the theme of repentance, renew the entire community along with those being prepared to celebrate the paschal mystery, in which each of the elect will share through the sacraments of initiation.[24] For both the elect and the local community, therefore, the Lenten season is a time for spiritual recollection in preparation for the celebration of the paschal mystery.

139. This is a period of more intense spiritual preparation, consisting more in interior reflection than in catechetical instruction, and is intended to purify

the minds and hearts of the elect as they search their own consciences and do penance. This period is intended as well to enlighten the minds and hearts of the elect with a deeper knowledge of Christ the Savior. The celebration of certain rites, particularly the scrutinies (see nos. 141–146) and the presentations (see nos. 147–149), brings about this process of purification and enlightenment and extends it over the course of the entire Lenten season.

140. Holy Saturday is the day of proximate preparation for the celebration of the sacraments of initiation and on that day the rites of preparation (see nos. 185–192) may be celebrated.

THIRD STEP: CELEBRATION OF THE SACRAMENTS OF INITIATION

206. The third step in the Christian initiation of adults is the celebration of the sacraments of baptism, confirmation, and eucharist. Through this final step the elect, receiving pardon for their sins, are admitted into the people of God. They are graced with adoption as children of God and are led by the Holy Spirit into the promised fullness of time begun in Christ[25] and, as they share in the eucharistic sacrifice and meal, even to a foretaste of the kingdom of God.

207. The usual time for the celebration of the sacraments of initiation is the Easter Vigil (see no. 23), at which preferably the bishop himself presides as celebrant, at least for the initiation of those who are fourteen years old or older (see no. 12). As indicated in the Roman Missal, "Easter Vigils" (no. 44), the conferral of the sacraments follows the blessing of the water.

208. When the celebration takes place outside the usual time (see nos. 26–27), care should be taken to ensure that it has a markedly paschal character (see *Christian Initiation, General Introduction, no. 6*). Thus the texts for one of the ritual Masses "Christian Initiation: Baptism" given in the Roman Missal are used, and the readings are chosen from those given in the Lectionary for Mass, "Celebration of the Sacraments of Initiation apart from the Easter Vigil."

CELEBRATION OF BAPTISM

209. The celebration of baptism has as its center and high point the baptismal washing and the invocation of the Holy Trinity. Beforehand there are rites that have an inherent relationship to the baptismal washing: first, the blessing of water, then the renunciation of sin by the elect, and their profession of faith. Following the baptismal washing, the effects received through this sacrament are given expression in the explanatory rites: the anointing with chrism (when confirmation does not immediately follow baptism), the clothing with a white garment, and the presentation of a lighted candle.

210. PRAYER OVER THE WATER: The celebration of baptism begins with the blessing of water, even when the sacraments of initiation are received outside the

Easter season. Should the sacraments be celebrated outside the Easter Vigil but during the Easter season (see no. 26), the water blessed at the Vigil is used, but a prayer of thanksgiving, having the same themes as the blessing, is included. The blessing declares the religious meaning of water as God's creation and the sacramental use of water in the unfolding of the paschal mystery, and the blessing is also a remembrance of God's wonderful works in the history of salvation.

The blessing thus introduces an invocation of the Trinity at the very outset of the celebration of baptism. For it calls to mind the mystery of God's love from the beginning of the world and the creation of the human race; by invoking the Holy Spirit and proclaiming Christ's death and resurrection, it impresses on the mind the newness of Christian baptism, by which we share in his own death and resurrection and receive the holiness of God himself.

211. RENUNCIATION OF SIN AND PROFESSION OF FAITH: In their renunciation of sin and profession of faith those to be baptized express their explicit faith in the paschal mystery that has already been recalled in the blessing of water and that will be connoted by the words of the sacrament soon to be spoken by the baptizing minister. Adults are not saved unless they come forward of their own accord and with the will to accept God's gift through their own belief. The faith of those to be baptized is not simply the faith of the Church, but the personal faith of each one of them and each one of them is expected to keep it a living faith.

Therefore the renunciation of sin and the profession of faith are an apt prelude to baptism, the sacrament of that faith by which the elect hold fast to God and receive new birth from him. Because of the renunciation of sin and the profession of faith, which form the one rite, the elect will not be baptized merely passively but will receive this great sacrament with the active resolve to renounce error and to hold fast to God. By their own personal act in the rite of renouncing sin and professing their faith, the elect, as was prefigured in the first covenant with the patriarchs, renounce sin and Satan in order to commit themselves for ever to the promise of the Savior and to the mystery of the Trinity. By professing their faith before the celebrant and the entire community, the elect express the intention, developed to maturity during the preceding periods of initiation, to enter into a new covenant with Christ. Thus these adults embrace the faith that through divine help the Church has handed down, and are baptized in that faith.

212. BAPTISM: Immediately after their profession of living faith in Christ's paschal mystery, the elect come forward and receive that mystery as expressed in the washing with water; thus once the elect have professed faith in the Father, Son, and Holy Spirit, invoked by the celebrant, the divine persons act so that those they have chosen receive divine adoption and become members of the people of God.

213. Therefore in the celebration of baptism the washing with water should take on its full importance as the sign of that mystical sharing in Christ's death and resurrection through which those who believe in his name die to sin and rise to eternal life. Either immersion or the pouring of water should be chosen

for the rite, whichever will serve in individual cases and in the various traditions and circumstances to ensure the clear understanding that this washing is not a mere purification rite but the sacrament of being joined to Christ.

214. EXPLANATORY RITES: The baptismal washing is followed by rites that give expression to the effects of the sacrament just received. The anointing with chrism is a sign of the royal priesthood of the baptized and that they are now numbered in the company of the people of God. The clothing with the baptismal garment signifies the new dignity they have received. The presentation of a lighted candle shows that they are called to walk as befits the children of the light.

CELEBRATION OF CONFIRMATION

215. In accord with the ancient practice followed in the Roman liturgy, adults are not to be baptized without receiving confirmation immediately afterward, unless some serious reason stands in the way. The conjunction of the two celebrations signifies the unity of the paschal mystery, the close link between the mission of the Son and the outpouring of the Holy Spirit, and the connection between the two sacraments through which the Son and the Holy Spirit come with the Father to those who are baptized.

216. Accordingly, confirmation is conferred after the explanatory rites of baptism, the anointing after baptism (no. 228) being omitted.

THE NEOPHYTES FIRST SHARING IN THE CELEBRATION OF THE EUCHARIST

217. Finally in the celebration of the eucharist, as they take part for the first time and with full right, the newly baptized reach the culminating point in their Christian initiation. In this eucharist the neophytes, now raised to the ranks of the royal priesthood, have an active part both in the general intercessions and, to the extent possible, in bringing the gifts to the altar. With the entire community they share in the offering of the sacrifice and say the Lord's Prayer, giving expression to the spirit of adoption as God's children that they have received in baptism. When in communion they receive the body that was given for us and the blood that was shed, the neophytes are strengthened in the gifts they have already received and are given a foretaste of the eternal banquet.

PERIOD OF POSTBAPTISMAL CATECHESIS OR MYSTAGOGY

244. The third step of Christian initiation, the celebration of the sacraments, is followed by the final period, the period of postbaptismal catechesis or mystagogy. This is a time for the community and the neophytes together to grow in deepening their grasp of the paschal mystery and in making it part of their lives through meditation on the Gospel, sharing in the eucharist, and doing the works of charity. To strengthen the neophytes as they begin to walk in newness of life, the community of the faithful, their godparents, and their parish priests (pastors) should give them thoughtful and friendly help.

245. The neophytes are, as the term "mystagogy" suggests, introduced into a fuller and more effective understanding of mysteries through the Gospel message they have learned and above all through their experience of the sacraments they have received. For they have truly been renewed in mind, tasted more deeply the sweetness of God's word, received the fellowship of the Holy Spirit, and grown to know the goodness of the Lord. Out of this experience, which belongs to Christians and increases as it is lived, they derive a new perception of the faith, of the Church, and of the world.

246. Just as their new participation in the sacraments enlightens the neophytes' understanding of the Scriptures, so too it increases their contact with the rest of the faithful and has an impact on the experience of the community. As a result, interaction between the neophytes and the faithful is made easier and more beneficial. The period of postbaptismal catechesis is of great significance for both the neophytes and the rest of the faithful. Through it the neophytes, with the help of their godparents, should experience a full and joyful welcome into the community and enter into closer ties with the other faithful. The faithful, in turn, should derive from it a renewal of inspiration and of outlook.

247. Since the distinctive spirit and power of the period of postbaptismal catechesis or mystagogy derive from the new, personal experience of the sacraments and of the community, its main setting is the so-called Masses for neophytes, that is, the Sunday Masses of the Easter season. Besides being occasions for the newly baptized to gather with the community and share in the mysteries, these celebrations include particularly suitable readings from the Lectionary, especially the readings for Year A. Even when Christian initiation has been celebrated outside the usual times, the texts for these Sunday Masses of the Easter season may be used.

248. All the neophytes and their godparents should make an effort to take part in the Masses for the neophytes and the entire local community should be invited to participate with them. Special places in the congregation are to be reserved for the neophytes and their godparents. The homily and, as circumstances suggest, the general intercessions should take into account the presence and needs of the neophytes.

249. To close the period of postbaptismal catechesis, some sort of celebration should be held at the end of the Easter season near Pentecost Sunday; festivities in keeping with local custom may accompany the occasion.

250. On the anniversary of their baptism the neophytes should be brought together in order to give thanks to God, to share with one another their spiritual experiences, and to renew their commitment.

251. To show his pastoral concern for these new members of the Church, the bishop, particularly if he was unable to preside at the sacraments of initiation himself, should arrange, if possible, to meet the recently baptized at least once in the year and to preside at a celebration of the eucharist with them. At this Mass they may receive holy communion under both kinds.

NOTES

1. See SC, 64–66; AG, 14; CD, 14.

2. See SC, 109.

3. See AG, 14.

4. See LG, 17.

5. See AA, 6.

6. See *Christian Initiation*, General Introduction, nos. 8 and 10.1.

7. See *Christian Initiation*, General Introduction, 12.

8. See *Christian Initiation*, General Introduction, 13–15.

9. See PO, 6.

10. See *Rite of Confirmation*, Introduction, no. 7b.

11. See *Rite of Confirmation*, no. 8.

12. See LG, 26; AG, 16.

13. See SC, 79.

14. See CIC, can. 874, §1, 2.

15. See AG, 13.

16. See AG, 14.

17. See AG, 13.

18. See LG, 14; AG, 14.

19. See *Rite of Marriage*, 55–66.

20. See AG, 14.

21. AG, 13.

22. See AG, 14.

23. See SC, 64.

24. See AG, 14.

25. See LG, 48; also Ephesians 1:10.

THE CHALLENGE
OF
ADOLESCENT CATECHESIS:
MATURING IN FAITH

1986

OVERVIEW OF *THE CHALLENGE OF ADOLESCENT CATECHESIS: MATURING IN FAITH*

by Carole M. Eipers

"Precisely because of the many different possibilities, the time of adolescence is a unique opportunity for the Catholic Christian community to affirm, support and challenge young people to grow as persons and believers." The introduction to *The Challenge of Adolescent Catechesis* (CAC) articulates our conviction that adolescence is a moment in life's journey when the potential for people to develop as disciples of Jesus is enormous. It hints also at our concern, given the developmental tasks of adolescence and the "different possibilities," that our young people may turn to sources other than the church community to satisfy their needs. The statement as well belies, perhaps, a communal self-doubt. Can we provide the resources required to enable our adolescents to flourish in their Christian commitment in a society that is increasingly hostile to the gospel?

Raising both the opportunities of adolescence and our fears for the futures of our young people is an appropriate opening for this document. The statement encapsulates the challenge of adolescent catechesis; the document then declares "a vision and direction for adolescent catechesis" to meet the challenge.

LINEAGE AND GENESIS

The Challenge of Adolescent Catechesis traces its genealogy to its roots in the scriptures; it is also related intimately to other key documents. *The Challenge of Adolescent Catechesis* both expands and distills elements from its predecessors. Understanding it and implementing its vision faithfully requires a working knowledge of the documents that informed its direction. *The Challenge of Adolescent Catechesis* includes citations from six documents that contribute to its perspective and its content: *The Pastoral Constitution on the Church in the Modern World* (Vatican II, 1965), the *General Catechetical Directory* (Congregation for the Clergy, 1971), *A Vision of Youth Ministry* (USCC, Department of Education, 1976), *On Catechesis in Our Time* (CT) (John Paul II, 1979), *Sharing the Light of Faith: National Catechetical Directory for Catholics of the United States* (NCD) (NCCB, 1979) and *The Christian Family in the Modern World* (John Paul II, 1981). The inclusion of most of these documents in this volume provides a unique opportunity to view the CAC within its context of documentary development. It relies most heavily on CT and the NCD as the bases for its catechetical foundations; other contemporary authors are used as resources concerning adolescent maturation and Christian faith development.

The Challenge of Adolescent Catechesis represents a consultative effort with many "levels" of ministry: parish, diocesan, regional and national. It represents grassroots input and the collaborative distillation of these practitioners' insights by four major agencies. Representatives from the National Conference of Diocesan Directors of Religious Education (NCDD, now the National Conference of Catechetical Leadership); the National Catholic Educational Association (NCEA); the Desk for Youth and Young Adult Ministry, Department of Education, United States Catholic Conference (USCC) and the National Federation for Catholic Youth Ministry (NFCYM). The effectiveness of their collaboration is evidenced in the inclusiveness of ministerial roles for adolescent catechesis. The document's simultaneous publication in English and Spanish demonstrates another dimension of its inclusivity.

INTRODUCTION

The introduction to the CAC reiterates several broad concepts regarding catechesis and their particular application to adolescents.

First, it acknowledges the primacy of catechesis for adults: "Effective catechesis with youth requires that the adult members of our community grow continually in their faith and in their ability to share it with others." Second, it sees adolescents in the context of their communities and families: Effective adolescent catechesis "can lead to a richer life for the entire Catholic Christian community and for the family." Third, it recognizes that the catechesis of adolescents must address their unique stages of development, which "can be exciting" but also "can be depressing, alienating and filled with self-doubt and anxiety." Fourth, it builds on the integrated approach to the catechesis of adolescents set forth in *A Vision of Youth Ministry* (USCC, 1976). This approach encompasses "a coordinated, multidimensional ministry of word, worship, justice/service, community life, guidance/healing, enablement and advocacy."

These concepts inform the development of the "vision and direction for adolescent catechesis." While these concepts are focused naturally on adolescents in this document, their application to all catechetical efforts is supported by prior documents.

FOUNDATIONS OF ADOLESCENT CATECHESIS

The initial section of the CAC sets forth six foundational themes: "Jesus, discipleship, mission and ministries, faith, the developing human person and the community."

Adolescent catechesis is first "rooted in Jesus Christ." This theme echoes the words of CT: "At the heart of catechesis we find, in essence, a person, the person of Jesus of Nazareth" (CT, 5). To set rootedness in Jesus Christ as the first of the faith themes is to remember that "the definitive aim of catechesis is to put people not only in touch but in communion, in intimacy, with Jesus Christ" (CT, 5). The document anchors the second theme, Christian discipleship, in the gospel call to repentance and faith. This theme notes the price of responding to Jesus' call and that all disciples share in Jesus' mission.

The third theme focuses on the role of the church to carry on Jesus' work of proclaiming the gospel, of building community, of worship and of service and healing. It then highlights catechesis, its vital relationship with other ecclesial ministries and the responsibility of the entire faith community concerning the catechesis of adolescents. This theme also addresses the relationship of catechesis to the broader ministry of evangelization. This relationship has now been elaborated more fully in a subsequent document, *The Challenge of Catholic*

Youth Evangelization (NFCYM, 1993), and is elucidated also in the NCD (34, 35) and in *On Evangelization in the Modern World* (44).

The fourth theme addresses three dimensions of Christian faith: affective, cognitive and behavioral. This section relies on the work of Thomas Groome to develop the catechetical activities of "trusting, believing and doing." This holistic thrust is crucial to the whole catechetical enterprise and certainly to adolescent catechesis. Neglect of any of these three activities makes for an unbalanced catechesis at best.

The fifth theme calls attention to the indispensable adaptation of catechesis to the development of those catechized. This section is rooted in the perspectives articulated in the NCD and CT. Adolescence, it reminds us, is appropriately a time for questioning; it also recalls that "maturity in Christian faith is a life-long journey." These two points call the catechist to be open to questions and patient as the young person comes to "personally owned" answers. Contemporary studies in psychology and sociology since the publication of this document call our attention to the multifaceted nature of human development. Effective adolescent catechesis will attend to these facets in designing programs and processes: human development, faith and moral development, cultural and ethnic influences, gender differences and socioeconomic factors. The young people to be catechized are not simply adolescents.

The sixth theme recognizes that life in community is integral to discipleship. This section is rooted again in scripture and cites documents that address various aspects of Christian community: *The Christian Family in the Modern World*, the NCD and the *Pastoral Constitution on the Church in the Modern World*.

The family is the primary Christian community. That "parents strengthen the faith of adolescents in many ways" is an underestimated fact in adolescent catechesis. An overemphasis on peer activities loses sight of a key point in this theme: "A family perspective needs to be woven throughout adolescent catechesis." Those who minister to adolescents do so to "assist parents," or guardians, not in their stead.

The parish community is the "permanent community." Youth groups, religious education programs and Catholic high schools are enjoined to engage youth in the parish and not become communities unto themselves. This theme also addresses the reality of our multicultural, multiethnic, multiracial church and society that places unique demands and offers unique opportunities for adolescent catechesis.

These foundational themes are more or less explicit in the remainder of the document, and some are more emphasized than others. It is good, therefore, to return to this section in planning and assessing efforts in adolescent catechesis.

THE MINISTRY OF ADOLESCENT CATECHESIS

This section of the document states the aim, the process and the principles for adolescent catechesis. The aim is "to sponsor youth toward maturity in Catholic Christian faith, as a living reality." This statement is a new articulation, one that resounds with CT (5), the NCD (32, 33), the *General Catechetical Directory* (89) and *On Evangelization in the Modern World* (72). A review of the aim and purpose of catechesis in these documents can illuminate the richness behind the aim as articulated in the CAC.

Using the work of John Nelson as a basis, the section on the "Aim of Adolescent Catechesis" presents two tasks for the adults: "to foster in youth a communal identity as Catholic Christians and to help them develop their personal faith identity."

The section identifies characteristics of adolescents that can help catechists understand some generalities about adolescent development. There is also a disclaimer that is critical: These characteristics "need to be adapted to the social and cultural settings of the ministry." The "characteristics of adolescents" are clues, not definitions, and still less are they to be seen as descriptions of individual adolescent persons. The clues direct us to listening attentively to real adolescent persons.

"The Process of Adolescent Catechesis" section draws heavily from the NCD. The process suggested attends to tradition and scripture, contemporary insights and life experience as sources of God's revelation to be exploited and interrelated through the catechetical process.

There are two sets of "Principles for Developing Adolescent Catechesis." The first set, the foundational principles, are "key understandings that shape adolescent catechesis." These principles reiterate concisely points that have been stated earlier in this document. The second set, the operational principles, "describe the processes for developing adolescent catechesis." These principles concretize what it means to provide a catechesis adapted to the needs of adolescents. The tenth operational principle lays the groundwork for the next section's faith themes. The principles included in this section, both formational and operational, are applicable to the catechetical enterprise for all ages.

A FRAMEWORK FOR ADOLESCENT CATECHESIS

The framework begins with "six integral dimensions" woven throughout each of the faith themes: Jesus Christ, scripture, church, prayer action and lifestyle, and interpretation and critical reflection. The section then introduces the faith themes for younger adolescents (11–12 to 14–15), giving a focus statement and suggested content for each. The same format follows considering the faith themes for older adolescents (14–15 to 18–19).

"A Framework for Adolescent Catechesis" can be of use to practitioners. It would be a mistake to take this section in isolation or without consideration of its explicit cautions: "The framework . . . is not intended to serve all needs of a given situation." Application of the framework "may also need to include additional faith themes not presented in this paper."

The framework attends to the major areas of content in adolescent catechesis from the NCD: "the study of scripture, the church, the sacraments and morality" (228). The major areas are not, however, equally attended to nor consistently present in the faith themes.

Adapting this framework to a local situation requires careful assessment of adolescent catechesis in a total catechetical plan. What catechesis have adolescents received prior to this time? What content has been stressed in their formation? What is offered for young adults? What themes will be emphasized in this later catechesis? The specific faith themes suggested presume prior catechesis and foundations of knowledge and experience. The framework provides a usable guide and format for local adolescent catechesis if the necessary assessment and adaptation occur.

LEADERS IN THE MINISTRY OF ADOLESCENT CATECHESIS

Recognizing the ideal of an adolescent catechesis that is well integrated and collaborative, this section outlines the responsibilities of "a variety of leaders with specialized roles": catechists and religion teachers, coordinators of youth ministry, directors of religious education, priests, pastoral associates, school principals, campus ministry coordinators, chairs of departments of religious studies, diocesan religious education personnel, youth ministry personnel of Catholic schools and bishops.

The section on catechists and religion teachers is the most fully developed. The qualities of catechists (NCD, 205–11) and their catechetical preparation are defined clearly. The section also draws on Charles Shelton's work *Adolescent Spirituality*. These same qualities, along with the knowledge and skills outlined, are applicable to all persons with catechetical responsibilities.

The treatment of the other roles focuses on programmatic responsibility rather than the competencies necessary to fulfill these roles effectively. Using the responsibilities as a basis, one could determine the qualities and competencies required and also define appropriate training for the roles.

Ministerial roles continue to develop and additional leaders in adolescent catechesis already are on the scene: permanent deacons, pastoral coordinators and administrators, chairpersons of religion departments in schools, catechumenate directors and coordinators, and catechists and sponsors. Defining these roles and responsibilities for adolescent catechesis will enable us to name the specific qualities and competencies required for them. The parental role, defined in the first paragraph, needs greater definition to aid with more intentional development in parish efforts.

IMPACT AND FUTURES

The preface to the CAC issues an invitation reiterated in its conclusion: "Readers of this paper are urged to reflect on the paper, react to it, criticize it and use it in assessing current efforts in adolescent catechesis and in designing and implementing new and/or renewed efforts." The first measure of the document's impact is how well we have responded to this invitation. The second measure is whether we have implemented the "vision and direction" of the document. Those parishes and schools that have effective adolescent catechesis have done their planning conscious that this ministry is "to, with, by and for youth" (*Vision*, 6).

Effective adolescent catechesis is attentive to the primacy of adult catechesis. "We cannot expect more of youth than we do of adults. The ways we adults learn about, express and live our faith is a vigorous support or a serious obstacle in effectively catechizing youth." The primacy of adult catechesis places the focus on the adult community of faith, particularly those with specific catechetical roles.

Effective adolescent catechesis is well-integrated. The dimensions of word, worship, community and service each nourish and give impetus to the others. This integration implies successful collaboration among those who have specific roles within these ministries.

Effective adolescent catechesis is developmentally sound but focused on the gospel message. While responding to the needs and experiences of adolescents, it is, nonetheless, "always an orderly and systematic initiation into the revelation that God has given of himself to humanity in Christ Jesus" (CT, 22). The employment of "minicourses" and "issue-oriented sessions" are in service to an overall plan for systematic catechesis. Those who have successfully implemented adolescent catechetical efforts have dedicated the necessary resources and personnel, chosen leaders wisely and prepared them thoroughly and continually.

The best measure of the impact of the CAC is its effect on the "young church of today." Those who were adolescents when this document was published are now 21–29 years old. How well these young adults exhibit "maturity in Catholic Christian faith as a living reality" is the litmus test of this document's impact and of the effectiveness of adolescent catechesis in the past decade.

On Catechesis in our Time states, "Catechesis is thus a permanent school of the faith and follows the major stages of life, like a beacon lighting the path." The Challenge of Adolescent Catechesis focuses the beam for the adolescent journey. If the path has been illuminated by our efforts so that adolescents see their direction as disciples and avoid the potholes, then this document has made a contribution.

These measures of the impact of the CAC are also its challenges for the future. Additionally, there are three significant issues to address for the future.

The first challenge harkens back to On Catechesis in our Time: "The catechesis of children and young people, permanent catechesis, and the catechesis of adults should not be separate watertight compartments. . . . There should be no break between them. On the contrary, their perfect complementarity must be fostered" (CT, 45). The integration and collaboration called for in the CAC needs expansion to include the catechesis that precedes and follows the adolescent period.

The second challenge is to see this document in the light of documents published after its arrival. The Revised Code of Canon Law, the Rite of Christian Initiation of Adults, the Catechism of the Catholic Church and The Challenge of Catholic Youth Evangelization offer valuable insights and further development of many catechetical areas.

The third challenge is one stated in the NCD. Its section on "Adolescence" begins with the phrase, "no specific age bracket" (180). Contemporary sociological phenomena have complicated further the stage known as "adolescence." These phenomena can accelerate the onset of adolescence and/or delay its completion. How shall we accurately define adolescence and so appropriately apply the CAC?

The conclusion of the CAC declares that "this paper is not the final word." It is, indeed, not the final word, but it is a good word. It deserves renewed attention and calls for renewed efforts at responding faithfully to the challenge of adolescent catechesis.

OUTLINE

I. INTRODUCTION

[1.]   All human beings experience change during adolescence. This change can be exciting if it awakens a deeper sense of self-identity, leads to the expansion of authentic freedom, enhances our ability to relate to others, and promotes greater maturity. However, the changes of adolescence can also be depressing, alienating, and filled with self-doubt and anxiety. Precisely because of the many divergent possibilities, the time of adolescence is a unique opportunity for the Catholic Christian community to affirm, support, and challenge young people to grow as persons and believers.

[2.]   Over the past decade, the Church has developed an all-embracing approach to ministry with youth. As articulated in A Vision of Youth Ministry (USCC, 1976), this comprehensive approach to youth recognizes their personal, familial, social, and spiritual needs and the environments that affect their lives. It also invites them into the life, mission, and work of the faith community. In the past 10 years, a coordinated, multi-dimensional ministry of Word, worship, justice/service, community life, guidance/healing, enablement, and advocacy has evolved in parishes and schools to respond to the needs of today's youth. The ongoing evangelization and catechesis of youth are essential and integral elements of fostering the maturing in faith of the "Young Church of Today."

[3.]   Adolescent catechesis is clearly in a state of transition, reflecting both the cultural and ecclesial shifts of the past two decades. The growth of catechetical theory and practice and the evolution of the Church's ministry with youth has forced Church leaders to rethink adolescent catechesis, to clarify its aim and scope, and to recognize its contribution within the broader context of ministry. Moreover, the dramatic increase in the number of coordinators of youth ministry and high school campus ministry has resulted in confusion and tension regarding responsibilities for adolescent catechesis at every level of the Church— schools, parishes, and diocesan offices. This changing and somewhat perplexing scene presents the Church with a marvelous opportunity to develop new initiatives in vision and practice that will shape adolescent catechesis.

[4.]   This paper is a serious and cooperative effort to speak in a fresh way to the needs and gifts of young people and to determine how the Church can respond to those needs and affirm those gifts through effective catechesis. God's Word when proclaimed, celebrated, shared, and lived in the Christian community is dynamic and fruitful. What an opportunity exists when the energy and giftedness of young people can be engaged with the vibrancy and richness of God's Word! The possibilities for personal development and growth in faith are then enormous and can lead to a richer life for the entire Catholic Christian community and for the family. The enthusiasm and challenge offered by young people who become more involved in the life of the Church can energize parish, home, and society.

The opportunity of engaging adolescents in the life of the Church challenges us. As youth experience and express their expanding freedom, they resist mediocre or halfhearted efforts. Effective catechesis with youth requires that the adult members of our community grow continually in their faith and in their ability to share it with others. This growth is especially necessary for the parents of adolescents. We cannot expect more of youth than we do of adults. The ways we adults learn about, express, and live our faith is a vigorous support or a serious obstacle in effectively catechizing youth.

This paper is addressed to leaders in ministry with youth and in catechetical ministry in parishes, Catholic schools, and diocesan offices. It is written to affirm, support, and encourage the creative initiatives of ministers with youth across this country and to challenge the Church in the United States to take seriously its catechetical ministry with "The Young Church of Today." By proposing the aim, process, and principles for adolescent catechesis and a framework of key faith themes for younger and older adolescents, and by identifying the roles and responsibilities of key leaders in ministry with youth, the paper sets forth a vision and direction for adolescent catechesis.

II. FOUNDATIONS OF ADOLESCENT CATECHESIS

[5.]   The Ministry of Adolescent Catechesis is rooted in the Church's understanding and experience of six foundational themes: Jesus, discipleship, mission and ministries, faith, the developing human person, and the community.

. . . ROOTED IN JESUS CHRIST

The essence of Christian faith is a living relationship with God—a God fully revealed by Jesus of Nazareth and present to us through the Holy Spirit. This Spirit fills and transforms the lives of his followers. When people encountered Jesus' sustaining love and transforming power they experienced the saving love of God. The very person of Jesus made the saving love of God accessible. The life, death, and resurrection of Jesus of Nazareth is the Revelation of God. If we want to learn how to relate to God, we focus on the person of Jesus—his life and message, his death and resurrection. A Christian disciple lives in relationship with God in Jesus Christ.

. . . ROOTED IN CHRISTIAN DISCIPLESHIP

[6.]   ". . . Jesus appeared in Galilee proclaiming the good news of God: 'This is the time of fulfillment. The reign of God is at hand! Reform your lives and believe in the gospel!'" (Mark 1:14–15)

The Gospel of Jesus is the Good News of the reign of God. Jesus used the image of the reign of God or the kingdom of God to reveal God's presence among people and God's promises for them. Jesus proclaimed this reign in his words and made it present in his actions. He called people to conversion and repentence. He asked them to turn away from sin, from all that bound and oppressed them and to turn toward faith and freedom. Jesus invited people to believe in, trust in, and live the Good News. Those who accepted the invitation experienced a new life—a life faithful to the values and vision of the reign of God.

Through his teachings, Jesus described the character, priorities, values, and norms of the reign of God. Jesus addressed the fundamental questions that each of us must face. Jesus summons us to journey with him. The relationship to which he call us defines us as his disciples—people who belong to the Lord and serve God alone. The first disciples joined Jesus, followed him, transferred their loyalty to him, and, in so doing, became a new people.

The first disciples shared in the mission of Jesus. While essential to the Christian experience, discipleship is costly, for the invitation to follow Jesus and to share in his mission demands total response and requires a lifelong conversion. Accepting the values and priorities of the reign of God forces us to break with many of the values of our culture. Only the power of grace can effect this profound social and personal transformation.

The Good News of Jesus and the dynamics of Christian Discipleship are the energizing core of catechesis "At the heart of catechesis, for all ages, is the person and message of Jesus of Nazareth" (CT, 5). Our catechetical task "has the twofold objective of maturing the initial faith and of educating the true disciple of Christ by means of a deeper and more systematic knowledge of the person and message of our Lord Jesus Christ" (CT, 19).

. . . ROOTED IN THE CHURCH'S MISSION AND MINISTRIES

[7.] "The spirit of the Lord is upon me; therefore he has anointed me. He has sent me to bring glad tidings to the poor, to proclaim liberty to captives, recovery of sight to the blind and release to prisoners, to announce a year of favor from the Lord" (Luke 4:18–19).

Through the power and presence of the Holy Spirit, the mission of Jesus is continued in the Church. Faithful to the mission of Jesus, the Church is called "to proclaim in word and in sacrament the definitive arrival of the Kingdom in Jesus of Nazareth; to offer itself as a sign of its own proclamation—to be a people transformed by the Spirit into a community of faith, hope, love, freedom, and truthfulness; and to enable and facilitate the coming of the reign of God through service within the community of faith and in the world at large."[1]

Four fundamental ministries that have their roots in the life of Jesus serve the mission of the Church: ministry of the Word, the ministry of community building, the ministry of worship, and the ministry of serving-healing. Each of these ministries continues the work of Jesus. The ministry of the Word takes many forms, among them evangelization or missionary preaching, catechesis, liturgy, and theology (GCD, 17). An integral element of the ministry of the Word is catechesis.

CATECHESIS — LINKED WITH THE OTHER MINISTRIES

[8.] All ministries have catechetical aspects. "Catechesis is intrinsically linked with the whole of liturgical and sacramental activity, for it is in the sacraments, especially in the Eucharist, that Christ Jesus works in fullness for the transformation of human beings" (CT, 23). "Catechesis is closely linked with the responsible activity of the Church and of Christians in the world. . . . If catechesis is done well, Christians will be eager to bear witness to their faith, to hand it on to their children, to make it known to others, and to serve the human community in every way" (CT, 24).

The interrelationship of catechesis with the other ministries of the Church is reflected in *A Vision of Youth Ministry* (USCC) which describes adolescent catechesis as one component of a multi-dimensional ministry with youth. Each component of this multi-dimensional ministry fosters maturing in faith.

CATECHESIS — A RESPONSIBILITY OF THE COMMUNITY

Responsibility for catechesis rests with the entire Church. "Catechesis always has been and always will be a work for which the whole Church must feel responsible and must wish to be responsible" (CT, 16). The entire faith community needs to be interested in, supportive of, and concerned about adolescent catechesis.

CATECHESIS AND EVANGELIZATION

[9.] *This paper elaborates an understanding and practice of catechesis as a systematic, planned, and intentional pastoral activity. This activity is directed toward the kind of teaching and learning which emphasizes growth in Christian faith through understanding, reflection, and transformation* (cf. CT, 19, 21). Although catechesis is a broad reality, this paper focuses on that aspect of catechesis that is systematic and intentional and that can be planned.

Catechesis is closely related to evangelization, which is the energizing core of all ministries. All ministries are elements in the evangelization/conversion process. As an evangelizing activity, catechesis promotes an ongoing conversion toward a permanent commitment to the Lord. " . . . within the whole process of evangelization, the aim of catechesis is to be the teaching and maturation stage" (CT, 20).

In a time when so many young people remain untouched by the Good News, initial evangelization is a priority. Through evangelization we invite young people into the community of faith, into a faith relationship with Jesus Christ, and into the lifestyle of the Good News. Catechesis then builds upon this faith by explaining more fully the Good News and by exploring the common faith that binds the Catholic Christian community together. Catechesis seeks to foster the maturing of faith of young people.

[10.] Christian faith is a gift of God inviting people to a living relationship with God in Jesus Christ. In the years since Vatican II, the Church has reiterated its belief that faith has affective (trusting), cognitive (believing), and behavioral (doing) dimensions. We remain firmly convinced that Christian faith must be lived. Catechesis that takes the Christian faith as its purpose intentionally promotes all three dimensions — trusting, believing, and doing.[2]

AN ACTIVITY OF TRUSTING

[11.] Christian faith is a response to an invitation to a loyal and trusting relationship with God. Developing and deepening the adolescent's relationship with God in Jesus requires particular attention to and catechesis on the activity of personal and communal prayer. Catechesis attempts to dispose young people to awe, reverence, and wonder at the goodness of God. The loving relationship adolescents develop with God will shape and be shaped by their relationship with other people. The affective dimension of the Christian faith helps young people develop and deepen their sense of belonging within the faith community. Catechesis has the task of enabling adolescents to develop friendship-making and maintenance skills. Such a catechesis seeks to promote in adolescents a deep and abiding bond of friendship and good will toward the whole human family.

AN ACTIVITY OF BELIEVING

[12.] The cognitive dimension of Christian faith — the activity of believing — requires that we provide opportunities for youth to deepen and expand their understanding of the scriptural/doctrinal expression of our faith tradition in ways appropriate to their readiness and maturity. We do this by showing the reasonableness of assenting to Catholic Christian beliefs, by helping youth draw on the wisdom of the Catholic Christian tradition to give meaning to their lives, and by enabling youth to think for themselves about matters of faith. We help them to articulate their understanding of the tradition in a language appropriate to their generation (cf. GCD, 88).

AN ACTIVITY OF DOING

[13.] Christian faith requires a catechesis that promotes a life based on the values of the reign of God. This means that we present the Christian story as Good News, thus enabling young people to live as a Christian people — joyfully, hopefully, peacefully, and justly. Catechesis challenges young people to respond to God's love by living a life of loving service to others and by working for peace and justice on all levels of human existence — the personal, the interpersonal, and the social/political. The "doing of faith" leads to a deepening of faith. Faith leads to doing and doing leads to renewed faith.

. . . ROOTED IN THE DEVELOPING HUMAN PERSON

[14.] A social and developmental understanding of the human person guides our ministry with youth. Through this ministry we seek to create a climate conducive to the healthy development of adolescents and providing them with multiple opportunities for growth in maturity. We want to help them interact with peers, acquire a sense of belonging, and develop self-worth and a healthy self-concept. They need to gain experience in decision-making, discuss diverse values, and formulate their own value system. We are challenged to help them explore different understandings of personal and vocational identity, to voice openly their questions in the area of sexuality, to develop a sense of accountability in the context of relationships, and to cultivate a capacity to enjoy life (cf. NCD, 180).

[15.] Maturing in Christian faith is a lifelong journey for everyone. It is a process of conversion, not a point of arrival. Adolescents are at a crucial point in this life-long journey. While younger adolescents build their faith identity upon the beliefs, attitudes, and values of the Christian community, older adolescents are beginning to reflect critically on the community's faith, seeking to establish a personally-owned faith identity. They are beginning to take seriously the burden of responsibility for their own commitments, lifestyle, beliefs, and attitudes. The journey from accepting the faith of the community to owning their own faith within the community is often a time of deeper questioning and of anguished or even frustrating searching (cf. CT, 38). It is a crucial time of maturing. "Catechesis cannot ignore these changeable aspects of this delicate period of life" (CT, 38). In fact, adolescent catechesis must view adolescents as maturing people who are growing in every way and who are experiencing their own questions, joys, struggles, and quests for meaning. Adolescent catechesis helps young people understand the relationship of Jesus and the Church to the important realities in their lives (cf. NCD, 174).

. . . ROOTED IN CHRISTIAN COMMUNITY

[16.] The call of Jesus was to a new commitment and a new companionship. The earliest Christians were a community of faith, sharing a new way of life. "They devoted themselves to the apostles' instruction and the communal life, to the breaking of bread and the prayers. . . . With exultant and sincere hearts they took their meals in common, praising God and winning the approval of all the people" (Acts 2:42, 46–47). They were known for the way they lived as well as what they believed. Their experience continues today. The Christian faith produces a discernible lifestyle, a way of life, a process of growth visible to all, a community of believers. The context for catechesis is this faith community.

This community shapes our self-identity. within this community, we encounter role models, a world view, and a value system that we can interiorize as our own Catholic Christian self-identity. These Catholic Christian environments include the family, the parish, ethnic culture, and ministry with youth in parishes and Catholic schools.

[17.] The family serves the life and mission of the Church by becoming an evangelizing and catechizing community (cf. FC, 51–54). Family relationships can support or hinder the faith growth of the young person. Moreover, family members catechize informally but powerfully. Parents strengthen the faith of adolescents in many ways — by showing love and affection, by nurturing their adolescents, by living their Catholic Christian moral beliefs, by responding to the needs of others and working for peace and justice, by helping their adolescents internalize moral beliefs, by developing a liberating rather than a restrictive faith life, by sharing their experiences of faith with members of the family, by discussing Scripture and praying with the family, and by reverently receiving the Eucharist and living its spirit (cf. NCD, 212).

Frequently stress, caused by separation or divorce, by living in a single parent or blended family, by unemployment or illness, or by family disunity, affects growth in faith. Adolescent catechesis acknowledges the varied family styles in the United States and the particular stresses experienced by the contemporary family and responds with new directions and strategies. Many parents recognize their need for assistance in fostering the faith of their adolescent children. When adolescents test their independence from the family, other adults may assist parents by serving as Christian role models. A family perspective needs to be woven throughout adolescent catechesis. Acknowledging the importance of the family in catechesis means sponsoring programs for parents around their areas of need, creating parent catechetical experiences that parallel the adolescent catechetical program, sponsoring intergenerational catechetical experiences, and supporting parents in their catechetical ministry. The Church of the Home needs to reclaim its own mission and task. Once this happens, the parish can initiate a process to deepen the family's ability to catechize effectively.

THE PARISH

[18.] The parish is constantly catechizing by its life, worship, actions, and service. Vibrant parishes nourish adolescent catechesis. Young people, who need to experience a sense of belonging to the parish community, must be integrated into the life, mission, and work of the Church for they bring important gifts and talents to the faith community. Often times this sense of belonging and involvement in mission is created in smaller communities of adults and youth. Through this active engagement, adolescents' faith matures and their Catholic Christian identity deepens. Meaningful involvement of the "Young Church of Today" lays the foundations for the adult church of tomorrow.

ETHNIC CULTURE

[19.] We live in a Church which is enriched by the cultural heritages of many people. These cultural heritages have an intimate link with faith. The Church has utilized the resources of different cultures to spread and explain the message of Christ and to express this message more perfectly in the liturgy and in various aspects of the life of the faithful (GS, 58). The strong sense of family, tradition, community, celebration, and art/music in these cultures provides building blocks for a catechesis which speaks to the experience of youth from these cultures. However, because these young people may have one foot in their ethnic culture and one foot in the dominant culture, they experience a tension that affects their growth in personal identity, values, and beliefs. This tension presents a serious challenge to adolescent catechesis.

The reality of a multicultural Church and society requires that we develop creative catechetical approaches to youth of ethnic cultures and a multicultural catechesis for all youth. We need to become aware of the riches of ethnic cultures and introduce that awareness into our catechesis. A multicultural catechesis brings youth of different cultures together to learn from each other, to develop respect for each other, and to experience Christians community with each other. Adolescent catechesis can provide a celebration of the many cultures as signs of the bountiful creation of God. We need to bring adolescents of various ethnic groups together in proper timing, in an open and non-threatening environment, and in a respectful manner. This can help them discover their unique riches and gifts and their commonalities and place them at the service of the entire Christian community.

A COMPREHENSIVE MINISTRY WITH YOUTH IN PARISHES AND CATHOLIC SCHOOLS

[20.] Adolescent Catechesis is an integral component of a broad-based comprehensive ministry with youth in a parish or Catholic school context. "Youth Catechesis is most effective within a total youth ministry" (NCD, 228). *A Vision of Youth Ministry* (USCC) outlines the components of this broader ministry with youth: Word, prayer and worship, community life, justice and service, guidance and healing, enablement, and advocacy. Faith is fostered through the entire communal life and programs of the Catholic school and of the parish youth ministry. The establishment of this broader ministerial context is essential for effective adolescent catechesis.

In developing a comprehensive ministry with youth, parishes and Catholic high schools need to collaborate. For young people, the experience of the Catholic high school can be an intense and enriching opportunity to grow in faith. Parish personnel need to recognize this reality, affirm the Catholic high school as an important resource, and develop close communication with it.

On the other hand, the Catholic high school is not a permanent experience in the life of young people because they will graduate from the school environment. Catholic high school personnel need to recognize the parish as a permanent community and seek to develop communication and coordination with parishes. The effective cooperation of parish and Catholic high school personnel can be a powerful factor in fostering the growth in faith of young people. This maturing in faith continues beyond the high school years, and parish and school leaders need to work together in ways that promote, rather than hinder, this continuing growth in faith.

III. THE MINISTRY OF ADOLESCENT CATECHESIS

[21.] The aim, process, and principles of the ministry of adolescent catechesis are built on the six foundational themes of adolescent catechesis.

A. THE AIM OF ADOLESCENT CATECHESIS

The primary aim of adolescent catechesis is to sponsor youth toward maturity in Catholic Christian faith as a living reality. We adults guide, challenge, affirm, and encourage youth in their journey toward maturity in faith. We have two tasks: to foster in youth a communal identity as Catholic Christians and to help them develop their own personal faith identity. To accomplish the first task, we present the faith convictions and values of the Catholic Christian tradition and invite adolescents to adopt and own these values and convictions. To effect the second, we help adolescents respond to God in faith, in prayer, in values, and in behavior. The sense of belonging experienced by youth in an active Christian community supports these two tasks of adolescent catechesis.[3]

Young people are on a journey toward the realization of a number of characteristics of Catholic Christian maturity. A systematic, planned, and intentional adolescent catechesis addresses these characteristics by blending knowledge and understanding with skills and attitudes and by emphasizing the believing, trusting, and doing dimensions of Christian faith. The following characteristics, which need to be adapted to the social and cultural settings of the ministry, provide a guide to direct the catechetical effort in the adolescent years:

- The maturing adolescent is developing a clear personal identity and is learning how to accept one's self as lovable and loved by God and others.

- The maturing adolescent is developing a commitment to a personal faith and taking responsibility for his or her own faith life and ongoing growth as a Catholic Christian, which involves the gradual realization and response to the plan, will, and purpose of God for the world.

- The maturing adolescent is developing a mature relationship with Jesus Christ whom the adolescent has come to know in a personal way in the Scriptures and in the life and teachings of the Catholic Christian community.

- The maturing adolescent is learning the skills of critical reflection that enables one to analyze life experience, society, culture, and Church in light of the Good News of Jesus Christ.

- The maturing adolescent is developing an appreciation for the importance of the Scriptures in the Christian life and learning the skills for reading and interpreting the Scriptures.

- The maturing adolescent is developing a personal pattern of personal and communal prayer and worship and understands and appreciates the sacramental life of the Church, especially the Eucharist.

- The maturing adolescent is developing an appreciation for and knowledge of the Catholic Christian tradition, its doctrinal expression, and its applicability to life in today's complex society.
- The maturing adolescent is actively engaged in the life, mission, and work of the Catholic Christian community and in particular his or her own family, the Church of the Home.
- The maturing adolescent is developing an interiorized, principled Catholic Christian moral value system and is able to confront moral issues using principles of Catholic Christian moral decision making.
- The maturing adolescent is integrating sexuality into his or her personality in a holistic way within the context of the sexual values of the Catholic Christian community and in particular his or her own family.
- The maturing adolescent is beginning to appreciate deeper relationships and is learning the skills for developing and maintaining relationships.
- The maturing adolescent is developing a life of Christian service modeled on Jesus' life and is learning that life is enriched when one gives one's self for others.
- The maturing adolescent is realizing that Christian faith means a commitment to justice and peace at the personal, interpersonal, and social/ political levels of one's life and is acquiring the tools to work for justice and peace.
- The maturing adolescent is discovering how one's spirituality can be lived out through a variety of adult lifestyles.

B. THE PROCESS OF ADOLESCENT CATECHESIS

[22.] The fundamental process of adolescent catechesis involves discovering the relationships among the Catholic Christian tradition; God's present activity in the life of the adolescent, family, community, and world; and the contemporary life experience of the adolescent. "Experience is of great importance in catechesis. Experiential learning, . . . gives rise to concerns and questions, hopes and anxieties, reflections and judgments, which increase one's desire to penetrate more deeply into life's meaning" (NCD, 176d). In this process, Scripture, tradition and the contemporary life experience of youth are honored and held in dialogue. Adolescent catechesis encourages young people "to reflect on their significant experiences and respond to God's presence there" (NCD, 176d). It enables young people to understand the meaning of their life experience in relation to the Christian faith. The Christian faith is a tool that helps adolescents interpret and test their experience; conversely, experience is a tool that helps them to understand the Christian faith. "Experience can also increase the intelligibility of the Christian message, by providing illustrations and examples which shed light on the truths of revelation. At the same time, experience itself should be interpreted in the light of revelation" (NCD, 176d).

[23.] Faith often needs to be personally held and critically appropriated. As we hand on the Catholic Christian tradition and discern the activity of God in the contemporary pluralistic and secular world and in young people's own experience, we invite them to find a vocabulary to articulate their beliefs, to examine it, and to own it. We invite them to think for themselves, to come to their own "faith knowing." We encourage them to critically reflect upon their own experience and to allow the wisdom of Scripture and tradition to inform and transform their lives.

Catechesis reads the signs of the times — in our cultural values, in our lifestyles, in media, and especially music, and utilizes the positive values, questions, and crises of these signs. It challenges young people to reflect actively on the impact of these signs in their lives, and consider how the Good News relates to them. Effective catechesis is in tune with the life situations of youth — their language, lifestyles, family realities, culture, and global realities. It identifies the core meanings of the signs, symbols, and images of youth today, explores how these surface in youth's lives, and relates them to the signs, symbols, and images of the Catholic Christian tradition.

C. PRINCIPLES FOR DEVELOPING ADOLESCENT CATECHESIS

[24.] This paper proposes ten principles to guide the work of developing adolescent catechesis in parishes and Catholic high schools. Flowing from the foundations of adolescent catechesis, the first set of five are foundational principles that describe the key understandings that shape adolescent catechesis. The second set of five are operational principles that describe the processes for developing adolescent catechesis.

FOUNDATIONAL PRINCIPLES

1. *Adolescent catechesis is situated within the lifelong developmental process of faith growth and of ongoing catechesis. The entire catechetical effort is committed to the continuing faith growth of the individual.*

2. *Adolescent catechesis fosters Catholic Christian faith in three dimensions: trusting, believing, and doing.*

3. *Adolescent catechesis supports and encourages the role of the family and in particular the role of the parent in the faith growth of the young person and involves the parent in formulation of an adolescent catechesis curriculum and in programs to strengthen their parenting role.*

4. *Adolescent catechesis respects the unique cultural heritages of young people and builds upon the positive values found in these cultural heritages, while at the same time engaging young people in examining their culture in the light of faith and examining their faith in the light of culture.*

5. *Adolescent catethesis is integrated and developed within a comprehensive, multifaceted approach to ministry with youth.*

6. Adolescent catechesis responds to the developmental, social, and cultural needs of adolescence. Related to that, the curriculum respects the changing developmental and social characteristics of the various stages of adolescence, providing a significantly different content and approach for younger and older adolescents.

Contemporary psychological and sociological research describes adolescence in distinct life phases and provides growth characteristics for each of these life stages. These characteristics serve as a guide to the learning needs of adolescents. In developing a framework for adolescent catechesis, this paper proposes catechetical faith themes for younger adolescents (11/12 – 14/15) and older adolescents (14/15 – 18/19) that draw on the psychological and sociological research. Research has also developed an understanding of family styles and life cycles. Adolescent catechesis needs to recognize and appreciate the tasks and life issues that families may be experiencing at home. In some households the parents or parent may be encountering their own mid-life transition as the adolescent is going through his or her transition.

Research also provides a guide for developing the content (key topics) and catechetical approach (focus) for exploring a specific faith theme. The content and approach to exploring the Jesus faith theme, for example, is developed differently for younger adolescents than it is for older adolescents. Research provides a guide for selecting the particular topics and for developing specific catechetical approaches that are in keeping with the adolescent's readiness level.

The ministry of adolescent catechesis is viewed through the prism of developmental research and the social/cultural analysis of youth today. Understanding Christian faith as a lifelong journey means that catechesis first discerns a young person's developmental journey and social/cultural situation and then designs catechetical experiences that respond to the young person's particular faith needs. Patience with the gradual progress of youth is a necessity in the ministry of adolescent catechesis.

7. Adolescent catechesis respects the variability in maturation rates and learning needs of adolescence.

Young people mature at varied rates. A ministry with youth recognizes the varying degrees of faith maturation in young people. Many young people are in need of evangelization experiences prior to catechesis. Such experiences are essential to foster the faith growth of adolescents.

A wide variability in maturation exists within adolescent catechesis. In adolescence as much as a four year difference in maturation rates can be seen within the same age group. In light of this, grouping only on the basis of age or grade involves serious complications for meeting the varied learning needs of youth. However, organizing adolescent catechesis around the learning needs of younger adolescents and older adolescents helps to overcome many of the difficulties of age-grading.

Implementing approaches such as individualized learning and interest grouping also helps to overcome the limitations of age-grading. Even though this principle is easier to implement in some settings than in others, we need to develop creative approaches in all settings to respect the variability in maturation and the learning needs of adolescents.

8. *Adolescent catechesis respects the expanding freedom and autonomy of adolescents.*

Adolescent catechesis is open to dialogue, question, and searching on the part of young people. It recognizes and respects the essential freedom of young people to question, doubt, rebut, and perhaps even temporarily reject the Catholic Christian faith. Catechesis must avoid coercion and manipulation.

In light of the faith readiness, learning needs, and expanding freedom and autonomy of young people, we need a variety of catechetical themes and forms of participation in adolescent catechesis. Parents and catechetical leaders can invite, encourage, and guide participation. But gradually the responsibility for participation in catechesis shifts from the family or adult authorities to the adolescent. While we can legitimately expect participation on the part of young people, we cannot manipulate or coerce a particular faith response. With adult guidance, adolescents can select meaningful faith themes that respond to their learning needs and the form of their participation in catechesis. In light of this, adolescent catechesis must be attractive, interesting, creative, and responsive to the adolescents' learning needs and must offer a variety of faith themes, learning formats, environments, schedules, and educational techniques to encourage participation.

This principle needs to be creatively implemented in response to the unique settings of the parish and Catholic high school.

9. *Adolescent catechesis uses a variety of learning formats, environments, schedules, and educational techniques.*

The varied learning needs, expanding freedom, and social/cultural situation of adolescents suggest that catechetical planners offer a variety of learning formats, environments, schedules, and techniques. In developing catechetical programming, planners can draw upon various learning formats (mini-courses, seasonal programming such as Advent and Lent, small group learning teams, youth fellowship, intergenerational programming, worship/celebration, action-learning, retreats, study tours/trips, individualized learning, and peer ministry) and various scheduling options (weekly, bi-weekly, full day, monthly, overnight, weekend, and week-long). Our selection of formats, environments, schedules, and techniques needs to fit local needs, circumstances, and resources.

Catholic schools have much experience in providing a variety of schedules and formats for responding to the differing abilities, needs, and interests of students. This experience can be a rich resource in designing a flexible and creative approach to the structure and scheduling of the catechetical program and curriculum. Core topics and electives presented in a variety of formats, such as long- and short-term courses, independent study, retreats, and service involvement, can provide a creative and flexible way to weave the various faith themes into the catechetical program of the school. In this way we can develop a comprehensive response to the varying maturation rates and the expanding freedom and autonomy of the students.

The particular needs of parish adolescent catechesis suggest short-term, rather than long-term, programming. Young people have increased demands placed upon their time. Catechesis adapts to their world by offering a diversity of faith themes in a variety of short-term formats. Short-term learning opportunities actually increase the participation of youth and encourage them to engage in multiple learning experiences throughout the year.

10. *Adolescent catechesis best responds to the learning needs of adolescents when it is focused on particular faith themes.*

A thematic approach to catechesis for younger and older adolescents draws faith themes from the Catholic Christian tradition and the developmental, sociological, and cultural research on youth. It focuses the exploration of a faith theme on selected topics (content) that provide possibilities for exploring the theme in some depth. Instead of surveying the broad scope of a particular faith theme, this approach selects a primary focus and key topics in keeping with the adolescent's developmental and social readiness. In the context of lifelong learning, these faith themes for young and older adolescents have been selected because of their particular importance at this stage of a person's life. This approach to adolescent catechesis builds on the foundations developed in childhood catechesis and looks to young adult and adult catechesis for continued opportunities for learning.

IV. A FRAMEWORK FOR ADOLESCENT CATECHESIS
AN INTEGRATED CATECHESIS

[25.] By focusing on key faith themes, adolescent catechesis provides a systematic, orderly, and focused presentation of the Catholic Christian tradition. Six integral dimensions are woven throughout each of these themes.

Jesus Christ—Every faith theme includes a discussion of its relationship to Jesus and the Gospel. Thus the adolescent develops an understanding of Jesus and his message and is invited to a personal response in faith to both.

Scripture—The catechesis for each faith theme is grounded in Scripture. This fosters in adolescents a deepening knowledge and appreciation of the Scriptures in the Church's tradition and in their own lives.

Church—Each faith theme affirms the vision of the Church as a historical community of people committed to the vision, values, and mission of Jesus. In seeking to create experiences of such a community, ministers establish this Church in the minds and hearts of the young people.

Prayer—Each faith theme leads to and flows from prayer. Adolescents learn to pray by personally and communally experiencing prayer.

Action/Lifestyle—Each faith theme leads to action that reflects a Christian lifestyle. This empowers young people to live a more faithful Christian life—personally, interpersonally, and socially/politically.

Interpretation and Critical Reflection—Each faith theme seeks to promote critical reflection and interpretion that affirms and critiques the values and behaviors of culture and society. This enables young people to interpret their own culture, ethnic culture, society, and life experience in the light of the Catholic Christian faith.

INTRODUCTION TO THE FRAMEWORK

This framework presents faith themes designed in light of the learning needs of younger adolescents and older adolescents. The framework, which can be used as the basis for developing the scope, sequence, and objectives of a curriculum, is not intended to serve all the needs of a given situation. Local leaders need to adapt the framework to the particular needs of their youth, and they may also need to include additional faith themes not presented in this paper.

The suggested content for the faith themes is drawn from the Catholic Christian tradition and the developmental, sociological, and cultural research on youth. The selection of each faith theme is designed to "shed the light of the Christian message on the realities which have greater impact on the adolescent" (GCD, 84). The catechetical focus for each faith theme is in keeping with the developmental and social readiness of the adolescent. Themes that occur for both younger and older adolescents are given new perspectives in light of the adolescent's experience.

FAITH THEMES FOR YOUNGER ADOLESCENTS (11/12–14/15)

Church

[26.] FOCUS: This faith theme helps younger adolescents understand and experience the Catholic Christian story and mission and become involved in the Christian community.

SUGGESTED CONTENT

- the story of the Church as related to the younger adolescent's story;
- Jesus' mission and ministry as these continue today through the Christian community's ministries of Word, worship, community building, and service;
- the global and multicultural reality of the Church;
- the community life and ministries in the other major Christian churches;
- involvement in the life, mission, and work of the parish community and the family.

Jesus & The Gospel Message

[27.] FOCUS: This faith theme helps younger adolescents follow Jesus, develop a more personal relationship with Him, concentrate on the person and teaching of Jesus, discover what a relationship with Jesus means, and respond to Jesus from a growing inner sense of self.

SUGGESTED CONTENT:

- Christian faith as a personal response to and relationship with Jesus;
- Gospel discipleship or the exploring of what following Jesus and living the Good News means;
- the person of Jesus—his values, intentions, motives, and attitudes;
- the key themes of the Good News (what Jesus teaches us about God, prayer, justice/peace, service, and moral life);
- the impact of the Good News on the adolescent's life;
- the response of the first disciples to Jesus and the Good News.

Morality & Moral Decision Making

[28.] FOCUS: This faith theme helps younger adolescents apply Catholic Christian moral values as maturing persons who are becoming increasingly capable of using decision-making skills to make free and responsible choices.

SUGGESTED CONTENT:

- Jesus' vision of being fully human as the foundation of Catholic Christian morality;
- the moral values in Jesus' teachings;
- Catholic Christian moral values that relate to the life of the adolescent;
- the basis of moral decision-making within a Catholic Christian context: conscience, sin, and reconciliation;
- four sources of moral maturing: mind, heart, family/other persons, and Catholic Christian tradition;
- skills for critically reflecting on self, youth culture, and media and society's values in light of Catholic Christian moral values.

Personal Growth

[29.] FOCUS: This faith theme helps younger adolescents develop a stronger and more realistic concept of self by exploring who they are and who they can become.

SUGGESTED CONTENT:

- the building of a strong and realistic concept of self with an emphasis on self-concept, growing autonomy, and self- determination;

- Jesus' vision of being fully human and its impact on the younger adolescent's growing identity as a Christian;
- the response of the Good News and tradition to adolescent struggles (isolation, loneliness, frustration, anger) and problems (suicide, substance abuse);
- the development of skills for handling peer pressure and values, and adolescent problems.

Relationships

[30.] FOCUS: This faith theme helps younger adolescents develop more mutual, trusting, and loyal relationships with peers, parents, and other adults by emphasizing skills that enhance and maintain relationships.

SUGGESTED CONTENT:

- the nature of relationships;
- Jesus' life of service and teaching on living a life of loving service;
- relationship in the Christian community;
- the development of responsible relationships with an emphasis on honesty, love, and respect;
- the development of skills, such as active listening and self disclosure, for communicating with peers, parents, and other adults.

Service

[31.] FOCUS: This faith theme helps younger adolescents explore Jesus' call to live a life of loving service, discover that such a life is integral to discipleship, develop a foundation for a social justice consciousness, and participate in service that involves relationships and concrete action.

SUGGESTED CONTENT:

- Jesus' life of service and his teaching on living a life of loving service;
- service as an essential element of discipleship;
- the development of knowledge and skills needed to engage in service;
- service projects;
- reflection on involvement in service projects.

Sexuality

[32.] FOCUS: This faith theme helps younger adolescents learn about sexual development, better understand the dynamics of maturing as a sexual person within a Catholic Christian's value context, and discuss sexuality with their parents using a Catholic Christian value-based approach.

SUGGESTED CONTENT:

- sexual development with an emphasis on accurate information;
- sexuality as integral to one's personal identity with an explanation of gender identity and roles;
- relationships and dating;
- Catholic Christian understanding of sexuality and sexual moral values.

FAITH THEMES FOR OLDER ADOLESCENTS (14/15 – 18/19)

Faith & Identity

[33.] FOCUS: This faith theme helps older adolescents explore what being a Christian, a Catholic, and a person of faith means; appraise the faith of the community; develop their own personally-held faith and own it; and grow in response to the Gospel challenge to be a person of faith.

SUGGESTED CONTENT:

- the meaning and experience of revelation and of God's actions in our lives;
- faith as a gift, as a process of understanding the basic questions that all persons face as a dynamic and positive force that can shape the adolescent's life and personality and ongoing process of conversion;
- reflection on present faith growth and struggles;
- the development of skills for reflection;
- Jesus as the model of a completely faithful person;
- Catholic Christian beliefs with an emphasis on integrating these beliefs into a personal identity;
- the beliefs and faith traditions of the major Christian churches — their uniqueness and what they share in common with the Catholic Christian church.

The Gospels

[34.] FOCUS: This faith theme helps older adolescents appreciate the historical and literary development, structure, and major themes of the Four Gospels; grasp insights that come from scriptural scholarship; and utilize these insights to interpret the Gospels.

SUGGESTED CONTENT:

- the three stages of Gospel development;
- revelation and inspiration;
- a study of the writing styles of the Evangelists and the structure of the Gospels;

- a study of the unique presentations of Jesus and the Good News in the gospels;
- an in-depth exploration of one particular Synoptic Gospel.

Hebrew Scriptures

[35.] FOCUS: This faith theme helps older adolescents appreciate the historical and literary development, structure, and major themes of the Hebrew Scriptures; grasp the insights that come from scriptural scholarship; and utilize these insights in interpreting the Scriptures.

SUGGESTED CONTENT:

- the growth, composition, historical development, writing styles and methods, and structure of the Hebrew Scriptures;
- Revelation, inspiration, and biblical interpretation;
- the reading and interpreting of the Hebrew Scriptures;
- exploration of the major themes and life-questions of the Hebrew Scriptures and their relevance to today.

Jesus

[36.] FOCUS: This faith theme helps older adolescents explore who Jesus Christ is, discover his meaning for their lives, and develop a personal, deeply relational experience of Him.

SUGGESTED CONTENT:

- the historical and social world of Jesus;
- Jesus' relationship with his Father and his image of God;
- Jesus' life, mission, and the key themes of his message;
- Jesus' death, resurrection, and ongoing presence;
- the Spirit and the church throughout history;
- new ways of thinking about Jesus today;
- ways to develop a richer, more mature relationship with Jesus.

Justice & Peace

[37.] FOCUS: This faith theme helps older adolescents develop a global social consciousness and compassion grounded in the Christian vision and attentive to the needs of those who are hurting and who are oppressed.

SUGGESTED CONTENTS:

- the Scriptural vision of life (justice, peace, equality, and stewardship);
- the call to conversion, to live the vision, values, and lifestyle of the reign of God;

- an analysis of the social problems and injustices in the world, such as hunger, poverty, war/peace, inequality, discrimination, and ecology;
- the determination of a constructive, Christian response to these problems on the personal, interpersonal, and social/political levels of one's life;
- the development of practical skills such as peaceful conflict resolution and organization for action;
- the recognition of the injustices experienced by young people themselves.

Love & Lifestyles

[38.] FOCUS: This faith theme helps older adolescents explore their maturing sexual identity; use skills for developing intimate, trusting, enduring relationships; and discover how their spirituality can be lived out through a variety of lifestyles.

SUGGESTED CONTENT:

- Christian view of sexuality and intimacy;
- how to build love relationships and develop intimacy;
- dating;
- development of a sexual identity;
- how single persons, priests, deacons, vowed religious, and married persons live as Christians;
- the choice of a lifestyle;
- the improvement of life decision-making skills;
- Christian marriage, love, and family life in today's world.

Morality

[39.] FOCUS: This faith theme helps older adolescents critique their personal and social values; develop and use an interiorized, principled moral value system, and understand the rule of Christian conscience and moral decision-making in the development of this interiorized moral value system.

SUGGESTED CONTENT:

- the development of an adult conscience based on Catholic Christian moral principles with emphasis on taking responsibility for one's moral values, actions, and lifestyles;
- how to interiorize a personally chosen set of moral principles and values;
- the confrontation and resolution of moral dilemmas;
- the development of skills for critically reflecting on self, youth culture, and media and society's values in the light of Catholic Christian moral values.

[40.] FOCUS: This faith theme helps older adolescents develop an understanding of the historical context, literary style, and major themes of Paul's Letters; utilize the insights of scriptural scholarship to interpret his writings; and discover Paul as apostle, preacher, theologian, and man of faith.

SUGGESTED CONTENT:

- the early church communities as the context and setting for Paul's letters;
- Paul's missionary journeys, sufferings, and trials;
- the major practical and pastoral problems to which Paul responded;
- the major theological themes of Paul's Letters as seen especially in his letters to the Galatians and Romans.

Prayer & Worship

[41.] FOCUS: This faith theme helps older adolescents develop a personally-held spirituality and a rich personal and communal prayer life.

SUGGESTED CONTENT:

- the nature of prayer;
- Jesus as a person of prayer;
- Jesus' teachings on prayer;
- an exploration of images and concepts of God;
- the development of a personal prayer life by exploring the who, what, when, where, why, and how of prayer and by experimenting with and experiencing a variety of prayer forms and styles;
- the Church's worship and sacramental life;
- an experience of the richness of the community's communal prayer.

ADOLESCENT CATECHESIS AND CONFIRMATION

[42.] There is much diversity in the age and practice of Confirmation in the United States. When Confirmation is celebrated in the adolescent years, it affords the parish a significant opportunity to foster the faith maturing of adolescents. This paper offers a catechetical context within which to view Confirmation preparation. The aim, process, and principles proposed in "The Ministry of Adolescent Catechesis" directly apply to the practice of confirmation. Confirmation catechesis needs to embody the process articulated by this paper. The ten principles developed in this paper are a guide to the development of the preparation process for Confirmation. Realizing that sacramental preparation for Confirmation has a distinct catechesis with its own focus and elements, this paper does not address that specific catechesis. It does propose that the fully initiated Christian is not the fully mature Christian. Catechesis is lifelong and the Christian community needs to provide learning opportunities for continuing growth in faith. Therefore, the faith themes presented in this paper can serve as a foundation prior to Confirmation catechesis and as a continuing catechesis after the celebration of the sacrament.

V. LEADERS IN THE MINISTRY OF ADOLESCENT CATECHESIS

[43.] The collaborative ministry of adolescent catechesis requires the integration of a variety of leaders with specialized roles. The effectiveness of adolescent catechesis relies on the contribution of all leaders. In "The Foundations of Adolescent Catechesis," this paper identified the important contributions that the family, in particular parents, and the parish community make to the faith maturing of adolescents. The parent is the primary educator. However, the roles identified in this section complement and support the parents role. This section examines the specific roles and responsibilities of catechists/religion teachers and of coordinators of adolescent catechesis in parish, school, and diocesan settings.

A. CATECHISTS/RELIGION TEACHERS

[44.] Catechists/religion teachers hold a central role within the ministry of adolescent catechesis, second only to the parents. They are formally involved in an actual learning setting with youth, sponsoring them in their journey to maturity in Catholic Christian faith. The role of catechist in a parish setting may be exercised by both pastoral leaders (priest, DRE, coordinator of youth ministry) and designated members of the Christian community. The Church calls catechists/religion teachers to work toward developing the following competencies, recognizing that growth as a catechist/religion teacher is an ongoing process.

Qualities of Catechists/Religion Teachers

Catechists/religion teachers are first and foremost Persons of Faith with a vibrant personal relationship with Jesus and a well-developed life of prayer. They recognize that they are called to exercise their gifts in catechetical ministry. Catechists/religion teachers are Witnesses of the Gospel who believe and live the Good News of Jesus within the Catholic Christian tradition and want to share that faith with others. They witness to the Good News in their life and teaching ministry. Catechists/religion teachers are Witnesses of the Church, committed to the Catholic Church and the Church's teaching mission. They are Sharers in the Fellowship of the Spirit, participating in the ongoing communal life of the parish, developing a spirit of community with other catechists, and dealing with conflict and disagreement in a sensitive and understanding manner. Catechists/religion teachers are Servants of the Community, responding to the needs of individuals and community. Catechists/religion teachers are knowledgeable of the Catholic Christian tradition and have a fundamental understanding of the scriptural, doctrinal, and moral expression of the Catholic faith. In addition, they are committed to continued growth as Catholic Christians and as catechists/religion teachers (cf. NCD, 205–211).

Above and beyond these qualities, catechists/religion teachers possess a genuine love for young people and display qualities that demonstrate this love: availability, acceptance, authenticity, and vulnerability. An encounter with an adolescent requires an openness, a presence, and real availability. Adolescents need to know that they are welcome to come and talk on their own terms. Catechists/religion teachers understand the questions, struggles, and concerns of youth and appreciate them for who they are — persons loved by God. These adolescents seek out catechists/religion teachers who can authentically share their own faith story — the struggles, hopes, and doubts that they experience in their own lives. By this interaction with adolescents, catechists/religion teachers quietly demonstrate an inner acceptance of the adolescents' journey for personal meaning. Catechists/religion teachers who are capable of being vulnerable provide a tremendous support to the adolescent, encouraging the adolescent's growth toward maturity as an adult. When the adolescent perceives a catechist/religion teacher who is comfortable with personal limitations and capable of admitting failure, the way is opened for the adolescent's own personal self-acceptance.[4]

Education of Catechists/Religion Teachers

[45.] "Because catechists approach their task with varying degrees of competence, programs should be designed to help individuals acquire the particular knowledge and skills they need" (NCD, 213). The entire Church through diocesan offices, parishes, schools, universities, formation centers, etc. needs to provide education for catechists/religion teachers. This education focuses on the spiritual and theological growth of the person and the development of understandings and skills necessary for adolescent catechesis.

A. Spirituality of the Catechist/Religion Teacher

The catechist/religion teacher demonstrates the following qualities:

- a willingness and ability to speak with conviction about his or her own experience and convictions as a Catholic Christian;
- continuing growth in his or her personal and communal prayer life;
- an ability to see God's activity in his or her experience, ministry, and lifestyle.

B. Knowledge of the Adolescent

The catechist/religion teacher demonstrates a fundamental understanding of the following:

- the characteristics of adolescent growth and development drawn from psychology, moral and faith development, sociology, and research on family life cycle, family systems, the socio-economic situation of the family, and how these relate to catechetical ministry with youth;
- the characteristics and values of our society, of youth culture, of ethnic culture, of media/music, etc. and their impact on the life of the adolescent and how it relates to catechetical ministry with youth;

- the signs, symbols, images, language, and culture of youth and how these surface in youths' lives and how these relate to catechetical ministry with youth.

C. Skills for Adolescent Catechesis

The catechist/religion teacher demonstrates the ability to do the following:

- design and conduct learning experiences for youth, utilizing a variety of learning processes, media, methods, and resources;
- relate the Gospel to the world of youth in the language, signs, symbols, and images understandable to youth;
- utilize communication, group discussion, community building, faith-sharing, and storytelling processes and skills;
- design and conduct worship, prayer, justice, and service experiences with youth.

D. Content of Catechesis

The catechist/religion teacher demonstrates a fundamental understanding of the following content:

- the development and key themes of the Hebrew and Christian Scriptures and the way to utilize the tools of scriptural scholarship to interpret the Scriptures for his or her life;
- Jesus Christ (his life, mission, message, death, and resurrection) and the historical development and contemporary approach to the Church's understanding of Jesus;
- the models of the Church as mystery, people of God, faith community, mystical body, and institution, and the Church's mission and ministries in today's world, a global, multicultural Church;
- contemporary sacramental theology and the role of the sacraments within the Christian life;
- Catholic Christian morality, conscience, personal and social sin, and moral decision making;
- the development and major themes of the Church's teachings on justice and peace and how they relate to our world;
- the core beliefs/doctrines (e.g. Trinity, Salvation, Grace) of Catholic Christianity and their expression within the contemporary Church.

B. COORDINATORS OF ADOLESCENT CATECHESIS IN A PARISH SETTING

[46.] The following brief descriptions of the coordinators in parish settings is offered as a means for clarifying the variety of coordination roles in adolescent catechesis. Each of these coordinators needs a thorough understanding of the adolescent and of the aims, processes, and principles of adolescent catechesis.

Those coordinators directly responsible for adolescent catechesis need the qualities, knowledge, and skills of the catechist.

Coordinator of Youth Ministry

The primary task of the coordinator of youth ministry (CYM) is to facilitate the harmonious working together of the various personnel and programs that embody the parish youth ministry efforts. These programs serve to develop a comprehensive ministry embracing Word, worship, community life, justice/service, guidance/healing, enablement, and advocacy. An integral dimension of this comprehensive ministry is catechesis. The harmonious functioning of a youth ministry requires the involvement of the CYM in adolescent catechesis.

Directors of Religious Education

The primary task of the director of religious education (DRE) is to facilitate the development of personnel and programs for lifelong catechesis in the parish. These programs span each age group from childhood catechesis through adolescent and adult catechesis. In addition the DRE is often responsible for sacramental preparation and is often involved in the adult catechumenate (RCIA). The integration of a lifelong catechesis requires the involvement of the DRE in adolescent catechesis (cf. NCD, 214).

Priests/Pastoral Associates

Priests/pastoral associates often exercise the role of CYM or DRE. They also "exercise a uniquely important role and have a special responsibility for the success of the catechetical ministry. They are a source of leadership, cooperation, and support for all involved in this ministry" (NCD, 217). Through preaching, liturgical sacramental ministry, and presence to young people, the priest and pastoral minister play a central factor in adolescent catechesis (NCD, 217). Among the parish leaders, the pastor is "primarily responsible for seeing to it that the catechetical needs, goals, and priorities of the parish are identified, articulated and met" (NCD, 217). A collaborative approach is needed to harmonize the role of priests/pastoral associates with the DRE and CYM.

A Collaborative Approach

[47.] Adolescent catechesis represents the intersection of the responsibility of the CYM and DRE. The DRE is responsible for catechesis throughout the life span. The CYM is responsible for a specific age group. The CYM brings the perspective of a comprehensive ministry to a wide set of youth needs and understands the integral place of catechesis within this ministry. The DRE brings the perspective of a lifelong approach to catechesis and understands the integral place of adolescent catechesis within this lifelong approach. From this perspective, both the DRE and CYM share responsibility for the adolescent catechesis program. This situation may cause tension that needs to be worked through. The clarification of responsibility for adolescent catechesis is based on the education, competence, and experience of the people involved in catechesis and ministry with youth. Using the four functions outlined below leaders can clarify the exact nature of that shared responsibility. Collaboration and teamwork are requirements for effective adolescent catechesis.

An essential ingredient in a collaborative approach is the involvement of parents and families in adolescent catechesis. Coordinators of adolescent catechesis in parish settings need to listen to families, involve parents and families in planning for adolescent catechesis, articulate what is happening with the families of the parish, and build in a family perspective within adolescent catechesis.

Clarifying Roles — Four Functions

[48.] Each of the above leadership roles (the coordinator of youth ministry, the director of religious education, and the priest/pastoral associate) are involved in the parish catechetical effort. The parish can use the following four functions to discuss and clarify the responsibilities of the CYM, DRE, and priest/pastoral associate in adolescent catechesis. Determining the pattern of relationships and responsibilities among these leaders is critically important. This clarification demands collaboration and teamwork by the CYM, DRE, and priest/pastoral associate. Through this process of clarification, a person(s) can be designated to develop and coordinate adolescent catechesis.

The Advocate works to educate the appropriate leadership about adolescent catechesis, about the needs of young people and their families, and about processes and programs that can be developed to meet these needs. The Advocate does not assume direct responsibility for developing programs but, rather, indicates continued growth possibilities. The Resource Person helps those involved in adolescent catechesis to become aware of diocesan services, newly published print and audio-visual materials, workshops, training programs, and conferences. The Resource Person keeps abreast of new resources and channels the information to other leaders. The Coordinator assumes organizational direction for the adolescent catechesis program, developing the program with a planning team, recruiting/training/supporting catechists, and administering the program. The Catechist is directly involved in designing and conducting learning experiences with youth.

C. COORDINATORS OF ADOLESCENT CATECHESIS IN A CATHOLIC SCHOOL SETTING

School Principals

[49.] As the primary administrator and coordinator of the school's ministry, the principal is primarily responsible for seeing to it that the catechetical needs, goals, and priorities of the school are identified, articulated, and met. He or she facilitates the development of a shared philosophy and shared planning among the administrators and faculty to build a faith community in the school and to provide for a holistic ministry with the students. The principal also provides opportunities for the ongoing education of faculty members by which they can deepen their faith and enhance their ministry with youth (cf. NCD, 215).

High School Campus Ministry Coordinator

The primary task of the high school campus ministry coordinator is to call forth the ministerial talents of those in the school community to help organize, motivate, and initiate a coordinated and holistic ministry at the high school level. This often involves a complex of programs and activities in each of the components of youth ministry: Word, worship, community life, justice/service, guidance/healing, enablement, and advocacy. All of these are aimed at building a living faith community among students, faculty, and administration. The high school campus ministry coordinator works with the religious studies department, the chaplain, and the guidance department to create an environment in which their respective programs are experienced by the students as complementary. The harmonious functioning of a high school campus ministry requires the collaboration of the coordinator with the religious studies department, the chaplain, and the guidance department. In addition, it is essential for the high school campus minister to be in close collaboration with parish youth ministry efforts.

Religious Studies Department Chairperson

The primary task of the department chairperson is to facilitate the development of curricula and personnel for catechesis in the high school. In addition to his or her responsibilities as a religion teacher, the chairperson shares responsibility for coordinating the ministry of catechesis within the school community. He or she often assumes the roles of advocate and resource person, in addition to those of religion teacher and coordinator. As one dimension of a broader ministry within the school, the chairperson collaborates with the coordinator of campus ministry, the chaplain, and the guidance department to provide an integrated, total ministry.

D. ADOLESCENT CATECHESIS IN THE DIOCESAN CHURCH

Diocesan Offices

[50.] Diocesan offices of religious education, youth ministry, and Catholic schools are catalysts for the vision and development of adolescent catechesis within the diocese. Through their training, consultation, and resourcing services they assist parishes and schools in the development of adolescent catechesis programs. These indirect services focus on the key leaders who have the responsibility for adolescent catechesis in parishes and schools. These diocesan offices must collaborate in formulating and implementing a plan for educating parish and school leaders to the foundations, aims, process, principles, and framework of adolescent catechesis contained in this paper. A collaborative effort is also needed in providing curriculum development assistance to parishes and schools, in making available current resources for adolescent catechesis, and in providing education programs for catechists/religion teachers. Special attention needs to be given to assisting parishes and schools in developing multicultural and multiracial catechetical programming, to making available multicultural and multiracial catechetical resources, and to educating coordinators and catechists/

religion teachers on the educational methods and techniques suited to the cultural, racial, and linguistic needs of the people in the diocese. Consultation services to assist parishes and Catholic schools in clarifying responsibility for adolescent catechesis may also be required (NCD, 238).

Bishops

The urgency of the present situation of adolescent catechesis necessitates the active encouragement and support of the bishop for new initiatives in adolescent catechesis. His active involvement through support of diocesan and local efforts, through his pastoral visits, and through his communication in pastoral letters and the media brings the Church's concern for adolescent catechesis to the forefront. As chief catechist in the diocese, he is "responsible for seeing to it that sound catechesis is provided for all people" (NCD, 218). The active support and involvement of the Bishop is essential for helping all ecclesial communities realize that youth are more than the church of the future — they are "The Young Church of Today."

VI. CONCLUSION

[51.] The content of this paper and the extensive consultation process through which it was prepared speak strongly about the need for, elements of, and principles for developing adolescent catechesis. However, this paper is not the final word. If the paper has validity, it will best be seen in effective implementation of adolescent catechesis in families, parishes, schools, diocesan programs, and national efforts. Readers of this paper are urged to reflect on the paper, react to it, criticize it, and use it in assessing current efforts in adolescent catechesis and in designing and implementing new and/or renewed efforts.

In striving to enrich and affirm the life and faith of young people through catechesis, it is humbling to realize that our best efforts may not always bring forth the fruit that was intended or hoped for. " . . . it (catechesis) is more difficult and tiring than ever before, because of the obstacles and difficulties of all kinds that it meets" (CT, 40). However, this should not cause us discouragement or laxity. Youth deserve our very best efforts, even if we do not often see the fruits of our efforts. Yet in the long run, we all must rely on the presence and power of the Spirit of God. Adults and youth are challenged to be open to the urging and movement of the Holy Spirit in the process of catechesis. Pope John Paul II has described this reality well. This paper concludes with his words. This is also the point where the next words and steps belong to us.

"Catechesis, which is growth in faith and the maturing of the Christian life toward its fullness, is consequently a work of the Holy Spirit, a work that the Spirit alone can initiate and sustain in the Church" (CT, 72).

NOTES

1. Richard McBrien, *Catholicism* (Winston Press, 1976): 716.

2. Thomas Groome, *Christian Religious Education* (New York: Harper & Row, 1981): chapter 5.

3. John S. Nelson, "Faith and Adolescents: Insight from Psychology and Sociology," in *Faith Maturing: A Personal and Communal Task* (NFCYM, 1985).

4. Charles Shelton, *Adolescent Spirituality* (Chicago: Loyola University Press, 1983): chapter 9.

THE
RELIGIOUS DIMENSION
OF EDUCATION
IN A
CATHOLIC SCHOOL

GUIDELINES FOR REFLECTION AND RENEWAL
1988

OVERVIEW OF *THE RELIGIOUS DIMENSION OF EDUCATION IN A CATHOLIC SCHOOL: GUIDELINES FOR REFLECTION AND RENEWAL*

by Fayette Breaux Veverka

Judging by the few references to "catechesis" in *The Religious Dimension of Education in a Catholic School: Guidelines for Reflection and Renewal* (RDE), one might wonder why this work by the Congregation for Catholic Education should be characterized as a "catechetical" document. The first time the term "catechesis" appears in the document is in part four of the five-part document (68 – 73). The purpose of this section, moreover, is to establish a "clear distinction" between "catechesis," whose aim is "maturity: spiritual, liturgical, sacramental and apostolic" that takes place in the "local church community" over "a whole lifetime," and "religious instruction" in Catholic schools, whose aim is systematic "knowledge" of Christian faith.

Examining the document's sources raises some additional questions. Issued April 7, 1988, on the feast of Saint John Baptist de La Salle, principal patron of teachers, the document links its work to other papers published by the Congregation for Catholic Education, *The Catholic School* and *Lay Catholics in Schools: Witnesses to the Faith.* Its main sources are the documents of the Second Vatican Council, especially the *Declaration on Christian Education;* Paul VI's apostolic exhortation *On Evangelization in the Modern World;* the *General Catechetical Directory,* issued by the Congregation for Clergy; and selected papal addresses and pastoral letters of bishops (3). It is worth noting that the RDE makes no mention of the church's *General Catechetical Directory* (1971) and quotes from *On Catechesis in Our Time* (1979) only once. The Congregation does not cite any of the major catechetical documents of the U.S. Catholic bishops, such as *To Teach as Jesus Did* (1972), *Basic Teachings for Catholic Religious Education* (1973) or *Sharing the Light of Faith: National Catechetical Directory for Catholics of the United States* (1978).

This paucity of references to the literature of catechesis occurs in part because the RDE is a contemporary expression of a philosophy of Catholic education, whose roots and traditions differ in significant ways from the modern catechetical movement. In terms of the purposes and goals of religious education, catechetical works focus on the task of fostering maturity in faith. The literature of Catholic education emphasizes a necessary and intrinsic relationship between religious formation and social, cultural and intellectual development. The language of catechesis reflects its biblical roots and pastoral orientation. The core principles of Catholic education reflect the systematic framework of neoscholastic philosophical sources.

The RDE is similar in purpose, though not in tone, to Pius XI's 1929 encyclical, *The Christian Education of Youth.* As a mission statement for Catholic education, the 1929 encyclical expressed fundamental convictions about the relationship of religion, education and culture that are affirmed and reinterpreted in the context of post-Vatican II theology in the RDE.

Less triumphalistic and defensive than its predecessor, the RDE is addressed to "local ordinaries and the superiors of religious congregations dedicated to the education of young people" (2). As the document's subtitle suggests, its purpose is to offer "guidelines for reflection and renewal" in Catholic schools at the "pre-university level," defined as all institutions "dependent on ecclesiastical authority and therefore falling within the competence of this dicastery" (i.e., The Congregation for Catholic Education) (4).

A brief introduction advances the document's central thesis. Citing Vatican II's *Declaration on Christian Education*, the document argues that though Catholic schools pursue cultural goals similar to other educational institutions, what makes them distinctive is a "religious dimension" found in the educational climate, the personal development of students, the relationship between faith and culture and the integration of all knowledge in the light of the gospel (1). Educational leaders are invited "to examine whether or not the words of the Council have become a reality" and to adapt these general guidelines to the specific needs of their local situations (2, 5). The major themes of this educational vision are developed in five major parts and a brief conclusion.

THE SITUATION OF YOUTH: READING THE SIGNS OF THE TIMES

One recognizes the spirit of Vatican II's admonition to read "the signs of the times" in part one: "The Religious Dimension in the Lives of Today's Youth." Here, the document establishes a context for the discussion of Catholic education by examining the "special situation of youth" (7). It describes the ambiguity and insecurity young people face in a world dominated by utilitarian and technological values (10). Though "surprisingly well-informed" about the world, many young people lack "the critical ability" to make moral judgments about the societies in which they live (8, 9). The document expresses concern for the "loneliness" and "depression" of youth suffering from the breakdown of family and community life. A range of social ills from the nuclear threat to poverty and unemployment foster reactions of violence, self-destructive escapist behaviors and widespread religious indifference among youth (11–15).

The document is realistic in recognizing that for some students "the years spent in a Catholic school seem to have scarcely any effect" (19) but also notes some positive signs that youth are "searching for a deeper understanding of their religion." Some have moved through their questions and are "ready to commit themselves . . . to a Christian way of life" (18). It is to this picture of hope and despair that Catholic educators must respond.

CATHOLIC SCHOOLS AS CENTRAL TO THE CHURCH'S EDUCATIONAL MISSION

Part two, "The Religious Dimension of the School Climate," and part three, "The Religious Dimension of School Life and Work," articulate the religious and educational vision that should distinguish the work of Catholic schools.

Central in this argument is the conviction that schools are necessary instruments for carrying out the church's educational mission. On this point the document is unambiguous: "The Catholic school is not a marginal or secondary element in the pastoral mission of the bishop" (33). Those looking to this document to support a vision of Catholic schools as part of a broader configuration of agencies, programs and approaches within the total mission of Catholic education will be disappointed. "Such things as film clubs and sports groups are not enough; not even classes in catechism instruction are sufficient. What is needed is a school" (41). While the document cites briefly the need for coordination between religious instruction in the school and catechesis "in parishes, in the family and in youth associations" (70), this is not a vision of schools as partners and collaborators but as a preferred model of religious formation.

PRINCIPLES OF A CATHOLIC PHILOSOPHY OF EDUCATION

The document's commitment to the priority of schooling rests on a cohesive set of principles fundamental to the tradition of a Catholic philosophy of education.

1. Catholic schools integrate the tasks of religious formation and human development because of a Christian understanding of the fundamental unity of the human person. "The believer is both human and a person of faith, the protagonist of culture and the subject of religion" (51). The scope of religious formation must embrace the whole of human life in a "movement or a growth process" (98) that "guides men and women to human and Christian perfection. . . . For those who believe in Christ, these are two facets of a single reality" (34).

2. Catholic schools perform a "specific pastoral function" as a mediator between faith and culture (31). Their particular responsibility is to "interpret and give order to human culture in the light of faith." They are central to the church's educational mission not because they merely "supplement" secular education with religious instruction but because they are "a privileged place" (52) where "faith, culture and life are brought into harmony" (34). In addition to this synthetic function, the schools also help students develop critical perspectives that enable them to "recognize and reject cultural counter-values which threaten human dignity" (52).

3. The intellectual and the religious work of the schools mutually enhance and illumine one another. While "being faithful to the newness of the gospel," Catholic schools at the same time respect "the autonomy and the methods proper to human knowledge" (31). While the academic disciplines cannot be seen "merely as subservient to faith," this does not mean that "one can negate spiritual values or prescind from them" (53).

4. The Catholic school maintains a dual identity as an agency of religious formation for life in the church and an agency of public education for life in the world. This imposes on the institution "enormous and complex" responsibilities that require careful and critical deliberation.

On the one hand, a Catholic school is a "civic institution": Its aims, methods and character are the same as those of every other school. On the other hand, it is a "Christian community" whose educational goals are rooted in Christ and his gospel. It's not always easy to bring these two aspects into harmony; the task requires constant attention, so that the tension between a serious effort to transmit culture and forceful witness to the gospel does not turn into a conflict harmful to both (67).

IMPLEMENTING THE VISION

The document suggests a number of concrete strategies for implementing this vision in the life and work of the school.

Among its most important recommendations are the following:

1. *A "permeation" theory of religious formation.* Students entering a Catholic school should experience an educational environment "illumined by the light of faith" and "permeated with the gospel spirit of love and freedom" (25). Not merely an institution, the school is a "community" that gives witness to the values of "simplicity and evangelical poverty" (29, 31). It is not just in the teaching of religion that faith is present; teachers in other subject areas "can help students to see beyond the limited horizon of human reality . . . God cannot be the Great Absent One or the unwelcome intruder" (51).

2. *The teaching of religion.* Those who teach religion must be trained professionally and competent for their task of communicating a "systematic presentation of religion" (96–97). One approach to this task is suggested in part four, "Religious Instruction in the Classroom and the Religious Dimension of Formation" (74–95), which outlines one approach to teaching religion centered on the person of Jesus. "It is possible to love a person; it is rather difficult to love a formula" (107). The authenticity of religious education is found among teachers "in their unity among themselves and their generous and humble communion with the holy father" (44).

3. *Respect for religious freedom.* Recognizing the presence of non-Catholic students in Catholic schools, the document emphasizes the need to respect the "religious freedom and personal conscience of individual students and their families." With a diverse student body, "evangelization . . . may not even be possible" (108). The "right and duty of the school to proclaim the gospel" is not the same as "the imposition" of faith, which the document condemns as a form of "moral violence which is strictly forbidden, both by the gospel and by church law" (6).

4. *Pursuit of social goals.* Catholic schools must promote "traditional civic values such as freedom, justice, the nobility of work," respect for the state and its laws, and commitment to social progress and the common good. At the same time, Catholic schools invite students to "develop a critical sense" (101) so they may evaluate their world and participate in its transformation toward greater "peace, justice, freedom and progress for all peoples" (45).

5. *Openness to a range of pedagogical theories and approaches.* The document accepts the premise "that every pedagogical current of thought contains things which are true and useful." Teachers must be exposed to various approaches from which they can "begin to reflect, judge and choose" (62).

6. *Respect for students.* Catholic schools need to create a "warm and trusting atmosphere" where teachers "accept the students as they are." Teachers can establish rapport with students by being available for personal conversation and by responding to them with "affection, tact, understanding, serenity of spirit, a balanced judgment, patience . . . and prudence" (71).

7. *Collaboration with families.* Recognizing parents as the primary educators of their children, the document encourages a strong "partnership between a Catholic school and the families of the students" (42).

8. *Leadership roles.* "Love for and fidelity to the church is the organizing principle and the source of strength of a Catholic school" (44). Religious communities are encouraged to persevere in "the fulfillment of an educational charism" and to draw from their own educational traditions (36). Lay teachers have an important role as "a concrete example of the lay vocation" and can even establish and run schools, with the recognition of "competent ecclesiastical authority" (37, 38). Catholic school leaders and church authorities must strive for "mutual esteem and reciprocal collaboration" (44).

CONCLUSION

The RDE offers both important contributions and significant challenges to the church's catechetical ministry. It represents a different voice in the conversation about the church's catechetical and educational mission. It is a voice that emphasizes the need to bring faith to bear on our common cultural, social, political and intellectual life. It reminds us that faith is both personal and public; the gospel must be lived in the world and not simply in the church. It insists that Christians cannot lead compartmentalized lives that separate the gospel from culture, intellect from faith and religion from life.

However, its identification of this vision of Catholic education with the structure of Catholic schooling poses significant challenges to catechetical leaders. Catechetical documents emphasize the priority of adult education and the life of the total community of faith as the locus of Christian formation. Can this vision of Catholic education enrich and complement non-schooling approaches such as the renewed Rite of Christian Initiation of Adults, parish-based renewal experiences, retreats, service and justice programs or adult leadership development? To what extent can these alternative strategies carry out the church's educational mission and collaborate rather than compete with one another for scarce resources and personnel? These are questions that remain to be answered.

OUTLINE

Introduction

PART ONE: THE RELIGIOUS DIMENSION IN THE LIVES OF TODAY'S YOUTH

    1. Youth in a changing world

    2. Some common characteristics of the young

PART TWO: THE RELIGIOUS DIMENSION OF THE SCHOOL CLIMATE

    1. What is a Christian school climate?

    2. The physical environment of a Catholic school

    3. The ecclesial and educational climate of the school

    4. The Catholic school as an open community

PART THREE: THE RELIGIOUS DIMENSION OF SCHOOL LIFE AND WORK

    1. The religious dimension of school life

    2. The religious dimension of the school culture

PART FOUR: RELIGIOUS INSTRUCTION IN THE CLASSROOM AND THE RELIGIOUS DIMENSION OF FORMATION

    1. The nature of religious instruction

    2. Some basic presuppositions about religious instruction

    3. An outline for an organic presentation of the Christian event and the Christian message

    4. An outline for a systematic presentation of the Christian life

    5. The religion teacher

PART FIVE: A GENERAL SUMMARY: THE RELIGIOUS DIMENSION OF THE FORMATION PROCESS AS A WHOLE

    1. What is a Christian formation process?

    2. Educational goals

Conclusion

INTRODUCTION

1.   On October 28, 1965, the Second Vatican Council promulgated the Declaration on Christian Education *Gravissimum educationis*. The document describes the distinguishing characteristic of a Catholic school in this way: "The Catholic school pursues cultural goals and the natural development of youth to the same degree as any other school. What makes the Catholic school distinctive is its attempt to generate a community climate in the school that is permeated by the Gospel spirit of freedom and love. It tries to guide the adolescents in such a way that personality development goes hand in hand with the development of the 'new creature' that each one has become through baptism. It tries to relate all of human culture to the good news of salvation so that the light of faith will illumine everything that the students will gradually come to learn about the world, about life, and about the human person."[1]

The Council, therefore, declared that what makes the Catholic school distinctive is its religious dimension, and that this is to be found in *a)* the educational climate, *b)* the personal development of each student, *c)* the relationship established between culture and the Gospel, *d)* the illumination of all knowledge with the light of faith.

2.   More than twenty years have passed since this declaration of the Council. In response to suggestions received from many parts of the world, the Congregation for Catholic Education warmly invites local ordinaries and the superiors of Religious Congregations dedicated to the education of young people to examine whether or not the words of the Council have become a reality. The Second Extraordinary General Assembly of the Synod of Bishops of 1985 said that this opportunity should not be missed! The reflection should lead to concrete decisions about what can and should he done to make Catholic schools more effective in meeting the expectations of the Church, expectations shared by many families and students.

3.   In order to be of assistance in implementing the Council's declarations the Congregation for Catholic Education has already published several papers dealing with questions of concern to Catholic schools. *The Catholic School*[2] develops a basic outline of the specific identity and mission of the school in today's world. *Lay Catholics in Schools: Witnesses to the Faith*[3] emphasizes the contributions of lay people, who complement the valuable service offered in the past and still offered today by so many Religious Congregations of men and women. This present document is closely linked to the preceding ones; it is based on the same sources, appropriately applied to the world of today.[4]

4.   The present document restricts its attention to Catholic schools: that is, educational institutions of whatever type, devoted to the formation of young people at all pre-university levels, dependent on ecclesiastical authority, and therefore falling within the competence of this Dicastery. This clearly leaves many other questions untouched, but it is better to concentrate our attention on one area rather than try to deal with several different issues at once. We are confident that attention will be given to the other questions at some appropriate time.[5]

5.   The pages which follow contain guidelines which are rather general. Different regions, different schools, and even different classes within the same school will have their own distinct history, ambiences and personal characteristics. The Congregation asks bishops, Religious superiors and those in charge of the schools to study these general guidelines and adapt them to their own local situations.

6.   Not all students in Catholic schools are members of the Catholic Church; not all are Christians. There are, in fact, countries in which the vast majority of the students are not Catholics—a reality which the Council called attention to.[6] The religious freedom and the personal conscience of individual students and their families must be respected, and this freedom is explicitly recognized by the Church.[7] On the other hand, a Catholic school cannot relinquish its own freedom to proclaim the Gospel and to offer a formation based on the values to be found in a Christian education; this is its right and its duty. To proclaim or to offer is not to impose, however; the latter suggests a moral violence which is strictly forbidden, both by the Gospel and by Church law.[8]

PART ONE
THE RELIGIOUS DIMENSION IN THE LIVES
OF TODAY'S YOUTH

1. YOUTH IN A CHANGING WORLD

7.   The Council provided a realistic analysis of the religious condition in the world today,[9] and paid explicit attention to the special situation of young people;[10] educators must do the same. Whatever methods they employ to do this, they should be attentive to the results of research with youth done at the local level, and they should be mindful of the fact that the young today are, in some respects, different from those that the Council had in mind.

8.   Many Catholic schools are located in countries which are undergoing radical changes in outlook and in life-style: these countries are becoming urbanized and industrialized, and are moving into the so-called "tertiary" economy, characterized by a high standard of living, a wide choice of educational opportunities, and complex communication systems. Young people in these countries are familiar with the media from their infancy; they have been exposed to a wide variety of opinions on every possible topic, and are surprisingly well-informed even when they are still very young.

9.   These young people absorb a wide and varied assortment of knowledge from all kinds of sources, including the school. But they are not yet capable of ordering or prioritizing what they have learned. Often enough, they do not yet have the critical ability needed to distinguish the true and good from their opposites; they have not yet acquired the necessary religious and moral criteria that will enable them to remain objective and independent when faced with the prevailing attitudes and habits of society. Concepts such as truth, beauty and goodness have become so vague today that young people do not know where to turn to find help; even when they are able to hold on to certain values, they do not yet have the capacity to develop these values into a way of life; all too often they are more inclined simply to go their own way, accepting whatever is popular at the moment.

Changes occur in different ways and at different rates. Each school will have to look carefully at the religious behavior of the young people "in loco" in order to discover their thought processes, their life-style, their reaction to change. Depending on the situation, the change may be profound, it may be only beginning, or the local culture may be resistant to change. Even a culture resistant to change is being influenced by the all-pervasive mass media!

2. SOME COMMON CHARACTERISTICS OF THE YOUNG

10.   Although local situations create great diversity, there are characteristics that today's young people have in common, and educators need to be aware of them.

Many young people find themselves in a condition of radical instability. On the one hand they live in a one-dimensional universe in which the only criterion is practical utility and the only value is economic and technological progress. On the other hand, these same young people seem to be progressing to a stage beyond this narrow universe; nearly everywhere, evidence can be found of a desire to be released from it.

11.   Others live in an environment devoid of truly human relationships; as a result, they suffer from loneliness and a lack of affection. This is a widespread phenomenon that seems to be independent of life-style; it is found in oppressive regimes, among the homeless, and in the cold and impersonal dwellings of the rich. Young people today are notably more depressed than in the past; this is surely a sign of the poverty of human relationships in families and in society today.

12.   Large numbers of today's youth are very worried about an uncertain future. They have been influenced by a world in which human values are in chaos because these values are no longer rooted in God; the result is that these young people are very much afraid when they think about the appalling problems in the world: the threat of nuclear annihilation, vast unemployment, the high number of marriages that end in separation or divorce, widespread poverty, etc.

Their worry and insecurity become an almost irresistible urge to focus in on themselves, and this can lead to violence when young people are together — a violence that is not always limited to words.

13.   Not a few young people, unable to find any meaning in life or trying to find an escape from loneliness, turn to alcohol, drugs, the erotic, the exotic, etc. Christian education is faced with the huge challenge of helping these young people discover something of value in their lives.

14.   The normal instability of youth is accentuated by the times they are living in. Their decisions are not solidly based: today's "yes" easily becomes tomorrow's "no."

Finally, a vague sort of generosity is characteristic of many young people. Filled with enthusiasm, they are eager to join in popular causes. Too often, however, these movements are without any specific orientation or inner coherence. It is important to channel this potential for good and, when possible, give it the orientation that comes from the light of faith.

15.   In some parts of the world it might be profitable to pay particular attention to the reasons why young people abandon their faith. Often enough, this begins by giving up religious practices. As time goes on, it can develop into a hostility toward Church structures and a crisis of conscience regarding the truths of faith and their accompanying moral values. This can be especially true in those countries where education in general is secular or even imbued with atheism. The crisis seems to occur more frequently in places where there is high economic development and rapid social and cultural change. Sometimes the phenomenon is not recent; it is something that the parents went through, and they are now passing their own attitudes along to the new generation. When this is the case, it is no longer a personal crisis, but one that has become religious and social. It has been called a "split between the Gospel and culture."[11]

16.   A break with the faith often takes the form of total religious indifference. Experts suggest that certain patterns of behavior found among young people arc actually attempts to fill the religious void with some sort of a substitute: the pagan cult of the body, drug escape, or even those massive "youth events" which sometimes deteriorate into fanaticism and total alienation from reality.

17.   Educators cannot be content with merely observing these behavior patterns; they have to search for the causes. It may be some lack at the start, some problem in the family background. Or it may be that parish and Church organizations are deficient. Christian formation given in childhood and early adolescence is not always proof against the influence of the environment. Perhaps there are cases in which the fault lies with the Catholic school itself.

18.   There are also a number of positive signs, which give grounds for encouragement. In a Catholic school, as in any school, one can find young people who are outstanding in every way — in religious attitude, moral behavior, and academic achievement. When we look for the cause, we often discover an excellent

family background reinforced by both Church and school. There is always a combination of factors, open to the interior workings of grace.

Some young people are searching for a deeper understanding of their religion; as they reflect on the real meaning of life they begin to find answers to their questions in the Gospel. Others have already passed through the crisis of indifference and doubt, and are now ready to commit themselves — or recommit themselves — to a Christian way of life. These positive signs give us reason to hope that a sense of religion can develop in more of today's young people, and that it can be more deeply rooted in them.

19. For some of today's youth, the years spent in a Catholic school seem to have scarcely any effect. They seem to have a negative attitude toward all the various ways in which a Christian life is expressed — prayer, participation in the Mass, or frequenting of the Sacraments. Some even reject these expressions outright, especially those associated with an institutional Church. If a school is excellent as an academic institution, but does not witness to authentic values, then both good pedagogy and a concern for pastoral care make it obvious that renewal is called for — not only in the content and methodology of religious instruction, but in the overall school planning which governs the whole process of formation of the students.

20. The religious questioning of young people today needs to be better understood. Many of them are asking about the value of science and technology when everything could end in a nuclear holocaust; they look at how modern civilization floods the world with material goods, beautiful and useful as these may be, and they wonder whether the purpose of life is really to possess many "things" or whether there may not be something far more valuable; they are deeply disturbed by the injustice which divides the free and the rich from the poor and the oppressed.

21. For many young people, a critical look at the world they are living in leads to crucial questions on the religious plane. They ask whether religion can provide any answers to the pressing problems afflicting humanity. Large numbers of them sincerely want to know how to deepen their faith and live a meaningful life. Then there is the further practical question of how to translate responsible commitment into effective action. Future historians will have to evaluate the "youth group" phenomenon, along with the movements founded for spiritual growth, apostolic work, or service of others. But these are signs that words are not enough for the young people of today. They want to be active — to do something worthwhile for themselves and for others.

22. Catholic schools are spread throughout the world and enroll literally millions of students.[12] These students are children of their own race, nationality, traditions, and family. They are also the children of our age. Each student has a distinct origin and is a unique individual. A Catholic school is not simply a place where lessons are taught; it is a center that has an operative educational philosophy, attentive to the needs of today's youth and illumined by the Gospel

message. A thorough and exact knowledge of the real situation will suggest the best educational methods.

23.   We must be ready to repeat the basic essentials over and over again, so long as the need is present. We need to integrate what has already been learned, and respond to the questions which come from the restless and critical minds of the young. We need to break through the wall of indifference, and at the same time be ready to help those who are doing well to discover a "better way," offering them a knowledge that also embraces Christian wisdom.[13] The specific methods and the steps used to accomplish the educational philosophy of the school will, therefore, be conditioned and guided by an intimate knowledge of each student's unique situation.[14]

PART TWO
THE RELIGIOUS DIMENSION OF THE SCHOOL CLIMATE

1. WHAT IS A CHRISTIAN SCHOOL CLIMATE?

24.   In pedagogical circles, today as in the past, great stress is put on the climate of a school: the sum total of the different components at work in the school which interact with one another in such a way as to create favorable conditions for a formation process. Education always takes place within certain specific conditions of space and time, through the activities of a group of individuals who are active and also interactive among themselves. They follow a program of studies which is logically ordered and freely accepted. Therefore, the elements to be considered in developing an organic vision of a school climate are persons, space, time, relationships, teaching, study and various other activities.

25.   From the first moment that a student sets foot in a Catholic school, he or she ought to have the impression of entering a new environment, one illumined by the light of faith, and having its own unique characteristics. The Council summed this up by speaking of an environment permeated with the Gospel spirit of love and freedom.[15] In a Catholic school, everyone should be aware of the living presence of Jesus the "Master" who, today as always, is with us in our journey through life as the one genuine "Teacher," the perfect Man in whom all human values find their fullest perfection. The inspiration of Jesus must be translated from the ideal into the real. The Gospel spirit should be evident in a Christian way of thought and life which permeates all facets of the educational climate. Having crucifixes in the school will remind everyone, teachers and students alike, of this familiar and moving presence of Jesus, the "Master" who gave his most complete and sublime teaching from the cross.

26.   Prime responsibility for creating this unique Christian school climate rests with the teachers, as individuals and as a community. The religious dimension of the school climate is expressed through the celebration of Christian values in Word and Sacrament, in individual behavior, in friendly and harmonious interpersonal relationships, and in a ready availability. Through this daily witness, the students will come to appreciate the uniqueness of the environment

to which their youth has been entrusted. If it is not present, then there is little left which can make the school Catholic.

2. THE PHYSICAL ENVIRONMENT OF A CATHOLIC SCHOOL

27.   Many of the students will attend a Catholic school—often the same school—from the time they are very young children until they are nearly adults. It is only natural that they should come to think of the school as an extension of their own homes, and therefore a "school-home" ought to have some of the amenities which can create a pleasant and happy family atmosphere. When this is missing from the home, the school can often do a great deal to make up for it.

28.   The first thing that will help to create a pleasant environment is an adequate physical facility: one that includes sufficient space for classrooms, sports and recreation, and also such things as a staff room and rooms for parent-teacher meetings, group work, etc. The possibilities for this vary from place to place; we have to be honest enough to admit that some school buildings are unsuitable and unpleasant. But students can be made to feel "at home" even when the surroundings are modest, if the climate is humanly and spiritually rich.

29.   A Catholic school should be an example of simplicity and evangelical poverty, but this is not inconsistent with having the materials needed to educate properly. Because of rapid technological progress, a school today must have access to equipment that, at times, is complex and expensive. This is not a luxury; it is simply what a school needs to carry out its role as an educational institution. Catholic schools, therefore, have a right to expect the help from others that will make the purchase of modern educational materials possible.[16] Both individuals and public bodies have a duty to provide this support.

Students should feel a responsibility for their "school-home"; they should take care of it and help to keep it as clean and neat as possible. Concern for the environment is part of a formation in ecological awareness, the need for which is becoming increasingly apparent.

An awareness of Mary's presence can be a great help toward making the school into a "home." Mary, Mother and Teacher of the Church, accompanied her Son as he grew in wisdom and grace; from its earliest days, she has accompanied the Church in its mission of salvation.

30.   The physical proximity of the school to a church can contribute a great deal toward achieving the educational aims. A church should not be seen as something extraneous, but as a familiar and intimate place where those young people who are believers can find the presence of the Lord: "Behold, I am with you all days."[17] Liturgy planning should be especially careful to bring the school community and the local Church together.

3. THE ECCLESIAL AND EDUCATIONAL CLIMATE OF THE SCHOOL

31.   The declaration *Gravissimum educationis*[18] notes an important advance in the way a Catholic school is thought of: the transition from the school as an institution to the school as a community. This community dimension is, perhaps, one result of the new awareness of the Church's nature as developed by the Council. In the Council texts, the community dimension is primarily a theological concept rather than a sociological category; this is the sense in which it is used in the second chapter of *Lumen gentium,* where the Church is described as the People of God.

As it reflects on the mission entrusted to it by the Lord, the Church gradually develops its pastoral instruments so that they may become ever more effective in proclaiming the Gospel and promoting total human formation. The Catholic school is one of these pastoral instruments; its specific pastoral service consists in mediating between faith and culture: being faithful to the newness of the Gospel while at the same time respecting the autonomy and the methods proper to human knowledge.

32.   Everyone directly involved in the school is a part of the school community: teachers, directors, administrative and auxiliary staff. Parents are central figures, since they are the natural and irreplaceable agents in the education of their children. And the community also includes the students, since they must be active agents in their own education.[19]

33.   At least since the time of the Council, therefore, the Catholic school has had a clear identity, not only as a presence of the Church in society, but also as a genuine and proper instrument of the Church. It is a place of evangelization, of authentic apostolate and of pastoral action — not through complementary or parallel or extra-curricular activity, but of its very nature: its work of educating the Christian person. The Words of the present Holy Father make this abundantly clear: "the Catholic school is not a marginal or secondary element in the pastoral mission of the bishop. Its function is not merely to be an instrument with which to combat the education given in a State school."[20]

34.   The Catholic school finds its true justification in the mission of the Church; it is based on an educational philosophy in which faith, culture and life are brought into harmony. Through it, the local Church evangelizes, educates, and contributes to the formation of a healthy and morally sound life-style among its members. The Holy Father affirms that "the need for the Catholic school becomes evidently clear when we consider what it contributes to the development of the mission of the People of God, to the dialogue between Church and the human community, to the safeguarding of freedom of conscience . . . ." Above all, according to the Holy Father, the Catholic school helps in achieving a double objective: "of its nature it guides men and women to human and Christian perfection, and at the same time helps them to become mature in their faith. For those who believe in Christ, these are two facets of a single reality."[21]

35.   Most Catholic schools are under the direction of Religious Congregations, whose consecrated members enrich the educational climate by bringing to it the values of their own Religious communities. These men and women have dedicated themselves to the service of the students without thought of personal gain, because they are convinced that it is really the Lord whom they are serving.[22] Through the prayer, work and love that make up their life in community, they express in a visible way the life of the Church. Each Congregation brings the richness of its own educational tradition to the school, found in its original charism; its members each bring the professional preparation that is required by the call to be an educator. The strength and gentleness of their total dedication to God enlightens their work, and students gradually come to appreciate the value of this witness. They come to love these educators who seem to have the gift of eternal spiritual youth, and it is an affection which endures long after students leave the school.

36.   The Church offers encouragement to these men and women who have dedicated their lives to the fulfillment of an educational charism.[23] It urges those in education not to give up this work, even in situations where it involves suffering and persecution. In fact, the Church hopes that many others will be called to this special vocation. When afflicted by doubts and uncertainty, when difficulties are multiplied, these Religious men and women should recall the nature of their consecration, which is a type of holocaust[24] — a holocaust which is offered "in the perfection of love, which is the scope of the consecrated life."[25] Their merit is the greater because their offering is made on behalf of young people, who are the hope of the Church.

37.   At the side of the priests and Religious, lay teachers contribute their competence and their faith witness to the Catholic school. Ideally, this lay witness is a concrete example of the lay vocation that most of the students will be called to. The Congregation has devoted a specific document to lay teachers,[26] meant to remind lay people of their apostolic responsibility in the field of education and to summon them to participate in a common mission, whose point of convergence is found in the unity of the Church. For all are active members of one Church and cooperate in its one mission, even though the fields of labor and the states of life are different because of the personal call each one receives from God.

38.   The Church, therefore, is willing to give lay people charge of the schools that it has established, and the laity themselves establish schools. The recognition of the school as a Catholic school is, however, always reserved to the competent ecclesiastical authority.[27] When lay people do establish schools, they should be especially concerned with the creation of a community climate permeated by the Gospel spirit of freedom and love, and they should witness to this in their own lives.

39.   The more the members of the educational community develop a real willingness to collaborate among themselves, the more fruitful their work will be. Achieving the educational aims of the school should be an equal priority for teachers, students and families alike, each one according to his or her own role,

always in the Gospel spirit of freedom and love. Therefore channels of communication should be open among all those concerned with the school. Frequent meetings will help to make this possible, and a willingness to discuss common problems candidly will enrich this communication.

The daily problems of school life are sometimes aggravated by misunderstandings and various tensions. A determination to collaborate in achieving common educational goals can help to overcome these difficulties and reconcile different points of view. A willingness to collaborate helps to facilitate decisions that need to be made about the ways to achieve these goals and, while preserving proper respect for school authorities, even makes it possible to conduct a critical evaluation of the school — a process in which teachers, students and families can all take part because of their common concern to work for the good of all.

40.   Considering the special age group they are working with, primary schools should try to create a community school climate that reproduces, as far as possible, the warm and intimate atmosphere of family life. Those responsible for these schools will, therefore, do everything they can to promote a common spirit of trust and spontaneity. In addition, they will take great care to promote close and constant collaboration with the parents of these pupils. An integration of school and home is an essential condition for the birth and development of all of the potential which these children manifest in one or the other of these two situations — including their openness to religion with all that this implies.

41.   The Congregation wishes to express its appreciation to all those dioceses which have worked to establish primary schools in their parishes; these deserve the strong support of all Catholics. It also wishes to thank the Religious Congregations helping to sustain these primary schools, often at great sacrifice. Moreover, the Congregation offers enthusiastic encouragement to those dioceses and Religious Congregations who wish to establish new schools. Such things as film clubs and sports groups are not enough; not even classes in catechism instruction are sufficient. What is needed is a school. This is a goal which, in some countries, was the starting point. There are countries in which the Church began with schools and only later was able to construct Churches and to establish a new Christian community.[28]

4. THE CATHOLIC SCHOOL AS AN OPEN COMMUNITY

42.   Partnership between a Catholic school and the families of the students must continue and be strengthened: not simply to be able to deal with academic problems that may arise, but rather so that the educational goals of the school can he achieved. Close cooperation with the family is especially important when treating sensitive issues such as religious, moral, or sexual education, orientation toward a profession, or a choice of one's vocation in life. It is not a question of convenience, but a partnership based on faith. Catholic tradition teaches that God has bestowed on the family its own specific and unique educational mission.

43. The first and primary educators of children are their parents.[29] The school is aware of this fact but, unfortunately, the same is not always true of the families themselves; it is the school's responsibility to give them this awareness. Every school should initiate meetings and other programs which will make the parents more conscious of their role, and help to establish a partnership; it is impossible to do too much along these lines. It often happens that a meeting called to talk about the children becomes an opportunity to raise the consciousness of the parents. In addition, the school should try to involve the family as much as possible in the educational aims of the school—both in helping to plan these goals and in helping to achieve them. Experience shows that parents who were once totally unaware of their role can be transformed into excellent partners.

44. "The involvement of the Church in the field of education is demonstrated especially by the Catholic school."[30] This affirmation of the Council has both historical and practical importance. Church schools first appeared centuries ago, growing up alongside monasteries, cathedrals and parish churches. The Church has always had a love for its schools, because this is where its children receive their formation these schools have continued to flourish with the help of bishops, countless Religious Congregations, and laity; the Church has never ceased to support the schools in their difficulties and to defend them against governments seeking to close or confiscate them.

Just as the Church is present in the school, so the school is present in the Church; this is a logical consequence of their reciprocal commitment. The Church, through which the Redemption of Christ is revealed and made operative, is where the Catholic school receives its spirit. It recognizes the Holy Father as the center and the measure of unity in the entire Christian community. Love for and fidelity to the church is the organizing principle and the source of strength of a Catholic school. Teachers find the light and the courage for authentic Religious education in their unity among themselves and their generous and humble communion with the Holy Father. Concretely, the educational goals of the school include a concern for the life and the problems of the Church, both local and universal. These goals are attentive to the Magisterium, and include cooperation with Church authorities. Catholic students are helped to become active members of the parish and diocesan communities. They have opportunities to join Church associations and Church youth groups, and they are taught to collaborate in local Church projects.

Mutual esteem and reciprocal collaboration will be established between the Catholic school and the bishop and other Church authorities through direct contacts. We are pleased to note that a concern for Catholic schools is becoming more of a priority of local Churches in many parts of the world.[31]

45. A Christian education must promote respect for the State and its representatives, the observance of just laws, to civic values such as freedom, justice, the nobility of work and the need to pursue social progress are all included among the school goals, and the life of the school gives witness to them. The national anniversaries and other important civic events are commemorated and celebrated in appropriate ways in the schools of each country.

The school life should also reflect an awareness of international society. Christian education sees all of humanity as one large family, divided perhaps by historical and political events, but always one in God who is Father of all. Therefore a Catholic school should be sensitive to and help to promulgate Church appeals for peace, justice, freedom, progress for all peoples and assistance for countries in need. And it should not ignore similar appeals coming from recognized international organizations such as UNESCO and the United Nations.

46.   That Catholic schools help to form good citizens is a fact apparent to everyone. Both government policy and public opinion should, therefore, recognize the work these schools do as a real service to society. It is unjust to accept the service and ignore or fight against its source. Fortunately, a good number of countries seem to have a growing understanding of and sympathy for the Catholic school.[32] A recent survey conducted by the Congregation demonstrates that a new age may be dawning.

PART THREE
THE RELIGIOUS DIMENSION OF SCHOOL LIFE AND WORK

1. THE RELIGIOUS DIMENSION OF SCHOOL LIFE

47.   Students spend a large share of each day and the greater part of their youth either at school or doing activities that are related to school. "School" is often identified with "teaching"; actually, classes and lessons are only a small part of school life. Along with the lessons that a teacher gives, there is the active participation of the students individually or as a group: study, research, exercises, para-curricular activities, examinations, relationships with teachers and with one another, group activities, class meetings, school assemblies. While the Catholic school is like any other school in this complex variety of events that make up the life of the school, there is one essential difference: it draws its inspiration and its strength from the Gospel in which it is rooted. The principle that no human act is morally indifferent to one's conscience or before God has clear applications to school life: examples of it are school work accepted as a duty and done with good will; courage and perseverance when difficulties come; respect for teachers; loyalty toward and love for fellow students; sincerity, tolerance, and goodness in all relationships.

48.   The educational process is not simply a human activity; it is a genuine Christian journey toward perfection. Students who are sensitive to the religious dimension of life realize that the will of God is found in the work and the human relationships of each day. They learn to follow the example of the Master, who spent his youth working and who did good to all.[33] Those students who are unaware of this religious dimension are deprived of its benefits and they run the risk of living the best years of their lives at a shallow level.

49.   Within the overall process of education, special mention must be made of the intellectual work done by students. Although Christian life consists in loving God and doing his will, intellectual work is intimately involved. The light

of Christian faith stimulates a desire to know the universe as God's creation. It enkindles a love for the truth that will not be satisfied with superficiality in knowledge or judgment. It awakens a critical sense which examines statements rather than accepting them blindly. It impels the mind to learn with careful order and precise methods, and to work with a sense of responsibility. It provides the strength needed to accept the sacrifices and the perseverance required by intellectual labor. When fatigued, the Christian student remembers the command of Genesis[34] and the invitation of the Lord.[35]

50. The religious dimension enhances intellectual efforts in a variety of ways: interest in academic work is stimulated by the presence of new perspectives; Christian formation is strengthened; supernatural grace is given. How sad it would be if the young people in Catholic schools were to have no knowledge of this reality in the midst of all the difficult and tiring work they have to do!

2. THE RELIGIOUS DIMENSIONS OF THE SCHOOL CULTURE

51. Intellectual development and growth as a Christian go forward hand in hand. As students move up from one class into the next, it becomes increasingly imperative that a Catholic school help them become aware that a relationship exists between faith and human culture.[36] Human culture remains human, and must be taught with scientific objectivity. But the lessons of the teacher and the reception of those students who are believers will not divorce faith from this culture;[37] this would be a major spiritual loss. The world of human culture and the world of religion are not like two parallel lines that never meet; points of contact are established within the human person. For a believer is both human and a person of faith, the protagonist of culture and the subject of religion. Anyone who searches for the contact points will be able to find them.[38] Helping in the search is not solely the task of religion teachers; their time is quite limited, while other teachers have many hours at their disposal every day. Everyone should work together, each one developing his or her own subject area with professional competence, but sensitive to those opportunities in which the can help students to see beyond the limited horizon of human reality. In a Catholic school, and analogously in every school, God cannot be the Great Absent One or the unwelcome intruder. The Creator does not put obstacles in the path of someone trying to learn more about the universe he created, a universe which is given new significance when seen with the eyes of faith.

52. A Catholic secondary school will give special attention to the "challenges" that human culture poses for faith. Students will be helped to attain that synthesis of faith and culture which is necessary for faith to be mature. But a mature faith is also able to recognize and reject cultural counter-values which threaten human dignity and are therefore contrary to the Gospel.[39] No one should think that all of the problems of religion and of faith will be completely solved by academic studies; nevertheless, we are convinced that a school is a privileged place for finding adequate ways to deal with these problems. The declaration *Gravissimum educationis*,[40] echoing *Gaudium et spes*,[41] indicates that

one of the characteristics of a Catholic school is that it interpret and give order to human culture in the light of faith.

53.   As the Council points out, giving order to human culture in the light of the message of salvation cannot mean a lack of respect for the autonomy of the different academic disciplines and the methodology proper to them; nor can it mean that these disciplines are to be seen merely as subservient to faith. On the other hand, it is necessary to point out that a proper autonomy of culture has to be distinguished from a vision of the human person or of the world as totally autonomous, implying that one can negate spiritual values or prescind from them. We must always remember that, while faith is not to be identified with any one culture and is independent of all cultures, it must inspire every culture: "Faith which does not become culture is faith which is not received fully, not assimilated entirely, not lived faithfully."[42]

54.   In a number of countries, renewal in school programming has given increased attention to science and technology. Those teaching these subject areas must not ignore the religious dimension. They should help their students to understand that positive science, and the technology allied to it, is a part of the universe created by God. Understanding this can help encourage an interest in research: the whole of creation, from the distant celestial bodies and the immeasurable cosmic forces down to the infinitesimal particles and waves of matter and energy, all bear the imprint of the Creator's wisdom and power. The wonder that past ages felt when contemplating this universe, recorded by the biblical authors,[43] is still valid for the students of today; the only difference, is that we have a knowledge that is much more vast and profound. There can be no conflict between faith and true scientific knowledge; both find their source in God.

The student who is able to discover the harmony between faith and science will, in future professional life, be better able to put science and technology to the service of men and women, and to the service of God. It is a way of giving back to God what he has first given to us.[44]

55.   A Catholic school must be committed to the development of a program which will overcome the problems of a fragmented and insufficient curriculum. Teachers dealing with areas such as anthropology, biology, psychology, sociology and philosophy all have the opportunity to present a complete picture of the human person, including the religious dimension. Students should be helped to see the human person as a living creature having both a physical and a spirit nature; each of us has an immortal soul, and we are in need of redemption. The older students can gradually come to a more mature understanding of all that is implied in the concept of "person": intelligence and will, freedom and feelings, the capacity to be an active and creative agent, a being endowed with both rights and duties, capable of interpersonal relationships, called to a specific mission in the world.

56. The religious dimension makes a true understanding of the human person possible. A human being has a dignity and a greatness exceeding that of all other creatures: a work of God that has been elevated to the super-natural order as a child of God, and therefore having both a divine origin and an eternal destiny which transcend this physical universe.[45] Religion teachers will find the way already prepared for an organic presentation of Christian anthropology.

57. Every society has its own heritage of accumulated wisdom. Many people find inspiration in these philosophical and religious concepts which have endured for millennia. The systematic genius of classical Greek and European thought has, over the centuries, generated countless different doctrinal systems, but it has also given us a set of truths which we can recognize as a part of our permanent philosophical heritage. A Catholic school conforms to the generally accepted school programming of today, but implements these programs within an overall religious perspective. This perspective includes criteria such as the following:

Respect for those who seek the truth, who raise fundamental questions about human existence.[46] Confidence in our ability to attain truth, at least in a limited way—a confidence based not on feeling but on faith. God created us "in his own image and likeness" and will not deprive us of the truth necessary to orient our lives.[47] The ability to make judgments about what is true and what is false, and to make choices based on these judgments.[48] Making use of a systematic framework, such as that offered by our philosophical heritage, with which to find the best possible human responses to questions regarding the human person, the world, and God.[49] Lively dialogue between culture and the Gospel message.[50] The fullness of truth contained in the Gospel message itself, which embraces and integrates the wisdom of all cultures, and enriches them with the divine mysteries known only to God but which, out of love, he has chosen to reveal to us.[51] With such criteria as a basis, the student's careful and reflective study of philosophy will bring human wisdom into an encounter with divine wisdom.

58. Teachers should guide the students' work in such a way that they will he able to discover a religious dimension in the world of human history. As a preliminary, they should be encouraged to develop a taste for historical truth, and therefore to realize the need to look critically at texts and curricula which, at times, are imposed by a government or distorted by the ideology of the author. The next step is to help students see history as something real: the drama of human grandeur and human misery.[52] The protagonist of history is the human person, who projects onto the world, on a larger scale, the good and the evil that is within each individual. History is, then, a monumental struggle between these two fundamental realities,[53] and is subject to moral judgments. But such judgments must always be made with understanding.

59. To this end, the teacher should help students to see history as a whole. Looking at the grand picture, they will see the development of civilizations, and learn about progress in such things as economic development, human freedom, and international cooperation. Realizing this can help to offset the disgust that comes from learning about the darker side of human history. But

even this is not the whole story. When they are ready to appreciate it, students can be invited to reflect on the fact that this human struggle takes place within the divine history of universal salvation. At this moment, the religious dimension of history begins to shine forth in all its luminous grandeur.[54]

60.   The increased attention given to science and technology must not lead to a neglect of the humanities: philosophy, history, literature and art. Since earliest times, each society has developed and handed on its artistic and literary heritage, and our human patrimony is nothing more than the sum total of this cultural wealth. Thus, while teachers are helping students to develop an aesthetic sense, they can bring them to a deeper awareness of all peoples as one great human family. The simplest way to uncover the religious dimension of the artistic and literary world is to start with its concrete expressions: in every human culture, art and literature have been closely linked to religious beliefs. The artistic and literary patrimony of Christianity is vast and gives visible testimony to a faith that has been handed down through centuries.

61.   Literary and artistic works depict the struggles of societies, of families, and of individuals. They spring from the depths of the human heart, revealing its lights and its shadows, its hope and its despair. The Christian perspective goes beyond the merely human, and offers more penetrating criteria for understanding the human struggle and the mysteries of the human spirit.[55] Furthermore, an adequate religious formation has been the starting point for the vocation of a number of Christian artists and art critics.

In the upper grades, a teacher can bring students to an even more profound appreciation of artistic works: as a reflection of the divine beauty in tangible form. Both the Fathers of the Church and the masters of Christian philosophy teach this in their writings on aesthetics — St. Augustine invites us to go beyond the intention of the artists in order to find the eternal order of God in the work of art; St. Thomas sees the presence of the Divine Word in art.[56]

62.   A Catholic school is often attentive to issues having to do with educational methods, and this can be of great service both to civil society and to the Church. Government requirements for teacher preparation usually require historical and systematic courses in pedagogy, psychology and teaching methods. In more recent times, educational science has been subdivided into a number of areas of specialization and has been subjected to a variety of different philosophies and political ideologies; those preparing to become teachers may feel that the whole field is confused and fragmented. Teachers of pedagogical science can help these students in their bewilderment, and guide them in the formulation of a carefully thought out synthesis, whose elaboration begins with the premise that every pedagogical current of thought contains things which are true and useful. But then one must begin to reflect, judge, and choose.

63.   Future teachers should be helped to realize that any genuine educational philosophy has to be based on the nature of the human person, and therefore must take into account all of the physical and spiritual powers of each individual, along with the call of each one to be an active and creative agent in service

to society. And this philosophy must be open to a religious dimension. Human beings are fundamentally free; they are not the property of the state or of any human organization. The entire process of education, therefore, is a service to the individual students, helping each one to achieve the most complete formation possible.

The Christian model, based on the person of Christ, is then linked to this human concept of the person — that is, the model begins with an educational framework based on the person as human, and then enriches it with supernatural gifts, virtues, and values — and a supernatural call. It is indeed possible to speak about Christian education; the Conciliar declaration provides us with a clear synthesis of it.[57] Proper pedagogical formation, finally, will guide these students to a self-formation that is both human and Christian, because this is the best possible preparation for one who is preparing to educate others.

64. Interdisciplinary work has been introduced into Catholic schools with positive results, for there are questions and topics that are not easily treated within the limitations of a single subject area. Religious themes should be included; they arise naturally when dealing with topics such as the human person, the family, society, or history. Teachers should be adequately prepared to deal with such questions and be ready to give them the attention they deserve.

65. Religion teachers are not excluded. While their primary mission must be the systematic presentation of religion, they can also be invited — within the limitations of what is concretely possible — to assist in clarifying religious questions that come up in other classes. Conversely, they may wish to invite one of their colleagues to attend a religion class, in order to have the help of an expert when dealing with some specific issue. Whenever this happens, students will be favorably impressed by the cooperative spirit among the teachers: the one purpose all of them have in mind is to help these students grow in knowledge and in commitment.

PART FOUR
RELIGIOUS INSTRUCTION IN THE CLASSROOM AND THE RELIGIOUS DIMENSION OF FORMATION

1. THE NATURE OF RELIGIOUS INSTRUCTION

66. The mission of the Church is to evangelize, for the interior transformation and the renewal of humanity.[58] For young people, the school is one of the ways for this evangelization to take place.[59] It may be profitable to recall what the Magisterium has said: "Together with and in collaboration with the family, schools provide possibilities for catechesis that must not be neglected . . . This refers especially to the Catholic school, of course: it would no longer deserve the title if, no matter how good its reputation for teaching in other areas, there were just grounds for a reproach of negligence or deviation in religious education properly so-called. It is not true that such education is always given *implicitly*

or *indirectly*. The special character of the Catholic school and the underlying reason for its existence, the reason why Catholic parents should prefer it, is precisely the quality of the religious instruction integrated into the overall education of the students."[60]

67.   Sometimes there is an uncertainty, a difference of opinion, or an uneasiness about the underlying principles governing religious formation in a Catholic school, and therefore about the concrete approach to be taken in religious instruction. On the one hand, a Catholic school is a "civic institution"; its aim, methods and characteristics are the same as those of every other school. On the other hand, it is a "Christian community," whose educational goals are rooted in Christ and his Gospel. It is not always easy to bring these two aspects into harmony; the task requires constant attention, so that the tension between a serious effort to transmit culture and a forceful witness to the Gospel does not turn into a conflict harmful to both.

68.   There is a close connection, and at the same time a clear distinction, between religious instruction and catechesis, or the handing on of the Gospel message.[61] The close connection makes it possible for a school to remain a school and still integrate culture with the message of Christianity. The distinction comes from the fact that, unlike religious instruction, catechesis presupposes that the hearer is receiving the Christian message as a salvific reality. Moreover, catechesis takes place within a community living out its faith at a level of space and time not available to a school: a whole lifetime.

69.   The aim of catechesis, or handing on the Gospel message, is maturity: spiritual, liturgical, sacramental and apostolic; this happens most especially in a local Church community. The aim of the school however, is knowledge. While it uses the same elements of the Gospel message, it tries to convey a sense of the nature of Christianity, and of how Christians are trying to live their lives. It is evident, of course, that religious instruction cannot help but strengthen the faith of a believing student, just as catechesis cannot help but increase one's knowledge of the Christian message.

The distinction between religious instruction and catechesis does not change the fact that a school can and must play its specific role in the work of catechesis. Since its educational goals are rooted in Christian principles, the school as a whole is inserted into the evangelical function of the Church. It assists in and promotes faith education.

70.   Recent Church teaching has added an essential note: "The basic principle which must guide us in our commitment to this sensitive area of pastoral activity is that religious instruction and catechesis are at the same time distinct and complementary. A school has as its purpose the students' integral formation. Religious instruction, therefore, should be integrated into the objectives and criteria which characterize a modern school."[62] School directors should keep this directive of the Magisterium in mind, and they should respect the distinctive characteristics of religious instruction. It should have a place in the weekly

order alongside the other classes, for example; it should have its own syllabus, approved by those in authority; it should seek appropriate interdisciplinary links with other course material so that there is a coordination between human learning and religious awareness. Like other course work, it should promote culture, and it should make use of the best educational methods available to schools today. In some countries, the results of examinations in religious knowledge are included within the overall measure of student progress.

Finally, religious instruction in the school needs to be coordinated with the catechesis offered in parishes, in the family, and in youth associations.

2. SOME BASIS PRESUPPOSITIONS ABOUT RELIGIOUS INSTRUCTION

71. It should be no surprise that young people bring with them into the classroom what they see and hear in the world around them, along with the impressions gained from the "world" of mass media. Perhaps some have become indifferent or insensitive. The school curriculum as such does not take these attitudes into account, but teachers must be very aware of them. With kindness and understanding, they will accept the students as they are, helping them to see that doubt and indifference are common phenomena, and that the reasons for this are readily understandable. But they will invite students in a friendly manner to seek and discover together the message of the Gospel, the source of joy and peace.

The teachers' attitudes and behavior should be those of one preparing the soil.[63] They then add their own spiritual lives, and the prayers they offer for the students entrusted to them.[64]

72. An excellent way to establish rapport with students is simply to talk to them — and to let them talk. Once a warm and trusting atmosphere has been established, various questions will come up naturally. These obviously depend on age and living situation, but many of the questions seem to be common among all of today's youth, and they tend to raise them at a younger age.[65] These questions are serious ones for young people, and they make a calm study of the Christian faith very difficult. Teachers should respond with patience and humility, and should avoid the type of peremptory statements that can be so easily contradicted.

Experts in history and science could be invited to class. One's own experiences and study should be used to help the students. Inspiration can be found in the numerous and carefully worked out responses which Vatican II gives to these kinds of questions. In theory at least, this patient work of clarification should take place at the beginning of each year, since it is almost certain that new questions and new difficulties will have come up during the vacation period. And experience suggests that every other opportune occasion should be taken advantage of.

73. It is not easy to develop a course syllabus for religious instruction classes which will present the Christian faith systematically and in a way suited to the young people of today.

The Second Extraordinary General Assembly of the Synod of Bishops in 1985 suggested that a new catechism be developed for the universal Church, and the Holy Father immediately created a commission to begin the preparatory work on this project. When the catechism becomes available, adaptations will be necessary in order to develop course outlines that conform to the requirements of education authorities and respond to the concrete situations that depend on local circumstances of time and place.

While we await the new synthesis of Christian doctrine — the completion of the work mandated by the Synod — we present by way of example an outline which is the fruit of experience. It is complete in content, faithful to the Gospel message, organic in form, and is developed according to a methodology based on the words and deeds of the Lord.

3. AN OUTLINE FOR AN ORGANIC PRESENTATION OF THE CHRISTIAN EVENT AND THE CHRISTIAN MESSAGE

74.   As expressed by Vatican II, the task of the teacher to summarize Christology and present it in everyday language. Depending on the level of the class, this should be preceded by a presentation of some basic ideas about Sacred Scripture, especially those having to do with the Gospels, Divine Revelation, and the Tradition that is alive in the Church.[66] With this as a base, the class begins to learn about the Lord Jesus. His person, his message, his deeds, and the historical fact of his resurrection lead to the mystery of his divinity: "You are the Christ, the Son of the living God."[67] For more mature students, this study can he expanded to include Jesus as Savior, Priest, Teacher, and Lord of the universe. At his side is Mary his Mother, who cooperates in his mission.[68]

The discovery process is an important pedagogical method. The person of Jesus will come alive for the students. They will see again the example of his life, listen to his words, hear his invitation as addressed to them: "Come to me, all of you . . . ."[69] Faith is thus based on knowing Jesus and following him; its growth depends on each one's good will and cooperation with grace.

75.   The teacher has a reliable way to bring young people closer to the mystery of the revealed God, to the extent that this can ever be humanly possible.[70] It is the way indicated by the Savior: "Whoever has seen me, has seen the Father."[71] Through his person and his message we learn about God: we examine what he has said about the Father, and what he has done in the name of the Father. Through the Lord Jesus, therefore, we come to the mystery of God the Father, who created the universe and who sent his Son into the world so that all men and women might be saved.[72] Through Christ we come to the mystery of the Holy Spirit, sent into the world to bring the mission of the Son to fulfillment.[73] And thus we approach the supreme mystery of the Holy Trinity, in itself and as operative in the world. It is this mystery that the Church venerates and proclaims whenever it recites the Creed, repeating the words of the first Christian communities.

The process has great educational value. Its successful completion will help to strengthen the virtues of faith and of Christian religion, both of which have God as their object: Father, Son and Holy Spirit; known, loved and served in this life as we await an eternal life in union with them.

76.   Students learn many things about the human person by studying science; but science has nothing to say about mystery. Teachers should help students begin to discover the mystery within the human person, just as Paul tried to help the people of Athens discover the "Unknown God." The text of John already cited[74] demonstrates that, in and through Christ, a close relationship has been established between God and each human being. The relationship has its beginning in the love of the Father; it is expressed in the love of Jesus, which led to the ultimate sacrifice of himself: "No one has greater love than this: to lay down one's life for one's friends."[75] A crowd of people constantly surrounded Jesus; they were of all types, as if representing all of humanity. As the students see this, they will begin to ask themselves why Jesus loves everyone, why he offers an invitation to all, why he gives his life for us all. And they will be forced to conclude that each person must be a very privileged creature of God, to be the object of so much love. This is the point at which students will begin to discover another mystery — that human history unfolds within a divine history of salvation: from creation, through the first sin, the covenant with the ancient people of God, the long period of waiting until finally Jesus our Savior came, so that now we are the new People of God, pilgrims on earth journeying toward our eternal home.[76]

The educational value of Christian anthropology is obvious. Here is where students discover the true value of the human person: loved by God, with a mission on earth and a destiny that is immortal. As a result, they learn the virtues of self-respect and self-love, and of love for others — a love that is universal. In addition, each student will develop a willingness to embrace life, and also his or her own unique vocation, as a fulfillment of God's will.

77.   The history of salvation continues in the Church, an historical reality that is visible to the students. They should be encouraged to discover its origins in the Gospels, in Acts, and in the Apostolic Letters; as they study these works they will see the Church at its birth, and then as it begins to grow and take its place in the world. From the way it comes into being, from its miraculous growth, and from its fidelity to the Gospel message the transition is made to the Church as a mystery. The teacher will help students to discover the Church as the People of God, composed of women and men just like ourselves, bringing salvation to all of humanity. The Church is guided by Jesus the Eternal Shepherd; guided by his Spirit, which sustains it and is forever renewing it; guided visibly by the pastors he has ordained: the Holy Father and the bishops, assisted by priests and the deacons who are their collaborators in priesthood and in ministry. The Church, called by God to be holy in all its members, continues to be at work in the world. This is the mystery of the One, Holy, Catholic, and Apostolic Church that we celebrate in the Creed.[77]

Ecclesiology has an extremely important educational value: the ideal of a universal human family is realized in the Church. As young people come to a better knowledge of the Church they belong to, they will learn to love it with a filial affection; this has obvious consequences for life, for apostolate, and for a Christian vision of the world.

78.   As they get older, many young people stop receiving the Sacraments; this may be a sign that their meaning has not been grasped. Perhaps they are seen as devotional practices for children, or a popular devotion joined to a secular feast. Teachers are familiar with this phenomenon and its dangers. They will, therefore, help students to discover the real value of the Sacraments: they accompany the believer on his or her journey through life. This journey takes place within the Church, and therefore becomes more comprehensible as students grow in an understanding of what it means to be a member of the Church. The essential point for students to understand is that Jesus Christ is always truly present in the Sacraments which he has instituted,[78] and his presence makes them efficacious means of grace. The moment of closest encounter with the Lord Jesus occurs in the Eucharist, which is both Sacrifice and Sacrament. In the Eucharist, two supreme acts of love are united: Our Lord renews his sacrifice of salvation for us, and he truly gives himself to us.

79.   An understanding of the sacramental journey has profound educational implications. Students become aware that being a member of the Church is something dynamic, responding to every person's need to continue growing all through life. When we meet the Lord in the Sacraments, we are never left unchanged. Through the Spirit, he causes us to grow in the Church, offering us "grace upon grace";[79] the only thing he asks is our cooperation. The educational consequences of this touch on our relationship with God, our witness as a Christian, and our choice of a personal vocation.[80]

80.   Young people today are assaulted by distractions; the circumstances are not ideal for reflecting on the last things. An effective way to approach this mystery of faith is, however, available to the teacher: the Lord proposes it in his own unique way. In the story of Lazarus, he calls himself "the resurrection and the life."[81] In the parable of the rich man he helps us to understand that a personal judgement awaits each one of us.[82] In the impressive drama of the last judgment he points to an eternal destiny which each of us merits through our own works.[83] The good or evil done to each human being is as if done to him.[84]

81.   Then, using the Creed as a pattern, the teacher can help students to learn about the Kingdom of Heaven: that it consists of those who have believed in him and spent their lives in his service. The Church calls them "saints" even if not all are formally venerated under that title. First among them is Mary, the Mother of Jesus, living a glorified life at the side of her Son. Those who have died are not separated from us. They, with us, form the one Church, the People of God, united in the "communion of saints." Those dear to us who have left us are alive and are in communion with us.[85]

   These truths of faith contribute to human and Christian maturity in several important areas. They provide a sense of the dignity of the person, as destined to immortality. Christian hope offers comfort in life's difficulties. We are personally responsible in everything we do, because we must render an account to God.

4. AN OUTLINE FOR A SYSTEMATIC PRESENTATION OF THE CHRISTIAN LIFE

82. As we have seen, each truth of faith has educational and ethical implications, and students should be helped to learn about these from the time when they first begin the study of religion. But a systematic presentation of Christian ethics is also needed; to assist in this task, we present here a sample outline.

As an introduction to a study of the relationship between faith and life through religious ethics it can be helpful to reflect on the first Christian communities, where the Gospel message was accompanied by prayer and the celebration of the Sacraments.[86] This has permanent value. Students will begin to understand the meaning of the virtue of faith helped by grace, to give complete, free, personal and active loyalty to the God who reveals himself through his Son.

This commitment is not automatic; it is itself a gift of God. We must ask for it and wait for it patiently. And students must be given time to grow and to mature.

83. The life of faith is expressed in acts of religion. The teacher will assist students to open their hearts in confidence to Father, Son, and Holy Spirit through personal and liturgical prayer. The latter is not just another way of praying; it is the official prayer of the Church, which makes the mystery of Christ present in our lives — especially through the Eucharist, Sacrifice and Sacrament, and through the Sacrament of Reconciliation. Religious experiences are then seen, not as something externally imposed, but as a free and loving response to the God who first loved us.[87] The virtues of faith and religion, thus rooted and cultivated, are enabled to develop during childhood, youth, and in all the years that follow.

84. The human person is present in all the truths of faith: created in "the image and likeness" of God; elevated by God to the dignity of a child of God; unfaithful to God in original sin, but redeemed by Christ; a temple of the Holy Spirit; a member of the Church; destined to eternal life.

Students may well object that we are a long way from this ideal. The teacher must listen to these pessimistic responses, but point out that they are also found in the Gospel.[88] Students may need to be convinced that it is better to know the positive picture of personal Christian ethics rather than to get lost in an analysis of human misery. In practice, this means respect for oneself and for others. We must cultivate intelligence and the other spiritual gifts, especially through scholastic work. We must learn to care for our body and its health, and this includes physical activity and sports. And we must be careful of our sexual integrity through the virtue of chastity, because sexual energies are also a gift of God, contributing to the perfection of the person and having a providential function for the life of society and of the Church.[89] Thus, gradually, the teacher will guide students to the idea, and then to the realization, of a process of total formation.

85. Christian love is neither sentimentalism nor humanitarianism; it is a new reality, born of faith. Teachers must remember that the love of God governs the

divine plan of universal salvation. The Lord Jesus came to live among us in order to show us the Father's love. His ultimate sacrifice testifies to his love for his friends. And the Lord's new commandment is at the center of our faith: "This is my commandment: that you love one another as I have loved you."[90] The "as" is the model and the measure of Christian love.

86. Students will raise the standard objections: violence in the world, racial hatred, daily crime, both young and old concerned only with themselves and what they can get for themselves. Teachers cannot avoid discussing these issues, but they should insist that the commandment of Christ is new and revolutionary, and that it stands in opposition to all that is evil and to every form of egoism. The new Christian ethic needs to be understood and put into practice.

87. It begins at the level of family and school: affection, respect, obedience, gratitude, gentleness, goodness, helpfulness, service and good example. All manifestations of egoism, rebellion, antipathy, jealousy, hatred or revenge must be rooted out. At the broader level of Church: a love for all that excludes no one because of religion, nationality or race; prayer for all, so that all may know the Lord; laboring together in apostolic works and in efforts to relieve human suffering; a preferential option for the less fortunate, the sick, the poor, the handicapped, the lonely. As love grows in the Church, more young people may choose a life of service in it, responding to a call to the priesthood or to Religious life.

As they begin to prepare for marriage: rejecting anything that would hint at a desecration of love; discovering the newness and the depth of Christian love between man and woman, including the mutuality and reserve with which it is expressed and the sincere tenderness by which it is preserved. Young people should experience love in this way from their first friendships, gradually leading to the possibility of a commitment, until finally love is consecrated for the whole of life in the Sacrament of Matrimony.

88. Christian social ethics must always be founded on faith. From this starting point it can shed light on related disciplines such as law, economics and political science, all of which study the human situation,[91] and this is an obvious area for fruitful interdisciplinary study. But it is important to remind ourselves that God has put the world at the service of the human family.[92] As our Lord pointed out,[93] violence and injustice in society come from men and women, and they are contrary to the will of God. But in saving us, God also saves our works: a renewed world flows from a renewed heart. The works of the new Christian order of humanity are love, justice, freedom and grace.[94]

89. These, then, are the basic elements of a Christian social ethic: the human person, the central focus of the social order; justice, the recognition of the rights of each individual; honesty, the basic condition for all human relationships; freedom, the basic right of each individual and of society. World peace must then be founded on good order and the justice to which all men and women have a right as children of God; national and international well-being

depend on the fact that the goods of the earth are gifts of God, and are not the privilege of some individuals or groups while others are deprived of them. Misery and hunger weigh on the conscience of humanity and cry out to God for justice.

90.   This is an area which can open up broad possibilities. Students will be enriched by the principles and values they learn, and their service of society will be more effective. The Church supports and enlightens them with a social doctrine which is waiting to be put into practice by courageous and generous men and women of faith.[95]

91.   The guidelines developed up to this point seem excessively optimistic. While the presentation of the Christian message as "good news" is pedagogically sound,[96] the realism of revelation, history and daily experience all require that students have a clear awareness of the evil that is at work in the world and in the human person. The Lord spoke about the "power of darkness."[97] Men and women wander far away from God, and rebel against the Gospel message; they continue to poison the world with war, violence, injustice and crime.

92.   A teacher can invite the students to examine their own consciences. Which one of us can honestly claim to be without sin?[98] Thus they will acquire a sense of sin: the great sin of humanity as a whole and the personal sin which all of us discover within ourselves. Sin drives us away from God, rejects the message of Christ, and transgresses the law of love; sin betrays conscience, abuses the gift of freedom, offends the other children of God, and harms the Church of which we are all members.

93.   But we are not in a hopeless situation. The teacher should help students to see, in the light of faith, that this reality has another side to it. On the world scale, the Gospel message continues to "die" as the "seed" in the soil of the earth only to blossom and bear fruit in due season.[99] At the personal level, the Lord waits for us in the Sacrament of Reconciliation. It is not just a devotional practice, but rather a personal encounter with him, through the mediation of his minister. After this celebration we can resume our journey with renewed strength and joy.

94.   These truths can lead to a new and more mature understanding of Christianity. The Lord call us to an endless struggle: to resist the forces of evil and, with his help, to have the courage to overpower it. This is a Christianity which is alive and healthy, at work in history and within the life of each individual.[100]

The call to be a Christian involves a call to help liberate the human family from its radical slavery to sin and, therefore, from the effects of sin in the cultural, economic, social and political orders. Ultimately, these effects all result from sin; they are obstacles which prevent men and women from living according to the dignity which is theirs.[101]

95.   Perfection is a theme which must be part of this systematic presentation of the Christian message. To pass over it would be disloyal; to the Lord, who calls

us to limitless perfection;[102] to the Church, which invites us all to perfection;[103] and to the young people themselves, who have the right to know what the Lord and the Church expect of them. The teacher will begin by reminding believing students that, through their baptism, they have become members of the Church. The Christian perfection to which we are all called is a gift of Jesus through the mediation of the Spirit; but the gift requires our cooperation. Our apostolic witness must make this perfection visible in the world, today and in the future.

Once they get beyond feeling that too much is being asked of them, students will realize that perfection is actually within their grasp. The only thing they have to do is live their lives as students as well as they can:[104] do their best in study and work; put into practice the virtues they already know in theory — especially love, which must be lived in the classroom, at home, and among friends; accept difficulties with courage; help those in need; give good example. In addition, they must find the inspiration for their daily lives in the words and the example of Jesus. They must converse with him in prayer and receive him in the Eucharist. No student can say that these are impossible demands.

The ideal would be for each student to have an opportunity for spiritual guidance, to help in interior formation. It is the best way of giving orientation and completion to the religious instruction given in the classroom and, at the same time, of integrating this instruction into the personal experiences of each individual.

5. THE RELIGION TEACHER

96. The fruits of an organic presentation of the faith and of Christian ethics depend in great part on the religion teachers: who they are and what they do.

The religion teacher is the key, the vital component, if the educational goals of the school are to be achieved. But the effectiveness of religious instruction is closely tied to the personal witness given by the teacher; this witness is what brings the content of the lessons to life. Teachers of religion, therefore, must be men and women endowed with many gifts, both natural and supernatural, who are also capable of giving witness to these gifts; they must have a thorough cultural, professional, and pedagogical training, and they must be capable of genuine dialogue.

Most of all, students should be able to recognize authentic human qualities in their teachers. They are teachers of the faith; however, like Christ, they must also be teachers of what it means to be human. This includes culture, but it also includes such things as affection, tact, understanding, serenity of spirit, a balanced judgment, patience in listening to others and prudence in the way they respond, and, finally, availability for personal meetings and conversations with the students. A teacher who has a clear vision of the Christian milieu and lives in accord with it will be able to help young people develop a similar vision, and will give them the inspiration they need to put it into practice.

97.   In this area, especially, an unprepared teacher can do a great deal of harm. Everything possible must be done to ensure that Catholic schools have adequately trained religion teachers; it is a vital necessity and a legitimate expectation. In Catholic schools today, these teachers tend more and more to be lay people, and they should have the opportunity of receiving the specific experiential knowledge of the mystery of Christ and of the Church that priests and Religious automatically acquire in the course of their formation. We need to look to the future and promote the establishment of formation centers for these teachers; ecclesiastical universities and faculties should do what they can to develop appropriate programs so that the teachers of tomorrow will be able to carry out their task with the competence and efficacy that is expected of them.[105]

PART FIVE
A GENERAL SUMMARY: THE RELIGIOUS DIMENSION OF THE FORMATION PROCESS AS A WHOLE

1. WHAT IS A CHRISTIAN FORMATION PROCESS?

98.   The declaration of the Council insists on the dynamic nature of integral human formation,[106] but it adds immediately that, from a Christian point of view, human development by itself is not sufficient. Education "does not merely strive to foster in the human person the maturity already described. Rather, its principal aims are these: that as the baptized person is gradually introduced into a knowledge of the mystery of salvation, he or she may daily grow more conscious of the gift of faith which has been received . . . ."[107] What characterizes a Catholic school, therefore, is that it guide students in such a way "that the development of each one's own personality will be matched by the growth of that new creation which he or she became by baptism."[108] We need to think of Christian education as a movement or a growth process, directed toward an ideal goal which goes beyond the limitations of anything human.[109] At the same time the process must be harmonious, so that Christian formation takes place within and in the course of human formation. The two are not separate and parallel paths; they are complementary forms of education which become one in the goals of the teacher and the willing reception of the students. The Gospel notes this harmonious growth in the child Jesus.[110]

99.   A Christian formation process might therefore be described as an organic set of elements with a single purpose: the gradual development of every capability of every of student, enabling each one to attain an integral formation within a context that includes the Christian religious dimension and recognizes the help of grace. But what really matters is not the terminology but the reality, and this reality will he assured only if all the teachers unite their educational efforts in the pursuit of a common goal. Sporadic, partial, or uncoordinated efforts, or a situation in which there is a conflict of opinion among the teachers, will interfere with rather than assist in the students' personal development.

2. EDUCATIONAL GOALS

100. The responsibility of a Catholic school is enormous and complex. It must respect and obey the laws that define methods, programmed structure, etc., and at the same time it must fulfil its own educational goals by blending human culture with the message of salvation into a coordinated program; it must help each of the students to actually become the "new creature" that each one is potentially, and at the same time prepare them for the responsibilities of an adult member of society. This means that a Catholic school needs to have a set of educational goals which are "distinctive" in the sense that the school has a specific objective in mind, and all of the goals are related to this objective. Concretely, the educational goals provide a frame of reference which:

—defines the school's identity: in particular, the Gospel values which are its inspiration must be explicitly mentioned;

—gives a precise description of the pedagogical, educational and cultural aims of the school;

—presents the course content, along with the values that are to be transmitted through these courses;

—describes the organization and the management of the school;

—determines which policy decisions are to be reserved to professional staff (governors and teachers), which policies are to be developed with the help of parents and students, and which activities are to be left to the free initiative of teachers, parents, or students;

—indicates the ways in which student progress is to be tested and evaluated.

101. In addition, careful attention must be given to the development of general criteria which will enable each aspect of school activity to assist in the attainment of the educational objective, so that the cultural, pedagogical, social, civil and political aspects of school life are all integrated:

a) Fidelity to the Gospel as proclaimed by the Church. The activity of a Catholic school is, above all else, an activity that shares in the evangelizing mission of the Church; it is a part of the particular local Church of the country in which it is situated, and shares in the life and work of the local Christian community.

b) Careful rigor in the study of culture and the development of a critical sense, maintaining a respect for the autonomy of human knowledge and for the rules and methods proper to each of the disciplines, and at the same time orienting the whole process toward the integral formation of the person.

c) Adapting the educational process in a way that respects the particular circumstances of individual students and their families.

d) Sharing responsibility with the Church. While school authorities are the ones primarily responsible for the educational and cultural activities of the school, the local Church should also be involved in appropriate ways; the educational goals should be the result of dialogue with this ecclesial community.

It is clear, then, that the set of educational goals is something quite distinct from internal school regulations or teaching methods; and it is not just a description of vague intentions.

102. The educational goals should be revised each year on the basis of experience and need. They will be achieved through a formation process which takes place in stages: it has a starting point, various intermediate points, and a conclusion. At each stage, teachers, students and families should determine the degree of success in achieving these goals; where there is insufficient progress they should look for the reasons and find suitable remedies. It is essential that this evaluation be seen as a common responsibility, and that it be carried out faithfully.

The end of each school year is one appropriate time for such an evaluation. From a Christian perspective, it is not enough to say that this is the time for examinations. The academic program is only one part of the process, and the end of the school year is also the time for a serious and intelligent examination of which educational goals have been achieved and which have not. A much more decisive time comes at the completion of a student's years in the school, because this is the moment when students should have reached the maximum level of an education that integrates the human and the Christian.[111]

103. The religious dimension of the school climate strengthens the quality of the formation process, so long as certain conditions are verified—conditions that depend both on teachers and students. It is worth noting, once again, that the students are not spectators; they help to determine the quality of this climate.

Some of the conditions for creating a positive and supportive climate are the following: that everyone agree with the educational goals and cooperate in achieving them; that interpersonal relationships be based on love and Christian freedom; that each individual, in daily life, be a witness to Gospel values; that every student be challenged to strive for the highest possible level of formation, both human and Christian. In addition, the climate must be one in which families are welcomed, the local Church is an active participant, and civil society—local, national, and international—is included. If all share a common faith, this can be an added advantage.

104. Strong determination is needed to do everything possible to eliminate conditions which threaten the health of the school climate. Some examples of potential problems are these: the educational goals are either not defined or are defined badly; those responsible for the school are not sufficiently trained; concern for academic achievement is excessive; relations between teachers and students are cold and impersonal; teachers are antagonistic toward one another; discipline is imposed from on high without any participation or cooperation from the students; relationships with families are formal or even strained, and families are not involved in helping to determine the educational goals; some within the school community are giving a negative witness; individuals are unwilling to work together for the common good; the school is isolated from

the local Church; there is no interest in or concern for the problems of society; religious instruction is "routine." Whenever some combination of these symptoms is present, the religious dimension of the school is seriously threatened. Religious instruction can become empty words falling on deaf ears, because the authentically Christian witness that reinforces it is absent from the school climate. All symptoms of ill health have to be faced honestly and directly, remembering that the Gospel calls us to a continuous process of conversion.

105. A school exerts a great deal of effort in trying to obtain the students' active cooperation. Since they are active agents in their own formation process, this cooperation is essential. To be human is to be endowed with intelligence and freedom; it is impossible for education to be genuine without the active involvement of the one being educated. Students must act and react: with their intelligence, freedom, will, and the whole complex range of human emotions. The formation process comes to a halt when students are uninvolved and unmoved. Experienced teachers are familiar with the causes of such "blocks" in young people; the roots are both psychological and theological, and original sin is not excluded.

106. There are many ways to encourage students to become active participants in their own formation. Those with sufficient knowledge and maturity can be asked to help in the development of educational goals. While they are clearly not yet able to determine the final objective, they can help in determining the concrete means which will help to attain this objective. When students are trusted and given responsibility, when they are invited to contribute their own ideas and efforts for the common good, their gratitude rules out indifference and inertia. The more that students can be helped to realize that a school and all its activities have only one purpose — to help them in their growth toward maturity — the more those students will be willing to become actively involved.

Even students who are very young can sense whether the atmosphere in the school is pleasant or not. They are more willing to cooperate when they feel respected, trusted and loved. And their willingness to cooperate will be reinforced by a school climate which is warm and friendly, when teachers are ready to help, and when they find it easy to get along with the other students.

107. One important result of religious instruction is the development of religious values and religious motivation; these can be a great help in obtaining the willing participation of the students. But we must remember that religious values and motivation are cultivated in all subject areas and, indeed, in all of the various activities going on in the school. One way that teachers can encourage an understanding of and commitment to religious values is by frequent references to God. Teachers learn through experience how to help the students understand and appreciate the religious truths they are being taught, and this appreciation can easily develop into love. A truth which is loved by the teacher, and communicated in such a way that it is seen to be something valuable in itself, then becomes valuable to the student. One advantage of the Christological approach to religious instruction is that it can develop this love more easily in young people. The approach we have suggested concentrates on the person of Jesus. It

is possible to love a person; it is rather difficult to love a formula. This love for Christ is then transferred to his message which, because it is loved, has value.

But every true educator knows that a further step is necessary: values must lead to action; they are the motivation for action. Finally, truth becomes fully alive through the supernatural dynamism of grace, which enlightens and leads to faith, to love, to action that is in accord with the will of God, through the Lord Jesus, in the holy Spirit. The Christian process of formation is, therefore, the result of a constant interaction involving the expert labor of the teachers, the free cooperation of the students, and the help of grace.

108. We have already referred to the fact that, in many parts of the world, the student body in a Catholic school includes increasing numbers of young people from different faiths and different ideological backgrounds. In these situations it is essential to clarity the relationship between religious development and cultural growth. It is a question which must not be ignored, and dealing with it is the responsibility of each Christian member of the educational community.

In these situations, however, evangelization is not easy — it may not even be possible. We should look to pre-evangelization: to the development of a religious sense of life. In order to do this, the process of formation must constantly raise questions about the "how" and the "why" and the "what" and then point out and deepen the positive results of this investigation.

The transmission of a culture ought to be especially attentive to the practical effects of that culture, and strengthen those aspects of it which will make a person more human. In particular, it ought to pay attention to the religious dimension of the culture and the emerging ethical requirements to be found in it.

There can be unity in the midst of pluralism, and we need to exercise a wise discernment in order to distinguish between what is essential and what is accidental. Prudent use of the "why" and the "what" and the "how" will lead to integral human development in the formation process, and this is what we mean by a genuine pre-evangelization. It is fertile ground which may, at some future time, be able to bear fruit.

109. In order to describe the formation process, we have had to proceed by an analysis of its various elements; this, of course, is not the way things happen in the real world. The Catholic school is a center of life, and life is synthetic. In this vital center, the formation process is a constant interplay of action and reaction. The interplay has both a horizontal and a vertical dimension, and it is this qualification that makes the Catholic school distinctive from those other schools whose educational objectives are not inspired by Christianity.

110. The teachers love their students, and they show this love in the way they interact with them. They take advantage of every opportunity to encourage and strengthen them in those areas which will help to achieve the goals of the educational process. Their words, their witness, their encouragement and help, their advice and friendly correction are all important in achieving these goals,

which must always be understood to include academic achievement, moral behavior, and a religious dimension.

When students feel loved, they will love in return. Their questioning, their trust, their critical observations and suggestions for improvement in the class-room and the school milieu will enrich the teachers and also help to facilitate a shared commitment to the formation process.

111. In a Catholic school, even this is not enough. There is also a continuous vertical interaction, through prayer; this is the fullest and most complete expression of the religious dimension.

Each of the students has his or her own life, family and social background, and these are not always happy situations. They feel the unrest of the child or adolescent, which grows more intense as they face the problems and worries of a young person approaching maturity. Teachers will pray for each of them, that the grace present in the Catholic school's milieu may permeate their whole person, enlightening them and helping them to respond adequately to all that is demanded of them in order to live Christian lives.

And the students will learn that they must pray for their teachers. As they get older, they will come to appreciate the pain and the difficulties that teaching involves. They will pray that the educational gifts of their teachers may be more effective, that they may be comforted by success in their work, that grace may sustain their dedication and bring them peace in their work.

112. Thus a relationship is built up which is both human and divine; there is a flow of love, and also of grace. And this will make the Catholic school truly authentic. As the years go by, students will have the joy of seeing themselves nearing maturity: not only physically, but also intellectually and spiritually. When they look back, they will realize that, with their cooperation, the educational objectives of the school have become a reality. And as they look forward, they will feel free and secure, because they will be able to face the new, and now proximate, life commitments.

CONCLUSION

113. The Congregation for Catholic Education asks local ordinaries and superiors of Religious Congregations dedicated to the education of youth to bring these reflections to the attention of all teachers and directors of Catholic schools. At the same time, the Congregation wishes to affirm once again that it is fully conscious of the important service they offer — to youth and to the Church.

114. Therefore the Congregation extends warm thanks to all those engaged in this work: for all they have done, and for all that they continue to do in spite of political, economic, and practical difficulties. For many, to continue in this mission involves great sacrifice. The Church is deeply grateful to everyone dedicated to the educational mission in a Catholic school; it is confident that,

with the help of God, many others will be called to join in this mission and will respond generously.

115. The Congregation would like to suggest that further study, research, and experimentation be done in all areas that affect the religious dimension of education in Catholic schools. Much has been done, but many people are asking for even more. This is surely possible in every school whose freedom is sufficiently protected by civil law. It may be difficult in those countries which allow the Catholic school as an academic institution, but where the religious dimension leads to constant conflict. Local experience must be the determining factor in such situations; however, to the extent that it is possible, a religious dimension should always be present — either in the school or outside its walls. There has never been a shortage of families and students, of different faiths and religions, who choose a Catholic school because they appreciate the value of an education where instruction is enhanced by a religious dimension.

Educators will know the best way to respond to their expectations, knowing that, in a world of cultural pluralism, dialogue always gives grounds for hope.

Rome, April 7, 1988, Feast of Saint John Baptist de La Salle, Principal Patron of teachers.

William Cardinal Baum

Prefect

+ Antonio M. Javierre Ortas

Titular Archbishop of Meta

Secretary

NOTES

1. GE, 8.

2. March 19, 1977.

3. October 15, 1982.

4. From Vatican Council II: GE; LG; GS; DV; SC; AA; AG; NA; UR; DH. From Paul VI, EN. From John Paul II, CT; in addition, a number of his talks given to educators and to young people will be cited below. From the Congregation for Clergy, GCD.

5. Note that the Congregation has also published *Educational Guidance in Human Love: Outlines for Sex Education*, November 1, 1983. This there, therefore, will receive only brief and passing mention in the present document.

6. GE, 9: "It is clear that the Church has a deep respect for those Catholic schools, especially in countries where the Church is young, which have large numbers of students who are not Catholics."

7. Cf. DH, 2, 9, 10, 12, *et passim*.

8. CIC, canon 748 § 2: "homines ad amplectendam fidem catholicam contra ipsorum conscientiam per coactionem adducere nemini unquan fas est."

9. Cf. GS, 4–10.

10. GS, 7: "The change of mentality and of structures often call into question traditional values, especially among the young . . . ."

11. Cf. EN, 20.

12. Cf. the *Annuario Statistico della Chiesa* published by the Central Statistical Office of the Church, an office within the Secretariate of State for Vatican City. By way of example, on December 31, 1985, there were 154,126 Catholic schools with 38,243,304 students.

13. Cf. 1 Corinthians 12:31.

14. Various aspects of the religious attitudes of young people developed in this section have been the object of recent statements of the Holy Father. A handy compilation of these numerous talks can be found in a book edited by the Pontifical Council for the Laity, *The Holy Father Speaks to Youth: 1980–1985*. The book is published in several languages.

15. Cf. GE, 8. For the Gospel spirit of love and freedom, cf. GS, 38: "[The Lord Jesus] reveals to us that God is love (1 John 4:8), and at the same time teaches us that the fundamental rule for human perfection, and therefore also for the transformation of the world, is the new commandment of love." See also 2 Corinthians 3:17: "Where the Spirit of the Lord is present, there is freedom."

16. This question was treated in *The Catholic School*, 81–82.

17. Matthew 28:20.

18. GE, 6.

19. Cf. the address of John Paul II to the parents, teachers and students from the Catholic schools of the Italian Province of Lazio, *Insegnamenti*, VIII/1 (March 9, 1985): 620.

20. Address of John Paul II to the bishops of Lombardy, Italy, on the occasion of their "Ad limina" visit, January 15, 1982, *Insegnamenti*, V/1 (1982): 105.

21. *Insegnamenti*, VIII/1: 618f.

22. Matthew 25:40: "For indeed I tell you, as often as you have done these things to one of these least of my brothers, you have done it to me."

23. Cf. PC, 8: "There are in the Church a great number of institutes, clerical or lay, dedicated to various aspects of the apostolate, which have different gifts according to the grace that has been given to each: 'some exercise a ministry of service; some teach' (cf. Romans 12:5–8)." Also see AG, 40.

24. *Summa Theologiae* II–II, q. 186, a. 1: "By antonomasis those are called 'religious' who dedicate themselves to the service of God as if they were offering themselves as a holocaust to the Lord."

25. *Summa Theologiae*, a. 2.

26. *Lay Catholics in Schools: Witnesses to the Faith.*

27. The norms of the Church in this respect are to be found in canons 800–803 of the Code of Canon Law.

28. Cf. the address of Pope Paul VI to the Nation Congress of Diocesan Directors of the Teacher's Organizations of Catholic Action, *Insegnamenti*, I, (1963): 594.

29. Cf. GE, 3.

30. GE, 8.

31. A number of recent documents from national Episcopal Conferences and from individual local ordinaries have had the Catholic school as their theme. These documents should be known and put into practice.

32. See, for example, the Resolution of the European Parliament on Freedom of education in the European Community, approved by a large majority on March 14, 1984.

33. Cf. Mark 6:3; Acts 10:38. Useful applications of the ethics of work to the work done in school can be found in the September 14, 1981, Encyclical *Laborem exercens* of John Paul II, especially in Part Five.

34. Genesis 3:19: "By the sweat on your face shall you get bread to eat."

35. Luke 9:23: " . . . let him take up his cross each day."

36. GE, 8: among the elements characteristic of the Catholic school, there is that of "developing the relationship between human culture and the message of salvation, so that the knowledge of the world, of life and of the human person which the students are gradually acquiring is illuminated by faith."

37. For a description of culture and of the relationship between culture and faith, see GS, 54ff.

38. Cf. DS 3016–3017 for the traditional doctrine on the rapport between reason and faith, as defined by Vatican Council I.

39. Cf. the address of Pope John Paul II to the teachers and students of Catholic schools in Melbourne, Australia, on the occasion of his pastoral journey to East Asia and Oceania: *Insegnamenti;* IX/2 (1986): 1710ff.

40. Cf. GE, 8.

41. Cf. GE, 53–62.

42. Pope John Paul II, speaking at the National Congress of Catholic Cultural Organizations: *Insegnamenti*, v/1 (1982): 131. See also John Paul II, *Epistula qua Pontificium Consilium pro hominum Cultura instituitur:* AAS 74 (1982): 685.

43. Wisdom 13:5: "Through the grandeur and beauty of the creatures we may, by analogy, contemplate their Author." Psalm 18 (19): 2ff: "The heavens tell of the glory of God . . . ."

44. Cf. Matthew 25:14–30.

45. Cf. GS, 12, 14, 17, 22.

46. Cf. GS, 10.

47. Cf. DS 3004 for the ability to know God through human reason, and 3005 for the ability to know other truths.

48. Cf. 1 Thessalonians 5:21: "Examine all things, hold on to what is good." Philippians 4:8: "Everything that is true, noble, or just . . . let all this be the object of your thoughts."

49. Cf. GS, 61, on the need to hold on to certain fundamental concepts.

50. GS, 44: "At the same time there should be a vital exchange between the Church and the diverse cultures of peoples."

51. Cf. DV, 2.

52. Cf. Blaise Pascal, *Pensées*, fr. 397.

53. GS, 37: "The whole of human history is permeated with the gigantic struggle against the powers of darkness."

54. Invaluable material for presenting the divine history of salvation can be found in LG and DV.

55. Cf. GS, 62.

56. Cf. St. Augustine, *De libero arbitrio*, II, 16, 42. PL 32: 1264. St. Thomas, *Contra gentiles*, IV, 42.

57. Cf. GE, 1–2.

58. EN, 18: "For the Church to evangelize is to bring the Good News to all aspects of humanity and, through its influence, to transform it from within, making humanity itself into something new."

59. EN, 44: "The effort to evangelize will bring great profit, through catechetical instruction given at Church, in schools wherever this is possible, and always within the Christian family."

60. CT, 69.

61. Cf. the address of Paul VI at the Wednesday audience of May 31, 1967, *Insegnamenti*, V (1967): 788.

62. Address of John Paul II to the priest of the diocese of Rome (March 5, 1981): *Insegnamenti*, IV/1: 629f.

63. Cf. Matthew 3:1–3 on the mission of the Precursor.

64. Cf. John 17:9, the prayer of the Lord for those entrusted to him.

65. Apart from strictly local concerns, these questions are generally the ones treated in university "apologetics" manuals, and are about the "preambles to the faith." But the questions acquire a specific nuance for today's students, because of the material they are studying and the world they are living in. Typical questions have to do with atheism, non-Christian religions, divisions among Christians, events in the life of the Church, the violence and injustice of supposedly Christian nations, etc.

66. Revelation, Scripture, Tradition and Christology are themes developed in DV, LG, and GS. Study of the Gospels should be extended to include a study of these documents.

67. Matthew 16:16.

68. Concerning the Blessed Virgin Mary in the life of the Pilgrim Church, cf. the encyclical *Redemptoris Mater* of Pope John Paul II, number 39.

69. Matthew 11:28.

70. Cf. DS 2854: one cannot speak about God in the same way that one speaks about the objects of human knowledge.

71. John 14:9.

72. Cf. Luke 12:24–28; John 3:16f.

73. Cf. John 16:13.

74. Cf. John 3:16f.

75. John 15:13.

76. From the point of view of Christian anthropology, it is essential that the history of salvation presented in LG and GS be a part of what is studied in class.

77. Important and valuable material for teaching about the Church can be found in LG.

78. SC, 7: "Christ is present in the sacraments with his own authority, so that when one baptizes it is Christ himself who baptizes . . . ."

79. John 1:16.

80. The content and the methods for teaching about the Sacraments can be enriched through studying parts of LG and SC.

81. John 11:25–27.

82. Cf. Luke 16:19–31.

83. Cf. Matthew 25:31–46.

84. Cf. Matthew 25:40.

85. Cf. LG, chapter VII on the estachological nature of the pilgrim Church and its union with the heavenly Church.

86. Cf. Ephesians 1:1–14 and Colossians 1:13–20 for doxologies which witness to the faith of the early communities. Acts 10 speaks of evangelization, conversion, faith, and the gift of the spirit in the house of the Roman official Cornelius. Acts 20:7–12 describes evangelization and the Eucharist in a house at Troas.

87. 1 John 4:10: "it is not we who have loved God, but God who first loved us . . . ."

88. Cf. Matthew 15:19f.

89. Cf. the document of the Congregation for Catholic Education already referred to— *Educational Guidance in Human Love: Outlines for Sex Education.*

90. John 15:12.

91. Cf. GS, 63–66 and related applications.

92. Cf. Genesis 1:27f.

93. Again cf. Matthew 15:19f.

94. Cf. GS, 93.

95. Students should become aware of at least some of the Church's major social documents.

96. Luke 2:10: "I bring you news of great joy . . . ."

97. Luke 22:53: "But this is your hour; this is the reign of darkness." Evidence of this

is easily found in various abuses, acts of injustice, attacks on freedom, the overwhelming weight o misery that leads to sickness, decline and death, the scandalous inequality between rich and poor, the lack of any equity or sense of solidarity in international relations. (Cf. *Some Aspects of the "Theology of Liberation,"* published by the Congregation for the Doctrine of Faith, Introduction and Part I).

98. John 8:7: "Let the one who is without sin cast the first stone . . . ."

99. Cf. Luke 8:4–15.

100. Cf. Ephesians 6:10–17, a characteristically vigorous Pauline description.

101. Cf. the Introduction of *Some Aspects of the "Theology of Liberation,"* published by the Congregation for the Doctrine of the Faith, August 6, 1984.

102. Matthew 5:48: "You must be perfect as your heavenly Father is perfect."

103. LG, 42: "All the faithful are invited and called to holiness and to perfection within their own state of live."

104. LG, 39: "This holiness of the Church . . . is expressed in various forms according to each individual, who in their lives and their activities join perfection to love."

105. Some aspects of this are treated in the documents already referred to: *The Catholic School,* 78–80; *Lay Catholics in Schools: Witnesses to the Faith,* especially 56–59. What is said there does not apply only to lay teachers.

106. GE, 1: "Children and young people should be assisted in the harmonious development of their physical, moral and intellectual gifts . . . They should be helped to acquire gradually a more mature sense of responsibility . . . ."

107. GE, 2.

108. GE, 8.

109. Cf. Matthew 5:48.

110. Luke 2:40: "The child grew and became strong, filled with wisdom; and the favor of God was upon him." Luke 2:52: "And Jesus grew in wisdom and in stature, and in favor with God and with men."

111. Cf. once again GE, 1–2.

ADULT CATECHESIS
IN THE
CHRISTIAN COMMUNITY

1990

PREFACE
1992

OVERVIEW OF *ADULT CATECHESIS IN THE CHRISTIAN COMMUNITY*

by Margaret N. Ralph

Both as individuals and as a community of baptized people we are well aware of a certain disparity between what we say and what we do. When it comes to adult catechesis we have been saying one thing and doing another for quite some time. As the introduction to *Adult Catechesis in the Christian Community* (ACCC) states, "The *Magisterium of the Church*, imbued with the spirit of renewal of the Second Vatican Council (see *Christus Dominus*, 14; *Ad Gentes*, 14) has constantly affirmed with authority, clarity and insistence the centrality and importance of the catechesis of adults" (ACCC, 4). And as the document also acknowledges,

> one must admit that in various communities, the formation of adults has been taken for granted or perhaps carried out in connection with certain events, not infrequently in an infantile way. Because certain external or traditional supports are sometimes lacking, a grave imbalance is created insofar as catechesis has devoted considerable attention to children while the same has not happened in the catechesis of young people and adults (ACCC, 21).

With the publication of ACCC in 1990, the International Council for Catechesis (COINCAT), a consultative body of the Congregation for the Clergy, hoped to contribute to remedying this imbalance by providing us with a document with the expressed purpose of promoting adult catechesis.

The subtitle of the document, "Some Principles and Guidelines," tells us a little about what the document is and is not. As the "Preliminary Remarks" explain, "This contribution does not intend to be an exhaustive directory for adult catechesis or a practical program ready for implementation. Rather, it simply offers some guidelines which, arranged in a systematic and organic way, reflect a rich world of experiences."

AUDIENCE AND ORGANIZATION

The guidelines are extremely helpful for their most specific audience, "those *lay catechists* who are already engaged in the catechesis of adults or who are preparing themselves for this service" (8). The guidelines will be less helpful for the broader intended audience, "the whole people of God" (8), because that intended audience has not yet understood the crucial nature of the subject at hand and so will probably not read them.

The document is divided into three sections: "The Adults to Whom Catechesis is Directed"; "Motivations, Criteria and Other Points of Reference for Adult Catechesis" and "Guidelines for Practical Implementation."

In this section the document mentions as one of a number of needs that "require a new approach in adult catechesis" a need for "a more visible expression of sensitivity, availability and openness on the part of clergy and church institutions toward adults, their problems and their need for catechesis" (17ff). While this statement is tucked away near the end of the section, the sentiment that it expresses seems to have inspired the whole section. If readers do not already know the burdens, challenges and needs of adults who wish to grow in their faith, reading this section would go a long way toward sensitizing them. The document focuses first on the "difficulties and sufferings" that are experienced universally, among which are political, social and even ecclesial conditions that fail to affirm human beings in their basic dignity as people who have been made in God's own image. After acknowledging so many difficulties that one might feel hopeless, the document goes on to affirm "the vigor of the gospel seed" and reminds us of Jesus' words, "Open your eyes and see! The fields are shining for harvest" (John 4:35; ACCC, 17). A great deal can be accomplished through adult catechesis.

SECTION TWO: MOTIVATIONS, CRITERIA AND OTHER POINTS OF REFERENCE

In this section the document states the fundamental reasons for adult catechesis, reasons that relate to "the faith life of the adult as such," to the "adult's public role in society and in ecclesial communities" and to "the greater glory of God and the good of the church." The document explains that adults have both a right and an obligation to be catechized, and where such catechesis does not take place, the individual is prevented from fulfilling "his or her adult duties toward others, as is required by the vocation given to each at baptism" (ACCC, 21). As is obvious throughout the document and is stated explicitly here, adult catechesis is seen not merely as the imparting of knowledge but as a process of formation that informs, inspires and equips one to live out one's vocation in private and public life. Adults are seen not just as the recipients of catechesis but as those who fulfill the mission of the church by giving witness to the good news in every setting in which they find themselves. So essential is adult catechesis that "a fully Christian community can exist only when a systematic catechesis of all its members takes place and when an effective and well-developed catechesis of adults is regarded as the *central task* in the catechetical enterprise" (ACCC, 25).

The basic criteria necessary for such a crucial undertaking are that the catechesis be "acutely sensitive to *men and women insofar as they are adults*" (ACCC, 26), that there be "full recognition and appreciation of the 'secular character which is proper and peculiar to the laity'" (LG, 31; ACCC, 27), that the catechesis involve the community (ACCC, 28), that the catechesis be *within the overall pastoral plan* of the local church communities" (ACCC, 29) and that the catechesis make all the adaptations necessary for a given setting while at the same time remaining faithful to the gospel message that is our common heritage (ACCC, 30).

This section discusses "four most important areas":

1. the qualities of the adult Christian,

2. the process involved in adult catechesis,

3. the catechists and

4. those responsible for adult catechesis in the community.

1. QUALITIES OF THE ADULT CHRISTIAN (GOALS)

In describing the qualities of the Christian adult in faith, the document of necessity ventures into an area that, in fact, causes a great deal of tension in adult educational settings. This tension is caused because, due to our past failures in adult education, many adults who attend, or fail to attend, adult education opportunities are literally unaware that the church actually does encourage adults to relate to both God and to the institutional church as seeking, intelligent adults rather than as unthinking and blindly obedient children. The document names as the essential characteristics of an adult Christian "an obedient listening to the word of God," "communion with the faith community" and "the service of charity and witness in the world." An adult who possesses these characteristics would function in the church as a listening pilgrim on both a journey and a mission with other disciples. Such a person would be light years removed from a legalistic person with a consumer mentality, characteristics that are sometimes seen in those who have never accepted the invitation to become adults in faith. In order to help form Catholics who are adults in their faith, catechesis will have to enable Catholics to achieve three stated goals: "to acquire an attitude of *conversion to the Lord*" (ACCC, 36), a conversion that leads to "membership in a community whose way of life as disciples of Christ is shared by all" (ACCC, 37), and that "gives a missionary purpose to those tasks for which it is responsible" (ACCC, 38).

Objectives Necessary to Achieve the Goals

How might one hope to achieve such results? The document next names specific objectives that are necessary stepping stones in the achievement of the goals. Such goals are unobtainable unless one has the opportunity to achieve a "basic understanding of the church's faith, presented in a sufficiently organic way together with the reasons for believing" (ACCC, 39), unless one succeeds in assimilating the "theological and cultural heritage in which faith is expressed" (ACCC, 40), unless one develops the "capacity of *Christian discernment*" (ACCC, 41) and unless one acquires "those *skills and abilities which allow the adult believer to carry out*" the Christian witness (ACCC, 42).

While a discussion of methodology comes later, the document touches on methodology here by emphasizing "elements in the presentation of content," which are all too often overlooked. The document states that catechesis "must deal with the many *questions*, difficulties and doubts which arise in the human heart" (ACCC, 48). Our failure to deal adequately with questions often causes thinking adults to become disenchanted with the teaching voice of the church. Catechesis must invite adults to name their experiences as well as to name the conclusions they have drawn from these experiences, even when their conclusions call into question the content of the teaching that we are presenting. Unless we are willing to engage in such discussion, we will not help adults reach the goal of integration, which is a necessary component of the faith life of an adult.

Other "constant elements" include teaching adults how to pray; encouraging adults to develop an ecumenical outlook; and encouraging them to be "open to the encounter between faith, culture and science, in which an attempt is made to integrate them with one another while respecting the specific identity of each" (Pope John Paul II to members of COINCAT; ACCC, 51). One can only surmise how much pain, misunderstanding and mistreatment of other Christians and of scholars we would have avoided if we had been able to act on such wise advice through past centuries!

2. METHODOLOGICAL CONSIDERATIONS (THE PROCESS OF ADULT CATECHESIS)

The "methodological considerations" that the document discusses grow naturally from the stated goals. Again there is the struggle to balance the fact that the church teaches truth, not opinion, while at the same time we are "pilgrims" on our way "toward the full revelation of truth and life," so the "path of research and investigation always remains open" (ACCC, 58). Given this posture, adult catechesis must use a dialogical approach that "respects the basic freedom and autonomy of adults and encourages them to engage in an open and cordial dialogue" (ACCC, 57).

It is the parish that has the task of providing appropriate catechesis in an organic, developmental way, not just episodically. The parish has this duty because all baptized Christians have a right to ongoing faith formation at every stage of life.

The document reminds us that "every form of catechesis should be inspired by the catechumenal model" (ACCC, 66). This model emphasizes formation over information and uses a variety of catechetical methodologies depending entirely on the stage and needs of those being served. In a catechumenate one does not speak of a "class" or a "syllabus," nor does one presume that people who accompany one another on a faith journey will be ready to "graduate" at the same time. Rather each individual is encouraged to grow at whatever rate the Holy Spirit sees fit, and there is no end to the process. As one grows in faith, one learns to reflect with others on the mystery of the sacramental life and to act with others to carry out the mission of the church. The importance of small groups to both the catechumenate and to all adult catechesis is emphasized.

3. THE CATECHIST

Obviously, skilled adult catechists are needed to facilitate such a process. The document next names characteristics of adult catechists that are considered "fundamental requirements." First, "catechists do not regard themselves as superior or extrinsic to the persons or groups to whom they minister. . . . They know how to recognize everyone and make them agents and participants in the faith journey" (ACCC, 71). This statement is equally true of ordained clergy and flows naturally from earlier statements regarding the value and dignity of each human being. It is very difficult for people to become adults in faith if those who minister to them feel superior and so, consciously or unconsciously, treat them as less than fully responsible adults.

Adult catechists must also be stable and living the Christian faith as members of an ecclesial community (ACCC, 72); they must be able to "critically interpret present day events and the 'signs of the time'" (ACCC, 73), and they must be flexible and adaptable. The requirements flow from the goals. Catechists cannot center catechesis around the needs of those being catechized if, instead of being responsive, they are merely carrying out their own preplanned agendas.

4. THOSE RESPONSIBLE

Finally the document addresses the question of who in the Christian community is responsible for catechesis. Again, with the catechumenate as the model, the document says that "the whole Christian community" should be involved in the catechesis of adults. The bishop, as chief catechist, should "take a keen interest" in seeing that adult educators, who are his collaborators, receive the necessary support and formation to carry out their responsibilities. Priests, who bear the primary responsibility at the local level, should directly involve themselves in the catechesis of adults. Therefore, seminaries should make sure that all priests have a "solid formation in catechesis" (ACCC, 83).

CONCLUSION

The document offers those of us who are involved in adult catechesis words of consolation and of inspiration. First, we are reminded to have patience. Then, Mary is presented as "the exemplary model of the adult who undertakes the journey of faith." Indeed, Mary serves as a truly inspirational model for those being catechized and for those doing the catechesis. Who more than Mary listened and responded to the word of God? Who more than Mary was thrown into complete mystery? Who more than Mary experienced both the exultant joy and the painful "giving up" that is part of the journey of each baptized Christian? Who more than Mary pondered the meaning of it all as she treasured God's presence in her heart? The document reminds each and every one of us that, like Mary, we are called to be catechists in word and deed, in order to be Christ-bearers to others.

When we hear and respond to this call there will be no more disparity between what we say and what we do in the area of adult catechesis.

OUTLINE

PREFACE

In 1990, the International Council for Catechesis published a notable document, *Adult Catechesis in the Christian Community: Some Principles and Guidelines.* The Council is a consultative body of the Congregation for the Clergy, which has as one of its responsibilities the promotion and organization of catechesis. The Council, which is made up of catechetical experts from all over the world, began preparing this document in October 1988. Sr. Maria de la Cruz Aymes, SH, and Msgr. Francis Kelly represent the United States on the Council.

The stated purpose of *Adult Catechesis in the Christian Community* is to stimulate a spirit of communion and solidarity among those responsible for the catechesis of adults. On the way to achieving that lofty goal, it seems to accomplish several others, not the least of which is the promotion of adult catechesis as the principal form of catechesis and an essential component in the Church's pastoral ministry.

While the document is addressed to the whole People of God, it is more specifically directed to "lay catechists who are already engaged in the catechesis of adults or who are preparing themselves for this service" (no. 8). The text is readable and understandable. I would like to highlight a few of its major points.

First of all, the document employs catechetical rather than educational language. Catechesis is a distinctive kind of education/formation process and, in my view, should employ its own vernacular system. Catechesis is a unique contribution the Church makes to the world. No one else offers such a gift. If catechetical language is rarely used, it will rarely be understood. The document shows respect for the "mystery of adulthood" (no. 31) and the intimate relationship between adult experience and adult catechesis. It reiterates the primacy of adult catechesis urging that "the catechesis of adults must be regarded as a preferential option" (no. 29). It recognizes the fact that adult catechesis is not easily identified, but happens in a variety of places, programs, events, and experiences. Adult catechesis is presented as the right of every believer and not as a reward for the adult's performance of any service.

The text encourages the use of adult methodology and the integration of adult catechesis with the process of evangelization. It emphasizes the revelatory nature of the experience of Christian living in ecclesial communities.

Let me now turn to a few of the more specific points made in *Adult Catechesis in the Christian Community.* It is divided into three parts: (1) "The Adults to Whom Catechesis Is Directed"; (2) "Motivations, Criteria and Other Points of Reference for Adult Catechesis"; and (3) "Guidelines for Practical Implementation."

Part One urges the Church to take into account "the actual situation, full of both serious drawbacks and positive opportunities, of accomplishments and expectations . . . when proposing the Gospel to adults" (no. 14). It also identifies a number of needs that require a new approach in adult catechesis, for example, "a more adequate language of faith comprehensible to adults at all - levels . . . more accessible places where unchurched adults feel welcomed . . . a wider variety of catechetical models responding to the local and cultural needs . . . the popular religiosity of the people, both in its content and expression, to be taken seriously . . . a more consistent effort to reach out to all adults, especially those who are unchurched, alienated or marginated . . . a more visible expression of sensitivity, availability and openness on the part of clergy and church institutions toward adults, their problems and their need for catechesis" (no. 17).

Part Two notes that "a grave imbalance has been created insofar as catechesis has devoted considerable attention to children while the same has not happened to the catechesis of young people and adults" (no. 21). It also underscores the primary role adults play in the coming of the Kingdom. "[I]t is not only legitimate, but necessary, to acknowledge that a fully Christian community can exist only when a systematic catechesis of all its members takes place and when an effective and well-developed catechesis of adults is regarded as the *central task* in the catechetical enterprise" (no. 25).

Part Three describes the qualities of the adult Christian especially emphasizing the fact that "catechesis must help adults to learn not only for themselves, but should prepare them to *communicate the contents of faith to others* . . . showing other adults what an impact the faith can have on their lives and on the world around them" (no. 52).

It also presents several methodological considerations for adult catechesis calling the parish "'the privileged place' where 'catechesis is realized not only through formal instruction, but also in the liturgy, sacraments and charitable activity.' . . . Catechesis allows adults to have 'a more direct and concrete perception of the sense of ecclesial communion and responsibility in the Church's mission' (*Christifideles Laici*, 61; henceforth as CL)" (no. 61).

In addition, it describes the identity of the adult catechist as "a sufficiently balanced human being with a flexibility to adapt to different circumstances" (no. 73). "Always and in every way [such] catechists should be *recognized, respected and loved* by their priests and communities. They should be supported in their formation and encouraged and helped to accomplish a task which is indispensable but far from easy" (no. 76). Finally, Part Three reminds us that, while the whole Christian community is responsible for adult catechesis, there are special responsibilities as well. "[T]he *bishop* as Teacher of the faith (cf. CT, 63) is the chief catechist of adults. . . . He should take a keen interest in the diocesan program of adult catechesis and keep abreast of its activities through meetings with the moderators or directors . . . " (no. 82). Priests "should be directly involved in the catechesis of adults . . . [and] it is essential that candidates for the priesthood have a solid formation in catechesis" (no. 83).

The Church has consistently taught that all forms of catechesis must be oriented to the catechesis of adults. In practice, however, this is rarely the case. As the body of church literature on adult catechesis grows, let us hope the resolve of pastoral leaders to regard the catechesis of adults as a preferential option will intensify.

As a means to that end, the National Advisory Committee on Adult Religious Education has prepared a discussion guide for use with parish education commissions, adult religious education committees, parish staffs, groups of catechetical leaders, and diocesan religious education staffs. While the format for use of the discussion guide is flexible, it provides outlines for six group sessions. Each group session is based on a section of the text itself. Therefore, if participants attend all six sessions, they will have had the opportunity to read the entire document and discuss its implications with other adults.

Those who are sometimes deterred from reading "official type" documents such as *Adult Catechesis in the Christian Community* will be encouraged by the inclusion of an extremely helpful glossary of terms at the end of the discussion guide. Since the success of the discussion sessions relies heavily on a clear and unambiguous understanding of some technical terms, the glossary is itself an instructive tool.

The Department of Education of the United States Catholic Conference is especially grateful to Jack McBride, associate director for adult/special religious education in the Office of Religious Education, Diocese of Madison, for serving as general editor of the discussion guide. We also want to acknowledge Matthew J. Hayes, director of religious education, Archdiocese of Indianapolis, and Sr. Maria de la Cruz Aymes, SH, Archdiocese of San Francisco, for serving as senior consultants for the project.

The Department of Education is also grateful to the following persons and organizations who made pivotal contributions to the development of the discussion guide:

Michael Carotta	Sr. Marita Maschmann
Margaret Borders	Sr. Mary Parry
Michael Dowling	Margaret Ralph, Ph.D.
Pat Davidson	Joseph Sinwell, D.Min.
Susan Genereaux	Daniel Sparapani
Carole Eipers, D. Min.	Joseph Streett
Mary Jo Klase	Michael Wagner
Eileen Loughran	John Zaums, Ph.D.

United States Catholic Conference, Department of Education
The National Advisory Committee on Adult Religious Education
The National Conference of Catechetical Leadership
The National Catholic Educational Association
The National Association of Parish Coordinators and Directors
The National Conference of Directors of Religious Education
The National Advisory Committee for Catechesis with Hispanics
The National Organization of Catechists for Hispanics

This new edition of *Adult Catechesis in the Christian Community*, with the discussion guide conveniently appended to the text, places in the hands of pastoral workers and catechists a truly valuable resource with which "to promote a deeper appreciation and implementation of adult catechesis" ("Preliminary Remarks"). In addition, the discussion guide, as edited by Sr. Maria de la Cruz Aymes, SH, will be available in a Spanish edition of *Adult Catechesis in the Christian Community* to be released later this year.

Reverend John E. Pollard
Department of Education
United States Catholic Conference
Washington, D.C.

PRELIMINARY REMARKS

The International Council for Catechesis (COINCAT) took as the theme for its sixth plenary session, held in Rome October 23 – 29, 1988, the "Catechesis of Adults in the Christian Community."

The results of this session have been summarized to the document which, after being reviewed by the Congregation for the Clergy, of which COINCAT is a consultative body, is now being published under the sponsorship of COINCAT.

This document hopes to contribute to the efforts being made in the Christian communities spread throughout the world to promote adult catechesis, in keeping with the "new evangelization" so often called for by Pope John Paul II.

With this purpose in mind, the suggestions made here, in keeping with the most important pronouncements of the Magisterium on this question, reflect the expertise of members of the various local Churches throughout the world. This has allowed a great variety of approaches to emerge, but it has also permitted the identification of certain principles and features common to every form of adult catechesis.

This contribution does not intend to be an exhaustive directory for adult catechesis or a practical program ready for implementation. Rather, it simply offers some guidelines which, arranged in a systematic and organic way, reflect a rich world of experiences. These reflections are presented to pastoral workers and catechists in order to promote a deeper appreciation and implementation of adult catechesis.

In composing this document, the contributions of all the members of COINCAT were utilized, but the actual organization of the material and the writing of the text were the work of the Secretary General, who was assisted in this task by various experts.

May the Lord bless the service rendered by adult catechesis and grant His Church the grace to proclaim the Kingdom of God in ever more incisive ways through adult believers living in adult communities.

Easter 1990.
Fr. Cesare Bissoli, S.D.B.
Secretary General of COINCAT

INTRODUCTION
FROM THE PERSPECTIVE OF THE KINGDOM

1.   "What comparison shall we use for the reign of God? What image will help to present it? It is like a mustard seed which, when planted in the soil, is the smallest of all the earth's seeds, yet once it is sown, springs up to become the largest of shrubs, with branches big enough for the birds of the sky to build nests in its shade" (Mark 4:30–32).

This parable of Jesus sums up nicely for our time the dynamism of faith which is evident among people of all ages. In a particular way, through the proclamation of the Word, which in the beginning is humble and often arduous, adults receive the grace to become a living part of the Kingdom of God, are able to recognize their Lord and Savior and become witnesses to Him among their brothers and sisters in the world.

This parable therefore captures succinctly the *fundamental traits* of adult catechesis: its ultimate and radical purpose (the definitive coming of the Kingdom), the completely transcendent power which sustains it, the collaboration to which adults are necessarily called, and its extraordinarily positive impact on adults and on others.

2.   Jesus said, "Only one is your Master and you are all brothers" (Matthew 23:8).

We recognize Jesus today as He was in His own time, as one who approaches every kind of person — women and men, the small and the great, the good and the evil, the poor and the rich — in order to proclaim the Good News of the Kingdom with truth, simplicity and love. In Him every adult finds the "Way, the Truth and the Life" (John 14:6). The catechesis of adults, therefore, draws its own inspiration, courage and joy from the *Gospel of Jesus.*

3.   The consciousness of just how complex the world is in which we live requires humility and realism on the part of pastoral workers and leads them to be ever attentive, in the proclamation of the Christian message, to the real conditions in which people live. This sensitivity helps to overcome the distance between Church and society, between faith and culture, which is an important issue in dealing with adults.

This means that adult catechesis, in pursuing its goals, must clearly discern the problems and expectations of people today and be alert to the positive elements in their situation which are emerging. With evangelical forthrightness, it must be able to show why the Kingdom of God announced by Jesus offers light and hope.

IN THE FOOTSTEPS OF THE COUNCIL

4. The *Magisterium of the Church*, imbued with the spirit of renewal of the Second Vatican Council (cf. CD, 14; AG, 14) has constantly affirmed with authority, clarity and insistence, the centrality and importance of the catechesis of adults.

John Paul II states that "one of the constant concerns whose urgency is confirmed by present day experience throughout the world, is the catechesis of adults. This is the principal form of catechesis because it is addressed to persons who have the greatest responsibility and the capacity to live the Christian message in its fully developed form" (CT, 43).

5. It is certainly a gift of the Holy Spirit to witness in these years after the Council *the development of initiatives* on behalf of a new catechesis of adults in the local Churches throughout the world. This is manifested in pastoral letters, reflections and programs offered by experts and study centers, the implementation of the RCIA (the *Rite of Christian Initiation of Adults*) and a wide variety of other pastoral initiatives, all sustained by a truly ecclesial and missionary spirit.

In this spring of the catechesis of adults, the most notable developments in the various local Churches are the growth in the number of lay catechists, both women and men, and the fruitful and original activity of new groups, movements and associations.

In this context of hope, the same Spirit makes us all the more painfully aware of the limits and difficulties with which we are faced: the many adults who are not reached by any kind of catechesis, Christian communities lacking in missionary spirit, pastoral workers not sufficiently motivated by a sense of pastoral love and patience, an inadequate catechesis which too often is not integrated into a broader program of evangelization, and the lack in number and in preparation of catechists.

6. For this reason the Church makes a renewed call to all those most directly involved in the faith education of its members to increase their efforts to find *new ways* to reach those adults who have not been touched by the message of Christ, or who having been evangelized, have left the Church.

Responding to this call, the *International Council for Catechesis*, a consultative body of the Congregation for the Clergy, made a special study of adult catechesis during its 1988 session. As a result, the present document was elaborated, based on the experience of its members, clerical, religious, lay men and women, who come from various regions of the world and represent different races and cultures.

THE PURPOSE AND AUDIENCE OF THIS DOCUMENT

7.   The present document intends to highlight only the most significant aspects of the catechesis of adults. It touches on *common issues,* common problems and probable solutions, which seem prevalent throughout the world, fully recognizing that inculturation will have to be made in the local Churches.

This document wishes therefore to stimulate a spirit of communion and solidarity with others, by encouraging the sharing of insights and resources necessary for carrying out the catechesis of adults.

8.   This document is addressed to the whole People of God, gathered in the diverse Christian communities throughout the world, under the guidance of their Pastors.

In a more direct way it has in mind those *lay catechists* who are already engaged in the catechesis of adults or who are preparing themselves for this service.

They are living proof of the action of the Spirit who in every community continues to call forth people who make themselves available to accompany their brothers and sisters on their faith journey.

9.   Certain elements in the Gospel Parable of the Sower provide a fitting way for articulating the three parts of this document:

—the "different kinds of terrain" on which the seed falls, i.e. the present situation and the signs of the presence and growth of adults in today's Church;

—the "seed" of the Word which is communicated by means of the catechesis of adults, together with the profound reasons which motivate its communication and the principles which govern it;

—the process of "sowing and reaping," in which some guidelines are offered for concrete action.

PART ONE
THE ADULTS TO WHOM CATECHESIS IS DIRECTED

10.   To become an adult and to live as an adult is a vocation given by God to human beings as illustrated in the very first pages of the Bible (cf. Genesis 1:27–28; 2:15). This vocation finds its most perfect model in Jesus of Nazareth who "was almost thirty when He began His ministry" (Luke 3:23) of proclaiming the Kingdom. To grow into and draw near to Him, the Perfect Man (cf. Ephesians 4:13–15) becomes accordingly a grace and a task for every creature.

But how does this actually take place? What "lights" and "shadows," in the world and in the Church, characterize the human and Christian growth of adults?

IN THE WORLD

11. Our attention is drawn right away to the *difficulties and sufferings* which weigh heavily on so many adults, including Christians, both men and women. Among these we would like to single out the insufficient and disproportionate means for self-development (humanization); lack of respect for the basic rights to freedom "among which religions freedom occupies a place of primary importance" (EN, 39), as well as the right to follow one's own conscience and the right to personal dignity, especially with respect to the poor; and the obstacles to carrying out one's responsibilities to society and the family.

The causes of these evils are multiple and complex, and from time to time must be investigated. Generally speaking, we can point to the enormous disproportion in the distribution of the world's goods, the diminished regard for the family, the insufficient appreciation of women, lack of work, racial discrimination, the lack of access to culture, the incapacity or impossibility on the part of the masses to participate in public decision making.

These distortions gravely deform the image of God which men and women, precisely as adults, are called to reflect and fully enjoy (Genesis 1:26–27).

12. At the same time, we are witnessing an awakening of the individual and collective consciousness with respect to personal dignity, mutual interdependence and communion, and the need to stand in solidarity with the weak and the poor.

Furthermore, respect for and interest in religion and spiritual values are on the rise among adults, who regard religion as a source from which their lives draw new strength. The awareness that the earth is a gift from God, which must be respected and protected from all forms of pollution, is also gaining ground.

Civil institutions for their part, have in some places made a serious attempt to protect the rights and the freedom of individuals. They help adults to carry out their responsibilities through programs of continuing education, which extend up through old age.

IN THE CHURCH

13. The Church, which lives in the midst of the human family and is engaged like its Founder in the service of people, contributes to humanity by *proclaiming the Good News* of the Kingdom of God in Jesus the Savior. In bringing about the ever more just and more fraternal human family, the Good News proclaimed by Jesus is indispensable.

Faithful to this task the Church which is always open to the contributions of human experience and science, regards adult catechesis as the path to follow as a disciple of Christ, a path which is incarnate in the concrete situations of life.

Thus, it is necessary at the start to recognize the various conditionings and challenges in the ecclesial communities which have the greatest influence on the growth of adults as Christians.

CONDITIONINGS AND CHALLENGES

14.   "Why have you been standing here idle all day?" asked the Lord of the vineyard to the men who had been standing around all day. "No one has hired us," they told him. He answered them, "You go to the vineyard too" (Matthew 20:6 – 7).

In the parable of Jesus which expresses the universal invitation to the Kingdom of God, we recognize the positive response of many but we cannot overlook those — and they are the majority — who have not heard the invitation, or have forgotten it or for various reasons cannot come to terms with it.

This is the actual situation, full of both serious drawbacks and positive opportunities, of accomplishments and expectations, which the Church has to take into account when proposing the Gospel to adults.

15.   On the *economic-social level*, large numbers of believers do not have access to religious formation through catechesis because of a relentless underdevelopment which, in fact, prevents the poor from being evangelized (Luke 4:18), though this is their sacred right.

One could add here the migrations of whole peoples going on at present. Uprooted and displaced from their homelands, they are deprived of the basic need of security and stability.

16.   On the *social-cultural level*, in light of the determining influence of culture in all its various expressions, a number of important factors which have a decisive impact should be noted:

a) With the growth and expansion of the process of *secularization*, the very possibility of catechesis is put in crisis, particularly among adults, because of the great changes in culture and customs which have had significant repercussions, at least in the recent past, on the organization of life and the availability of time.

Much has also been said about the spiritual difficulties which adults have to face, such as the absence of human and religious certitudes, the loss of individual and collective identity, and the burden of loneliness.

b) Adults who are fervent in their faith sometimes find themselves in countries where the number of believers is small and resources are lacking, and where, on the other hand, *other great religions or value systems* exercise the predominant influence, which is not infrequently hostile to Christians. Under these circumstances, catechesis encounters great difficulties in reconciling an authentic and original faith journey with the legitimate local culture.

It should also be remembered that in certain countries, because of the reigning ideology, religious gatherings are forbidden or prevented and pastoral and catechetical services in public places are seriously obstructed.

c) Everywhere, *technological development* applied to the problems of life and exacerbated beyond all hounds by the media, poses new problems, particularly for adults, which the Christian faith must address.

This challenge requires a new way of formulating and resolving the perennial problems, such as the meaning and value of life, the destiny of human beings and the world, living together with others, the relationship between faith and the moral life, and the primacy of religious and spiritual values.

17. On the *level of the ecclesial communities*, it would be an oversight not to acknowledge the vigor of the Gospel seed in the realization of adult catechesis in the context of parishes, families, movements and groups, and in many other situations which will be discussed in Part Three.

Indeed, in taking to heart the invitation of Jesus, "Open your eyes and see! The fields are shining for harvest!" (John 4: 35), our attention is focussed on what it is possible to accomplish in the catechesis of adults.

There are, in fact, a number of identifiable needs which require a new approach in adult catechesis. These needs can only be met within the context of an adult Christian community.

There is a great needs for:

a) a more adequate language of faith, which will be comprehensible to adults at all levels, from those who are illiterate or quasi-literate to those who are highly educated; unless this language is addressed to them, they will feel alienated from the Church and perceive catechesis as irrelevant;

b) more accessible places where un-churched adults will feel welcomed, and where adults who have gone through their catechumenate or some other form of initiation can continue their faith journey in a Christian community;

c) a wider variety of catechetical models responding to the local and cultural needs of the people;

d) the popular religiosity of the people, both in its content and expression, to be taken seriously; the aspects which reflect the Gospel should be prudently incorporated in catechesis;

e) a more consistent effort to reach out to all adults, especially those who are un-churched, alienated or marginated, responding to their needs, so as to counteract the widespread proselytizing by sects;

f) a more visible expression of sensitivity, availability and openness on the part of clergy and Church institutions toward adults, their problems and their need for catechesis.

18. By way of conclusion to this analysis and with a view to what follows, we can group the adults who need catechesis into the following categories, keeping in mind *Catechesi Tradendae*, 44:

— adults in places which have become dechristianized, who have not been able to deepen their knowledge of the gospel message;

— adults who were catechized beginning in childhood, but who have fallen away from the faith;

—adults who have benefitted little from catechesis, either because they absorbed little or were incorrectly catechized;

—adults who were baptized as children but were not subsequently catechized, and who find themselves as adults, to a certain extent, in the situation of catechumens.

PART TWO
MOTIVATIONS, CRITERIA AND OTHER POINTS OF REFERENCE FOR ADULT CATECHESIS

19. "If one of you decides to build a tower, will he not first sit down and calculate the outlay to see if he has enough money to complete the project?" (Luke 14:28).

In the exhortation of the Master to acquire the evangelical wisdom needed for every undertaking on behalf of the Kingdom of God, we are invited to recognize and state the fundamental reasons for adult catechesis in the Church, all the more so as its importance becomes recognized.

MOTIVATIONS

20.   Theological-pastoral reflection proposes a number of different, complementary motives for catechesis: some in relationship to the faith life of the adult as such; others in relationship to the adult's public role in society and in ecclesial communities; and finally those which outrank the others in importance because they aim at the greater glory of God and the good of the Church.

21.   Adults in the Church, that is, all Christians — men and women, lay people, priests and religious — are people who have a *right and an obligation to be catechized, just like everyone else* (CT, c.v.; can. 217, 774; CL, 34).

This reason does not derive from any kind of service which the adult Christian is called to render. It springs instead directly from the "seed" of faith planted within and which hopes to mature as the adult grows in age and responsibility. "When I was a child I used to talk like a child, think like a child, reason like a child. When I became a man I put childish ways aside" (1 Corinthians 13:11).

Only by becoming an adult in the faith is one able to fulfill his or her adult duties toward others, as is required by the vocation given to each at baptism.

One must admit that in various communities, the formation of adults has been taken for granted or perhaps carried out in connection with certain events, not infrequently in an infantile way. Because certain external or traditional supports are sometimes lacking, a grave imbalance is created insofar as catechesis has devoted considerable attention to children while the same has not happened in the catechesis of young people and adults.

22.   The need for personal formation is necessarily bound up with the role which adults assume in *public life.* They share with all Christians the task of witnessing to the Gospel in words and deeds, but they do this with undeniable

authority and in a specifically adult way. This is true in the family context in which many adults, precisely as parents or other relatives, become both by nature and grace the first and indispensable catechists of their children. Adults also serve as role models for young people who need to be confronted with and challenged by the faith of adults.

In the context of society, the role of adults is crucial in the workplace and in the academic, professional, civil, economic, political and cultural spheres, and wherever responsibility and power are exercised. This is the case because the believing adult is so often the only one who can introduce the leaven of the Kingdom, express the novelty and beauty of the Gospel, and demonstrate the will for change and liberation desired by Jesus Christ.

The simple, faith-filled actions by which adults give witness to the Gospel in these situations require a great effort on their part to inwardly appropriate what they are called to pass on to others in a convincing and credible way.

23. This missionary task assumes greater weight in the context of the Christian community, which is called to acquire an adult faith.

It will be helpful to recall that this necessarily involves the intelligent and harmonious collaboration of all those who make up the Church, from children and young people to adults and the elderly.

In this context of communion, adults are asked in a special way to commit themselves to the *catechetical service and, in a broader sense, the pastoral care* of their brothers and sisters, both the little ones and grown-ups, always keeping in mind the different situations, problems and difficulties with which they are confronted.

It is not difficult to imagine what level of competence — and hence of previous formation — is required of adults in such a complex world, which is at one and the same time open to and wary of the Gospel of Jesus Christ.

24. A number of other motivations of a socio-religious, psychological and pedagogical-pastoral nature could be added. But all motivations converge on the most eminent and radical reason which is the basis of their validity and meaning. This is the reason which derives from *the order of faith:* the glory of God, the building of the Kingdom and the good of the Church. Indeed, God is fittingly honored by the person who is fully alive, and all the more so if the person is a mature adult. The Kingdom of God, like the seed in the field, grows above all through the activity of its adult members.

The Church herself, as well as every form of catechesis, are enriched by the charism of maturity and wisdom which comes from adults, and in this way the Church is helped in the effort of understanding the truth which is in gestation among the People of God.

A great number of adults, women and men, have offered a brilliant example of the contribution adults make when they collaborate with God in shaping the history of salvation, both in the constitutive period of the Bible and in the time of the Church, which actualizes Christ's salvation in her life.

25. In summary, in order for the Good News of the Kingdom to penetrate all the various layers of the human family, it is crucial that every Christian play an active part in the coming of the Kingdom. The work of each will be coordinated with and complementary to the contribution of everyone else, according to the different degrees of responsibility each one has. All of this naturally requires adults to play a primary role. Hence, it is not only legitimate, but necessary, to acknowledge that a fully Christian community can exist only when a systematic catechesis of all its members takes place and when an effective and well-developed catechesis of adults is regarded as the *central task* in the catechetical enterprise.

BASIC CRITERIA

In light of the motivations which we have just set forth, it will be possible to identify some criteria which support an effective and valid catechesis of adults.

We will single out five particularly important criteria, whose application in practice will be taken up in Part Three.

26. A catechesis of adults will be acutely sensitive to *men and women insofar as they are adults.* It will approach them in their adult situation, which is for the most part the lay state, and will be attentive to their problems and experiences. It will make use of their spiritual anti cultural resources, always respecting the differences among them. Finally, adult catechesis will stimulate the active collaboration of adults in the catechesis which involves them.

27. This implies, as a second criterion, that the catechesis of adults is realized with full recognition and appreciation of the "secular character which is proper and peculiar to the laity," which qualifies them "to seek the Reign of God in temporal affairs, putting them into relationship with God" (LG, 31).

In this regard, it is worth remembering what the Apostolic Exhortation *Evangelii Nuntiandi* and later, in the same words, *Christifideles Laici,* described as the responsibilities of the Christian laity: "Their own field of evangelizing activity is the vast and complicated world of politics, society and economics, as well as the world of culture, of the sciences and the arts, of international life, of the mass media. It also includes other realities, which are open to evangelization, such as human love, the family, the education of children and adolescents, professional work, and suffering. The more Gospel-inspired lay people there are engaged in these realities, clearly involved in them, competent to promote them and conscious that they must exercise to the full their Christian powers which are often repressed and buried, the more these realities will be at the service of the Kingdom of God and therefore at the service of salvation in Jesus Christ, without in any way losing or sacrificing their human content but rather pointing to a transcendent dimension which is often disregarded" (EN, 70; CL, 23).

28. One of the most valid criteria in the process of adult catechesis, but which is often overlooked, is the *involvement of the community* which welcomes and sustains adults. Adults do not grow in faith primarily by learning concepts, but by sharing the life of the Christian community, of which adults are members who both give and receive from the community.

29. The catechesis of adults, therefore, can bear fruit only *within the overall pastoral plan* of the local Church communities. It must have its own distinctive place in the whole, since it aims at making adults constructive participants in the life and mission of the community.

This implies two fundamental principles operative in all forms of adult catechesis:

—Even considering the autonomy of the process of adult catechesis, we must keep in mind that it must be integrated with liturgical formation and formation in Christian service.

—Adult catechesis cannot be conducted to the exclusion or slighting of catechesis for other age groups. When coordinated with them, it becomes the catechesis of Christian maturity and the goal of other kinds of catechesis.

By reason of its special position and the contribution it makes to the growth of the whole community's faith journey, the catechesis of adults must be regarded as a preferential option.

30. Finally, following the example of Jesus, who taught the people "the message in a way they could understand" (Mark 4:33), the catechesis of adults must recall in a particular way the responsibility of the local Churches, on the one hand, to remain united with the whole People of God, on the basis of the unique Gospel message authentically proclaimed in all its integrity and, on the other hand, to reflect on their own local situations in order to adapt the presentation of the message of salvation to the needs of the people.

The wisdom that is the fruit of experience, prayer and study will guide catechists to maintain a balance between making all the necessary *adaptations* and *being faithful* to what constitutes the common heritage of catechesis.

POINTS OF REFERENCE

31. Attempting to define adulthood in an univocal way is quite complex, given the number of factors at play in different, complementary interpretations. The contributions of the psychological, social and pedagogical sciences must all be carefully considered, although always directly in rapport with the specific life context, in which the ethnic, cultural and religious factors peculiar to that environment play a significant role.

Particularly today, it is essential to keep in mind the relationship between the young generation and that of adults, since the two groups influence and condition each other in a wide variety of ways.

To respect the "mystery of adulthood" and to organize well all forms of pastoral service for adults means keeping in mind all these factors and the vary diverse ways of speaking about and being an adult.

32. It is not at all easy, from a practical viewpoint, to provide a precise and uniform definition of the *catechesis of adults.* The reasons and criteria for its significance and necessity have already been pointed out. There are differences over the best way to put adult catechesis into practice, with respect to the scope of the subject matter, the length of time needed, and the most suitable arrangement of the material for a given audience.

Here, in light of recent Church documents, we understand catechesis as one moment in the total process of evangelization (EN, 17; CT, 18).

The specific role of the catechesis of adults consists in an initial deepening of the faith received at baptism, in an elementary, complete and systematic way (CT, 21), with a view to helping individuals all life long grow to the full maturity of Christ (cf. Ephesians 4:13).

Catechesis *per se* has to be *distinguished* therefore from other activities, even though it cannot be separated from them;

— it is different from evangelization, which is the proclamation of the Gospel for the first time to those who have not heard it, or the re-evangelization of those who have forgotten it;

— it is different from formal religious education, which goes beyond the basic elements of faith in more systematic and specialized courses;

— it is also different from those informal occasions for faith awareness in God's presence, which arise in fragmentary and incidental ways in the daily life of adults.

At the same time, adult catechesis remains *closely related* to all the above aspects of faith development;

— it makes explicit in the life of adults the reality of God's message *(kerygma),* taking into consideration concrete human situations, and "translating" it into the cultural language of the people;

— it goes to the core of the doctrinal content of our Catholic faith, presenting the fundamental beliefs of the creed in a way that relates to the life experience of people, instilling in them a faith mentality;

— it calls for a structured and organized, though perhaps very elementary, faith journey, which is expressed and sustained by listening to the Word of God, by celebration (liturgy), by charitable service *(diakonia),* and by a forthright witness in the various situations in which adults find themselves.

PART THREE
GUIDELINES FOR PRACTICAL IMPLEMENTATION

33. The common operative features of adult catechesis are presented here according to the four most important areas:

—the qualities of the adult Christian, which constitute the objective of catechesis and determine its content as well as certain constant factors in the way it is presented;

—the process involved in adult catechesis, with special reference to its methodological principles, forms and models;

—catechists of adults and their formation;

—those responsible for adult catechesis in the community.

QUALITIES OF THE CHRISTIAN ADULT IN THE FAITH

34. St. Paul admonishes the Christians of Ephesus in a fatherly way "to be children no longer, tossed here and there." As he goes on to explain, this is because it is our vocation to become the "perfect man," worthy of the infinite riches of Christ, who fills the universe (cf. Ephesians 4:13–14; 1:23; 3:8).

The ultimate and unifying goal of adult catechesis is to help the mature Christian to live as an adult by acquiring certain qualities. These qualities can be grouped around three major goals, which are in turn rooted in a common vision and then articulated in certain objectives and specified in content.

A) GOALS

35. Everywhere in the Church, the need to build *adult Christian communities* has been noticed. These communities must express a clear faith identity and must be centered on a clear proclamation of the Gospel, a meaningful celebration of the liturgy and a courageous witness in charity.

All catechesis must be directed to this goal, beginning with the catechesis of little children. Obviously, in the catechesis of adults the effects are more immediate and incisive.

Only in this way can we create convincing signs and effective conditions for an adherence to the faith which is stable and fruitful.

36. "The Reign of God is at hand. Reform your lives and believe in the Gospel!" (Mark 1:15).

These words of Jesus establish the first and enduring goal of anyone who wishes to be one of his mature disciples: to acquire an attitude of *conversion to the Lord*.

The catechesis of adults promotes an openness of the heart to the mystery of the Lord's greatness and grace by encouraging sincere reconciliation with the Lord and with one's brothers and sisters. Adults are led to recognize and accept the Lord's call and His salvific plan by living a life which is pleasing to God and which aims at holiness (cf. CL, 16–17). Adult catechesis is an invitation to faithfully practice the discipleship of Jesus and to judge all personal, social and spiritual experiences in the light of faith.

37.   "They devoted themselves to the apostles' instruction and the communal life, to the breaking of bread and the prayers" (Acts 2:42).

The conversion to the Lord at baptism leads to membership in a community whose way of life as disciples of Christ is shared by all. The catechesis of adults aims at bringing to fruition a conscious and firm decision to live the gift and choice of faith through *membership in the Christian community*. Adults who are mature in the faith understand what it means to be in communion with others and accept their coresponsibility for the community's mission and internal life.

38.   "You are the salt of the earth . . . You are the light of the world. In the same way, your light must shine before men so that they may see goodness in your acts and give praise to your heavenly father" (Matthew 5:13–16).

Recognizing the strong commitment to the new evangelization to which the Spirit is calling the Church today everywhere in the world, adult catechesis gives a missionary purpose to those tasks for which it is responsible.

Adult catechesis makes one more willing and able to be a *Christian disciple in the world* in that it helps to differentiate between good and evil, especially in the most significant expressions of one's culture, and to recognize and accept "all that is true, all that deserves respect, all that is honest, pure, admirable, decent, virtuous, or worthy of praise" (Philippians 4:8). Adult catechesis also draws others into one's faith-working-in-love (Galatians 5:6), and provides reasons for the hope that one has (1 Peter 3:15). It knows how to come to terms with the longings for liberation and salvation of people in every age, especially the poor, and then it takes effective steps in favor of the transformation of family, social and professional life in the light of the Gospel.

In this way, a harmonious and vital synthesis of the essential characteristics of the Christian, appropriate for adults, is being brought about. These characteristics are an obedient listening to the Word of God, communion with the faith community, and the service of charity and witness in the world.

B) OBJECTIVES

The goals which have been mentioned can be attained through *objectives* which specify more concretely the catechetical journey.

Recalling that the catechetical apostolate aims at active participation in the life and mission of the Church, including direct participation in the pastoral programs of the Church, we propose the following objectives to be of particular relevance and universal application.

39. A *basic understanding of the Church's faith, presented in a sufficiently organic way together with the reasons for believing.* It should be drawn directly from the sources of Revelation; that is, the Bible, the Liturgy, the Fathers, the Magisterium of the Church, other great documents of the Tradition, and the experience of Christian living in the ecclesial communities.

40. *An appropriate assimilation of the theological and cultural heritage in which faith is expressed.* This implies a knowledge of the major religious signs and symbols of faith, the role and use of the Bible, a grasp of the significance and practice of liturgical and private prayer, and an awareness of the impact of religious belief on culture and its institutions.

41. The capacity of *Christian discernment* in various situations, particularly regarding ethical principles which bear on human life and dignity and which have to do with respect for justice and the cause of the weak and the poor. Always in a spirit of respect for others, one also needs to develop a critical sense in the face of other religions or ways of life which people find meaningful.

42. Finally, the acquisition of those *skills and abilities which allow the adult believer to carry out his Christian witness* in the most diverse circumstances, in the community and in society.

c) CONTENTS

The contents of adult catechesis must be as comprehensive and exhaustive as possible. It is important to adapt the didactic methodology employed to the situations and needs of any given audience. Corresponding to the objectives indicated and the major common needs of adult believers today, these are the basic components of adult catechesis:

43. Catechesis has to present in a comprehensive and systematic way the *great themes of the Christian religion* which involve faith and reasons for believing: the mystery of God and the Trinity, Christ, the Church, the sacraments, human life and ethical principles, eschatological realities and other contemporary themes in religion and morality. It will respect the hierarchy of truths and their interrelationship.

44. In the context of a more than ever complex and pluralistic society, particular importance will be attached to a knowledge of the truths of the Gospel, and to the Church's duty to enlighten and educate the moral conscience. Catechesis presents the *ethical implications* of the Christian vision for major problems which emerge in personal and collective situations, such as the dignity of every person, the inviolable right to life, the transmission and protection of human life, the promotion of social justice, solidarity and peace, as well as concern for the poor, the powerless and the forgotten (CL, 37–41).

45. Catechesis must lead to a knowledge and evaluation, in the light of faith, of the *socio-cultural order* and of the changes that are taking place in the world today and in the life of individuals, affirming what is good but also pointing out

what is harmful and contrary to the Gospel. It has to clarify the distinction between action in the temporal order and in the ecclesial order, between political commitment and the commitment to evangelization, while drawing attention to the various ways they can influence one another (GCD, 97; CL, 42–43).

46.   To help bring adults to completeness and full maturity in their knowledge of the Christian faith, catechesis must include an *introduction* to the reading and use of Sacred Scripture, both private and communal, as well as the most important expressions of liturgy and prayer. It would also be most useful if catechesis presented the major moments in the history of the Church, both universal and local, as well as the principal documents of the Church's Magisterium, especially regarding social doctrine.

d) CONSTANT ELEMENTS IN THE PRESENTATION OF CONTENT

47.   "All the people made a great feast for they had understood the meaning of the words they heard" (Nehemiah 8:12). These words describe the joy the people experienced when, after returning from exile, they were able to understand the Scriptures. Later, Jesus and the apostles imparted their message in an exemplary way so that the people could understand (Mark 4:33; 1 Corinthians 14:19). Hence, we should consider it the Lord's will that in teaching the faith, we present it in a readily understandable way.

The contents of adult catechesis are offered to men and women of every social and cultural background as the nourishing and satisfying bread of life so that, filled with divine wisdom, they might radiate this wisdom in all areas of life.

These considerations allow us to identify certain principles which govern the presentation of content and which concretize the basic criteria enunciated above (nn. 26–30).

48.   In the presentation of the Christian religion, catechesis must deal with the many *questions*, difficulties and doubts which arise in the human heart. Indeed, these questions should be brought to light when they have been obscured or confused by ignorance or indifference. The faith response to these questions will appear meaningful if it is rooted in the Bible and in concrete historical life, and if it is respectful of reason and attentive to the signs of the times.

49.   Precisely because the principal content of adult catechesis is the revelation of the living God who saves human beings and helps them to realize their full potential, this catechesis must be dynamic and relevant so that adults, to their own satisfaction, can become gradually more aware of *their value and dignity as human beings*, as a result of a careful and stimulating exposition of the great truths of faith.

50.   Conscious of how secularized and pluralistic the world of the adult can be, the catechesis of adults seeks to provide solid formation *in a spirituality suitable for the Christian laity* (cf. n. 27). The special tasks of the Christian lay

person in the Church and in society, which vary according to the widely different situations in which adults find themselves, should be given a prominent place in the formation program. Special attention should be reserved for teaching adults how to pray.

51.   Catechesis of adults must encourage *an ecumenical outlook* (CT, 32–34). It must be open to *confronting and entering into dialogue* with the great religions and with those attitudes, theories and practices which constantly seek to attract adults. "The catechesis of adults will be surer of success when it is open to the encounter between faith, culture and science, in which an attempt is made to integrate them with one another while respecting the specific identity of each" (John Paul II, Discourse to the members of COINCAT, in *L'Osservatore Romano*, 30 October 1988, p. 4).

Hence, whatever knowledge and methodologies allow a more adequate reading of historical, social and religious phenomena, both in their negative and positive aspects, have a right to a place in adult catechesis. With their help, catechesis will be able to provide a more enlightened Christian interpretation of reality.

52.   Since the constructive contribution of adults in giving witness to their faith in the family and in many other areas of life is clearly recognized, catechesis must help adults to learn not only for themselves, but should prepare them to *communicate the contents of faith to others.* They can make an important contribution in showing other adults what an impact the faith can have on their lives and on the world around them. In a particular way, they have a responsibility for the disadvantaged, especially the poor and marginated, and all who find themselves in especially trying circumstances.

53.   Finally, as an underpinning for the needs just mentioned, the *communitarian dimension* of the contents of faith will be thoroughly developed. In this way, adults will come to know and experience the "mystery of the Church," which is incarnate in a particular community and history and which is characterized by particular needs, initiatives and pace of life. Catechesis will help adults see how they can fit in and participate in the life of the Church.

METHODOLOGICAL CONSIDERATIONS

54.   The widely varying kinds of adults and life circumstances which adult catechesis must take into consideration make it impossible to provide a catalogue of fixed norms applicable to every program of adult catechesis. Nevertheless, the results of our reflection on adult catechesis permit us to identify several reference points which are valid for all situations. These common features apply to the recipients of catechesis, organizational principles, and the forms and models of catechesis.

We have repeatedly stressed that the adult formation process has its own particular characteristics. A central feature is the establishment of a friendly and dialogical rapport. This means that the didactic moment must be integrated into a broader and more elaborate faith journey, of which we would like to point out a number of aspects.

55.   There are certain *special categories* which deserve attention because of their intrinsic value, both from a merely human as well as an evangelical perspective. Here we have in mind those whose need for the consolation of the Christian message is all the greater because of the intensity of their isolation and suffering. These include the disabled, the elderly, the sick, and all who find themselves on the fringes of society (refugees, immigrants, nomads and prisoners). The possibility of their involvement in the Christian community is often underestimated and unappreciated. With the solicitude of Christ, catechesis will also show special concern for those living in irregular situations.

56.   Above all, one must begin by *accepting adults where they are*. To make more explicit what was said in n. 26, it is essential to keep in mind the specific adults with whom one is working, their cultural background, human and religious needs, their expectations, faith experiences, and their potential. It is also important to be attentive to their marital and professional status.

Individual groups should be as homogeneous as possible so that their participants will benefit from their experience.

57.   Of fundamental importance is the *dialogical approach* which, while recognizing that all are called to the obedience of faith (Romans 1:5), respects the basic freedom and autonomy of adults and encourages them to engage in an open and cordial dialogue. In this way, they can make known their needs and can participate, as they should, as subjects or agents in their own catechesis and in that of others.

58.   On a more practical level, to maintain a good relationship with adults, their catechesis must include a clear witness to the Christian life and must focus on the essential issues, as it seeks to express itself in a solid and convincing way. Moreover, the truths of faith should be presented as certitudes, without taking away from the fact that for pilgrims on their way toward the full revelation of truth and life, the path of research and investigation always remains open.

B) ORGANIZATIONAL PRINCIPLES

59.   Practically speaking, under the term "adult catechesis" a variety of programs can be grouped. Some are traditional; others are new. They can be structured or more spontaneous, permanent or temporary, widely used or restricted in number and frequency.

One often has the impression that there is a wealth of initiatives, which however are wasteful of resources and badly organized, and do not match the sort of catechesis outlined so far.

To guarantee an effective catechetical program, the interaction of a number of factors, assisted by God's grace, is necessary: a good pastoral plan, the participation of the Christian community, the creation of positive experiences.

Moreover, in order for this interaction to work, catechesis must have an organic development and cannot be merely episodic. To this end, every program or journey must be *systematic and organic,* and structured around precise goals. It must ensure continuity in regularly scheduled meetings and must be clear about what is to be accomplished, even in only occasional or one-time programs.

In order to ensure unity in faith and life, when there are a number of different catechetical programs within the same community, all the programs need to contain certain common elements; namely, communion centered on the Word, participation in the liturgy, charitable service, and attentiveness to the Church's life.

60. Certain *forms* of adult catechesis seem particularly suitable because of the impact they have and should therefore not be neglected. Among these are programs aimed at families (parents, couples, . . .), student groups, parish organizations or other associations, and groups which gather on the occasion of a significant event (preparation for the sacraments, funerals, community celebrations, popular feast days, etc.).

61. The *parish* has "the essential task of a more personal and immediate formation of the lay faithful" (CL, 61).

Since it is in a position to reach out to individual persons and groups, it is the "privileged place" where "catechesis is realized not only through formal instruction, but also in the liturgy, sacraments and charitable activity" (John Paul II, Discourse to the members of COINCAT; cf. CL, 26–27; 61). Catechesis allows adults to have "a more direct and concrete perception of the sense of ecclesial communion and responsibility in the Church's mission" (CL, 61).

A typical pattern for adult catechesis is the structuring of programs in certain clearly defined periods of time, particularly during the important seasons of Advent and Lent. In this way, catechesis recognizes the true value of the liturgical year, which is an important element in the Church's educational process.

62. In various places, *small communities* of adults (basic Christian communities) have emerged. Here the members carry out catechesis through praying and reflecting together on the Word of God. They strive to discover the relevance of the Word for their everyday life and particularly for their society, to whose service they have lovingly and generously dedicated themselves.

Organized by good leaders who are in harmony with the local Church, these communities can be a powerful and effective way by which adults can bring the Gospel to the world, as the leaven of holiness and liberation.

63.   As for the kinds of catechesis carried out by the *various movements and associations*, a plurality of approaches is legitimate. Their programs offer " . . . the possibility, each with its own method, of offering a formation through a deeply shared experience in the apostolic life . . . " (CL, 62). Yet no movement should consider itself the only valid one and, above all, none should forget the principles of ecclesial communion (CL, 30). As an act of the Church, catechesis must everywhere express the fullness of the Christian faith and should be in the service of ecclesial communion. It is important to keep in mind the great majority of the People of God who do not belong to any movement.

In light of the tremendous spiritual and apostolic impact which the movements have had, it is appropriate to inform adults about them and encourage their participation.

64.   Undoubtedly a useful instrument for imparting a knowledge of the faith and for maintaining communion in the faith are *adult catechisms*, approved by the proper ecclesiastics authority (cf. can. 775, §§ 1–2). In conjunction with them, the resources of the sciences of communications and language should be utilized in order to communicate the Christian message with greater facility and effectiveness. We can never recall too often that "the language used must elicit the attention and interest of modern adults. The best forms of communication for reaching them, including signs, gestures and symbols, must be employed" (John Paul II, Discourse to the members of COINCAT).

65.   The *mass media*, when used skillfully, are effective means of adult catechesis. The most prominent means of social communication are the press, radio and television, but videotapes, audiotapes, films, comic books, and other forms of the "minimedia" are also useful.

Professional Catholic lay people should be encouraged by all means to serve in news agencies and production centers, especially when these belong to the Church. They should strive to produce high quality resource materials.

c) MODELS AND ITINERARIES

In recent times, various models have been proposed for adult catechesis, some of which transcend parish boundaries and may even have an international character. It has been said that the various itineraries are tailored to the spiritual condition of adults.

To assist the implementation of the various models, some clarifications and suggestions are in order.

66.   The Synod of 1977 affirmed that "the model of all catechesis" is the catechumenate which culminates in baptism (*Synod Message* 8; cf. EN, 44; CL, 61). According to ancient tradition, every form of catechesis should be inspired by the catechumenal model. Precisely because the catechesis of adults aims at living the Christian life in all its fullness and integrity, the process outlined in the *catechumenate* seems the most appropriate model and should be encouraged everywhere, though it cannot be considered the exclusive model.

67. In the Church, the classic *catechumenal model* consists in a number of stages (cf. RCIA). The three which are considered most important are:

—the pre-catechumenate, which concentrates on the conversion of adults by presenting them with the kerygma or first proclamation of the Gospel;

—the catechumenate which forms adults in the basic components of the Catholic faith, summed up in the Creed, the liturgical celebration, and Christian living;

—the mystagogy, through which the neophytes deepen their knowledge of Christian doctrine and build on the basic catechesis already received.

68. The decision as to *which itineraries* are to be taken will depend on the situation in which adults find themselves. As already pointed out in Part One (n. 18), some need pre-evangelization to stimulate an interest in the faith. Others are ready for evangelization, the "kerygmatic moment" in which the Gospel is proclaimed. Finally, those who are farthest along are ready for catechesis in the strict sense.

In pastoral planning, the specific itinerary needed for a particular group of adults must be identified and the specifically catechetical dimension in programs for adults should be respected.

69. Adult catechesis necessarily aims at making the adult a member of and a participant in the community. This means that adults must not only know the community, but must also actively participate in its various faith expressions and accept some form of responsibility for community life. For this reason, the building of *small communities or ecclesial groups* is conducive to the strengthening of adult catechesis (cf. CT, 24).

THE IDENTITY AND FORMATION OF THE CATECHIST OF ADULTS

70. "The harvest is good but laborers are scarce. Beg the harvest master to send out laborers to gather the harvest" (Matthew 9:37–38).

The harvest is the seed of the Kingdom which has grown to maturity, that is, the crowds which, though "prostrate from exhaustion," are eager for a shepherd who will take pity on them (Matthew 9:35–36; Mark 6:34). Jesus says that generous harvesters are needed.

In the light of faith, we can see a marvelous response to this invitation at work in the Church today in the emergence of a large number of *catechists*, particularly from among the laity. They are involved with every age group, including the often challenging category of adults.

The requirements of adult catechesis described above highlight the decisive role of catechists as well as the qualities they must possess. "Forming those who, in turn, will be given the responsibility for the formation of the lay faithful, constitutes a basic requirement of assuring the general and widespread formation of all the lay faithful" (CL, 63).

71.   In general, the catechist of adults, whether a priest, religious or lay person, must have an *adult faith* and be capable of supporting and leading other adults on their journey of growth in the faith. If a catechist is not a natural leader, it will be necessary for him or her to acquire certain basic leadership skills.

Catechists do not regard themselves as superior or extrinsic to the persons or groups to whom they minister. Rather, in the process of growing in the faith, they feel one with and indebted to everyone, and they know how to recognize everyone and make them agents and participants in the faith journey.

72.   Stability and living the Christian faith as a member of the ecclesial community are basic requirements for catechists. They must mature as spiritual persons in the concrete tasks they perform, in such a way that the "first word" they speak is that of personal witness. To this must be added a professional competence, or the ability to sustain a catechetical journey with their brothers and sisters.

73.   More precisely, an indispensable quality of catechists is the wise insight which allows them to go beyond the interpretation of texts to a deep grasp of vital issues and contemporary problems, and to be able to critically interpret present day events and the "signs of the times." Other requirements are the ability to listen and dialogue, encourage and reassure, form relationships, work in teams, and build community. There must also be a sense of being sent by the Church and of being accepted by the community, whose journey they share in a fraternal spirit.

In a word, the catechist of adults will be a sufficiently balanced human being, with the flexibility to adapt to different circumstances.

B) PLURALITY IN THE TYPES OF CATECHISTS

74.   Room should be made for a *plurality of types* among adult catechists, in relationship to the needs of the community and according to the Spirit which each receives. There is a primary need for catechists who know how to work with families, persons or groups with particular needs, such as the disabled, the poor, the marginated, and those in irregular situations.

75.   A true sign of God's love in our time is the emergence of *lay catechists of adults*, whose growth in number and competence we have identified as one of the most reassuring developments in the Church today (cf. n. 5). Precisely because of the charism of the lay state, they are in a better position than anyone else to accompany adults along their faith journey since they share the same tasks and problems in the family, society and the Church. They can also render a service which is essential in the catechesis of adults: the inculturation of the faith.

76. For all these reasons, the number of lay catechists—women and men, singles and married couples—will have to continue to grow since their number is not yet equal to the demand for them. At times, according to the need, they will require specialized training.

Always and in every way, lay catechists should be *recognized, respected and loved* by their priests and communities. They should be supported in their formation and encouraged and helped to accomplish a task which is indispensable but far from easy. Theirs is a genuine service through which God in Christ continues His work of mercy and salvation in the world.

c) FORMATION

77. More than ever we are aware that catechists, and particularly catechists of adults, are not born as such, but become catechists in two stages: *the initial formation program followed by continuing education.*

The development of a program must take into consideration the particular circumstances of the local Church, the people's needs, the catechists' skills and abilities, and the resources available. In a realistic, well thought out plan, there will be an initial formation program for future catechists, which lays the foundation for possible specialization. Later on, periodic updating will take place, in which instruction in theory will be supplemented by the insights of experience and a supervised apprenticeship.

78. Since the primary purpose of formation is growth in the faith, the core of the catechists' formation will be identical with that of the adult Christian. This includes a solid theological, anthropological and cultural preparation, carried out with the catechetical mission in mind and, hence, with particular attention to didactic-pedagogical questions.

79. Especially for the lay catechist, formation will be at one and the same time theoretical and practical, intellectual and spiritual. It will insist on the development of interpersonal relationships and a community-oriented attitude, always keeping in mind methods suitable for adult formation. Only in this way can the secular character of the lay catechist's identity and mission he expressed.

80. The formation of catechists must be responsibly directed by the local Church, under the guidance of the bishop and the appropriate offices, commissions and institutes of formation, in accordance with approved principles and programs.

One can be recognized as an adult catechist only after the required introductory formation program, as approved by the local church, and after receiving a mandate from the bishop.

THOSE RESPONSIBLE FOR CATECHESIS IN THE COMMUNITY

81. The catechesis of adults, as a service of the Church on behalf of the Kingdom of God, is conceived and nurtured in the womb of Mother Church. For this reason, the *whole Christian community* should be involved in it, all the more so because adults determine the quality of Church life and guarantee its smooth operation. For this reason, adult catechesis should be carefully planned in the parish, advertized in advance and supervised as it unfolds in its various stages. The community should pray for its success and joyfully offer its encouragement and support.

82. Within the Christian community, the *bishop* as Teacher of the faith (cf. CT, 63), is the chief catechist of adults. He brings to this service the contribution of his own charism and personal witness. He should take a keen interest in the diocesan program of adult catechesis and keep abreast of its activities through meetings with the moderators or directors and with the catechists themselves, whom he should treat as close collaborators. The bishop should also devote care and attention to the formation of adult catechists.

Because of the responsibility he bears, the bishop will also follow, in a spirit of fraternal charity, the various forms of adult catechesis which do not originate within the diocese.

Because of the complexity and importance of adult catechesis, it is recommended that the bishop appoint at least one person to direct and coordinate the various initiatives on behalf of adult catechesis in the diocese.

It is only right to acknowledge that, in some countries, well-trained lay people serve as directors of adult catechesis on the diocesan and parish levels. Their contribution should be encouraged and supported.

83. What the bishop assumes responsibility for on the diocesan level, *priests assume responsibility for in the local communities.* They should be directly involved in the catechesis of adults, and as directors of lay catechists, they should treat them with concern and respect.

Since the role of the priest in the community is irreplaceable, it is essential that *candidates for the priesthood have a solid formation in catechetics.* This is particularly true with respect to adult catechesis, for which they need to learn to direct and collaborate with lay catechists.

84. The present document, within the limits it has set for itself, may be a useful instrument for existing *national, regional and diocesan programs* in the various local Churches, which will naturally adapt the suggestions made here to their own pastoral circumstances.

This is also true for the various groups, movements and associations which offer catechesis for adults. Through close association with the pastors of the Church, a true spirit of ecclesial communion can be created in the various forms of catechesis and so they will be sure that their apostolic endeavors are authentic and constructive.

CONCLUSION

85.   Since there are many obstacles to adult catechesis in our times, there must be a willingness to accept even modest success and to exercise utmost *courage and patience* in the face of the failure of even the finest initiatives. Through repeated efforts and, above all, through an unshakable faith in God, one is drawn into the Mystery of the Kingdom: a small seed which slowly but surely grows, for the joy and salvation of all.

86.   In the light of all these reflections, it is fitting to turn our attention to the *Virgin Mary,* as she is repeatedly described in the Gospels as one who listens attentively and knows how to meditate in the depths of her heart (cf. Luke 1:29; 2:19. 51; Acts 1:14). we rightly see in Mary the exemplary model of the adult who undertakes the journey of faith. She listens to the Word of God and knows how to discover it in the complex events in which her life is caught up from the beginning. She listens, and as an adult person, she meditates at length; she searches within herself and seeks to understand the Will of God. Once she knows it, she generously accepts it and puts it into practice.

Later on, with utmost human sensitivity and a true missionary spirit, Mary knows how to interpret and respond to the questions of the various people she encounters, like those of the couple at the wedding feast of Cana. Through her, a catechist as much in deeds as in words, the grace of Christ could reach all these people.

May Mary of Nazareth, the faithful and courageous servant of God and of human beings, whom we see present as the Church begins her mission of evangelization and catechesis, inspire every adult who sets out on the journey of faith. At the same time, may she be the teacher and model of catechists who, like her, with their store of knowledge and wisdom, cheerfully put themselves at the service of their adult brothers and sisters.

GUIDELINES
FOR
DOCTRINALLY SOUND
CATECHETICAL MATERIALS

1990

OVERVIEW OF *GUIDELINES FOR DOCTRINALLY SOUND CATECHETICAL MATERIALS*

by Eva Marie Lumas, sss

Considering the numerous catechetical directives published for the worldwide and American Catholic community since the Second Vatican Council, the need for *Guidelines for Doctrinally Sound Catechetical Materials* (GDSCM) seemed questionable to everyone on the NCCB/USCC task force except the bishops. The task force consisted of three bishops and a multicultural group of 15 catechetical professionals. Some of the catechetical professionals had contributed to the development of *Sharing the Light of Faith: National Catechetical Directory for Catholics of the United States* (NCD). Some were (arch)diocesan personnel engaged actively in promoting the NCD as the definitive guide for parish catechetical efforts. Still others were nationally renowned catechetical innovators who relied on the NCD to direct their ministry. Moreover, everyone on the task force was aware that the NCCB/USCC had made a commitment to revise the NCD as needed, and everyone knew the *Catechism of the Catholic Church* (CCC) was forthcoming soon.

For these reasons, the catechetical professionals questioned the publication of the GDSCM on the grounds that it might undermine the catechetical renewal promoted by the NCD. More specifically, they were concerned that the GDSCM might prompt a return to a pre-NCD catechetical model that was primarily intellectually focused and did little to foster an integration of faith and life. As a result, this group of catechetical scholars and practitioners strongly encouraged the bishops to invest their resources in promoting the previously published catechetical documents rather than in promulgating yet another document. It was also recommended that the American bishops publish a composite text that would highlight and possibly embellish the doctrines previously published in *Basic Teachings for Catholic Religious Education* (BT) and "Principal Elements of the Christian Message for Catechesis" in the NCD (chapter 5). But the bishops maintained that neither of these suggestions would address fully their concerns regarding the practice of contemporary catechesis.

The bishops endorsed fully the catechetical renewal engendered by Vatican II and most of the parish catechetical materials it had spawned. In fact, they intended that the GDSCM be an affirmation of the previous catechetical documents and a support for the "admirable dedication and zeal" demonstrated by contemporary catechetical publishers. At the same time, the bishops believed the GDSCM would contribute toward the development of "an informed laity, people of faith who know their religion and can give an account of it" (9). Simply stated, the GDSCM was written for two specific purposes: First, it sought to strengthen the influence of individual bishops and the American episcopacy as a whole over the doctrinal content of parish catechetical curricula. Second, it sought to provide the bishops with a means of identifying "certain doctrines that seem to need particular emphasis in the life and culture of the United States."

This commentary on the GDSCM will review the major principles and guidelines addressed in the document, discuss the general strengths and weaknesses of the GDSCM and conclude with a statement regarding the ongoing need for episcopal direction in the development of effective catechetical curriculum materials.

MAJOR PRINCIPLES AND GUIDELINES

The GDSCM consists of three major sections. The first of these is the introduction, which begins by clarifying the bishops' concerns regarding the presentation of doctrine in catechetical materials. It then describes the specific kind of catechetical materials to which the GDSCM is to be applied and emphasizes the integral link between doctrinal soundness and the fourfold task of catechesis. The closing segment of the introduction delineates principles and criteria to be used for determining the doctrinal soundness of catechetical materials.

The bishops' concerns for doctrinal soundness in catechetical materials arise from the challenge posed by the vast quantity and diversity of parish catechetical curricula that are currently being produced. While acknowledging that most of these resources have contributed greatly to the advancement of the church's catechetical mission, the bishops also imply that they regard some of these resources as unsuitable for the task. Particular attention is therefore given to stating two of the bishops' most basic expectations of Catholic catechetical materials: They are expected to adhere faithfully to the teaching authority of the magisterium. They are also expected to facilitate a communally shared understanding of the faith among the intergenerational and culturally diverse American Catholic community.

One of the primary strengths of the introduction is to be found in its presentation of the interdependent relationship between catechesis and the other four primary ministries of the church—proclamation of the word, worship, community and service. Unfortunately, however, the bishops' acuity regarding effective catechesis is not evident in their description of catechetical materials presented in the GDSCM. The document describes these materials as "printed and audiovisual materials, and textbooks and programs that utilize such learning strategies as role playing, crafts and other supportive educational activities" (5).

The description is simplistic as it reduces faith formation to education. For that matter, it also reflects a reductionist view of cogent educational resources and methodologies.

The most instructive segment of the introduction is its concluding segment, which presents a clear statement of the principles and criteria of doctrinally sound catechetical materials. The first principle is that the presentation of doctrine "be both authentic and complete." For their authenticity, these presentations are expected to reflect accurately the bishops' teachings on matters of faith, morals and church tradition. In order to be complete, catechetical curricula are expected to present the teachings of the church in their entirety while observing the integral relationship and balance among the respective parts and being attentive to the capacity of the learners.

The second principle of doctrinal soundness is the presentation of the church's teachings in ways that depict clearly the incarnate and dynamic nature of the Christian faith. Toward this end, the document speaks eloquently to the ongoing activity of God in the world that is "mediated" through human experience, personal and social relationships, culture, science, technology, scripture, liturgy, the teachings and life of the church and the "signs of the times."

Four criteria for determining the doctrinal soundness of catechetical materials are then derived from these two general principles. First, catechetical texts and programs are to utilize a holistic approach for nurturing the life of faith such that children, youth and adults are engaged in an ever-deepening and lifelong conversion process. Second, these texts and programs should highlight the church's foundational doctrines and thereby demonstrate an acknowledgement of a certain hierarchy of truths. Third, catechetical materials are expected to develop meaningful ways of presenting the teachings of the church in ways that resonate with the "language, customs and symbols" of diverse cultural groups. Finally, the fourth criterion for doctrinal soundness calls for catechetical texts and programs that cultivate "a healthy and vital Catholic identity" among American Catholics by engaging them in common experiences, investing them with a common language and promoting some common expressions of the faith.

The clarity, coherence and scope of these principles and guidelines single them out as the most important contribution of the GDSCM to contemporary catechesis. The benefits of providing authors, editors and publishers with a single set of episcopal norms to guide the creation of Catholic catechetical curriculum materials notwithstanding, this segment of the document also provides diocesan and parish catechetical ministers with a concise, yet definitive, guide to assist their selection and use of current catechetical curricula.

The first chapter of the GDSCM, which bears the same name as the document itself, begins by restating the primary sources and purposes that influenced the publication of the document. Then, using the same literary genre as the CCC, that is, short summary statements, this chapter presents a list of nine general principles that should undergird the doctrinal content of all catechetical texts and a list of 60 doctrines and doctrinal issues that the bishops believe need "particular emphasis" in contemporary catechesis. To some degree, these summary statements are simple paraphrases of principles, doctrines or doctrinal issues addressed in the documents of Vatican II as well as more recent episcopal documents and insights regarding catechesis. In addition, the statements are divided into the same topical categories found in the NCD's chapter on doctrine, except for the few references to "creation" that are subsumed into other topical categories.

However, a critical reading of these 69 summary statements reveals that they were written to address the inability of some catechetical materials to cultivate the religious identity and literacy of the American Roman Catholic community. In light of this, the statements can be grouped easily according to the doctrinal issues the bishops intended them to address: Three of the statements call for an explicit acknowledgment of the teaching authority of the magisterium (22–23, 31). Another six statements call for greater emphasis to be given to the authoritative teachings of the magisterium. Of particular note are the statements regarding the interpretation of scripture (5), theological opinion (6), the use of traditional language when speaking of the three persons of the Trinity (17), compliance with liturgical norms (45), the formation of conscience (53) and Christian morality (59). And while three statements highlight a legitimate diversity of faith expressions with the church (6, 26–27), ten statements are written explicitly as correctives for deficiencies that the bishops believe to be evident in current catechetical curricula regarding the full, balanced and inter-related presentation of doctrine (2–3), the Trinitarian and Christocentric nature of the faith (10, 12–14), the divine nature of Jesus (15), the distinctive "marks" of the church (24) and original sin (51).

Nine statements speak to the distinctive nature of the Christian message, especially as it is taught and practiced within the Catholic Church (9, 18–21, 28–30, 32), and two statements validate the ongoing development of church doctrine and practice (7–8).

While a significant number of the summary statements are devoted to affirming the constitutive role of prayer and the sacraments in the formation of faith (25, 34, 38–43, 45–47), the preponderance of them affirm the inherent dignity of the human person as a creation of God, the integral link between faith and life and the social responsibilities of the Catholic Christian (4, 11, 16, 52, 54–58, 60–69).

Chapter one also includes five statements that focus on the vocation of all the baptized while making a strong exhortation for nurturing vocations to the priesthood and vowed religious life (48–50). There is one statement that encour-ages a fuller appreciation for the intercessory role of angels and saints in peo-ple's lives (37). There is also a statement that affirms the value of sacramentals and popular devotions for nurturing faith (44).

Also included in chapter one are two statements regarding the veneration of Mary. The document advocates participation in the "liturgical cult of Mary" and other Marian devotions as a means of promoting Marian theology (35–36). The manner in which these two statements are written casts their value to the GDSCM in a dubious light. Here, the bishops seem to be safeguarding a tradition-ally favored cultic practice, rather than addressing a doctrinal issue. If indeed there are episcopal concerns regarding the presentation of Marian doctrine in catechetical materials, those issues should have been stated clearly. And the value of Marian devotions could have been included in the statement on sacra-mentals and popular devotions (44).

In light of the diversity of catechetical practitioners, this chapter will undoubtedly evoke mixed reviews as a support for the catechetical ministry of the church. Some persons may very well agree with the bishops that the doctrinal precepts and issues addressed are given insufficient attention in contemporary catechetical materials. Others may be disheartened by the chapter's restrained endorsements of inclusive language. Some may even be alarmed by those state-ments that describe the church in terms that are explicitly reminiscent of the pre-Vatican II axiom that referred to Roman Catholicism as "the one, true faith." Still others may conclude that this chapter is praiseworthy for the balanced emphasis it places on knowing and living the faith, as well as the balanced impor-tance it ascribes to participating in the cultic practices as well as the social mis-sion of the church as requisites for mature faith. To some extent each of these critiques is justified.

The last chapter of the GDSCM is the smallest of the document's three sec-tions. It highlights pastoral principles that should undergird the presentation of doctrine and also outlines 18 ministerial strategies. Here the bishops affirm the need for the presentation of doctrine to be "attractive, appealing and understandable," as well as accurate and complete. Following from this general principle, they call for the development of catechetical curricula that resonate with the life experience and culture of the learners (70, 72, 74, 80–81).

The bishops stress also the use of a variety of pedagogical methods including memorization (71, 75, 83), the importance of scripture (73, 77), private prayer and communal worship (76), the need to foster community-building and service (78–79) and involving parents in the catechesis of their children (84).

This chapter encourages also the development of catechetical curricula that facilitates the ministry of catechists and teachers with (a) more "user-friendly" materials, (b) practical suggestions for catechizing persons with special needs and (c) facilitating their own faith development (82, 85, 87). And, in accord with the previous two sections of the document, the chapter contains an inference regarding the teaching authority of the bishops by calling for catechetical curricula to better enable catechists and teachers to differentiate between church doctrine and the interpretations and/or opinions of theologians (86). Moreover, it speaks to the formation of a Catholic identity by recommending that catechists maintain a "judicious balance" between personalized and traditional expressions of the faith among their learners (75).

GENERAL STRENGTHS AND WEAKNESSES OF THE DOCUMENT

Taken as a whole, the GDSCM succeeds in supporting the catechetical renewal initiated by Vatican II and affirms many of the catechetical documents that preceded it. The most essential contribution the document makes to contemporary catechesis is to be found in the statement of general principles and guidelines for doctrinal soundness. Besides the obvious benefits of providing publishers and catechetical practitioners with a pragmatic tool for developing their ministries, this delineation of guidelines and principles also gives the bishops a common frame of reference for discerning the doctrinal merit of catechetical texts.

The GDSCM also presents an insightful synopsis of the fourfold task of catechesis that brings the teachings of the church out of the realm of theory or abstraction and grounds them firmly into the existential realities of people's lives. Coupled with chapter two's statements on the "life of grace and moral issues" and the pastoral considerations addressed in the last chapter, these insights illustrate the interrelationship of faith development and human dignity, personal integrity and social ethics.

Another strength of the document is the few but compelling statements it makes regarding the relationship between faith and culture. These pastoral insights give further testimony to the fact that effective catechesis must honor the intentionality of each person's humanity. It must speak to the person's heart as well as intellect. It must also be appropriated to the urgent concerns and noble ambitions that distinguishes persons as a people. In this way, catechesis achieves its primary goals of enabling each person to rise to his or her full stature as an image and likeness of God and to participate meaningfully in the ongoing activity of God in the world.

The fourth strength, however, is concomitantly its major weakness. This matter has to do with the listing of doctrinal precepts and issues in chapter one.

The strength of this segment of the document is that it elucidates concretely the mind of the bishops regarding the doctrinal precepts and issues they believe to need "particular attention." But because these precepts and issues are extracted out of their broader context, the listing actually countermands the bishops' directives for a full and balanced presentation of doctrine. The substantive impact of this listing is further detracted from because there is no uniformity in the manner the statements are written. Some of the statements cite specific issues to be addressed, as in article 15:

> Present Jesus as true God, . . . highlighting the uniqueness of his divine mission so that he appears as more than a great prophet and moral teacher.

On the other hand there are a significant number of statements that simply refer the reader back to previous documents, as does article 42:

> Explain the liturgical year, with special attention to the seasons of Advent-Christmas, Lent-Easter (see NCD, 144c).

There are also a number of statements that offer no suggestions or references for enhancing the representation of a specific doctrine, for example:

> Promote lifelong conversion and an understanding of the need for reconciliation that leads to a renewed appreciation of the sacrament of penance (47).

Admittedly, the GDSCM does not purport to be a comprehensive presentation of Catholic doctrine, and the reader is encouraged to study the document in conjunction with the NCD's chapter on doctrine and with the CCC. However, the bishops' desire for a full, balanced and integrally related presentation of doctrine might have been better served if the GDSCM had incorporated the bishops' doctrinal concerns into a narrative embellishment of the "Principal Elements of the Christian Message for Catechesis" presented in the NCD. The primary merit of such a narrative is that it would have afforded the bishops an opportunity to redress the deficiencies of current catechetical texts while affirming their strengths. As it is, the GDSCM most assuredly leaves the door open for authors, editors, publishers and practitioners to overcompensate for their previous mistakes or to miscalculate their doctrinal presentations in other ways that could have been avoided.

CONCLUSION

The simple fact is that we no longer live in an age when "quick fixes" or simple solutions can address adequately the spiritual hungers or influence the spiritual quests of the American Catholic community. The vast quantity and diversity of catechetical materials give evidence of the vast and divergent spiritual sensibilities of contemporary Catholics. These are the core issues that the American episcopacy must address, and it cannot be done by listing doctrinal precepts and issues, however valid or urgent they may be. A "list" of statements cannot inspire the heart or stimulate the imagination. To do that, the bishops will have to rely on the experience and expertise of catechetical professionals and practitioners. And if the GDSCM can in fact lead to an ongoing dialogue in the American episcopacy and their colleagues in the field, it will have served the catechetical ministry of the church well.

OUTLINE

Preface

Introduction
  Catechetical Materials
  Dimensions of Catechesis
  Principles and Criteria of Doctrinally Sound Catechetical Materials

I. Guidelines for Doctrinally Sound Catechetical Materials
  General Doctrinal Content
  Father, Son, and Holy Spirit
  Church
  Mary and the Saints
  Liturgy and Sacraments
  Life of Grace and Moral Issues
  Death, Judgment, and Eternity

II. Guidelines for Presenting Sound Doctrine

PREFACE

As shepherds of the People of God, and by reason of their unique teaching office, bishops have the responsibility of preserving the deposit of faith and ensuring that it is passed on so that the faith of individuals and the community becomes "living, conscious and active, through the light of instruction" (CD, 14). According to the *Decree on the Bishops' Pastoral Office in the Church* of Vatican II, this responsibility implies the use of publications and "various other media of communication" that are helpful in proclaiming the Gospel of Christ (CD, 13).

From time to time, the National Conference of Catholic Bishops issues pastoral letters and statements on specific issues of national concern, but it is individual bishops who must provide guidance and oversee catechetical programs and materials in their dioceses. Diocesan bishops, acting alone, are not in a position, however, to influence publishers outside their jurisdiction. And for their part, publishers have on occasion asked for national norms and standard criteria that can help them in presenting the Church's doctrine on faith and morals while taking into account "the natural disposition, ability, age, and circumstances of life" of their audiences (CD, 14). Accordingly, the NCCB/USCC adopted as one of its objectives for the years 1988–1990:

> to support the catechetical ministry of the Church in the United States by developing policy guidelines for the creation of doctrinally sound textbooks and by providing for their implementation.

The Division of Catechesis/Religious Education of the USCC's Department of Education was given the assignment to implement this objective. The plan of action called for the formation of a task force, chaired by Bishop John Leibrecht of Springfield-Cape Girardeau. Included among its eighteen members were Bishop Donald Wuerl of Pittsburgh and Auxiliary Bishop Robert Banks of Boston. The task force members brought varied professional and personal experiences to the work and were generally representative of the geographic, cultural, and social profile of the Church in the United States.

The task force met between June 1988 and May 1990. Evolving through several drafts, the guidelines benefitted from consultations with publishers of catechetical materials, members of the NCCB Committee on Doctrine, and members of the NCCB Committee on the Liturgy. The task force submitted its work to the USCC Committee on Education which, after amending it, presented it for adoption to the full body of bishops. The bishops, after making several recommendations for text improvements, approved the document at their meeting on November 14, 1990.

INTRODUCTION

Since the Second Vatican Council, the Church has experienced a remarkable renewal in catechesis. This renewal has been encouraged and guided by the *General Catechetical Directory* (1971); the third and the fourth general assemblies of the Synod of Bishops (1974, 1977); Paul VI's apostolic exhortation *Evangelization in the Modern World* (1975); John Paul II's *Catechesis in Our Time*; and, in the United States, by *Sharing the Light of Faith: National Catechetical Directory for Catholics of the United States* (1979). In 1985, the Extraordinary Synod of Bishops proposed a *Catechism for the Universal Church* that will offer a presentation of doctrine, inspired by Scripture and the liturgy, and "suited to the present life of Christians" (II, B.4). In recent years, the on-going effort toward renewal of catechesis in the United States has been nowhere more evident than in the area of religion textbooks and catechetical materials. Each year many new materials for children, youth, and adults appear on the market. Publishing companies, with admirable dedication and zeal, make significant investments in researching, testing, editing, and marketing catechetical tools. They employ writers and editors with the finest credentials, and they seek the guidance of theologians, biblical scholars, specialists in pastoral liturgy, professional educators, and catechetical experts. Most of these materials advance and enrich the Church's catechetical mission, but their diversity and quantity present a new challenge. The faithful expect the bishops—and we recognize it as our responsibility—to assure them that these materials express the teaching of the Church as faithfully as possible.

The traditional way for bishops to exercise supervision in this ecclesial process is through the granting of an *imprimatur* to catechetical works. The 1983 *Code of Canon Law* directs that "catechisms and other writings dealing with catechetical formation or their translations need the approval of the local ordinary for their publication" (c. 827.1). The *Code* further states, that "it is the responsibility of the diocesan bishop to issue norms concerning catechetics and to make provision that suitable instruments for catechesis are available . . . " (c. 775.1). It is with this latter directive in mind that the National Conference of Catholic Bishops, with due regard for the responsibility and prerogatives of the local ordinary, responding to the desire of publishers for guidance and concerns of the faithful, outlines a number of principles and offers a series of guidelines.

These guidelines are intended to provide direction to the publishers, particularly in the area of Catholic doctrine regarding both faith and morals. Based on the major catechetical documents of the Church and the teachings of Vatican II, they highlight essential components of the documents that relate to doctrinal soundness in catechetical materials. *Doctrinal soundness* implies, first of all, a complete and correct presentation of church teaching, with proper attention to its organic unity. In the context of catechesis, doctrinal soundness also requires that church teaching be presented clearly and in a manner that can be readily understood. Language and images must be adapted to the capacity of the learners in accord with their age levels and cultural backgrounds.

Catechesis is a pastoral ministry "which leads both communities and individual members of the faithful to maturity of faith" (GCD, 21). John Paul II reminds us that early in the Church's history

> ... the name of *catechesis* was given to the whole of the efforts within the Church to make disciples, to help people believe that Jesus is the Son of God, so that believing they might have life in his name, and to educate and instruct them in this life and thus build up the Body of Christ (CT, 1).

Thus, it is part of the mission of the Church and a significant concern of the bishops that catechesis be provided for all members of the Catholic community.

The faith that the Church seeks to strengthen is the free acceptance of the mystery of God and the divine plan of salvation offered in revelation to all peoples. The act of faith has two aspects that by their nature are inseparable. Faith includes both the firm adherence given by a person "under the influence of grace to God revealing himself (the faith *by which* one believes) [and] the content of revelation and of the Christian message (the faith *which* one believes)" (GCD, 36) This latter aspect has a communal dimension insofar as it is handed on by the Church and shared by the Catholic faithful. These guidelines pertain chiefly to the Christian message as it is dealt with in catechetical materials.

CATECHETICAL MATERIALS

Catechetical materials are intended as effective instruments for teaching the fullness of the Christian message found in the Word of God and in the teachings of the Church. They include many kinds of resources: printed and audiovisual materials, and textbooks and programs that utilize such learning strategies as role playing, crafts, and other supportive educational activities. They are prepared for groups and persons of diverse interests, needs, ages, and abilities. Although the *National Catechetical Directory* recognizes that catechists are more important than their tools, it acknowledges that "good tools in the hands of skilled catechists can do much to foster growth in faith" (NCD, 249).

DIMENSIONS OF CATECHESIS

Catechesis nurtures the faith of individuals and communities by integrating four fundamental tasks: (1) proclaiming Christ's message; (2) participating in efforts to develop community; (3) leading people to worship and prayer; and (4) motivating them to Christian living and service (cf. NCD, 213). Catechetical materials aid this process. First, catechesis, a form of ministry of the word, supposes that the hearer has embraced the Christian message as a salvific reality. It is the purpose of catechesis and, by extension, of catechetical materials to motivate the faithful to respond to the message in an informed way, both personally and in community. Catechesis takes place within the Church, and catechetical materials reflect the beliefs, values, and practices of the Christian community.

Second, catechetical materials develop community by keeping traditions alive and recommending activities that build up the Church, making it a "community of believers [striving to be] of one heart and mind" (Acts 4:32).

Third, the Church, from its earliest days, has recognized that liturgy and catechesis are supportive of one another. Catechetical materials can be expected, therefore, to explain how liturgical celebrations deepen the community's knowledge of the faith and to "promote an active, conscious, genuine participation in the liturgy of the Church . . ." (GCD, 25). Sound catechetical materials provide examples of ways that the Christian community prays together, with particular emphasis on forms of devotional prayer inspired by and directed toward the liturgy itself (SC, 13).

Fourth, in calling upon Christians to serve others, catechetical materials should explain clearly the Church's moral teaching. They should emphasize the twofold responsibility of individuals and communities to strive for holiness and to witness to Christian values. This includes respect for life, service to others, and working to bring about peace and justice in society (cf. NCD, 38).

In short, catechetical materials should present the story of salvation and the Church's beliefs according to the principles of doctrinally sound catechesis that we describe below.

PRINCIPLES AND CRITERIA OF DOCTRINALLY SOUND CATECHETICAL MATERIALS

The first principle of doctrinal soundness is that the Christian message be both *authentic* and *complete*. For expressions of faith and moral teachings to be authentic, they must be in harmony with the doctrine and traditions of the Catholic Church, which are safeguarded by the bishops who teach with a unique authority. For completeness, the message of salvation, which is made up of several parts that are closely interrelated, must, in due course, be presented in its entirety, with an eye to leading individuals and communities to maturity of faith. Completeness also implies that individual parts be presented in a balanced way, according to the capacity of the learners and in the context of a particular doctrine.

The second principle in determining the doctrinal soundness of catechetical materials is the recognition that the mystery of faith is *incarnate* and *dynamic*. The mystery of the divine plan for human salvation, revealed in the person of Jesus Christ and made known in the Sacred Scriptures, continues as a dynamic force in the world through the power of the Holy Spirit until finally all things are made subject to Christ and the kingdom is handed over to the Father "so that God may be all in all" (1 Corinthians 15:28). God's creative power is mediated in the concrete experiences of life, in personal development, in human relationships, in culture, in social life, in science and technology, and in "signs of the times." The *National Catechetical Directory* refers to the Scriptures, the teaching life and witness of the Church, the Church's liturgical life, and life experiences of various kinds as "signs of God's saving activity" in the world (NCD, 42). These biblical, ecclesial, liturgical, and natural signs should inform the content and spirit of all catechetical materials.

From these two basic principles flow several criteria that describe doctrinally sound catechetical materials.

First, a holistic approach to catechesis reflects the progressive, step-by-step initiation of the believer into the church community, and the lifelong conversion that is required of individuals and communities if they are to mature in faith. Catechetical materials should relate to the age, ability, and experience of those being catechized. The principal form of catechesis is catechesis of adults, for adults are those "who have the greatest responsibilities and the capacity to live the Christian message in its fully developed form" (CT, 43). Catechesis for children and other age groups is always necessary and should in some way lay the foundation for adult catechesis (cf. GCD, 20; NCD, 32).

Second, proper expression of our faith highlights the centrality of fundamental doctrines of the Christian tradition. Both the *General Catechetical Directory* and the *National Catechetical Directory* offer valuable guidance in this regard, as will a *Catechism for the Universal Church*. The trinitarian structure of the Apostles' Creed and the Nicene Creed is an example that offers helpful guidance in ordering the hierarchy of truths. In presenting the Christian message, catechetical materials take into account the developmental nature of the learner and the particular circumstances of the local church community, but they cannot be selective as to content and emphasis in ways that compromise the authentic and complete teaching of the Church (cf. GCD, 46; NCD, 47).

Third, authentic catechesis recognizes that Christian faith needs to be incarnated in all cultures; accordingly, it is expressed in diverse ways that witness to the catholicity of the Church without endangering its unity. John Paul II has stated, "The Gospel of Christ is at home in every people. It enriches, uplifts and purifies every culture" (*Meeting with Native Americans*, September 14, 1987). Catechetical materials not only alert the faithful to the full meaning of catholicity and the cultural dimensions of the Christian faith experience, but they also facilitate the assimilation of the gospel message, using language, customs, and symbols familiar to those being taught.

Fourth, the fruit of effective catechesis is unity "among all who hold and teach the Catholic faith that comes to us from the apostles' *(Eucharistic Prayer I)*. The common faith is shared and celebrated most perfectly in the eucharist. Biblical, creedal, and prayer formulas are also essential to the unity of the faith community. There is "one Lord, one faith, one baptism; one God and Father of all, who is over all and through all and in all" (Ephesians 4:5). For believers to share their faith, they must have common experiences and a shared language in which to express and celebrate it. Some common expression of faith is essential to the unity of the believing community. Without a shared language, the faithful cannot profess and celebrate their faith in communion with one another. Catechetical materials, taken as a whole, need to promote a healthy and vital Catholic identity in such a way that the believer hears the message clearly, lives it with conviction, and shares it courageously with others.

In the NCCB document *Basic Teachings for Catholic Religious Education*, the bishops of the United States expressed a desire for an informed laity, people of faith who know their religion and can give an account of it (see BT, introduction). But now, as then, this means a Church transformed by the gospel message for Christians who bring the Gospel into their daily lives; for faithful men and women whose zeal for peace and justice, joy and simplicity, witness to Christ's continuing presence in the world while we await his return in glory, when every tear will be wiped away and death will be no more. It is our hope that these *Guidelines for Doctrinally Sound Catechetical Materials* will contribute to these goals.

I. GUIDELINES FOR DOCTRINALLY SOUND CATECHETICAL MATERIALS

The following guidelines are based on major catechetical documents of the Church; the constitutions, decrees, and declarations of Vatican II; recent papal encyclicals and apostolic exhortations; and the pastoral letters of the U.S. bishops. The guidelines, even taken as a whole, are not a synthesis of the gospel message nor an exhaustive list of Catholic beliefs. They are not intended to supplant—and in fact should be studied in conjunction with—the outline of the "Principal Elements of the Christian Message for Catechesis" (NCD, chapter V) and any exposition of doctrine found in a future *Catechism for the Universal Church.*

The guidelines differ from the *National Catechetical Directory* and our earlier document *Basic Teachings for Catholic Religious Education* in two ways: First, they incorporate teachings and principles stated in recent papal encyclicals and in pastoral letters issued by the National Conference of Catholic Bishops; second, they single out certain doctrines that seem to need particular emphasis in the life and culture of the United States at this time. The guidelines take into account a hierarchy of truths of faith insofar as they give priority to the foundational mysteries in the Creed, but they do not prescribe a particular order in which the truths are to be presented (cf. GCD, 46). The guidelines are intended to present church teachings in a positive and meaningful way so that authors, editors, and publishers of catechetical materials can better assist the faithful to integrate the truth of Catholic doctrine and moral teachings into their lives.

GENERAL DOCTRINAL CONTENT

DOCTRINALLY SOUND CATECHETICAL MATERIALS . . .

(1) help the baptized, as members of the Church founded by Christ, appreciate Catholic tradition, grounded in the Scriptures and celebrated in the Divine Liturgy, in such a personal way that it becomes part of their very identity.

(2) present the teaching of the Church in a full and balanced way that includes everything necessary for an accurate understanding of a particular doctrine and express it in a manner appropriate to the audience and purpose of a given catechetical text.

(3) situate the teachings of the Church in the context of God's saving plan and relate them to one another so that they can be seen as parts of an organic whole and not simply as isolated and fragmented truths (see GCD, 39).

(4) describe the many ways that God has spoken and continues to speak in the lives of human beings and how the fullness of revelation is made known in Christ (see Hebrews 1:1–2; CT, 20, 52).

(5) explain the inspired Scriptures according to the mind of the Church, while not neglecting the contributions of modern biblical scholarship in the use of various methods of interpretation, including historical-critical and literary methods (see *1964 Instruction*, Pontifical Biblical Commission).

(6) are sensitive to distinctions between faith and theology, church doctrine and theological opinion, acknowledging that the same revealed truth can be explained in different ways. However, every explanation must be compatible with Catholic tradition (see NCD, 16).

(7) reflect the wisdom and continuing relevance of the church Fathers and incorporate a sense of history that recognizes doctrinal development and provides background for understanding change in church policy and practice.

(8) explain the documents of the Second Vatican Council as an authoritative and valid expression of the deposit of faith as contained in Holy Scripture and the living tradition of the Church (see 1985 Extraordinary Synod of Bishops, *The Final Report*, n. 2).

(9) present the uniqueness and preeminence of the Christian message without rejecting anything that is true and holy in non-Christian religions, show a high regard for all religions that witness to the mystery of divine presence, the dignity of human beings, and high moral standards (see NA, 2).

FATHER, SON, AND HOLY SPIRIT

DOCTRINALLY SOUND CATECHETICAL MATERIALS . . .

(10) are trinitarian and christocentric in scope and spirit, clearly presenting the mystery of creation, redemption, and sanctification in God's plan of salvation (see NCD, 47).

(11) help Christians contemplate with eyes of faith the communal life of the Holy Trinity and know that, through grace, we share in God's divine nature (see GCD, 47).

(12) arouse a sense of wonder and praise for God's world and providence by presenting creation, not as an abstract principle or as an event standing by itself, but as the origin of all things and the beginning of the mystery of salvation in Jesus Christ (see GCD, 51; NCD, 85).

(13) focus on the heart of the Christian message: salvation from sin and death through the person and work of Jesus, with special emphasis on the paschal mystery — his passion, death, and resurrection.

(14) emphasize the work and person of Jesus Christ as the key and chief point of Christian reference in reading the Scriptures (see JJPC, II:5, 6).

(15) present Jesus as true God, who came into the world for us and for our salvation, and as true man who thinks with a human mind, acts with a human will, loves with a human heart (see NCD, 89), highlighting the uniqueness of his divine mission so that he appears as more than a great prophet and moral teacher.

(16) describe how the Holy Spirit continues Christ's work in the world, in the Church, and in the lives of believers (see NCD, 92).

(17) maintain the traditional language, grounded in the Scriptures, that speaks of the Holy Trinity as Father, Son, and Spirit and apply, where appropriate, the principles of inclusive language approved by the NCCB (see *Criteria for the Evaluation of Inclusive Language Translations of Scriptural Text Proposed for Liturgical Use* [Washington, D.C.: USCC Office for Publishing and Promotion Services, 1990]).

CHURCH

DOCTRINALLY SOUND CATECHETICAL MATERIALS . . .

(18) recognize that the Church, a community of believers, is a mystery, a sign of the kingdom, a community of divine origin, that cannot be totally understood or fully defined in human terms (see NCD, 63).

(19) teach that the Church's unique relationship with Christ makes it both sign and instrument of God's union with humanity, the means for the forgiveness of sin as well as a means of unity for human beings among themselves (see NCD, 63).

(20) emphasize the missionary nature of the Church and the call of individual Christians to proclaim the Gospel wherever there are people to be evangelized, at home and abroad (see NCD, 71; 74e).

(21) nourish and teach the faith and, because there is often a need for initial evangelization, aim at opening the heart and arousing the beginning of faith so that individuals will respond to the Word of God and Jesus' call to discipleship (see CT, 19).

(22) emphasize that Jesus Christ gave the apostles a special mission to teach and that today this teaching authority is exercised by the pope and bishops, who are successors of St. Peter and the apostles.

(23) highlight the history and distinctive tradition of the Church of Rome and the special charism of the pope as successor of St. Peter in guiding and teaching the universal Church and assuring the authentic teaching of the Gospel.

(24) explain what it means when the Church professes to be "one, holy, catholic and apostolic" (see NCD, 72, 74i, ii).

(25) show how the Church of Christ is manifest at the local level in the diocesan church and the parish, gathered in the Holy Spirit through the Gospel and the eucharist (see CD, 11; LG, 26).

(26) present the Church as a community with a legitimate diversity in expressing its shared faith according to different ages, cultures, gifts, and abilities.

(27) foster understanding and unity by accurately presenting the traditions and practices of the Catholic Churches of the East (see NCD, 73, 74g).

(28) are sensitive in dealing with other Christian Churches and ecclesial communities, taking into account how they differ from the Catholic tradition while at the same time showing how much is held in common (see NCD, 76).

(29) foster ecumenism as a means toward unity and communion among all Christians and recognize that division in the Church and among Christians is contrary to the will of Christ (see UR, 1).

(30) integrate the history of the Jews in the work of salvation so that, on the one hand, Judaism does not appear marginal and unimportant and, on the other hand, the Church and Judaism do not appear as parallel ways of salvation (see JJPC, I:7).

(31) explain the pastoral role and authority of the magisterium — the bishops united with the pope — in defining and teaching religious truth.

(32) emphasize that individuals reach their full potential and work out their salvation only in community — the human community and the community that is the Church (see EJFA, 63, 65, and passim).

(33) support the family as the basic unit of society and underline its role as "domestic church" in living the Gospel (see FC, 12).

MARY AND THE SAINTS

DOCTRINALLY SOUND CATECHETICAL MATERIALS . . .

(34) explain the sacramental meaning of "communion of saints," linking it to the eucharist which, bringing the faithful together to share the "holy gifts," is the primary source and sign of church unity.

(35) explain the biblical basis for the liturgical cult of Mary as Mother of God and disciple *par excellence* and describe her singular role in the life of Christ and the story of salvation (see LG, 66, 67).

(36) foster Marian devotions and explain the Church's particular beliefs about Mary (e.g., the Immaculate Conception, Virgin Birth, and Assumption) (see GCD, 68; NCD, 106).

(37) explain the Church's teaching on angels and its veneration of saints, who intercede for us and are role models in following Christ (see GCD, 68).

LITURGY AND SACRAMENTS

(38) present the sacraments as constitutive of Christian life and worship, as unique ways of meeting Christ, and not simply as channels of grace.

(39) emphasize God's saving and transforming presence in the sacraments. In the eucharist, Christ is present not only in the person of the priest but in the assembly and in the Word and, uniquely, in the eucharistic species of bread and wine that become the Body and Blood of Christ (see SC, 7).

(40) link the eucharist to Christ's sacrifice on the cross, explaining it as a sacrament of his presence in the Church and as a meal of communal solidarity that is a sign of the heavenly banquet to which the faithful are called (see SC, 7, 47; GS, 38).

(41) call attention to the special significance of Sunday as the day of the Lord's resurrection, emphasizing active participation in Sunday Mass as an expression of community prayer and spiritual renewal.

(42) explain the liturgical year, with special attention to the seasons of Advent–Christmas, Lent–Easter (see NCD, 144c).

(43) promote active participation in the liturgy of the Church not only by explaining the rites and symbols but also by fostering a spirit of praise, thanksgiving, and repentance, and by nurturing a sense of community and reverence (see NCD, 36).

(44) explain the Catholic heritage of popular devotions and sacramentals so that they serve as a means "to help people advance towards knowledge of the mystery of Christ and his message . . . " (CT, 54).

(45) embody the norms and guidelines for liturgy and sacramental practice found in the *praenotanda* of the revised rites, with special attention to those that preface the sacraments of initiation.

(46) assist pastors, parents, and catechists to inaugurate children into the sacraments of penance and eucharist by providing for their proper initial preparation according to Catholic pastoral practice as presented by the magisterium.

(47) promote lifelong conversion and an understanding of the need for reconciliation that leads to a renewed appreciation of the sacrament of penance.

(48) establish the foundations for vocational choices — to the married life, the single life, the priesthood, the diaconate, and to the vowed life of poverty, chastity, and obedience — in the framework of one's baptismal commitment and the call to serve.

(49) respect the essential difference between the ministerial priesthood and the common priesthood, between the ministries conferred by the sacrament of orders and the call to service derived from the sacraments of baptism and confirmation (see CL, 22, 23).

(50) foster vocations to the priesthood and religious life in appropriate ways at every age level.

(51) teach that from the beginning, God called human beings to holiness, but from the very dawn of history, humans abused their freedom and set themselves against God so that "sin entered the world" (Romans 5:12), and that this "original sin" is transmitted to every human being (see GS, 13).

(52) introduce prayer as a way of deepening one's relationship with God and explain the ends of prayer so that a spirit of adoration, thanksgiving, petition, and contrition permeates the daily lives of Christians (see NCD, 140).

(53) promote the continual formation of right Catholic conscience based on Christ's role in one's life; his ideals, precepts, and examples found in Scripture; and the magisterial teaching of the Church (see NCD, 190).

(54) cultivate the moral life of Christians by inculcating virtue and nurture a sense of responsibility that goes beyond external observance of laws and precepts.

(55) discuss the reality and effects of personal sins, whereby an individual, acting knowingly and deliberately, violates the moral law, harms one's self, one's neighbor, and offends God (see GCD, 62).

(56) make it clear that the dignity of the human person and sanctity of life are grounded in one's relation to the Triune God, and that individuals are valued not because of their status in society, their productivity, or as consumers but in themselves as beings made in God's image (see EJFA, 28, 78).

(57) go beyond economic and political concerns in describing ecological and environmental issues and define human accountability for the created universe in moral and spiritual terms (see SRS, 38).

(58) present a consistent ethic of life that, fostering respect for individual dignity and personal rights, highlights the rights of the unborn, the aged, and those with disabilities and explains the evils of abortion and euthanasia.

(59) explain the specifics of Christian morality, as taught by the magisterium of the Church, in the frame-work of the universal call to holiness and discipleship; the Ten Commandments; the Sermon on the Mount, especially the Beatitudes; and in Christ's discourse at the Last Supper (see NCD, 105).

(60) include the responsibilities of Catholic living, traditionally expressed in the precepts of the Church.

(61) present Catholic teaching on justice, peace, mercy, and social issues as integral to the gospel message and the Church's prophetic mission (see NCD, 170).

(62) explain that the Church's teaching on the "option for the poor" means that while Christians are called to respond to the needs of everyone, they must give their greatest attention to individuals and communities with greatest needs (see EJFA, 86–87).

(63) state the Church's position on moral and social issues of urgent concern in contemporary society, for example, the developing role of women in the Church and in society, racism and other forms of discrimination.

(64) present human sexuality in positive terms of life, love, and self-discipline, explain the responsibilities of a chaste Christian life, and teach that love between husband and wife must be exclusive and open to new life (see FC, 29).

(65) link personal morality to social issues and professional ethics and challenge the faithful to make responsible moral decisions guided by the Church's teaching (see NCD 38, 170).

(66) teach that all legitimate authority comes from God and that governments exist to serve the people, to protect human rights and secure basic justice for all members of society (see EJFA, 122).

(67) teach that though sin abounds in the world, grace is even more abundant because of the salvific work of Christ (see NCD, 98).

DEATH, JUDGMENT, AND ETERNITY

DOCTRINALLY SOUND CATECHETICAL MATERIALS . . .

(68) explain the coming of Christ "in glory" in the context of the Church's overall teaching on eschatology and final judgment (see NCD, 110).

(69) teach, on the subject of the last things, that everyone has an awesome responsibility for his or her eternal destiny and present, in the light of Christian hope, death, judgment, purgatory, heaven, or hell (see NCD, 109; GCD, 69).

II. GUIDELINES FOR PRESENTING SOUND DOCTRINE

A second set of guidelines—no less important than the first if catechesis is to be effective—are based on pastoral principles and practical concerns. They are reminders that catechetical materials must take into account the community for whom they are intended, the conditions in which they live, and the ways in which they learn (cf. GCD, foreword). Publishers are encouraged to provide catechetical materials that take into consideration the needs of the Hispanic community and other ethnic and culturally diverse groups that comprise the Church in the United States. No single text or program can address the many cultures and social groups that make up society in the United States, but all catechetical materials must take this diversity into account. Effective catechesis, as we have noted above, requires that the Church's teaching be presented correctly and in its entirety, and it is equally important to present it in ways that are attractive, appealing, and understandable by the individuals and communities to whom it is directed.

To present sound doctrine effectively, catechetical materials . . .

(70) take into account the experience and background of those being catechized and suggest ways that the Christian message illumines their life (see NCD, 176e).

(71) must be based on accepted learning theory, established pedagogical principles, and practical learning strategies (see NCD, 175).

(72) use language and images appropriate to the age level and developmental stages and special needs of those being catechized (see NCD, 177–188).

(73) integrate biblical themes and scriptural references in the presentation of doctrine and moral teaching and encourage a hands-on familiarity with the Bible (see NCD, 60a).

(74) challenge Catholics to critique and transform contemporary values and behaviors in light of the Gospel and the Church's teaching.

(75) maintain a judicious balance between personal expression and memorization, emphasizing that it is important both for the community and themselves that individuals commit to memory selected biblical passages, essential prayers, liturgical responses, key doctrinal ideas, and lists of moral responsibilities (see CT, 55; NCD, 176e).

(76) provide for a variety of shared prayer forms and experiences that lead to an active participation in the liturgical life of the Church and private prayer (see NCD, 145, 264).

(77) continually hold before their intended audience the ideal of living a life based on the teachings of the Gospel.

(78) include suggestions for service to the community that is appropriate to the age and abilities of the persons who are being catechized.

(79) stress the importance of the local church community for Christian living, so that every Catholic contributes to building up the spirit of the parish family and sees its ministries as part of the Church's universal mission.

(80) are sensitive to the appropriate use of inclusive language in the text and avoid racial, ethnic, and gender stereotypes in pictures (see NCD, 264).

(81) reflect the catholicity of the Church in art and graphics by presenting the diverse customs and religious practices of racial, ethnic, cultural, and family groups (see NCD, 194, 264).

(82) assist catechists by including easy-to-understand instructions regarding scope, sequence, and use of texts.

(83) suggest a variety of strategies, activities, and auxiliary resources that can enrich instruction, deepen understanding, and facilitate the integration of doctrine and life.

(84) include material that can be used in the home to aid parents in communicating church teaching and nurturing the faith life of the family.

(85) instruct teachers and catechists on how to respond to the needs of persons with disabilities and individuals with special needs (see NCD, 195, 196, 264).

(86) help teachers and catechists distinguish between church doctrine and the opinions and interpretations of theologians (see NCD, 264).

(87) help develop the catechists' own faith life, experience of prayer, and mature commitment to the Church and motivate them toward ongoing enrichment.

GUIDE

FOR

CATECHISTS

DOCUMENT OF VOCATIONAL, FORMATIVE AND
PROMOTIONAL ORIENTATION OF CATECHISTS IN THE
TERRITORIES DEPENDENT ON THE CONGREGATION
FOR THE EVANGELIZATION OF PEOPLES

1993

OVERVIEW OF *GUIDE FOR CATECHISTS*

by Marina Herrera

In the *Guide for Catechists* (GC), the Congregation for the Evangelization of Peoples (CEP) addresses the issue of the nature, role, function and formation of catechists in mission lands. The *Guide for Catechists* does not break new ground; it depends for its wisdom on previously issued church documents, beginning with those of Vatican II, and on the statements and exhortations of Pope Paul VI and Pope John Paul II. Yet the GC serves a very useful purpose in that it draws these sources together and adds its own practical observations based on "information and suggestions that came in from a wide-ranging consultation with bishops and catechetical centers in mission territories" (GC, 1). In his preface, Jozef Cardinal Tomko, the cardinal prefect of the CEP, notes that the *Catechism of the Catholic Church* was published before the GC was issued. The catechism serves as an authoritative reference source for the GC and reinforces its themes.

The *Guide for Catechists* is addressed to diocesan ordinaries and their associates, as well as to catechists. But it has a much wider audience than mission personnel; all those engaged in ministry can learn from its practical wisdom.

The mission lands referred to in the GC are lands that, although they might now have their own church hierarchy, still fall under the jurisdiction of the CEP. This may be because their populations are still largely unevangelized or because they are still dependent on the support of older churches for personnel and resources. As those older churches have found it increasingly difficult to meet their own needs, however, the mission churches have had to draw much more upon their own resources and have found them to be much richer than they had imagined.

High on the list of resources are the mission catechists themselves, who have always been essential in sustaining first evangelization. Emphasizing this fact, the CEP cites the Second Vatican Council's *Decree on the Church's Missionary Activity*, which states that "from the very beginning of Christianity and wherever there has been missionary activity, catechists have made, and continue to make, an outstanding contribution to the spread of the faith and of the church" (AG, 17).

The GC is divided into three parts, plus a brief introduction and a brief conclusion in the form of "a hope for the mission of the third millennium." The most important section is part 1, "An Apostle Ever Relevant," which inquires into the identity and spirituality of the catechist as well as the appropriate attitude the catechist should have toward contemporary issues such as ecumenism — a critical area in most foreign lands where religions older than Christianity command the fidelity of millions of believers.

PART I: AN APOSTLE EVER RELEVANT

1. THE CATECHIST IN A MISSIONARY CHURCH

The *Guide for Catechists* states a fundamental principle of faith when it says that "every baptized Catholic is personally called by the Holy Spirit to make his or her contribution to the coming of God's kingdom" (GC, 2). However, beyond this general vocation of every baptized Christian, the GC sees in the catechist a specific call from the Holy Spirit, "a special charism recognized by the Church" and confirmed by the bishop's mandate. Mission catechists have a special identity corresponding to the particular needs of the mission territories: "Apart from the explicit proclamation of the Christian message and the accompaniment of catechumens and newly baptized Christians on their role to full maturity in the faith and in sacramental life, the catechist's role comprises presence and witness, and involvement in human development, inculturation and dialogue." The document notes that while catechetical activity derives its legitimacy "from the official permission granted by the pastors," "the catechist is not a simple substitute for the priest, but is by right a witness of Christ in the community" (GC, 3).

Mission catechists can be either men or women, working full-time or part-time. Their activities are in accordance with local customs and sensibilities and cover a wide range of apostolic endeavors that in older churches are performed as specialized ministries, such as DRES, religion teachers, eucharistic ministers and others.

One catechetical role, though it is referred to only in the conclusion in passing, is crucial to successful evangelization: the role of interpreter for the foreign missionary, whose knowledge of the local language and culture may not be equal to the task of proclaiming and explaining the gospel. The missionary may not have the aptitude or time to develop more than a rudimentary level of communication. He or she is very dependent on the skills of the catechist as interpreter.

The message of the missionary priest sometimes reaches his hearers through the interpreter quite differently from what he intended. This may be particularly true in a mission station where the full-time catechist is a community leader and in practice is vicar for the pastor for weeks or months at a time. The catechist might edit the words of the missionary if he disagrees with the message. Aware of this and other pitfalls, the CEP insists that "absolute precedence must be given to quality" in the selection of catechist candidates, just as elsewhere in its guidelines for foreign missionary priests and religious it urges immersion in the language and culture of the indigenous people in order to facilitate direct contact between pastor and people. In Part II, the GC deals more fully with the question of the "Choice and Formation of Catechists," insisting on high quality.

2. THE CATECHIST'S SPIRITUALITY

As is true for all evangelizers, the success of the catechist's mission depends on the depth of his or her spirituality. "They must live in the Spirit who will help them to renew themselves continually in their specific identity" (GC, 6). Their spirituality is linked to their status as lay Christians who share by baptism in Christ's prophetic, priestly and kingly offices. As laity they have a special role in witnessing to Christ in the secular world. Citing Pope John Paul II, the GC reminds us that an integral part of married catechists' spirituality is formed by matrimonial life. Catechists' spirituality is conditioned specifically by their apostolic vocation, which is marked by openness to God's word, to the church and to the world, authenticity of life, missionary zeal and devotion to Mary as an exemplar of the Christian disciple.

For the mission catechist, openness to the world brings a special challenge because the world of Asia and Africa is mostly non-Christian. Christian witness there will certainly involve the cross. The catechist is reminded that "the preaching of the word is always connected with prayer, the celebration of the eucharist and the building of community" (GC, 10). This was true of the earliest Christian community, united as it was around Mary, the mother of Jesus.

3. THE CATECHIST'S ATTITUDE TO SOME CONTEMPORARY ISSUES

Because the community the catechist serves is made up of a wide variety of groups, each with their own needs, the GC advocates, in addition to catechists' general training, instruction in dealing with groups with specific needs (such as the sick and the elderly).

The very complex question of the inculturation of the gospel is raised briefly: "Like all forms of evangelization, catechesis, too, is called to bring the gospel into the heart of the different cultures" (GC, 12).

The dialogue between the gospel and culture began when Jesus proclaimed the kingdom of God. His proclamation challenged the Jewish religion/culture to see in the gospel the meaning of its own tradition. A dialogue was set in motion leading to either acceptance or rejection. With acceptance, a new way of thinking came into being — the Christian way.

In one of his most eloquent parables, Jesus warned that the new wine of his truth could not be put into old wineskins of preconceived beliefs and habits. The transition from the old way of thinking and being would not be a smooth or instantaneous process, even for the apostles. As Jesus continued his dialogues with the disciples and the Jewish people in his public ministry, they gradually became more and more enlightened. Finally, Jesus told them the Spirit would enlighten them when his mission was complete in his death and resurrection. In the atmosphere of prayer with Mary, the mother of Jesus, Pentecost brought them to an understanding of what Jesus had taught and preached. They went forth to preach in his name.

The more they preached, the more the dialogue between gospel and culture presented new challenges. The principal challenge came with the preaching of the gospel to the non-Jewish peoples, the Gentiles. Were the prescriptions of the Jewish law to be imposed on non-Jewish converts? What were the requirements of Christian discipleship? These difficult questions found a first answer in a meeting of the apostles and elders in Jerusalem, in the middle of the first century, some time after the death of Jesus. Leading to the solution they proposed was the very human experience Peter and his companions had in the conversion of the centurion Cornelius. Here, even Peter required a heavenly vision to accept the pagan soldier as a brother in the faith and not as an unclean outcast (see Acts 11:1–18).

The church has addressed the issue of faith and culture at great length in the era of the Second Vatican Council. The Council's documents, especially the *Decree on the Church's Missionary Activity* and the *Pastoral Constitution on the Church in the Modern World*, brought a fresh way of thinking. Modern means of transportation and communication make possible not only the extraordinary phenomenon of the missionary journeys of Pope Paul VI and Pope John Paul II in the tradition of Paul the Apostle but also the constant stream of religious and political leaders of all faiths who visit the pope in the Holy See. The two very important synods on evangelization and catechesis, and the encyclicals on evangelization and catechesis, expressed the contemporary understanding of the church on these topics. In Latin America, Africa, and Asia, Pope John Paul II has continued to probe the relationship of faith and culture ever more deeply during his frequent apostolic travels.

In the short space the GC allots to this need for inculturation, it notes that although the gospel can never be identified with any one culture, it has in its history been incarnated in specific cultures, beginning with the culture of the Chosen People. The history of the spread of the gospel constitutes a heritage to be shared with the new churches, who in turn enrich that heritage and enable the universal church to see new facets of its faith, ever old, ever new. The gospel is also a force for renewal that can purify cultures of elements that are incompatible with it. Popular piety, when it is based on a sound understanding of the faith, "is a privileged form of inculturation of the gospel."

The *Guide for Catechists* specifies human development and the option for the poor, the spirit of ecumenism and dialogue with other religions as areas of which the catechist should be aware. Connected with human development is "the preferential option for the poor," whose need is greatest. The poor include all marginalized groups in society.

An ecumenical spirit aimed at promoting a spirit of Christian unity is important in mission territories. Also important is dialogue with non-Christian religious bodies, which includes practical cooperation but does not diminish Christian convictions. In conclusion, catechists, living as they do at the grassroots among the people, are seen as "particularly suitable for counteracting the influence of the sects" that are hostile to the Catholic Church.

PARTS II AND III:
CHOICE AND FORMATION OF CATECHISTS
AND
THE RESPONSIBILITIES TOWARDS CATECHISTS

Part II, "Choice and Formation of Catechists," develops at greater length the qualities the CEP requires in candidates seeking to become catechists. Recognizing the wide variety of conditions and needs in mission lands, it offers practical but general advice on the doctrinal, spiritual and pastoral formation of catechists. Part III considers the "Responsibilities Towards Catechists" on the part of church leaders and the Christian communities in which they work. Catechists deserve respect and appreciation and, depending on the extent of their services, they also deserve remuneration "which must be considered a matter of justice and not of benevolence" (GC, 32). The *Guide for Catechists* recognizes that the problem of remuneration has to be solved by the local church but according to precise norms.

In a brief conclusion, the GC affirms the role of catechists in the mission of the church for the third millennium. The theme of the third millennium is dear to Pope John Paul II, who is cited here in the GC's appreciation of the work of catechists. As we enter Christianity's third millennium, the number of ordained ministers in many parts of the world is decreasing. As a result, catechists, both here and in mission lands, will play an ever greater role in the proclamation and nurturing of the faith. The *Guide for Catechists* highlights for those charged with their formation the importance of this ministry and the care that should be given to their preparation. The churches that pay attention to the meaning of this document and develop local and concrete responses to its recommendations will be beacons sending light to all who care to see.

OUTLINE

INTRODUCTION

1. AN INDISPENSABLE SERVICE

The Congregation for the Evangelization of Peoples (CEP) has always had a special concern for catechists, convinced as it is that these are, under the direction of their Pastors, a factor of prime importance in evangelization. In April 1970 it published some practical directives for catechists,[1] and now, conscious of its responsibility and of radical changes in the missionary world, the CEP would like to call attention to the present situation, the problems that arise, and prospects for the development of this *"praiseworthy army"* of lay apostles.[2] It is encouraged in this project by the many pressing interventions of His Holiness Pope John Paul II, who, during his apostolic voyages, makes use of every opportunity to stress the importance and relevance of the work of catechists as a *"fundamental evangelical service."*[3] Our task is a demanding but also a necessary and an attractive one,[4] seeing that, from the very beginning of Christianity and wherever there has been missionary activity, catechists have made, and continue to make, *"an outstanding and indispensable contribution to the spread of the faith and of the church."*[5]

And so, having examined, in its Plenary Assembly of April 27 – 30, 1992, the information and suggestions that came in from a wide-ranging consultation with bishops and catechetical centers in mission territories, the CEP has drawn up this *Guide for Catechists*, which treats in a doctrinal, existential and practical way the principal aspects of the catechists' vocation, identity, spirituality, selection and training, missionary and pastoral tasks, and remuneration, along with the responsibility of the People of God towards them, in today's conditions and those of the immediate future.

Under each heading we will try to give the ideals to be aimed at, along with the essential considerations, while taking account of the difficulty, in certain missionary situations, of defining who exactly can be called a catechist. The directives are deliberately given in general terms, so as to be applicable to all catechists in the young Churches. It is up to the respective Pastors to make them more specific, in keeping with the requirements and possibilities of the individual Churches.

The Guide is addressed first of all to the lay catechists themselves, but also to the bishops, priests, religious, formators and the faithful, by reason of the strong links between the various components of the ecclesial community.

Before this Guide could see light, the Holy Father John Paul II had approved the *Catechism of the Catholic Church*[6] ordering its publication. The extraordinary importance, for the Church as well as for every man of good will, of this rich and synthetic "exposition of the faith of the church and of catholic doctrine, verified and enlightened by the Sacred Scripture, by the apostolic Tradition and by the Magisterium"[7] is well known. Even though this is a document of different aim and content, it becomes immediately evident that the new catechism could offer some special enlightenment at different points of the Guide and, above all, that it could be a sure and authentic point of reference for the formation and for the activities of the catechists. In the final edition of the text, therefore, care has been taken to point out, particularly in the notes, the principal connections with the themes exposed in the catechism.

It is our hope that this Guide will be used as a reference book and will be a source of unity and encouragement for catechists and, through them, for their ecclesial communities. The CEP offers it, therefore, to the Episcopal Conferences and to individual bishops as an aid to the life and apostolate of their catechists and as a basis for the renewal of national and diocesan catechetical programs and directors.

PART I
AN APOSTLE EVER RELEVANT
I. THE CATECHIST IN A MISSIONARY CHURCH

2. VOCATION AND IDENTITY

Every baptized Catholic is personally called by the Holy Spirit to make his or her contribution to the coming of God's kingdom. Within the lay state there are various *vocations*, or different spiritual and apostolic roads to be followed by both individuals and groups. Within the general vocation of the laity there are particular ones.[8]

At the origin of the catechist's vocation, therefore, apart from the sacraments of baptism and confirmation, there is a specific call from the Holy Spirit, a *"special Charism recognized by the Church"*[9] and made explicit by the bishop's mandate. It is important for the catechist candidate to recognize the supernatural and ecclesial significance of this call, so as to be able to respond, like the Son of God, *"Here I come"* (Hebrews 10:7), or, like the prophet, *"Here I am, send me"* (Isaiah 6:8).

In actual missionary practice, the catechist's vocation is both *specific*, i.e. for the task of catechizing, and *general*, for collaborating in whatever apostolic services are useful for the building up of the Church.[10]

The CEP insists on the value and distinctiveness of the catechist's vocation. Each one, therefore, should try to discover, discern and foster his or her own particular vocation.[11]

From these premises it can be seen that catechists in mission territories have their own identity, which characterizes them in respect to those working in the older Churches, as the Church's magisterium and legislation clearly recognize.[12]

In short, the catechist in mission territories is identified by four elements: a call from the Holy Spirit; an ecclesial mission; collaboration with the bishop's apostolic mandate; and a special link with missionary activity *ad gentes*.

3. ROLE

Closely linked to the question of identity is that of the role of the catechist in missionary activity, a role that is both important and many-sided. Apart from the explicit proclamation of the Christian message and the accompaniment of catechumens and newly baptized Christians on their road to full maturity in the faith and in sacramental life, the catechist's role comprises presence and witness, and involvement in human development, inculturation and dialogue.[13]

Thus the Church's Magisterium, when it speaks of catechists *"in mission lands,"*[14] treats the subject as an important one and gives space to it. The Encyclical Redemptoris Missio, for instance, describes catechists as *"specialized workers, direct witnesses, indispensable evangelizers, who represent the basic strength of Christian communities, especially in the young Churches."*[15] The *Code of Canon Law* has a canon on catechists involved in strictly missionary activity and describes them as *"lay members of Christ's faithful who have received proper formation and are outstanding in their living of the Christian life. Under the direction of missionaries, they are to present the Gospel teaching and engage in liturgical worship and in works of Charity."*[16]

This description of the catechist corresponds with that of the CEP in its 1970 Plenary Assembly: *"The catechist is a lay person specially appointed by the Church, in accordance with local needs, to make Christ known, loved and followed by those who do not yet know Him and by the faithful themselves."*[17]

To the catechist, as indeed to other members of the faithful, may be entrusted, in accordance with the canonical norms, certain functions of the sacred ministry which do not require the character of Holy Orders. The execution of these functions, when a priest is not available, does not make a pastor of the catechist, inasmuch as he or she derives legitimation directly from the official permission granted by the pastors.[18] However, we may recall a clarification made in the past by the CEP itself: in his or her ordinary activity, *"the catechist is not a simple substitute for the priest, but is, by right, a witness of Christ in the community."*[19]

4. CATEGORIES AND TASKS

Catechists in mission territories are not only different from those in older Churches, but among themselves vary greatly in characteristics and modes of action from one young Church to another, so that it is difficult to give a single description that would apply to all.

There are two main types of catechist: full-time catechists, who devote their life completely to this service and are officially recognized as such; and part-time catechists, who offer a more limited, but still precious, collaboration. The proportion between the two categories varies from place to place, but in general there are far more part-time than full-time catechists.

Various tasks are entrusted to both types of catechist, and it is in these tasks that one can see the great diversity that exists between different areas. The following outline would seem to give a realistic summary of the main functions entrusted to catechists in Churches dependent on the CEP:

—Catechists with the specific task of catechizing, which includes educating young people and adults in the faith, preparing candidates and their families for the sacraments of Christian initiation, and helping with retreats and other meetings connected with catechesis. Catechists with these functions are more numerous in Churches that have stressed the development of lay services.[20]

—Catechists who collaborate in different forms of apostolate with ordained ministers whose direction they willingly accept. The tasks entrusted to them are multiple: preaching to non-Christians; catechizing catechumens and those already baptized; leading community prayer, especially at the Sunday liturgy in the absence of a priest; helping the sick and presiding at funerals; training other catechists in special centers or guiding volunteer catechists in their work; taking charge of pastoral initiatives and organizing parish functions; helping the poor and working for human development and justice. This type of catechist is more common in places where parishes cover a large area with scattered communities far from the center, or where, because of a shortage of clergy, parish priests select lay leaders to help them.[21]

The dynamism of the young Churches and their socio-cultural situation give rise to other apostolic functions. For instance, there are *religion teachers* in schools, teaching both baptized and non-Christian students. These can be found in government schools, where the State allows religious instruction, as well as in Catholic schools. There are also *Sunday catechists*, who teach in Sunday schools organized by the parish, especially where the State does not allow religious instruction in its schools. And in large cities, especially in the poorer quarters, there are lay apostles doing excellent work among the destitute, immigrants, prisoners and others in need. Such functions are considered, according to the sensibilities and experience of the different Churches, as either proper to the catechist or as a general form of lay service to the Church and its mission. The CEP considers the multiplicity and variety of these tasks as an expression of the richness of the Spirit at work in the young Churches, and recommends them all to the attention of the bishops. It asks them to foster especially those that best respond to present needs and to the immediate future, in so far as this can be foreseen.

There is another consideration. Catechists may be old or young, male or females, married or single, and these factors should be taken into account in assigning tasks in the various cultural settings. Thus, a married man seems most indicated to be the community leader, especially in societies where men still have a dominant role. Women would seem to be the natural choice for educating the young and working for the Christian promotion of women. Married adults have greater stability and can give witness to the values of Christian marriage. The young, on the other hand, are to be preferred for contact with youth and for activities that take up more time.

Finally, one should bear in mind that, beside the lay catechists, there is a great number or religious men and women, who carry out catechesis and, because of their special consecration, are able to bear a unique witness in the capacity of their mission and consequently are called to be available and prepared in their own way for this task. In practice they take on many of the tasks of the catechist and, because of their close cooperation with the priests, often play a directing role. The CEP, therefore, strongly recommends the involvement of religious men and women, as is already the practice in many places, in this important sector of ecclesial life, especially in the training and guidance of catechists.[22]

5. PROSPECTS FOR DEVELOPMENT IN THE NEAR FUTURE

The tendency in general, and one which the CEP approves of and encourages, is for the figure of the catechist as such to be affirmed and developed, independently of the tasks he or she performs. The value of catechists and their influence on the apostolate are always decisive for the Church's mission.[23]

Basing itself on its own worldwide experience, the CEP offers the following suggestions to help promote reflection on this subject:

— Absolute precedence must be given to quality. A common problem is certainly the scarcity of properly trained candidates. The character of the catechist is of prime importance and this must influence the criteria for selection and the program for training and guidance. The words of the Holy Father are illuminating: "For such a fundamental evangelical service a great number of workers are necessary. But, while striving for numbers, we must aim above all today at securing the quality of the catechist."[24]

— In view of the present impetus towards a renewed mission *ad gentes*,[25] the future of the catechist in the young Churches will certainly be marked by missionary zeal. Catechists, therefore, should be ever more fully qualified as lay pioneers of the apostolate. In the future, as in the past, they should be distinguished by their indispensable contribution to missionary activity *ad gentes*.

— It is not enough to fix an objective, but suitable means must be chosen for attaining the goal, and this holds true also for the training of catechists. Concrete programs should be drawn up, adequate structures and financial support provided, and qualified formators secured, so as to provide the catechists with a solid formation. Obviously the scale of the facilities and the level of study will vary according to the real possibilities of each Church, but certain standards should be attained by all, without giving in to difficulties.

— The cadres in charge to be strengthened. Everywhere there should be at least a few professional catechists who have been trained in suitable centers and who, placed in key posts of the catechetical organization under the direction of their pastors, see to the preparation of new candidates, introduce them to their functions and guide them in their work. These cadres should be found at all levels — parish, diocesan and national — and will be a guarantee of the good functioning of such an important sector of the Church's life.

—The CEP expects that in the near future the work of catechists will be still further developed, and we should try to see from now how tomorrow's protagonists will act.

Special encouragement will be given to catechists with a marked missionary spirit, who *"will themselves become missionary animators in their ecclesial communities and would be willing, if the Spirit so calls them and their Pastors commission them, to go outside their own territory to preach the gospel, prepare catechumens for baptism and build new ecclesial communities."*[26]

Catechists who are involved in the catechesis will have a developing future, because the young Churches are multiplying the services of the lay apostolate, which are distinct from those of the catechists.[27] Hence it will be of great use to have specialized catechists, for instance, those who promote Christian life where the majority of the people are already baptized but where the level of religious instruction and of the life of faith is not high. Catechists should also be trained for challenges which already face us today and will become even greater in future: urbanization, increasing numbers going on to third-level education, the world of youngsters, migrants and refugees, growing secularization, political changes, the influence of the mass media, etc.

The CEP draws attention to these future prospects and the need to face up to them, while realizing that it is up to the local pastors to see how best to go about it. Episcopal Conferences and individual bishops should draw up a program for the preparation of catechists for the future, giving special attention to the missionary dimension in both their training and activity. These programs should not be vague, but specific and adapted to local conditions, so that each Church will have both the catechists it needs today and those that will be necessary in the near future.

II. THE CATECHIST'S SPIRITUALITY

6. NECESSITY AND NATURE OF SPIRITUALITY FOR THE CATECHIST

Catechists must have a deep spirituality, i.e. they must live in the Spirit, who will help them to renew themselves continually in their specific identity.

The need for a spirituality proper to catechists springs from their vocation and mission. It includes, therefore, a new and special motivation, a call to sanctity. Pope John Paul II's saying: *"The true missionary is the saint,"*[28] can be applied without hesitation to the catechist. Like every member of the faithful, catechists are *"called to holiness and to mission,"*[29] i.e. to live out their own vocation *"with the fervor of the saints."*[30] Their spirituality is closely bound up with their status as lay Christians, made participants, in their own degree, in Christ's prophetic, priestly and kingly offices. As members of the laity, they are involved in the secular world and have, *"according to the condition of each, the special obligation to permeate and perfect the temporal order of things with the spirit of the gospel. In this way, particularly in conducting secular business and exercising secular functions, they are to give witness to Christ."*[31]

For married catechists, matrimonial life forms an integral part of their spirituality. As the Pope justly affirms *"married Catechists are expected to bear witness constantly to the Christian value of matrimony, living the sacrament in full fidelity and educating their children with a sense of responsibility."*[32] This matrimonial spirituality can have great impact on their activity, and it would be good for them to involve their spouse and children in the work, so that the whole family radiates apostolic witness.

Catechists' spirituality is also conditioned by their apostolic vocation, and therefore should bear the marks of: openness to God's word, to the Church and to the world; authenticity of life; missionary zeal; and devotion to Mary.

7. OPENNESS TO THE WORD

The office of catechist is basically that of communicating God's word, and so the fundamental spiritual attitude should be one of openness to this word, contained in revelation, preached by the Church, celebrated in the liturgy and lived out in the lives of saints.[33] This is always an encounter with Christ, hidden in his word, in the eucharist and in our brothers and sisters. Openness to the word means openness to God, to the Church and to the world.

—Openness to God *Uno et Trino*, who is in the most intimate depths of each person and gives meaning to his or her life: convictions, criteria, scale of values, decisions, relationships, behavior, etc. Catechists should allow themselves to be drawn into the circle of the Father, who communicates the word; of the Son, the incarnate Word, who speaks only the words He hears from the Father (cf. John 8:26; 12:49); and of the Holy Spirit, who enlightens the mind to help it understand God's words and opens the heart to receive them with love and put them into practice (cf. John 16:12 – 14).

It is a spirituality, therefore, that is rooted in the living word of God, with a Trinitarian dimension, like the universal mission itself with its offer of salvation. It requires a corresponding interior attitude which shares in the love of the Father, who wishes that all should come to the knowledge of the truth and be saved (cf. 1 Timothy 2:4); which seeks communion with Christ, so as to share his own *"mind"* (Philippians 2:5) and experience, like Paul, his comforting presence: *"Do not be afraid . . . because I am with you"* (Acts 18:9 – 10): which allows oneself to be molded by the Spirit and transformed into a courageous witness of Christ and enlightened preacher of the word.[34]

—Openness to the Church, of which catechists are living members, which they strive to build up, and from which they receive their mandate. The word is entrusted to the Church, so that it may keep it faithfully, deepen its understanding of it with the help of the Holy Spirit, and proclaim it to the whole World.[35]

As People of God and the Mystical Body of Christ, the Church requires from catechists a deep sense of belonging and responsibility, inasmuch as they are living and active members of it; as universal sacrament of salvation, it elicits the will to live its mystery and its manifold grace so as to be enriched by it and become a visible sign to the community. The catechist's service is never an individual or isolated act, but is always deeply ecclesial.

Openness to the Church expresses itself by filial love, dedication to its service and a willingness to suffer for its cause. In particular, it is expressed in the attachment and obedience to the Roman Pontiff, the center of unity and the bond of universal communion, so also to the bishop, the father and guide of the particular Church. Catechists should share responsibly in the earthly vicissitudes of the pilgrim Church, which is by nature missionary,[36] and aspire with it towards the final reunion with Christ the Spouse.

The ecclesial sense that is proper to the catechist's spirituality expresses itself, therefore, in sincere love of the Church, in imitation of Christ, who *"loved the Church and sacrificed himself for her."* It is an active and total love which becomes a sharing in the Church's mission of salvation to the point even of giving one's life for it if necessary.[37]

— Missionary openness to the world, finally — the world which is offered the salvation that springs from *"that fountain of love or charity within God the Father"*;[38] the world in which historically God's Word came to live among us to redeem us (cf. John 1:14), and in which the Holy Spirit was poured out to sanctify men and women and gather them into the Church, to have access to the Father through Christ in the one Spirit (cf. Ephesians 2:18).[39]

Catechists, therefore, will be open and attentive to the needs of the world, knowing that they are called to work in and for the world, without however belonging completely to it (cf. John 17:14 – 21). This means that they must be thoroughly involved in the life of the society about them, without pulling back from fear of difficulties or withdrawing through love of tranquillity. But they must keep a supernatural outlook on life and trust in the efficacy of God's word, which does not return to Him without *"succeeding in what it was sent to do"* (Isaiah 55:11).

Openness to the world is a characteristic of the catechist's spirituality in virtue of the apostolic love of Jesus the Good Shepherd, who came *"to gather together in unity the scattered children of God"* (John 11:52). Catechists must be filled with this love, bringing it to their brothers and sisters as they preach to them that God loves and offers his salvation to all.[40]

8. COHERENCE AND AUTHENTICITY OF LIFE

The work of catechists involves their whole being. Before they preach the word, they must make it their own and live by it.[41] *"The world (. . .) needs evangelizers who speak of a God that they know and who is familiar to them, as if they saw the Invisible."*[42]

What catechists teach should not be a purely human science nor the sum of their personal opinions but the Church's faith, which is the same throughout the world, which they themselves live and whose witnesses they are.[43]

Hence the need for coherence and authenticity of life. Before doing the catechesis one must first of all be a catechist. The truth of their lives confirms their message. It would be sad if they did not *"practice what they preached"* and spoke about a God of whom they had theoretical knowledge but with whom they had no contact. They should apply to themselves the words of St. Mark concerning the vocation of the apostles: *"He appointed twelve, to be his companions and to be sent out to preach"* (Mark 3: 14 – 15).

Authenticity of life means a life of prayer, experience of God and fidelity to the action of the Holy Spirit. It implies a certain intensity and an internal and external orderliness, adapted to the various personal and family situations of each. It might be objected that catechists, being members of the laity, cannot have a structured spiritual life like that of religious and that therefore they must content themselves with something less. But in every life situation, whether one is engaged in secular work or in the ministry, it is possible for everyone, priest, religious or lay person, to attain a high degree of communion with God and an ordered rhythm of prayer, including the finding of times of silence for entering more deeply into the contemplation of God. The more intense and real one's spiritual life is, the more convincing and efficacious will one's witness and activity be.

It is also important for catechists that they grow interiorly in the peace and joy of Christ, so that they may be examples of hope and courage (cf. Romans 12:12). For Christ *"is our peace"* (Ephesians 2:14), and he gives his apostles his joy that their *"joy may be full"* (John 15:11).

Catechists, therefore, should be bearers of paschal joy and hope, in the name of the Church. In fact, *"the most precious gift that the Church can offer to the bewildered and restless world of our time is to form within it Christians who are confirmed in what is essential and who are humbly joyful in their faith."*[44]

9. MISSIONARY ZEAL

In view of their baptism and special vocation, catechists who live in daily contact with large numbers of non-Christians, as is the case in mission territories, cannot but feel moved by Christ's words: *"Other sheep I have that are not of this fold and these too I must lead"* (John 10:16); *"go out to the whole world and preach the gospel to every creature"* (Mark 16:15). To be able to affirm, like Peter and John before the Sanhedrin, *"we cannot but speak of what we have seen and heard"* (Acts 4:20), and to realize with Paul the ideal of apostolic ministry: *"the love of Christ overwhelms us"* (2 Corinthians 5:14), catechists should have a strong missionary spirit—a spirit that will be all the more effective if they are seen to be convinced of what they say and are enthusiastic and courageous, without ever being ashamed of the gospel (cf. Romans 1:16). While the wise ones according to this world seek immediate gratification, the catechist will glory only in Christ, who gives strength (cf. Colossians 1:29), and will wish to know and preach only *"Christ the power of God and the wisdom of God"* (1 Corinthians 1:24). As the *Catechism of the Catholic Church* rightly affirms, from *"the loving knowledge of Christ springs out the irresistible desire to announce, to 'evangelize' and to lead others to the 'yes' of the faith in Jesus Christ. At the same time, one also feels the need to know this faith ever better."*[45]

Catechists will try to be like the shepherd who goes in search of the lost sheep *"until he finds it"* (Luke 15:4), or like the woman with the lost drachma who would *"search thoroughly until she had found it"* (Luke 15:8). Their convictions should be a source of apostolic zeal: *"I have made myself all things to all in order to save some at any cost. I do it all for the sake of the gospel"* (1 Corinthians 9:22–23; cf. 2 Corinthians 12:15). And again St. Paul says: *"Woe to me if I do not preach the gospel"* (1 Corinthians 9:16). The burning zeal of St. Paul should inspire catechists to stir up their own zeal, which should be the response to their vocation, and which will help them to preach Christ boldly and work actively for the growth of the ecclesial community.[46]

Finally, one should not forget that the stamp of authenticity on the missionary spirit is that of the cross. The Christ whom catechists have come to know is *"a crucified Christ"* (1 Corinthians 2:2): he whom they preach is *"Christ crucified, a stumbling block to Jews and folly to Gentiles"* (1 Corinthians 1:23), whom the Father raised from the dead on the third day (cf. Act: 10:40). They should be prepared, therefore, to live in hope the mystery of the death and resurrection of Christ in the midst of difficult situations, personal suffering, family problems and obstacles in their apostolic work, as they strive to follow the Lord on his own difficult road: *"in my own body I complete what is lacking in Christ's afflictions the sake of his body, the Church"* (Colossians 1:24).[47]

10. DEVOTION TO MARY

Through her own special vocation, Mary saw the Son of God *"grow in wisdom, in age and in grace"* (Luke 2:52). She was the teacher who *"trained Him in human knowledge of the Scriptures and of God's loving plan for his people, and in adoration of the Father."*[48] She was also *"the first of his disciples."*[49] As St. Augustine boldly affirmed, to be his disciple was more important for Mary than to be his mother.[50] One can say with reason and joy that Mary is a *"living catechism,"* *"mother and model of catechists."*[51]

The spirituality of catechists, like that of every Christian and especially those involved in the apostolate, will be enriched by a deep devotion to the Mother of God. Before explaining to others the place of Mary in the mystery of Christ and the Church,[52] they should have her present in their own soul and should give evidence of a sincere Marian piety,[53] which they will communicate to the community. They will find in Mary a simple and effective model, for themselves and others: *"The Virgin Mary in her own life lived an example of that maternal love by which all should be fittingly animated who cooperate in the apostolic mission of the Church on behalf of the rebirth of humanity."*[54]

The preaching of the word is always connected with prayer, the celebration of the eucharist and the building of community. The earliest Christian community was a model of this (cf. Acts 2–4), united around Mary the mother of Jesus (cf. Acts 1:14).

III. THE CATECHIST'S ATTITUDE TO SOME CONTEMPORARY ISSUES

11. SERVICE TO THE COMMUNITY AS A WHOLE AND TO PARTICULAR GROUPS

There are various groups in the community that may require the services of catechists: young people and adults, men and women students and workers, Catholics, other Christians and non-Christians. It is not the same thing to be a catechist for catechumens preparing for baptism as to be community leader for a village of Catholics, with responsibility for various pastoral activities, or to be a religion teacher in a school, or to be charged with preparing people for the sacraments, or to be assigned to pastoral work in an inner-city area, etc.

Catechists will try to promote communication and communion between the members of the community, and will devote themselves to the groups committed to their care, trying to understand their particular needs so as to help them as much as possible. As the needs differ from group to group, so the training of catechists will have to be adapted for the groups envisaged. It would be useful, therefore, for catechists to know in advance the sort of work they will be called to and make acquaintance with the groups concerned. Some useful suggestions in connection with this have already been offered by the Magisterium, especially in the *General Catechetical Directory*, nos. 77 – 97, and the Apostolic Exhortation *Catechesi Tradendae*, nos. 34 – 35.

Special attention should be paid to the sick and aged, because their physical and psychological weakness calls for greater charity and concern.[55]

The sick should be helped to understand the redemptive value of the cross,[56] in union with Jesus, who took upon himself the weight of our infirmities (cf. Matthew 8:17; Isaiah 53:4). Catechists should visit them frequently, offering them the comfort of God's word and, when commissioned to do so, the eucharist.

The aged too should be followed with special care, for they have an important role in the community, as Pope John Paul II recognizes when he calls them *"witnesses of the tradition of faith* (cf. Psalm 44:1; Exodus 12:26 – 27), *teachers of wisdom* (cf. Sirach 6:34; 8:11 – 12), *workers of charity.*"[57] Families should be encouraged to keep their elderly members with them, to *"bear witness to the past and instill wisdom in the young."*[58] The aged should feel the support of the whole community and should be helped to bear in faith their inevitable limitations and, in certain cases, their solitude. Catechists will prepare them for their meeting with the Lord and help them experience the joy that comes from our hope in eternal life.[59]

Catechists will also show sensitivity in dealing with people in difficult situations such as those in irregular marriages, the children of broken marriages, etc. They must be able to share in and express the immense compassion of the heart of Jesus (cf. Matthew 9:36; Mark 6:34; 8:2; Luke 7:13).

12. NEED FOR INCULTURATION

Like all forms of evangelization, catechesis too is called to bring the gospel into the heart of the different cultures.[60] The process of inculturation takes time, as it is a deep, gradual and all-embracing process. Through it, as Pope John Paul II explains, *"the Church makes the gospel incarnate in different cultures and at the same time introduces peoples, together with their cultures, into her own community; she transmits to them her own values, at the same time taking the good elements that already exist in them and renewing them from within."*[61]

Catechists, like all missionary personnel, will play an active part in this process. They should be specifically prepared for it, with courses on the elements of cultural anthropology and on their own culture, and should be aware of the guidelines that the Church has laid down on this matter[62] and which may be summarized as follows:

—The gospel message, though it can never be identified with any one culture, is necessarily incarnated in cultures. From its very beginnings it was incarnated in certain specific cultures, and one must take account of this if one is not to deprive the new Churches of values which are now the patrimony of the universal Church.

—The gospel is a force for renewal, and can rectify elements in cultures which do not conform to it.

—The local ecclesial communities, which are the primary subjects of inculturation, live out their daily experience of faith and charity in a particular culture, and the bishop should indicate the best ways to bring out the positive values in that culture. The experts give incentive and support.

—Inculturation is genuine when it is guided by two principles: it must be founded on the word of God, revealed in the Scriptures, and must follow the Church's tradition and the guidance of the Magisterium; and it must never go against the Church unity that was willed by the Lord.

—Popular piety, understood as an expression of Catholic devotion colored by local values, traditions and attitudes, when purified of defects caused by ignorance and superstition, expresses the wisdom of God's people and is a privileged form of inculturation of the gospel.[63]

Following the above directives, catechists should contribute to inculturation by fitting into the overall pastoral plan drawn up by the competent authorities and avoiding adventures into particular experiments that might upset the faithful. They should be convinced that the gospel is strong enough to penetrate any culture and enrich and strengthen it from within.

13. HUMAN DEVELOPMENT AND OPTION FOR THE POOR

There is a *"close connection"* between the preaching of the gospel and the promotion of human development.[64] They are both included in the Church's mission. *"Through the gospel message, the Church offers a force for liberation which promotes development precisely because it leads to conversion of heart*

and of ways of thinking, fosters the recognition of each person's dignity, encour-
ages solidarity, commitment and service of one's neighbor, and gives everyone
a place in God's plan, which is the building of his kingdom of peace and jus-
tice, beginning already in this life. This is the biblical perspective of the new
heavens and a new earth (cf. Isaiah 65:17; 2 Peter 3:13; Revelation 21:1), *which*
may been the stimulus and goal for humanity's advancement in history.[65]

It is well known that the Church claims for itself a mission of a *"religious"*[66] nature, but this has to take place, to be incarnated, in the real life and history of humanity.

To take the values of the gospel into the economic, social and political fields is a task especially for the laity.[67] Catechists have an important role in the field of human development and the promotion of justice. Living as lay people in society, they can well understand, interpret and try to bring solutions to personal and social problems in the light of the gospel. They should there-fore be close to the people, help them to understand the realities of social life so as to try to improve it, and, when necessary, they should have the courage to speak out for the weak and defend their rights.

When it is necessary to take practical initiatives in this area, they should act in union with the community, in a program drawn up with the approval of the bishop.

Connected with human development is the question of the preferential option for the poor. Catechists, especially those engaged in the general aposto-late, have a duty to make this ecclesial option, which does not mean that they are interested only in the poor, but that these should have a prior claim on their attention. The foundation of their interest in the poor must be love, for, as Pope John Paul II explicitly says, *"love has been and remains the driving force of mission."*[68]

By the poor should be understood especially the materially poor, who are so numerous in many mission territories. These brothers and sisters of Christ should be able to feel the Church's maternal love for them, even when they do not yet belong to it, so as to be encouraged to accept and overcome their diffi-culties with the help of Christian faith and themselves become agents of their own integral development. The Church's charitable activity, like all pastoral activity, *"brings light and an impulse towards true development"* to the poor.[69]

Apart from the financially deprived, catechists should pay special attention also to other groups in need: those who are oppressed, persecuted or marginal-ized, the handicapped, the unemployed, prisoners, refugees, drug addicts, those suffering from AIDS, etc.[70]

14. SPIRIT OF ECUMENISM

Discord among Christians *"openly contradicts the will of Christ, provides a stumbling block to the world, and inflicts damage on the most holy cause of proclaiming the good news to every creature."*[71]

All Christian communities should *"participate in ecumenical dialogue and in other initiatives designed to promote Christian unity."*[72] In mission territories this task assumes special urgency so that Jesus' prayer to his Father should not be in vain: *"may they be one in us . . . so that the world may believe it was you who sent me"* (John 17:21).[73]

Catechists, by their very mission, are necessarily involved in this aspect of the apostolate and should promote an ecumenical spirit in the community, beginning with the catechumens and newly baptized.[74] They should have a deep desire for Christian unity, should willingly engage in dialogue with Christians of other denominations, and should commit themselves generously to ecumenical initiatives,[75] keeping to their particular role and following the Church's directives as specified by the Episcopal Conference and the local bishop.[76] Their catechetical activity, therefore, and their teaching of religion in schools should instill an openness to ecumenical cooperation.[77]

Their activity will be truly ecumenical if they can both courageously *"teach that the fullness of the revealed truths and of the means of salvation instituted by Christ is found in the Catholic Church"*[78] and also *"give a correct and fair presentation of the other Churches and ecclesial communities that the Spirit of Christ does not refrain from using as means of salvation."*[79]

They should try to have good relations with catechists and leaders of other denominations, in accord with their Pastors and, when so charged, as their representatives. They should avoid stirring up useless rivalries; should help the faithful to live in harmony with and respect for Christians of other denominations, while fully maintaining their own Catholic identity; and should join other believers in working for peace.[80]

15. DIALOGUE WITH THOSE OF OTHER RELIGIONS

Inter-religious dialogue forms part of the Church's evangelizing mission. Like preaching, it is also a way of making Christ known, and it is essential that the Catholic Church maintain good relations and contact with those of other faiths. It should be a saving dialogue, approached in the spirit of Christ himself.

Catechists, with their task of communicating the faith, should be open to this kind of dialogue and be trained to take part in it. They should be taught to realize its value and put it into practice in accordance with the guidelines of the Magisterium, especially those of *Redemptoris Missio*, of the subsequent document *Dialogue and Proclamations*, which was drawn up jointly by the Pontifical Council for Inter-religious Dialogue, and the CEP, and of the *Catechism of the Catholic Church*.[81] These guidelines include:

—Listening to the Spirit, who blows where He wills (cf. John 3:8); respecting his work in souls; and striving for inner purification, without which dialogue cannot bear fruit.[82]

—Accurate knowledge of the religions practiced in the area: their history and organization; the values in them which, like *"seeds of the Word,"* can be a *"preparation for the gospel"*;[83] their limitations and errors which are not in conformity with the gospel and which should be respectively completed and corrected.

— A conviction that salvation comes from Christ and that, therefore, dialogue does not dispense one from proclamation,[84] that the Church is the ordinary way of salvation and that only she possesses the fullness of revealed truth and salvific means.[85] As Pope John Paul II confirmed, while referring to *Redemptoris Missio: "One cannot place on the same level God's revelation in Christ and the scriptures or traditions of other religions. A theocentrism which did not recognize Christ in his full identity would be unacceptable to the Catholic Faith. (. . .) Christ's missionary command remains permanently valid and is an explicit call to make disciples of all nations and to baptize them, in order to bring them the fullness of God's gift."[86]* Dialogue should not, therefore, lead to religious relativism.

— Practical cooperation with non-Christian religious bodies in facing the great challenges to humanity such as the bringing about of peace, justice, development, etc.[87] There should always be an attitude of esteem and openness towards persons. God is the Father of all, and it is his love that should unite the human family in working for good.

In taking part in such dialogue, catechists should not be left on their own but should be integrated in the community. Initiatives in this area should be undertaken in the context of programs approved by the bishop and, when necessary, by the Episcopal Conference or the Holy See. Catechists should not act unilaterally, and especially should do nothing against the norms laid down. Finally, one should continue to believe in dialogue, even when it seems difficult or misunderstood. In certain conditions, it is indeed the only way to bear witness to Christ; it is always *"a path towards the Kingdom and will certainly bear fruit, even if the times and seasons are known only to the Father"* (cf. Acts 1:7).[88]

16. ATTENTION TO THE SPREAD OF SECTS

The rapid spread of sects of both Christian and non-Christian origin presents a pastoral challenge for the Church throughout the world today. In mission territories they are a serious obstacle to the preaching of the gospel and the orderly growth of the young Churches because they damage the integrity of faith and communion.[89]

Certain regions and persons are more vulnerable and more exposed to the influence of these sects. What the sects offer seems to work in their favor as they present apparently simple and immediate answers to the felt needs of the people, and the means they use are adapted to local sensibilities and cultures.[90]

As is well known, the Church's Magisterium has often given warnings about the dangers posed by sects, and called for *"serious reflection"* in view of their rapid spread.[91] Rather than a positive campaign against them, however, what is called for in mission territories is a renewal of mission itself.[92]

Catechists would seem to be particularly suitable for counteracting the influence of the sects. As they have the task of teaching the faith and of fostering the growth of Christian life, they can help both Christians and non-Christians understand what the real answers to their needs are, without having recourse to the pseudo-securities of the sects. Also, being members of the laity, they are closer to the people and can know their direct and lived situations.

The preferential work-lines for the catechists should be: to study first of all what exactly the sects teach and the points on which they particularly attack the Church, so as to be able to point out the inconsistencies in their position; to forestall their encroachment by giving positive instruction and encouraging the Christian community to greater fervor; and to proclaim clearly the Christian message. They should give personal attention to people and their problems, helping them to clarify doubts and to be wary of the specious promises of the sects.

It must not be forgotten that many of the sects are intolerant and are particularly hostile to Catholicism. Constructive dialogue is often not possible with them, even though here too one must have respect and understanding for persons. The Church's position must be made clear in this and also in an ecumenical way, for the spread of the sects poses a danger to the other Christian denominations as well.[93] Here, as in other areas, catechists should remain firmly within the common pastoral program approved by the Church authorities.[94]

PART II
CHOICE AND FORMATION OF CATECHISTS
IV. CHOICE OF CANDIDATES

17. IMPORTANCE OF A PROPER CHOICE

It is difficult to lay down rules as to the level of faith and the strength of motivation that a candidate should have in order to be accepted for training as a catechist. Among the reasons for this are: the varying levels of religious maturity in the different ecclesial communities, the scarcity of suitable and available personnel, socio-political conditions, poor educational standards and financial difficulties. But one should not give in to the difficulties and lower one's standards.

The CEP insists on the principle that a good choice of candidates is essential. Right from the beginning, a high quality must be set. Pastors should be convinced of this as the goal to be aimed at and, even though it may be achieved only gradually, they should not easily settle for less. They should also prepare the community, and especially the young, by explaining the role of catechists, so as to awaken an interest in this form of ecclesial service. It should not be forgotten either that the community's esteem for this service will be directly proportional to the way in which pastors treat their catechists, giving them worthwhile tasks and respecting their responsibility. A fulfilled, responsible and dynamic catechist, working enthusiastically and joyfully in the tasks assigned,[95] appreciated and properly remunerated, is the best promoter of other vocations.

18. CRITERIA FOR SELECTION

In choosing candidates, some criteria should be considered essential while others might be optional. It is useful to have a list of criteria for the whole Church, which could be referred to by those with the charge of choosing candidates. These criteria, which should be sufficient, precise, realistic and controllable, could be adapted to local conditions by the local authorities, who are the ones best able to judge the needs and possibilities of the community.

The following general considerations should be kept in mind, so that there may be a common policy in all mission areas while respecting inevitable differences.

— Some criteria concern the catechist's person. A basic rule is that no one should be accepted as a candidate unless he or she is positively motivated and is not seeking the post simply because another suitable job is not available. Positive qualities in candidates should be: faith that manifests itself in their piety and daily life; love for the Church and communion with its pastors; apostolic spirit and missionary zeal; love for their brothers and sisters and a willingness to give generous service; sufficient education; the respect of the community; the human, moral and technical qualities necessary for the work of a catechist, such as dynamism, good relations with others, etc.

— Other criteria concern the actual process of selection. As it is a question of ecclesial service, the decision belongs to the pastor, which in this case usually means the parish priest, but the community should be involved in the proposal of candidates and their evaluation. At a later stage, the parish priest should present the candidates chosen to the bishop or his representative, to confirm the choice and eventually give them their official mandate.

— There should also be special criteria for the acceptance of candidates in catechetical centers. Apart from the general criteria, each center, in keeping with its character, will have its own requirements concerning the level of scholastic achievement needed for entry, its conditions for participation, its formation program, etc.

These general guidelines will have to be made more specific for local conditions and applied to the particular circumstances in each area.

V. PROCESS OF FORMATION

19. NEED FOR PROPER FORMATION

In order to have a sufficient number of suitable catechists for the communities, besides a careful selection, it is indispensable to stress on the training to which the quality is connected. This has often been stressed by the Magisterium, because every apostolic activity *"which is not supported by properly trained persons is condemned to failure."*[96]

The relevant documents of the Magisterium require both a general and a specific formation for catechists: general, in the sense that their whole character and personality should be developed; and specific, with a view to the particular tasks they will be charged with in a supplementary way: preaching the word to both Christians and non-Christians, leading the community, presiding when necessary at liturgical prayers, and helping in various ways those in spiritual or material need. As Pope John Paul II said: *"To set high standards means both to provide a thorough basic training and to keep it constantly updated. This is a fundamental duty, in order to ensure qualified personnel for the Church's mission, with good training programs and adequate structures, providing for all aspects of formation — human, spiritual, doctrinal, apostolic and professional."*[97]

It will be a demanding training program therefore, both for the candidates and for those who have to provide it. The CEP entrusts its realization to the bishops as part of their pastoral task.[98]

20. UNITY AND HARMONY IN THE PERSONALITY OF CATECHIST

In living out their vocation, catechists, like all members of the Catholic laity, *"must be formed according to the union which exists from their being members of the Church and citizens of human society."*[99] There cannot be separate parallel lives: a *"spiritual"* life with its values and demands, a *"secular"* life with its various forms of expression, and an *"apostolic"* life with its own requirements.[100]

To bring about unity and harmony in one's personality, certain obstacles of a temperamental, intellectual or emotional nature must first of all be overcome, and an ordered life style established. But what will be decisive will be the ability to reach into the depths of one's soul and find there the principle and source of the catechist's identity, namely the person of Christ himself.

The first and essential object of catechesis is, of course, the person of Jesus of Nazareth, the only begotten of the Father, *"full of grace and truth"* (John 1:14), *"the way, the truth and the life"* (John 14:6). It is the *"mystery of Christ"* (Ephesians 3:4) in its integrity *"hidden for generations and generations"* (Colossians 1:26), which must be revealed. It follows that the catechists' concern should be to transmit, through their teaching and behavior, the doctrine and life of Christ. Their mode of being and of working should depend entirely on that of Christ. The unity and harmony in their personalities should be Christocentric, built upon *"a deep intimacy with Christ and with the Father,"* in the Spirit.[101] This cannot be too strongly insisted upon, when there is question of the catechist's role and importance in these decisive times for the Church's mission.

21. HUMAN MATURITY

From the beginning it should be clear that the candidate possesses basic human qualities that can be further developed. What is to be aimed at is a person with human maturity suitable for a responsible role in the community.

The following qualities should be taken into consideration: in the purely human sphere: psychophysical equilibrium: good health, a sense of responsibility, honesty, dynamism; good professional and family conduct; a spirit of sacrifice, strength, perseverance, etc.; with a views to the functions of a catechist: good human relations, ability to dialogue with those of other religions, grasp of one's own culture, ability to communicate, willingness to work with others, leadership qualities, balanced judgement, openness of mind, a sense of realism, a capacity to transmit consolation and hope, etc.; with a view to particular situations or roles: aptitudes for working in the fields of peacemaking, development, socio-cultural promotion, justice, health care, etc.

The aim of catechetical formation will be to build on the human qualities already present, to develop them and add the necessary skills for a fruitful ministry.

22. DEEP SPIRITUAL LIFE

To be able to educate others in the faith, catechists should themselves have a deep spiritual life. This is the most important aspect of their personality and therefore the one to be most stressed in formation. The real catechist is a saint.[102] Their spiritual life should be based on a communion of faith and love with the person of Jesus, who calls them and sends them on his mission.[103] Like Jesus, the only Master (cf. Matthew 23:8),[104] catechists serve their brothers and sisters by their teaching and works (cf. Acts 1:1), which are manifestations of love. To do the will of their Father, which is an act of salvific love for others, is their food, as it was that of Jesus (cf. John 4:34). Sanctity of life, lived as a lay apostle,[105] is the ideal to be striven for. Spiritual formation should be a process of listening *"to Him who is the principle inspiring all catechetical work and all who do this work — the Spirit of the Father and of the Son, the Holy Spirit."*[106]

The best way to attain this interior maturity is an intense sacramental and prayer life.[107]

Basing itself on the actual experiences of catechists, the CEP proposes the following practices as key elements in the prayer life at least of the catechists who guide the community in a supplementary way, full-time catechists and those working closely with the parish priest, especially of the cadres:

— Regular, even daily, reception of the Eucharist, so as to nourish oneself with the "bread of life" (John 6:34), to form *"a single body"* with the community (cf. 1 Corinthians 10:17) and offer oneself to the Father along with the Lord's body and blood.[108]

— Lived liturgy in its various dimensions for the personal growth and for the help of the community.[109]

— Recital of part of the Divine Office, especially Lauds and Vespers, in union with the song of praise that the Church addresses to the Father *"from the rising of the sun to its setting"* (Psalm 113:3).[110]

— Daily meditation, especially on the word of God, in an attitude of contemplation and response; experience shows that, even for lay people, regular meditation and *lectio divina* bring order to one's life and guarantee spiritual growth.[111]

— Personal prayer, which ensures contact with God during one's daily occupations, with special attention to Marian prayer.

— Frequent reception of the sacrament of penance, to ask pardon for faults committed and renew one's fervor.[112]

—Participation in spiritual retreats, for personal and community renewal.

It is through such a life of prayer that catechists will enrich their interior life and attain the spiritual maturity required by their role. Prayer is also necessary for their ministry to be fruitful, for communication of the Christian faith depends less on the catechist's ability than on God's grace working in the hearts of those who hear the message.[113]

If a sufficient number of suitable candidates cannot be found, there may be a risk of settling for catechists who are not spiritual enough, but the CEP would not encourage such pragmatic solutions, for mission in the world today requires that the catechist hold a place of honor in the Church.

To help catechists in their spiritual life, spiritual direction should be made available. Dioceses are encouraged to name specific priests to interest themselves in the catechists and their work and provide spiritual guidance. But it is important that each catechist should choose a personal spiritual director from among the priests who are easily accessible. Parish priests in particular should be close to their catechists and help them even more in their spiritual growth than in their work.

Also to be encouraged are parish or diocesan initiatives for catechists, such as prayer groups, days of recollection together, or spiritual retreats, which will help them to share with each other on a spiritual level.

Catechists should also realize that the Christian community itself is a place where they can cultivate their own interior life. While they lead others in prayer, they will receive from them a stimulus and example to maintain their own fervor and grow in apostolic spirit.

23. DOCTRINAL TRAINING

The need for doctrinal training is obvious, as catechists must first understand the essentials of Christian doctrine before they can communicate it to others in a clear and interesting way, without omissions or error.

All candidates should have attained a certain level of education, in keeping with the standards of the country. As mentioned above, there can be problems where the general standard is not high, but facile solutions should be resisted. On the contrary, standards for admission should be above average, as candidates should be able to follow a course of *"higher religious education."* Without this, they would feel inferior to those who have done higher studies and would be ill at ease in educated circles and unable to face certain issues.

As for the contents of the course, they should be based on the program for *"doctrinal, anthropological and methodological formation"* presented in *the General Catechetical Directory*, published by the Congregation for the Clergy in 1971.[114] For mission territories, however, there should be certain adaptations and additions, as the CEP had indicated in part at its 1970 Plenary Assembly and which it now summarizes and develops on the basis of the encyclical *Redemptoris Missio:*

—in view of the specific aims of missionary activity, the doctrinal formation of catechists will be based especially on theology of Trinity, Christology and Ecclesiology, presented in a systematic and progressive synthesis of the Christian message. As they have the task of making Christ known and loved, they will strive to know Him doctrinally and on a personal level; and in order to make the Church known and loved, they will study its tradition and history, and the witness of its great figures, the Church Fathers and the Saints.[115]

—The level of religious and theological training will vary from place to place and will also depend on whether it is given in a catechetical center or in short courses. A minimum standard, however, will be set by the Episcopal Conference or individual bishops, to ensure that the training will qualify as *higher* religious education.

Sacred Scripture will always be the main field of study and will be the soul of the program. Around it will be structured the other branches of theology. It should be born in mind that the catechist must be qualified in the biblical pastoral, also in view of the comparison with the non-Catholic confessions and with the sects which often use the Bible in an incorrect way.

—The main elements of Missiology will also be studied, as this is an important subject for the mission.

—Liturgy must also, obviously, be given a prominent place, as catechists are to be leaders of community prayer.

—According to local circumstances, it may be necessary to study the beliefs and practices of other religions or Christian denominations in the area.

—Attention should also be given to other subjects connected with local conditions: the inculturation of Christianity in the country or region; the promotion of justice and human development in the local socio-economic situation; the history of the country; the religious practices, language, problems and needs of the area in which the catechist is to work.

—Regarding the methodological training one should bear in mind that many catechists will be working in various pastoral fields, and almost all will be in contact with people of other religions, they will be taught not only how to teach the catechism but also how to go about the various tasks connected with the proclamation of the Christian message and the life of an ecclesial community.

—It will also be important to grant the catechist contents and materials connected to their new and emerging life situations. The programs of study, which have a starting point in the actual reality and from foresight, can also include subjects that help them to face the phenomena of urbanization, secularization, industrialization, emigration, socio-political changes, the world of youngsters, etc.

—In spite of the diversity of subjects, one should aim at a global and not compartmentalized theological formation, i.e. there should be an overall vision of faith that brings unity and harmony to the knowledge acquired, to the catechists' personalities and to their apostolic service.

—At this point, it is necessary to emphasize the special importance the *Catechism of the Catholic Church* assumes for the doctrinal preparation of the catechists. In it, in fact, is contained an orderly synthesis of the Revelation and of the perennial catholic faith, as the Church would propose to herself and to the community of men of our time. As the Holy Father John Paul II affirms in the Apostolic Constitution *Fidei depositum*, in the catechism there are *"new things and old things* (cf. Matthew 13:52), *since the faith is always the same and at the same time it is the source of the lights which are ever new."* The service which the catechism aims at pertains and is relevant to each catechist. The same Apostolic Constitution attests that it is offered to the pastors and to the faithful, so that it may help them to fulfill, inside and outside the ecclesial community, *"their mission to announce the faith and to call to the evangelical life."* Moreover, it *"is offered to each man who may ask us the reason for the hope in us* (cf. 1 Peter 3:15) *and who may desire to know what the Church believes."* There is no doubt that the catechists will find in the new Catechism a source of inspiration and a mine of knowledge for their specific mission.

Training courses for catechists are best given in centers built for this purpose. Where these are not available, shorter courses may be provided in other locations by dioceses or parishes, and individual instruction could be given by a priest or an expert catechist. The courses should include lectures, group discussions and practical exercises, as well as personal study and research.

To provide adequate training is not easy and will require personnel, structures and financial support. But, in view of the importance of catechists, the challenge should be faced courageously, with realistic and intelligent planning.

Catechists should dedicate themselves to their studies so as to become lamps to light the way of their brothers and sisters (cf. Matthew 5:14–16). They should be joyful in their faith and hope (cf. Philippians 3:1; Romans 12:12), with the wisdom to transmit the authentic teaching of the Church, in fidelity to the Magisterium, without disturbing consciences, and especially those of the young, with theories that *"are only likely to raise irrelevant doubts instead of furthering the designs of God which are revealed in faith"* (1 Timothy 1:4).[116]

They should submit their minds and hearts to Christ, who is the one Teacher, and be aware that *"anyone else teaches to the extent that he is Christ's spokesman, enabling Christ to teach with his lips."*[117]

24. PASTORAL SPIRIT

The pastoral dimension of formation concerns the exercise of the prophetic, priestly and royal functions of the baptized lay person. Catechists will be taught, therefore, how to proclaim the Christian message and teach it, how to lead others in community and liturgical prayer, and how to carry out various other pastoral services.

Qualities to be developed for these tasks are: a spirit of pastoral responsibility and leadership; generosity, dynamism and creativity; ecclesial communion and obedience to pastors.

The theoretical part of the pastoral course will deal with the different types of pastoral work to be undertaken and also with the different groups of people to be addressed: children, adolescents, young people or adults; students or workers; baptized or unbaptized; healthy or sick; rich or poor; individuals or members of particular movements or groups, etc.

The practical part of the course will include practical exercises especially at the beginning, under the direction of the teacher or a priest or an experienced catechist.

Special attention will be paid to the sacraments, so that catechists will learn how to help the faithful to understand the religious meaning of these signs and approach them with faith in their supernatural efficacy. The sacrament of the anointing of the sick should not be forgotten, as catechists will often have to help the sick and dying to accept their sufferings in a spirit of faith.

For training in the specific field of catechesis, it would be well to consult the *General Catechetical Directory*, particularly the section on *"elements of methodology."*[118]

25. MISSIONARY ZEAL

The missionary dimension is an essential part of a catechist's identity and work, and so should be given a prominent place in the formation program. Catechists should be taught, theoretically and practically, how to devote themselves as lay Christians to the missionary apostolate, which includes the following elements:

— Being actively present in society, offering true Christian witness, entering into sincere dialogue with others, and cooperating in charity to resolve common problems.[119]

— Proclaiming boldly (cf. Acts 4:13; 28:31) the truth about God and his Son Jesus Christ, whom He sent into the world for the salvation of all (cf. 2 Timothy 1:9–10), so that those of other religions whose hearts are opened by the Holy Spirit (cf. Acts 16:14) may be able to believe and be freely converted.[120]

— Meeting followers of other religions in a spirit of openness and dialogue.

— Introducing catechumens to the mystery of salvation, the practice of evangelical norms and the religious, liturgical and community life of the People of God.[121]

— Building community and helping candidates prepare for the reception of baptism and the other sacraments of Christian initiation, as they become members of the Church of Christ which is prophetic, priestly and royal.[122]

— With dependence on the Pastors and in collaboration with the faithful, fulfilling those practices, which according to the pastoral design are destined to the maturing of the particular Church. These services are connected with various necessities of each Church and mark the catechist of the mission territories. As a result the formative activity must help the catechist to improve his own missionary sensibility, enabling him to discover and be involved in all the favorable situations at the first proclamation.

We have already quoted words of Pope John Paul II concerning catechists who are well trained in a missionary spirit and who themselves become missionary animators in their community, work for the evangelization of non-Christians, and are willing to do so outside of their own region or nation when sent by their pastors. Pastors will make the most of these zealous apostles and encourage them in their missionary work.

26. ATTITUDE TO THE CHURCH

The fact that the Church is missionary by nature and is sent to evangelize the whole world means that apostolic activity is not something individual or isolated, but is always carried out in communion with the local and universal Church.

This remark was made by Pope Paul VI concerning evangelizers,[123] but it also can be applied fully to catechists, whose role is eminently ecclesial.[124] They are sent by their pastors and act in virtue of a mandate given them by the Church. Their activity is part of the Church's activity and shares in its grace.

The following points should be stressed when training catechists in this area:

—An attitude of apostolic obedience to one's pastors, in a spirit of faith, just as Jesus *"emptied himself, taking the form of a servant . . . and became obedient unto death"* (Philippians 2:7–8: cf. Hebrews 5:8; Romans 5:19). Obedience should be accompanied by a sense of responsibility, as catechists in their ministry are called upon to respond to the grace of the Holy Spirit.[125]

In view of this, the canonical mandate or mission which is conferred in certain Churches is something to be encouraged, as it brings out the link between the catechist's mission and that of Christ and his Church. It should take place during a liturgical or liturgically inspired ceremony, at which the bishop or his delegate will confer the mandate, accompanied by some suitable sign, such as the presentation of a crucifix or a bible. There could be different grades of solemnity for full-time and part-time catechists.

—An ability to work with others at all levels is essential. Catechists should work in harmony with the local priests and religious, and especially with other members of the laity involved in the apostolate. They should fit into the overall pastoral plan and should meet from time to time with the others to discuss matters of common interest and review the work. The bishops should promote this type of work in common.

Catechists will be prepared to suffer for the Church, accepting the difficulties of work in common and the imperfections of others, and imitating Christ, who *"loved the Church and gave himself up for her"* (Ephesians 5:25).[126]

Training in this community spirit will be part of the catechists' training course from the beginning, with practical exercises carried out in groups.

27. AGENTS OF FORMATION

One of the problems of paramount importance in the field of formation of catechists is that of having suitable and sufficient formators. When we speak about the agents of formation, we should keep in mind all persons involved in formation.

The catechists should be convinced that: the most important formator is Christ himself, who forms them through the Holy Spirit (John 16:12–15). To hear God's voice requires a spirit of faith and an attitude of prayer and recollection. The education of apostles, in fact, is primarily a supernatural activity.

The catechists themselves can also be considered formators, in that they are responsible for their own interior growth through their response to God. They should be aware of this and should strive to listen always to the Divine Master so as to grow in wisdom and love.

Catechists work in communion with, at the service of and with the help of the ecclesial community. The community as a whole, therefore, is called to cooperate in the formation of its catechists, providing them with an atmosphere of acceptance and encouragement, welcoming them for what they are and offering them help. In the community, the bishop and parish priests hold a special place as formators. They will take an interest in the candidates, who in turn will be happy to learn from them.

Formators in the strict sense, i.e. those designated by the Church to train the catechists, have a most important role entrusted to them. They may be directors and staff of catechetical centers or may be charged with providing initial or ongoing formation outside of these centers. They should be chosen with care, and should be good Christians, loyal to the Church, with proper intellectual qualifications and personal experience in the catechetical field. It would be good if they could work as a team, made up of priests, religious and lay men and women, chosen especially from among experienced catechists. Candidates should be able to trust their formators and respect them as guides offered by the Church to help them in their growth.

28. INITIAL FORMATION

The initial or basic training period that precedes the beginning of a catechist's ministry is not the same in every Church, on account of the varying local conditions, but, whether the training is given in a catechetical center or in other ways, it should meet certain requirements. The following criteria should be born in mind:

— Knowledge of the candidates: they should be known personally and in their cultural milieu, not only so as to avoid making mistaken choices, but also for the formation to be personalized and adapted to the needs of each one.

— Attention to the actual conditions of the local Church and society. The training given should be not only theoretical but practical and rooted in the real life situations of the people.

—A step-by-step approach. The program should be methodical and gradual, respecting each candidate's progress and growth. One should not pretend to have a perfect catechist from the beginning, but should assist him to grow without interruption and incompleteness.

—Orderly and complete method: taking into consideration the situations of mission and of the pedagogy, the training should be based on experience: should aim at developing the whole personality: should promote a continuous dialogue between the candidate and God, the formators and the community: should be liberating, freeing the catechist from conscious or unconscious obstacle, to God's action; and should promote unity and harmony.

—The candidates should be helped to draw up a life program, with goals to be aimed at and means to achieve them, but in a realistic spirit. The goals should include identity and lifestyle, and also the qualities needed for the apostolate.

—There should be continual personal dialogue between the candidates and formators, who should be looked upon not merely as teachers but as friends and guides. As mentioned above, spiritual direction is very important, as it touches the depths of a person's soul and helps open it to God's grace.

—The Christian community in which the catechists live and work will also contribute to their formation, for no true apostolic education can take place outside of it. They will be constantly discovering how God's plan for salvation is being worked out in the community.

These guidelines should be taken into account where there are proper structures for initial formation, but even where these have not been established they can serve as a stimulus for both pastors and candidates. The training should not be improvised or left to the initiative of the candidates themselves.

29. ONGOING FORMATION

The fact that persons should never stop growing interiorly, the dynamic nature of the sacraments of Baptism and Confirmation, the process of continual conversion and growth in apostolic love, changes in culture, the evolution of society and constant updating of teaching methods, all mean that catechists should keep themselves in a process of ongoing formation during the whole course of their service. It should include human, spiritual, doctrinal and apostolic formation, and they should be helped in this and not merely left to their own devices.[127]

In the early period of their apostolate, ongoing formation will be largely the reinforcement of the basic training and its application in practice. Later it will entail updating on various points, so as to keep in touch with developments in theology and changing circumstances. In this endeavor one can ensure the quality of catechists, avoiding the risk of wearing down. In certain cases of special difficulty, such as discouragement or a change of work, it will entail a process of renewal and revitalization.

Ongoing formation is not the responsibility of the pastoral centers only, but should be attended to in each local community, especially as needs differ from person to person and place to place.[128]

Besides, one should guarantee the use of the means of the ongoing formation. Obstacles to ongoing formation may come from lack of funds, of books and other teaching aids, of qualified personnel, of transport for distances that can often be considerable, etc. But, as with initial formation, every effort should be made to overcome such obstacles, as it is important that each catechist should be helped towards continual progress and growth. The catechetical centers are certainly the most suitable agencies for promoting ongoing formation. They should follow up their former students, especially soon after they graduate, through circulars and individual letters, teaching aids, visits from formators, refresher courses or meetings at the centers, etc.

Where there are no centers, the diocesan authorities will try to ensure ongoing formation by means of short courses or renewal days directed by qualified personnel. Likewise individual parishes, or groups of parishes cooperating with each other, should organize such courses.[129]

For proper ongoing formation, haphazard individual initiatives are not enough. There should be an organized program covering the various aspects of catechists' work, the development of their personalities and, above all, their spiritual growth.

In spite of going from time to time to catechetical centers or other meeting places, catechists will necessarily accomplish most of their ongoing formation in their local communities and will derive support from them. But wider horizons should also be opened, with opportunities for catechists to meet those of other local Churches.

Finally, ongoing formation will depend to a large extent on the catechists themselves. They should be aware of the need for constant renewal and updating, and should seek out the means for this in reading, prayer and contacts with others.

30. MEANS AND STRUCTURES OF FORMATION

Where possible, catechists should be trained in their own special centers or schools. Church documents from *Ad Gentes* to *Redemptoris Missio* stress the importance of making efforts *"to establish and support schools for catechists, which are to be approved by the Episcopal Conferences and confer diplomas officially recognized by them."*[130]

The centers are very different entities: some of them being large residential centers with a team of formators and well organized training programs, while others are smaller centers for restricted groups or short courses. Most centers are diocesan or interdiocesan, some of them national or international.

There are common elements to these centers, such as a formative program, which makes the center a place of growth in faith, a possibility of residence, school teaching combined with pastoral experiences and, above all, the presence of the team of formators. There are also some proper elements which distinguish one center from the other: among them, for example, the minimum qualification and other conditions for entry, the length of the course, the methods employed, with a view to local conditions, and the categories of students: men or women or both; young people or adults; married or unmarried people or couples. Some centers will include training for the wife or husband of the candidate and issuing of diplomas.

It is important to promote contacts between catechetical centers, especially at a national level, under the guidance of the Episcopal Conference. Formators from the different centers should meet from time to time to exchange ideas and teaching methods and learn from the experiences of others.

Centers should aim not merely at training their students but at being places of research and reflection on themes connected with the apostolate, such as: catechesis itself, inculturation, interreligious dialogue, pastoral methods, etc.

Besides the centers or schools, there should also be courses and encounters of diverse duration and composition organized by the dioceses and parishes, particularly those in which the bishop and the parish priests participate. These are very significant means of training and, in certain zones and situations, they become the only way of formation. These courses do not counteract the programs of the centers, but help them keep on the impact or, as very often happens, compensate for deficiency.

Each diocese should make sure that it provides the books, audiovisual material and other teaching aids necessary for catechetical training, and it would be good if there could be a pooling of ideas, information and teaching aids between centers, dioceses and neighboring countries.

The CEP insists on the fact that it is not sufficient to propose high objectives in formation, but one should identify and use efficacious means. Therefore, besides confirming the absolute priority of formators, who must be well prepared and sustained, the CEP asks that a strengthening of centers should be at work everywhere. Here too, a healthy realism is essential in order to avoid a theoretical discourse. The objective is to do things in such a way that all the dioceses have the possibility to train a certain number of their catechists, at least the *cadres*, in a center. Besides this, fostering the initiatives on the post, particularly the guided and programmed meetings, because they are indispensable for the first training of those [who] were not able to frequent a center, and for the permanent formation of all.

PART III
THE RESPONSIBILITIES TOWARDS CATECHISTS
VI. REMUNERATION FOR CATECHISTS

31. THE FINANCIAL QUESTION IN GENERAL

The question of proper remuneration for catechists is generally agreed to be one of the most difficult to solve. The problem, obviously, does not arise for religion teachers in schools where their salaries are paid by the State. But when catechists are paid by the Church, especially when they have a family to support, their salary must be adequate and must take full account of the cost of living.

If the salary is not high enough, there will be several negative consequences: on the choice of candidates, because capable persons will prefer better paid jobs; on commitment, because it might be necessary to take on other work to make up the deficit; on formation, because some might not be able to attend the training courses; on perseverance and on relations with the pastors. Also, in many cultures a job is respected only if it is a well-paid one, so if catechists are not well paid they risk being looked down upon.

32. PRACTICAL SOLUTIONS

Remuneration for catechists must be considered a matter of justice and not of benevolence. Both full-time and part-time catechists must be paid according to precise norms, drawn up at diocesan and parish levels, taking account of the local Church's financial situation, that of the catechist and his or her family, and the general economic conditions of the country. Special consideration has to be given to old, invalid and sick catechists.

The CEP, for its part, will continue, in so far as it can, to raise and distribute subsidies for catechists, but each diocese should try to arrive at a more stable solution of the problem.

Dioceses and parishes, therefore, should set aside a reasonable proportion of their budgets for catechists, and in particular for their formation.[131] The faithful too should contribute to their support, especially when it is a question of the village leader. The quality of persons, in particular those involved in direct apostolate, takes precedence over structures, and so funds earmarked for catechists should not be diverted to other purposes.

Money put into catechetical centers will be well spent, as these will certainly contribute to the *active and effective catechesis* of the community and therefore to its spiritual growth.[132]

The good will of voluntary catechists, who have another job but are willing to devote part of their free time to catechetical work, is certainly to be encouraged, and indeed many such generous workers are to be found in the more developed Churches. The faithful should be taught, in fact, to look upon the vocation of a catechist as a mission rather than a job. Further it may be necessary to rethink the organization and distribution of catechists. The problem of remuneration, therefore, is one that has to be solved basically by the local Church. Subsidies from abroad can help, but it is up to the local Church to find a place in its budget for this important apostolic work and to educate the faithful to contribute to its support.

VII. RESPONSIBILITY OF THE PEOPLE OF GOD

33. RESPONSIBILITY OF THE COMMUNITY

The CEP would like to make a public declaration of gratitude to the bishops, priests and communities of faithful for the care and support they have given to catechists. Their attitude is a guarantee for the future of evangelization and the growth of the young Churches. For catechists are, indeed, front-line apostles without whom *"Churches that are flourishing today would not have been built up."*[133] They are essential to the Christian community and are rooted in it through their baptism, confirmation and special vocation. They should be given respect and responsibility in their work and should be able to achieve personal growth through it.

It is important to note that in his encyclical letter *Redemptoris Missio* Pope John Paul II, says: *"Among the laity who become evangelizers, catechists have a place of honor . . . Even with the extension of the services rendered by lay people both within and outside the Church, there is always need for the ministry of catechists, a ministry with its own characteristics."*[134] And in his apostolic exhortation *Catechesi Tradendae* the same Pontiff remarked that *"the term 'catechists' belongs above all to the catechists in mission lands."*[135] Catechists are among those who have received Christ's command to *"go and teach all nations"* (Matthew 28:19) and, according to Vatican II, they are *"legitimately active in the ministry of the word."*[136]

They should have a place of honor, therefore, in their communities and should be well represented in pastoral councils and other organizations of the parish and diocese. They are growing in number throughout the Church, and the future of Christian communities will depend on them to a considerable extent. In the secularized atmosphere of the modern world, as lay people they will have a particular role to play in bringing the light of the gospel to bear on various situations.[137] In any discussion on the theology of the laity, catechists will necessarily occupy a special place.

All these considerations converge on the urgency to strengthen the catechists with an adequate vocational promotion in number as well as, and above all, in quality, which calls for a careful and global formation program.

34. RESPONSIBILITY OF THE BISHOPS IN PARTICULAR

The bishops, as *"the ones primarily responsible for catechesis,"*[138] are also those primarily responsible for catechists. Recent documents of the Magisterium and the new Code Of Canon Law stress this responsibility, based on the bishops' role as successors of the Apostles, both collegially and as pastors of local Churches.[139]

The CEP urges individual bishops and the Episcopal Conferences to continue and even increase their attention and care for catechists, making sure that there are definite criteria for selection, developing programs and structures for formation, seeing to questions of remuneration, etc. They should take an interest in their catechists and, as far as possible, have a personal relationship with each of them. Where this is not possible, an episcopal vicar should be named for them.

From its own experience, the CEP suggests the following points for special attention:

—Making the faithful, and especially priests, aware of the importance and role of catechists.

—Drawing up or renewing catechetical directories on a national or diocesan level, so as to apply and adapt to local conditions the guidelines of the *General*

Catechetical Directory, the Apostolic Exhortation *Catechesi Tradendae* and the present *Guide for Catechists*.

—Guaranteeing a minimum of teaching aids and equipment for the formation of catechists, so that they will be properly trained for their task; also, if possible, founding or improving catechetical centers.[140]

—Encouraging the preparation and selection of cadres, i.e. catechists who have been well trained in a center and who have had a certain amount of experience, to work closely with the bishop and priests, to help in the training and guidance of volunteer catechists, and to take leading roles in the application of the catechetical program.

—Providing, with the help of the community, a budget for the training, activities and maintenance of catechists.

Above all, bishops will express their responsibility for catechists through paternal love, attention to their needs and personal acquaintance with them.

35. RESPONSIBILITY OF THE PRIESTS

Priests, and parish priests in particular, as teachers of the faith and immediate collaborators of the bishops have a special responsibility for catechists. As pastors, who should recognize, promote and coordinate the various charisms in the community, they should have a particular interest in that of catechists, who share with them the task of instructing people in the faith. They should look on them as cooperators, responsible for the ministry entrusted to them, and not as subordinates carrying out instructions. They should encourage them to be creative and show initiative. They should also educate the community to respect their catechists, help them in their work and contribute to their support, especially if they have a family.

Future priests should be taught in the seminary to value and respect catechists as apostles and fellow-workers in the Lord's vineyard.

36. RESPONSIBILITY OF THE FORMATORS

The training of catechists is usually entrusted to qualified persons, either in special centers or in the parishes. These formators have an important role and make a valuable contribution to the Church. They should be aware, therefore, of the responsibility that is theirs.

When a person accepts the mandate to train the catechists, he should consider the concrete expression of the care of pastors and should seriously follow their directives. In the same way, he should live the ecclesial dimension of this mandate, realizing it in a communitarian spirit and following the programs therein.

As was mentioned above, formators should be chosen for their spiritual, moral and pedagogical qualities. They should be exemplary Christians, able to educate others by the witness of their own lives. They should be close to their students and should communicate their own fervor and enthusiasm to them.

Every diocese will do its best to have a team of formators, made up possibly of priests, brothers, sisters and lay people, who could be sent to parishes to help in the selection and training of catechists.

CONCLUSION

37. A HOPE FOR THE MISSION OF THE THIRD MILLENNIUM

The directives contained in this *Guide* are proposed as a general model, to serve as an ideal and be adapted where necessary.

The catechists are held in great esteem for their participation in missionary activities and for their characteristics which are rarely found in the ecclesial communities outside the mission.

Their number continues to grow and in recent years has been between 250,000 and 350,000. For many missionaries they have been absolutely indispensable, serving as their close assistants and at times interpreters. They have often been able to keep the faith of a community alive during trying periods, and their families have given priestly and religious vocations.

We cannot but have the greatest respect for these *"fraternal animators of young communities,"*[141] and feel that we should place the highest ideals before them, while recognizing that, because of objective difficulties or personal limitations, ideals are not always attained.

By way of conclusion, we may quote the words of Pope John Paul II to the catechists of Angola during his visit to that country: *"So many times it has fallen to you to strengthen and build up the young Christian communities, and even to found new ones through the first proclamation of the gospel. If missionaries could not be there for this first proclamation or had to leave before it could be followed up, it was you, the catechists, who instructed the catechumens, prepared people for the sacraments, taught the faith and were leaders of the Christian Community (. . .) Give thanks to the Lord for the gift of your vocation, through which Christ has called you from among other men and women to be instruments of his salvation. Respond with generosity to your vocation and your names will be written in heaven"* (cf. Luke 10:20).[142]

The CEP hopes that, with God's help and that of the Virgin Mary, this *Guide* will give new impulse to the promotion of catechists so that their generous contribution will continue to bear fruit for the Church's mission in the third millennium.

The supreme Pontiff John Paul II, during the course of the Audience granted to the undersigned Cardinal Prefect on June 16th, 1992, approved the present Guide for Catechists and gave consent to its publication.

Rome, from the Office of the Congregation for the Evangelization of Peoples, December 3rd, 1993, Feast of Saint Francis Xavier.

Jozef Card. Tomko, *Prefect*

Giuseppe Uhac, Arch. tit. of Tharros, Secretary

NOTES

1. Cf. Plenary Assembly of the Congregation for the Evangelization of Peoples, April 14–16, 1970, and its final report: *Bibliografia Missionaria* 34 (1970): 197–212, and *s.c. de Propaganda Fide Memoria Rerum.* 111/2 (1976): 821–831.

2. Cf. AG, 17.

3. Pope John Paul II, *Address* to the Plenary Assembly of the CEP (April 30, 1992, *or* May 1, 1992): 4; cf. also the addresses to the catechists of Guinea at Conakry (February 25, 1992), and to those of Angola in the Benguela cathedral (June 9, 1992 or June 11, 1992): 6.

4. Cf. John Paul II Encyclical Letter *Redemptoris Missio* (December 7, 1990): 73: AAS 83 (1991): 320.

5. AG, 17; 8.

6. *Catechism of the Catholic Church* (CCC), Vatican City, 1992.

7. John Paul II, Apostolic Exhortation *Fidei Depositum* (October 11, 1992): 4.

8. Cf. John Paul II, Apostolic Exhortation CL, 56.

9. Cf. Plenary Assembly cit., I.2.

10. Cf. AG, 15.

11. CL, 58.

12. Cf. CIC, cc. 773–780 and c. 785.

13. Cf. CCC, 6.

14. CT, 66.

15. RM, 73.

16. CIC, c. 785, 1.

17. Plenary Assembly cit., 1.

18. CL, 23; CIC, c. 230, 2.

19. Plenary Assembly cit., I. 4.

20. Cf. RM, 73; CCC, 4–5, 7–8, 1697–1698.

21. Cf. John Paul II, *Address* to the Plenary Assembly cit., 2; CCC, 6.

22. Cf. CT, 65.

23. Cf. RM, 73.

24. John Paul II, *Address* to the Plenary Assembly cit., 3; Cf. GCD, 108.

25. Cf. RM, 31.

26. John Paul II, *Address* to the Plenary Assembly cit., 4.

27. Cf. RM, 74.

28. RM, 90.

29. RM, 90.

30. EN, 80.

31. CIC, c. 225, 2.

32. John Paul II, *Address* to the Plenary Assembly cit., 2.

33. Cf. CT, 26–27.

34. CIC, 225, 2; RM, 87; CCC, 2653–2654.

35. Cf. CIC, c. 747, 1.

36. Cf. AG, 2, 6, 9.

37. Cf. RM, 89.

38. Cf. AG, 2.

39. Cf. LG, 4; AG, 4.

40. EN, 76; CT, 57.

41. Cf. CT, 27.

42. EN, 75; CT, 57.

43. Cf. Irenaeus, *Adv. Haer. I*, 10, 1–3; PG 7: 550–554; CT, 60–61; RM, 11.

44. CT, 61.

45. CCC, 429.

46. Cf. RM, 89.

47. CCC, 853.

48. CT, 73.

49. CT, 73.

50. Cf. *Sermo* 25, 7: PL 46: 937–938.

51. CT, 73; RM, 92; EN, 82.

52. Cf. CCC, 487–507, 963–972.

53. Cf. CCC, 2673–2679.

54. LG, 65.

55. Cf. John Paul II, *Address* to the third International Conference on Longevity and Quality of Life: *Dolentium Hominum:* Church and Health in the World, 10 (1989): 6–8.

56. SD, 19.

57. Cf. CL, 48.

58. FC, 27.

59. Cf. GCD, 95.

60. Cf. CT, 53.

61. RM, 52.

62. Cf. AG, 9, 16, 22; GS, 44, 57ff; ES, III, 18, 2; Pope Paul VI, Address at Kampala, August 2, 1969; EN, 62ff; FC, 10; CL, 44; RM, 52–54; CCC, 854, 1204–1206, 1232.

63. Cf. CCC, 2628.

64. RM, 59; EN, 31.

65. RM, 59; CA; CCC, 1939–1942.

66. GS, 42; EN, 25–28; 32–34; CCC, 2443–2449.

67. CL, 41–43; CCC, 1908, 2442.

68. RM, 60; CCC, 2443–2449.

69. RM, 59.

70. SRS, 42; CT, 41, 45; RM, 60; CA, 57.

71. UR, 1; AG, 6; RM, 36, 50; CCC, 817, 885.

72. Cf. UR; GCD, 27.

73. Cf. CCC, 820–822.

74. Cf. AG, 15.

75. Cf. RM, 50.

76. Cf. CIC, c. 753.

77. Cf. CT, 33.

78. Cf. CT, 32; UR, 3–4, 11; GCD, 27.

79. Cf. CT, 32; GCD, 27.

80. Cf. CT, 32; RM, 50.

81. Cf. RM, 55–56; Pontifical Council for Inter-Religious Dialogue — Congregation for the Evangelization of Peoples, *Dialogue and Proclamation*, May 19, 1991; cf. Secretariat for Non-Christians, *The Church's attitude to followers of other religions* (September 4, 1984); CCC, 839–845, 856, 1964.

82. Cf. RM, 56; Pontifical Council for Inter-Religious Dialogue — Congregation for the Evangelization of Peoples, *Dialogue and Proclamation*, 40–41.

83. Cf. Eusebius of Caesarea, *Praeparatio Evangelica*, 1, 1: PG 21: 28; St. Irenaeus, *Adv. Haer.* III, 18, 1: PG 7: 932; St. Irenaeus PG 7: 943, III, 20, 2; St. Justinus, *1 Apol.* 46: PG 6: 395; AG, 3, 11.

84. Cf. RM, 55.

85. Cf. LG, 14; UR, 3; AG, 7.

86. Cf. John Paul II, *Address* to the Urban University (April 11, 1991, or April 13, 1991): 5; cf. CCC, 846–848.

87. Cf. AG, 12; CA, 60.

88. Cf. RM, 57.

89. Cf. RM, 50.

90. Cf. Secretariat for Christian Unity — Secr. for Non-Christians — Pont. Council for Culture, *The phenomenon of sects and new religious movements* (May 7, 1986: or May 7, 1986), tabloid supplement.

91. Cf. John Paul II, *Address* to the Bishops of Zaire (April 24, 1988): 4.

92. Cf. RM, 50.

93. Cf. RM, 50.

94. Cong. for the Evangelization of Peoples, *Pastoral Guide for Diocesan Priests,* (October 1, 1989): 17; EV, 2579–2581.

95. Cf. St. Augustine, *De catechizandis rudibus*, PL 40: 310–347.

96. GCD, 108.

97. John Paul II, *Address* to the Plenary Assembly cit., 3; AG, 17; CD, 14; RM, 73; CL, 60; CIC, c. 785.

98. Cf. CD, 40; GCD, 108, 115.

99. CL, 59.

100. Cf. CL, 59.

101. Cf. CT, 5–6, 9.

102. Cf. RM, 90.

103. Cf. CCC, 428.

104. Cf. St. Ignatius of Antioch, *Epistula ad Magnesios*, IX 1.

105. Cf. LG, 41.

106. CT, 72; cf. St. Augustinus, *In Joannis Evangelium Tractatus*, 97, 1: PL 35: 1887.

107. Cf. GCD, 114; CCC, 2742–2745.

108. Cf. LG, 34; CCC, 1324–1327, 1343.

109. Cf. CCC, 1071–1075, 1136ff, 2655.

110. Cf. CCC, 1174–1178.

111. Cf. CCC, 2653–2654, 2705–2708.

112. Cf. CCC, 1446–1456.

113. Cf. GCD, 71.

114. Cf. GCD, 112–113.

115. Cf. Plenary Assembly cit., II, 1–2.

116. Cf. EN, 78; CT, 61.

117. CT, 6.

118. GCD, 70ff.

119. Cf. AG, 12; RM, 44–45; CCC, 854.

120. Cf. AG, 13; RM, 44–45; CCC, 854.

121. Cf. AG, 14; RM, 46–47; *Ordo Initiationis Christianae*; CCC, 854.

122. Cf. AG, 15; RM, 48; CCC, 854.

123. Cf. EN, 60.

124. Cf. CT, 24.

125. Cf. LG, 12.

126. Cf. RM, 89.

127. Cf. GCD, 110.

128. Cf. GCD, 110.

129. Cf. AG, 17.

130. Cf. RM, 73; AG, 17; CT, 21; CIC, c. 785.2.

131. CT, 63.

132. CT, 63.

133. CT, 66.

134. RM, 73.

135. CT, 66; cf. *Angelus*, (October 18, 1987, or October 19–20, 1987): 5.

136. DV, 25.

137. Cf. John Paul II, *Address* to the Plenary Assembly cit., 2.

138. CT, 63.

139. CD, 14; CT, 63; GCD, 108; CIC, cc. 773, 780.

140. Cf. RM, 71.

141. John Paul II, *Address* to the catechists of Guinea, cit.

142. John Paul II, *Address* to the catechists of Angola, cit.

INTRODUCTION TO THE *CATECHISM OF THE CATHOLIC CHURCH:* ON CATECHESIS, CATECHISMS AND CATECHETICAL DIRECTORIES

by Michael P. Horan

In the apostolic constitution that accompanied the publication of the *Catechism of the Catholic Church*, Pope John Paul II set the context for the writing of the *Catechism* by situating the document in the history of catechesis since the Second Vatican Council.[1] Other documents on catechesis since the Council were for the most part statements aimed at addressing the *why* of catechesis and the *who* of this essential ministry of the word. Chief among them are catechetical directories, which are official statements aimed at describing the context, goals and elements, as well as the desired qualities of personnel for the catechetical ministry. These official statements resulted from long and wide and rich processes of consultation among bishops, practitioners and theorists, who elaborated the why and the who of the ministry. A catechism, or compendium of the content of Christian belief, articulates the *what* of catechesis in a succinct way. The pope's words set the stage for the publication and reception of the *Catechism*. His message, given on the thirtieth anniversary of the opening of Vatican II, serves as a reminder that the content of catechesis resides in a large home, constructed by many people in the field who have attempted to craft a meaningful contemporary theory for this essential pastoral activity.

This introduction attends to the concerns of people who wonder about the use and usefulness of a catechism at this time in the history of the church and who question whether an item such as a catechism properly belongs tucked away in the attic of our memories. Some of the related questions that the introduction of the *Catechism* addresses are a) the meaning of terms (How shall we understand a catechism in the context of the activity of catechesis?), b) the historical context for the literary genre itself (From whence the relatively new genre of a catechism?), and c) the particular characteristics and distinguishing features of catechisms in relation to catechetical directories (Why and how does a new catechism differ from the ones used by aging Catholics in their pre–Vatican II childhood and the more recently published catechetical directories of the postconciliar church?). It concludes with several questions that remain unanswered as the church witnesses the reception of the *Catechism of the Catholic Church*.

CATECHESIS

The term catechism is related to the term catechesis. In the secular literature of ancient Greece, the term refers to the activity of "sounding from above," as a poet or actor might perform from a stage.[2] From the origins of the term one can discern a connection between the activity of hearing and seeing, and an implicit sense of the aesthetic dimensions of receiving a message. Employed by the early followers of the new movement that came to be known as Christianity, the term catechesis suggests the activity of communicating, between poet and listener, between actor and audience, in the context of the aesthetic.

The liturgy of the church was the aesthetic forum in which the message was shared in the process that came to be known as the catechumenate. The term catechumenate is more familiar to members of the Catholic Church since the Vatican's promulgation in January 1972 of the *Rite of Christian Initiation of Adults*. The catechumenate, the process and period of preparation to become a Christian, was not uniform in the early churches. The diary entries of the Spanish nun Egeria provide clues to understanding the delicate relationship between message and aesthetics suggested in the catechesis of Cyril of Jerusalem.[3] The lectures were addressed to the initially curious, the *photizomenoi*, or "those who have come to be enlightened." In addition, Cyril's mystagogical catecheses, addressed to the newly baptized, employ rich imagery and refer directly to the ritual actions culminating in the sacraments of initiation. While the term catechesis denotes the general activity and the term catechumenate connotes that activity of initiation within the context of liturgy, "catechism" is a rather specific term that carries a focused interest in the content of the message shared.

CATECHISM

The Historical Context for the Genre of Catechism

From the earliest moments of the Christian movement, there was a concern for the content of the message. In hindsight, historians can see that the tension between the content of the message and the act of communication was, and continues to be, a healthy one, but the history of catechesis shows that there is no formula for success in offering the "audience" a message that is both delightful and clear, at once inspiring and solid. The need for a summary of the content of catechesis is as ancient as the activity itself. The story of the catechumenate found in Jerusalem demonstrates that the first summaries of the content of catechesis, the creed and the Lord's Prayer, may have included other formulas often associated with the worship of the community of faith. But to speak directly of catechisms (printed books that summarize the content of Christian faith) is to note that catechisms have been produced in two distinct styles, addressed to two audiences. The large catechism is a compendium designed as a reference for clergy and other leaders; the small catechism is a brief work that can be memorized by children and uneducated adults.

Josef Jungmann's history of catechesis notes that the confessional books that predate catechisms function as a model for large catechisms, which were designed to aid the clergy. It was assumed that these texts did not circulate among the general population.[4] The *ABC des Simples Gens*, written by Jean Gerson, was an example of the small catechism, designed to address directly the faithful who were semiliterate adults and children, who could memorize simple formulas. It contained the Lord's Prayer and other lists of virtues and vices.[5] The invention of the printing press not only made books accessible but also had a profound impact on the ministry of catechesis during the Reformation.

Reformation and the Use of Large and Small Catechisms

Catechisms as we have known them in recent times really began with the sixteenth-century reform. In 1529, Martin Luther wrote two catechisms that advanced his agenda and that persuasively argued his theological concerns to the people as well as to the leaders in the new movement. The *Grosse Katechismus* (Large Catechism) by Luther, aimed at the clergy, elaborated the notions of grace and the place of the sacramental life of the church in a way that advanced the ideas he had set forth in other theological treatises.[6] The *Kleiner Katechismus* (Smaller Catechism) simplified the program for children, so that they could memorize questions and answers.

The Catholic leaders at the Council of Trent responded to the aggressive work of Luther and other reformers by commissioning the large catechism of the Council of Trent. While the original plan called for a catechism for children and uneducated adults, little was done on that matter. Instead, the large *Catechism of the Council of Trent for the Clergy* appeared in Latin in 1566 and was translated into several languages by 1569. The large catechism was intended to help the members of the clergy in their responsibilities; like the penitential books of the early centuries, the large catechism was a reference and guide for the parish priests who may not have received a great deal of preparation for their duties. The large catechism advanced this interest in uniformity of expression and thus met a need of the time. The project for a universal small catechism would have to be taken up by a later council.

Universal Small Catechisms: Trent to Vatican I

When Vatican I convened on December 8, 1869, one of the issues to be considered was the composition of a universal small catechism. The schema that the bishops debated was entitled "The Compilation and Adoption of a Single Short Catechism for the Universal Church." Surprisingly, the issue surrounding this schema occupied more attention than any single issue at Vatican I except, of course, the issue of infallibility. It was the only pastoral issue that was completely explored and decided upon at the Council.[7] The idea was strongly supported by Spanish and Italian bishops, led by Bishop Juan Ignacio Moreno of Valladolid. Moreno argued that one faith could be expressed in a uniform way, and he assumed that Trent's decision for a large catechism provided the model for the small catechism.[8] Bishops in support of Moreno's position pointed out that the patterns of immigration left societies unsettled; people moved either from rural areas to the newly industrialized cities or from one continent to the other (from Europe to North America) and had to make considerable adjustments. This unsettled state tugged at the fabric of family life and challenged patterns of learning for immigrant peoples. The situation warranted a uniform catechism that would transcend place.[9]

Those bishops who opposed the adoption of a uniform catechism did so for two reasons; the first was pedagogical, and the second, ecclesiological. On the grounds of practical pedagogy, Bishop Felix Dupanloup of Orleans, France, an author of several works on catechesis, noted that a multilingual society comprised of various cultures could not receive or esteem one uniform text. It seemed to Dupanloup and his supporters that a complex world demanded a variety of texts for catechesis, with the specifics left to be worked out best by individual bishops. The bishops were the ones with the intimate knowledge of the pastoral situation in each location.

Dupanloup's first concern, practical and pedagogical in nature, was related to the second more subtle ecclesiological concern: the role and the authority of the bishop.[10] This point of view can be summed up in reviewing the words of Archbishop Haynald of Hungary, who stated the position strongly: "To catechize the people is one of the great duties and rights of a bishop; if a catechism is dictated to us, our sermons will be dictated next."[11] With Haynald, several bishops believed that a small common catechism compromised their authority and the authority of the bishop in the church. Historians of catechesis have suggested that the concerns expressed over the issue of a catechism functioned in part to air analogous concerns about papal infallibility as the core issue for the First Vatican Council.[12] The Council passed a resolution, but no action was actually taken; no small universal catechism was ever written.

The familiar *Baltimore Catechism* exemplifies the small catechism genre, employing the usual question-answer format and encouraging memorization. While it never became a national catechism, it continues to function as a cultural item in the memories of many Catholics whose education in faith took place in Catholic schools or religious instruction programs in the years before the Second Vatican Council. The *Baltimore Catechism* was commissioned at the Third Plenary Council of Baltimore in 1885, and despite dissatisfaction expressed by several bishops and catechetical writers,[13] the catechism was used in many parts of the United States. One unfortunate outgrowth of its use was the popular equation of catechesis with the small catechism, leaving the impression that catechesis is for children alone and carrying forward the accompanying assumption that memorization of content could function as the standard for initiation into the community of faith.

CATECHETICAL DIRECTORIES FOR THE MINISTRY OF THE WORD:
VATICAN II ON CATECHESIS

Before the question of a catechism gained the attention of the bishops at the Second Vatican Council, Bishop Pierre Lacointe of Beauvais, France, proposed the composition of a catechetical directory rather than a catechism. He assumed correctly that the unfinished work of Vatican I, the construction of a universal catechism for children, would be in the minds of some bishops at Vatican II. Lacointe's reasoning in proposing a directory rather than a catechism echoed some of the concerns expressed by Bishop Dupanloup nearly a century earlier, namely, that the complexity of the modern world in its variety and multiplicity of cultural and linguistic expression made the construction of a single catechism impractical and undesirable.[14] In the years just before the opening of Vatican II, both France and Italy had developed directories treating the basic principles of catechesis, so there had been precedents and a measure of success for this new genre. A general directory would function "to provide the basic principles of pastoral theology . . . by which pastoral action in the ministry of the word can be more fittingly directed and governed."[15] The directory as conceived at Vatican II placed the responsibility for catechesis in the hands of the bishops through the national bishops' conferences, which the Council also advocated. The commission that prepared the *General Catechetical Directory* completed its work in 1971, and the effort to compose national directories was then assumed by the national conferences of bishops. A wide process of consultation among bishops and catechetical personnel in the United States resulted in the publication of *Sharing the Light of Faith: National Catechetical Directory for Catholics of the United States.*[16] That publication could not have occurred had it not been for the *General Catechetical Directory.*

CONCLUSION

The story of catechesis is an ancient and rich one. The story of the genre of the catechism makes sense only in that older and broader history. Throughout Catholic history, especially since the sixteenth-century reform, printed books in two styles (large and small) have been available to people as resources for summarizing the content of Christian faith. They have not been free from bias or agendas, functioning for the sixteenth-century reformers and counter-reformers as media through which to advance the spirit of the times and the concerns of their authors for living the Christian life in a particular era, church and culture.

With the pope, readers of the *Catechism of the Catholic Church* can place this large compendium in the larger context of the movements and intentions of the pastoral ministers and church leaders who have provided the ministry and the theory to support pastoral activity since the Council. The genre of the catechetical directory reminds us of the efforts and the insights that catechists have shared through the centuries. Directories also call our attention to the renewal of Vatican II with respect to understanding catechesis as a lifelong activity, intricate in practice, rich in meaning and aimed at fostering mature faith. The *Catechism* reminds us as well that there has been consistent attention to summarizing the content of the message in a language and style that attempt to meet the needs of the people in the spirit of the times. One thing is clear: Neither genre is likely to mitigate the other, either in the interests each genre represents or in the insights that each carries forward. That simple truth may aid bishops, catechetical leaders and publishers as they try new approaches, prepare new materials and attempt to work in service of catechesis, a ministry of the word.

NOTES

1. "Apostolic Constitution Fidei Depositum, On the Publication of the *Catechism of the Catholic Church* Prepared Following the Second Vatican Council," as in *Catechism of the Catholic Church* (Vatican City: Libreria Editrice Vaticana, 1994). English translation printed by St. Paul Books and Media.

2. See Herman Wolfgang Beyer's analysis of the term in Gerhard Kittel, ed., *Theological Dictionary of the New Testament*, trans. Geoffrey W. Bromiley, Vol. III (Grand Rapids: Eerdmans, 1964): 638.

3. Leonel L. Mitchell, "The Development of Catechesis in the Third and Fourth Centuries: From Hippolytus to Augustine," in John H. Westerhoff and O. C. Edwards, eds., *A Faithful Church: Readings in the History of Catechesis* (Wilton CT: Morehouse Barlow, 1981): 55.

4. Josef Andreas Jungmann, *Handing on the Faith: A Manual of Catechetics*, trans. A. N. Fuerst (New York: Herder and Herder, 1959): 13–16.

5. For an account of this historical period and the use of the catechism genre, see Milton McC. Gatch, "Basic Christian Education from the Decline of Catechesis to the Rise of the Catechisms," in John H. Westerhoff and O. C. Edwards, eds., *A Faithful Church: Issues in the History of Catechesis* (Wilton CT: Morehouse Barlow, 1981): 79–108.

6. For example, the arrangement of the material itself communicated a theological agenda. Luther placed the commandments and the moral life before the life of grace, leaving the learner clear on the fact that the life of the Christian cannot be lived on one's own merit or human effort but must rely on the grace of God, which is neither earned nor deserved.

7. Mary Charles Bryce, *Pride of Place: The Role of the Bishops in the Development of Catechesis in the United States* (Washington DC: The Catholic University of America Press, 1984): 78. Bryce's work establishes the context for the bishops' involvement in decisions like the one at Vatican I, and it offers important data regarding the vote of the bishops on the schema, as well as an analysis of the reactions of United States bishops in light of their experience in a democratic society. See also Michael T. Donnellan, *Rationale for a Uniform Catechism* (Ann Arbor MI: University Microfilms, 1972).

8. Mary Charles Bryce, *Pride of Place*: 79–87, narrates the decisions of Vatican I regarding a small catechism and includes the U.S. bishops' voting record on the proposal to create one catechism.

9. Mary Charles Bryce, *Pride of Place*: 79.

10. See Michael Donnellan, "Bishops and Uniformity in Religious Education: Vatican I to Vatican II," in Michael Warren, ed., *Sourcebook for Modern Catechetics* (Winona MN: St. Mary's Press, 1983): 232–37; also Mary Charles Bryce, *Pride of Place*: 82. Bryce developed the objections of Bishop Dupanloup and includes those of Bishop Augustin David of Saint-Brieuc, France, who insisted on the impracticality of one common catechism.

11. J. D. Mansi, *Sacrorum conciliorum nova et amplissima collectio*, vol. 50: 849. Cited in Michael Donnellan, "Bishops and Uniformity: Vatican I to Vatican II": 235.

12. Donnellan states, "[A]s [the catechism] debate wore on, the problem centered more on the relationship of bishops to the Holy See than on improvement of religious education." Michael Donnellan, "Bishops and Uniformity in Religious Education: Vatican I to Vatican II": 235.

13. For an analysis of the contents of and the critiques of bishops and other writers, see Mary Charles Bryce, "Happy Birthday Baltimore Catechism," *Catechist* (April 1972): 6–9, 25.

14. For an analysis of the arguments that led to the writing of the *General Catechetical Directory*, see Berard L. Marthaler, *Catechetics in Context* (Huntington IN:

Our Sunday Visitor, 1973) and the essay in this book that specifically treats the GCD.

15. "Foreword" to the *General Catechetical Directory*, in Marthaler, *Catechetics in Context*: 4.

16. *Sharing the Light of Faith: National Catechetical Directory for Catholics of the United States* (Washington DC: United States Catholic Conference, 1979). For a detailed narrative and analysis of the consultation for and composition of the national directory, see Mary Charles Bryce, "*Sharing the Light of Faith:* Catechetical Threshold for the U.S. Church" in *Sourcebook for Modern Catechetics*, Michael Warren, ed. (Winona MN: St. Mary's Press, 1983).

AUTHORS

Carole M. Eipers is the director of the Office for Religious Education for the archdiocese of Chicago.

Marina Herrera is a theologian, catechist and writer specializing in the preparation of ministers and of new immigrants for full participation in the multicultural church.

Michael Horan is assistant professor of theological studies at Loyola Marymount University in Los Angeles, where he also directs the graduate program in pastoral studies.

John E. Pollard, former director of the Office for Religious Education for the archdiocese of Chicago, directs the U.S. Bishops' Office for the Catechism. Pope John Paul II recently appointed him a permanent member of the International Catechetical Council.

Eva Marie Lumas, SSS, assistant professor of religious education and culture at the Franciscan School of Theology in Berkeley, California, was a member of the USCC/NCCB taskforce that produced GDSCM.

Anne Marie Mongoven, OP, is associate professor of catechetics in the graduate program in pastoral ministry at Santa Clara University in Santa Clara, California.

Margaret N. Ralph is secretary of educational ministries in the diocese of Lexington. She is the author of six books for adults on scripture, including *And God Said What!*"

Jane E. Regan teaches pastoral theology in the school of theology at Saint John's University in Collegeville, Minnesota. Her most recent publication is *Exploring the Catechism* (Liturgical Press, 1995).

Fayette Breaux Veverka is an assistant professor in the department of theology and religious studies at Villanova University in Villanova, Pennsylvania.

Richard Walsh serves as the secretary of education in the diocese of Joliet. He is an adjunct faculty member at Catholic Theological Union in Chicago and at Saint Mary's University, Minnesota.

Thomas P. Walters is professor of religious education in the school of theology at Saint Meinrad Seminary in Saint Meinrad, Indiana.

John R. Zaums is a professor in the religious studies department, Marywood College, Scranton, Pennsylvania, and a consultant for the diocese of Scranton on matters concerning adult religious education.

INDEX

References are to paragraph or section numbers of individual documents. For a list of abbreviations of document names, see page vii. As appropriate, the following abbreviations denote unnumbered sections of text: intro (introduction), conc (conclusion), n (note), add (addendum) and app (appendix).

in catechesis and evangelization, TJD 21–
26; EN 13–16, 23; NCD 25; CAC 8, 16;
ACCC 28, 35, 37, 62, 69, 81
in Catholic schools, TJD 21–26, 108, 126,
139; RDECS 42–46

CONFESSION.
See Penance, sacrament of

CONFIRMATION,
sacrament of, GCD 57; BT 10, appB; NCD
118–19, appB; RCIA 215–16; CAC 47

**CONFRATERNITY OF
CHRISTIAN DOCTRINE (CCD),**
GCD 126; TJD 85; BT intro; NCD 8

**CONGREGATION FOR
CATHOLIC EDUCATION,**
RDECS 2–3, 113–15

**CONGREGATION FOR THE
EVANGELIZATION OF PEOPLES
(CEP),**
GC 1, 5, 15, 17, 23, 30, 32, 37

CONSCIENCE,
development of. *See* Morality, Catholic
teachings about

COUNCIL OF TRENT,
CT 13

CREATION,
BT 5; NCD 51, 85

CREEDS,
NCD 36, 45; CT 28, 59; RDECS 81;
ACCC 32

**CULTURAL DIFFERENCES AND
SPECIAL NEEDS,**
sensitivity to, GCD 1–5, 8, 34, 37, 132;
TJD 98, 109; BT 22; EN 20, 52–58, 63;
NCD 3, 8, 9, 12–16, 73, 95, 137, 192–
96, 231, 237–38, 264; CT 31, 51–54;
RCIA 32, 34; CAC 19, 23–24, 28;
RDECS 8, 45, 57, 108; ACCC 3, 11–12,
16a–b, 17a–c, 26, 32, 38, 44–45, 47,
56; GDSCM intro, 26, 70. *See also*
Missionary activity, catechists in

CYRIL OF JERUSALEM, SAINT,
CT 12

DEATH,
judgment, and eternity, BT 25; NCD 108–
10; GDSCM 68–69

**DIOCESAN CATECHETICAL
OFFICE,**
GCD 126; NCD 238

DIVORCE.
See Families; Matrimony, sacrament of

EASTER TRIDUUM,
NCD 144c; RCIA 7–9, 12, 17–30, 207–8,
249

EASTERN CHURCH,
relationship to. *See* Ecumenism

ECUMENISM,
GCD 66; BT 22; EN 53; NCD 3, 14–15,
73, 75–81; CT 32–34; ACCC 51;
GDSCM 27–30; GC 14–16

EDUCATION, CATHOLIC.
See Catechesis; Colleges and universities,
Catholic education in; Schools, Catholic

EUCHARIST,
sacrament of, GCD 57–58, add1–5;
BT 12, appB; NCD 72a, 120–22, appB;
RCIA 217; RDECS 78; GDSCM 39–40

EVANGELIZATION
beneficiaries of, EN 49–58
content of, EN 17–39
increased emphasis on, GCD 9; EN 1–5;
ACCC 38
methods of, EN 40–48
and pre-evangelization, EN 51; NCD 34;
ACCC 68
relationship to catechesis, GCD 17–18;
NCD 34–35; CT 18, 20; CAC 9;
ACCC 32, 68
in Rite of Christian Initiation of Adults,
RCIA 36–40
workers for, EN 59–73, 76–80
See also Catechesis

FAMILIES,
GCD 59; BT 13; NCD 21, 131, 226;
RDECS 87; ACCC 22, 52; GDSCM 33;
GC 6
contemporary changes in, NCD 25–29,
197–203; CAC 17
education for, TJD 49–51; NCD 9
role in catechesis and education, TJD 25,
52–59; EN 71; NCD 9, 119, 126, 177–
81, 191, 212, n265; CT 68–69; CAC 17,
24, 48; RDECS 42–43
See also Sexuality, Catholic teachings
about

FATHERS OF THE CHURCH,
CT 12; ACCC 39

**FIRST INTERNATIONAL
CATECHETICAL CONGRESS,**
CT 2

FOURTH GENERAL ASSEMBLY.
See Synod of Bishops (1977)

FREEDOM.
See Liberation

GOD THE FATHER,
GCD 41–43, 47; BT 1, 19; NCD 49–55, 83–84; RDECS 75; GDSCM 10–17

GOSPELS.
See Scripture

HOLY ORDERS,
sacrament of, GCD 57; BT 10; NCD 132–33

HOLY SPIRIT,
GCD 13, 22, 41–42, 47, 60, 65; NCD 54
in catechesis and evangelization, TJD 14; EN 74–76; CT 72–73
central Catholic teachings about, BT 4, 9–10, 14, 20; NCD 83, 84, 92; GDSCM 10–17

HOMILIES,
TJD 45; EN 43; CT 48; RCIA 125

IGNATIUS, SAINT,
GCD 53

INFANTS.
See Baptism, sacrament of; Children, catechesis and education of

INTERNATIONAL COUNCIL FOR CATECHESIS,
CT 2; ACCC 6

JESUS CHRIST,
BT 10–11; EN 75
central Catholic teachings about, BT 1, 4–8; NCD 83, 87–91; GDSCM 10–17
as central element of catechesis, GCD 40–43, 47, 50, 52–54; NCD 47; CT 5–9; CAC 5–7, 30, 31–32, 41; RDECS 25, 74, 107; GC 20
as primary evangelizer, EN 6–12, 15–16, 31, 49; NCD 8, 154; CT 1, 5–9, n20, n27; RDECS 48; ACCC 10, 30, 47
and revelation, GCD 12, 16; NCD 53

JEWISH PEOPLE,
relationship to. *See* Ecumenism

JOHN XXIII,
NCD 169

JOHN PAUL I,
CT 4

JOHN PAUL II,
ACCC 4, 51, 64; GC 1, 6, 11, 15, 19, 23, 25, 33–34

JOHN THE BAPTIST,
EN 12, 80

LAITY,
role of, EN 70–73; NCD 9; CT 66–71; RCIA 38; RDECS 3, 37–38; ACCC 5, 8, 27, 50, 65, 70–80; GDSCM intro. *See also* Missionary activity, catechists in

LENT,
NCD 144c; RCIA 7–9, 17–30, 125–28, 138; ACCC 61

LEO XIII,
NCD 9, 164

LEO THE GREAT, SAINT,
EN 67; NCD 162

LIBERATION,
GCD 61; BT 15; EN 29–39; NCD 101; CT 14

LITURGICAL YEAR,
BT intro; NCD 44, 144; ACCC 61; GDSCM 42

LITURGY,
BT intro, NCD 9, 36, 44, 60a, 112–13, 134–39; GDSCM 38–50. *See also* Eucharist, sacrament of; Word, ministry of the

MAGISTERIUM OF THE CHURCH,
GCD 13, 38, 45, 59, 63; BT 17; EN 43, 64–65; NCD n123; CT 6, 46, 49, 52, 61; RDECS 44, 66, 70; ACCC 4, 39, 46; GDSCM 31; GC 1, 3, 12, 15, 16, 19, 34. *See also* Bishops, role of; Pope, role of

MANUALS.
See Catechetical materials

MARRIAGE.
See Families; Matrimony, sacrament of

MARY, VIRGIN,
GCD 43, 68, 78; BT 24; EN 82; NCD 77, 78, 87, 106; CT 30, 73; RDECS 29, 74, 81; ACCC 86; GDSCM 35–36; GC 10

MASS.
See Eucharist, sacrament of; Liturgy

MASS MEDIA,
role of, GCD 123; TJD 34–35; EN 45; NCD 20, 22, 251–62; CT 14, 46; ACCC 16c, 65

RECONCILIATION,
sacrament of. *See* Penance, sacrament of

REVELATION,
GCD 10–16, 33, 37–38; TJD 16–18;
NCD 48–61; CT 52

RITE OF CHRISTIAN INITIATION
OF ADULTS (RCIA),
GCD 96; NCD 9, 115; RCIA 2–3; ACCC 5
adaptations of, RCIA 32, 34–35
candidates for, RCIA 1, 32
godparents and sponsors in, RCIA 10–11,
80, 119–23
stages of, RCIA 4–8, 17–31, 35–47, 75–
80, 118–28, 138–40, 206–17, 244–51;
ACCC 66–67

SACRAMENTALS,
NCD 147; GDSCM 44

SACRAMENTS,
GCD 55–59; RDECS 78–79
and catechesis and evangelization, EN 28,
46–47; NCD 36, 44, 55, 114–33; CT 23
central Catholic teachings about, BT 10–
13; NCD 97; GDSCM 38–50
order of reception, GCD add1–5;
NCD 118–20, 126
See also individual sacraments by name

SACRED CONGREGATION FOR
DIVINE WORSHIP,
NCD 135

SACRED CONGREGATION FOR
THE CLERGY,
GCD 134; CT 2; ACCC 6

SACRED CONGREGATION FOR
THE EVANGELIZATION OF
PEOPLES,
CT 66

SAINTS,
BT 24; NCD 107; RDECS 81; GDSCM 34–
37. *See also* Mary, Virgin, *and various
other individual saints by name*

SALVATION,
GCD 16, 37–44, 47, 62; BT 5–6, 8, 22,
23; EN 27, 34; NCD 85, 96

SCHOOLS, CATHOLIC,
GCD 79–80, 109; TJD 84, 101–26;
NCD 8, 9, 215, 232–33; CT 69; CAC 20;
RDECS 18–19, 22–23
approach to academic disciplines,
RDECS 49–65
climate of, RDECS 24–65, 103–4

philosophy and goals of, TJD 102–11;
RDECS 1–6, 33–34, 98–112
religious instruction in, TJD 84, 94–95,
101–26; CAC 54; RDECS 66–97
See also Adolescents and youth,
catechesis and education of; Children,
catechesis and education of; Colleges
and universities, Catholic education in

SCIENCE AND TECHNOLOGY,
GCD 4–5, TJD 33–41, 73; NCD 9, 17–22,
37, 46, 175; RDECS 20, 54–55, 76. *See
also* Mass media, role of

SCRIPTURE,
as source of catechesis and
evangelization, GCD 14, 32; BT intro,
19; EN 18–22, 43; NCD 9, 41, 43, 55,
60a, 151–54; CT 11, 27; RCIA 38;
CAC 6, 30, 32, 39–40; RDECS 25, 47;
ACCC 2, 13, 39, 46, 62; GC 23

SECOND VATICAN COUNCIL,
GCD 7, 9, 66, 67; BT 24; NCD 1, 106;
CT 61; CAC 10; GDSCM 8
on catechesis and evangelization,
GCD 20; EN 2, 15, 17, 55, 59, 67, 71,
76, 77; NCD 2, 9; CT 2, 13, 22, 27, 63;
RCIA 2; ACCC 4–6
on ecumenism, BT 22; NCD 73; CT 32
on education and Catholic schools,
TJD 57, 66, 76, 85, 101; NCD 233;
RDECS 1–3, 6, 33, 44
on marriage and morality, BT 13, 18;
NCD 191; CT 68
reaction to, NCD 23–24
on study of Scripture, BT intro; NCD 60a

SEMINARIES,
NCD 241

SERMON ON THE MOUNT,
BT 19, appA; NCD 105; GDSCM 59

SERVICE TO COMMUNITY,
TJD 27–32, 106, 118; NCD 162, 210;
CAC 13, 36; ACCC 29, 32; GC 11

SETON, SAINT ELIZABETH ANN,
NCD conc

SEXUALITY,
Catholic teachings about, TJD 52–58;
BT 13, 18–19; NCD 105b, 130–31,
191; CT 38; CAC 37, 43; RDECS 83, 87;
GDSCM 65

SIN,
GCD 62; TJD 9; BT 10, 15–16, 19;
NCD 98–99, 165b, n138; RCIA 211;
GDSCM 51

SOCIAL PROBLEMS,
addressing, TJD 10, 26, 29, 60–61; NCD 105b, 149–71, 233; CAC 13, 42; RDECS 88; ACCC 12, 15, 52, 55; GDSCM 57; GC 13

STEPHEN, SAINT,
CT 11

SYNOD OF BISHOPS (1971),
NCD 160, 165b

SYNOD OF BISHOPS (1974),
EN 2, 4, 7, 14, 15, 24, 30–31, 38, 50, 53, 55, 58, 65, 75, 77, 81

SYNOD OF BISHOPS (1977),
NCD 4; CT 2–5, 16, 17, 18, 21, 25, 29, 33, 35, 40, 43, 50, 55, 63, 66, n6; ACCC 6

SYNOD OF BISHOPS (1985),
RDECS 2, 73

TECHNOLOGY.
See Science and technology

TEN COMMANDMENTS,
BT 19, appA; NCD 105, appA; GDSCM 59

TEXTBOOKS.
See Catechetical materials

THEOLOGY,
TJD 67, 77–81; NCD 16, 37; CT 60–61

TRANSUBSTANTIATION,
GCD 58; BT 11. *See also* Eucharist, sacrament of

TRINITY,
GCD 41–42, 47, 60; BT 1; NCD 47, 83; RDECS 75; GDSCM 10–17; GC 7

TRUTHS,
hierarchy of, GCD 43; BT intro; NCD 47; GDSCM intro

UNITED STATES CATHOLIC CONFERENCE (USCC),
NCD 222b–223, 240, 250, 257, 266

UNITED STATES CENTER FOR THE CATHOLIC BIBLICAL APOSTOLATE,
NCD 223

VATICAN II.
See Second Vatican Council

VIOLENCE AND WAR,
EN 37; NCD 18; RDECS 86, 91

VIRGIN MARY.
See Mary, Virgin

WITNESSING TO THE GOSPEL,
GCD 35, 49; BT intro, 3, 20; EN 21, 26, 41; NCD 45, 207; CT 1, 13, 18, 24; ACCC 22, 32, 42

WORD, MINISTRY OF THE,
GCD 10–17; NCD 30–38; CAC 7. *See also* Catechesis; Evangelization

YOUTH,
catechesis and education of. *See* Adolescents and youth, catechesis and education of; Children, catechesis and education of

NOTES

NOTES

NOTES